MW01038907

THE FACE OF THE LORD

THE FACE OF THE LORD

Contemplating the Divine Son through the Four Senses of Sacred Scripture

STEVEN C. SMITH

Foreword by Rev. John Kartje

FRANCISCAN UNIVERSITY PRESS

Franciscan University Press
1235 University Boulevard
Steubenville, OH 43952
740-283-3771

Distributed by:
The Catholic University of America Press
c/o HFS
P.O. Box 50370
Baltimore, MD 21211
800-537-5487

Library of Congress Cataloging-in-Publication Data
Names: Smith, Steven C. (Ph.D.), author.
Title: The face of the Lord : contemplating the divine son through the four senses of sacred scripture / Steven C. Smith with an introductory essay by Bogdan G. Bucur ; foreword by Rev. John Kartje.
Description: Steubenville : Franciscan University Press, [2020] | Includes bibliographical references and index. | Summary: "Is it possible to "see God"? A close examination of the Bible suggests that answering this question is more complex-and interesting-than one might imagine. Following The Word of the Lord and The House of the Lord, this sweeping conclusion to the trilogy asks whether it is possible to see God. After properly framing the question and citing scriptural examples, author Steven C. Smith takes the reader on an epic journey into the literal and spiritual meanings of biblical interpretation. Smith's thesis is that the multiplicity of "senses" is a pathway and progression toward the face of the Lord. He leads the reader through five Old Testament theophany scenes, beginning with the patriarch Jacob "wrestling" with God and concluding with Job's contending with the Voice from the Whirlwind. These five encounters span all three parts of the Old Testament: the Law, the Prophets, and the Writings. A tour de force much like Smith's previous books, The Face of the Lord thoroughly examines each biblical episode from the standpoint of the Literal, Allegorical, Tropological (Moral), and Anagogical (Heavenly) senses. Smith engages all of the relevant literature—from ancient Jewish sources to Christian medieval masters to present-day theologians—without taking his eye off the central question: Can we see God? The result is a fresh, robust exploration of Sacred Scripture, drawing upon ancient, medieval, and contemporary exegesis in pursuit of this fascinating biblical question"—Provided by publisher.
Identifiers: LCCN 2019060187 | ISBN 9781733988940 (hardback)
Subjects: LCSH: Theophanies in the Bible. | Bible. Old Testament—Criticism, interpretation, etc. | Jesus Christ—Face. | Typology (Theology)
Classification: LCC BS1199.T45 S84 2020 | DDC 221.6—dc23
LC record available at https://lccn.loc.gov/2019060187

Cover Design: Kachergis Book Design
Cover Image: *Transfiguration*, by Jonathan Pageau
Printed in the United States of America.

To Bishop Robert Barron and Jordan B. Peterson,
two brilliant men who have challenged my
understanding of Scripture in old and new ways.

And to Isabelle and Olivia, for helping
me to seek the face of the Lord in our family
and in the everyday moments.

CONTENTS

ACKNOWLEDGMENTS

There are numerous people that need to be recognized for their contributions to this book. I first wish to express my gratitude to the faculty and seminarians at Mount St. Mary's Seminary (Emmitsburg, MD), where I began my research on this enormous project. And to the faculty and seminarians at the University of Saint Mary of the Lake (Mundelein, IL), where, by the grace of God, it now continues. Without the generosity, resources, and kindness of the both major seminaries, this work could not have been accomplished.

I am indebted to my publisher, Franciscan University Press, for their belief in the project, for all of their dedication, and for countless acts of generosity. In particular I wish to thank Sarah Wear, general editor, and with her all of the dedicated folks of this fine academic press. This book would not have been possible were it not for her confidence in me and her leadership in coordinating so many moving parts. Final work on the book was completed on retreat at the Sea of Galilee. I especially owe a debt of gratitude to Ashleigh McKown, for her tireless efforts in reviewing and editing the manuscript back in the United States. As with her work on *The House of the Lord*, the editing of this book involved large text files, often filled with technical and theological data. Ashleigh never missed a beat, and her suggestions for improving the manuscript were brilliant. Likewise, I wish to thank Catholic University of America Press, and especially John Martino, for the wide distribution of *The Face of the Lord.*

I am thankful for those who reviewed drafts of the work, for their time and smart input on the book, especially Fr. John Kartje, Matthew Levering, Michael Barber, Hans Boersma, Michael Foley, and Bogdan Bucur.

Lastly, and after a decade of work on a trilogy of books, I am eternally grateful for my beloved girls Isabelle and Olivia Smith. Words cannot convey the depth of love and thanks I owe both of you; for your goodness, kindness, patience, and tenderness to me over the years. I love you all.

ILLUSTRATIONS

ABBREVIATIONS

Catechism of the Catholic Church	*CCC*
English Standard Version	ESV
King James Version	KJV
New American Bible	NAB
New Jerusalem Bible	NJB
Revised Standard Version	RSV
Septuagint	LXX

FOREWORD

For those perusing modern biblical scholarship with the desire to both learn about the Scriptures *and* pray with them, we might well imagine them echoing Tertullian's famous query: What has Athens to do with Jerusalem? One often finds a gap between careful, critical exegesis of the Bible and prayerful, contemplative encounter with it. This is clearly in evidence among many of today's seminary students, who are expected to apply their intellects in the classroom during "academic" Scripture courses and then perhaps engage in *lectio divina* in the chapel during "prayer time." Beyond the realm of seminary education, anyone seeking an author who is versed enough in biblical scholarship to present insightful exegesis and familiar enough with (and respectful toward) the rich tradition of Catholic biblical spirituality to serve as a guide into sacred mystery is faced with relatively few choices. In the face of such disappointment, Steven Smith sounds a welcome voice.

I had the pleasure of meeting Steve several years ago at a spiritual retreat being offered for seminary academic faculty. I was familiar with some of his scholarly writing and was pleasantly surprised to find that this accomplished exegete was also a man whose personal spirituality was steeped in his passion for the Bible. He found no conflict between a critical reading of the texts and a spiritual encounter with them. Furthermore, he did not find these two approaches to be simply parallel and nonconflicting but rather to be profoundly integrated, each dependent upon the other and both dependent upon the primary truth that the texts are divinely inspired. Although the acknowledgment of such inspiration may not be considered scholarly in certain exegetical circles, it nevertheless demands just as much rigor (if not more so) as a purely secular approach, as any reader of the present work will quickly find.

Contemporary Catholics, and others, have an abiding desire to encounter God more intimately and at the same time to become better informed about the deep intellectual tradition of their faith. While myriad blogs, podcasts, and videos abound, there yet remains a hunger that can only be satisfied by learning about our sacred texts. Once acquired, this knowledge of the Word facilitates a direct engagement with the one who *is* the living Word. But a frustrating disconnect is sometimes perceived between what the Scriptures seem to say and what one longs to hear. Such a perception lies at the core of the lament of many of today's "nones," who have forsaken any religious affiliation.

Considering such frustration, Smith calls for nothing less than a modern reclaiming of the medieval fourfold sense of Scripture and an unapologetic admission that the spiritual sense provides a necessary complement to the literal sense. Beyond simply citing complementarity, Smith challenges us to understand the dual senses as part of a natural progression along a directional pathway, beginning with the literal sense and necessarily culminating in the spiritual sense. And at that culmination point, one reaches a personal encounter with the living face of God. This progression would doubtless resonate profoundly with many Catholics today, if only they could appreciate that the literal sense of Scripture is not meant to be an end in itself. Rather, it exists to elevate the reader beyond the written word and to invite him to embrace the natural pairing of the exegetical tools at his disposal with the deepest longing of his heart: "may his face shine upon us" (Ps 67:2).

A clear example of this dynamic from the early Church is manifested by the meeting between the disciples on the road to Emmaus and the unrecognized risen Jesus. He first takes them on an exegetical tour through the Hebrew Scriptures, interpreting how all recorded salvation history related to his life and ministry. Only then does he engage them in a typological reenactment of the Last Supper, during which they gain recognition of whose face upon which they have been gazing. As they recall the lesson in exegesis they were given, they receive a deeper spiritual understanding of the same texts, and they now fully appreciate in whose divine presence they have been journeying (and presumably will continue to encounter, whenever the same texts are read).

In modern times, such encounters are found in diverse settings. For example, they are witnessed in the growing prevalence of Eucharistic Adoration as a preferred devotion in many parishes. But they are also glimpsed in the heeding of Pope Francis's clarion call to accompany those who are precariously huddling at the margins of society. Indeed, to seek the Lord's face is an inherent desire of the human condition—if only we could recognize the inexhaustibly diverse miens he presents.

Throughout the present work, Steven Smith reminds us that the serious study of Scripture is also a vital and privileged avenue into the presence of the divine face. Contrary to any purported dichotomy between the classroom and the chapel, an exegesis that is faithful to the fourfold sense of Scripture invites one into the practice of biblical contemplation. Smith precipitates such contemplation by confronting his readers with the "theophany" presented within the text itself, and also by offering a series of meditative reflections interspersed among the exegetical passages. He does this with the pedagogical skill and pastoral sensitivity one would expect from a seminary Scripture professor with over a decade of teaching experience at Mount St. Mary's Seminary and Mundelein Seminary, plus extensive public outreach ministry.

It is a rare biblical scholar who can not only inflame both the mind and heart, but also do so in a way that helps the reader to transcend from the profane study of biblical texts into a sacred encounter with the divine. St. Jerome rightly proclaimed that it is impossible to truly know Jesus Christ without knowing Scripture. Steven Smith reminds us that it is impossible to truly know Jesus Christ without knowing his face.

Fr. John Kartje
Rector, Mundelein Seminary

THE FACE OF THE LORD

Praefatio

Contemplating the Divine Son through the Four Senses of Sacred Scripture

> Since we cannot deceive the whole human race all the time, it is most important to cut off every generation from all others . . . thanks to Our Father and the Historical Point of View, great scholars are now as little nourished by the past as the most ignorant mechanic who holds that "history is bunk."
>
> —C. S. Lewis, *The Screwtape Letters*

The Word, House, and Face of the Lord

This book helps readers encounter the Bible in a fresh and invigorating way, yet its approach is different than one may be accustomed to. By the book's conclusion, this approach may well change the way the Bible is read, studied, and prayed. What is it about *The Face of The Lord* that makes its content *frais et vivifiant*? Will it strengthen or challenge one's beliefs about Scripture, about God? These are good questions, the right sort to ask when picking up a new book. There are several ways to address them, and so prepare for what lies ahead. Neither answer pays much attention to Screwtape's nefarious advice.

First, a bit of context. This book is the third and final part of a trilogy concerning Sacred Scripture.[1] It's unnecessary to have read the previous volumes, yet it is worth knowing how the present book is related

Epigraph. C. S. Lewis, *The Screwtape Letters*, 265.

1. Unless specified, all Scripture citations are from the Revised Standard Version–Catholic Edition.

to the previous two. For those who've read one or both, it will be helpful to understand where the project is now headed. The first volume in the trilogy is *The Word of the Lord* (2012).[2] Since its release, many have found it to be a clear, concise, and reliable introduction to biblical study from a Catholic perspective. It explains the principles that govern sound biblical interpretation, including the dynamic interplay between the divine and human authors (inspiration and inerrancy), the relationship of Sacred Scripture to Sacred Tradition, the unity of the Old and New Testaments, and so on. No introductory work can cover every topic one needs to know. Still, the seven principles articulated within it get the reader moving in the right direction.[3]

2. Smith, *Word of the Lord*. The seven principles are: (1) Catholic biblical interpretation [CBI] is rooted in the firm belief that in Scripture, God speaks to us in human language. God's Word was written under inspiration of the Holy Spirit and by true human authors, with their capacities and limitations. All Scripture comes simultaneously from God and the inspired authors. 2. CBI affirms God's intervention in history. The incarnation of Jesus, the Living Word, reveals 'God in the flesh' (Jn 1:14). Exegesis searches for the meaning expressed by the authors in their ancient context. 3. CBI affirms one source of Divine revelation: Scripture and Tradition 'flow from the same one divine wellspring' and 'form one sacred deposit of the word of God' (DV 9, 10). Through apostolic Tradition, the Church discerned the canon (DV 8), and with the Magisterium, it helps us comprehend Scripture. 4. CBI affirms the coherence of the Old and New Testaments. This 'unity of the Word' is evident in: (i) the covenants, (ii) typology; and (iii) recapitulation in Christ. In these and other ways, we affirm that "The New Testament lies hidden in the Old, and the Old is unveiled in the New" (Augustine). 5. CBI affirms Scripture's rich meaning. No one 'sense' or method can adequately plumb its depths. Ancient, medieval, and modern approaches illuminate the text, provided one appropriates them within Tradition and a hermeneutic of faith. 6. CBI strives for wisdom and excellence in scholarship: anchored in robust faith, and grounded in pastoral concern for God's people. Three rules govern proper exegetical control: (i) the unity of the Bible; (ii) the Church's living Tradition; and (iii) the analogy of faith. 7. CBI affirms Scripture's life-giving, foundational, and authoritative role in the Church. Exegesis doesn't stop with the text, but strives for the transcendent reality of which the Bible speaks: communication with God. The Church continually actualizes the Sacred Page as 'the Word for today,' embodying it in all situations and cultures. Competence in these principles assist one to study, pray, and proclaim Scripture faithfully and clearly, with full confidence in their transformative power.

3. Additionally, see Carbajosa, *Faith*; idem, "Nine Theses on the Interpretation of Scripture," in Davis and Hays, *Art of Reading Scripture*. Among the nine are the following: (1) Scripture truthfully tells the story of God's action of creating, judging, and saving the world; (2) Scripture is rightly understood in light of the Church's rule of faith as a coherent dramatic narrative; (3) faithful interpretation of Scripture requires an engagement with the entire narrative; (4) the New Testament cannot be rightly understood apart from the Old, nor can the Old be rightly understood apart from the New; (7) the saints of the Church provide guidance in how to interpret and perform Scripture. For the complete list, see pp. 1–5.

This second book of the trilogy is *The House of the Lord* (2017).[4] It was met with immediate and surprising success.[5] At nearly twice the length of the first volume, it is a more ambitious project. It puts the above principles into practice by moving to the Scriptures themselves. Specifically, *The House of the Lord* presents a Catholic biblical theology of the Old and New Testaments—through the lens of the Jerusalem Temple. The first half of the book investigates God's "temple presence" in the Old Testament.[6] In the second half of *The House of the Lord*, the emphasis turns from the Old Testament to the New. Here, the central message of the book emerges: *Jesus is the New Temple,* symbolically prefigured in all of the previous sanctuaries of ancient Israel.[7]

The Face of the Lord shares many qualities with the two previous volumes, but it is more like *The House of the Lord* in scope and substance. Both build upon foundation of *The Word of the Lord*, employing its principles through careful exegesis of biblical texts. There are differences, too. For starters, *The House of the Lord* focuses upon the Temple as its central theme. In contrast, *The Face of the Lord* investigates the recurrent desire, expressed in a number of Scripture texts: the desire to "see" God, to look upon his face. Additionally, the previous volume was a work of *biblical theology*. *The Face of the Lord* has a different focus and is more

4. Smith, *House of the Lord*.

5. The immense popularity of *The House of the Lord* was something of a surprise. Within weeks of its initial release in hardcover, it became a best seller in numerous categories, and a second printing was necessary. A social media site called "The Outer Court" was launched to provide community and book discussion, along with a weekly podcast by the author, called *Solomon's Porch* (see Facebook.com/TheOuterCourt). *Solomon's Porch* is available at The Outer Court, on iTunes: https://itunes.apple.com/us/podcast/solomons-porch-hotl-podcast/id1281370322?mt=2, and at https://www.spreaker.com/show/solomons-porch-hotl-podcast. In 2019, *The House of the Lord* was re-released in paperback.

6. Beginning with the cosmological temple of Mt. Eden, the book explores the intrinsic connection between the Creation narratives of Genesis and the rest of Scripture, with the Jerusalem Temple at the center. Discussions of priesthood, sacrifices, the building and destruction of the Temple, etc. all underscore the raison d'être of the book: God's "temple presence" remains steadfast with his people throughout salvation history. To the reader: the phrase "temple presence," which recurs throughout the book, is not capitalized to distinguish it from the (Jerusalem) Temple proper. As such, temple presence is the theological notion of God-with-his-people, whether in Eden, the wilderness, the Jerusalem Temple, and so on.

7. Through extensive research of the Four Gospels and the remainder of the New Testament, the book explains how Jesus—*Verbum caro factum est* "the Word made flesh" (Jn 1:14)—recapitulates the plan of the Father begun in Genesis; namely, to sanctify his people and through them to spread his temple presence throughout all Creation until the end of time.

a work of *biblical contemplation.* There are several ways of addressing what sort of book this is, and what the reader can expect to get out of it. Consider the book's subtitle, "Contemplating the divine Son through the Four Senses of Sacred Scripture."

Two Distinctive Features of This Book

This book offers more opportunities than previous ones for the reader's intellectual and spiritual involvement. New features make this possible, as the reader is afforded opportunities to actually seek the face of the Lord, and not merely think about it in a cerebral fashion. Four such opportunities are mentioned here.

1. *Biblical contemplation.* First and most importantly, the central aim of the book is to help the reader "contemplate the face of the Lord" in Scripture. This phrase may be new for some. The reader is invited to "put out into the deep"[8] with Christ in a participative way. To accomplish this goal, a series of theophanies—or, more precisely, "encounter" scenes—have been carefully chosen from across the Old Testament.

The Old Testament needs to be reclaimed by Catholics and all readers of the New Testament. It's not an option. There is no such thing as "New Testament Christians," as is sometimes heard. For those disinterested or put off by some of its content, the Old Testament is dismissed as dry, dull, or irrelevant when compared with the New. At the extreme end, however, such dismissal morphs into the ancient heresy of Marcionism, which involved the outright rejection of the God of the Old Testament. This heresy was a profound distortion of Christianity, and it was unequivocally condemned by the second-century Church just as quickly as it arose. Yet some traces lingered on. Even today, there are no small number of Christians dismiss the Old Testament as the record of a legalistic, judgmental people and their violent, merciless God. Often, such misgivings are the result of misinterpretations or simple ignorance

8. "And when he had ceased speaking, he said to Simon, 'Put out into the deep and let down your nets for a catch'" (Lk 5:4). Unless specified, all Scripture translations are taken from the Revised Standard Version–Catholic Edition (RSV–CE), 2nd ed. (San Francisco: Ignatius Press, 2005). A number of other translations are engaged throughout the book: from the King James Version to the New Jerusalem Bible, among others. At times, I provide my own translations or modifications of translations. When any other translations than the RSV–CE are employed, they will be noted accordingly.

about the true contents of the Old Testament and the loving and merciful God within them.

Such apathy or wariness about the Old Testament may be understandable in our skeptical age, yet it must be overcome. The Scriptures are a dynamic unity, a totality of revelation, that converge at the Cross. It is essential for Christians to robustly embrace the Old Testament, first for its own truth, beauty, and covenantal story, but above all because it is the road that leads to the Savior.[9] Such has been and remains the constant teaching of the Catholic Church.[10] The Creator in Genesis is the One true God and the Father of Jesus Christ. The story that Jesus the Jew steps into is a Jewish story, the story of Yahweh and his covenant people Israel, told on all the pages of the "Hebrew Scriptures," the Scripture that along with Fleming Rutledge, we will respectfully refer to as the "Old Testament" throughout this book.[11]

Though an array of Catholic sources, both ancient and modern, could be marshalled to underscore our point about the ongoing value of the Old Testament, let us stay for the moment with Rutledge, an Anglican theologian and preacher. As she puts it,

9. *Catechism of the Catholic Church*, §122. "Indeed, 'the economy of the Old Testament was deliberately so oriented that it should prepare for and declare in prophecy the coming of Christ, redeemer of all men.' 'Even though they contain matters imperfect and provisional,' the books of the Old Testament bear witness to the whole divine pedagogy of God's saving love: these writings 'are a storehouse of sublime teaching on God and of sound wisdom on human life, as well as a wonderful treasury of prayers; in them, too, the mystery of our salvation is present in a hidden way." *CCC* §337. See also Pope Paul VI, *Dei Verbum*, November 18, 1965, http://www.vatican.va/archive/hist_councils/ii_vatican_council/documents/vat-ii_const_19651118_dei-verbum_en.html, 15.

10. "Christians venerate the Old Testament as true Word of God. The Church has always vigorously opposed the idea of rejecting the Old Testament under the pretext that the New has rendered it void (Marcionism)." *CCC* §123; also see §121–22, *Dei Verbum*, 14–16.

11. "It has become the vogue in many mainline churches to refer to the Old Testament as the 'Hebrew Scriptures.' One's intentions in doing so are generally of the best, for they arise out of a wish to honor the primacy of the Jews in God's plan of salvation. However, as a number of Old Testament specialists have recently pointed out, the Old Testament is not the same thing as the Hebrew Scriptures; the books are arranged in a different order and give a quite different impression for that reason. It is verging on presumption for Christians to appropriate the Tanakh (Hebrew Bible) by calling the Old Testament the Hebrew Scriptures, even with the best of intentions. It might be more respectful to acknowledge the differences and allow for the distinction. The real challenge for the church is not terminology. It is recovering—in preaching, teaching, and worship—the place of honor that the Old Testament should have. If it is not intentionally and consistently preached and taught, the current practice of reading selections from it in worship along with two New Testament readings will not take us very far." Rutledge, *Crucifixion*, 214n1.

The importance of what Christians know as the Old Testament can hardly be overstated. The Hebrew Scriptures were mined by the apostolic authors as they proclaimed the gospel of the cross and resurrection. The Old Testament is not just a source of further information for the New Testament, or an interesting sideshow attached to it, or even the indispensable prelude to it. The New Testament *will not work* without the Old Testament. Jesus of Nazareth knew no other Scriptures than the Law and the Prophets. The apostles knew no other Scriptures. The New Testament is inconceivable without the First Testament. It was not simply a history book. It was the living lode from which to discover the meaning of what the God of Israel had done among them.[12]

As but one example of Rutledge's fine reasoning, consider the Jerusalem Temple. Unless one comprehends the meaning of the Temple in the Old Testament, then St. John's declaration that "Jesus was speaking of the temple of his body" simply won't make much sense.[13] Jesus came to fulfill the Scriptures and declared, "If you don't believe Moses's words, how will you believe mine?"[14]

This book puts the reader in contact with "Moses's words," in order *to embrace Jesus's words—and deeds more fully.* A number of Old Testament scenes—five in all—will be broken open through what are known as the "Four Senses" of meaning in Scripture. These are subdivided into the *literal* sense and the *spiritual* sense. The latter is further subdivided into three specific types of spiritual senses: the *allegorical*, the *tropological*, and the *anagogical*. Each of the Four Senses represents a distinct approach to extract meaning from a given biblical text.[15] The approach in this book is more inclusive than those that rely strictly upon modern critical methods. To apprehend meaning from Scripture in this study, I draw from an array of sources: ancient, medieval, and modern. This polyvalent approach may challenge some readers' expectations as to what the Bible means. Drawing on methods from antiquity, I map the meaning of Scripture in ways that are uncharted for some readers. But are these methods credible today?

12. Rutledge, *Crucifixion*, 214–25; emphasis original.

13. See Jn 2:21.

14. Jn 6:47.

15. Some readers may be familiar with the idea of the Four Senses of Scripture, or have at least heard that there is both a literal and spiritual dimension of biblical interpretation. Others may be less familiar with this concept. Regardless, all readers will receive an explanation of these terms, how they work, and so on. Those who read *The Word of the Lord* may recall that the Four Senses were discussed, albeit succinctly. By way of contrast, in this book, they play an immensely vital role.

In a thought-provoking essay, Brian Daley asks whether "patristic exegesis" is still usable and relevant today. In his strong affirmation of such approaches, Daley in no way negates modern biblical criticism. He writes, "Historical criticism will obviously continue to play *an indispensable role* in any sophisticated modern interpretation of biblical texts."[16] Daley adds, "That role, first of all, must be to free readers from *the same destructive literalism* that Origen recognized as the basis for most false interpretation of the Bible—taking the apparent face value so seriously, so much in isolation from the rest of the canon, that we invest it with a meaning at odds with both its probable original sense and its traditional Christian application."[17] Daley believes that "having a historically sophisticated sense of where a text comes from" allows readers to better appreciate "*the distance the text has traveled* to be God's word for us" today.[18] Finally, he stresses that, "As Christians, we need to rediscover the implicit sense of the mutual dependence between theology and biblical interpretation, of the fluid and often imperceptible border between them, that characterized the patristic era."[19]

In full agreement with Daley's analysis, let us move on to the topic of the "encounter" scenes that lay ahead. First, the five episodes are dissimilar from one another. Each was selected from a particular book of the Old Testament: Genesis, Exodus, Isaiah, Song of Songs, and Job. Second, and related, the scenes are drawn from all three parts of the Old Testament—Law, Prophets, and Writings. Third, the episodes represent distinct literary forms (genres). Consequently, they need to be approached on their own objective terms. Fourth and importantly, these texts share one key criterion: each is a sort of "theophany,"[20] they are *theophanic* in nature. In each, a person longs to see God, draws near to him, and in some sense the prayer is answered.

Theophanies are among the most stirring texts within the Old Testament. They involve an episode where the veil is lifted between God and man, if just a bit. And we have the privilege of peering over the shoulder

16. Brian E. Daley, "Is Patristic Exegesis Still Usable?," in Ellen and Hays, *Art of Reading Scripture*, 86; emphasis added.

17. Daley, "Is Patristic Exegesis Still Usable?," 86–87; emphasis added.

18. Daley, "Is Patristic Exegesis Still Usable?," 87; emphasis added.

19. Daley, "Is Patristic Exegesis Still Usable?," 87.

20. Later, additional remarks will be made about theophanies, including a definition of the term and descriptions of the kind found in the Old Testament.

of a biblical giant—no, not the *Nephilim* of the early biblical world,[21] but the *other sort* of giants in Scripture: towering figures like Jacob and Moses. Such figures loom over the rest because they were permitted a kind of "proximity" to the Lord. For some reason, they were allowed a rare, "close encounter" with Almighty God.

By nature, theophanies are mysterious and paradoxical.[22] The problem? *They might be giants, but they are still not holy enough to gaze upon the face of God.* In every biblical theophany, a sort of wall in placed between the Lord and those seeking his face. Recall that in the Day of Atonement liturgy, even the (presumably) holiest man in Israel—the High Priest—had to shield his face from accidentally "seeing God" in the Holy of Holies.[23]

Elsewhere, even God's holy angels could not look upon his face. Recall the Temple vision described by the prophet Isaiah, early in the book attributed to him: "Above him stood the seraphim; each had six wings: with two he covered his face, and with two he covered his feet, and with two he flew."[24] Borrowing a line from the Great Apostle in Romans, we

21. Gn 6:1–4: "When men began to multiply on the face of the ground, and daughters were born to them, the sons of God saw that the daughters of men were fair; and they took to wife such of them as they chose. Then the Lord said, 'My spirit shall not abide in man forever, for he is flesh, but his days shall be a hundred and twenty years.' The *Nephilim* [Hebrew for "giants, rebels"] were on the earth in those days, and also afterward, when the sons of God came in to the daughters of men, and they bore children to them. These were the mighty men that were of old, the men of renown." About this enigmatic text, John Walton writes, "Genesis 6:1–4 has long been considered one of the most controversial and difficult passages of the OT. This difficulty is due to four problems. First, the brevity of the pericope with its lack of much explanatory detail leaves large interpretive holes that must be filled in by the interpreter. Whether one describes the narrative as laconic, terse, elliptical or fragmented, the point remains that the character of the text undermines the confidence with which it can be deciphered. Second, the connections of the passage to the surrounding context have been seriously questioned. Does the account relate to what is positioned before it or after it? Or is it independent of both? Additionally, does it relate yet another narrative of offense committed by transgressing boundaries, or is it simply setting up a situation with no offense described? Third, what mythical connections have been retained or expunged? What level of interaction between supernatural beings and humans can the text absorb or tolerate? Finally, there are numerous lexical problems in the short passage." "Sons of God, Daughters of Man," in Alexander and Baker, *Dictionary of the Old Testament*, 793–94.

22. One recent work on theophanies and their interpretation is Bogdan Gabriel Bucur's *Scripture Re-envisioned*, an important book that informs this study.

23. See Lv 16, 23:26–32; Num 29:7–11. Also, see Smith, *House of the Lord*, chap. 6; Milgrom, *Leviticus 1–16*.

24. See Isa 6:1–5. The reference to the seraphim covering their faces is clear enough and requires no further explanation. With regard to their covering their faces, it is plausible that it actually refers to their genitalia: "Another pair covers their feet. The precise meaning

can say that "all have sinned and fallen short of the ability to see the face of the Lord."[25] As the Lord abruptly warned perhaps the most gigantic of them all, the great Lawgiver, Moses: "*No one shall see God and live.*"[26]

And yet it is not as though these theophany scenes disappoint or fail to deliver the goods. True, there is no unabated gazing upon "the face of the Lord" in any of them. Even so, one cannot come away from such episodes without concluding *that something happened, that some sort of seeing of God* appears to have taken place. So, describing exactly what happened in these scenes is complex. Did they actually see the Lord? What did they see? What can we learn from their close encounter? These are the right questions to have, to ask. Unquestionably, these giants went further than all others; they were given a "higher access" to God than all the rest of humanity.

In sum, the careful reader is left with a strong impression that these figures "saw God" in such theophanies. And yet each scene intelligently and quickly pulls the rug out from under the reader's feet, lest one come away with an overly simplistic conclusion about what actually took place. As Jordan Peterson might say, "*Gotcha.*"[27]

As we examine the data in each biblical encounter scene, it will be of paramount importance to discover how God reveals (or does not reveal) himself, to whom, and any accompanying explanation. Like Jacob, we must learn how to "wrestle" with such questions in the Scriptures and "not let go" until we are blessed with insight about seeking the face of God.[28]

Readers will be challenged to assess for themselves what is to be

---

of this action is not clear. The Targum has 'body' for 'feet' and says the body was covered so that it might not be seen. 'Feet' is sometimes used in ancient Near Eastern literature as a euphemism for genitalia, and it is possible that such a meaning is intended here (cf. also Ruth 3:4, 7, 8). In any case, the sense is the same, with the part standing for the whole body." Oswalt, *Book of Isaiah*, 178–79.

25. See Rom 3:23, where Paul describes humanity as having fallen short of the *doxa*—the "glory" of God.

26. Ex 33:20; emphasis added.

27. "Jordan Peterson Debate on the Gender Pay Gap, Campus Protests and Postmodernism," YouTube video, 29:55, posted by Channel 4 News, January 16, 2018, https://www.youtube.com/watch?time_continue=8&v=aMcjxSThD54. This interview between Channel 4 news anchor Cathy Newman and Jordan B. Peterson has been viewed millions of times. Jordan Peterson has experienced a meteoric rise—from relative obscurity to nearly a household name—in just several years' time. Later in the book, more will be said about Peterson as it relates to our topic.

28. See Gn 32:26.

gleaned from these biblical episodes. What change, if any, does the divine encounter bring about for the recipient(s)? How does it affect the person's behavior, his relationships? With good fortune, the reader's own "name" may even be changed in the process, to *one who struggles with biblical texts and prevails*, or perhaps *one who has come closer to the face of the Lord.*[29]

2. *Meditatio*. We discussed the notion of "biblical contemplation" and the important role it plays in this book. Let us turn to a second new feature: *Meditatio*. A number of "meditations" are interspersed at strategic points, six in all. They are concise, compared with the exegetically thick material they follow.[30] Each meditation is an opportunity to breathe, intellectually speaking. Their purpose is to slow one's pace, and for just a few moments enter into the Scriptures in a more reflective manner. Through them, the reader is encouraged to intuit what response is called for. *Does the text console, confound? What aspirations does it raise?* And so on.

It is hoped that each brief meditation is a chance for the reader to pause and, aided by the Spirit,[31] to sort out one's own personal search for the face of the Lord. As Robert Cardinal Sarah wrote, "Like a living presence, the Word does not let go of us, and we do not let go of it, either.... Through it, he who seeks my soul is there. He meets me, and I meet him. He reveals himself to me, and *he reveals me to myself.* Then prayer can be lost in silence; not the silence of the absence of the other or of myself... but the silence that comes above and beyond the Word when it has affected us."[32]

With these two particular features, this book plunges the reader into deeper and more contemplative waters than previous volumes. And as anyone whose attempted to scuba dive in the ocean or launch a sailboat upon it will tell you, it's a serious business. Think of swimming in the ocean. At first, quiet waters dance about one's toes, and every footstep in the sand below the shallow waters is visible. Quickly, though, one's

29. See Gn 32:28: "Then he said, 'Your name shall no more be called Jacob, but Israel, for you have striven with God and with men and have prevailed (*tûkāl*).'"

30. E.g., following the chapter on Jacob is a meditation on the episode. After the chapter on Moses is a meditation on the scene, and so on.

31. As with the other chapters in the book, each *Meditatio* is annotated with Scripture texts and bibliographic sources. If these are a distraction, set them aside and let the meditation guide you toward the face of Christ.

32. Sarah, *Power of Silence*, 241; emphasis added.

body is surrounded by darker and deeper waters, and simply standing amid the tide becomes a daunting challenge. With a few more steps into its depths, one cannot see or even touch the sandy bottom that once danced between the toes so innocently. As one first steps in the water, there is a feeling of control; once in the deeper waters, this illusion washes away. Much more so with actual *diving*. Yes, one may summon forth experience and human strength. But these skills cannot dominate the immense ocean. They can only assist the diver to cooperate with it, respond to it, and make their way within it.

Though more mechanics and greater skills are involved, a similar phenomenon holds true for the sailor. Recall the intense fury of Poseidon in Homer's great works. It was this Greek god of the sea, not the fittest nor most experienced sailor, who determined whereabouts he traveled. The sea, with all of its magnificent beauty, beckons man's curiosity to chart a course and set sail. Yet the ablest sailor must come to grips with its power over him and his vessel. He must renounce any capricious or egotistical nonsense about mastering the sea. Man sets out not as the sea's master but as its curious and attentive pupil, confidant that it always has something to teach him, as the classic novel *Moby Dick* attests: "Why did the old Persians hold the sea holy? Why did the Greeks give it a separate deity, and own brother Jove? Surely all this is not without meaning. And still deeper the meaning of that story of Narcissus who, because he could not grasp the tormenting mild image he saw in the fountain, plunged into it, and was drowned. But that same image, we ourselves see in all rivers and oceans. *It is the image of the ungraspable phantom of life*; and this is the key to it all."[33]

Moving from fiction to divine revelation, the deuterocanonical Wisdom of Solomon (14:1–4) describes something similar:

> Again, one preparing to sail and about to voyage over raging waves
> calls upon a piece of wood more fragile than the ship which carries him.
> For it was desire for gain that planned that vessel,
> and wisdom was the craftsman who built it;
> but it is thy providence, O Father, that steers its course,
> because thou hast given it a path in the sea,
> and a safe way through the waves,
> showing that thou canst save from every danger,
> so that even if a man lacks skill, he may put to sea.

33. Melville, *Moby Dick*, chap. 1.

Unlike Melville's novel, this inspired biblical text is not prescribing nautical advice. What it poetically describes is the way to chart one's course in the great mystery, of knowing and doing God's will.

Being Broken Open by the Word

Our primary objective is not, as is sometimes overheard today, to "master" the Scriptures. It is to be mastered by them. In *The Word of the Lord*, we spoke of "breaking open" the Word. In fact, it is really the other way around. True biblical contemplation does not merely entail breaking open the Scriptures. It requires *a willingness to be broken by them*, allowing them to shape and transform us.[34] Like the humble sailor, the reader must confidently rest in the power of the Spirit-inspired Scriptures. Only then can one begin to see the One gazing at him. A text from the Psalter beautifully conveys this phenomenon. The psalmist writes, "By the Word of the Lord the heavens were made, and all their host by the breath of His mouth. He gathered the waters of the sea as in a bottle; He put the deeps in storehouses. Let all the earth fear the Lord, let all the inhabitants of the world *stand in awe* of Him! For He spoke, and it came to be; He commanded, and it stood forth."[35]

The Revised Standard Version translates the Hebrew verb *gūrū* in verse 8 as "stand in awe." The New American Bible has something equivalent, "show him reverence."[36] These are good. Yet no English translation approaches the sheer trepidation that is evoked by *gūrū* in Psalm 33. Its lexical form is precisely rendered as "to be afraid or in dread." The psalm conveys the idea of our frail humanity in holy dread before the immortal Creator and Lord of heaven and earth. If we wish to gaze upon the face of the Lord in Scripture or otherwise, it is best to know the *dread* that truly awaits us. Encountering God is a profound, transformative event. One that involves life and death. As God himself told Moses, *non poteris videre faciem meam; non enim videbit me homo et vivet* "you cannot see

34. Smith, *Word of the Lord*, 204. According to Paul Claudel, "It would be more exact to acknowledge that it is Scripture which is questioning us, and which finds for each of us, through all time and all generations, the appropriate question." De Lubac, *Sources of Revelation*, 73.

35. Ps 33:6–9.

36. Regrettably, the New International Version Reader's Edition is considerably more diluted: "Let all of the people in the world *honor him*."

my face; for man shall not see me and live."[37] This is about as definitive a declaration one will find on the matter. And yet the biblical figures do look. And we look with them, hoping to see what they see. Somehow, something mysterious and paradoxical does happen.

We can hear it in Jacob, who with full-throated confidence dares to say, "I have seen God face-to-face (*pānîm 'el*), and yet my life is preserved."[38] Every ancient Jewish reader worth his salt knew that Jacob's statement is fraught with impossibility, and yet there it is in the Scripture. And it is not as though this scene is wedged in a nook or cranny that few people pay attention to in the Bible, say, in Obadiah or some such place.[39] The point is simply that that is not where the biblical saying is located, that is, in a relatively obscure book. It is front and center in the Torah, in a pivotal scene in the life of the great patriarch. Did Jacob "see God face-to-face?" If so, why him. And why not Moses? If not, how can he—*how can anyone*—get away with such a thing? Such questions will be addressed in time.

But death? Those who look upon God, or attempt to, will die? Isn't hoping to see God a virtuous thing, borne of a good desire? Perhaps the point is not to get too caught up in the declaration too literally. Nor should one be, let's say, filled with a mortal terror that disables. That is not the point either. The point is to be alert: *the God of the universe is near, and he just may invite us to gaze at him.* The point is expressed well by the ancient Israelite psalmist: "*Let all of the people in the world honor him*" (emphasis added). To kneel in holy reverence before our Lord and to begin our search with humility as well as with joy. Filled with confidence and with the Easter joy of the Apostle John, we long to cry out *It is the Lord!* as we draw near to Jesus.[40] Upon hearing this Good News, Peter "sprang into the sea"—and we with him as we launch out on our journey.

Like the sea, the Scriptures are a great mystery before us. We must decide to "put out into the deep" with Christ.[41] But unlike the sea, the Scriptures have the supernatural capacity to carry us toward God him-

37. Ex 33:20.

38. Gn 32:30.

39. I revere the book of Obadiah, but it is not, in truth, a book most read today. In biblical times, it was considered inspired and revered as the Word of God—which it is.

40. See Jn 21:7.

41. Lk 5:4.

self, to the face of the Lord. Realizing this, how should one prepare for the journey? *The Face of the Lord* should be engaged in a spiritual and not merely an academic way. Although "the how" is left to the freedom of the reader, this may be facilitated by reading at a slightly slower than usual pace, along with attentive prayer.[42]

Finally, because the *Meditationes* are interspersed at strategic points in the book, they offer a lighthouse effect, helping the reader synthesize and make sense of the whole. As noted, they offer the reader periodic "breathers" to integrate a multitude of biblical insights and to turn one's gaze from the written Word to the Living Word in a reflective way.

As to the overall aims of this book, two further points are helpful.

3. *Doctrinal, not devotional. The Face of the Lord* is rigorously exegetical and analytical. At the same time, it allows for and in fact invites deliberate contemplation, as discussed above. In this sense, it aims for the sweet spot of both/and: intellectual engagement and spiritual engagement. Despite this contemplative element of the book, it should in no way be seen as a sort of "beefed-up devotional." While we would be encouraged to learn that this book aided the prayer of certain readers, it should not be confused with a devotional. Rather, *The Face of the Lord* is an exercise in biblical contemplation.

To be fair, regular devotional reading is to be praised. It is vital in the life of the growing Christian, a most worthy habit. There certainly are an array of options to select from today. And the reader is advised to exercise prudence in choosing wisely. Those looking for such might do well to begin with the classics, such as St. Francis de Sales's *Introduction to the Devout Life,* which are readily available today. Among more modern works, one thinks almost immediately of St. Thérèse of Lisieux's *The Story of a Soul*[43] or, more recently, Pope Benedict XVI's *Jesus of Nazareth* series[44] and Robert Cardinal Sarah's *The Power of Silence*.[45] All of the above are truly exceptional for spiritual devotional reading. There are others, too, that are rich and edifying.

42. Additionally, numerous scriptural texts are cited in every chapter of this book. For that reason, it is highly recommended to have a Bible at the ready when reading the book.

43. St. Thérèse of Lisieux, *Story of a Soul.*

44. Joseph Ratzinger (Pope Benedict XVI), *Jesus of Nazareth*; *Jesus of Nazareth, Part Two*; *Jesus of Nazareth: The Infancy Narratives*

45. St. Francis De Sales, *Introduction to the Devout*; St. Augustine, *Confessions*; Sarah, *Power of Silence.* Other translations of *Confessions* include: Chadwick, *Saint Augustine*; Boulding, *Confessions.*

In truth, however, far too many only end up muddying the waters between Christian devotional and self-help books. (The latter have been euphemistically rebranded as "personal development," much like used cars being euphemistically referred to as preowned.) And rather than fixing the mind and heart on the eternal—on the Blessed Trinity and Christ crucified—self-help books entice the reader with tired clichés. Such Osteen-esque pseudo-spirituality is not much more than "feel good" pop psychology. Avoid such material and stick with the classics; there is a reason St. Augustine's *Confessions* is a perennial favorite among the spiritually hungry.

What is remarkable about these works of St. Thérèse, Pope Benedict, and Cardinal Sarah is that they did not start out as devotionals. They are not merely esteemed authors; they are *disciples* who know Christ personally. This shows through on every page of their work. They had something to say about Christ because *Christ had something to say to them*. Such is our aim.[46]

The present book is a work of exegesis. The reader will have to roll up the sleeves to get the most out of it. If it aids in true biblical contemplation, all the better. This book focuses keenly on the Scriptures, desiring to traverse their wondrous depth, and invites the reader to gaze upon the face of the Lord Jesus, primarily in the Old Testament. It is possible to read it purely within an intellectual framework. Spiritually motivated readers are encouraged to allow it to penetrate the heart as well, however.

In sum, *The Face of the Lord* engages the reader in rigorous exegesis and analysis of texts, requiring concentrated effort. Even so, it is hoped that this book assists the reader's spiritual growth by being more doctrinal than devotional. How is this possible? Academic books are supposed to teach us something new, to instill knowledge—not open our souls—*aren't they*? Yes.

C. S. Lewis offers a more nuanced and helpful answer. In his marvelous preface to St. Athanasius's *De Incarnatione* (*On the Incarnation*), Lewis described the paradox: "For my own part, I tend to find the doctrinal books often more helpful in devotion than the devotional books, and I rather suspect the same experience may await others. I believe that many who find that nothing happens when they sit down, or kneel

46. I do not dare place the present book in such great ranks but speak with reverence and in aspirational terms.

down, to a book of devotion, would find that the heart sings unbidden while they are working through a tough bit of theology with a pipe in their teeth and a pencil in their hand."[47] Lewis's words are salient. His descriptions of the mystery and the paradox are apt. This is precisely the experience of biblical contemplation that *The Face of the Lord* offers the reader. Pipe tobacco optional; pencils mandatory.

4. *An ancient, well-worn path*. Finally, this book does not claim to present "the right way" to best seek the face of the Lord in Scripture, as if there is merely one. Rather, there is a personal quality to this endeavor. Much like Ratzinger's trilogy of *Jesus* books, the present book is borne of our own struggle with Scripture and of our "*personal search for the face of the Lord*."[48]

Final edits of this book were completed on the north Pacific Ocean, just off the coast of Alaska. This is the sort of place where the veil between the spectacular beauty of God's majestic creation and the face of the Lord is astonishingly thin. Seeing a humpback whale breach the surface of the icy waters for the first time is *unforgettable*. It is yet another echo of the goodness and beauty of God manifest in nature. A breaching whale is truly a sight to behold. It remains etched in the memory long after the moment of wonder passes.

Still more of the final work was done at the famed Storyville Coffee in Seattle. No Orcas were spotted. Yet, as a self-described espresso snob, I experienced an exhilarating, nearly transcendent rush in sipping what is arguably one of the best mugs of coffee around.

The list is nearly endless: a summer wedding, a newborn baby, a multigenerational family reunion, serving the poor and sharing a meal with them, the sun rising over the Rockies, Wagner's *Der Ring des Nibelungen*, Michelangelo's notebooks, a Dostoevsky novel, hiking in a rainforest. How could one omit the architecture of the still-unfinished Sagrada Familia of Barcelona? *Schindler's List*? These and many other human experiences truly stir the soul in profound ways. Every reader likely has a list of wonders—of memories or future aspirations of seeing and encountering *the true, the good, the beautiful*. Yet for all the marvel involved in such experiences, they are surpassed, infinitely so, by seeing the face of the Lord in Scripture.

47. C. S. Lewis, "Preface," 11.

48. Ratzinger, *Jesus of Nazareth*, 1:xxiii; emphasis added.

This is because Scripture is not merely one more "God moment" among so many others. True, all of these are inspiring encounters. But the Bible alone is *inspired.* As St. Paul tells us, "all of Scripture is *theopneustos*—God-breathed."[49] There is no competition to be had here. It is not a matter of Scripture "topping" such moments in some sort of emotive way. The breaching whale or Appalachian mission trip may evince more tears or feelings of joy, than, say, reading the Gospel According to Luke. Even so, reading the memoirs of the Apostles ought not be "one more thing" on one's spiritual to-do list.

Scripture involves an ongoing dialogue with God, not unlike the continuing conversation between a husband and wife who've been married for decades. Yet it is *even more than a dialogue.* It is a *gazing,* often in stillness, in silence, at the countenance of the Creator. We are invited—summoned, really—to gaze at God. *We see and are met in the act of seeing. There we are seen, there we are united to God, there we are known.* God can be met in all of the above ways, and countless others.[50] Even so, in an utterly unique way, *the God of heaven and earth speaks to us and invites us to speak with him in Scripture*:

> The word of God draws each of us into a conversation with the Lord: *the God who speaks teaches us how to speak to him.* Here we naturally think of the Book of Psalms, where God speaks forth his word—words with which we speak to him. As we utter the words of a psalm, we are drawn to God by his own voice.
>
> In the Psalms we find expressed every possible human feeling set masterfully in the sight of God; joy and pain, distress and hope, fear and trepidation: here all find expression. Along with the Psalms we think too of the many other passages of sacred Scripture which express our turning to God in intercessory prayer, in exultant songs of victory or in sorrow at the difficulties experienced in carrying out our mission. *In this way our word to God becomes God's word, thus confirming the dialogical nature of all Christian revelation, and our whole existence becomes a dialogue with the God who speaks and listens, who calls us and gives direction to our lives.* Here the word of God reveals that our entire life is under the divine call.[51]

49. See 2 Tm 3:16.

50. "While the Christ event is at the heart of divine revelation, we also need to realize that creation itself, the *liber naturae*, is an essential part of this symphony of many voices in which the one word is spoken." Pope Benedict XVI, *Verbum Domini*, 7.

51. *Verbum Domini*, 24; emphasis added.

To read Luke—or for that matter Joshua, Job, Jonah, or Jude—is to peer over the shoulder of the prophets and Apostles upon the divine Son himself. Doing so knits together all of our life experiences. Every moment of time—jubilant delight and excruciating pain, boredom and doubt, temptation and holiness, are all laid to rest at the feet of the Savior. Every search for meaning *leads here*; forgiving our sin, restoring our purpose, leading us home.

We believe that encountering the divine Son in Scripture is a privileged meeting. Every moment that we turn to the *Sacra Pagina*, the *Sacred Page* opens up the opportunity to become more of who we are, more of who we were created to be: to sit at his feet, to "rest upon the heart of Christ."[52] And although we cannot see Jesus of Nazareth in the flesh, we really do gaze upon him in Scripture. Every open Bible is potentially a theophanic experience for the expectant reader.

Still, the reader should understand that this book does not promise novelty or innovation. To the contrary, the approach taken here is quite ancient. Apart from the *Meditationes*, our tack draws profusely upon the masters of centuries past. More specifically, *The Face of the Lord* is an invitation to receive the mystery that is the Word of God according to the ancient and medieval pattern of reading according to the Four Senses. It is specifically through the lens of the Four Senses—the *literal*, *allegorical*, *tropological*, and *anagogical*—that we approach the mysteries and paradoxes involved in the theophanic episodes in the book. The Four Senses provide *the fuller calculus*, and are the matrix through which all biblical texts will be carefully consider read. Reading the Bible through the Four Senses takes us to the thesis of the book: the *Four Senses of Sacred Scripture represent a pathway and a progression toward the face of the Lord.* What does this mean, that the Four Senses are a "pathway and progression" to the face of God?

To begin with, ample evidence from the primitive Church through the twelfth to thirteenth centuries indicates that the literal and spiritual senses were not viewed as diametrically opposed ends. In this larger period, stretching past the first millennium of Christianity, it was broadly understood that the search for the deeper meaning of the Scriptures was

52. I am grateful to Dcn. James Keating for this phrase. See his *Resting upon the Heart of Christ.*

only revealed by engaging both the literal and the spiritual senses.[53] Yet our thesis demands something more.

In 2015, historian Andrew Willard Jones gave a series of lectures at Franciscan University of Steubenville. These lectures focused on what he called the "Liturgical Cosmos," the worldview of the High Middle Ages, specifically at the time of the Fourth Lateran Council (1215). Jones laid out a vision of reality that was based on the Four Senses of the Scripture. He showed how, through these senses, the Medievals brought together revelation, history, their social and political lives, and their pursuit of spiritual perfection into one dynamic whole. The Four Senses of Scripture allowed the Medievals to apply Scripture not only to different aspects of their historical lives, but also to different levels of spiritual ascent.[54] Working from Jones's insights, in the current book, I will show how, specifically, the Four Senses are not be merely various approaches to read the Scriptures, nor are they utterly different paths, to be kept apart from one another. Rather, they may be engaged in relation to one another. And when one successively reads Scripture "through" the totality of the Four Senses, something happens. When one considers them in a sequential fashion—from the literal clear through to the anagogical—there is a dynamism, a rolling tide that carries one closer to the face of

53. There was considerable diversity as to how the Four Senses were engaged in the ancient and medieval Church. Biblical exegesis was not uniform in this period; even a cursory examination reveals otherwise. This is to be expected, and I readily concede this point. Some assume that Origen *only dealt with the allegorical sense* and no others. This is not the case. In fact, he implemented *all Four Senses* on various occasions. I provide textual data showing that Origen clearly distinguished between the allegorical and the anagogical senses. Though he often operated within an allegorical framework, Origen fully recognized the distinctions between the two senses and did not conflate them. Ancient and medieval commentators did not apply the Four Senses in a "slavish" manner in their work. Across the first millennium, the Four Senses were, broadly speaking, appropriated in a fluid and multifarious way.

54. Andrew Willard Jones's lectures can be found online: "The Liturgical Cosmos: The Worldview of the High Middle Ages (Part 1 of 3)," YouTube video, 1:01:37, posted by Franciscan University of Steubenville, January 15, 2016, https://www.youtube.com/watch?v=GpdD6a-TYss; "The Liturgical Cosmos: The Worldview of the High Middle Ages (Part 2 of 3)," YouTube video, 1:01:29, posted by Franciscan University of Steubenville, January 15, 2016, https://www.youtube.com/watch?v=wdy6PjqTgyc&t=3s; "The Liturgical Cosmos: The Worldview of the High Middle Ages (Part 3 of 3), YouTube video, 1:06:43, posted by Franciscan University of Steubenville, January 15, 2016, https://www.youtube.com/watch?v=XA1C7U8TdbM. He is currently in the process of revising them into a book length treatment. I am indebted to Jones's insights throughout the current work, as he provided me with a pad from which to launch my own research.

God. As Jones has demonstrated was the general understanding in the twelfth and thirteenth centuries, my thesis is that the Four Senses are meant to be experienced in an integrative way, so that the contemplative reader is lifted higher and higher, to the face of the Lord.

The above proposal—that together the Four Senses are a "pathway and progression," an exegetical ascension to God's presence—is the raison d'être of the entire book. This is the essential takeaway for the reader. It is the crux of this project, with an aim toward affecting the way that the Bible is read, studied, and prayed by many for years to come.

Dei Verbum: An Integrative Approach

Over the course of this book, the reader will gaze at God through a plethora of biblical episodes. In the company of the great Fathers, Doctors, and Mystics of (roughly) the first millennium of Christianity, the reader will consider each theophany, make the journey. This is not to say that historical-critical approaches are shunned. Hardly. To the contrary, modern critical methods are engaged seriously and thoroughly in the examination of each of the five encounter scenes. Nevertheless, such methodologies are accompanied by theological and contemplative approaches. By bringing them together, we engage in a more integrative and inclusive analysis of scriptural texts, with respect to history and theology.

From this perspective, there is no danger in introducing historical-critical approaches into our study. Likewise, investigating biblical texts with the apparatus of the spiritual sense poses no harm to the project at hand. Both are of benefit, both are needed. Every distinct method of biblical inquiry, *sui generis*, is subject to deficiencies, limitations, errors. But to exclude a method out of hand reflects an unwarranted bias and a predetermined conclusion that it has nothing to offer. All approaches, however legitimate they may be, are subject to misuse in the hands of the interpreter. The value of a given method can be exaggerated as "the way to do it," to the exclusion of all others. I would certainly advise against such prejudices, exegetically speaking. And I would caution against a shortsightedness that praises one method while excluding another, out of hand. This holds true both ways, that is, whether one is praising strictly historical or strictly spiritual methods over the other.

Most historical-critical approaches to Scripture essentially set aside all spiritual (and even theological) dimensions of the text. At times, for example, in an academic journal, such a narrowly critical approach may be called for or even required. Nevertheless, by and large the anti-supernatural basis upon which much biblical exegesis has been exercised over the past several hundred years has severely torn the spiritual sense away from the Scriptures. So much is this the case that in reading certain commentaries of this sort, one wonders if there is *anything spiritual* to be said about the Institution of the Eucharist in the Upper Room, about Jesus's dialogue with Pilate, or even the Resurrection of Jesus.

Some believers, however, out of frustration and dissatisfaction with this sort of biblical criticism, fail in the opposite direction. They leap over the literal sense in hopes of quickly extracting the spiritual riches from a text. Again, in liturgical and devotional contexts, such as *Lectio divina*, this too may well be entirely appropriate. Yet serious study of the Bible *requires* historical inquiry. It demands it. One cannot omit the literal in the hopes of arriving at a sound spiritual insight by extraction. To do so would involve mere luck—and make the reader culpable of *eisegesis*, that is, "reading into the text" that which is not present. Throwing the baby out with the bathwater is a grievous mistake, whether from one side of the basin or the other.

There is—and must be—a place for biblical exegesis and theological contemplation to coexist. Not all Scriptural studies can or should necessarily attempt to integrate them. Obviously, there are profound biblical deficiencies in our day—including such disintegration of biblical interpretation. It is not the objective of this book to correct what may be deemed as "deficient hermeneutics" of one kind or another. We would much rather focus on the Scriptures, breaking them open with humility, curiosity, and great care. As this project unfolds, its *integrative* approach is a strong and positive step in the right direction.[55] *Dei Verbum* got it exactly right in its concise summary of the role of the exegete:

> To search out the intention of the sacred writers, attention should be given, among other things, to "literary forms." For truth is set forth and expressed differently in texts which are variously historical, prophetic, poetic, or of other

55. I have argued elsewhere that *methods* are not enough in the approach of Scripture. More important than one's methodology are the "principles" which they rest upon. For more, see my *Word of the Lord.*

forms of discourse. The interpreter must investigate what meaning the sacred writer intended to express and actually expressed in particular circumstances by using contemporary literary forms in accordance with the situation of his own time and culture. For the correct understanding of what the sacred author wanted to assert, we must learn about the context, and the customary styles of speaking and narrating which prevailed at the time of the sacred writer. We must learn to place ourselves in the text, and become attentive to the thoughts and patterns with which the sacred writers communicated.

But, since Holy Scripture must be read and interpreted in the sacred spirit in which it was written, no less serious attention must be given to the content and unity of the whole of Scripture if the meaning of the sacred texts is to be correctly worked out. The living tradition of the whole Church must be taken into account along with the harmony which exists between elements of the faith. It is the task of exegetes to work according to these rules toward a better understanding and explanation of the meaning of Sacred Scripture, so that through preparatory study the judgment of the Church may mature. For all of what has been said about the way of interpreting Scripture is subject finally to the judgment of the Church, which carries out the divine commission and ministry of guarding and interpreting the word of God.[56]

In the first paragraph of the above quoted text, one hears a definitive endorsement of several types of modern methodological approaches, for example, form and source criticism, and seeking the *intention* of the human authors of a biblical text and all that such entails. Similarly, the subsequent paragraph extols the "living tradition of the whole Church"—of the unity of the Scriptures and, in fact, the wisdom of the Church as final arbiter in the discovery of meaning. These paragraphs are the lodestar by which we will navigate.

Operating within an integrative framework, we draw upon the best practices of literal and spiritual exegesis. In *The Face of the Lord*, we attend to both the *Letter* and *Spirit*. Ultimately, this book serves as an excellent example of, if not a cohesive model for, the interpretation of Sacred Scripture today according to all Four Senses.

Why the *Exordium*?

Having clarified the larger aims of this book, I now invite the reader to join the effort. And make no mistake: there is work involved in learning

56. *Dei Verbum*, 11. I have slightly altered the translation for the sake of readability.

to gaze upon *the face of the Lord* in Scripture. For example, before turning to the theophany scenes, some preliminary effort is necessary, taken up in the first part of the book.

Why is this initial work necessary? Why not just dive right into the Scriptures, as was the case with the previous volume, *The House of the Lord*? There, the reader was immediately plunged into the Book of Genesis and the temple theology within it.[57] This was fitting. It is likewise fitting that this book begin with a slightly different bearing—asking the reader to take in the *Exordium* before moving directly to the biblical encounter scenes. The reason for this initial step is that there is much to learn about the Four Senses before diving in and wielding them in the study of Scripture. In fact, there is more to each of them than one might imagine at the outset. The Four Senses developed over a period of one thousand years and were accessed by the greatest thinkers, philosophers, and theologians in Christian history. It would be premature to employ them without first learning something about their form and function.

This preparatory work, of growing in understanding of the literal and spiritual senses, is the focus of the first part of the book. The *Exordium* is composed of three foundational chapters. Together, they arm the reader with exactly the sort of insight that is needed to engage Scripture according to the Four Senses in a prescient and astute way.

Chapters 1–3 lay out what is involved, scripturally speaking, in seeking the face of God. Additionally, they undergird the methodological approach of the book. In sum, the *Exordium* is absolutely vital to assure that, from the outset, we stride with clarity and confidence toward the Old Testament in the remainder of the book. For these reasons, the reader is encouraged not to skip over or rush through this material.

Chapter 1 is a clarion call for the reader to prepare to seek the face of the Lord in Scripture. It is an invitation to gaze upon Jesus, to "gaze upon him who gazes at the Father." Here, some preliminary questions are raised: *Can we really "see" God? Has anyone really done so? What steps are involved in "seeing" God?* This is a complex topic, and the reader will not receive spoon-fed or simplistic, pat answers. For support, I draw upon the wisdom of one of the most brilliant and trustworthy theologians of the twentieth century, the great Romano Guardini. With Guardini as a guide, I put forth a few scriptural hints, including Jesus's

57. See Smith, *House of the Lord*, chaps. 1–3.

own words from the Parable of the Prodigal Son (Lk 15) and a text from the Gospel According to John (Jn 14). Throughout I contemplate Jesus and, scripturally speaking, *gaze upon him who gazes at the Father.*

Chapters 2 and 3 are especially crucial. They are packed with insights on the Four Senses. Chapter 2, "*De Spiritu et Littera* I," deals with the necessity of the Four Senses. Whereas chapter 1 lays a biblical foundation for "seeking the face of the Lord," chapter 2 introduces the reader to the true depth of the Four Senses. Here, the reader discovers their immense historical and theological value of sound biblical interpretation. Methodologically, this book simply could not proceed without the involvement of the Four Senses. They are the heart of the book, as chapter 2 makes abundantly clear. Without them, it is unlikely that we would be able to extract the rich potential of meaning within each theophany. With the Four Senses, the project can make genuine progress in this respect. With them, we can metaphorically sail toward the horizon on the deep sea of meaning. Without them, we would do well to barely leave the port.

Chapter 3, "*De Spiritu et Littera* II," builds upon the previous chapter and takes the discussion of the Four Senses to a higher level. Those who are only vaguely familiar with the Four Senses may be taken aback at how much is involved with each of them. Here, we learn about the dynamic relationship that exists between the Four Senses and how, together, they lead us toward the face of God.

Turning to chapter 3 and switching metaphors, we climb higher up the mountain of biblical meaning. A key takeaway for the reader will be understanding the Four Senses as the ancient and medieval theologians did: *as a true ascent to the face of God.* We learn about the relationship between the senses and why it is that the spiritual senses can be accessed *only by going through the literal sense.* There are no shortcuts up to the mountain's mystical peak. This places a burden on the literal sense. Objectively speaking, it is *la première priorité.* It cannot be omitted or set aside. As important as the literal sense is, however, the search for meaning does not end with it. It merely begins there. From the literal sense we cross over a great threshold into the spiritual senses. Once there, we truly "enter the mystery" and ascend higher still, closer to the face of God.

This ascent requires a certain maturity and patience. We make considerable contact with the vast, great Tradition of the Church. In addition, we encounter an array of insights from Jewish, Orthodox, and

Protestant/Evangelical Christian scholars. *Faith* and *sound reasoning* are necessary to sort through these sources and traditions. We must act responsibly with these texts and traditions, respecting their contributions while being mindful of their limitations.

Given all of this, is learning about the Four Senses worth the trouble? This is a question the reader will answer over the course of the book. At present, we respectfully yet unabashedly place own our cards on the table face-up. Unequivocally, yes. It is worth it. How could it not be worth it? The reader will contemplate the face of Christ in communion with Origen, St. Augustine, St. Gregory the Great, St. Ephrem, Hugh of St. Victor, St. Bernard of Clairvaux, St. Thomas, and a host of other trustworthy ancient and medieval guides. This is not to suggest that this or that figure has "the answer." We will have to learn how to evaluate individual interpretations wisely and fairly. Collectively, they open up entirely new worlds of meaning, beyond what one believed a biblical text was about. From these dynamic encounters the reader comes to appreciate how, together, the Four Senses really do represent *a pathway and a progression toward the face of God.*

Perhaps it is becoming clear that ascending the mountain of biblical meaning involves risk. Mistakes are increasingly costly up in the thin atmosphere. Take heart: the diligent climber will "receive blessings" for the effort:

> *Who shall ascend the hill of the Lord*?
> And who shall stand in his holy place?
> He who has clean hands and a pure heart,
> who does not lift up his soul to what is false,
> and does not swear deceitfully.
> He will receive blessing from the Lord,
> and vindication from the God of his salvation.
> Such is the generation of those who seek him,
> who seek the face of the God of Jacob.[58]

"How Medieval Are You?"

Such a question almost sounds like an insult, fired off at a pesky Neanderthal at the local watering hole. It is in fact an intelligent question, es-

58. Ps 24:3–6; emphasis added.

pecially when approaching Scripture in a meaningful way. Developing a "medieval mind-set" is crucial. A medieval mind-set is one that respects and appreciates the distinct qualities of each of the Four Senses. Additionally, regarding the spiritual senses, it means not dismissing them prematurely, as precritical sermonizing or outdated, syrupy subjectivity.

Recovering the Four Senses and properly engaging them are vital to everything that follows in the book. This cannot be more stressed. Collectively, the *Letter* and the *Spirit* form a "hermeneutical continuum" in unlocking greater biblical meaning, more abundant biblical meaning. With the ancient and medieval masters of Scripture, we traverse a well-worn path to scriptural illumination. This classical principle, known as *sensus plenior*—of Scripture having a polyvalence of meaning has its roots in ancient Judaism and earliest Christianity—is at the heart of this project.[59] The point cannot be emphasized enough, and without a clear grasp of it, understanding and appreciating the remainder of the book may be seriously jeopardized. To ensure that the reader is clear on this concept—of the *Four Senses as a pathway and a progression toward the face of God*—a number of illustrations are provided along the way. The reader is asked to study them with care, and to refer back to them as needed.

Once the reader has digested the material presented in the three preliminary chapters, the greater voyage of contemplating the divine Son through the Four Senses of Scripture truly begins. *Vetus Testamentum* is the heart of the book, and it invites the reader to truly set sail and grapple with five encounter scenes located within the Old Testament in fresh and unexpected ways.

Collectively, the aim of the *Exordium* is *a threefold preparation*: (1) a

59. "The concept of the *sensus plenior*, the 'fuller sense,' was first proposed by Andrea Fernández in 1925. Fernández' reasons were apologetic: he sought a basis for theological exegesis in light of the rejection of the traditional Four Senses by the Reformation and critical scholarship. Later advocates included Joseph Coppens, Pierre Benoit and Raymond Brown. The *sensus plenior* permitted interpreters to acknowledge the limited knowledge and intention of the human authors of Scripture, and, at the same time, to affirm the deeper meaning of texts, e.g., the fulfillment of the Old Testament in Christ, as a meaning placed in Scripture by its divine author. It also opened the way to the acceptance of other later applications of texts in the Fathers of the Church, the liturgy, and in theological authors. This deeper meaning was not seen as accessible through the historical-critical method, which derives the literal sense, but through consideration of later texts in the progression of revelation and theological reflection." Williamson, *Catholic Principles for Interpreting Scripture* 208. See also Pontifical Biblical Commission, *Interpretation of the Bible*, para. 3.

summons to "seek his face," (2) a strategy session in method, and (3) an immersion into the Four Senses. Together, chapters 4–6 are a pedagogical portal through which the wise reader is asked to pass through, *to gaze with all of one's being*—intellect, heart, and spirit—at the face of the Lord in each encounter that follows.

Receiving the Mystery

Proper methodology is critical. Yet it is not the *entirety* of the matter. Putting forth a sound approach must be joined by the reader's full attention and true participation in seeking the face of the Lord. There can be no half measures when dealing with such a great mystery. And let us not mince words or pussyfoot around: a recovery is needed. A recovery of the biblical notion of mystery must take place if this journey is to be considered successful by any measure, if we are to make legitimate progress in biblical interpretation today. But recovery from what? Oddly, from "too much clarity." To be fair, lucidity, strictly speaking, is not the problem. If the Bible has meaning at all, then it should be and is quite clear in most cases. As modern readers of Scripture, we crave clarity to such a degree that, ironically, once we believe we have discovered *what a text meant*, we stop searching for *what it means*. This is not gibberish nor fancy wordsmithing, though it is our namesake.

Modern approaches have truly helped us to achieve greater precision about the historical contexts in which the Scriptures gradually emerged. And this is good. Yet strict dependence upon such methods can—and have—created a kind of biblical myopia, so that history is all we see: "scholars read ancient Christian texts differently than their ancient Christian authors would have recommended. The discrepancy between the implied readers of much of early Christian literature and the actual readers in academia is especially evident in the case of theophanic texts and their Christian interpretation as Christophanies. The theological, ascetical, and liturgical interpretative context, shared by ancient Christian exegetes with their ideal readers and facilitating the reader's dynamic assimilation of the writer's theological mystagogy, is, to a large extent, lost to us and remains, at best, the object of tentative scholarly reconstruction."[60]

60. See Bucur, *Scripture Re-envisioned*.

Bogdan Bucur's insight about Christian interpretation of Scripture is extraordinarily important. Texts are not merely a string of words in a certain order. There is more than meets the eye in every biblical text. We would do well to make wise use all of the best *modern* as well as *ancient* tools. To master them. Yet once we've discovered what the text *meant*, we need to continue to ask what lies beneath the surface, beyond understanding, technically speaking. For well over the first thousand years of Christianity, the holy Scriptures were not so capriciously or cavalierly dismissed, as is too often the case today, with regard to the other question: *What does it mean?*

Here is a metaphor. For the ancient and medieval masters, once the literal sense was dealt with, that was not the end of the matter. It marked *a fresh new beginning*, the true start of the search for Christ. In a sense, it was for them as if the literal sense was a signpost indicating a deep mine: *You have found its precise literal location. Now, enter in—if you dare.*

And if you enter, you will be plunged into the depths of the earth. You don't know what you will find, or where, or when. You will frequently move in darkness, and it will all be a bit odd. Yet the light of God—the illumination of the Spirit of Christ—will be with you. With humility, time, prayer, and Scripture—new light, divine light—will begin to flicker and glow. And its light will intensify. As you draw nearer, this holy light will expand, radiate, burn. Soon, new vistas will be revealed. Connections between the Old and New Testaments will present themselves, and you won't be able to "unsee" them. *In this deep mine are the mysteries of Christ; first hidden, then glowing bright.* And with Christ, the Church, the sacraments, the moral life, your heavenly home. Now you are truly seeing, and you will not be able to, nor wish to, unsee what holy light from God has made known. This is the journey we will make—in moving from the literal to the spiritual senses. And we will make it no less than five times.

In examining five encounter scenes in Scripture, we will seek with critical precision, along with modern, technical craft, the location of the "mine." All of the resources of historical-critical methods will be at our disposal. Yet once we locate the mine, a new journey begins—a journey toward Lady Wisdom, God's divine wisdom.[61] We will be led to the place that "is hid from the eyes of all living, and concealed from the

61. See Prv 8:22–30; Sir 1:1; 24:8–11; Wis 7:22–8:1.

birds of the air."[62] And where it ultimately leads is known to God alone: "God understands the way to it, and he knows its place."[63]

Today, we have all but lost the medieval notion that the Scriptures have a cryptic meaning. This is a related aim of the book: we can and must rekindle this sense of "the mystery of the Word" that was commonplace throughout the whole of ancient Judaism and early Christianity. Do we still believe that "there is a God in heaven who reveals mysteries?"[64] Do we believe that the mysteries of Christ are hidden in the Old Testament?

That a biblical text could *simultaneously have multiple meanings* was also a given. That the Old Testament was ultimately about Christ was for Origen and Augustine hallowed ground. These beliefs were widely embraced and passed on in the cathedrals and catechetical schools of the medieval Church.[65] Regrettably, and broadly speaking, such is not the case today.

Here is an illustration. A young girl went for her annual eye exam before the start of the schoolyear. Previously, however, a different ophthalmologist had misdiagnosed a considerable myopia that had developed in the girl's right eye. That doctor reported to her parents that only a minimal correction was called for. Her vision was impaired, and the

62. Jb 28:21.

63. Jb 28:23.

64. Dn 2:28.

65. This is not to say that allegory was universally accepted in the patristic period. It wasn't. In fact, there was considerable conflict between the Alexandrian school, which embraced the allegorical method, and the Antiochene school, which vehemently opposed it: "In Eastern exegesis of the 4th and 5th centuries, the emergence of the so-called Antiochene school with a programme antagonistic to the allegorising exegesis of the Alexandrian school, is of fundamental importance." Simonetti, *Biblical Interpretation in the Early Church*, 59. Commenting on Theodore of Mopsuestia, one of the greatest figures of the literalist, Antiochene approach, Simonetti writes: "In the introduction to his commentary on John, Theodore observes that *the business of exegesis is to explain difficult expressions in the biblical text*, without superfluous digressions, which are permitted, even required of the preacher. He is obviously alluding to the verbose commentaries of the Alexandrian exegetes, and the contrast between the conciseness of Antiochene commentaries and the prolixity of the Alexandrians (Origen, Didymus) does indeed highlight their divergent approach to Scripture. *The Antiochene perceives in the sacred text a precise meaning to be illustrated without frills in a reading which adheres to the literal sense. The Alexandrian sees it as pregnant with meaning and with depth of mystery, to be read at several levels, and needing patient excavation to uncover, at least partly, its richness of meaning.*" Simonetti, *Biblical Interpretation in the Early Church*, 71–72; emphasis added. See also Altaner and Stuiber, *Patrologie*; di Berardino, *Encyclopedia of the Early Church*; Ferguson, *Encyclopedia of Early Christianity*; Kannengiesser, *Handbook of Patristic Exegesis*; Quasten, *Patrology*.

muscles in her right eye had begun to atrophy and became "lazy." Thankfully, a recent exam with a more thorough doctor detected the true problem. Closing in on the problem, the good doctor had the girl read many sets of letters. "Can you read this set?" the doctor asked. "No," the young lady responded, "all I can see is Superman." On a side wall was a poster of the Man of Steel. It seems that the sight in her right eye had so deteriorated that *it couldn't even see the correct wall*, the one with the letters. Her eye muscles were so out of sorts that they fixated instead on *the nearer object*—a poster of Superman on the side wall. Once the seriousness of the myopia became evident to the good ophthalmologist, new lenses were made. Now the girl began to see properly, and she cried with joy at her newly corrected vision. Not only this—the new lenses were "retraining" the muscles in her eyes, so that with time she was able to see all the things that she had previously missed.[66]

Engaging the Bible with the Four Senses is similar: they offer the reader a lens that allows one to see more of the truth and meaning of Scripture than ever before. Muscles that have been underutilized will be stretched. Yet once one "peers" with this new lens, it may be unthinkable to return to the old ones. To our detriment, we have been conditioned to read Scripture within a narrow, postmodern lens.[67] As a result, we are missing out of some of the richest insights ever produced about the Sacred Page. And, sadly, many do not even know that they are missing out on such treasures! This book is our attempt to disrupt, at least a bit, the momentum of modern myopia regarding Scripture study.

Some years ago, folk-rock singer Sarah McLachlan had success with her song "Building a Mystery."[68] It is a fairly well-crafted, catchy tune that includes references to Jesus, churches, and crosses. Sounds promising. The song certainly advanced McLachlan's career. Sadly, though, much like modernity itself, the song's lyrics are a tangled web of words that convey little about "mystery" in the classical sense. Likewise, one may hear a celebrity proudly claim that he or she is "spiritual but not re-

66. This is a true story; the girl in the illustration is my daughter.

67. For an introduction to postmodernism and its detrimental effects, see Collins, *The Bible after Babel*; Legaspi, *Death of Scripture*; Hicks, *Explaining Postmodernism*; Vanhoozer, *Is There a Meaning in This Text?* For a discussion between Hicks and Jordan Peterson on postmodernism, see "Stephen Hicks: Postmodernism. Reprise," YouTube video, 1:39:21, posted by Jordan B. Peterson, May 27, 2019, https://youtu.be/BwW9QV5Ulmw.

68. Sarah McLachlan, "Building a Mystery," on *Surfacing*, Arista Records, 1997.

ligious." This notion is commonplace among many in contemporary life, especially among the so-called none's[69] (i.e., religiously nonaffiliated) of our time. Yet, like the catchy song lyrics, it is simply more gibberish, devoid of substance. These sorts of vague, modernistic biases will not assist us in getting at the biblical concept of *musteriōn* (mystery), nor in seeking the face of the Lord.[70] What we need is the kind of faith of Daniel, who boldly proclaimed to "there is a God who reveals mysteries"[71] and did so in a darkened culture. But not so fast.

The biblical notion of *musteriōn* is not something one discovers on one's own, much less "builds." No—the mysteries of God, and the mysteries in holy Scripture, *build us*, if we allow it room to move in our mind, our heart, our soul. In the Hebrew Bible, *musteriōn* is equated with the Torah itself, revealed by God on Mt. Sinai (or at Creation).[72] Daniel and the other prophets grasped that, whatever it amounts to, it is rooted in the Divine: "*there is a God in heaven who reveals mysteries*."[73] Elsewhere in the writings, *musteriōn* takes the form of *Hagia Sophia*, Lady Wisdom.[74] She is the personification of the wisdom of God, divine wisdom, hidden from and revealed to man by the Father alone. According to the Scriptures, such holy wisdom is a treasure. But not one "pulled out of the mines" of men.[75] It is a gift, given by God.

In the New Testament, Jesus is proclaimed by the Four Evangelists as the Son of God and Mystery-in-Person.[76] As St. John poetically reveals, Jesus is divine wisdom in the flesh.[77] Accordingly, to the church

69. By "none's," we mean those who self-identify as having no religious affiliation. See especially Drescher, *Choosing Our Religion*; Putnam, *American Grace*; Barna Research Group, *Barna Trends 2018*; Haidt, *Righteous Mind*. See also the work of Jordan B. Peterson, especially his lectures on YouTube concerning religion and in particular the "archetypal" stories of Genesis. Whatever one thinks of his ideas, there is little doubt that they have electrified many people today, including many of the "none's." Peterson, *Twelve Rules for Life*. See esp. chap. 7, "Rule 7: Pursue What Is Meaningful, Not What Is Expedient."

70. In the Septuagint of the Old Testament as well as in the New Testament, the term *musteriōn* is used. In the Hebrew Bible, however, a distinct term is used to convey the idea of "mystery," *rāz*. Canonically, this term is found only in the Book of Daniel (2:18–19, 2:27, 2:30, 2:47, 4:9). For a thorough treatment on the biblical notion of "mystery," see Beale and Gladd, *Hidden but Now Revealed*.

71. See Dn 2:28.

72. See Ex chaps. 20–24. See Beale and Gladd, *Hidden but Now Revealed*.

73. See Dn 2:28; emphasis added.

74. See Prv 8:22–30; Wis 7:22–8:1.

75. See Jb 28:12.

76. Mk 1:1; Mt 27:54; Lk 1:35.

77. See Jn 1:1–18.

at Colossae, St. Paul explains his apostolic mission in precisely this manner: "to make the word of God fully known, the *musterion* hidden for ages and generations but now made manifest to his saints."[78] About the saints, Paul adds, "God chose to make known how great among the Gentiles are the riches of the glory of this *musterion*, which is Christ in you, the hope of glory" (vv. 27–28). *Musterion* is at the heart of seeking the face of the Lord in the Scriptures.

To ponder the mystery of "Christ in you," which is the "hope of glory,"[79] the Scriptures must be approached with the greatest degree of confidence in their divine authorship and in the charism of inspiration by which the human authors composed them.[80] This is truly how the Fathers and Doctors received the Scriptures—as a divinely revealed mystery being opened, and into which they stepped with an assurance that the Holy Spirit would lead them ever closer to Christ. It was not nearly enough to approach the Scriptures from a historical plateau. For the ancient and medieval theologians, every word of the Old and New Testament was Spirit infused with *musterion*, and every word revealed something about Jesus Christ, crucified and Risen.

What would it look like if modern students of Scriptures heeded this ancient and sage advice? Louis Bouyer eloquently captures this idea in an important essay on the relationship between the Bible and the liturgy.[81] In explaining the role that the Old and New Testament played in the primitive Church, Bouyer writes:

> The Word of God in the celebrations of the ancient Church remained the saving event, the personal intervention of God in the history of men, choosing and setting apart for Himself a people, then forming them little by little and enlightening them at the same time, to lead them to what Saint Paul calls the intelligence of the mystery. *The "mystery," in the sense that Paul gives to this word in the First Epistle to the Corinthians and in the Epistle to the Ephesians, this is what the proclamation of the Word of God in His Church opens out on.*[82]

78. Col 1:25–26.

79. See Col 1:27.

80. For a fairly recent treatment of the topic of biblical inspiration—and, more particularly, the development of the doctrine in *Dei Verbum,* the Catholic Church's Dogmatic Constitution on Divine Revelation (Second Vatican Council)—see Farkasfalvy, *Inspiration and Interpretation*; idem, *Theology of the Christian Bible.*

81. Bouyer, "Word of God."

82. Bouyer, "Word of God," 61; emphasis added.

Touching on the Old Testament in particular, Bouyer adds:

The "mystery"—that is to say, the proclamation of Christ and of His victorious Cross coming as the achievement and the key of human history, as also the fullness and the core of all divine words which little by little and step by step were communicated by the prophets. The "mystery"—that is to say, the saving event sketched out and prepared by the first Pasch, the first deliverance; more profoundly approached in the sorrowful and radiant experience of the exile in Babylon and the return of the captives, that first resurrection after death hailed by an Ezekiel; finally carried out in the "passage" of Jesus through death, His "exodus" to the Father, containing in Himself in advance our own victory over sin and death, our own accession to the freedom of sons in glory.[83]

We seek the face of the Lord in such ways as these, as Bouyer advocates.

Finally, to better handle the enormity of this task, we have chosen a trusted guide to accompany us up the mountain. Specifically, we rely considerably upon the great French Jesuit theologian of the mid-twentieth century Henri de Lubac. Among many distinguished achievements,[84] de Lubac catalogued the insights of the fathers and doctors on the Four Senses of Scripture more thoroughly than any modern scholar. The result is truly a modern masterpiece of biblical insight, a four-volume opus called *Medieval Exegesis*. This book is indebted to this achievement and will interact with his project extensively throughout the book.[85]

83. Bouyer, "Word of God," 61.

84. First and foremost, one thinks of de Lubac's *Catholicism*; *Splendor of the Church*; and the "controversial" *Surnaturel*. For a complete bibliography of de Lubac through 1974, see Neufeld and Sales, *Bibliographie Henri de Lubac*; for later works, see K. H. Neufeld and M. Sales, "Bibliographie Henri de Lubac, S.J., 1970 to 1990," in de Lubac, *Théologie dans l'histoire*, 408–37. See also von Balthasar, *Henri de Lubac*; Chantraine, "Beyond Modernity and Postmodernity"; D'Ambrosio, "*Ressourcement* Theology, *Aggiornamento* and the Hermeneutics of Tradition."

85. De Lubac, *Medieval Exegesis*, vols. 1–3. Originally published as *Exégèse Médiévale: Les quatre sens de l'Écriture*, 4 vols. (Paris: Aubier, 1959–1964). At present, vol. 4 has not been translated. Several remarks as to the manner of citation adopted in the book: (1) Scripture references are abbreviated when used parenthetically and in footnotes (e.g., Jn 1:1–3). (2) Every effort was taken to properly cite all sources, whether ancient or modern. At times, this is more complicated with the former. The translators of *Medieval Exegesis* had the unenviable task of translating hundreds and hundreds of pages of de Lubac's handwritten notes. This was made more formidable given that de Lubac had drawn from a vast ensemble of ancient and medieval sources, the majority of which were hastily abbreviated in the French original. Moreover, the publisher did not provide an index of the abbreviations used. The result is admirable, yet imperfect, as to be expected. The reader will be referred to the appropriate sections of de Lubac for reference. (3) In certain instances, a volume or translation of a patristic/medieval source is cited in complete bibliographic fashion. Most often, however,

At one point in the work, de Lubac summons a crucial Latin phrase that gets at the heart of our book: *mysticant nobis aliquid.* The phrase—which de Lubac admits requires diligence to translate into English with clarity and without losing the original essence—is something like the Scriptures are "*conveying to us a mystery.*"[86] De Lubac explains that the verb *mysticare* is "untranslatable into English." At any rate, he offers several imperfect renderings, among them "they *mysticate* something to us" and "they *en-mystery* us something."[87] These phrases, as unusual as they may be, nevertheless describe the task of *The Face of the Lord:* to allow the Scriptures *to break us open* so that we may *receive* the mystery of Christ. But to do so, we must move beyond the historical horizon of modern, critical exegesis. We must enter into the fullness of the Four Senses of Scripture. As de Lubac insists, "our faith depends upon it. It imposes itself; we cannot elude it is we want to produce a *Christian* exegesis."[88]

We look to St. Gregory the Great, who in his *Moralia in Iob* robustly makes this same point: "Now the order of exposition *requires* us to lay bare the secrets of the allegories."[89] Here, de Lubac adds, "We do not have the right through negligence to deprive ourselves of the many allegories of which history is so full."[90]

Lord, as we seek your holy face, *en-mystery* yourself to us through your Word.

Steven C. Smith, The Solemnity of the Mother of God
January 1, 2020

---

an abbreviated form will be adopted (e.g., St. Augustine, *Confessions*, VIII, 3). The primary aim of this book is not to provide an encyclopedic reference work of patristic exegesis, but is rather a volume of *biblical contemplation*. Throughout the book, I have sought to strike a reasonable balance between proper annotation and simplicity and ease of reading. See the bibliography for more extensive references.

86. De Lubac, *Medieval Exegesis*, 2:84; emphasis added.

87. De Lubac, *Medieval Exegesis*, 2:310n21.

88. De Lubac, *Medieval Exegesis*, 2:84.

89. St. Gregory the Great, *Moralia in Iob*, XXI, 1,1.

90. De Lubac, *Medieval Exegesis*, 2:84; emphasis added.

PART I

Exordium

CHAPTER 1

"He Who Has Seen Me Has Seen the Father"

The final end of human beings is the vision of God.

—Hans Boersma

Heaven Is Right Here

In the mid-1950s, the Veronese-born German Catholic priest Romano Guardini (1885–1968) began composing what would become his magnum opus, *The Lord.*[1] This modern gem has tremendous staying power well into the present century, and with good reason: *The Lord* is a historically sound and intelligently written life of Christ.

What's more, Guardini managed to produce a grand, reintegrated portrait of the divine Son. For much of the twentieth century, the image of Jesus was in broken shards, sadly obscured beneath higher criticism. The true portrait of Jesus was replaced by a false bifurcation of "the Jesus of history" and "the Christ of faith."[2] The grand hopes of the rationalist critics—of removing the ecclesial varnishes of faith that had "distorted" the Jesus of history—had failed miserably. And this failure was costly. The fallout is still being felt today. Mostly what those efforts yielded was a fragmented Savior and generations of bewildered believers.

1. Guardini, *The Lord*. See also idem, *End of the Modern World*; idem, *Spirit of the Liturgy*; idem, *Letters from Lake Como*. Additionally, see Robert Krieg's biography *Romano Guardini*.

2. The phrase originated with Martin Kähler, the German theologian who in 1892 published *Der sogenannte historische Jesus und der geschichtliche, biblische Christus* (*So-Called Historical Jesus*).

Guardini distinguished himself from the rationalist glut of biblical critics of his generation, such as Strauss, Schweitzer, and Bultmann,[3] among so many others. He developed his Jesus portrait from a *hermeneutic of faith*[4] and not of unwarranted suspicion.[5] Guardini's primary source material was not the overly complex hypotheses of form critics. It was the Gospels themselves. By no means was Guardini alone in his faith-informed approach to Scripture. Nevertheless, in the first half of the twentieth century, the number of like-minded biblical scholars was relatively small, compared with the predominance of historical-critical practitioners across Europe and in America.

To solidify our understanding of Guardini's overall approach, we can compare it to that of one of his contemporary theologians, for instance, Jean Daniélou (1905–74). Just a few remarks about Daniélou will help flesh out the "hermeneutic of faith" that such scholars held in common. Daniélou, like his mentor, the French Jesuit Henri de Lubac, made his mark in Catholic theology in the decades leading up the Second Vatican Council. In an important essay called "The Historical Approach," Daniélou asserted that the historical deposit of the Gospel is vindicated in opposition to any such "literary decomposition."[6]

In eschewing the deconstruction of the Four Gospels by rationalist critics like Bultmann in his day (one lamentably thinks of figures such

3. Strauss, *Das Leben Jesu*; Bultmann, *Die Geschichte der synoptischen Tradition*; idem, *History of the Synoptic Tradition*.

4. "The mere objectivity of the historical method does not exist. It is simply impossible to completely exclude philosophy or hermeneutical foresight ... it has become evident that the pure historical method–as in the case of secular literature as well–does not exist." Joseph Cardinal Ratzinger, "The Relationship between the Magisterium and Exegetes," 100th Anniversary of the Pontifical Biblical Commission, Vatican website, accessed January 26, 2018, http://www.vatican.va/roman_curia/congregations/cfaith/pcb_documents/rc_con_cfaith_doc_20030510_ratzingercomm-bible_en.html.

5. As I laid out in the introduction to *House of the Lord*, operating within a hermeneutic of faith is not over or against the pursuit of knowledge about the "historical Jesus." Such requires diligent and careful use of historical methods of inquiry. On the contrary, to believe that seeking the face of Jesus within the context of *both faith and history* is an unattainable goal is to succumb to the perils of a "hermeneutic of suspicion." As the past several hundred years has proven, following such a pathway of skepticism yields more hypotheses yet less meaning. According to Ratzinger, "I have tried to maintain a distance from any controversies over particular points and to consider only the essential words and deeds of Jesus—guided by the hermeneutic of faith, but at the same time adopting a responsible attitude toward historical reason, which is a necessary component of that faith." *Jesus of Nazareth, Part Two*, xvii. See also Benedict XVI's *Verbum Domini*, 31, 39, 47.

6. Daniélou, "The Historical Approach," in *Christ and Us*, 10.

as Bart Ehrman in our time),[7] Daniélou did not shrink from addressing historical questions head-on. He was one of the earliest scholars to publish his findings on the Dead Sea Scrolls,[8] and later he developed a thoughtful study of Christian faith within its historical context.[9] His various monographs dealt with topics such as biblical typology, the Church Fathers, and Scripture and its relationship to liturgy.[10] Yet even in those volumes he engaged the Bible according to the "letter" (history) and the "spirit" (theology).

Lastly, for Daniélou, it was always a grave mistake to impugn the veracity of the Gospels and their authors, as a goodly number of his contemporaries had done: "We need to remind ourselves that Christianity does not primarily rest upon *the evidence of dead books, but of living men.*"[11] Daniélou clearly gave proper attention to both the historical horizon and the spiritual horizon. He was well armed with an insatiable curiosity about history, coupled with an intelligent, mature, and stable faith in a time of shifting sands. Pope John XXIII had noted these and other achievements and invited Daniélou to the council, where he served as *peritus*.[12] Following the council, in 1969, Pope Paul VI appointed him cardinal.

These remarks about Daniélou will suffice. They remind the reader that even in such a rationalistic period, Guardini was by no means alone in operating within a hermeneutic of faith. And during this time, there were others that embraced such an approach to Scripture. But let us stay for the moment with Guardini. Just about the time he was putting the finishing touches on his masterpiece, Guardini was invited to speak at Berlin University on the life of Christ. What an event that must have been! Fortunately, the lectures were eventually transcribed and translated into English as *Jesus Christus*[13] and are highly recommended reading.

After considering various dimensions of the person of Christ—

7. See Ehrman, *Jesus before the Gospels*; idem, *Jesus, Interrupted*.

8. Daniélou, *Les manuscrits de la Mer Morte*.

9. Daniélou, *Lord of History*.

10. See Daniélou, *From Shadows to Reality*; idem, *Bible et liturgie*; idem, *Théologie du Judéo-Christianisme*.

11. Daniélou, *Christ and Us*, 12. He adds, "If, then, it is upon the authority of the Apostles that our knowledge of the life of Jesus rests, we may say that our knowledge receives from that source an essential guarantee ... The Gospels are the outward expression of what for the Apostles Jesus *was*" (12–13; emphasis added).

12. Latin for "expert." During the council, a number of theological advisors took part in plenary sessions and smaller meetings.

13. Guardini, *Jesus Christus*.

including his healing ministry, his relationship with his Mother, and his glorious Resurrection—Guardini turned in his final essay to the theme of heaven. Several of his insights on the reality of heaven will illuminate our path moving forward. First, Guardini was thoughtful and serious in his answer to a question posed to a child: *Where is heaven? Up there.* For a small child, "up there" is wholly sensible, for up there is "where God lives."[14] From this elemental stage, Guardini plunged deeper into the mystery and challenge of seeing God: "But if Heaven is where God lives, and God is everywhere," he writes, "then it must follow that Heaven is everywhere. That is quite true, Heaven is everywhere ... That is the first and greatest answer. *Heaven is right here.*"[15] Guardini likely had in mind Jesus's response to the Pharisees in the Gospel According to Luke: "Being asked by the Pharisees when the kingdom of God was coming, He answered them, 'The kingdom of God is not coming with signs to be observed; nor will they say, "Lo, here it is!" or "There!" for behold, the kingdom of God is *in the midst of you.*'"[16]

With Jesus, Heaven Is Right Here

As to this Lucan text, Guardini showed how the Vulgate is, in some sense, even more illuminative than the original Greek (*entos hymōn*), which is often put into English as "in the midst of you."[17] The Vulgate renders this phrase as *intra vos,* as in "within" or "inside" you. Accordingly, the Latin rendering seems to bring out the interior dimension of the kingdom of God within *each disciple*, rather than the impression from the Greek, of the kingdom's presence "amongst all the disciples as a group." From these Greek and Latin details, we come to see what Guardini is getting at. There are two dimensions of God's nearness to humanity—both the corporate sense and the personal sense. Guardini then made a second observation as salient as his first. Not only is Heaven in the midst of us and within us. Importantly, he stressed that it must first be opened *for us* before we can truly receive it: "We cannot get in. It is all about us, yet it is closed."[18]

14. Guardini, *Jesus Christus*, 106.

15. Guardini, *Jesus Christus*, 106; emphasis added.

16. Lk 17:21.

17. In Lk 17:19, the personal pronoun *sū* is conjugated in its second person plural form, *hymōn*, or "you all."

18. Guardini, *Jesus Christus*, 107.

Do you see his point? It is not that God shuts himself off from us, or that he closes off access to himself, away from humanity. No—it is God who pursues us and opens the connection between us and himself. It is he who seeks us, he who invites us, he who takes the initiative for us. It is God who makes it possible for us to encounter him in a personal way. His way is Jesus. Heaven "was open around Jesus."[19]

To advance his point about heaven being closed off, Guardini offered an illustration. Suppose a certain person wants to visit another who is far off. He may travel to the town where he lives and locate his house. Yet if the other is unavailable or uninterested, he remains closed off to the one searching: "It would open up, as it were, *if he takes notice of me, felt some sympathy for me*, trust, affection—then this presence would be an open thing, and he alone can create this condition of accessible proximity. *It can only come from him.*"[20]

Decades after Guardini's book was published, Denis Farkasfalvy stressed this same principle: "No matter how true it is that man seeks God, *God seeks man first and addresses him;* when deciding to disclose himself, he invites man to listen; *God is the one who both initiates and commands*, while, from the beginning of human history, the human being appears to be endowed with a desire for God, which one may even call *natural*, though it is rooted not in man's physical nature *but in a grace that elevates him.*"[21] "Most importantly," Farkasfalvy adds, "any actual and personal contact between God and man produced by a divine deed *comes from unmerited grace*."[22]

It Is God Who Must Reveal His Face to Us

Here is a marvelous insight: God is the Person whom we travel to see. Even so, *it is he who must avail himself to us.* He must open himself to us *if we are to encounter him at all.* This situation is not a result of any selfishness or disinterest on God's part. It is simply the consequence of our fallen human condition.[23]

As in Guardini's illustration, God's presence is at first closed off from

19. Guardini, *Jesus Christus*, 107.
20. Guardini, *Jesus Christus*, 107; emphasis added.
21. Farkasfalvy, *Theology of the Christian Bible*, 12; emphasis added.
22. Farkasfalvy, *Theology of the Christian* Bible, 12; emphasis added.
23. See Gn 3:1*ff*.

the one seeking him. When it opens—through Jesus—a response is demanded. When, through Jesus, man receives access to God's presence, he must respond. He chooses to get involved: "I must notice how he directs his attention towards me, I must respond to his affection and trust."[24] This interplay of action and response is, as Guardini's illustration makes clear, what opens all genuine encounters with God: "Then, when one has become *inwardly involved with the other*, has developed sympathetic response to the other's thoughts and emotions, then there is true proximity."[25]

Salvation History, "Drawn into the Womb of Mary"

Armed with Guardini's insights, we turn to the Scriptures to pray with Moses, and with all humanity, fully opened to the possibilities present in Moses's cry, "Lord *show me Your glory*."[26] These words give voice to the whole of salvation history and resonate throughout the biblical narrative. They are at the bedrock of our deepest human needs: "The primordial human longing to see God had taken, in the Old Testament, the form of 'seeking the face of God.'"[27] But even Moses—the great Lawgiver, the courageous Deliverer, the one who both the books of Exodus[28] and Deuteronomy say God knew *pānîm 'el pānîm* ("face-to-face")[29]—did not in truth "see" the glory of God. Instead, God instructs Moses that "You cannot see my face; for man shall not see me and live."[30]

It is only when we come to the New Testament that Moses's prayer—and all of humanity with him—is definitively answered: "And the Word became flesh and dwelt among us" (Jn 1:14a). God taking on human flesh. This is the one way, the decisive way, recalling Guardini's illustration, that the Father has "turned His attention towards us." The Incarnation of the divine Son is the Father's opening up the life of God to us—his taking notice of us. More than *noticing*: redeeming, sacrificing, and offering his greatest gift, his one and only Son.[31]

24. Guardini, *Jesus Christus*, 107.
25. Guardini, *Jesus Christus*, 107; emphasis added.
26. Ex 33:18; emphasis added.
27. Ratzinger, *On the Way to Jesus Christ*, 14.
28. Ex 33:11.
29. See Dt 34:10.
30. Ex 33:20.
31. Greek = *monōgenes* ("only begotten"). See Jn 1:18, 3:16.

It is this mystery—the Incarnation of the divine Son—that makes whole the New Testament Good News. And not only it, but by way anticipation, the entirety of the Old Testament too. There, Jesus is present "Christophanically," in a hidden yet real way.[32] Thomas Weinandy put it this way: "In the incarnating act, *the whole previous salvific history of Israel is drawn into the womb of Mary*, the wife of Joseph, and the child she carries will be the fulfillment *of* that salvific history—Jesus Christ, the Father's Son, the Lord and Savior."[33]

Above I highlighted the work of Bogdan Bucur and his recent book *Scripture Re-envisioned.* It is a bright achievement that asks us to rethink how Old Testament theophanies—like the Burning Bush—are to be interpreted. He shows that in the primitive Church they were received "Christophanically," that is, as manifestations of the to-be-incarnate Logos. Moreover, he shows how, in their reception history, the primitive Church employed these Christophanies for doctrinal reflection, apologetics/polemics, in liturgy and in doxological praise. Another important, fresh in biblical Christology, is Thomas Weinandy's *Jesus Becoming Jesus.* In it, Weinandy explains how, through the Incarnation, the Holy Spirit even "knits together names, titles, and concepts of the Old Testament with the New."[34] The result is that "they depict a new revelational tapestry that was previously unimaginable."[35]

Jacob, Moses, Isaiah, Solomon, and Job—all of the figures that we will peer at in our theophany scenes—are woven into this rich Christological (or, in Bucur's language, *Christophanic*) tapestry with the divine Son. And not only such male figures. There is also a dazzling array of female figures. One only needs to recall the role of Rachel, Miriam, Hannah, Ruth, and Esther in the story of the Bible. When read Christophanically, they too are, in Weinandy's expression, part of this "revelational tapestry."

How does one come to know Jesus in Scripture? As Weinandy explains, in and through "all salvific deeds." He writes, "To know the Christ, the Son of God, the Holy One of God, the Son of the Most High, the Lord, the Savior, the King of David—and so to know the Father, the Most High, the Holy One, the Lord, *the source of all holi-*

32. See Bucur, *Scripture Re-envisioned.*

33. Weinandy, *Jesus Becoming Jesus*, 68; emphasis added.

34. Weinandy, *Jesus Becoming Jesus*, 69.

35. Weinandy, *Jesus Becoming Jesus*, 69.

ness and the author of all salvific promises and their fulfillment as well as to know the Holy Spirit, the Father's Spirit of Sonship, the one who anoints and makes holy, the one who empowers, and in whom all *salvific deeds* are done—*is simply to know the man Jesus.*"[36] Weinandy's excellent description of what it means to know "the man Jesus" could possibly be mistaken for the words of Guardini and Daniélou. Far from the rationalistic bifurcation, of "the Jesus of history" and the "Christ of faith," Weinandy's approach is precisely the sort of "knowing" that is advocated in the present book.

There are at least three things that are particularly appealing about Weinandy's distillation of seeking Christ in the Scriptures, as "Jesus becoming Jesus." First, Weinandy's approach is grounded on the reality of the Incarnation. This is the most significant point. And it leads to two closely related points, the second of which is that it brings *all of salvation history* into sharp focus—from the Creation to the Christ. On this footing, the Church's patristic and medieval theologians saw Christ on every page and in every episode of the Old Testament.

The third point that commends itself about Weinandy's approach is that it pays particular attention to God's "salvific acts" throughout the Old Testament, leading up to the Christ event: "Amid this long history of revelatory acts, *God was advancing the future when he would reveal himself fully* by making a new covenant with his people whereby they would be truly cleaned of their sin and interiorly sanctified in his Spirit and so empowered to live hoy lives in the kingdom. Now, as evident from the Gospel, *all these revelatory divine acts find their climax and end in the Father sending into the world his Son,* who became incarnate in the womb of Mary through the overshadowing of the Holy Spirit."[37]

36. Weinandy, *Jesus Becoming Jesus*, 69; emphasis added.

37. "Thus, for example, within the Old Testament history, *God* acts to establish a unique relationship with Abraham and the nation he would father. He makes a covenant with Moses and the Hebrew people so that they might be singularly his people and he might be singularly their God. He anoints kings, prophets, and priests with his Spirit so that they might lead the people in holiness; speak his words of condemnation, correction and admonition as well as those of forgiveness, comfort, and encouragement; and so gather them together in worshipping and glorifying him as the one true Lord God of Israel." Weinandy, *Jesus Becoming Jesus*, 466, emphases added.

Accessible Proximity to the Face of the Lord

The "salvific acts" of the Word made flesh is told in one of Jesus's best-known parables, that of the Lost Son.[38] Everyone knows the story. But not everyone sees what Guardini happens to see. Near the climax of the parable, the pattern that Guardini has laid out is again evident in the father's movement toward his son. As the wayward son's journey into sin and isolation finally reaches the lowest depths in his self-imposed pit, he arrives at a self realization: his father, from whom he is now estranged, *is and always has been good.* It occurs to him that even to return as a mere servant in his father's house is infinitely better than the darkness and emptiness—the meaninglessness that is now all about him. He rehearses his speech of remorse and sets out.

Yet, before the son can reach his father, and the son's astonishment, the father already is out searching for him! St. Luke records these memorable, grace-filled words of Jesus: "And he arose and came to his father. But while he was still at a distance, *his father saw him and had compassion,* and ran and embraced him and kissed him."[39] What is striking is not only that the father sees the prodigal son before notices his father. It is also that the father *takes the initiative* and displays a love without limitations. As Guardini wrote in *Jesus Christus,* if there is to be a divine encounter at all, it is His initiative. God alone "can create this condition of *accessible proximity*. It can only come from him."[40] "Accessible proximity." This is a helpful phrase, one we will hold on to throughout the remainder of the book.

The divine initiative leading to our accessible proximity is an important insight that will accompany our us throughout the book. Here is another way to think about it: the Word becoming flesh[41] is the Father's plea, the Father's running out to meet his prodigal children, to invite us into his loving mercy. The Father's initiative, granting to his children the Word made flesh, the divine Son—*yes, this is the supreme act of God that opens our accessible proximity back to him.* And the patristic and medieval masters *cannot but see* the Word made flesh upon all the pages of the Old Testament.

38. See Lk 15:11–32.

39. Lk 15:20; emphasis added.

40. Guardini, *Jesus Christus,* 107, emphasis added. For reasons that will become clear, "accessible proximity" is a key phrase in the remainder of the study.

41. Jn 1:14.

Just before turning to St. John's prologue for a closer look at the mystery of the Incarnation, one further point may be added about Jesus's parable in Luke 15: the father, who runs toward his lost son and receives him back with kisses, "had compassion" on him (v. 20). The Greek is more graphic, in fact bodily so: *splanchnizomai*. This biblical expression is worth looking at more closely, in the form of word study.

Both noun and verb forms of the Greek term carry the meaning of the viscera (i.e., "entrails") of an animal or person. By at least the fourth century BC, the noun *splanchna* had come to be associated with temple sacrifices and signified "the internal parts of a sacrificial victim, mentioned in cultic regulations as part of the compensation of priests.[42] As a verb, *splanchnizomai* often referred to consuming such. Helmut Köster is correct when he states that in the Parable of the Prodigal Son, Jesus describes the compassion of the father "in the strongest of terms *in order to bring out the totality of mercy* ... with which God claims man in His saving acts."[43]

A totality indeed. Turning from its wider Hellenistic usage to first-century Judaism, the Jewish philosopher Philo of Alexandria lists seven interior organs among human viscera: "If any one were to set about investigating the different parts of the body, he will in each case find seven divisions. Those which are visible are as follow—the head, the chest, the belly, two arms, and two legs; the internal parts, or the viscera, as they are called, are *the stomach, the heart, the lungs, the spleen, the liver, and the two kidneys*."[44] In modern, everyday language, Philo means "the guts" of a person. In the canon of the Old Testament, *splanchnizō* and *splanchna* hold true to the broader meaning just described.[45]

The noun form, a rare one in the Four Gospels, is found at the culmination of the *Benedictus* of Zechariah: "through the tender mercy (*splanchna*) of our God, when the day shall dawn upon us from on high to give light to those who sit in darkness and in the shadow of death, to guide our feet into the way of peace."[46] Similarly, in another parable, that

42. Spicq and Ernest, *Theological Lexicon of the New Testament*, 273. See also Sokolowski, *Lois sacrees des cites grecques*, n. 151, 14.

43. Köster, Σπλαγχνίζομαι, 554; emphasis added.

44. See Philo of Alexandria, *De opificio mundi*, 118.

45. E.g., Sir 30:7: "He who spoils his son will bind up his wounds, and his feelings (*splanchna*) will be troubled at every cry." Likewise, in Proverbs and 2 Maccabees, the term designates "bowels" (see Sir 30:7; 2 Mc 9:5).

46. See Lk 1:78–79. The term "viscera" appears in the Vulgate: *per viscera misericordiae Dei nostri.*

of the Wicked Tenant,[47] Jesus uses the term to describe the divine pity shown to the remorseful, praying servant: "And out of pity (*splanchnizomai*) for him the lord of that servant released him and forgave him the debt."[48] Elsewhere, in Mark's account of the Feeding of the Five Thousand, it is this same divine pity that Jesus felt in his most interior being, which leads to an outpouring of compassion: "As he went ashore he saw a great throng, and he had compassion (*esplanchnisthē*) on them, because they were like sheep without a shepherd."[49]

What does our brief word study of *splanchnizomai* reveal about God? How does it aid our investigation, in seeking the face of the Lord, seeking "*Jesus have become Jesus*"? In precisely this way: in every search for the face of God, we begin with the realization that it is he who first searches for us, from all of eternity—and more, that *his search proceeds from the innermost dimension of divine compassion*. It is the heart of Jesus that searches for us, with the Father's tenderness. And it is Jesus's divine will, perfectly aligned the Father's,[50] that graciously directs his *compassionate gaze* upon us.

All that is required is for us to return our gaze to him, only to discover that, like the father in Luke 15, he is already looking upon us with divine compassion. The tender mercy of God, evident in every gaze of the Father, revealed "in the flesh" through his divine Son, only becomes evident *if* we return his gaze with our own. And this is where Guardini's logic returns to us with its simplicity and truth: "we must respond to his affection and trust … then, when one has become inwardly involved with the other, has developed sympathetic response to the other's thoughts and emotions, then there is true proximity."[51]

The One Who Gazes at God Now Gazes at Us

All of these observations—from Guardini to our study of the Parable of the Prodigal Son—now lead us to one of the most salient scenes of "accessible proximity" within the Gospel According to St. John. Our

47. Mt 21:33–44; Mk 12:1–11; Lk 20:9–18.
48. Mt 18:27.
49. Mk 6:34.
50. See Jn 5:30, 10:30.
51. Guardini, *Jesus Christus*, 107.

discussion turns in a decisive way upon the Gospel's prologue.[52] At the heart of the prologue is a text so central to the Christian faith, so well known, that it almost requires no special introduction: "*The Word became flesh and dwelt among us.*"[53]

This text, embedded as it is in the epicenter of the prologue, is at the heart of biblical Christology and biblical faith. If the text is hurt by anything, perhaps it is overfamiliarity. How much theological ink has been spilt on this infamous Scripture? Even at an everyday level, the text looms over the Christian conscience. In fact, until the time of Vatican II, the entire prologue was professed at the end of the Holy Liturgy. With such a text it may be asked, Has everything of weight already been expressed about it? No—and by God's grace, every encounter with his Word is weighty, ripe for further digging, for it is where "the God who speaks" speaks to us. And so we turn our attention to it again, armed with our earlier insights, to meditate upon John 1:14 anew.

The first point to be made about this remarkable text is that, like any biblical expression, it is best grasped when placed within its proper literary context. In this case, that immediate context is the entire prologue of the Gospel (Jn 1:1–18). From its opening words, we are attuned to this distinctive start this Gospel has made, apart from the others.

St. John's account of the Good News is, in at least a dozen ways, a remarkable and unique contribution among the four canonical Gospels. Recall the starting point of each of the Synoptic Gospels, which, in their own ways, put forth beautiful and provocative beginnings of their particular portrait of Jesus. Yet they are unlike the prologue of St. John's Gospel. To begin, the Gospel According to St. Mark plunges the reader quickly into the action, within the context of Jesus's preaching and his Baptism.[54] By verse 12, one is already in the wilderness with Jesus, whereas at the same point in John, one is knee-deep into the second of three strophes of his opening poem!

Distinguishing themselves from Mark, both Matthew and Luke each begin with this in common: they allow us to peer into the birth of the divine Son.[55] Additionally, both offer a divergent, theologically

52. Jn 1:1–18.
53. Jn 1:14a; emphasis added.
54. Mk 1:1–11.
55. See Mt 1:18–22; Lk 2:1–20.

driven[56] *generatio* (Latin for "genealogy")[57] of Jesus.[58] Luke adds unique material, such as the "Annunciations" of Jesus, as well as John the Baptist, the Visitation of Mary to Elizabeth, and the Temple scenes.[59]

In developing his unique portrait of Jesus, however, it is St. John who invites the reader to *ascend* higher still, to the heights of heaven. In unprecedented ways, John unveils the divine Son, the eternal Logos, and his relation to the Father: "*In the beginning was the Word, and the Word was with God, and the Word was God.*"[60]

God Was Never without His Logos

The prologue is, as Benedict XVI, expressed, "a magnificent text, one which offers a synthesis of the entire Christian faith."[61] In fact, he structured his Apostolic Exhortation *Verbum Domini* around the theology of the prologue. From it we take away three keen insights.

First, commenting on its opening verse, Benedict XVI writes, "The Johannine Prologue makes us realize that the Logos is truly eternal, and from eternity is *himself God*. God was never without his *Logos*."[62] Indeed, John's Logos Christology emerges as a distinctive element of this Gospel. This is not to suggest for a moment that the Synoptic Gospels do not proclaim the divinity and eternality of Jesus—they do, and this point needs no further defense here. The Johannine prologue adds a datum that truly distinguishes it from the larger Gospel tradition. St. John

56. "It seems to me utterly futile to formulate hypotheses on this matter. Neither evangelist is concerned so much with the individual names as with the symbolic structure within which Jesus' place in history is set before us: the intricacy with which he is woven into the historical strands of the promise, as well as the *new beginning* which paradoxically characterizes his origin side by side with the *continuity* of God's saving action in history." Ratzinger, *Jesus of Nazareth: The Infancy Narratives*, 8–9; emphasis original.

57. See Mt 1:1–17; Lk 3:23–38.

58. A number of exegetes, Catholic and otherwise, agree with Benedict XVI's assessment: "Scholars have increasingly argued that the primary purpose of the NT genealogies is theological and thus they contend that the key to understanding the divergences between the genealogies is to probe their distinct Christological emphases." In Green et al., *Dictionary of Jesus and the Gospels*, 2nd ed., s.v. "Genealogy," 302. See also Nolland, *Luke 1–9:20*, 174–75; Brown, *Birth of the Messiah*, 70–71, 93–94; Keener, *Commentary on the Gospel of Matthew*, 75–76.

59. See Lk 1–2.

60. Jn 1:1; emphasis added.

61. Benedict XVI, *Verbum Domini*, 5.

62. Benedict XVI, *Verbum Domini*, 6; emphases added.

unveils details about the Son's preexistent life with the Father[63]—and it is his relationship to the Father that concerns us. Above all, what John reveals is this: *God was never without his Logos.* The Father loves the Son and gives all his love to him, and the divine Son does the same. Echoing Guardini's earlier point, Benedict XVI explains that "The Word, who from the beginning is with God and is God, reveals God himself *in the dialogue of love between the divine persons*, and invites us to share in that love."[64] God was never without his Logos. And in Scripture, neither are we. Even in the deepest recess of the Old Testament, the Word made flesh is with us, in mystery.

Second, and related to the above, is an insight that we have discussed elsewhere and is worth emphasizing here.[65] St. John's phrase in John 1:1, *kai hō lōgos ēn pros tōn theōn* ("and the Word was with God"), does not merely indicate that Jesus, the Logos, was "with" God, as opposed to being without or apart from God. The fuller meaning of the phrase has to do with his "accompanying" the Father always, his "being at" the Father's side. It is precisely because Jesus, the Logos, who alone was "in the bosom of the Father" from all eternity,[66] uniquely reveals the Father to humanity.

It is the divine Son alone who sees God, who from all eternity has been continually "gazing at the Father."[67] And yet, simultaneously, the Son, in his flesh, "gazes at His Apostles." John boldly testifies to this: "*we beheld Him*!"[68] Is this not some of the most exciting news of the Gospel?

63. Our emphasis upon the relationship of the Son to the Father and the Father to the Son follows the Johannine pattern as laid out in the prologue (Jn 1:1–18). It is in no way to the exclusion of the third Person of the Holy Trinity: "God makes himself known to us as a mystery of infinite love in which the Father eternally utters his Word *in the Holy Spirit*... Created in the image and likeness of the God who is love, we can thus understand ourselves only in accepting the Word *and in docility to the work of the Holy Spirit*" (*Verbum Domini*, 6).

64. This "dialogue of love between the divine Persons reminds us that while we love and venerate the Sacred Scriptures, it is the *Holy Spirit* and not the *Holy Scriptures* that complete the Blessed Trinity." As Benedict XVI writes, "All this helps us to see that, while in the Church we greatly venerate the sacred Scriptures, the Christian faith is not a 'religion of the book': Christianity is the 'religion of the word of God' not of 'a written and mute word, but of the incarnate and living Word'" (*Verbum Domini*, 6, emphasis added).

65. See Smith, *House of the Lord*, 290.

66. Jn 1:18.

67. See Smith, *House of the Lord*, 290–94, where I credit Ignace De La Potterie's significant essay in *Biblica* ("L'emploi dynamique de eis sans Saint Jean et ses incidences théologiques"), 1962.

68. Jn 1:14b; emphasis added.

As Benedict XVI explains, being a Christian "is not the result of an ethical choice or a lofty idea, *but the encounter with an event, a person*, which gives life a new horizon and a definitive direction."[69]

Still, there are dangers with texts such as this, texts that have become overly familiar. One tendency is that we may hear a bit of it and, in relishing it, fail to take in rest. Specifically, in our haste to take in the joyful news—*Verbum caro factum est* ("The Word became flesh")—we risk losing site of the apostolic "response"—*et vidimus gloriam eius* ("we beheld His glory"). And it is precisely this response that Guardini would have us not lose sight of, for it is only through it that divine proximity becomes accessible. *The Word became flesh and dwelt among us*. This is the epicenter of Christian joy, of human hope and possibility! But only when coupled with what follows—*we beheld his glory*—does the mystery of the Incarnation coalesce as St. John intends. The Word revealed himself to John, to his Apostles. Their eyewitness testimony is so vital precisely because they "*beheld His glory.*"[70]

What exactly is John indicating in this statement? Does "beheld His glory" refer to Jesus's entire ministry, or to some specific incident? Is it, as the French Dominican Marie-Émile Boismard suggests in his theological reflection on the prologue, the transfigured Christ on Mt. Tabor?[71] The answers are unclear, but what is clear is that John *beheld the One who saw God from "the beginning."*[72] He gazed upon the One who gazed upon the Father, and continued to for about three years. Elsewhere, St. John reflects on the mysterious privilege he and the other Apostles were given—of gazing upon him who has been gazing at the Father from all eternity.

For instance, in his *First Epistle*, which is entirely reminiscent of his Gospel's prologue, John writes: "That which was from the beginning, which we have heard, which we have seen with our eyes, which we have looked upon and touched with our hands, concerning the word of life."[73] From the opening words of his letter, John instructs the Church as to why his testimony matters: his own encounter with the Lord was

69. Benedict XVI, *Verbum Domini*, 6; see also Benedict XVI, Encyclical Letter *Deus Caritas Est*, 1.

70. Jn 1:14b; emphasis added.

71. Boismard, *St. John's Prologue*, 138–39.

72. Jn 1:1, 1:18.

73. 1 Jn 1:1.

quod vidimus oculis nostris, that "which we have seen with our own eyes." These words guide us today as well. With every inspired word of the Apostle John, we peer over his shoulder as he gazes upon the Word, as he gazes at the Father from all eternity. And not only John. All of the Apostles experience this divine encounter. They all "beheld" him and *bear witness* to this transhistoric truth. And this is indeed what the Gospels really are: *the witness of the Word made flesh, by those who truly gazed upon "the face of the Lord."*

We may now carry Guardini's suggestion one crucial step further. We have seen that the Father's pity (*splanchnizomai*) upon fallen humanity's condition—which led to his revelation of the divine Son, the Word made flesh—required the "response" of the Apostles in order for it to become a true encounter, as "accessible proximity," in Guardini's phraseology. So, too, we must likewise respond to the Apostolic *witness*. And we must wrestle with and meditate upon their Apostolic *response*—the Gospel—if, in turn, it is truly to become an accessible encounter that we are engaged in and not merely one kept at a distance in a removed, disinterested way.

A third and final insight from Benedict XVI is that the great lawgiver spoke *facie ad faciem* ("face-to-face") with God.[74] Yet it is Jesus, the new Moses, who alone reveals God. In his discussion of the Word of God and the Eucharist, the pope highlights this important distinction: "I am the bread of life."[75] Here *the Law has become a person*. "When we encounter Jesus, we feed on the living God himself, so to speak; we truly eat the Bread from Heaven."[76] This insight—of the Law becoming a Person—is no clearer anywhere in John than near the conclusion of the prologue: "For the law was given through Moses; grace and truth came through Jesus Christ."[77]

At first, this text appears a bit out of sorts with the Christology that predominates the prologue until this point. Why in verse 17 does St. John abruptly change course? Is the Evangelist distracting us away from the

74. Ex 33:11: "Thus the Lord used to speak to Moses *face-to-face*, as a man speaks to his friend" (emphasis added). See also Dt 34:10.

75. Jn 6:33–35.

76. Benedict XVI, *Verbum Domini*, 54: "The mystery of the Eucharist reveals the true manna, the true bread of heaven: it is God's *Logos* made flesh, who gave himself up for us in the paschal mystery."

77. Jn 1:17.

mystery of the Logos, with this contrast of Moses to Jesus? To press the point, is verse 17 an unnecessary intrusion, pulling the focus away from the Incarnation? No. To the contrary, this apparent intrusion, when read in concert with the following verse, raises the entirety of the prologue to an even higher level: "No one has ever seen God; the only Son, who is in the bosom of the Father, *he has made him known.*"[78] It is he and he alone who has made God known to humanity; he is "the one, definitive word given to mankind."[79]

With these final words, the Johannine logic becomes clear. As Benedict XVI underscores, it is through the divine Son alone that vv. 17–18 become fully intelligible. Rather, with them, the entire prologue reaches its theological destination. In "coupling John 1:1 and 1:18 ... St. John's dynamic, relational Christology of the divine Logos begins to emerge."[80] John has established Jesus's unique credentials as "*the eternal Life which was with the Father and was made manifest to us.*"[81] Jesus is the One who in every way surpasses every other revelation or vision of God. Here, in verses 17–18, Moses represents not only himself but also all biblical figures who in some sense "saw God." Indeed, a host of biblical figures fit this Christophanic category. One thinks of Adam, who had unique access to God in "the Holy Place" of the Temple of Eden.[82] Nevertheless, he "hid himself" from God at the opportune moment.[83] Indeed of Abraham too, whom God called to begin a new humanity. And his grandson Jacob, who wrestled with the angel of God and was so moved by the experience that he renamed the place of this encounter *Peni'el* (literally, "*the face of God*").[84] Later still was Elijah, the great prophet who leered out of the cave in his encounter with God's still small voice,[85] surely desiring to "see God." A comprehensive study of Scripture would undoubtedly include many others.

78. Jn 1:18; emphasis added.
79. Benedict XVI, *Verbum Domini*, 14.
80. Smith, *House of the Lord*, 291.
81. 1 Jn 1:2; emphasis added.
82. See Smith, *House of the Lord*, chaps. 1–2.
83. See Gn 3:10.
84. Gn 32:30; emphasis added.
85. 1 Kgs 19:12.

No One Has Ever Seen God

None of these holy encounters rises to the stature of the Christophanies that Moses experienced. From the Burning Bush[86] and the revelation of the Divine Name,[87] to his "beholding God" atop Sinai,[88] to his seeing God pass by later in the wilderness[89] and in the Glory Cloud of the Tabernacle,[90] no biblical figure surpassed or even comes close to Moses's experiences of "seeing the face of the Lord." This is the point that John wishes to convey in his prologue, that in the figure of the great Lawgiver, all these theophanies are consolidated and find their expression in Moses. Then, in verse 18, John insists in the strongest possible Greek term, *oudeis*, that *absolutely no one* has "seen God." Not even Moses? No, not even Moses.

Now all becomes clear. John did not introduce Moses into his prologue at the climax to distract us. To the contrary—by summoning Moses to the fore, John swept away all possibilities that *anyone has actually seen God*, not even the great Lawgiver himself. As God declared to Moses himself, "no one can see God and live."[91] Biblically speaking, John's declaration in verse 18 is a challenge for us.

Here, at the conclusion of his prologue, John has smartly recast the Old Testament Christophanies mentioned above (and any others that we might add) as what they really are: close encounters with God—but in which the Divine Face *remained hidden*. St. John's strategy now becomes crystal clear: those in his audience who rejected Christ claiming the Jewish patriarchs had already in fact "seen God" are entirely mistaken. Neither Moses, nor Jacob, nor Elijah—nor any human person—has "seen God." Only the God-Man, God's *Verbum*, who was "gazing at God" from all of eternity,[92] has seen God *face-to-face*. St. John concludes his prologue with the verb *exēgēsato*—Jesus alone *has made God known*.

As Benedict XVI writes, "Jesus of Nazareth is, so to speak, the 'exegete' of the God whom no one has ever seen."[93] Only the Exegete of

86. See Ex 3:1–7.
87. See Ex 3:14.
88. See Ex 24:9–11.
89. See Ex 33:17–23.
90. See Ex 40:34–35.
91. Ex 33:20.
92. See Jn 1:1.
93. Benedict XVI, *Verbum Domini*, 90.

God can separate the waters above from the waters below and take us to the Father. Only he can reveal the Father. This fact—the uniqueness of the divine Son as the one true Revealer of God—is decisive in our project. Still, it does not diminish the significance of the various Old Testament theophanies/Christophanies we will encounter in this book. On the contrary, it only enhances them. With the reality of the Word made flesh, we may place these various encounter scenes in their proper Christological context. Together, they anticipate the One who truly gazes at God. Moreover, it means that St. John and all of the Twelve Apostles are in a privileged position over the great Jewish patriarchs of the Old Covenant.

The revelation of the Word made flesh among the Apostles is Christologically decisive. It places them over and above Moses and every other Old Testament counterpart. Consider it: on his own, John, the son of Zebedee, was merely a Galilean fisherman. Compared to Moses, the great Lawgiver who saw God more clearly than any other, John is insignificant. Nevertheless, as a called Apostle, as one who was "with Jesus," John experienced something Moses only dreamed of. He actually beheld God face-to-face. Only the Apostles can reveal the face of God to us, for he who has seen Jesus, the divine Son, has indeed "seen the Father."[94]

One more point must be added about the Apostle's encounter with the face of God in Jesus. Later in the Gospel, we find another plea that again recalls Moses's prayer, "Lord, show me your glory." This time, however, it does not come to us dressed in the poetic language of the prologue but in a direct statement to Jesus by Phillip: "*Lord, show us the Father*, and we shall be satisfied."[95] Jesus's response upbraids Phillip with several direct questions of his own: "Have I been with you so long, and yet you do not know me, Philip? . . . and "How can you say, 'Show us the Father?'" (v. 9). Between these questions, Jesus declares to Phillip—and all who cry "show us the Father"—a univocal pronouncement: *Qui vidit me, vidit Patrem* "*He who has seen me has seen the Father.*"

So, what does Jesus really mean when he says, "He *who has seen me* has seen the Father"? Can we hope to answer the question, or it is purely rhetorical? Surely, "seeing Him" must involve something beyond merely looking upon him. Many who did so would later turn their backs upon

94. See Jn 14:9.
95. Jn 14:8; emphasis added.

him and give no indication of "seeing the Father." One thinks of the Rich Young Ruler, Judas, and many others.[96] Pontius Pilate looked upon Jesus, he "saw" Jesus, and still cried out, "Behold the man!" How is it that Pilate "saw" Jesus and yet ordered Jesus's death by Crucifixion?[97] What did Pilate not see? What do we fail to see?

Behold the Pierced One

Surely, something other, something greater must be involved in gazing at Jesus, such that "the way to the Father" is definitively opened to man. Again, we return to the Beloved Disciple to contemplate what it means to really see Jesus and thus to see the Father. What precisely is involved? St. John hints at it in recording these words of Jesus: "Unless a grain of wheat falls into the earth and dies, it remains alone; but if it dies, it bears much fruit."[98]

Here as elsewhere, Jesus calmly and boldly predicts his coming Passion, preparing his disciples for when he is "lifted up" in glory. These words are given in the immediate aftermath of the Greeks who come to Phillip and entreat him, *Kyrie thēomen idein ton Ieosoun* ("Sir, we wish to see Jesus").[99] For St. John, to *truly* see Jesus in his glory is to see him "lifted up" on the Cross.

Only in gazing at the Word made flesh, crucified in the flesh, can one *really* see his glory. There, atop Calvary, one definitively encounters the face of the divine Son, fulfilling the will of the Father for the sake of his own. As Ratzinger stresses, "The glorification occurs in the Passion. This is what will produce 'much fruit'—which is, we might add, the Church of the Gentiles . . . Jesus' answer transcends the moment and reaches far into the future: Indeed, the Greeks shall see me, and not only these men who have come now to Philip, but the entire world of the Greeks. They shall see me, yes, but not in my earthly, historical life, 'according to the flesh', *they will see me by and through the Passion.*"[100]

In fact, such insights are not restricted to the second half of the Gos-

96. "After this many of his disciples drew back and no longer went about with him, Jesus said to the Twelve, 'Do you also wish to go away?'" (Jn 6:66–67). See also Mt 19:16–30 (and parallels); Jn 18:1–15.

97. See Jn 19:5.

98. Jn 12:24.

99. Jn 12:21.

100. Ratzinger, *On the Way to Jesus Christ*, 15; emphasis added.

pel, the so-called Book of Glory.[101] The entire "Book of Signs"[102] that proceeds it is, in some sense, a meditation on the glorification of the Word made flesh, who took our human nature upon himself to raise it up to the Father in glory. Consider Jesus's first miracle recorded in the Gospel, the Wedding Feast at Cana.[103] John's concluding statement does not concern the sign itself. Rather, John focuses attention on the *doxa* ("glory") of Jesus, just now beginning to be revealed. Through this first sign, Jesus's eternal glory is now beginning to be revealed: "This, the first of his signs, Jesus did at Cana in Galilee, *and manifested his glory; and his disciples believed in him*" (v. 11; emphasis added).

Another example is seen in the next chapter of the Gospel. In his discourse with Nicodemus, Jesus declares: "And as Moses lifted up the serpent in the wilderness, *so must the Son of man be lifted up*, that whoever believes in him may have eternal life."[104] In these and other ways, St. John is expanding our knowledge of *doxa*, of glory, from its various manifestations throughout the Old Testament, to its climax in the Word made flesh. St. John beheld Jesus's glory in the flesh.[105] And he could not be clearer; the *doxa* of the Father is "seen" in the Incarnate Word, who, as St. Paul writes, was willingly made flesh, and made to suffer: "And being found in human form he humbled himself and became obedient unto death, even death on a cross."[106]

These Johannine reflections help us understand Jesus's response to Phillip when he said, *Qui vidit me, vidit Patrem* ("He who has seen me has seen the Father"). To see Jesus in all his glory is to gaze at him, arms outstretched, and ever faithful to the Father's plan—*even to death on a Cross.* The paradox of the Cross is at the epicenter of St. John's "beholding His glory." To Caiaphas, Pilate, the bitter thief, and the large throng that yelled "crucify Him," Jesus's death was a fitting execution for a blasphemous man—a "lifting up" of shame and defeat. For the Apostle, however, it was only the first stage of his glorious ascent—a "lifting up" of selfless love, of God's triumph over the miserable stain of sin, and the hopelessness of death.

As Brown summarizes, "In John 'being lifted up' refers to one contin-

101. Jn 13–21.
102. Jn 1–12.
103. See Jn 2:1–2:11.
104. Jn 3:14; see also 8:28, 12:32.
105. Jn 1:14c.
106. Phil 2:8.

uous action of ascent: Jesus begins his return to his Father as he approaches death (13:1) and completes it only with his ascension (20:17). It is the upward swing of the great pendulum of the Incarnation corresponding to the descent of the Word which became flesh. The first step in the ascent is when Jesus is lifted up on the cross; the second step is when he is raised up from death; the final step is when he is lifted up to heaven."[107]

St. John gazed upon the One who has gazed at God from all of eternity. Intriguingly, he paints his portrait with a certain restraint, in a manner that is mysterious in its selectivity. John carefully chooses just seven *seimeion* (Greek for "signs") out of the dozens recorded in the Synoptic Gospels, and more still that he witnessed. Similarly, in presenting the Passion, the Apostle's brushstrokes are characteristically bold, deeply symbolic, and filled with mystery. In John, there is no mention of Jesus before the accusing Sanhedrin.[108] And while all Four Gospels record the either-Jesus-or-Barabbas question posed by Pilate,[109] John's version is much more concise. Unlike them, he does not explicitly tell of Barabbas's release.[110] Unlike the Synoptic accounts, John does not include Simon the Cyrene, carrying Jesus's cross,[111] the darkness covering the earth at the moment of Jesus's death,[112] nor the *kerygma* in the mouth of the Roman Centurion.[113]

There are a number of other significant details altogether absent from the Synoptic Gospels that are recorded in John, but the breadth of these Gospel distinctives cannot be traced here.[114] One thinks of particularly Johannine signatures, such as Pilate's utterance of *Ecce homo* (Greek for "Behold the man!"),[115] Jesus's entrusting the "Woman" to the Beloved Disciple,[116] and the "blood and water" pouring from the side

107. Brown, *Gospel According to John (I–XII)*, 146.

108. Cf. Jn 18:24 with Mt 27:1, Mk 15:1, and Lk 22:66–71.

109. Mt 27:15–23; Mk 15:6–14; Lk 23:17–23; Jn 18:39–40.

110. See Mt 27:26; Mk 15:15; Lk 23:24–25.

111. See Mt 27:32; Mk 15:21; Lk 23:26.

112. See Mt 27:45; Mk 15:33; Lk 23:44–45.

113. Mt 27:54; Mk 15:39; Lk 23:47.

114. For more on this issue, see "The Value of the Information Found Only in John" (xlii–xliv) and "The Question of Dependency upon the Synoptic Gospels" (xviv–xlvii), in Brown, *Gospel According to John (I–XII)*. See also Barrett, "John and the Synoptic Gospels"; idem, *Testimony of the Beloved Disciple*; Dodd, *Historical Tradition in the Fourth Gospel*; Kysar, *John*; Smith, *John among the Gospels*; von Wahlde, *Gospel and Letters of John*. In full disclosure, von Wahlde was my mentor (2003–8) and directed my doctoral dissertation.

115. Jn 19:5.

116. Jn 19:26–27.

of the crucified Lord.[117] There is something in this last, distinctly Johannine, scene of the blood and water pouring from Jesus's side that draws our attention. There, John concludes with reference to a text from the prophet Zechariah: "And again another scripture says, 'They shall look on him *whom they have pierced*.'"[118] What is Jesus really getting at when he says, "He who has seen me has seen the Father"?

Seeing Jesus Is Seeing the Father

St. John's portrait provides a clear answer: to truly see Jesus is to see the One who was "despised and rejected by men," and as one *et quasi abscondebamus vultum coram eo—"from whom men hide their faces."*[119] It is to gaze upon the "Lamb of God"[120] who was "led to the slaughter."[121] It is to behold the One who "poured out His soul unto death,"[122] death even on a Cross,[123] held there by divine love, a supernatural love by which he "bore the sins of many."[124]

St. John is selective in his brushstrokes, leading directly to *the heart of Jesus*, who was "pierced for our transgressions."[125] In the Upper Room Discourse, recall the profound statement of Phillip that John records: "Lord, *show us the Father,* and we shall be satisfied."[126] "*He who has seen Me has seen the* Father," Jesus responds.[127] Yet again we press further and inquire as to what Jesus precisely meant—and just what sort of "seeing" was involved.

It is only by working through the remainder of the Gospel and con-

117. Jn 19:31–37.

118. Cf. Jn 19:37 with Zec 12:10: "And I will pour out on the house of David and the inhabitants of Jerusalem a spirit of compassion and supplication, so that, when they look *on him whom they have pierced*, they shall mourn for him, as one mourns for an only child, and weep bitterly over him, as one weeps over a first-born" (emphasis added). See also Rv 1:7: "Behold, he is coming with the clouds, and every eye will see him, *everyone who pierced him*; and all tribes of the earth will wail on account of him. Even so. Amen" (emphasis added).

119. Is 53:3; emphasis added.

120. Jn 1:29, 1:36.

121. Is 53:7.

122. Is 53:12.

123. Phil 2:8.

124. Is 53:12. The Fourth Servant Song of Isaiah will be examined in great detail in the third encounter scene below.

125. Is 53:5.

126. Jn 14:8; emphasis added.

127. Jn 14:9; emphasis added.

templating the Pierced One that we truly "see" him as John wishes us to see. To behold the Crucified Jesus is to see the Father more fully than that offered to us in any other portraiture. Ratzinger explains it like this: "The disciples of Jesus are men who are seeking God's face. That is why they joined up with Jesus and followed after him. Now Philip lays this longing before the Lord and receives a surprising answer, in which the novelty of the New Testament, the new thing that is coming through Christ, shines as though in crystallized form: *Yes, you can see God. Whoever sees Christ sees him.*"[128]

Another insight from Ratzinger's essay on "Seeing Jesus in the Gospel of John" presents itself for our consideration: "The New Testament texts about seeing God in Christ are deeply rooted in the piety of Israel; by and through it they extend through the entire breadth of the history of religion or, perhaps to put it better: They draw the obscure longing of religious history upward to Christ and thereby guide it toward his response."[129] This is helpful, and here is why.

This book is not merely an exercise in gazing at the face of the Lord from the vista of the New Testament *alone*. It begins with the Old Testament and moves to the New Testament: "If we want to understand the New Testament theology of the face of Christ, we must look back into the Old Testament. *Only in this way can it be understood in all its depth.*"[130] We began this chapter with a deceptively simple question posed by Romano Guardini: "Where is Heaven? Up there." Now, as the chapter draws to a close, the question (and answer) comes back to us, full circle. Through our contemplation of the divine Son, it returns to us with fresh clarity, renewed urgency, and profound depth. Receiving the biblical revelation of the Beloved Disciple, who "beheld" him[131] in the flesh, who gazed upon him as he was "lifted up" in glory upon the Cross, we can say with confidence that we too have *seen Jesus*, and in him and with him, the face of the Lord.

We give the last word to Guardini as well: "God is always accessible and everywhere near to man. But His presence is inaccessible. We believe He did this. That presence of the Father was all about Jesus. The Father was completely open with Him, and one with Him in an infinity of

128. Ratzinger, *On the Way to Jesus Christ*, 14; emphasis added.
129. Ratzinger, *On the Way to Jesus Christ*, 17.
130. Ratzinger, *On the Way to Jesus Christ*, 17; emphasis added.
131. Jn 1:14c.

love ... *Heaven surrounded Jesus, the accessible presence of the Father.*"[132] Guardini adds that it is the Father who brings Jesus to us: "We know the Father loves us in Jesus. We have confidence in the grace of His love for us; *we know His eyes see us*, His heart is turned towards us, His hand leads us. We believe Heaven is about us."[133]

132. Guardini, *Jesus Christus*, 108; emphasis added.
133. Guardini, *Jesus Christus*, 108; emphasis added.

CHAPTER 2

De Spiritu et Littera I

On the Necessity of the Four Senses

From Seen to Unseen

The aim of this chapter and the next is for the reader to become comfortable with—and competent in—a fresh idea about the Bible and its interpretation. When conceived of as a whole, the Four Senses are bigger than any of them individually. When integrated, they form a fuller way of receiving the Scriptures, a totality of interlocked meanings. Together, the Four Senses coalesce into a *definitive pathway* and a *true progression* toward the face of God.

Even so, some modern readers will immediately dismiss them: Why place such emphasis on them? Isn't it possible to explore this topic in biblical theology without resorting to outdated modes of interpretation, such as allegory and the like? How can *The Face of the Lord* offer the reader anything fresh if it merely rehashes such antiquated approaches as the Four Senses? One could go further and ask: Is this book imposing an uncritical lens upon the reader, and if so, how is that preferred? These questions are not irrelevant. It is fair to ask about the approach of this book at the outset. Ultimately, each reader will decide whether it is an asset or a liability, and I accept fair-minded criticism. In fairness, inherent in such modern concerns are certain prejudgments about the intrinsic worth of the Four Senses in biblical interpretation today.

It is not my aim to mount a full response to such questions here; the subsequent exegesis will be sufficient. Yet neither can such go entirely unanswered, and four points of rebuttal are necessary as to our reliance upon the Four Senses of Scripture.

1. First, to suggest that anything other than modern biblical criticism is useful for breaking open the Word—to the exclusion of all other methodologies—is unreasonable and without merit, historically speaking. In fact, if we look carefully, the authors of the Old and New Testaments reveal time and again their direct embrace of symbolism. Moreover, if left unchallenged, such approaches risk evolving into a hermeneutic of postmodern authoritarianism.

2. Literary elements such as typology and allegory are not at all uncommon within the Scriptures themselves. St. Paul made use of such figural readings in his discussion of Sarah and Hagar in Galatians.[1] There, Paul uses the Greek term *allēgoroumena*, from which we derive our English word "allegory." Paul's treatment of the Hagar-Sarah story is explicitly and undisguisedly allegorical.[2]

3. There is always the risk that interpreting the Word in a "literal only" fashion may lead some to force a kind of literalism upon certain texts that can *only* be unpacked in light of the symbols and figures placed there by the author. Yet the true literal sense is not at all the same as an overwrought, wooden "literalism." An example springs quickly to mind: Genesis 1 and 2. While exegetes may disagree over the details, any "forcing" of a literalism into the text often results in a kind of biblical fundamentalism.[3] Evidently, the text was meant to be read and interpreted figurally,[4] without conceding or diminishing the truths expressed in the inspired text.

4. Finally, the notion of interpreting the Scriptures "beyond than the literal" happens to be a Jewish idea. Here one thinks, for example, of

1. See Gal 4:21–31.

2. Paul's use of the participle *allēgoroumena* here is the only occurrence in the New Testament. For more on the text, see Barrett, "Allegory of Abraham, Sarah, and Hagar"; Longenecker, *Galatians*, 208; Martyn, *Galatians*, 432–57; Hays, *Echoes of Scripture*.

3. See Smith, *House of the Lord*, chaps. 1–2 on the temple theology in Gn 1–3. *CCC* §337: "God himself created the visible world in all its richness, diversity, and order. Scripture presents the work of the Creator symbolically as a succession of six days of divine 'work,' concluded by the 'rest' of the seventh day."

4. *CCC* §390: "The account of the fall in Genesis 3 *uses figurative language*, but affirms a primeval event, a deed that took place *at the beginning of the history of man*" (emphasis added; see also *CCC* §362). See also Beale, *The Temple and the Church's Mission*; Clifford, *Creation Accounts*; Congar, *Mystery of the Temple*; Levering, *Christ's Fulfillment of Temple and Torah*.

Jewish philosopher Philo of Alexandria. Even prior to Origen, the first full-fledged Christian allegorist, Philo composed a number of rather complex allegorical interpretations of the Hebrew Scriptures, such as *On the Creation*, *On Dreams*, *Special Laws*, and *The Decalogue*, among others.[5] This is not to imply that all meaning derived from the spiritual senses is equally sound.[6] Nevertheless, the numerous, authentic gains that flow from the spiritual senses far exceeds any of their limitations.

By way of summary, in the interpretation of Scripture, there is a decisive role for "figural" readings, using Anglican scholar Ephraim Radner's language. Moreover, both the literal and spiritual senses are indispensable and will be treated as such in this study. They have different ends and are attained by different methods. "Their relative autonomy must be preserved. Spiritual exegesis must not interfere with or try to substitute for historical science."[7]

St. Augustine and Boethius

In early Christianity, the idea of allegorical and figural readings of Scripture took root in Alexandria as early as the second century BC as the way to break open Holy Writ.[8] But while the spiritual senses were

5. Philo of Alexandria, *Philo*, vol. 1. See also *Philo*, vol. 2, no. 227, which contains *On the Cherubim, the Flaming Sword, and Cain*; *On Abel and the Sacrifices Offered by Him and Cain*; and *On the Giants*; *Philo*, vol. 3, no. 247, which contains *On the Decalogue*; *Abraham*; *Joseph*; *Moses*; *On Special Laws*; and *Philo: Questions and Answers on Exodus*. For analysis of Philo, see Daniélou and Colbert, *Philo of Alexandria*; Borgen, *Philo of Alexandria*; Tobin, *Creation of Man*. See also Sheridan, *Language for God in Patristic Tradition*; Radner, *Time and the Word*.

6. "While de Lubac does not deny that there are some spiritual interpretations of Scripture which have more objective validity than others, he frankly admits that spiritual understanding has an inherently subjective aspect which cannot be excised without neutralizing the entire process and rendering it spiritually profitless. Thus, it can never be judged from a purely objective viewpoint or reduced to a scientific discipline." D'Ambrosio, "Spiritual Sense in de Lubac's Hermeneutics of Tradition," 154.

7. D'Ambrosio, "Spiritual Sense in de Lubac's Hermeneutics of Tradition," 155. "Though many features of ancient exegesis inevitably succumb to the critique of modern historical science, the fundamental principles and structure of the traditional hermeneutic emerge from the crucible virtually intact. The primary impact of modem scientific exegesis upon this ancient hermeneutic is to increase the sophistication and religious value of this first phase of exegesis. As significant as this is, de Lubac contends that a focus on sound literal interpretation is not per se modern, and constitutes no contradiction with ancient exegesis" (156). See Radner, *Time and the Word*, chap. 1.

8. Although at times overstated, there is something to be said for a Christian appropriation of Jewish allegory. Philo of Alexandria and other Diaspora writers had already

flourishing early in the primitive Church, it was not until the fourth and fifth centuries that theories of the "meaning" of words would be more fully developed. Along these lines, it was from St. Augustine's *De Doctrina Christiana* (*On Christian Doctrine*)[9] and Boethius's commentaries on Aristotle's *De Interpretatione* (*On Interpretation*)[10] that the notion of "words and their signification" became highly developed in the patristic period.

For St. Augustine, "All instruction is either about things (*res*) or about signs (*signum*). No one uses words except as *signum* of something else. So, they may be understood as *signum*: those things which are used to indicate something else. Accordingly, every *signum* is also a *res*, and what is not a *res* is nothing at all. Every *res*, however, is not also a *signum*."[11]

As Levering helpfully explains,

> They key to a right reading of Scripture is to realize that God can and does use things as signs ... All signs are signs of things; but not all things are signs. It should be noted that even God is a thing (*res*), although he is most certainly not a thing like other things and he is never a sign of another thing ... when we imagine God as a finite thing, we show that *our minds need purification so as to see the divine light. This purification is the first step of our journey to our homeland, to God himself.*[12]

---

invested themselves in the *allegoria* of the various Platonic schools. Such Hellenistic Jews adapted such approaches to conform to the personal monotheism of Judaism. See Hengel, *"Hellenization" of Judea*; idem, *Judaism and Hellenism*; Barclay, *Jews in the Mediterranean Diaspora*; Stone, *Jewish Writings of the Second Temple Period*; Tcherikover, *Hellenistic Civilization and the Jews*; Tcherikover and Fuks, *Corpus Papyrorum Judaicarum*. See also Bickerman, *Jews in the Greek Age*; Boccaccini, *Middle Judaism*; Collins, *Between Athens and Jerusalem*; Feldman, *Jew and Gentile in the Ancient World*; Goodenough, *Jewish Symbols in the Greco-Roman Period*; Momigliano, *Alien Wisdom*; Neusner, *Jerusalem and Athens*; Nickelsburg, *Jewish Literature*; Rutgers, *Jews in Late Ancient Rome*; Sanders, *Jewish and Christian Self-Definition*; Schürer, *History of the Jewish People*; Smallwood, *Jews under Roman Rule*.

9. St. Augustine of Hippo, *De Doctrina Christiana* (*On Christian Doctrine*), in Schaff, *St. Augustin's City of God and Christian Doctrine*. See also these translations: Green, *Augustine*; Gavigan, *Christian Instruction*; Hill, *Teaching Christianity*; Green, *Saint Augustine*.

10. Boethius, *On Aristotle on Interpretation 1–3*.

11. St. Augustine, *De Doctrina Christiana*, I.2.2: "And so, in regard to this distinction between things and signs, I shall, when I speak of things, speak in such a way that even if some things may be used as signs also, that will not interfere with the division of the subject according to which I am to discuss things first and signs afterward" (my translation). See Levering, "On Christian Doctrine," in *Theology of Augustine*, 1–19; Van Fleteren, "Principles of Augustine's Hermeneutic: An Overview," in Van Fleteren and Schnaubelt, *Augustine*, 1–32.

12. Levering, *Theology of Augustine*, 3, 5; emphasis added.

Meanwhile, Boethius (480–524) would approach the subject in the manner of Aristotle. Boethius differentiated between "noise" and "words": *vox significativa per seipsam alquid significans*, meaning a sound is a word *only if it means something.*[13] The way that Augustine and Boethius conceptualized words and their respective meaning was instrumental in consolidating earlier advances. Although their arguments were distinct from one another, they were developing theories about *signification* that would have remarkable influence long after the four and fifth centuries. This is especially the case with Augustine's method of biblical interpretation, and his argument, laid out in *De Doctrina Christiana*, was of enormous impact.[14] In fact, in the High Middle Ages, Hugh of St. Victor was known as "the New Augustine." In no small way, Hugh's methodology was a result of his looking back to Augustine's biblical hermeneutic in *De Doctrina Christiana.*

Words signify things, and in Holy Scripture, these things in turn signify *still greater things*, by virtue of their divine authorship. All of this means, in turn, that the Scriptures are a *sacrament* and must be received accordingly. They are pregnant with meaning(s) that must take the literal into account, but only before plunging into the sacramental mystery that lies beyond it, in and through the spiritual senses: "*The sacraments exist to make contact between men and the Word of God at the point when that Word is pronounced for our salvation: in the man Jesus and in his action redeeming us*. Their name, 'sacraments,' means 'mysteries,' because by them the mystery of the redemption that is in Christ Jesus is accessible to mankind."[15]

Ephraim Radner and "Figural Readings" of Scripture

In his recent and well-articulated defense of what he calls "figural" readings of Scripture, Radner brings this out brilliantly.[16] Early in *Time and*

13. Boethius, *I Commentarii; De Interpretatione*, 37. See also Evans, *Language and Logic of the Bible*, esp. chap. 6, "Exegesis and the Theory of Signification."

14. Much of what Augustine discusses in *De Doctrina Christiana* is his own development of Tyconius's *Book of Rules* for the proper interpretation of Sacred Scripture. For a recent biography on Augustine, see Brown, *Augustine of Hippo*.

15. Durrwell, "Sacrament of Sacred Scripture," 167; emphasis added. This last point—the sacramental nature of Sacred Scripture—is highly significant. This topic will be discussed at greater length in chap. 3.

16. See Radner, *Time and the Word*.

the Word, Radner takes the example of St. Augustine's *Literal Commentary on Genesis.* Radner explains how interpreting Genesis was a philosophical as well as exegetical challenge, even for St. Augustine. By his own admission, Augustine found it difficult to comment on the mysteries of the Creation in his *Literal Commentary on Genesis.* Understandably so! How can temporal, time-bound creatures begin to grasp the eternal Creator, who *created* time: "*You are my eternal Father, but I am scattered in times whose order I do not understand.*"[17]

Drawing on Augustine's own words, in which he puzzled over such things, Radner stresses that Augustine's *Literal Commentary on Genesis* posed certain interpretative dilemmas: "How could an effort that is *so explicitly geared towards avoiding allegory* end up mired in so much metaphysical brush?"[18] That's a good question. Radner's analysis is as smart as it is clear: "The divine-human and eternal-temporal divide is so drastic that inevitably any discussion of, in this case, 'creation' or 'the world' must engage the foundational mysteries of this chasm as to impinge on any 'literal' reading. *What, after all, is the 'literal meaning' of the creation of 'time?*'"[19] What is the plain and accurate meaning of *that*?

Let us suppose one is determined to analyze Genesis 1 and 2 in a strictly literal way. How could one "break open" the text properly?[20] How could one discuss the creation of time, according to the literal sense? Augustine did, and he accomplished this by accounting for certain textual symbols within the literal sense. He was able to locate them *within the author's original intent.* This was an epic discovery. As Radner explains, Augustine did so without any vacillation or indecisiveness in his *Literal Commentary on Genesis*. Nor was there any dichotomy between his *Literal Commentary* and his work on the text in *Confessions*.[21]

17. St. Augustine, *Confessions*, 11.29; emphasis added. Radner's translation, in *Time and the Word*, 51. The Latin reads: "Et tu solacium meum, domine, pater meus aeternus es; at ego in tempora dissilui, quorum ordinem nescio, et tumultuosis varietatibus dilaniantur cogitationes meae, intima viscera animae meae, donec in te confluam purgatus et liquidus igne amoris tui." In *St. Augustine's Confessions*, 280.

18. Radner, *Time and the Word*, 53; emphasis added.

19. Radner, *Time and the Word*, 53; emphasis added.

20. Radner is not attempting to diminish the literal sense or suggesting that the way forward is to embrace "figural" readings at the expense of the literal. Later in the text, he raises a number of intriguing questions in the form of "lists" by which one may at least begin to sort out such matters, without compromising either the literal or the spiritual senses. See *Time and the Word,* 100–106.

21. Radner, *Time and the Word*, 55; emphasis original.

Following Augustine, what Radner claims is significant: figural readings are necessary because "Scripture is our access to the mind of God."[22] Scripture is not only a sensible text. It is the text that makes our lives sensible, the text that tells us that life is not senseless. It is the text that tells us, in Fulton Sheen's phrasing, that *life is worth living*; or, in Peterson's language, how to put ourselves together and orient ourselves in the world. In Augustine's terms, Scripture makes it possible to hear from God, it is "*our life with God*."[23] Not only this; the example Radner offers from St. Augustine's own explorations of Genesis 1 and 2 also make abundantly clear that for him figural readings "are necessary . . . simply by the nature of things. The literal gives rise to, *even demands logically*, figural investigation of the Scripture . . . The predestined truth of the eternal Word—infinitely fertile—is put into the world through time; and thus, gives rise to spiritual readings."[24] As Augustine wrote, "We have also looked at these things with an eye to their figurative meaning, *which Thou didst intend*, either in the order of their coming into being, or in the order in which they were written."[25] All of these insights—from Augustine to Radner—are vital as we move forward.

Jordan Peterson—and Exegesis on One's Knees

Moving on from Radner's contributions, we turn to another contemporary reader of the Old Testament and his insights on locating "meaning" in Scripture, Jordan Peterson. Peterson experienced an astonishing rise from relatively unknown clinical psychologist to sort of a worldwide media phenomenon. His now-infamous interview with Cathy Newman lit the fuse, and the proliferation of his book *Twelve Rules for Life* cemented things further.[26] I would argue, however, that his ongoing YouTube and podcast lectures on "meaning" are in fact what continually fuel the growing interest in Peterson.

It is intriguingly coincidental that the present book is being released in the era of Peterson's surprising fame.[27] At first, this may seem like a

22. Radner, *Time and the Word*, 55.

23. Radner, *Time and the Word*, 55; emphasis original.

24. Radner, *Time and the Word*, 55; emphasis added.

25. Augustine, *Confessions*, 13.24.49, ed. Deferrari, 453; emphasis added.

26. The interview, noted above, was about the content of Peterson's *Twelve Rules For Life*.

27. The research for this book was undertaken long before 2018, when Jordan Peterson first became relatively known.

rather idiosyncratic comment. Yet there is a curious connection between the two. To the point, many of Peterson's lengthy podcasts are dedicated to the exploration of Scripture. Indeed, Peterson's "biblical lectures" have, at this point, been heard by millions and millions.[28] Dealing with themes like "Genesis: Chaos and Order," "Cain and Abel: The Hostile Brothers," and "Jacob's Ladder," Peterson discusses Scripture from a psychological viewpoint. And these lectures have garnered interest—from delight to disdain—by religious and nonreligious alike.

In March 2019, Bishop Robert Barron was interviewed by Peterson on the latter's podcast. At least in the Catholic cultural landscape, this was a highly anticipated event. It might not have been the "rumble in the jungle," but for some it was comparable to the famed bout between Ali and Foreman. In any event, one of Barron's comments stands out. In talking about Peterson's biblical series, he drew a (relative) correlation between Peterson's psychological approach to Scripture and the allegorical insights of the great Origen.[29] This may seem like a bit of a leap. *Is this ascribing too much influence—too much of a complement—to Peterson?* No. Barron's loose comparison is not without warrant. In fact, it makes a good deal of sense. The point is not for critics of Peterson to be upset at such a suggestion; neither should his supporters ready the bronze statue just yet. But we should pay close attention to what Peterson is saying about Scripture, and how to interpret and engage it.

What Barron was getting at is precisely this: the ancients believed that there was a "deep intelligence" with which Scripture were written, and they interpreted in such a way. So does Peterson.[30] Not merely with cerebral acumen, but also with "spiritual" wisdom. Origen, Augustine,

28. See "The Psychological Significance of the Biblical Stories," JordanBPeterson.com, accessed November 7, 2019, https://www.jordanbpeterson.com/bible-series/.

29. "Bishop Barron: Catholicism and the Modern Age," *The Jordan B. Peterson Podcast*, accessed November 7, 2019, https://podcasts.apple.com/ca/podcast/bishop-barron-catholicism-and-the-modern-age/id1184022695?i=1000442430783.

30. I chose the phrase "deep intelligence" carefully. Barron and Peterson have distinct points of reference as to the authorship of Scripture. For Barron, authorship undoubtedly involves the inspired human authors, and goes beyond them to the "ultimate" author, the Holy Spirit. For Peterson, these are monumentally important texts of profound significance. Peterson believes the human authors were writing in response to God—beginning and ending with God in mind. And he believes we must take the Scriptures seriously and ponder their bountiful meaning. He believes they were composed with a deep intelligence. Yet here I refrain from answering the question, Were the Scriptures inspired by God? and await his further reflection on this crucial question.

Gregory the Great, and a great many others did *exegesis on their knees*, with prayer, humility, a sense of reverence for the Sacred Page. In the patristic and medieval eras, the Scriptures were met with "struggle." One might say that they "suffered with the text" beyond their literal meaning. In addition to the allegorical sense, Barron, in this interview, mentions "tropology." He rightly notes that for Origen and others, one of the deepest meanings of Scripture was the *moral dimension*. Therein lies Barron's comparison between what Origen did so many centuries ago and what Peterson is doing today, looking at Genesis and Exodus in a psychological fashion.[31] Barron's impressions are sound: the ancients grappled with the Scriptures on a deeply spiritual level.

To borrow Peterson's phraseology, Origen and Gregory and the rest were as interested in the believer "cleaning up his room" and growing as disciples as a result of encountering the text. One may hope that Peterson's efforts will reinvigorate interest in the Bible, especially for the "none's," that is, the religiously unaffiliated that frequently are a part of Barron's cultural observations.

The "Indispensability" of the Literal and Spiritual Senses

The goal is not to get "beyond the literal" as quickly as possible, as if it is to be dispensed with in a hurry. On the contrary, each of the senses—beginning with the literal and culminating in the anagogical—has a unique and crucial role to play in approaching the face of the Lord. Here, we agree with Ratzinger, who in the first of his three-volume *Jesus of Nazareth* series was unequivocal: "the historical-critical method—specifically because of the intrinsic nature of theology and faith—is and remains an *indispensable* dimension of exegetical work."[32] Why "indis-

31. One may balk at a comparison between "moral" and "psychological," but the reader should not be distressed. Barron makes a general comparison. He is not engaging in naive equivocation and understands the complexities of each category.

32. Ratzinger, *Jesus of Nazareth*, xv, emphasis added. "One of the more prominent attempts in recent years to synthesize the theological principles of premodern Christian exegesis with modern biblical criticism for the theological interpretation of Scripture is Pope Benedict XVI/Joseph Ratzinger's *Jesus of Nazareth*. Throughout *Jesus of Nazareth*, Ratzinger often appeals to the biblical interpretation of various Church Fathers as a resource for drawing out 'the abiding theological significance of the Gospels.' While he regards patristic exegesis as making a valuable theological contribution, his appropriation of

pensable"? There are many ways to respond to this question. One way ascends high above all others: *the Incarnation of the divine Son*. It is the Incarnation—the enfleshment of Jesus—that demands that Christianity in general, and Scripture in particular, be engaged with authentic historical rigor. In Jesus, God has broken into human history, taking on flesh, in space and time, so that history can never been set aside from biblical meaning.

Yet in the same breath we equally agree with the esteemed Bavarian scholar in his decidedly more critical assessment of the historical-critical method that appeared in his subsequent volume. Ratzinger writes, "One thing is clear to me: in two hundred years of exegetical work, historical-critical exegesis has already yielded its essential fruit. If scholarly exegesis is not to exhaust itself in constantly new hypotheses, becoming theologically irrelevant, it must take a methodological step forward and see itself once again as a theological discipline, without abandoning its historical character."[33] This remark does not discard the historical-critical method to a status of "dispensability." Rather, it balances his previous observations. The historical-critical method is essential. Yet it can only deliver to us, in a limited way, what the Bible means.

This method, while crucial to the task of interpretation, does not have within itself the capacity to *transcend* history. And Scripture is *transhistorical* by virtue of its divine authorship. Historical approaches are finite, limited in scope. By definition, they are unable to reveal the transcendent, present in the Word in a more hidden way. Make no mistake: the transcendent, apprehended primarily through the spiritual sense, is no less "dispensable" to the uncovering the text's meaning than the literal. As is often the case, it is a matter of both/and, not either/or. No one sense has the "the market cornered" when it comes to biblical meaning. The literal and spiritual senses are not opposed. They are not enemies, nor are they even strange bedfellows. They are more like siblings of the same parent: each an offspring, each a son of the same Father. Each "child" bears the same surname ("Meaning"), even as each possesses its own attributes and personality, and is called by a different personal name.

---

it is neither uncritical nor nostalgic." Wright, "Patristic Biblical Hermeneutics in Joseph Ratzinger's Jesus of Nazareth."

33. Ratzinger, *Jesus of Nazareth, Part Two*, xiv–xv. See also Ratzinger's 1988 Erasmus Lecture in *Biblical Interpretation in Crisis*.

A second point may be added to the above and requires a bit more explanation. This book has no interest in placing one sense over another. Rather, it aims at recognizing the vital role played by each of them, in breaking open the Word within the totality of the Four Senses. This book seeks to be part of the "methodological step forward" so eloquently called for by Ratzinger. We will insist that the literal be seen as the primary sense. Still, given our aim, we will not give it undue priority over the other senses. To the contrary, while we underscore the "pole position" of the literal, it is not the end of the matter. The literal is essential in its own right. Yet it is part of a larger equation. It is a threshold that we will pass through; the gateway through which we will pass on our way to the spiritual senses.

Sadly, far too many historical-critical approaches determinedly set aside the spiritual dimension of biblical texts. Raymond Brown, for instance, passed on most spiritual/theological questions a priori. He saw them as matters of "faith" to be taken up by systematic theologians.[34] Such theological bifurcation would have been utter nonsense to Origen, Augustine, or Thomas Aquinas. In a helpful essay, Bishop Robert Barron argues for an approach that embraces the literal *and* the spiritual senses: "There is a growing consensus that a one-sidedly historical-critical approach to the interpretation of Sacred Scriptures is inadequate. Figures as diverse as Brevard Childs, Walter Brueggemann, Jon Levenson, Gary Anderson, Francis Martin, Robert Louis Wilken, and Joseph Ratzinger have indicated how, in various ways, the dominance of historical criticism in the post-conciliar period has led to a diminishment of the Bible in the life of the Church."[35]

34. This isn't to say that Brown never engaged in questions of theology. In fairness, he did, in separate works apart from his biblical commentaries. Yet such discussions were usually limited to reconstructive hypotheses, e.g., his theories about the "Johannine community" and the like. Scarcely did he engage in matters of "dogmatic" theology in his biblical commentaries. See Brown, *Gospel According to John (I–XII)*, esp. xli–li; Francis Moloney, "Excursus: Theories of Johannine Community History," in Brown and Moloney, *Introduction to the Gospel of John*, 69–79. Francis Moloney, a student of Brown, composed this section after Brown's unexpected death. See also Brown's classic on the topic, *Community of the Beloved Disciple*.

35. See esp. Barron, "Biblical Interpretation and Theology." See also Childs, *Biblical Theology*; Bruggemann, *Creative Word*; Levenson, *Hebrew Bible*; Anderson, *Christian Doctrine and the Old Testament*; Martin, *Sacred Scripture*; Wilken, *Spirit of Early Christian Thought*; Ratzinger, "Biblical Interpretation in Crisis."

How Ancient Rabbis and Church Fathers Read Scripture

Barron's essay argues that in much modern biblical exegesis there has been "a severing of the ties" between the literal and the spiritual senses. He concludes that this trend is unhealthy, to say the least.[36] Barron advocates for a rediscovery of St. Irenaeus's biblical theology, with its emphasis on *anakephalaiosis* ("recapitulation").[37] He concludes his essay by looking at the precepts of *Dei Verbum,* which he describes as a "participatory"[38] model of reading and interpreting Scripture. Like Radner, Barron is not interested in diminishing historical-critical efforts.[39] In his balanced critique, Barron expresses confidence that historical-critical study of Scripture need not be at odds with the likes of Origen or Hugh, to name just two.[40]

The "participatory" approach is one in which *all the senses play their role*—from the literal through the various spiritual senses. St. Augustine did not abandon his project of composing a *Literal Commentary on Genesis*. Rather, he sensibly integrated figural readings as demanded by the nature of the biblical text. Augustine well understood that the inspired authors infused their works with both literal and spiritual depth. Such a polyvalent methodology is central to this project, too.

36. Barron, "Biblical Interpretation and Theology," 173. See also Levering, *Participatory Biblical Exegesis*.

37. See Barron, "Biblical Interpretation and Theology," 178–79. "The notion of *anakephalaiosis*, rendered in Latin as *recapitulatio* is the master idea of Irenaeus' biblical theology. Jesus draws all of the strands of history and revelation together in himself, preserving and repeating them even as he brings them to fulfillment. Thus, he is the new Adam, the one who participates fully in the reality of Adam, including physicality and alienation from God, even as he draws all that was implicit and potential in Adam to completion." See also *CCC* §518.

38. See Barron, "Biblical Interpretation and Theology," 186. "When Thomas and the Fathers before him were endeavoring to exegete the Scripture, they were not going after, primarily, what the historical authors intended, but rather what the divine author intended. They realized, of course, that God worked through the secondary causality of intelligently engaged human beings, but their real focus was on the God in whom both history as such and the biblical authors participated." See also Levering, *Participatory Biblical Exegesis*, 198.

39. "What I want to do in this article is to argue for the reintegration of exegesis and theology in the spirit of the Fathers and the medieval masters of the *sacra pagina* ["the sacred page"], fully acknowledging as I do so the legitimate gains of the modern historical-critical approach." Barron, "Biblical Interpretation and Theology," 173.

40. The choice of Origen and Hugh is not incidental; in some sense, they are like bookends that frame the periods from which most references (at least as they pertain to the spiritual senses) will be drawn.

Another helpful insight from Barron's essay has to do with how one approaches the Bible in the first place. Is it or isn't it the Word *of God*? Sure, it comes to us from "true" human authors, to recall *Dei Verbum*'s language.[41] Yet Scripture is not merely a human enterprise. Its origins are heavenly: *Divinitus revelata, quae in Sacra Scriptura litteris continentur et prostant, Spiritu Sancto afflante consignata sunt.*[42]

Mysteriously, all Scripture comes to us in a way that is *simultaneously* from the *human* authors and its *ultimate* author, the Holy Spirit. The prophets and apostles are "true authors," as they are *spiritu Sancto inspirante conscripti*, inspired by the Holy Spirit.[43] In a technical way, Farkasfalvy unpacks what biblical inspiration means. It is "the divine action stimulating the human authors of the biblical books to produce their work, and the divine charism bestowed upon the biblical authors, enabling them to produce those literary works that make up part of the Bible."[44]

As a result, Barron stresses the "coherence and consistence" of Scripture. This inexplicable continuity unfolds across the scores of books of the Bible, and it is the result of their coming to us from the divine Author: "The Bible, consequently, ought never to be read simply as a congeries of unrelated tales, prophecies, histories, and words of wisdom, drawn from a variety of sources and in response to differing historical situations. Though it might seem that way 'from the ground,' it takes on *coherence and consistency* when read from the standpoint of the divine author. Thus, the Bible is a *symphonos*, a sounding together of tones and melodies, under the direction of the supreme artist."[45] Here, Barron proposes that we read Scripture with much greater care. In light of the

41. *Dei Verbum*, 11: "In composing the sacred books, God chose men and while employed by Him they made use of their powers and abilities, so that with Him acting in them and through them, they, as true authors, consigned to writing everything and only those things which He wanted."

42. *Dei Verbum*, 11: "Those divinely revealed realities which are contained and presented in Sacred Scripture have been committed to writing under the inspiration of the Holy Spirit."

43. *Dei Verbum*, 11: "under the *inspiration* of the Holy Spirit."

44. Farkasfalvy, *Inspiration and Interpretation*, 211. Elsewhere, Farkasfalvy adds: "In Catholic theology, *divine revelation* is a specific, almost technical concept about God's self-manifestation to the world by means of words and deeds in salvation history. The process constitutes a sequence of divine interventions in history for the sake of human salvation, soliciting the recipient of the divine word to respond by faith and understanding through acts of *perception*, *belief*, and *reflection* as well as deliberate free decisions of obedience and through announcing publicly God's message by human verbal expressions and activities." *Theology of the Christian Bible*, 19–20; emphasis added.

45. Barron, "Biblical Interpretation and Theology," 177; emphasis added.

symphonic nature of the Scriptures, and by virtue of their divine authorship, we must become much more attentive to the distinctive patterns in which God speaks. "We should not be surprised to find a whole set of figural or typological correspondences throughout the Scriptural witness."[46] Additionally, Barron explains that there is proximity between the way in which ancient Jewish commentators read the Bible and that of the early Church Fathers. Barron, drawing on the research of Jewish scholar James Kugel, identifies four fundamental convictions shared in common: "These hermeneutical assumptions bring Irenaeus quite close to the rabbis of the inter-testamental period who, as James Kugel argues, operated out of four fundamental convictions—namely, *that God in a very real sense is the author of the whole Scripture, that the Bible is consistent with itself, that its meaning is often cryptic, and that it has relevance for us today*."[47] These four criteria—shared by early Jewish and Christian exegetes, are consistent with our aims and warrant further clarification.

The first conviction is that above and beyond the human author, it is God who speaks to us in his Word. He speaks in and through them, but he speaks. Despite certain distinctions between early Jewish and Christian exegetes, this central and unshakable belief—*that the Scriptures are of divine origin*—unified them. And this same conviction has the capacity to transform how exegesis is performed even today: "There is no greater priority than this: to enable the people of our time once more to encounter God, the God who speaks to us and shares his love so that we might have life in abundance."[48]

The second conviction of early Jewish and Christian exegetes flows directly from the first. The Bible is consistent within itself. As *Dei Verbum* states, "Since Holy Scripture must be read and interpreted in the sacred spirit in which it was written, no less serious attention must be given to the content and unity of the whole of Scripture if the meaning of the sacred texts is to be correctly worked out."[49]

46. Barron, "Biblical Interpretation and Theology," 178.

47. Barron, "Biblical Interpretation and Theology," 178; emphasis added. See Kugel, *How to Read the Bible*, 14–17. See also Kugel's much more comprehensive volume, *Traditions of the Bible*.

48. *Verbum Domini*, 2.

49. *Dei Verbum*, 12. I wrote about this at length in *The Word of the Lord*. See chap. 6, "Principle 4: God's Word Is Revealed in the Unity of the Old and New Testaments," 109–22. Three particularly important means of unity between the testaments are discussed: (1) the theme of "covenant," (2) biblical prophecy and typology, and (3) recapitulation.

The third conviction is particularly suspect today: that the meaning of Scripture is often "cryptic" or hidden. For de Lubac, one cannot make any real progress with the Word of God unless and until one searches for the meaning that is present but hidden: "It is a question of the change, which governs everything. Our faith depends upon it. It imposes itself; we cannot elude it if we want to produce a Christian exegesis. Gregory [the Great] indicates it for us using the strongest possible terms: *'we are forced,' 'we are compelled,' 'it is necessary,'* 'now the order of exposition requires us to lay bare the secrets of the allegories.'" De Lubac adds, "We do not have the right through 'negligence' to deprive ourselves of the many allegories of which history is so full."[50]

The fourth conviction builds upon and flows from the previous three—that the Bible has "meaning" for us today. As God's own words to us, Scripture is consistent within itself and has a cryptic meaning. Therefore it is ever new, ever creative, ever speaking to us, *even now*. Raymond Brown (1928–98), to whom Barron refers as "the dean of contemporary exegesis,"[51] would not deny this. Still, he placed certain restrictions on the role of exegesis to reveal meaning. As Barron observes,

> [Brown] spoke readily enough of the *sensus plenior*, the fuller sense, corresponding to what God intended to communicate through a text, even beyond the explicit intention of the author, but he never developed this in his own exegetical writings, leaving its explication to theologians and spiritual writers. Proper biblical scholarship, he felt, is limited to the determination of "what a given text meant," while theology or spirituality can sort out what a text might mean in the present situation. In quoting Brown, the bifurcation (whether intended or not) becomes clear: "The meaning of the Bible . . . goes beyond what the authors meant in a particular book. Not only scholarship but also Church teaching and tradition enters into the complex issue of what the Bible means to Christians."[52]

50. De Lubac, *Medieval Exegesis*, vol. 1, 84; emphasis added. Allegorical interpretation leads to a plurality of meaning. There may be more than one allegorical possibility for a text. This is not a problem, as Hans Boersma explains: "Plurality of meaning is *not a danger to be avoided* and does not constitute an argument against spiritual exegesis; rather, plurality of meaning is something to be *expected,* precisely because exegesis is the *Spirit-guided means that enables human participation in the heavenly realities." Heavenly Participation*, 149; emphases added.

51. Barron, "Biblical Interpretation and Theology," 185.

52. Brown et al., *New Jerome Biblical Commentary*, 1154. See Barron, "Biblical Interpretation and Theology," 185.

Modern-Day Marcionism

These four points are not endemic to the patristic and medieval periods. Indeed, they are at home in our overall methodology. From a Catholic perspective, these four criteria are not the vestige of bygone eras. We do not cling to them in a half-afraid, nostalgic way. *The Benedict Option* is not operable here; it is not a helpful paradigm for sound exegesis today.[53] Moreover, each of the four criteria should be taken seriously, intelligently, thoughtfully. There is nothing about them that ought to be seen as in conflict with modern critical approaches.

Sadly, however, modern scholars do not widely embrace these time-honored criteria. In fact, they are dismissed by many as precritical, antiquated obstacles to historical exegesis. One might understand a modern scholar who, let's say, does not often engage these criteria, who does not specialize in them, or for a variety of reasons simply does not "fly in their direction." This is not the state of exegesis today. Would that it were so! Where we find ourselves today is in a place of tremendous cynicism and skepticism about any sort of methodological approach that was developed *prior to the past two or three centuries.* Much modern scholarship simply acts as if any sort of achievement in biblical interpretation prior to 1780 or so *simply doesn't exist.*

Consider Origen of Alexandria. The depth and breadth of his contributions to biblical interpretation can hardly be summarized without leaving out a fact or accomplishment, simply by oversight of their voluminous nature. He was a pioneer, an intellectual, a theological giant. Yet, outside of a few specialists, modern biblical scholars don't cite him, much less pay attention to anything pertaining to Origen. Like James Stewart's "George Bailey," it is as if Origen never existed on this earth at all. Such myopia it is commonplace. And it is not Origen alone who suffers from modern scholarly stigmatization. The same is true of so many other early biblical masters. Astonishingly, the achievements of

53. See Dreher, *Benedict Option*, which has received much attention and has divided readers into positive and critical camps. I do not intend to wade into these waters too deeply and will instead simply state my view. As appealing as some its concepts may be, I am unconvinced that it doesn't amount to believers sticking their heads in the sand. A mindset of retreating, or hunkering down, is not concomitant with the message of the Gospel. Christ and his Kingdom are always advancing, even when its message is "out of season," as St. Paul writes (2 Tim 4:2).

Ambrose, Augustine, Gregory the Great, Irenaeus, and others are often impugned as *precritical.*

Numerous other scholars, including Radner and Barron, share this opinion. Barron's sharpest criticism is reserved for the sort of modern exegesis that dismisses figural or spiritual readings out of hand. He points to an essay by Brown in the *New Jerome Biblical Commentary*: "Brown laid out and defended his vision of modern historical criticism. He construed it as the attempt to discover, through philology, literary analysis, historical investigation, redaction criticism, and other tools, what precisely was the communicative intention of the author or redactor of a biblical text as he addressed his audience. This intention Brown identified with the literal sense of the Scriptural text."[54] In the same essay, however, Brown all but sets aside the allegorical approach of Origen, stating, "this writer does not share the view that Origen's exegesis can really be revived for our time."[55] Brown's suggestion that Origen's exegesis cannot be "revived" implies two things: (1) it is dead, an approach bound to antiquity and (2) it is irrelevant and useless to modern biblical interpretation.

Both of these implications are beset by the prevailing winds of exegesis. Today, scholars search out *what a text meant*. And they do so with modern critical ground rules. These rules are helpful to a point. Yet they can and do stifle any notion of *what a text means* in a theologically or spiritually rich way. This is highly problematic. Origen's understanding cannot, nor should not, be compressed into the narrow bandwidth of historical-critical methods of interpretation.

Barron writes, "There is, of course, something breathtaking, and typically modern, about this blithe dismissal of 1,500 years of biblical interpretation."[56] Breathtaking indeed. He adds, "From the standpoint of a participatory exegesis, which places a stress on the divine authorship of both the Bible and of the history of salvation itself, the Christological character of the Old Testament is taken for granted as the indispensable propaedeutic to the appearance of the Word made flesh."[57] He con-

54. Brown, *New Jerome Biblical Commentary*, 1154. Cited in Barron, "Biblical Interpretation and Theology," 185.

55. Brown, *New Jerome Biblical Commentary*, 1154. Cited in Barron, "Biblical Interpretation and Theology," 186.

56. Barron, "Biblical Interpretation and Theology," 186.

57. Barron, "Biblical Interpretation and Theology," 185.

tinues, "Thus, for Saint Irenaeus (as well as his patristic counterparts, to say nothing of the medieval interpreters that succeeded them), such denials of the Christological within the Old Testament was tantamount to Marcionism: I would like to draw attention to another strain of modern biblical interpretation which has had a rather massive impact on much theologizing—both Catholic and Protestant—over the last two centuries. It runs from Friedrich Schleiermacher, the founder of liberal Protestantism, through Adolf Harnack and Rudolf Bultmann, and its chief characteristic is neo-Marcionism, or a radical 'de-Judaizing' of the Scripture."[58]

Schleiermacher, upon Barron's assessment,

> dismisses the patristic and medieval method of interpretation with the back of his hand: "To those who would seek to restore the fallen walls of their Jewish Zion and its Gothic pillars, I say that we must discover the essence of religion in personal experience." Indeed, so dispensable is the Old Testament that Schleiermacher can say, "Christianity does indeed stand in a special historical connection with Judaism; but as far as concerns its historical existence and aim, its relations to Judaism and heathenism are the same." *It would be hard to imagine any of the first Christians finding that last statement anything but breathtakingly wrongheaded.* What this signals is the keynote for most of the theological liberalism of the past two centuries, that is to say, the disassociation of Christianity from its Old Testament roots.[59]

In other words, with due respect to Brown, it's much larger than the view of a single biblical scholar, dean though he was. This is a point worth stressing. There has been a trajectory, a pattern, that extends back hundreds of years. This trajectory has led to a bifurcation of the Gospels from their Jewish, Old Testament roots out of which they developed.[60] This interpretative move has had devastating effects for the

58. Barron, "Biblical Interpretation and Theology," 183–84; emphasis added. "N. T. Wright has commented that most of the christology of the modern period has been essentially Marcionite in form, and we can see the truth of this assertion borne out in the remarkably unbiblical christologies of Tillich, Karl Rahner, and David Tracy to name just a few representative cases" (184). See Wright, *Jesus and the Victory of God*, 26; Tracy, *Analogical Imagination*.

59. Barron, "Biblical Interpretation and Theology," 184; emphasis added.

60. "In the practice of the apostolic Church the Scriptures were not only regarded as tools to prove the truth of Christianity. The arguments were also used in the opposite direction: believing in Christ provided the key to the Scriptures . . . Indeed, as our earliest sources testify, *the Church of the Apostles considered itself a fully entitled proprietor of the Scriptures of old, capable of understanding and announcing their meaning. Thus not only is*

proper interpretation of *both testaments.* This modern-day Marcionism has produced all sorts of inadequate Christologies[61] and profound misunderstandings of Pauline theology,[62] to name just two tragic effects. A third and fourth might include the diminishment of the Old Testament priesthood and the negation of the "priesthood of Jesus." I have written previously about these last two unfortunate trends.[63]

Reclaiming "Participatory Exegesis" Today

Returning now to Barron's critique of Raymond E. Brown, we can add a few additional remarks. Some readers, especially those who have learned a good deal from Brown—as one surely can—may understandably consider Barron's criticism to be harsh. Barron's appraisal of one of the leading biblical scholars of the twentieth century is factually and historically fair. This by no means is to suggest that Brown—of one of the leading Catholic biblical scholars of the twentieth century—is unhelpful or irrelevant to our project. But it is a salient reminder that even the most capable of modern exegetes, and one of the most celebrated, stands on the shoulders of the ancient and medieval masters, and this should not be forgotten. Let's call it a limitation in Brown's work; all interpreters have limitations. If one is aware of Brown's interpretative oversights, there is much to be learned from his analysis of the Gospels, the death of Jesus, and a number of other critical topics.

The Fathers and Doctors of the Church rightly understood that dis-

---

faith in Christ built upon the Scriptures, but correspondingly, this faith introduces the believer into a full and authentic understanding of the Old Testament . . . The conviction by which the primitive Church considered the Scriptures of the Old Testament its own is rooted in Jesus' own thought and preaching. During his ministry, he often started from scriptural passages and continually referred back to biblical texts." Farkasfalvy, *Inspiration and Interpretation*, 16–17; emphasis added. See also pp. 53–62, where Farkasfalvy takes the reader through several important texts of the New Testament that concern inspiration: 2 Tm 3:16 and 2 Pt 1:21. (I have also written about these passages; see *Word of the Lord*, chap. 2.)

61. Fortunately, in the past few decades, there have been a number of rich works of biblical Christology and "historical Jesus" studies along the same lines. A few are strongly recommended: Keener, *Christobiography*; idem, *Historical Jesus of the Gospels*; Pitre, *Jesus and the Last Supper*; Sanders, *Historical Figure of Jesus*; Wright, *Jesus and the Victory of God*.

62. As to the latter, see especially two recent volumes not of the "Schleiermachian" school: Pitre et al., *Paul*, and Gorman, *Participating in Christ*. In addition, one might begin with E. P. Sanders's classical study, *Paul and Palestinian*. Of a similar magnitude as Sanders's work, see Wright, *Paul and the Faithfulness of God*.

63. Smith, *House of the Lord*, chap. 4.

pensing of such essentials would lead to skewed and spurious interpretations of the Scriptures. Such has become almost the norm today. We suspect that Brown, were he alive today, might well agree and lament where such "exegetical myopia" has led. Brown's phraseology is instructive. He believed that figural readings of Scripture, such as Origen's, are dead in our time. If they were *ever* useful for Brown remains unclear. He certainly expressed no confidence in their being "revived." Presumably, he'd prefer that they remained in the past. Yet there is a much larger point to see here, beyond what one thinks of Raymond Brown and his historically focused approach to biblical interpretation. The point is that the spiritual senses have been set aside in contemporary exegesis. In place of the fourfold "hermeneutic of faith," embraced throughout antiquity (as summarized by Barron and Kugel), is a "hermeneutic of suspicion."

Such suspicion—deep suspicion—ought not be confused with, let's say, a "hermeneutic of curiosity." One can and indeed should be curious about the many details out of which a given biblical text emerged. Intellectual curiosity is crucial to the science of biblical exegesis. Yet curiosity is not at all the same as imposing a lens of mistrust, of apprehension upon the text itself. The approach of source and redaction critics, among others, effectively turns the criteria of the rabbis and Church fathers on their head. Recall the four imperatives of ancient interpreters of the Word: (1) God is truly is the author of the whole Scripture; (2) the Bible is consistent with itself; (3) its meaning is often cryptic, hidden, and in need of being brought out; and (4) the Bible has relevance for us today.

Today, paradoxically, the imperatives of many historical-critical exegetes amounts to the *full reversal of those of the rabbis and Fathers of the Church*. At first, such a statement may seem unwarranted and even harsh. And yet, if one considers the hermeneutic of many modern interpreters of Scripture, the claim is less severe than it may first appear. For a majority of historical-critical scholars today, (1) the authorship of the Scriptures is an open question and, strictly speaking, a question of purely *human* authorship, often involving layers of redaction over long periods of time; (2) any notions of a larger narrative within the canon need to be deconstructed, replaced by microanalysis of the smallest units in a text; (3) deriving meaning in biblical texts is not a matter of discovering the mystery within but is accessed through historical and linguistic tools and subject to scholarly reconstructions of the text (since this is an impossible task, the "Jesus of history" remains an unsolvable riddle); and (4) whatever personal insight one may derive from a biblical text is a private matter and is unrelated to the task of historical inquiry.

Despite such an implosion in modern criticism, the fourfold imperatives that guided the ancient rabbis and patristic writers are thankfully accessible today. These tried and true criteria, which guided a thousand years or more of exegetes—from Origen to Hugh—are accessible today, provided one is open to such a participatory approach, and has "ears to hear."[64] Even so, by and large, the anti-supernatural basis upon which much biblical exegesis has been exercised over the past several hundred years has severely torn the spiritual sense away from the Scriptures. In reading certain academic commentaries of this sort, one wonders if there is *anything spiritual at all* to be said about, for example, Jesus's dialogue with Pilate.

One modern question is the determination of whether Pilate actually said *Ecce homo* ("behold the man"), since it is singly attested in John.[65] While such approaches are bound up with the aims of much historical criticism, the answers they yield don't necessarily help one to behold Jesus. Rather, they engender unnecessary skepticism. Indeed, the Four Gospels reveal Jesus of Nazareth, who is the divine Son—and not merely a historicized rabbi, far apart from "the Christ of faith."

But this schism between the literal and the spiritual—the latter being the "door to deeper meaning"—was unknown to patristic and medieval interpreters. And it is justly rejected by biblical scholars today who operate within a participatory framework. Along these lines, consider Ratzinger's assessment of John 19:5: "Thus caricatured, Jesus is led to Pilate, and Pilate presents him to the crowd—to all mankind: '*Ecce homo*,' 'Here is the man!'" The Roman judge is no doubt distressed at the sight of the wounded and derided figure of this mysterious defendant. He is counting on the compassion of those who see him. The expression *Ecce homo* spontaneously takes on a depth of meaning that reaches far

64. In calling for a return to "participatory" exegesis, there are undoubtedly contexts where one or another sense may need to recede and remain in the background. This is certainly the case with *Lectio Divina*. Laboring over a verb and why it is in the aorist tense would not likely prove fruitful in the "spiritual reading" of Scripture. Similarly, think of a linguistic or technical essay in an academic journal. It would be grossly unfair to dismiss its conclusions for not incorporating the tropological sense, for example.

65. Jn 19:5.

beyond this moment in history.[66] As Ratzinger stresses, "In Jesus, it is man himself that is manifested. In him is displayed the suffering of all who are subjected to violence, all the downtrodden. His suffering mirrors the inhumanity of worldly power, which so ruthlessly crushes the powerless. In him is reflected what we call 'sin': this is what happens when man turns his back upon God and takes control over the world into his own hands."[67]

In the patristic and medieval ages, even those sympathetic to one particular sense (e.g., Origen and allegory) held *all the senses* in high regard and as wholly necessary. Whether or not they discussed each sense at length, they reverenced them. The Four Senses were the software application "running in the background" of their intellect. More specifically, it would be wrong and fallacious to infer that Origen had no interest in the literal sense: "The sacred text must therefore be 'sounded' everywhere with the greatest care. That is what Origen repeats with respect to everything, and it is what immediately strikes the reader."[68] And yet, as de Lubac stresses, this dimension of the Bible "is not affirmed to the detriment of its historical character."[69]

Such inferences misunderstand the context in which Origen approached the Scriptures or of what lay in the background. As is well known, Origen often contrasted the "flesh" and the "spirit" in his writings and sought to move his readers from the former into the latter. If one is incessantly looking as to how Origen "dealt with the literal," however, there may be disappointment. It is there, but it is overshadowed by his exposition of Scripture allegorically. Such disappointment soon fades as one becomes attuned to Origen's strategic intentions, moving his readers from the surface of the text, with all of its fleshly inhibitions, up into the mystery of the text. It is here that the greater meaning lies. There, the faith-filled reader ascends with the Spirit and is able to contemplate Christ himself. In fact, "there are so many mysteries that it is impossible to explain them all. *Their grandeur surpasses our strength. Their density is crushing.*"[70]

Origen wasn't interested in negating the literal. He was interested in

66. Ratzinger, *Jesus of Nazareth, Part Two*, 199.
67. Ratzinger, *Jesus of Nazareth, Part Two*, 199.
68. De Lubac, *History and Spirit*, 103.
69. De Lubac, *History and Spirit*, 104; emphasis added.
70. De Lubac, *History and Spirit*, 104; emphasis added.

moving his readers from the flesh and into the mystery, from the *letter* to the *spirit.* He no more wanted to "'*curse the letter*' any more than '*blaspheme the spirit.*'"[71] As Radner summarizes, "The key to both history and to reading the Scriptures for Origen, then, is bound to the movement from the 'seen' to the unseen,' from the 'flesh' to the 'spirit.'"[72]

Turning from Origen at the start of the first millennium to St. Thomas Aquinas at the start of the second, we find a similar inclusivity at play. Thomas is rightly recognized for insisting that all biblical interpretation begins with the literal sense. Yet, just as it is false to assume Origen had no use for the literal, it is equally wrong to imagine Thomas had no use for the spiritual sense. In his *Commentary on Job*, Thomas sets out his exposition on the book with a prologue. There, he states his purpose, which is primarily an exploration of Job according to the literal sense: "With trust in God's aid, I intend to explain this book . . . as far as I am able *according to the literal sense.* The mystical sense has been explained for us both accurately and eloquently by the blessed Pope Gregory so that nothing further need be added to this sort of commentary."[73] The mystical (by which he means the spiritual) sense has already been elaborated both accurately and eloquently, he writes. Surprisingly, then, one encounters many spiritual elements in Thomas's commentary. How is this possible?

As was the case with St. Augustine's *Literal Commentary on Genesis*, here St. Thomas is dealing with complex questions in Job, including the apparent absence of God amid deep human suffering. As one reads his literal commentary on the Book of Job, such metaphysical questions are not left behind. As we learned in our discussion of Augustine's *Literal Commentary*, the literal sense does not only concern those things that may be called historical datum, that is, things constrained by the tempo-

71. De Lubac, *History and Spirit*, 105; slightly modified, with emphases added.

72. Radner, *Time and the Word*, 58.

73. Aquinas, *Commentary on the Book of Job*, 8; emphasis added. Here, in the prologue, Thomas is referring to St. Gregory the Great's *Moralia in Iob* that proceeds him. He describes Gregory's approach as the "mystical" (Latin = *mysteria*) sense. As we will see throughout the course of the book, numerous terms were used to describe the spiritual senses. While the allegorical and anagogical senses can be detected at various places in *Moralia in Iob*, Gregory's approach decidedly unfolds according to the tropological sense. (Emmaus Academic Press is now overseeing and completing the publishing of Thomas's works begun by the Aquinas Institute; see "Aquinas Institute's *Opera Omnia* Series," Emmaus Academic, accessed November 7, 2019, http://www.emmausacademic.com/aquinas-institutes-opera-omnia.)

ral and accessible only through empirical means. For his part, Augustine clearly engages figural elements. In exegeting Genesis 1 and 2, he places them "at the service" of the literal.

St. Augustine on Authorial Intent in Scripture

In his important treatise *De Doctrina Christiana* (*On Christian Doctrine*), St. Augustine describes the two tasks in biblical interpretation, specifically, what is required is: "discovering what there is to be learned and teaching what one has discovered."[74] Augustine emphasized the necessity of the interpreter to search for that meaning which the biblical author intended:

> For if he takes up rashly a meaning which the author whom he is reading did not intend, he often falls in with other statements which he cannot harmonize with this meaning. And he admits that if these statements are true and certain, then it follows that the meaning he had put upon the former passage cannot be the true one. And so, it comes to pass that out of love for his own opinion, he begins to feel angrier with Scripture than with himself. And if he should permit that evil to creep in, it will utterly destroy him.[75]

In other words, Augustine understood that without searching for the objectivity that rests in *the author's intentions*, one is left flailing about in the subjectivity of one's own opinion as to what Scripture means. For Augustine, to understand the Scriptures, "God has required that we learn from others. Even in speaking to us directly in Jesus Christ, God ensured that we would learn Jesus's words and deeds from others, *who would have to interpret them*. The divinity of Jesus Christ is mediated through his humanity, and the biblical signs that testify to him are mediated through Israel and the Church."[76] Augustine recognized the human authors, who were given the task of interpreting Jesus's words and deeds: "The guidance of the Holy Spirit does not take away from the profound presence of human mediation and interpretation at the heart of God's work of salvation."[77]

74. Levering, *Theology of Augustine*, 3. See also Arnold and Bright, *De Doctrina Christiana*.

75. St. Augustine, *On Christian Doctrine*, I.37, in Schaff, *St. Augustin's City of God and Christian Doctrine*, 533. Augustine explains that it is not only a lack of proper biblical exegesis that is at stake. It is also the interpreter's progress in the theological virtues.

76. Levering, *Theology of Augustine*, 17; emphasis added.

77. Levering, *Theology of Augustine*, 17.

Matthew Levering appropriately asks, "Why did God choose this way to reveal himself?"[78] As he explains, Augustine's response has to do with the limitations upon human nature as a result of the Fall: "*God reveals himself through signs so as to train us in love.* Since we must learn about God through signs that have been given in history, we can come to God only within the community of wisdom and love built up by Christ and the Holy Spirit. To learn from Christ in the Church means to learn how to move *from sign to thing, so as to cleave in love to the unseen God who is revealed through signs.*"[79]

St. Thomas's commentary works slightly differently than Augustine's treatise, though in the end both are consistent with one another. Thomas explained in his prologue that he was not writing the sort of commentary on Job as Gregory the Great did, that is, from the spiritual (tropological) sense. And that is true—his is a literal commentary. In approaching Job, he understands (as St. Augustine does with *Genesis*) that he is attempting to interpret a text from a *divine author*, not merely a human one. This being the case, Thomas does not restrict his exegesis to nonspiritual matters (e.g., names, places, events, and the like). Rather, he plunges deep into the mysteries of Job. How is this possible, given that by his own admission he is developing a *literal* commentary?

In part, it is because Thomas is interpreting Job as the inspired Word of God. He recognizes that the Spirit participates in the Word: both at its origins, inspiring the human authors, and in Thomas's own lived encounter with the Word. And so Thomas is not bound by the limitations imposed upon the text, in the manner that someone like Raymond Brown or another historical-critical scholar might approach the text today.[80] Nor should we be today.

When one reads the biblical commentaries of Origen, Augustine, and Thomas—and begins to compare them—it soon becomes clear that there are plenty of distinctions to be seen! Even so, our discussion underscores a common thread among them: they understood that *there are things both "seen" and "unseen" in the Word of God.* And this is true not only in the case of these three masters. We could quickly add a cacoph-

78. Levering, *Theology of Augustine*, 17.

79. Levering, *Theology of Augustine*, 17; emphases added.

80. "Without either a return to archaic forms or servile mimicry, often by totally different methods, it is a spiritual movement that we must reproduce above all." De Lubac, *History and Spirit*, 431.

ony of ancient and medieval thinkers: SS. Basil, Bernard of Clairvaux, Ephrem, Gregory of Nazianzus, Irenaeus, John Chrysostom, and Hugh and Richard of St. Victor, to list just a few. There are numerous reasons why the ancient and medieval masters firmly held this position and why it was a driving force in their respective hermeneutic. At the heart of it are the four incontrovertible criteria that the ancient rabbis and patristic writers held in common. Armed with these trustworthy criteria—as helpful today as in ancient Judaism and medieval Christianity—we turn our focus to the Four Senses themselves.

The Four Senses Defined

What are the Four Senses of Sacred Scripture? A clear and concise definition is offered in the universal *Catechism of the Catholic Church:* "According to an ancient tradition, one can distinguish between two *senses* of Scripture: the literal and the spiritual, the latter being subdivided into the allegorical, moral, and anagogical senses."[81] It then further delineates the literal from the spiritual senses: "The *literal sense* is the meaning conveyed by the words of Scripture and discovered by exegesis, following the rules of sound interpretation: 'All other senses of Sacred Scripture are based on the literal.'"[82] What the *Catechism* adds about the spiritual sense is brief yet significant: "Thanks to the unity of God's plan, not only the text of Scripture but also the realities and events about which it speaks can be *signs*."[83]

Here is a crucial concept: the words of Scripture not only convey meaning by pointing to "things" (i.e., by discovering the literal sense), but also the things that are referred to by the literal sense are themselves conveying deeper meaning. They function as signs of still deeper and

81. *CCC* §115. What follows immediately after gets to the epicenter of this book: "The profound concordance of the four senses guarantees all its richness to the living reading of Scripture in the Church."

82. *CCC* §116, citing St. Thomas Aquinas, *Summa Theologica* I, q. 1, a. 10, ad 1; emphasis added. Unless noted, all citations from the *ST* are from the edition translated by the Fathers of the English Dominican Province.

83. *CCC* §116. The *Catechism* expands upon this elsewhere: "The Holy Spirit gives a spiritual understanding of the Word of God to those who read or hear it, according to the dispositions of their hearts. *By means of the words, actions, and symbols* that form the structure of a celebration, the Spirit puts both the faithful and the ministers into a living relationship with Christ, *the Word and Image of the Father*, so that they can live out the meaning of what they hear, contemplate, and do in the celebration" (*CCC* §1101).

greater realities. This is a mystery with which we will further concern ourselves, in dealing with the various spiritual senses.

Finally, the *Catechism* distinguishes between the three spiritual senses: "The *allegorical* sense. We can acquire a more profound understanding of events by recognizing their significance in Christ; thus, the crossing of the Red Sea is a sign or type of Christ's victory and of Christian Baptism. The *moral sense*. The events reported in Scripture ought to lead us to act justly. As Saint Paul says, they were written 'for our instruction.'"[84] The *anagogical sense* (Greek = *anagoge*, "leading"). We can view realities and events in terms of their eternal significance, leading us toward our true homeland: thus the Church on earth is a sign of the heavenly Jerusalem."[85]

Picking up on the last image involving Jerusalem, we can use it to illustrate the basic distinctions between the Four Senses. Consider the phrase "Jesus went up to Jerusalem," which occurs twice in the Gospel According to St. John.[86] What is the literal meaning of Jerusalem in this sentence? First, the precise literal meaning is predicated upon one's ability to discover what the author wished to "convey by the words of Scripture and discovered by exegesis, following the rules of sound interpretation."[87]

Second, and following this definition, such may involve examining the original Greek text and investigating the literary and historical context. For the sake of this illustration, let us forgo such necessities and assume that here that the term Jerusalem connotes actual the city of Jerusalem, founded by David. It has walls and gates, and Herod's Temple sits atop Mt. Zion. In other words, the physical and historical entity that is the city of Jerusalem is, in this case, the literal sense of the term.

What about the allegorical, tropological, and anagogical meanings of Jerusalem? As the *Catechism* summarizes, the way that all the spiritual senses work is this: they are signs that convey a reality beyond the literal

84. 1 Cor 10:11: "Now these things happened to them as a warning, but they were written down for our *nouthesian* [Greek for "instruction, admonition") upon whom the end of the ages has come." See Heb 3:4–11.

85. *CCC* §117.

86. See Jn 2:23, "The Passover of the Jews was at hand, and *Jesus went up to Jerusalem*," and Jn 5:1, "After this there was a feast of the Jews, and *Jesus went up to Jerusalem*" (emphasis added).

87. *CCC* §116.

sense. And so a number of other meanings begin to emerge beyond the literal. Does this multiplicity of meaning imply that the borders defining the spiritual senses are permeable? Is it "anything goes?" No. There indeed patterns and rules evident across the clear majority of its practitioners.

As a matter of practice, virtually everything in the Old Testament pointed to Christ in according to the allegorical sense. Other possibilities existed: the Church, the Cross, Mary or the disciples, the sacraments, and so on. Within allegory, Jerusalem might point to the Church, that is, the unified body of believers, or something similar.

According to the tropological sense, the term "Jerusalem" might connote something like the interior Jerusalem of the believer's heart, out of which flow virtuous behavior and spiritual sacrifices. Here, it is the moral Jerusalem that is in view. Finally, as to the anagogical, the *Catechism* itself supplies a helpful example: "the Church on earth is a sign of the heavenly Jerusalem." It becomes clear that one word in Scripture—Jerusalem—may elicit at least four levels of meaning: the actual city of David, into which Jesus and the disciples walked; the Church as the well-ordered city; the virtuous believer; and the heavenly city above.

This simple illustration serves our purpose well as to the "how" of the Four Senses. Elsewhere, however, the Four Senses are employed in more intricate, even sophisticated ways. What makes biblical interpretation so fascinating is the complexity and multiplicity of meaning in Sacred Scripture. Often, two patristic figures will look at the same biblical text in the allegorical or tropological sense yet derive vastly different meanings. Such apparent lack of uniformity is often baffling to those newer to the Four Senses. This is understandable, but it should not keep the reader at bay. With the literal sense, there are certain rules that need to be respected—linguistically, semantically, contextually, and so on. Even a newer student of Scripture might spot a faulty conclusion with the literal sense. One can check it out, historically speaking.

What about the spiritual senses? Is it similarly possible to corroborate one's conclusions within the spiritual senses? There is a twofold answer: both "no" and "no." First, no: it is not possible to apply the criteria that govern the literal sense to the spiritual senses, to adjudicate their validity. This ought to be clear enough, as the literal sense points to *things*. In contrast, the spiritual senses view these same things as *signs* that in turn point to *other things* beyond them. Still, this is helpful and begins to point us to the coherence of the Four Senses. The first step, before touching the spiritual senses, is to establish the literal meaning properly. And this first stage takes us closer to answering our question with "yes" than we might imagine.

If this first step is executed properly, we may safely formulate our answer of what "thing" is conveyed by the biblical word. In the above example, Jerusalem signifies the City of David. The next step is to move to the spiritual senses, following the pattern described above. Here, one begins to ascertain, according to the nature of the various spiritual senses, what the "thing" signifies at the deeper level. For example, if one scans the allegorical sense as employed in patristic and medieval Christianity, it points consistently to the *Person of Christ*—to the Man, his words, his works, his Passion, and so on.

Likewise, if one examines the Fathers and Doctors and Mystics, one discovers that, over and over, the tropological takes up the *moral life in Christ*: the ethical choices facing the believer, the social dimension of discipleship, the virtues, the heart, and the like. Finally, if one examines the history of exegesis, again and again, the anagogical sense concerns the *destiny of the believer*, eschatological realities, one's heavenly hope, Christ the bridegroom of the soul, and so on. Clearly, the literal and spiritual senses have their own set of rules. And in working with the spiritual senses, it is crucial to develop an awareness of their common ancient and medieval usage and to avoid aberrant appropriations of them.

Being attuned to such patterns will aid the reader in following the logic in a patristic or medieval commentary. For instance, within such works, one may periodically encounter obscure terms or lengthy arguments that may jumble one's ability to follow along. Even so, the well-established patterns by which the spiritual senses tend to operate will carry the reader forward to the ancient writer's conclusions. The clearer one is as to how the spiritual senses generally work in patristic and medieval thinkers (or, better still, within a particular author or work) and aid the reader in apprehending the message being expressed by the biblical author.

Although there is a diversity of terms that have been used to distinguish the Four Senses from one another over the centuries,[88] we will

88. See de Lubac, *Medieval Exegesis*, vol. 2, 37.

consistently employ the medieval Latin of *littera*, *allegoria*, *tropologia*, and *anagoge*—that is, the *literal*, *allegorical*, *tropological*, and *anagogical*. By the time of St. Nicholas of Lyra, in the thirteenth century, the terminology deployed by so many figures had begun to settle down with the aforementioned fourfold formula of *littera*, *allegoria*, *tropologia*, and *anagoge*. To flesh these out, we turn to Nicholas, who in his prologue to the *Glossa Ordinaria* provides a classical expression of the threefold spiritual sense of Scripture: "If the things signified by the words are referred to as to signify the things that are believed in the new law, this amounts to the allegorical sense; if they are referred to so as to signify things to be done by us, this is tropological sense; and is they are referred to as to signify things to be hoped for in the beatitude to come, this is the anagogical sense."[89] Having defined the Four Senses and provided examples to answer initial questions, let us proceed by considering each in a more thorough way. We begin with the literal.

Littera

On the importance of the literal sense, de Lubac wrote, "Indeed, considered both in its totality and in its letter, Scripture first delivers us *facts*."[90] And this is where the search for biblical meaning must begin and rest upon factual knowledge that may be drawn from a biblical text. As he helpfully explained, the *littera* "recounts a series of events which have really transpired . . . It is neither an exposition of abstract doctrine, nor a collection of myths, nor a manual of the inner life. *It has nothing atemporal about it.*"[91]

De Lubac rightly cautioned that the literal can never be glossed over in haste to get to the spiritual sense. Rather, it must be encountered for its own primordial virtues[92] and has "no little instruction to offer."[93] Western and Eastern Fathers alike agree on the intrinsic value of the *Letter*. Representing the West, St. Jerome described the literal sense as

89. In de Lubac, *Medieval Exegesis*, vol. 2, 37, citing St. Nicholas of Lyra, *Glossa Ordinaria* (prologue).

90. De Lubac, *Medieval Exegesis*, vol. 2, 44; emphasis added.

91. De Lubac, *Medieval Exegesis*, vol. 2, 44; emphasis added.

92. See de Lubac, *Medieval Exegesis*, vol. 2, 45.

93. Rabanus Maurus, *Homilies on Leviticus*, Book VII, chap. 6, in de Lubac, *Medieval Exegesis*, vol. 2, 263n62.

having its own "beauty."[94] And in the East, even Origen insisted that the *littera* "builds us up."[95]

École de St. Victor was one of the most prolific communities of the High Middle Ages. This Augustinian abbey near Paris advanced the mystical interpretation of Sacred Scripture. The school was founded in 1108 by the French bishop and thinker William of Champeaux. Outside of medieval history and theology, William is an obscure figure. Yet among his close friends were the likes of St. Bernard of Clairvaux. In the ranks of his students were leading theologians such as Peter Abelard and Hugh of St. Victor, among others.

To its visitors, such as Bernard, the exterior of École de St. Victor was a quiet countryside abbey. But within was a bustling center of learning and prayer. Hugh and other Victorine thinkers, such as Andrew and Richard of St. Victor, composed philosophical and theological treatises. In them, they dealt with emerging questions of the day: natural law, categories of knowledge, an introduction to Scripture, treatises on the Trinity and Creation, music and the visual arts, the Blessed Sacrament, and much more. Though École de St. Victor produced many masters, none surpassed the philosophical clarity and theological depth of Hugh (d. 1141), whose works of great significance include the *Didascalion* (*On Sacred Reading*),[96] *De Arca Noe Mystica* (*Noah's Mystic Ark*), and *De sacramentis christianae fidei* (*On the Mysteries of the Christian Faith*).[97]

For numerous reasons, Hugh of St. Victor represents the pinnacle of biblical interpretation in the High Middle Ages. This is a fact. Today, however, there is some fiction surrounding Hugh. For example, though his works were filled with spiritual and mystical insights, Hugh neither diminished nor sacrificed the primary role of the *littera*. In fact, in *De Sacramentis*, he speaks of the spiritual senses of Scripture as *secunda eruditio*, the "second instruction."[98] In the same passage he refers to the literal sense as *prima erudition*, the "first instruction" in sacred elo-

94. St. Jerome, *Homilies on the Psalter*, LXVII, in de Lubac, *Medieval Exegesis*, vol. 2, 263n61.

95. Origen, *Homilies on Leviticus*, in de Lubac, *Medieval Exegesis*, vol. 2, 263n64.

96. Hugh of St. Victor, *Didascalion*.

97. For an English translation of *De Sacramentis*, see Hugh of St. Victor, *On the Sacraments of the Christian Faith*. For a theological introduction to Hugh, see Coolman, *Theology of Hugh of St. Victor*. I am grateful for his expertise on Hugh.

98. Hugh of St. Victor, *On the Sacraments of the Christian Faith*, prologue.

quence.[99] This is a substantial endorsement of the primacy and weight of the literal sense, especially since it comes from the pen of Hugh, champion of *interprétation mystique*, the mystical interpretation of Scripture. Even so, Hugh's ringing endorsement of the *littera* did not diminish his commitment to the divine knowledge opened up through the spiritual senses. In fact, when properly understood (and some do misunderstand him), it is clear that Hugh affirms both the *littera* and *sensus spiritualis*: "Upon the foundation of the literal sense is constructed an edifice of doctrine through allegorical interpretation, which is then decorated and adorned with the beauty of the tropological or moral meaning. This tripartite architectural structure—foundation, superstructure, adornment—is a kind of master-form for Hugh, and recurs frequently."[100]

Like Augustine before him, Hugh understood that to deal hastily with the literal in pursuit of the spiritual was to omit the "first instruction." Hugh grasped that one passes to the spiritual senses and all that they offer only by way of the literal sense. It could never be omitted nor diminished. To do so would compromise the discoveries that await the attentive reader, when one finally arrives at the threshold of the spiritual senses. And so it is only by attending diligently to the literal sense than one may enter into what Benedictine Mystic Rupert of Deutz (ca. 1080) called the "door of intelligence."[101] On a theological level, the spiritual sense is precisely that. To cross the threshold to Rupert's door of intelligence—as every interpreter hoped to do—one must step toward it through the literal sense.

There Is No Other Way but through This Door

About the same time as Hugh, another theologian in Paris stressed the importance of the literal: the Angelic Doctor St. Thomas Aquinas. Near the beginning of the *Summa Theologica*, in article 10, Thomas raises the objection that the Four Senses only produce confusion: "It seems that

99. Hugh of St. Victor, *On the Sacraments of the Christian Faith*, prologue; see de Lubac, *Medieval Exegesis*, vol. 2, 311n32.

100. Coolman, *Theology of Hugh of St. Victor*, 21. For Hugh, "there are two spiritual senses in addition to the literal, namely, the allegorical and the tropological" (128). This is not to say his interpretation of Scripture had no place for the anagogical. He stressed that the human person is fundamentally "formed by Wisdom for beauty" (168).

101. De Lubac, *Medieval Exegesis*, vol. 2, 85.

in Holy Writ a word cannot have several senses, historical [or literal], allegorical, tropological [or moral], and anagogical. *For many different senses in one text produce confusion and deception and destroy all force of argument.* Hence no argument, but only fallacies, can be deduced from a multiplicity of propositions. But Holy Writ ought to be able to state the truth without any fallacy. *Therefore, in it there cannot be several senses to a word.*"[102]

Thomas's answer is decisive in refuting the objection: "I answer that, the author of Holy Writ is God, in whose power it is to signify His meaning, not by words only (as man also can do), but also by things themselves. So, whereas in every other science, things are signified by words, this science has the property that the things signified by the words have themselves also a signification."[103] Here, Thomas makes the point underscored above, as presented in the *Catechism*: with God, there is more than one way in which things may be signified or signed. He contrasts the way meaning is signified for man and for God. For the former, meaning is limited to words themselves. Yet not with the latter. If Scripture were merely a human book, there would be no other meaning other than that provided by the words themselves. In our above example, Jerusalem would signify the City of David and nothing more.

Yet Holy Writ (by which Thomas means Sacred Scripture) is inspired by God.[104] What this means for Thomas is that there are several layers of signs. The literal sense is the *first and immediate signification.* And so a given biblical word has its literal (or historical) meaning, that is, that which is signified by the word itself. As he instructs, "the things signified by the words have themselves also a signification."[105] Thomas's sound logic not only provides the basis for the spiritual senses. It also dispels the notion that there is any confusion as a result. In light of this, all of the Four Senses are entirely valid. They do not produce confusion, nor do they replicate one another.[106] Thomas concludes, "*all*

102. *ST* I, q. 1, a. 10, obj. 1; emphasis added.

103. *ST* I, q. 1, a. 10, resp.

104. 2 Tm 3:16: "All scripture is inspired by God and profitable for teaching, for reproof, for correction, and for training in righteousness." Here, "inspired" is from the Greek *theosneustos*, or "God-breathed." See the discussion of biblical inspiration in my *Word of the Lord*, chaps. 1–2.

105. Latin: *quod ipsae res significatae per voces etiam significant aliquid.*

106. "The multiplicity of these senses does not produce equivocation or any other kind of multiplicity" (*ST* I, q. 1, a. 10, ad 1). See Augustine, *Letter* XLVIII.

the senses are founded on one—the literal—from which alone can any argument be drawn, and not from those intended in allegory, as Augustine says."[107] Thomas's explanation is undoubtedly the best articulation of the literal sense—and its primacy. In turn, the literal lays the foundation for the multiplicity of senses without confusion or redundancy, opening the horizon to the spiritual senses. In sum, the literal sense is the meaning signified by a Scriptural word—by the historical person, place, thing, or idea that the word is directly pointing to. For this reason, Thomas (and so many others) often refers to it as the historical sense.

Thomas makes another helpful point that further clarifies scope of the literal. At times, there are things like figures of speech, similes, and metaphors in the Word of God. What about them? Are these other spiritual senses, or something beyond the four altogether? No—they are contained *within* the literal sense: "The parabolical sense is contained in the literal, *for by words things are signified properly and figuratively*. Nor is the figure itself, but that which is figured, the literal sense."[108]

Elsewhere, in St. Thomas's *Expositio super Iob litteram* commentary (the *Literal Commentary on Job*), he makes precisely the same point as in the *Summa*. Specifically, Thomas articulates—and in a way not done prior to him, not even by Augustine—what might be called the "procedures of biblical language."[109] In explaining how the Book of Job works on a literal level, Thomas argues that the book "is written in the manner of a poem. Hence, through this whole book the author uses *the figures and styles which poets customarily use.*"[110]

With numerous puzzling texts in the Book of Job, which confounded many earlier interpreters as to how to deal with them at the literal level, Thomas applies this same logic. As he writes,

> Now although spiritual things are proposed under the figures of corporeal things, nevertheless the truths intended *about spiritual things through sensible figures belong not to the mystical but to the literal sense*, because the literal sense

107. *ST* I, q. 1, a. 10, ad 1; emphasis added. Latin: *Quia vero sensus literalis est, quem auctor intendit: auctor autem sacrae Scripturae Deus est, qui omnia simul suo intellectu comprehendit; non est inconveniens.*

108. *ST* I, q. 1, a. 10, ad 3; emphasis added. Latin: *nam per voces significatur aliquid proprie, et aliquid figurative.*

109. See Dahan, "Commentary of Thomas Aquinas in the History of Medieval Exegesis on Job," 1064. I am grateful to Dahan for the excellent phrase.

110. As cited in Dahan, "Commentary of Thomas Aquinas in the History of Medieval Exegesis on Job," 1065; emphases added. See 1065n44 for the original Latin.

is that which is primarily intended by the words, *whether they are used properly or figuratively.*[111]

This is a powerful and lasting insight, that we should expect to find various kinds of figurative language *within the literal sense*: we should expect to find various kinds of figurative language *within the literal sense.* St. Thomas is advising that, to get to the roots of the literal, it may be necessary to unpack a metaphor, or figure of speech. For example, if Scripture speaks of "God's arm," it must logically signify something else: his might and might. This too is part of the search for the literal since we are still asking what the words themselves signify.[112] If we are involved in that endeavor, we haven't left the literal for the spiritual sense.

Again, in his response, Thomas stresses that the above expression ("God's arm") is not itself the literal sense. Rather, it is a piece of the puzzle that needs to be put into its proper position to get to the full meaning within the literal sense, that is, to "solve for *x*." And, importantly, all of this takes place within the literal sense. Once we arrive at the "thing" signified by the words (whatever that thing is), we can ask questions about that thing. We are able to move beyond the words themselves. We have solved for *x* and now grasp what the words point to in the Scripture. Now we are free to ask, "What does this thing in turn point to?" This second question represents the crucial turn—the pivot from the literal to the spiritual senses. For this reason, the literal cannot be neglected nor rushed through prematurely. To do so could compromise any further discoveries of meaning derived from the spiritual senses. Worst of all, such carelessness could render such discoveries invalid!

Armed with this clear explanation of the literal as the primary sense of Scripture, let us go further by illuminating it with additional insights.

111. As cited in Dahan, "Commentary of Thomas Aquinas in the History of Medieval Exegesis on Job," 1067; emphases added. See 1067n49 for the original Latin.

112. St. Augustine, *On Christian Doctrine*, Book III.5.9: "But the ambiguities of metaphorical words, about which I am next to speak, demand no ordinary care and diligence. *In the first place, we must beware of taking a figurative expression literally*. For the saying of the apostle applies in this case too: 'The letter killeth, but the spirit giveth life.'" *St. Augustin's City of God and Christian Doctrine*, 559. See also *On Christian Doctrine*, Book III. 29.40: "Moreover, I would have learned men to know that the authors of our Scriptures use all those forms of expression which grammarians call by the Greek name *tropes* and use them more freely and in greater variety than people who are unacquainted with the Scriptures and have learnt these figures of speech from other writings, can imagine or believe. Nevertheless, those who know these tropes recognize them in Scripture, and are very much assisted by their knowledge of them in understanding Scripture."

Hugh of St. Victor taught us that *littera gesta docet—the letter teaches us what was done.*[113] Hugh has given us a deceptively simple truth: salvation history is filled with "things that have transpired," and the literal sense attends to these things.

Sometimes we hear expressions like "we shouldn't take the Bible too literally." This is a muddled claim and confuses the literal sense with "literalism." The former is essential. The latter to be avoided. To suggest that one shouldn't take the Bible literally is to imply that it does not have meaning, or much meaning. To diminish or negate the literal sense is in fact to relinquish the hope of discovering any meaning in the text. Once understood, we assert that we should not read the Bible in a "literalistic" fashion. It must be read it in a literal fashion, according to the literal sense. The latter is indispensable. The former twists one up in knots and conundrums. For example, the now-tired trope that the earth—indeed, all of Creation—is a mere six thousand years old. This opinion continues to be held by biblical literalists, despite genuine and overwhelming scientific data to the contrary. Taken to such a laughable extreme, literalism yields nothing but absurdity, for example, Jesus is literally a wooden door.[114]

Keeping these two terms clear and distinct from one another is vital. One can never—no, not ever—dispense with the literal sense. Why, once it is properly understood, would anyone want to do so? "Scripture first delivers us *facts.*"[115] As de Lubac points out, "To suppress this truth of history in practice, *even without intending to deny it,* or to dissolve it in fact by too much haste, would at very least be a blunder."[116]

Richard, also of the Parisian school of St. Victor, operated like Hugh at a highly elevated level of spiritual exegesis. Nevertheless, Richard insisted upon the literal as the text's true foundation: "The letter builds me up . . . before I come to the spiritual understanding, I marvel within the letter."[117] Elsewhere, he adjures us to attend to the literal, as there is nothing as sure as that which is "in the soil the historical sense." With

113. See de Lubac, *Medieval Exegesis*, vol. 2, 41: "The two words *littera* and *historia* are practically interchangeable, and we pass easily from the one to the other."

114. See Jn 10:7.

115. De Lubac, *Medieval Exegesis*, vol. 2, 44; emphasis added.

116. De Lubac, *Medieval Exegesis*, vol. 2, 45; emphasis added.

117. De Lubac, *Medieval Exegesis*, vol. 2, 45. De Lubac cites Richard, yet the source from which it is derived is unclear.

the literal sense, he adds, our efforts in the Scriptures would stand "upon what is empty and void."[118] Nevertheless, it is true that some medieval commentators move quickly through the literal sense to attend to the spiritual. Moreover, one may encounter works of exegesis that do not exemplify any tangible evidence of the literal. Is this a problem within patristic exegesis?

There are several possibilities. The first is that the interpreter deliberately evaded the literal, without any interest in seeking to establish the intent of the author at the primary, foundational level. This is problematic, as the reader may rarely encounter it. The second possibility is that the exegete did not step over the literal meaning, even if evidence of it is sparse. The two positions are not the same and may lead to a false assumption, that the commentator simply did not investigate the literal. Such is a rash judgment, interpretatively speaking, and should be avoided.

Part of its rashness is that, as moderns, we are conditioned to spend most if not all our time preoccupied within the literal sense. Fair enough. Yet this preoccupation may cloud expectations about premodern biblical interpreters and how they went about their task. For some, it is nearly the opposite of our historical-critical age. That is, their aim was to attain the literal meaning and then to proceed through the "door of intelligence" as expeditiously as possible, so that most of the time is spent there. Again, the former approach, of wholly omitting the literal, needs to be called out as insufficient and lopsided. Yet the latter approach, with its heavier emphasis upon the spiritual than the literal—requires a more nuanced investigation. There is likely much more going on with the latter than may be initially seen.

In a Sunday homily, St. Bernard of Clairvaux explains this well: "In the works of God, there are both things delightful in external appearance, and much more delightful with inner power . . . The surface, when considered from the outside, is very handsome; *but if anyone should crack the nut, he will find something more pleasant and delightful* . . . Of the signs of the Lord, whose history is quite admirable enough, and whose significance *is still more delightful*."[119] We have been conditioned to study the facts, the exterior. The Fathers, Doctors, and Mystics are not

118. De Lubac, *Medieval Exegesis*, vol. 1, xvii.

119. De Lubac, *Medieval Exegesis*, vol. 2, 62; emphasis added.

telling us to stop doing so. With Bernard, they are urging us to "crack the nut" and examine the truest riches that are only gleaned when we move from the literal to the spiritual senses.

Bernard was widely recognized as a purveyor of the spiritual senses, especially the *tropological* and *anagogical*, and in that order. Even so, it would be completely mistaken to imagine that he had no concrete knowledge or, worse, no interest in determining the literal sense. For example, in his magnificent commentary on the Song of Songs, it is likely that his attendance to "the letter" proceeded his writing. In any event, it wasn't something he neglected or took no interest in, as the above quote makes clear. To assert that those ancient and medieval theologians who tended to operate in one of the spiritual senses were ignorant of the literal is an absurd claim. Sadly, it is heard today. It falsely impugns the name and reputation of St. Bernard and all the premodern masters of the Scriptures.

De Lubac sets the record straight: "If our first concern is with history, the primary condition of a more exact understanding is for us *to banish the cliché that speaks of the 'naivety of the Middle Ages.' We must lay aside all our scornful or derisive attitudes about the men of this era*. What is more, we must abandon a certain tone, all too frequent, of *smirking condescension*."[120]

It is not only Catholic theologians who have lamented the "smirking condescension" of many moderns and their opinion about the Middle Ages. A recent monograph by Evangelical scholar Chris Armstrong raises concerns like those of de Lubac. Along with a growing chorus of Protestant theologians and historians—such as Thomas Oden,[121] Robert Webber,[122] Greg Peters,[123] Dennis Ockholm,[124] and especially Hans

120. De Lubac, *Medieval Exegesis*, vol. 2, 49; emphasis added.

121. In addition to his own scholarship, Oden (1931–2016) was general editor of the *Ancient Christian Commentary on Scripture* (InterVarsity Press), a multivolume patristic commentary on Scripture from the second through the eight centuries. Some consider him the leader of "paleo-Orthodoxy," a movement of Protestant theologians who incorporated ancient Christian practices and wisdom into their own writings and worship.

122. Robert E. Webber (1933–2007) was a Baptist author and professor deeply interested in liturgical renewal in Evangelicalism. He founded the Convergence Movement, which integrated charismatic worship with ancient liturgical practices. He spoke of the "ancient Evangelical future." See *Ancient-Future Worship*; Webber and Ruth, *Evangelicals on the Canterbury Trail*.

123. Peters, *Story of Monasticism*.

124. See Ockholm and Norris, *Monk Habits for Everyday People*.

Boersma[125]—Armstrong is engaging the ancient and medieval Church for its many riches.

In *Medieval Wisdom for Modern Christians,*[126] Armstrong warns of an "Evangelical Identity Crisis"[127] and suggests that, at present, much of Protestantism is locked into what he calls "evangelical immediatism,"[128] which is disconnected from the sacramental worldview of medieval Christianity. Positively, he calls for a robust reengagement with the rich spirituality of the monastic period, including *Lectio Divina* and immersion in the writings of theologians of the Middle Ages. Like de Lubac, Armstrong sets the record straight about the supposed "naivety of the Middle Ages," with its flat-earth cosmology, harsh dogma, and oppressive spirituality. These are modern myths, and not even well-constructed ones. Even so, by the nineteenth century, much of the gold from these periods of great illumination—intellectually, sacramentally, scripturally—had been long buried deep in the ground. It is time to unearth them.

For de Lubac, intrinsic to biblical interpretation in the ancient and medieval periods is the notion of the dual meanings of Scripture—they are an "inalienable datum of tradition."[129] De Lubac distinguishes the "sense of history" that characterized ancient and medieval theologians, in contrast to nineteenth-century historical-critical scholars. He adjures the reader to not impose modernity's preoccupation with historical inquiry upon second-, fifth-, or eleventh-century commentators who operated from within a theological sense of history. They dealt with the facts of history, yet they did so with far more restraint. And, frankly, with better discernment than their modern counterparts.

In *De Doctrina*, St. Augustine did not discourage exegetes from en-

125. See Boersma, *Scripture as Real Presence*; idem, *Heavenly Participation*; idem, *Nouvelle Theologie and Sacramental Ontology*. Boersma is one of the leading Protestant theologians to engage patristic and medieval beliefs about Scripture in a deep and sustained way. In his writings, Boersma frequently interacts with de Lubac, Daniélou, and other ressourcement theologians. Like them, he is committed to a recovery of Origen, SS. Irenaeus, Augustine, Gregory the Great, Bernard of Clairvaux, and all of the masters of the Sacred Page. Broadly speaking, his approach to Sacred Scripture is sacramental and liturgical. Among non-Catholic theologians, Boersma's liturgical and "Eucharistic" lens into Scripture, the Church, and the Christian's experience of the world as a sacrament is rare. As a result, his insights do not play an insignificant role in the book.

126. Armstrong, *Medieval Wisdom for Modern Christians.*

127. See Armstrong, *Medieval Wisdom for Modern Christians*, 45–47.

128. See Armstrong, *Medieval Wisdom for Modern Christians*, 18–20.

129. De Lubac, *Sources of Revelation*, 158. See also D'Ambrosio, "Henri de Lubac."

gaging historical questions, from digging deep into linguistic matters, and appropriate engagement of the sciences. But he cautions against the use of natural fields of knowledge, strictly speaking: "Accordingly, I think that it is well to warn studious and able young men, who fear God and are seeking for happiness of life, not to venture heedlessly upon the pursuit of the branches of learning that are in vogue beyond the pale of the Church of Christ, as if these could secure for them the happiness they seek; but soberly and carefully to discriminate among them."[130] Augustine's call for moderation regarding historical inquiry was broadly heeded by all that followed him, as de Lubac observes. It was the hermeneutic of faith that guided patristic and medieval commentators through the literal to the deeper mysteries that are encountered only by peering into the spiritual sense: "Only faith anticipates the future with security. Only an explication *founded on faith* can invoke a definitive principle and appeal to ultimate causes."[131] Anticipating the modern criticism that may arise from this, he adds, "If they rise a bit too fast to the absolute for our taste, *they at least have the merit of rising there within the faith.*"[132]

One final remark may be added to what has been said about the literal before turning to the spiritual senses. As modern exegetes, we have the ability to bring together the riches of the past ages (especially the commitment to the spiritual senses) with the best methods of our own age (which gives pride of place to historically-rooted inquiry). We have the capacity *to reconnect them*, and such reintegration is at the heart of *The Face of the Lord.* This book will examine the exterior in a sufficient and adequate way. Nevertheless, the method of approach embraced here is interested, in St. Bernard's words, in "cracking the nut" to gaze more deeply at the face of God. Only through *an examination of the exterior, leading to the deeper interior* will we demonstrate the sort of reintegration that is desirable today in biblical interpretation.

Here, we are reminded of some later words of Pope Emeritus Benedict XVI. In his afterword to Cardinal Sarah's *The Power of Silence*, he writes,

Certainly to interpret Jesus' words, historical knowledge is necessary, which teaches us to understand the time and the language at that time. That alone is

130. St. Augustine, *On Christian Doctrine*, II.58, in *Christian Instruction*, 110.
131. De Lubac, *Medieval Exegesis*, vol. 2, 71; emphasis added.
132. De Lubac, *Medieval Exegesis*, vol. 2, 81; emphasis added.

not enough if we are really to comprehend the Lord's message in depth. *Anyone who today reads ever-thicker commentaries on the Gospels remains disappointed in the end.* He learns a lot that us useful about those days and a lot of hypotheses that contribute nothing at all to an understanding of the text. In the end you feel that in all the excess of words, *something essential is lacking: entrance into Jesus' silence, from which his word is born.* If we cannot enter into this silence, we will hear the word only on the surface and thus not really understand it.[133]

This is sound advice. As the ancient and medieval mind understood, the *Letter* alone was not enough. Yes, the Scriptures needed to be engaged on the historical level. But from their divine origins—having been given to the Church by the Holy Spirit, and not merely by human authors—the *Letter* was not sufficient. From it, one moves to the mystery that is discovered in the *Spirit*. The *Letter* probed into the history. Ancients and medievals embraced the Word as *transhistoric*. We too must again receive the Scriptures as a *transhistoric event*. The *Letter* was a threshold through one stepped into the Mystery, into the cryptic, hidden, treasures that the Holy Spirit was waiting to unveil—to the holy reader. Let us turn now from the Letter to the Spirit.

Allegoria

Beryl Smalley (1905–84) was a gifted tutor at St. Hilda's College in Oxford in the mid-twentieth century. Her *Study of the Bible in the Middle Ages*, first published in 1940 (and reproduced many times over), is something of a classic in the field. In it, she sums up the attitude of the medieval period as it concerned the spiritual sense: "In in rare moments of skepticism, a medieval scholar questioned the truth of Scripture, he never doubted that it had letter *and* spirit; he only feared that the spirit might be bad."[134]

133. Pope Emeritus Benedict XVI, "Afterword," in Sarah, *Power of Silence*, 243; emphasis added.

134. Smalley, *Study of the Bible in the Middle Ages*, 1. Smalley recognized the many contributions of the so-called Victorine School (Hugh, Andrew, Richard, etc.) and allocates a sizable portion of the text to their discussion as it relates to biblical interpretation in the medieval period. Later referring to Andrew of St. Victor, Smalley writes, "A survey of medieval scholarship must include a reassessment of Andrew. The last ten years have made it possible to see him in better perspective. A study of thirteenth century postils [i.e., marginal notes] has disclosed the extent of his influence and has shown how far he was imitated. My conclusion is that he was even more significant that I thought at first" (365).

This is quite true. Certainly, it is not the rule in our own age. Yet, as Smalley wrote, it *was* the case in the ancient and medieval periods. For the masters of the Sacred Page, the literal sense was the starting place for the discovery of meaning, but it was never the only way in which meaning is drawn out of the Scriptures. To engage the hidden and cryptic, embedded in the text through its divine authorship, one had to make the move "from the *Letter* to the *Spirit*," from the literal to the spiritual senses. This first move, then, from the literal to the allegorical, is the most important of all: here one passes from fact to mystery.[135] We began our discussion of the literal sense with Hugh of St. Victor. Let us now return to him by looking at the first of the spiritual senses, the allegorical.

First, Hugh admitted only three senses: the literal, the allegorical, and the tropological.[136] In Hugh's writings, "the letter is constantly stressed."[137] His emphasis on the literal was grounded in his philosophy of history, which was something he learned from Augustine. His *De Sacramentis Christianae Fidei* (*Concerning the Sacraments of the Christian Faith*) was a *summa* of the faith. Yet, unlike the *summa* of his day, it was constructed on historical and not merely theological lines: "the work of Creation and the work of Restoration."[138]

Smalley summarizes, "The inspired history of Scripture, therefore, is the primary source of world history for Hugh ... Hence the importance of investigating and establishing every [sort of historical] detail."[139] The exegete, Hugh believed, could not neglect pertinent facts drawn out through the literal sense: language, grammar, historical events, and geography were all necessary tools. "Hugh himself prepared two chronicles and a world map."[140] However accurate this may be, Smalley clearly misunderstood certain key aspects of medieval biblical interpretation.

Strikingly, she added that each time she consulted Andrew's works, "I fall under the spell of his pages. There is really nothing quite like them."

135. For these reasons, this section is the most extensive of the discussions of the spiritual senses.

136. Smalley, *Study of the Bible in the Middle Ages*, 87. All Victorine thinkers were convinced, Smalley writes, of the Trinitarian order of the cosmos: "all good things go in threes" (86).

137. Smalley, *Study of the Bible in the Middle Ages*, 89.

138. Smalley, *Study of the Bible in the Middle Ages*, 90.

139. Smalley, *Study of the Bible in the Middle Ages*, 90.

140. Smalley, *Study of the Bible in the Middle Ages*, 90.

In particular, she misread elements of Hugh and the Victorine school. We will now discuss her understanding in an attempt to see what the issue is, and why it matters.

Smalley creates a false impression that there was a sort of contempt for the literal sense, among Christian commentators of Scripture, "up to the work of sanitation which would be due to the quite unexpected Latin translations of Aristotle and Maimonides."[141] De Lubac makes this bias clear in a few places, beginning with in his discussion of St. Paschasius Radbertus (785–865), the great Carolingian, in his *De Corpore et Sanguine Domini*, on the nature of the Eucharist. Summarizing her analysis, de Lubac states: "Miss Smalley brings Paschasius Radbertus's exegetical method together with his eucharistic doctrine. [Her] preliminary findings made on the subject are correct. Yet, the conclusion drawn from them does not seem to me necessarily to follow."

Paschasius teaches that the Eucharist *is at the same time both truth and figure*, for, he explains, a figure is not necessarily something illusory and fallacious. The figures that fill the Old Testament were real persons and facts that, in their real reality, presignified the realities of the New Testament. "*In the Bible there is a primary sense, the literal sense, prior to the allegorical sense in which one finds the fullness of Christian teaching.*"[142]

The issue is not Smalley's denial of Paschasius's apprehension of the literal sense. It is her characterization of it that is remarkable and rare: "Miss Smalley wants us to see an exceptional evaluation of the letter, whereby Paschasius would stand a cut above his age."[143] Similarly, in reviewing her analysis of Paschasius's commentary on the Book of Lamentations, de Lubac points out a similarly deficient understanding of the importance of both the literal and the spiritual senses at play. Paschasius treats the text according to both the Letter and the Spirit, and he recognizes in Lamentations both Jeremiah's own personal sufferings and the mourning over Jerusalem: "According to the history [literal sense], Jeremiah is shown to deplore no less the fall and ruin of his own people than the straits of *his own tribulation*," and "it is clear *that it happened to Jerusalem.*"[144]

141. De Lubac, *Medieval Exegesis*, vol. 2, 59.

142. De Lubac, *Medieval Exegesis*, vol. 3, 151; emphasis added.

143. De Lubac, *Medieval Exegesis*, vol. 2, 59.

144. Cited in de Lubac, *Medieval Exegesis*, vol. 3, 151; emphasis added.

As de Lubac writes (with some perturbation), "Once again, is anything out of the ordinary here? Ought we suppose the men of the ninth century so stupid as to be completely unaware of the tragic fate of Jerusalem or to find no echo of it in the writings of Jeremiah? ... Miss Smalley observes that *none of Paschasius's contemporaries had said anything of the sort*."[145] De Lubac then offers proof to the contrary from Rabanus Maurus, among others, that Smalley's assessment mischaracterizes the age.[146]

In moving to Hugh and the Victorine school, Smalley again draws similarly mischaracterized conclusions: "Hugh of Saint Victor had taught exegetes to distinguish between the literal and spiritual exposition, not to begin on the second until they had considered the first. Neither expositors nor glossators had been as alive as to the distinction between the letter and spirit as Hugh."[147] This is partially true but a bit misleading: "No one had distinguished them so methodologically in fact, because no one had organized a complete program of sacred studies on their basis. In the thought of Master Hugh, however, *this meant much less the abandonment or the loosening of the traditional doctrine of the senses of the Scripture than its consolidation, and if one can say so, its promotion.*"[148] Carrying this further, de Lubac writes that Hugh understood these distinctions as well or better than any previous commentator, but that "he began to exploit it more."[149]

Regarding the literal and spiritual senses, for Hugh it was not an either/or situation. Rather, he advocated both/and: *Primo historialiter, deinde mystice*. That is, "first in history, then in mystery." Moreover, just as was the case for Origen, Jerome, and Augustine, Hugh's objectivity consisted of "constructing a spiritual building on the foundation of the history."[150] Hugh considered the shift from the literal to the allegorical as momentous as it was necessary and not something to be taken lightly. He desired exegetes to be balanced in their handling of the spiritual senses. There was no place for excess or sloppiness in the spiritual sense. The exegete needed to be prudent in explicating only that which was

145. De Lubac, *Medieval Exegesis*, vol. 3, 151–52; Smalley, *Study of the Bible in the Middle Ages*, 41–42.

146. See de Lubac, *Medieval Exegesis*, vol. 3, 152, citing Rabanus Maurus's *Exposito*.

147. Smalley, *Study of the Bible in the Middle Ages*, 230.

148. See de Lubac, *Medieval Exegesis*, vol. 3, 236; emphasis added.

149. See de Lubac, *Medieval Exegesis*, vol. 3, 236.

150. See de Lubac, *Medieval Exegesis*, vol. 3, 250.

essential in the "first instruction," the literal sense. Restraint was necessary in examining the "second instruction,"[151] by which he meant the spiritual senses.

Just as one needed to have the necessary tools to draw out meaning according to the literal, the same was true regarding the allegorical and tropological senses. Hugh believed one needed *doctrine*—sound doctrine was the greatest aid regarding the allegorical sense.[152] For the latter, Hugh stressed the study of morality, of vice and virtue.[153] In setting these expectations for exegetes, Hugh was just as rigorous with the allegorical and tropological senses as he was with the literal sense.

Long before the New Augustine, St. Augustine made a similar point: "Just as human custom speaks with words, so does the divine power speak with deeds as well."[154] Augustine, while recognizing the primary position of the literal, did not content himself with history alone. But he only moved to the spiritual senses after dealing with the literal. A good example is seen in his examination of the text of John 12:3. There, the Evangelist reports that Mary, Lazarus's sister, "took a pound of costly ointment of pure nard and anointed the feet of Jesus and wiped his feet with her hair." As earlier in the scene at Cana, with his report of the considerable quantity of water turned into wine in Jesus's first sign, here at Bethany, John captures the scope of Mary's gesture with this sensory detail: "and the house was completely filled (*eplērthē*) with the fragrance of the ointment."

Preparing his readers for the move from the *littera* into the *sensus spiritualis*, Augustine writes, "We have heard the *fact*, now let us look into the *mystery*."[155] For Augustine, Mary's anointment signifies righteousness and therefore, he adds, that it weighed a full pound. Still alert to the literal as he moves forward, Augustine observes that the ointment was *pistikēs nardou*—pure nard. Noting this, he suggests that "there was some locality from which it derived its preciousness: *but this does not exhaust its meaning*."[156]

151. In de Lubac, *Medieval Exegesis*, vol. 2, 85.
152. In de Lubac, *Medieval Exegesis*, vol. 2, 87.
153. In de Lubac, *Medieval Exegesis*, vol. 2, 89.
154. In de Lubac, *Medieval Exegesis*, vol. 2, 88.
155. St. Augustine, *Homilies on the Gospel According to St. John*, 50.6, in Rettig, trans., *Tractates on the Gospel of John*, 78, 79, 88, 90, 92; emphasis added.
156. St. Augustine, *Homilies on the Gospel According to St. John*, 50.6; emphasis added.

Pressing forward into the spiritual sense, Augustine notes the close connection between *pistikēs* (pure) in verse 3 and its relation to *pistis*, the Greek term for "faith." Just as Mary's nard was pure, so must be the faith of the believer. And what does such faith look like according to Augustine? Drawing on St. Paul's admonition that "the just will live by faith,"[157] Augustine suggests that all Christians should "wipe the Lord's feet" with our own hair by caring for the poor and the giving of alms. Just as Mary did not spare the pure nard, so must we pour out what we have on the feet of the poor, as onto Christ: "Thou hast something to spare of thy abundance: it is superfluous to thee, but necessary for the feet of the Lord. Perhaps on this earth the Lord's feet are still in need."[158]

During the vast time between St. Augustine and Hugh of St. Victor, many echoes of this sort are heard among those that handled the Sacred Page. The Frankish Benedictine monk of the medieval period Rabanus Maurus (780–856) said it concisely: "*The history ... requires the mystery.*"[159] The letter is not enough for the true interpretation of Scripture. It is the beginning step and requires entering into the mystery that is encountered only when one crosses the threshold into the Spirit. A large chorus of patristic and medieval voices could easily be added to Rabanus. And modern voices, too. De Lubac is as adamant as Origen or Gregory the Great when he adds that "we do not have the right through negligence to deprive ourselves of the many allegories of which history is so full."[160]

The allegorical sense is particularly operative in the texts of the Old Testament, when one reads them in the light of Christ: "One is led by a series of singular facts up to one singular Fact ... everything culminates in one great Fact, which in its unique singularity, has multiple repercussions; which dominates history and which is the bearer of all light as well as all spiritual fecundity: *the fact of Christ.*"[161] Likewise, de Lubac adds: "Let us then seek, let us explore, let us dig deep: but let us not entertain the hope of exhausting the depths of Scripture. We cannot ever come to the end of the investigations that Scripture demands."[162]

157. Rom 1:17.
158. St. Augustine, *Homilies on the Gospel According to St. John*, 50.6.
159. In de Lubac, *Medieval Exegesis*, vol. 2, 84; emphasis added.
160. De Lubac, *Medieval Exegesis*, vol. 2, 84.
161. De Lubac, *Medieval Exegesis*, vol. 2, 101; emphasis added.
162. De Lubac, *Medieval Exegesis*, vol. 1, 76.

For all these reasons and more, it must be stressed that, among the spiritual senses, the allegorical is the floor upon which the others are raised up. Allegory is first among the spiritual senses. The literal alone deserves to be called the primary sense, as it truly is. Yet it is equally true that it is within the spiritual sense that the door to mystery opens. Metaphorically, the allegorical is the doorknob that leads inside to Christ himself.

Following the allegorical, one moves to the latter two spiritual senses of biblical interpretation. Of these, it is the *tropological* that informs one how to grow in charity with Christ. It shapes moral progress in the Christian life. Finally, it is through the last of the three spiritual senses—the *anagogical*, that one ascends the highest rungs on the ladder of meaning. It points the soul upward to the eternal hope of union with Christ and the Father, through the action of the Spirit. Sequentially, the tropological and anagogical follow the first great spiritual journey—that of allegory. As Wilken summarizes, "Allegory is the Church's love affair with the Bible. It is the oldest and most enduring way of interpreting the Bible and is very much alive today in the selection of scriptural readings in the liturgy, in the Church's daily praying of the psalms, and in classic works of devotion, such as St. Gregory of Nyssa's *Life of Moses* or St. Bernard's *Homilies on the Song of Songs.*"[163]

Commenting on the way in which the allegorical sense is penetrates to the heart of the mystery of the Old Testament—Christ himself—Hans Boersma describes a "sacramental hermeneutic" that was embraced by the Church Fathers. By this, Boersma means that they saw the entire mystery of Christ in the entirety of the Old Testament: "For the church fathers, *the hidden presence of the reality was finally revealed at the fullness of time, in the Christ event*—along with everything else it entails: Christ's own person and work; the church's origin; the believers new, Spirit-filled lives in Christ; and the eschatological renewal of all things in and through Christ."[164]

The primitive Church saw this entire new-covenant reality as "the *hidden treasure already present in the Old Testament.* In other words, the reason the fathers practiced … allegory is that they were convinced that the reality of the Christ event was *already* present (sacramentally) within the history described within the Old Testament narrative."[165]

163. Wilken, "Allegory and the Interpretation of the Old Testament," 11.
164. Boersma, *Scripture as Real Presence*, 336; emphasis added.
165. Boersma, *Scripture as Real Presence*, 12; emphasis added.

To this we can add that it was, in Boersma's phrase, "the Christ event" that fueled this entire process for the Church Fathers and medieval theologians. They were transformed by Christ and participated in his life and in the life of the Church sacramentally. Their exegesis of the Old Testament involved not just a spiritual reading. It was also a *true participation* in the text. For these masters of the Sacred Page, the allegorical sense was a true participation in Christ, the Logos, who himself participated in the Creation, and in all of salvation history:

> As the divine *Logos* incarnate, as the culmination of the process of the shaping of Israel to God's friendship, Jesus is, in person, the "recapitulation" of time and history. The notion of *anakephalaiosis*, rendered in Latin as *recapitulatio* is the master idea of Irenaeus' biblical theology. *Jesus draws all the strands of history and revelation together in himself, preserving and repeating them even as he brings them to fulfillment.* Thus, he is the new Adam, the one who participates fully in the reality of Adam, including physicality and alienation from God, even as he draws all that was implicit and potential in Adam to completion ... In his resurrection from the dead, he heals, renews, and elevates the fallen world. *The recapitulating Christ is himself the interpretive key of the whole Scripture, since he is the Logos made flesh.*[166]

As our understanding of allegory deepens, it only becomes clearer that it is rooted in the Old Testament. Undoubtedly, it involves *reading the Old Testament with Christ*. Given this, two related questions of biblical theology arise: First, what is typology? And are allegory and typology one and the same, and if not, what distinguishes them from one another?

While it is beyond our purpose to deal with such questions extensively here, a few remarks are necessary to provide clarity. First, a basic definition of typology is as follows: "The study of persons, places, events, and institutions in the Bible that foreshadow later, and greater realities made known by God in history. The basis of such study is the belief that God, who providentially shapes and determines the course of human events, infuses those events with a prophetic and theological significance. Typology thus reveals the unity of salvation history as a carefully orchestrated

166. Barron, "Biblical Interpretation and Theology," 178–79; emphases added. He adds: "And Mary the mother of Jesus is the new Eve, sharing in the reality of the first Eve even as she redirects the momentum of her forebear's sin. Jesus too is the recapitulation of creation." See Irenaeus, *Against Heresies*, III.19.3. On "recapitulation," see *CCC* §518 and Smith, *House of the Lord*.

plan that God unfolds in stages of ever-increasing fulfillment. The movement from 'types' to the realities they signify, called 'antitypes, is always a movement from the lesser to the greater."[167]

Although there are examples of *types* and *antitypes* within the Old Testament itself, the most lively and abundant examples of typology are seen in the movement from the Old to the New Testament: "Many typological themes of the Hebrew Scriptures, which were fulfilled in partial degrees in the history of Israel, give way to the definitive antitypes that God had intended to prefigure from the beginning. *In the Person and work of Jesus Christ, the full significance of the persons, places, events, and institutions of biblical history is finally revealed.*"[168] This definition of typology is clear and helpful. A third question is as follows. Do allegory and typology refer to the same thing, and if not, what distinguishes them from one another? A concise answer is that the terms "allegory" and "typology" are often used today in a way that is nearly interchangeable. They are not the same, though they are closely related.

A slightly longer answer begins with the adage *well, it depends upon whom you ask.* Henri de Lubac and his student Jean Daniélou shared much in common in this regard. But not everything. Whereas de Lubac would insist on the more ancient terminology of allegory, Daniélou used the more modern term, typology.[169] Such differences may seem slight, yet they are crucial for maintaining precision in our study.

De Lubac's view is illuminated by a well-known quote from St. Greg-

167. "Typology," in Hahn, *Catholic Bible Dictionary*, 929. "Jesus found in the Bible a treasury of types that prepared the way for his coming. Several examples of this appear in Matthew 12, where he claims, *'something greater than the temple is here'* (Mt 12:6), and *'something greater than Jonah is here'* (Mt 12:41), and again *'something greater than Solomon is here'* (Mt 12:42). His words indicate what is intrinsic to all typology, namely, that antitypes resemble the types that foreshadow them, *yet they also surpass them because they are something greater than the original.* In this case, Jesus placed himself above the holiest place known to Israel (the Temple), above the prophet who miraculously emerged from a three-day entombment (Jonah), and above the wisest king ever to rule the People of God (Solomon). Christ is a new and living temple, for in him dwells the divine presence more intensely than in the sanctuary (cf. Jn 2:21). He is likewise a new Jonah, for his Resurrection after three days in the grave would be the one miracle that outshines all others (cf. Mt 16:4). And he is also a new Solomon, a king from the royal line of David and a man of legendary wisdom who will draw the world closer to the Lord (Lk 11:31)" (930–31; emphases added).

168. Hahn, *Catholic Bible Dictionary*, 930; emphasis added.

169. "*'Typology' is a modern construct.* Ancient exegetes did not distinguish between typology and allegory, and it is often difficult to make the distinction, the one shading into the other all too easily." Young, *Biblical Exegesis and the Formation of Christian Culture*, 152; emphasis added.

ory the Great: "The Old and New Law are to be understood as *a double wheel*: The outside wheel is the covering one, while the second, covered wheel, is the wheel that does the uncovering."[170] Gregory's inner and outer wheels are a reference to the prophet Ezekiel.[171] This was an appealing image to de Lubac, and he used it to draw a contrast between the main division in meaning, between *letter* and *spirit*. De Lubac believed that the entire reality of Christ was present in the Old Testament people and events that signified him allegorically—a wheel in a wheel.

Moses, Joshua, David, the ark, the manna, the Temple, and so on—for de Lubac, such did not merely symbolize or point forward to Christ, as with typology's types and antitypes. Instead, in a mysterious way, Christ was already present in them. De Lubac's understanding of allegory is *sacramental* in nature. Boersma: "By endorsing the 'spiritual movement' of pre-modern exegesis, de Lubac hinted at a link between *spiritual interpretation and a sacramental view of reality*. The entire Tradition, he pointed out, had argued for a sacramental understanding of the historical facts related in the Old Testament."[172]

De Lubac rallied an impressive array of witnesses—a hallmark of his historical scholarship—and demonstrated that medieval interpreters had equated mystery and allegory; the terms *mysterium* and *sacramentum* had often been used interchangeably, "both of them referring to *the spiritual, allegorical, or mystical meaning of the Scriptures.*"[173]

About this, Boersma adds: "In terms of biblical interpretation, de Lubac was convinced that problems arose if and when the historical meaning was treated *as strictly autonomous and separate from the other levels of interpretation* or perhaps was even regarded as providing the sole meaning of the text. What he objected to was the reduction of history to *mere history* and the restriction of Old Testament exegesis to its literal meaning."[174]

In contrast to his mentor, Daniélou absolutely disdained the idea of Four Senses of Scripture and cautioned against reading Scripture along

170. St. Gregory the Great, *In Ezekiel*, Book 1, h. 7, n. 15. See Moorhead, *Gregory the Great*; emphasis added.

171. Ezek 1:16: "As for the appearance of the wheels and their construction: their appearance was like the gleaming of a chrysolite; and the four had the same likeness, their construction being as it *were a wheel within a wheel*" (emphasis added).

172. Boersma, *Scripture as Real Presence*, 12; emphasis added.

173. Boersma, *Nouvelle Theologie and Sacramental Ontology*, 155; emphases added.

174. Boersma, *Nouvelle Theologie and Sacramental Ontology*, 159; emphases added.

such lines. Why? For him, there are only two senses: the literal and the typological:

> There are, in the strict sense of the word, *only two meanings of Scripture. The one is the literal meaning, which is that of the text.* It is the meaning desired by the author and which the study of the text merely must explain. Further, this meaning can either be its own or figured, depending on whether it concerns the literal meaning of history or a parable. *The other is the typological meaning.* It is not another meaning of the text. There is nothing in the text except what the author has wished to place there. But it is a meaning of the things themselves, of which the author speaks. It is a relation between the realities of the Old Testament and those of the New.[175]

This is a striking quote. First, Daniélou insists that there are only two meanings in Scripture: the literal and the typological. And he stressed that typology is "*not another meaning of the text.*" There is nothing in the text except what the biblical writer intended to place there, seemingly indicating that the only true sense of Scripture is that supplied by the author—the literal. For Daniélou, typological meaning is that which is discovered in the New Testament through that which is being signifying, that is, the Old Testament type: "Thus, [Daniélou] reinforced the impression that he regarded the Old Testament types and their New Testament realities as *separate historical events*."[176]

This discussion indicates that the two great Catholic exegetes were colliding about something more than terminology. De Lubac embraced the classical term *allegoria*, as used by Philo of Alexandria, St. Paul, and Origen, to name a few. Moreover, he embraced the patristic and medieval concept of a "multiplicity of meaning" through the Four Senses. In contrast, Daniélou held a relatively narrower view of things. Strictly speaking, the only meaning for Daniélou was located within the literal. Typological meaning was simply that to which the Old Testament pointed forward—to Christ. Although the Fathers didn't distinguish between allegory and typology, this may often have been because the Fathers thought of what we call typology as belonging to the literal sense.

To be clear, the chief concern that Daniélou had with the allegorical sense was allegory's ability to set aside history and the historical foundation of the Word. This nonhistorical—or, better, ahistorical—dimen-

175. Daniélou, *Les divers sens de l'écriture*, 119–20; emphases added.
176. Boersma, *Nouvelle Theologie and Sacramental Ontology*, 185; emphasis added.

sion of allegorical interpretation was problematic for Daniélou in a way that biblical typology was not. To this end, in *The Bible and the Liturgy*,[177] Daniélou examined numerous biblical types from the Old Testament to the New—and into the primitive Church. With ample support from St. John Chrysostom, Tertullian, St. Gregory of Nazianzus, and others, Daniélou traced the trajectory of typology from Scripture into the sacramental and liturgical practices in early Christianity.

For example, in explaining the baptismal liturgies in the fourth century, he describes the rituals that were begun well in advance of the Easter Vigil, clear back to the initial preparation at the beginning of Lent.[178] One aspect of the preparation involved "a kind of examination to ensure the purity of [the candidate's] motives."[179] Only after this scrutiny would the bishop inscribe the candidate's name in the registers.

Commenting on this, Daniélou states that the literal meaning of these rites was for Theodore of Mopsuestia an escape of the domination of Satan: "The baptismal rites constitute a drama in which the candidate, who up to this point belonged to the demon, strives to escape his power."[180] For Daniélou, however, the entire rite was also saturated with typology. Following Theodore, Daniélou sees in this rite a figure of the biblical "battle" of Adam's contest with the serpent and, later, of Christ's temptation in the wilderness. As Daniélou sums up, "*We are now in the center of biblical typology.*"[181] The above example illustrates Daniélou's disdain for allegory and his clear preference for typology. For him, it is not a matter of mere semantics or definitions at stake. Rather, it is of how biblical types in many ways *led into the liturgical history* of the Church. In other words, for Daniélou, allegory remains questionable. This is primarily because of what Daniélou views as allegory's "ahistorical" aspect. It could and often did operate apart from history.

Yet typology, Daniélou stressed, was not merely historical but *his-*

177. Daniélou, *The Bible and the Liturgy*.

178. "This remote period of preparation as we know, could last for a long time; and the Fathers often protested against those who thus put off their entrance into the Church. But from the time of their enrollment at the beginning of Lent, the candidates constituted a new group, the *photizomenoi* ('those coming into the light'). The ceremonies of these forty days form a whole, of which our ceremony makes a single ceremony." Daniélou, *The Bible and the Liturgy*, 19.

179. Daniélou, *The Bible and the Liturgy*, 20.

180. Daniélou, *The Bible and the Liturgy*, 21.

181. Daniélou, *The Bible and the Liturgy*, 21; emphasis added.

torically centered. Two questions emerge: What does this mean? And why is it important?

1. By historically centered, and not merely historical, Daniélou means to say that typology is a kind of unfolding of theological patterns in salvation history—from the pages of the Old Testament to the New, and ultimately into the sacramental life of the Church: "The temptation of the [baptismal] candidate is, in turn, a participation in the temptation of Christ."[182]

2. This is significant because this participation is, for Daniélou, a real encounter, experienced in time, by the Church and her members. This encounter gives it a practical and personal meaning, unfolding in the liturgy. Salvation history in Scripture gives way to the history of the Church in its early baptismal rites.[183]

Despite Daniélou's insistences, there was less distance between the two theologians than one might imagine: (1) both de Lubac and Daniélou made vast contributions in *ressourcement*, or toward the recovery of patristic thought; (2) both wholeheartedly affirmed that the Old Testament needed to be read Christologically; and (3) both affirmed the integral unity that exists between Scripture and liturgy.[184] For all three reasons, as well as many other lasting contributions, both de Lubac

182. Daniélou, *The Bible and the Liturgy*, 21, emphasis added.

183. Daniélou's discussion was not restricted to the rite of Baptism. In subsequent chapters, he treats Confirmation (chap. 7), Eucharist (chaps. 8 and 9), the Lord's Day (chap. 150), and Easter (chap. 17), all in a similar light.

184. Summing up the main differences between the two views, Boersma writes: "de Lubac and Daniélou certainly had their hermeneutical differences. First, de Lubac's emphasis on multiplicity of meaning ensured his openness to the free rein of a biblically shaped imagination in support of the edification of the Church. Daniélou tended to disqualify spiritual interpretation as 'allegorical' when he could not find a clear biblical precedent or foundation for a particular patristic Christological or sacramental reading of the text. Second, de Lubac insisted that while a historical foundation and a literal reading were indispensable the purpose of spiritual reading was to move beyond history. Daniélou was wary of such 'vertical' interpretation and insisted that typology was based on a prophecy-fulfillment scheme that was thoroughly historical in character. Third, and most significantly, de Lubac's sacramental hermeneutic regarded the spiritual meaning as internal to the historical event, so that one could never separate these two main levels of reality. The spiritual level was 'a wheel within a wheel.' Daniélou, while agreeing that spiritual interpretation was sacramental in character, did not always make clear that he believed type and antitype to have such a 'perichoretic' relationship, emphasizing instead the temporal distance given with the historical development from the Old Testament to Christ and the Church." Boersma, *Nouvelle Theologie and Sacramental Ontology*, 189–90.

and Daniélou remain colossal figures in Catholic biblical theology. Both have significant insights to offer the present study. Even so, *The Face of the Lord* is aligned with the more classical understanding of the Four Senses, that is, the view articulated by de Lubac himself, rather than his preeminent student.[185]

The Lubacian approach is, at least between the two modern masters, the one that represents the view of meaning in Scripture throughout the patristic and medieval periods. Regardless of the precise terms patristic theologians used, they embraced the twofold sense of Scripture—the literal and the spiritual. Likewise, whether medieval exegetes spoke of two, three, or even more spiritual senses than that (St. Bonaventure conjectured that there were more than a dozen), they did not restrict all "true" meaning to the literal. The Scriptures were indeed cryptic, and one needed to move from the Letter to the Spirit if one was, in Origen's phraseology, "to draw out the honey" from the Word.

This widely held ancient conviction—that all of Scripture had a multiplicity of meanings—was no mere maxim. It truly set the course for ancient and medieval interpretation of the Bible for ages: "I think each word of divine Scripture is like a seed whose nature is to multiply diffusely, reborn into an ear of corn or whatever its species be when it has been cast into the earth. Its increase is proportionate to the diligent labor of the skillful farmer or the fertility of the earth. So, therefore, it is brought to pass that, by diligent cultivation, a little 'mustard seed,' for example, 'which is least of all, may be made greater than all herbs and become a tree so that the birds of heaven come and dwell in its branches.'"[186] These are the words of Origen, the pupil of Clement of Alexandria and the single greatest purveyor of allegory in the entire patristic period—and perhaps of all time. Origen's metaphor is an apt one. Not only for approaching his method of biblical interpretation, but also in our discussion of allegory as it relates to the Four Senses.

The Word is a seed, and this divine seed has within its constitution

185. We view Daniélou in the highest regard and appreciate the manner in which he articulated the "thread of continuity" between biblical typology and the liturgical and sacramental life of the Church. That said, de Lubac discusses allegorical interpretation in a way that properly that enfolds it into the classical formula of the "four senses." For this reason, de Lubac's treatment is most fitting for this work. The differences between the two scholars outlined here are real and not insignificant. Yet it is not as though the two were diametrically opposed, nor should these nuances be exaggerated.

186. Origen, *Homily One on Genesis*, in *Homilies on Genesis and Exodus*, 227.

a propensity to multiply. And multiply it does. Yet its fecundity is, in some sense, contingent upon the "skillful farmer." In other words, Origen rightly grasped that the fruitfulness of the Word is contingent upon the diligent and humble interpreter who cultivates and nurtures it with diligent care. Only then does he encounter its truth and witnesses its manifold increase. This Spirit-infused nature of both the Word and the faithful hearer of the Word is at the foundation of Origen's allegorical interpretation of Scripture.

Still, and this point must be stressed, Origen did not set aside the literal for the allegorical. He recognized that the literal sense was the starting position for the one seeking deeper meaning in the Scriptures, as did Hugh long after him: "Nor do I think that you will be able to become perfectly sensitive to allegory unless you have first been grounded in history."[187]

True, Origen believed that the literal sense was for the simpler minded; something to be worked through so that the more able reader is taken into the spiritual depths that figural readings yield: "That we may profit by *the primary sense* of Scripture, even if we go no further, is evident from the multitudes of true and simple-minded believers. Let us, however, take what Paul says in his first epistle to the Corinthians as an example of the higher 'soul' interpretation."[188] Even so, for Origen, the whole Scripture—every divine word—was saturated with meaning, with Christ-meaning. Much of this meaning was hidden below the surface. By virtue of their divine authorship, all the Scriptures, from beginning to end, had Christ within them, often in cryptic ways. And this deeper understanding was only available for those "with eyes to see." The onus was on the skilled interpreter, who approached the Word of God with faith, confident in that the text is like a husk that needed to be peeled back.

Confident, too, Origen believed that the faithful and attendant recipient will be filled with its sweet riches by the selfsame Spirit who breathed life into the Word: "Do not despair of finding meanings in the stone of stumbling and rock of offence, so that the saying may be fulfilled, 'He that believeth shall not be ashamed.' First believe, and thou shalt find beneath what is counted a stumbling-block much gain in god-

187. Hugh St. Victor, "To the New Student of Sacred Scripture."
188. Origen, *Philocalia*, 1.13; emphasis added.

liness."[189] This is precisely what the ancient and medieval commentators did when reading the Old Testament and saw Christ signified in the sacrifice of Abel, the water from the rock in the wilderness, and other scenes. Here, some may protest: What about context? Where is it in the mix of things? Were such masters of the Sacred Page merely ignoring the past context of the Scripture, bending it forward to make it say what they wish?

To answer these important questions, we return to Wilken, who explains that context need not—in fact ought not—be restricted to the past:

> Context is, however, an elusive category. In dealing with ancient texts it is often assumed that what went before or what is contemporaneous with the text set the terms of interpretation. One might ask why context should be restricted to what happened earlier. *Is what went before more significant than what occurred afterward or what came about because of what happened, was said, or was written down?* With great political ideas, for example, it is only as they are played out in history that we know what they mean. In the telling of American history, President John Kennedy's achievements during his presidency would be remembered much differently had he not been assassinated in his first term.[190]

Wilken's point may be a new and challenging one, and too provocative for some, particularly for those accustomed to thinking of the historical context, as in past context, as the definitive shovel that enables one to dig into the context of the past to illuminate a biblical passage. "Context is king" in approaching Scriptural interpretation in true, exegetical fashion. And this sort of contextual digging is right, sound, and necessary, and it is something I have strongly advocated for elsewhere.[191] But it is not necessarily the only tool. Nor should the notion of context be strictly limited to looking back. True, one must exercise a great deal of caution about anachronistically reading data back into the text, from a time longer after it is written.

Nevertheless, Wilken is not speaking of reading anachronistically.

189. Origen, *Philocalia*, 1.28. Origen's reference is to Rom 9:33. In in turn, Paul is the prophet Isaiah: "he who believes in him will not be put to shame" (Isa 28:16). I am indebted to Peter Leithart with regard to the expression "the text is a husk." See his excellent monograph *Deep Exegesis*, from which the phrase is derived. Chapter 1 of Leithart's book is "The Text Is a Husk" (1–34).

190. Wilken, "In Defense of Allegory," 201; emphasis added.

191. See Smith, *Word of the Lord*, esp. chap. 3.

His point is that context ought not be narrowly restricted to past events. Consider that "Even in our personal lives and in relations with others *we are constantly adjusting our view of the past and of the lives of others as new experiences unfold*. We view a close friend who has patiently and heroically endured a grave illness differently than we did before his illness. Even the things done or said earlier appear different."[192] All of this has the propensity to open new, groundbreaking horizons for the biblical reader. One may need to revisit his or her understanding of context and, if necessary, fine-tune it to allow for context to inform the present as well as the past. Wilken refers to this as type of interpretative approach as "reading forward."[193] As he helpfully explains, "There is then a realism in allegory as well as spiritual depth. The mystery of which the Bible speaks is realized historically and socially. Saint Paul was not interested in ephemeral 'meanings' that could be attached *ad libitum* to the ancient texts. He sought to discover what the authoritative documents of his religious tradition (and ours) meant in light of '*the things that have been accomplished among us*,' to invoke Luke's memorable words."[194]

Engaging texts from the Old Testament in an allegorical way allows the Word to speak anew, revealing Christ in myriad fresh ways in the New Testament. Origen offers this argument for the harmony between the Old and New Testaments, aptly using a musical motif: "But if a reader comes who has been instructed in God's music, a man who happens to be wise in word and deed, and on that account, it may be, called *David*, which being interpreted is 'a cunning player,' he will produce a note of God's music, for he will have learned from God's music to keep good time, playing now upon the strings of the Law, now upon those of the Gospel in harmony with them."[195]

192. Wilken, "Allegory and the Interpretation of the Old Testament"; emphasis added.

193. Wilken, "Allegory and the Interpretation of the Old Testament."

194. Wilken, "Allegory and the Interpretation of the Old Testament"; emphasis added (see also Lk 1:1–4). "Allegory's playfulness and inventiveness grows out of the certainty of faith formed by a community of shared beliefs and practices. *It keeps words from evaporating into nothing, from simply becoming things, not signs*. It also introduces a welcome and necessary obliqueness into our reading of the Scriptures. Remember that according to Exodus, God showed only his back to Moses. Metaphor, symbol, image are the natural clothing of religious thought. '*Tell all the truth but tell it slant*,' wrote Emily Dickinson, the American poet. By likening what is known to unexpected words or images within the Bible, allegory gave Christian thinkers a more subtle and versatile vocabulary to speak of the things of God. The language of the Bible became a vehicle of discovery" (20; emphasis added).

195. Origen, *Philocalia*, 6.2; emphasis added.

So far, we have been considering allegory as it pertains to the Old Testament. What about the New Testament? Does allegory work the same way as in the Old? Not exactly, no. This distinction is important and needs to be addressed here. In so doing, we will identify a key distinction between the Old and New Testaments with respect to allegorical sense. The distinction may be seen by posing another question: If the function of the allegorical sense is to "signify" Christ in the Old Law, what happens when we turn from the Old to the New Testament, where Christ is truly present? In a manner of speaking, allegory loses its raison d'être in moving from the Old to the New Testament. The necessity of seeing Christ in allegorical ways within the Old Testament has given way to the Word made flesh.[196]

Here, Wilken explains, "In its original sense, Christian allegory as an interpretative technique is a way of interpreting the Old Testament in light of the new things that have taken place with the coming of Christ. The New Testament does not need an allegorical interpretation because it speaks directly of Christ."[197] The logic is clear: "The death and Resurrection of Christ do not point to something else; they are the mystery hidden before the ages."[198]

Elsewhere, Wilken writes, "The term allegory is used so loosely today that it is sometimes forgotten that it is primarily a technique for interpreting the Old Testament, the Jewish Scriptures that the early Christian community made its own. In the words of a medieval Spanish exegete: The New Testament '*pro se stat sicut auditur; non est allegoria*,' stands on its own, it does not need allegory."[199] As Wilken sums up, "Allegory, then, is a term to refer to the 'Christological' dimension of the Old Testament, what came to be called the 'spiritual sense.'"[200] Wilken's logic is sound. The allegorical sense is active in the Old Testament when read in the light of the coming Christ. Even so, it needs to be stressed that allegory and allegorical interpretation is not altogether "off limits" regarding the New Testament. Two points underscore this fact.

196. Jn 1:14.

197. Wilken, "In Defense of Allegory," 201.

198. Wilken, "In Defense of Allegory," 201.

199. Wilken, "Allegory and the Interpretation of the Old Testament," 12. "The epistles of St. Paul do not call for allegory, and only occasionally is it appropriate for passages in the gospels, for example, in dealing with certain parables."

200. Wilken, "In Defense of Allegory," 201.

First, St. Paul himself develops his contrast between the Old and New Law in his *Epistle to the Galatians.*[201] "It was Saint Paul who taught the earliest Christian to use allegory . . . and pointed the way forward toward a rationale for the use of allegory."[202] Second, numerous Church fathers have drawn out allegorical interpretations of New Testament texts. One thinks almost immediately of St. Augustine's allegorical treatment of the Parable of the Good Samaritan, for example.[203] Still, the allegorical sense is primarily associated not with the New Testament, but with the Old Testament. Why? A way of getting at this disparity—of the abundant use of allegorical interpretation of the Old Testament and its virtual lack in regard to the New Testament—is as follows.

In a sense, there is a twofold dimension to allegory. The first element is the this-for-that aspect: a certain person, place, thing, or event from the Old Testament signifies Christ. But this is only the first element of allegory—identifying the signification. The decisive element is what follows this identification; namely, the spiritual interpretation that flows out of this connection. Without such explanation, one has, so to speak, allegory without allegorical interpretation. The two elements belong together. Wilken gets at this when he writes, "Allegory resists the tyranny

201. See Gal 4:21–31.

202. Wilken, "In Defense of Allegory," 200. He discusses a number of Pauline texts that provide "a biblical foundation for the practice of allegory" (200). Among them are Eph 5, 1 Cor 10, and Gal 4.

203. See Lk 10:25–37. "A certain man went down from Jerusalem to Jericho; Adam himself is meant; Jerusalem is the heavenly city of peace, from whose blessedness Adam fell; Jericho means the moon, and signifies our mortality, because it is born, waxes, wanes, and dies. Thieves are the devil and his angels. Who stripped him, namely; of his immortality; and beat him, by persuading him to sin; and left him half-dead, because in so far as man can understand and know God, he lives, but in so far as he is wasted and oppressed by sin, he is dead; he is therefore called half-dead. The priest and the Levite who saw him and passed by, signify the priesthood and ministry of the Old Testament which could profit nothing for salvation. Samaritan means Guardian, and therefore the Lord Himself is signified by this name. The binding of the wounds is the restraint of sin. Oil is the comfort of good hope; wine the exhortation to work with fervent spirit. The beast is the flesh in which He deigned to come to us. The being set upon the beast is belief in the incarnation of Christ. The inn is the Church, where travelers returning to their heavenly country are refreshed after pilgrimage. The morrow is after the resurrection of the Lord. The two pence are either the two precepts of love, or the promise of this life and of that which is to come. The innkeeper is the Apostle. The supererogatory payment is either his counsel of celibacy, or the fact that he worked with his own hands lest he should be a burden to any of the weaker brethren when the Gospel was new, though it was lawful for him 'to live by the gospel'" (St. Augustine, *Quaestiones Evangeliorum*, II, 19). See *Sermon* 299, in which Augustine provides a typological treatment of the text.

of historicism and invites us to see things as they are, not as we imagine them to have been centuries ago. This is one reason for the formative power of the liturgy on interpretation. The Church at prayer spans the great divide separating what the text *meant* from what it *means*. Allegory is about what has come to be, the accommodation that is inevitable because of what happened in Christ, in the Church, and what continues to unfold."[204]

All things point forward to Christ, so allegorical possibilities abound in the Old Testament. Yet it can cease once one opens to the pages of the New Testament. In reading the Sermon on the Mount, or looking on at one of Jesus's miracles, allegory has lost its raison d'être. As Daniélou put it, in the move from the Old Testament to the New, we pass "from shadows to reality." Along similar lines, Wilkens is correct: the *need* for allegory elides when we come to the Gospels. At the same time, the second element of allegory, that of interpretation, need not evaporate. In a manner of speaking, allegorical interpretation—so critical to the Old Testament—gives way to mystical interpretation. One may think of the mystical sense as allegory without the this-for-that aspect.

Often, in their dealing with New Testament texts, the ancient and medieval exegetes simply set the allegorical aside and turn instead to the other spiritual senses, that is, the tropological or the anagogical (or perhaps both). This is logical, as the allegorical has all but lost its raison d'être in the New Testament. At other times, however, one may detect a sort of spiritual interpretation in play, which is neither tropological nor anagogical. This is an intriguing development, and it is not uncommon. But such spiritual interpretation can no longer be identified as allegorical by our definitions. What is it then? What should it be called? For our purposes, we will refer to such exegesis as the mystical or sacramental sense.[205] More will be said about the mystical/sacramental sense—that which is spiritual in nature yet not necessarily allegorical—at the end of the book.[206]

204. Wilken, "In Defense of Allegory," 203.

205. Interestingly, such terminology is found among the ancient and medieval theologians in some instances (see de Lubac, *Medieval Exegesis*, vol. 2, 83–128). I am not claiming any sort of uniformity in the usage of this term or related terminology. As stressed, the terminology employed in discussions of the Four Senses was fluid throughout the ancient and medieval periods.

206. This book focuses on encounter scenes exclusively found in the Old Testament. It is beyond its scope to deal with encounter scenes in the New Testament and examining

In any event, the allegorical sense has within it powerful interpretive possibilities: "Allegory is about privileging the language of the Bible. It assumes that it is better to express things in the language of the Scriptures than in another idiom. As the Church's great preachers have always known metaphors drawn from elsewhere, no matter how apt, lack the power of the biblical language to enlighten the mind and enflame the heart. Like rhetorical ornaments that momentarily delight the hearer, they are ephemeral and soon forgotten."[207] In contrast, "the words of the Bible, however, are emblematic and weighted with experience. Unlike words taken from elsewhere, their meanings cannot be disengaged from the biblical narrative, from God's revelation in Israel, the sending of Christ and the pouring out of the Spirit on the Church. The range of possible meanings is never exhausted."[208] Among the spiritual senses, none has been subject to more criticism and even ridicule than the allegorical sense. This is the case not only in biblical studies today, but also in the field of literary criticism.

In an excellent study called *Allegory and Enchantment*,[209] Jason Crawford laments what Max Weber called "the disenchantment of the world" in postmodernism. There, he vigorously and persuasively advocates for a "poetics of enchantment."[210] He describes enchantment as "that old magic"[211] whose spell has been broken by modernity.[212] One thinks too of the view of C. S. Lewis on allegory, along with that of his Oxford colleague J. R. R. Tolkien, as it relates to the role of myth.[213]

Putting allegory back into the game today is no easy task, as Craw-

---

them according to the Four Senses. Yet, to provide understanding of the differentiation between the two testaments, some remarks about approaching the New Testament are offered in the "meditations" and in the closing chapter of the book.

207. Wilken, "Allegory and the Interpretation of the Old Testament."

208. Wilken, "Allegory and the Interpretation of the Old Testament."

209. Crawford, "Introduction: A Poetics of Enchantment," in *Allegory and Enchantment*, 1–44.

210. See Crawford, *Allegory and Enchantment*, 1–44.

211. Crawford, *Allegory and Enchantment*, 2.

212. Crawford, *Allegory and Enchantment*, 17.

213. See esp. J. R. R. Tolkien, "On Fairy-Stories," in *The Monster and the Critics*, 109–61. See the discussion on Lewis and Tolkien in Smith, *House of the Lord*, 56, 59–60. Tolkien disdained the kind of oversimplification involved in allegory. Unlike Lewis, Tolkien did not employ it in *The Hobbit* or *The Lord of the Rings*. But "myth," which involved a deep symbolism, archetypes, and the like, inhabited the Legendarium of Tolkien's work. See Fleiger, *Tolkien on Fairy Stories*; idem, *Splintered Light*. See also Bernthal, *Tolkien's Sacramental Vision*.

ford realizes. Even so, his project contains many notes of optimism. Although some might decry the use of literary criticism in discussing the Word of God, Crawford's articulate voice on the significance of allegory is worthy of inclusion here: "The very term 'allegory' . . . 'to speak other' yokes together the opposed orders of *narrative and of significance*. The 'other' which is spoken might seem to cancel or to transcend the material stuff of time and narrative, but allegory as other-speaking *embeds that transcendent other in the 'speaking,'* in a discourse that must unfold in time. Allegory allows neither of its diametrically opposed halves to escape from the other but rather forces them into a dialectic negotiation that opens narrative to meaning and meaning to narrative."[214]

De Lubac cites the four great Doctors, who all affirm the need to plunge into the mysteries of allegory: St. Jerome, "We have drawn the thin lines of history, now let is set our hand to allegory"; St. Augustine, "We have heard the fact; let us look into the mystery"; St. Ambrose, "A higher sense calls us forth"; and St. Gregory the Great, "But since we have discussed the surface of the history, let us weigh carefully what lies hidden within them within the mystic understanding."[215] This was not only the conviction of these doctors. It was a certainty among the vast majority of patristic and medieval theologians. In truth, it was a nearly universally held truth throughout the past the first millennium, and strongly the case well up to the Reformation.

Yet the idea of "setting the hand to allegory," as St. Jerome put it, had lost its ubiquitous appeal long before Vatican I. The encroachment of rationalism and scientific empiricism led to a widespread biblical skepticism in the eighteenth and nineteenth centuries, and the idea of *any senses* beyond the literal and historical was greatly diminished, if not nearly extinguished:

> For generations, indeed centuries, biblical scholars have scorned allegory. With the triumph of the historical approach to the Bible in the universities and colleges and seminaries many took it as self-evident that only the original meaning of the text, presented to us with the tools of historical criticism, can claim the allegiance of modern readers of the Bible. Yet, literary critics have always realized that the notion of a single sense does not carry us very far in the in-

214. Crawford, *Allegory and Enchantment*, 17; emphasis added.

215. De Lubac, *Medieval Exegesis*, vol. 2, 83. See St. Jerome, *Select Letters*, 52; St. Augustine, *Tractates on the Gospel of St. John*, 50.6; Ambrose of Milan, *Treatise on Paradise, Noah, and the Ark*, 9.38; St. Gregory the Great, *Morals on the Book of Job*, II.3.8.

terpretation of great works of literature. One reason that the "classics" of our civilization endure is because each generation is able to discover in the texts depths of meaning that were not discerned by earlier readers.[216]

But a renewed interest in patristic exegesis was about to dawn in the early twentieth century. This was particularly the case in Catholic circles, due in no small part to magisterial attention. Through various encyclicals as well as the establishment of the early Pontifical Biblical Commission and other means, the Catholic Church responded to rationalism and Protestant liberalism. Here, the so-called Catholic Scripture documents (i.e., papal encyclicals and exhortations) are of significance.

These documents provided magisterial guidance for Catholic exegetes on such things as biblical inspiration and inerrancy, the proper interpretation of Sacred Scripture, the unity of the Old and New Testaments, and, among other things, the crucial role of the Church Fathers and medieval theologians. Prior to *Dei Verbum*, the two most significant documents of this sort came in the form of papal encyclicals, specifically Pope Leo XIII's *Providentissimus Deus* (1893) and Pope Pius XII's *Divino Afflante Spiritu*.[217] Fanning the flames of these Scripture documents came later, especially in the 1930s through the 1960s, through the bib-

216. Wilken, "Allegory and the Interpretation of the Old Testament," 205.

217. See Bechard, *Scripture Documents*. *Providentissimus Deus* (*PD*), 14: "For the language of the Bible is employed to express, under the inspiration of the Holy Ghost, many things which are beyond the power and scope of the reason of man ... There is sometimes in such passages a fullness and a hidden depth of meaning which the letter hardly expresses and which the laws of interpretation hardly warrant." See also *Divino Afflante Spiritu* (*DAS*), 25–26: "Doubtless all spiritual sense is not excluded from the Sacred Scripture. For what was said and done in the Old Testament was ordained and disposed by God with such consummate wisdom, that things past prefigured in a spiritual way those that were to come under the new dispensation of grace. The exegete, just as he must search out and expound the literal meaning of the words, intended and expressed by the sacred writer, so also must he do likewise for the spiritual sense, provided it is clearly intended by God. For God alone could have known this spiritual meaning and have revealed it to us ... *Let Catholic exegetes then disclose and expound this spiritual significance, intended and ordained by God, with that care which the dignity of the divine word demands; but let them scrupulously refrain from proposing as the genuine meaning of Sacred Scripture other figurative senses*" (emphasis added). Despite its affirmation of the spiritual senses of Scripture, *DAS* clearly offered a more cautious endorsement of them, compared with *PD*, fifty years earlier. Additionally, the literal sense was continually reemphasized in this encyclical (see paras. 23, 36, 54). This was because of certain excesses at the time, especially in certain circles in Italy. Still, *DAS* stood shoulder-to-shoulder with *PD* and its insistence upon all four senses. In providing corrective to abuses, *DAS* brought the literal and spiritual senses back into alignment and urged that the Four Senses be appropriated with the same care and sense of mystery as in the primitive Church.

lical the theologians that were part of the so-called Nouvelle Théologie movement.[218]

In terms of its biblical dimensions, a number of theologians played influential roles in promoting *ressourcement.*[219] This was an important renewal, a bringing forth of the living Tradition. These theologians include Louis Bouyer, Yves Congar, Jean Daniélou, Henri de Lubac, Joseph Ratzinger (Pope Benedict XVI), and Hans Urs von Balthasar.[220] Through an onslaught of skeptical biblical criticism swirling around them, these theologians were important guideposts as Catholic biblical theology edged closer to Vatican II. There, at the Council, the most decisive and weighty of all the Catholic Scripture documents would—in no less than a Dogmatic Constitution—give the highest papal expression to the need for a return to the sources in biblical theology: "For as the centuries succeed one another, the Church constantly moves forward toward the fullness of divine truth until the words of God reach their complete fulfillment in her. The words of the holy fathers witness to the presence of this living tradition, whose wealth is poured into the practice and life of the believing and praying Church."[221]

Dei Verbum underscored the dynamic of Sacred Scripture and Sacred Tradition as the "one divine wellspring" of divine revelation: "Hence there exists a close connection and communication between sacred tradition and Sacred Scripture. For both of them, flowing from the same divine wellspring, in a certain way merge into a unity and tend toward the same end ... Therefore, both Sacred Tradition and Sacred Scripture are to be accepted and venerated with the same sense of loyalty and reverence. Sacred Tradition and Sacred Scripture form one sacred deposit of the word of God, committed to the Church."[222]

218. *Nouvelle théologie* means "new theology."

219. *Ressourcement* means "a return to the sources."

220. For a thorough review, see Boersma, *Nouvelle Theologie and Sacramental Ontology;* de Lubac, *Sources of Revelation.*

221. *Dei Verbum*, 8: "Through the same tradition the Church's full canon of the sacred books is known, and the sacred writings themselves are more profoundly understood and unceasingly made active in her."

222. *Dei Verbum*, 9: "For Sacred Scripture is the word of God inasmuch as it is consigned to writing under the inspiration of the divine Spirit, while sacred tradition takes the word of God entrusted by Christ the Lord and the Holy Spirit to the Apostles, and hands it on to their successors in its full purity, so that led by the light of the Spirit of truth, they may in proclaiming it preserve this word of God faithfully, explain it, and make it more widely known."

Near the end of *Dei Verbum*, the constitution draws together so many crucial themes—the divine authorship of the Scriptures and the retrieval of the living Tradition while embracing the legitimate gains of modern approaches—into one galvanizing phrase: *Sacrae Paginae studium sit veluti anima Sacrae Theologiae* "the Sacred Page is the soul of theology."[223]

Commenting on the way that it "tells God's story," as he puts it, Barron sums up the immense contributions of *Dei Verbum*:

> In the sixth and final chapter of *Dei Verbum* we find a discussion of the role of Scripture in the life of the Church today. The Council fathers ... explicitly recommend the study of the Church Fathers, both east and west, as a privileged way of coming to know the meaning of Scripture. How at odds this is with Raymond Brown's blithe dismissal of patristic analysis. And they call for a sort of mutual co-penetration of biblical exegesis and theology, each one conditioning and informing the other. When they speak of the Bible as the 'soul of theology, they imply that Scripture animates theology and that theology instantiates and gives concrete expression to the meaning of Scripture.[224]

And while *Dei Verbum* does not explicitly mention allegory, its merits are embedded in the larger notion of *ressourcement*, of a recovery of patristic biblical interpretation that the constitution advocated. The allegorical sense was part of the fabric of the Church's great Tradition of approaching the Scriptures with a robust confidence that Christ is present, somehow, on every page. The allegorical is that vital sense that animates theology—to seeing the New Testament hidden in the Old, to seeing Christ in both and, above all, to embracing him as the Lord of history and Lord of the Church.

One last point needs to be made as it relates to *Dei Verbum* and the recovery of *ressourcement* today. Again we turn to Barron's essay, in which he commends the sort of patristic-modern assimilation that characterizes *Dei Verbum* and which is central to *The Face of the Lord*:

> Like so many of the other texts of Vatican II, *Dei Verbum* is best read under the rubric of *ressourcement*, the recovery of the Biblical and patristic roots of the Christian faith. The great *ressourcement* theologians of the twentieth century, many of whom were *periti* ("experts") at the Council, tended to engage modernity in an oblique manner. Unlike their liberal colleagues who endeav-

223. *Dei Verbum*, 24.

224. Barron, "Biblical Interpretation and Theology," 190.

ored to present Christian theology in a straightforwardly modern form, the *ressourcement* masters—Henri de Lubac, Hans Urs von Balthasar, Ratzinger, Jean Daniélou—attempted to assimilate the best of modernity to the patristic form of the faith. They took modernity in, but they adapted and corralled it, making it ancillary to classical Christianity. This is just the method followed by the authors of *Dei Verbum* in regard to characteristically modern modes of biblical analysis.[225]

This is the method advocated here: one begins with the literal and draws upon all the resources available to us today, to come as close as possible to the intentions of the author. Next, this same method makes the decisive move—from the literal to the spiritual—to advance from fact to mystery.

In concluding this discussion of the allegorical sense, I give the last word to the Church Father who was the pioneer and greatest advocate of *allegoria*. In his *Philocalia*, Origen summons the student of Sacred Scripture to not merely read. He urges them to read with faith, to seek to understand the deeper mysteries. Even without receiving greater insight, one should keep reading just the same:

> If anyone has ever seen an asp or some other venomous creature under the spell of the charmer, I would have you look to that as an illustration of the Scripture. If it is read and not understood, the hearer may grow limp and weary ... Let us not tire when we hear Scriptures which we do not understand; but let it increase our faith by which we believe that all Scripture is inspired by God and profitable. *So*, have this sort of faith with regard to inspired Scripture; believe that your soul profits by merely reading it, even if your understanding has not yet received the fruit of these passages. Our soul is charmed; its better elements are nourished, the inferior weakened and brought to nothing.[226]

We now turn from the first to the second of the spiritual senses—from the allegorical to the tropological.

Tropologia

The *tropological* is that spiritual sense that moves from Christ himself (i.e., allegorical) to Christ within the soul of the believer. Three medieval examples of tropology will suffice; the first is from St. Ambrose:

225. Barron, "Biblical Interpretation and Theology," 190.
226. Origen, *Philocalia,* 12.2; my translation.

"And so in the *Canticles* the bride says, concerning the bridegroom, 'Behold, you are comely, my beloved—beautiful indeed! Our bed is shaded, the beams of our houses are cedar, our rafters, cypresses.'[227] We can interpret this *in a moral sense*. For where do Christ and his Church dwell except in the works of His people? Therefore, where there was impurity, or pride, or iniquity, there, says the Lord Jesus, 'the Son of Man has nowhere to lay his head.'"[228]

Here, Ambrose explains a text from the Song of Songs topologically; the bride signifies the pure disciple of Christ. The expression of the Shulamite is placed in the mouth of the devout Christian, who has made a home for Christ in the heart, exemplified by right moral action. To further the trope, Ambrose lists certain vices, such as impurity, pride, and sin. Using a common technique in spiritual exegesis, Ambrose brings in a second biblical text—this time, from the Gospel According to St. Matthew—to complete his tropological interpretation: "the Son of Man has nowhere to lay his head" in such a home as that.

A second example of tropological interpretation is from the Venerable Bede. Commenting on Jesus's Parable of the Vineyard,[229] he writes,

> But the Chief Priests showed that those things which the Lord had spoken were true; which is proved from what follows: "And they sought to lay hold on him;" for He Himself is the heir, whose unjust death He said was to be revenged by the Father. Again, in a moral sense, each of the faithful, when the Sacrament of Baptism is entrusted to him, receives on hire a vineyard, which he is to cultivate. But the servant sent to him is evil intreated, beaten, and cast out, when the word is heard by him and despised, or, what is worse, even blasphemed; further, he kills, as far as in him lies, the heir, who has trampled underfoot the Son of God. The evil husbandman is destroyed, and the vineyard given to another, when the humble shall be enriched with that gift of grace, which the proud man has scorned.[230]

Before turning his attention to the spiritual sense, Bede deals with the literal sense, explaining the connection between Jesus and the parable he told: "*for He Himself is the heir*, whose unjust death He said was to be revenged by the Father." Next, Bede interprets the parable to-

227. Song 1:15–16.

228. St. Ambrose of Milan, *Isaac, or the* Soul, 4.27, in *Seven Exegetical Works*, 27; emphasis added. See Mt 8:20.

229. See Mk 12:1–12.

230. Venerable Bede, in Thomas Aquinas, *Catena Aurea*, 240.

pologically, seeing in the text a signification between the hired servant and the recently baptized: "each of the faithful, when the Sacrament of Baptism is entrusted to him, receives on hire a vineyard, which he is to cultivate." The remainder of his commentary builds upon this connection, asking, for example, What sort of servant has the baptized allowed into the vineyard? As with the previous example from Ambrose, there is a *kerygmatic* dimension to these two tropological interpretations.

Here is a key insight: the ancient and medieval practitioners of the spiritual senses—of the allegorical, tropological and the anagogical—often laid their exegesis at the feet of *preaching.* A considerable number of patristic and medieval commentaries are, in one form or another, homilies. This is logical. The spiritual sense allowed the preacher to not merely admonish the Church in a general sense. Rather, he admonished the baptized souls seated directly in front of him, as he poured out the Word of God.

The third and final example of the tropological sense is from the High Middle Ages and one of its greatest practitioners, St. Bernard of Clairvaux. Like St. Ambrose and the Venerable Bede before him, St. Bernard scrutinizes the Scriptures and from them draws interpretations that concern the moral life. Like St. Gregory the Great did with his *Moralia in Iob*, much of Bernard's *Commentary on the Canticle of Canticles* is tropological in nature: "'Do not touch me,' says the resurrected Jesus to Magdalen; Grow unaccustomed to this seducible sense; strive for the Word; grow accustomed to faith."[231]

De Lubac summarizes, citing St. Bernard as he does, "The 'Divine fire' makes him 'burn with love:' it produces in him 'an extraordinary expansion of the mind;' then his understanding is flooded clarity that comes forth 'from the eye of the Bridegroom,' [and his soul] 'scrutinizes the mysteries of the Scriptures,' in the 'caves of rocks,' emboldened by a purified conscience, [penetrating] 'the secrets of wisdom.'"[232]

Having illustrated how tropology works from the above examples, we turn to de Lubac for additional analysis. In his chapter on the subject, titled "Mystical Tropology," he begins with a helpful distinction between the allegorical and the tropological senses: "In passing from

231. St. Bernard, *Commentary on the Canticle of* Canticles, 28.9, in de Lubac, *Medieval Exegesis*, vol. 2, 161.

232. De Lubac, *Medieval Exegesis*, vol. 2, 161.

history to allegory we passed, as it were, from the letter to the spirit. The passage from allegory to tropology *involves no such jump*. After the historical sense, all those that can still be counted belong to the spiritual sense, since they have been signified not through the letter but through the spirit of the letter."[233]

Even as he stresses its significance in the "edification of morals,"[234] de Lubac asserts that the tropological sense follows the allegorical. "It is no less dispensable," he writes; however, "it can only come in third place: it constitutes 'the third exposition.'"[235] Typical of his love for metaphors, de Lubac adds that "the fruits of tropology can only come after the flowers of allegory."[236] This point is valid—there is a sort of hierarchical structure within the Four Senses. The reader may have detected this hierarchy already; its full import is the subject of chapter 3.

Most often, this sense under consideration was called the tropological in the ancient and medieval periods. It originates from the Greek term *trope*, meaning "a turn or turning" around of something else. As de Lubac clarifies, tropology did not have to do with "moral conversion" any more than allegory did in the pre-Christian period, even within the primitive Church. The etymological story of the terms that specify the three spiritual senses is interesting. Initially, allegory, tropology, and even anagogy were used interchangeably.[237]

Gradually though steadily, in early Christianity, *allegoria* came to have pride of place among the spiritual senses. This was chiefly due to St. Paul's use of the term in Galatians. It would also come to function as "the head of the other two" spiritual senses.[238] What about the other two? Given its function as the heavenly sense, *anagogue* fit into the final position. "All that was left for [*tropologia*] was third place; it took it and kept it."[239] These terms and their respective order solidified, as did their usage.

What else may be said about the tropological to further distinguish it from allegory? First, as Andrew Willard Jones has developed De

233. De Lubac, *Medieval Exegesis*, vol. 2, 127; emphasis added.

234. De Lubac, *Medieval Exegesis*, vol. 2, 127.

235. De Lubac, *Medieval Exegesis*, vol. 2, 127. As he observes, Origen referred to the tropological sense as the "third topic of explanation."

236. De Lubac, *Medieval Exegesi*, vol. 2, 128.

237. See de Lubac, *Medieval Exegesis*, vol. 2, 129.

238. De Lubac, *Medieval Exegesis*, vol. 2, 129.

239. See de Lubac, *Medieval Exegesis*, vol. 2, 129.

Lubac's analysis, tropology does not deal with Christ in an objective sense, but more subjectively. Its concern is *the interiority of Christ within*, as one conforms oneself to him in word and deed. Make no mistake: it does put one in touch with Christ, and not merely one's own thoughts. Yet the move from the allegorical to the tropological is marked by a shift from *the person of Christ* to the experience of Christ *in one's own person.* If allegory is concerned with the Head, then tropology is concerned with the Body. Tropology is "the mystic sense of morality."[240]

No doubt there is a "seam" that hems the two senses together, and that seam is Christ. One encounters Christ—his life, his words and works, his Passion and Resurrection—in the allegorical sense. Then, one walks with Christ, draws ever closer to him through right worship and right moral deeds in the tropological sense. As de Lubac advises, after "the mystery of faith" comes "the works of faith."[241] Despite its third position behind the literal and the allegorical, the tropological is in no way insignificant. Its aim is to help the believer conform him- or herself into the image of Christ. How needed this is today![242] It is the sense that summons the believer to action and to charity. Without the tropological, one would leap over its central aim—moral perfection. Without it, one would contemplate the person of Christ in the allegorical sense, and then attempt to ascend to the heaven in the anagogical sense without striving for moral perfection, for sanctification.

This is the fruit of topological, to strive to become the "New Creation"[243] that St. Paul speaks of in Romans: "I appeal to you therefore, brethren, by the mercies of God, to present your bodies as a living sacrifice, holy and acceptable to God, which is your spiritual worship. Do

240. De Lubac, *Medieval Exegesi*, vol. 2, 132. See also "The Liturgical Cosmos: The Worldview of the High Middle Ages (Part 1 of 3)," YouTube video, 1:01:37, posted by Franciscan University of Steubenville, January 15, 2016, https://www.youtube.com/watch?v=GpdD6a-TYss; "The Liturgical Cosmos: The Worldview of the High Middle Ages (Part 2 of 3)," YouTube video, 1:01:29, posted by Franciscan University of Steubenville, January 15, 2016, https://www.youtube.com/watch?v=wdy6PjqTgyc&t=3s.

241. De Lubac, *Medieval Exegesis*, vol. 2, 133.

242. See the discussion above, of Barron likening Jordan Peterson's "psychological" impressions of the stories of Genesis and Exodus to the tropological interpretations of Origen and others. Again, Barron is not equivocating between them, nor am I. Still, his point is well taken. There is a broad interest in Peterson's lectures on these biblical stories, as he has found a way to tap into the deeper possibilities that involve their power to move a person to action and change.

243. See 1 Cor 5:17.

not be conformed to this world· but *be transformed by the renewal of your mind*, that you may prove what is the will of God, what is good and acceptable and perfect."[244] In this text, the verb that Paul uses is *metamorphousthe* (Greek for "transformed"). It refers to the full transformation that active faith demands and with which the Holy Spirit assists in the lives of Christ's disciples. With aid from the Pauline text, the role of the tropological sense becomes clearer: nothing less than the step-by-step *metamorphosis* of the believer into a "little Christ." Again, the move is from *the person of Christ* to *Christ within the person*.

The tropological sense should not be restricted to the transformation of individuals. Rather, its final aim is the conversion of the entire Bride of Christ, the universal Church. As Pascal once said, "Everything that happens to the Church happens to each Christian in particular."[245] And the reverse is true: everything good that happens to the believer is emblematic of the total transformation to which the entire Church is called. This is an important insight that should be recalled when dealing with texts tropologically.

What about the sense that follows it—the *anagogical*? Doesn't it have to do with heaven, and therefore the total metamorphosis of the Church in Christ? Yes, and as such, both the tropological *and* the anagogical concern "Christian perfection." But there is less overlap between the tropological and the anagogical than appears at first glance.[246]

On one hand, the tropological is primarily concerned with "the pilgrim's progress" in the here and now. On the other hand, the anagogical sense is primarily directed at our future perfection and with eschatological realities, such as Christ's glorious return, the Final Judgment, the Beatific Vision, the Wedding Feast of the Lamb, the communion of saints, the eternal state of the soul, and so on. In short, the anagogical sense concerns our destiny, whereas the tropological sense summons each Christian to do one's part in reaching this destiny with Christ's help.

A text from the First Epistle of St. John is helpful in distinguishing between the two senses: "Beloved, we are God's children now; it does not yet appear what we shall be, but we know that when he appears we

244. Rom 12:1–2; emphasis added.

245. Cited in de Lubac, *Medieval Exegesis*, vol. 2, 135.

246. At times, when reading a patristic or medieval commentator, it is unclear which spiritual senses is being invoked. In instances where that is not the case, or otherwise unclear, there are ordinarily enough clues within a text to make a prudential judgment.

shall be like him, for we shall see him as he is. And everyone who thus hopes in him purifies himself as he is pure."[247] The heart of the anagogical sense is seen in verse 2: "it does not yet appear what we shall be." Not yet; what we shall become in Christ is not yet realized in the here and now. Nevertheless, St. John assures that "we shall see him as he is."

In what follows, in verse 3, the tropological sense is evident: "everyone who thus hopes in him purifies himself as he is pure." Here, St. John summons the church to "continually purify himself" in the perfection of Christ. Stepping back from this Johannine example, we can see the power of Andrew Willard Jones's contention that each of the spiritual senses (*allegorical, tropological, anagogical*) enjoy, by their nature, a respective correlation to the theological virtues (*faith, hope, charity*).[248]

Recall that the allegorical sense signifies the person of Christ—it is the spiritual sense of *faith*. The tropological sense builds upon the allegorical and is concerned with the person of Christ being built up in the soul—it is the spiritual sense of *charity*. Lastly, and most obviously, the anagogical sense signifies our eternal destiny with the glorified Christ—it is the spiritual sense of *hope*. This notion of charity, and growing in charity, is the main thrust of the tropological sense. As de Lubac summarizes, "In everything, Scripture invites us to conversion of heart … All this teaching of Scripture, all this strength which shapes me to the divine likeness, is summarized in a single word: charity."[249]

Scripture is a mirror that reveals our moral progress toward the Blessed Trinity:

> In this mirror we learn to know our nature and our destiny; in it we see the different stages through which we have passed since creation, *the beautiful and ugly features of our internal face*. It shows us the truth of our being by pointing it out in relation to the Creator. It is a living mirror, a living and efficacious Word, a sword penetrating at the juncture of soul and spirit, which makes our secret thoughts appear and *reveals to us our heart*. It teaches us to read in the book of our own experience and makes us, so to speak, our own exegesis.[250]

We now turn to the last of the spiritual senses—the anagogical.

247. 1 Jn 2:2–3.

248. "The Liturgical Cosmos: The Worldview of the High Middle Ages (Part 1 of 3)," YouTube video, 1:01:37, posted by Franciscan University of Steubenville, January 15, 2016, https://www.youtube.com/watch?v=GpdD6a-TYss.

249. De Lubac, *Medieval Exegesis*, vol. 2, 141.

250. De Lubac, *Medieval Exegesis*, vol. 2, 142; emphases added.

Anagoge

Henri de Lubac begins his chapter "Anagogy and Eschatology" with this salient quote from Origen: "*Let us expand the extent of the mystery still higher.*"[251] This is a helpful description of the anagogical sense; it is a deepening of the mystery, of contemplating Christ in the Scriptures, and seeing that through to its end, when we will see him face-to-face: "For now we see in a mirror dimly, but then face to face. Now I know in part; then I shall understand fully, even as I have been fully understood."[252]

Expanding on this description, de Lubac explains the logic of the three spiritual senses and how the allegorical leads to the tropological and finally to the anagogical: "The first advent, 'humble and hidden,' ... performs the work of redemption, which is pursued in the Church and in her sacraments: this is the object of allegory in the proper sense of the word. The second advent, entirely interior, takes place within the soul of each of the faithful, and is unfolded by *tropology*."[253]

De Lubac's descriptions of the allegorical and tropological senses are fitting and concisely summarize what we have learned about them. He continues, "The third and last advent is saved up for the 'end of the age,' when the Christ will appear in his glory and will come to look for his own to take them away with him: such is the object of *anagogy*."[254] For the ancient and medieval mind, to read the Scripture without anagogy "was literally to profane it, since it was but a primer, a tool of elementary instruction, from which one entered into the silence of God in a state of contemplation completely purified."[255] Thinking of the three spiritual senses spatially may be helpful. If allegory leads to Christ *up on the Cross*, and tropology to Christ within, then anagogy leads to Christ above, in all of His glory. The directional pull of anagogy is upward.

Whereas the theological virtue of allegory is faith and of tropology is charity, the virtue of anagogy is most certainly *hope*. St. Ambrose wrote that "Through the Gospel we see on earth pre-figurations of the heavenly mysteries."[256]

251. De Lubac, *Medieval Exegesis*, vol. 2, 179, citing Origen; emphasis added.
252. 1 Cor 13:12.
253. De Lubac, *Medieval Exegesis*, vol. 2, 179; emphases added.
254. De Lubac, *Medieval Exegesis*, vol. 2, 179.
255. Chenu, *Nature, Man, and Society*, 124.
256. De Lubac, *Medieval Exegesis*, vol. 2, 182, citing St. Ambrose.

In *The City of God*, his student would carry this even further. St. Augustine writes:

> A shadow of the eternal City has been imaged on earth, *a prophetic representation of something to come* rather than a real manifestation in time. But this shadow, being symbolic and not the reality that is yet to come, is properly called the holy City … This exegesis, which comes to us with apostolic authority, opens for us a way to understand much that is in the Old and New Testaments. We see that the earthly city became a symbol of the heavenly City … its significance was not in and of itself but in signifying the other city. It was founded not for its own sake, but as the shadow of another reality, a shadow foreshadowed by the previous symbol.[257]

For St. Augustine, then, the anagogical sense allows one to see both the reality of a thing—and through that same thing, a "shadow" of something greater that is still to come at the end of the age. Whereas many patristic writers kept their anagogical interpretation within the Scriptures, St. Augustine extended it all of history as well: "In the world we find two realities of the city: one is the visible, earthly city which is visible; the other serves as a shadow of the heavenly City."[258]

Adding further understanding to this spiritual sense, St. Gregory the Great stressed that the anagogical is *aspirational*. Gregory sees this sense as calling believers to be transformed in the here and now—by the hope that is yet to come: "What is the holy Scripture but a letter of the omnipotent God to His creature? Therefore, I beg of you, try to meditate upon the words of your Creator every day … *Learn the heart of God in the words of God, so that you may strive for things eternal.*"[259] St. Gregory's expression represents the prevailing way in which the anagogical sense operated among patristic and medieval interpreters. Sacred Scripture was how one learned the heart of God, and this divine knowledge enabled one aim for one's eternal perfect in the present age.

The point was not that such perfection—that of the age to come—could be fully realized *now*, in the present moment. Rather, it was setting one's mind and heart on eternal things in the here and now and growing in sanctity as a result. In his Epistle to the Romans, St. Paul writes, "Do not be conformed to this world but be transformed by the

257. St. Augustine, *City of God*, XV.2, 415–17; translation slightly modified.
258. St. Augustine, *City of God*, XV.2; translation slightly modified.
259. De Lubac, *Medieval Exegesis*, vol. 2, 406n75; emphasis added.

renewal of your mind, that you may prove what is the will of God, what is good and acceptable and perfect."[260]

Regarding this text, N. T. Wright observes that "when Paul speaks of being 'conformed' (*syschematizesthe*) and 'transformed' (*metamorphousthe*) in verse 2, he uses similar language to what we find in Philippians 3:21, where he promises that Jesus will 'transform' (*metaschematisei*) the present body to be like his glorious body."[261] This phenomenon—of participating in the future glory within the present age—is known as "inaugurated eschatology." It is in play in Romans 12, as Wright explains: "Body and mind together, then, must live according to the new age, the period that has now begun with Jesus."[262]

Another clue that points to St. Paul's inaugurated eschatology comes at the end of verse 2, in the phrase "good and acceptable and perfect." The first two terms, good and acceptable, are straightforward, but the last term, perfect, points in the eschatological direction. The Greek term from which perfect is translated is *telos*, meaning the end of a thing, its purpose or destiny.[263] This is the same term used in the Gospel According to St. John. There, in the Upper Room, St. John declares that Jesus loved his own who were in the world, he loved them *to the end*.[264] The distinction between Jesus and the disciple is clear at this point: Jesus's *telos* was fulfilled perfectly, throughout the entirety of his earthly mission in the flesh. In contrast, for the believer, there is progress as well as fits and starts. And so the classical and biblical concept of *telos*—the realization of one's heavenly end—is for the Christian a work in progress, a striving toward.

In a fallen world, is the idea of setting before oneself one's *telos* a fool's errand? Not at all, least of all in the eyes of SS. Paul, Augustine, and Gregory the Great. To the contrary, aiming for the *telos* of Christian perfection clarifies and strengthens one's vocation and diligence. One

260. Rom 12:2.

261. Wright, *Resurrection of the Son of God*, 264.

262. Wright, *Resurrection of the Son of God*, 264. Elsewhere, Wright deals with Paul's inaugurated eschatology: "For Paul, then, the coming restoration of God's glory has been accomplished in Jesus Christ. This is at the heart of his solidly inaugurated eschatology, as well as of his nascent trinitarian monotheism. But this is only one part of Paul's redefinition of the Jewish eschatology of the return of God's glory." *Pauline Perspectives*, 384. See also Jewett and Kotansky, *Romans*, 725–35.

263. See Jewett and Kotansky, *Romans*, 735.

264. Jn 13:1.

strives for heavenly perfection in this age, so that with Christ's help, one is gradually drawn toward its full realization in the age to come. This is the raison d'être of the anagogical sense. Armed with this Pauline understanding of *telos* as it relates to the spiritual life further underscores why the anagogical sense is the last of the spiritual senses.

Let us continue our discussion with three patristic examples of anagogical interpretation: the first from Origen, the second from St. Augustine, and the third from St. Bernard of Clairvaux.

First, in the midst of his *Commentary on the Gospel According to Saint John*, Origen brings up a text from 2 Corinthians: "For it is the God who said, 'Let light shine out of darkness,' who has shone in our hearts to give the light of the knowledge of the glory of God in the face of Christ."[265] Three things are striking here, given what we have already learned about Origen's method of biblical interpretation.

1. Origen's approach is in no way bound to the allegorical sense alone. This is a common misconception. Although Origen explained the Scriptures a considerable amount through the allegorical sense, he did not restrict himself to only that sense. Rather, he held that there was the primary, twofold division in Scripture, between History and Spirit. By the former, Origen meant the literal sense, and by the latter, the spiritual senses—plural. In other words, for Origen, all three spiritual senses, taken together, comprise Spirit.[266]

2. In his discussion of the biblical text, Origen moves directly from the literal to the anagogical: "So far as the literal sense is concerned, there was a divine epiphany in the tabernacle and in the temple, which were destroyed, and in the face of Moses when he had conversed with the Divine Nature. But so far as the anagogical sense is concerned, the things that are accurately known of God might also be referred to as the visible glory of God that is contemplated by that mind which has the aptitude for such contemplation because of its pre-eminent purification."[267] In fairness, Origen argues that the "plain sense" of the Word needs to be "exchanged," because it cannot mean what it appears to mean. One example is the case of God's commands to slay everyone in

265. 2 Cor 4:6.

266. See de Lubac, *History and* Spirit, esp. 159–71.

267. Origen, *Commentary on John*, 32.338–39, in *Commentary on the Gospel According to John, Books 13–32*, 406.

Joshua. So, in some instances, the literal sense was exchanged or "supplanted" by an allegorized interpretation.

3. A third and decisive point about Origen's anagogical interpretation of the Pauline text is seen in what he concludes about it: "Since the mind that has been purified and has ascended above all material things, that it may scrupulously contemplate God, *is made divine by what it contemplates*. We must say that this is what is meant when it is said that the face of the one who contemplated God, conversed with him, and spent time with such a vision, was glorified."[268]

Consequently, the figurative meaning of the glorification of Moses's face is that "*his mind was made godlike*."[269] In expositing the text according to the anagogical sense, Origen anchors the future hope of divinization in the present age. As Moses contemplated God, his mind is in some sense "divinized." Moses remains mortal, yet his theophanic experience brings about a supernatural "perfecting" of his mind, according to Origen. Whatever one thinks of Origen's partial divinization of Moses at Sinai, the takeaway is that anagogy is not restricted to eschatology, that is, the "last things." No—the anagogical sense is about *appropriating future hopes in the present age*. This point cannot be stressed enough. Its import will be discussed in chapter 3.

A second example of anagogical interpretation is taken from St. Augustine. In Book 13 of *City of God*, he takes up the subject of the Fall of Man. Here, Augustine deals with original sin and its dreadful implications for humanity.[270] In his ensuing discussion of death—examined in the light of the resurrected Christ—Augustine looks to Genesis 1–3 and St. Paul's epistles, where he contrasts the First and Last Adam.[271] Working through various questions about death, he contrasts the Christian hope with the Platonic tradition. Augustine is concerned here about those "*who have allegorized the entire Garden of Eden* where, according to Holy Scripture, the first parents of the human race actually lived. The trees and fruit-bearing shrubs are turned into symbols of virtues and

268. Origen, *Commentary on John*, 32.338–39, 406; emphasis added.

269. Origen, Commentary on John, 32.338–39, 406; emphasis added.

270. St. Augustine, *City of God*, XIII.1: "Now that I have discussed the intricate problem about the origin of the world and the beginning of the human race, a proper order calls for a study of the fall of the first man, in fact, of the first parents, and of the origin and transmission of human mortality" (299).

271. See esp. Rom 5:12–20.

ways of living, as though they had no visible and material reality and as if Scripture had no purpose but to express meanings for our minds."[272]

Three observations can be made from the above text. First, St. Augustine does not reject allegorical meaning. He endorses them: "There is no reason, then, for anyone forbidding us to see in the Garden, symbolically, the life of the blessed; in its four rivers, the four virtues of prudence, fortitude, temperance, and justice; in its trees, all useful knowledge; in the fruits of the trees, the holy lives of the faithful; in the tree of life, that wisdom which is the mother of all good; and in the tree of the knowledge of good and evil, the experience that results from disobedience to a command of God."[273] Nevertheless, he presses beyond the immediate symbolic interpretation and sees an even deeper allegory at work: "This account can be even better read as an allegory of the Church, prophetical of what was to happen in the future. Thus, the Garden is the Church itself, as we can see from the *Canticle of Canticles*; the four rivers are the four Gospels; the fruit-bearing trees are the saints, as the fruits are their works; and the tree of life is, of course, the Saint of saints, Christ; and the tree of the knowledge of good and evil is the free choice of our own will."[274]

This should not surprise us. For Augustine, the Garden of Eden was an allegory of the future Church—this is how the Old Testament was often interpreted in ancient and medieval Christianity.[275] What needs to be emphasized here is the *future orientation* in Augustine's allegorical reasoning. This future dimension that characterizes allegorical interpretation of the Old Testament is paralleled by anagogical interpretation in the New Testament.

A second point emerges from the *City of God* passage. When one looks at the Old Testament allegorically, one sees Christ (and the Church) in the New Testament. In a comparable way, when one looks at the New Testament anagogically, one sees the eternal realities—union with the glorified Christ and the saints. This shines through in Book 13 of *City of God*:

272. St. Augustine, *City of God*, XIII.21, 330; emphasis added.

273. St. Augustine, *City of God*, XIII.21, 331.

274. St. Augustine, *City of God*, XIII.21, 331.

275. It should come as no surprise that St. Augustine's allegory points to *the Church* instead of *Christ*. As stressed above, with allegory, to speak of the Church is to speak of Christ; he is the Head of the Body.

Now, as we bear the likeness of the earthly man because of the inheritance of sin and death which we have received through generation, so, too, we bear the likeness of the heavenly man because of the grace of forgiveness and of life eternal, that is to say, because of the regeneration which is possible only through the "Mediator between God and men, himself man, Christ Jesus."[276] It is He whom the Apostle wishes us to understand as the heavenly man because He came down from heaven to be clothed with an earthly and a mortal body in order that later He might clothe it with a heavenly immortality.[277]

Augustine's thought reveals a significant pattern—one we must pay attention to in our study of Scripture according to the Four Senses. There is a basic correspondence between allegorical interpretation of the Old Testament and anagogical interpretation of the New. But even anagogical treatments of the Old Testament should not be unexpected. In dealing with an Old Testament text, an ancient or medieval interpreter might move from the allegorical to the anagogical, as Augustine does.[278]

Finally, and straightforwardly, this text from *City of God* not only reveals a similarity between allegory and anagogy. It also exemplifies the primary aim of the anagogical sense: the heavenly destination of the believer. As the saying goes, "The Letter shows us what God and our fathers did; the Allegory shows us where our faith is hid, the [Tropological] gives us the rule of daily life; *the Anagogy shows us where we end our strife.*"[279]

The third and final example of anagogical interpretation comes from the High Middle Ages. Specifically, it is from St. Bernard of Clairvaux's masterful *Commentary on the Canticle of Canticles.*[280] In our discussion of *City of God*, we noted an intriguing connection between the allegorical and the anagogical senses. We will see another one with Bernard, between the tropological and the anagogical senses.

Today, Bernard's *Commentary on the Canticle of Canticles* is often read as a devotional—a spiritual classic to help the dedicated believer grow in charity and moral excellence. This is certainly true and commendable, but he did not intend his *Commentary on the Canticle of*

276. See 1 Tm 2:5.

277. St. Augustine, *City of God*, XIII.21, 337–38.

278. As noted in the selections from *City of God,* Augustine's treatment is complex. He draws upon both Old and New Testament texts, making use of allegory and anagogy in establishing his argument.

279. Grant and Tracy, *Short History of the Interpretation of the Bible*, 85; emphasis added.

280. St. Bernard of Clairvaux, *St. Bernard's Sermons on the Canticle of Canticles.*

Canticles to be read as series of mere moral suppositions. It often weaves together the tropological and the anagogical in a sophisticated way. Recall the aim of tropology: to expand the charity in one's soul, and so conform oneself to Christ. And why does one desire to conform his or her soul to Christ? Because the Bridegroom is coming! In other words, the tropological sense prepares one's soul to be unified with Christ in the here and now, *as one prepares to be wedded to the risen Christ in Heaven*. Bernard integrates both the tropological and the anagogical seamlessly.

The goal of moral progress is not human development in and of itself. The true aim is *unity with Christ*. And so the tropological and the anagogical—and the allegorical with them—are all members of a larger enterprise. As Origen conceived of it nearly a millennia earlier, they are all a part of *Spirit*. For Bernard, as for Origen, *History* is the foundation and starting point. From there, one moves into the *Spirit* and into mystery. From all three spiritual senses, one perceives how to better prepare one's soul for unification with Christ.

In *Homily* 62 of his commentary, Bernard examines a text from the Song of Songs that is examined later in this present volume, "O my dove, in the clefts of the rock, in the covert of the cliff, *let me see your face*, let me hear your voice, for your voice is sweet, and your face is comely" (2:14; emphasis added). Meditating on this, Bernard writes, "Therefore, when the Spouse is herself pure she will be able to contemplate the pure and naked truth. Then she will desire to see the Face of her Bridegroom, and also to hear His voice."[281]

For Bernard, there is a deep connection between one's purity—and looking after it—and the ability to "see" God more clearly: "*What can be the comeliness of the interior face except purity*? The comeliness of purity pleases Him in many without the sweet voice of preaching."[282] Here, morality, hope, and preaching are all tied together—the tropological, the anagogical, and the pastoral—in his discussion of the biblical text.

The above examples from Origen, St. Augustine, and St. Bernard of Clairvaux have provided numerous insights about the anagogical sense. The reader should have a clear idea of what it is and how it works. And considerably more, too. Of highest importance is the close relationship

281. St. Bernard of Clairvaux, *Homily* 62, in *St. Bernard's Sermons on the Canticle of Canticles*, 215.

282. St. Bernard of Clairvaux, *Homily* 62, in *St. Bernard's Sermons on the Canticle of Canticles*, 215; emphasis added.

that exists between the spiritual senses. This development is critical to the following sections of the book and is further developed in chapter 3.

Concluding Remarks

This chapter offers a clear understanding of the Four Senses. Each of the Four Senses brings something unique to the study of the Bible, apart from the other three. Still, it is understandable if some may feel less certain about their particularities. As the reader spends time with them, the distinctions of the Four Senses will only become better defined.

We made headway by defining terms and providing an illustration of how they work in Scripture. Drawing upon the archetypal biblical term, Jerusalem, we distinguished the Four Senses from one another. We the examined each of them in considerable detail. Incorporated into these discussions were numerous examples from patristic and medieval writers. They helped to further delineate one sense from another, and allowed the reader to peer into them from the classical age of biblical interpretation.

But it is not enough merely to understand them. They are not museum pieces from ages past, but a way forward in extracting true depth from the Bible. The Four Senses need to be reawakened in our day. We discussed Raymond Brown's dismissive response about the recovery of allegory today. In a way, Brown's instincts were right. He correctly intuited that there are large gaps between patristic/medieval exegesis and modern biblical criticism. We sharply disagree with Brown's prognosis, however; not only do we believe that in our time the spiritual sense of Scripture *can* be retrieved, but we also believe it *must* if biblical interpretation is to take a major step forward. As we hope it shall.

For far too long, the participatory model, advocated by St. Irenaeus and countless masters of the Sacred Page, has been set aside. Here, Barron's assessment is entirely correct. It is only through such participatory approaches that we, with God's grace, can gradually fuse together what has been historically severed—namely, biblical exegesis and biblical theology.

In the postmodern age, the intrinsic connection between exegesis and theology (like faith and reason) has been measurably thinned. But it is equally true that the connection has not been severed through. There is reason for genuine optimism. Much has been accomplished to stem the tide over the past century. In this chapter we noted key contributions of the Catholic Church, from the Scripture documents and especially Vatican II's *Dei Verbum.* In addition, the past hundred years has brought forth a wealth of theological achievements. Along with these magisterial documents, they are once again placing the participatory model on *terra firma.* Along these lines, theologians from the *ressourcement* movement, such as Daniélou, de Lubac, and Ratzinger, all played decisive roles. More recently, the work of Matthew Levering and Hans Boersma, among others, has kept the flame burning brightly

As the Church moves forward in the twenty-first century, legitimate progress has been made on the way to a full and robust revival of the Four Senses. Nevertheless, much more needs to be done. *The Face of the Lord* is one step further in the direction of a renewal of biblical theology built upon both the historic horizon—and upon the participatory model of the patristic and medieval masters. This book helps to fan the flames of a broad and deep recovery of the Four Senses today: in ecclesial life and preaching; in academic study; and in the lived experience of individual readers of Sacred Scripture.

Ephraim Radner expresses the far-reaching implications of such a recovery in our times: "Part of the challenge is simply that, however much one might wish to rail against the *coercive historical-critical reduction of scriptural meaning,* historicism remains the working metaphysical assumption of most modern readers, even those with respect and affection of Patristic thinking ... And the history of [the spiritual senses] does locate at least one area we must engage if 'respect' is somehow to inform understanding and practice."[283] As Radner stresses, there is indeed a practical dimension to all of this. Recall the fourth criterion of the ancient rabbis and Church fathers, that the Scriptures have relevance today: "This understanding and practice are not simply of antiquarian interest: the moral foundation of scriptural reference, if nothing else, has grounded its credibility in the claim ... that God is creator of the very times in which we seek to find our meaning ... If we are to know God, we will do so through the dissolution of [our temporal framework's] priority; and within that dissolution, the Scriptures will be rightly heard, and our own lives rightly ordered."[284]

283. Radner, *Time and the Word,* 81–82; emphasis added.
284. Radner, *Time and the Word,* 81–82.

That the Scriptures will be rightly heard, and our own lives rightly ordered. In chapter 3, the discussion of the Four Senses continues and deepens. Now that their individual characteristics and fundamental value are better understood, our focus turns to a more advanced topic; namely, the integration of the Four Senses in contemplating the face of the Lord.

CHAPTER 3

De Spiritu et Littera II

The Four Senses and the Soul's Ascent to God

> There is a very sweet drink in history; but still sweeter in allegory; most sweet, however, in [tropology]; but incomparably sweetest by far is the one in anagogy, that is, in contemplation.
>
> —St. Bernard of Clairvaux

Recovering the Unity of the Four Senses Today

From the outset, the goal of this book has been clear: to seek *the face of the Lord*—to contemplate the divine Son through the Four Senses of Sacred Scripture. We are about ready to gaze at him precisely in this way in the Old Testament. Only one crucial step remains.

In chapter 2, I defined the Four Senses and considered each of them in their own light. Yet this does not go far enough; chapter 2 was merely the meridian point in this exploration of the Four Senses. There is a dynamic bond between them; they do not function in isolation from one another, nor as alternative paths. Classically, throughout Church history, the Four Senses were recognized as a unified body, as a totality. This bond between them has been hinted at but not fully developed. The present chapter takes this discussion of the Four Senses to its climax, and it is central to all that follows. The conclusions developed here have a direct bearing on the five encounter scenes that follow in Part II.

Before recalling the book's thesis, I must first press a point made at the end of the last chapter. It's not enough to intellectually grasp the Four Senses as a concept and to occasionally access them in one's study of the Bible. Even among those who do respect the Four Senses today, few possess a clear understanding of the Four Senses as a totality. They can. They must.

The Literal as the Starting Point

This book's thesis, restated, is this: together, *the Four Senses of Sacred Scripture represent a pathway and a progression toward the face of the Lord.* This is the raison d'être of the book as a whole. A mountain of literary data from roughly the second century AD through the thirteenth centuries makes clear that for exegetes of this period, Letter and Spirit were not seen as opposed ends. To the contrary, across the first millennium, the evidence is overwhelming that the *Letter* was merely the starting point. Not the end of the matter. Rather, it was recognized that the truest meaning of a text was discovered only by following the Letter with the Spirit, by engaging the various spiritual senses.

Only through the spiritual senses—and not the literal alone—was the fuller mystery of Christ made known.[1] Accordingly, the Four Senses were a pathway and a progression of true spiritual ascent that culminated with anagogical hope. The hope of seeing God in all his heavenly glory. The hope that anchored the fears and concerns of the present experience of the believer. This is how the Scriptures were read clear through the first millennium of Christianity.

This is not to suggest that they were elucidated in an entirely consistent manner in these former ages. Such was not at all the case. In the patristic and medieval periods, there were numerous terms used to designate the various senses (e.g., literal, letter, history/historical; allegorical, mystical, "spiritual"; tropological, moral; anagogical, heavenly, leading). Additionally, there were various formulations of the senses—sometimes three, other times four: "To the eager student, first of all it ought to be

1. I am aware of the distinctions between the Alexandrian and Antiochene Schools, and their vigorous debates about the allegorical versus literal approaches to Scripture, respectively. I do not diminish the importance of such conflicting views, but over the first millennium the prevailing consensus was a "both/and," not an "either/or" view of the literal and spiritual senses. For more on the history of these two catechetical schools in the primitive Church, see Pelikan, *Christian Tradition*, esp. chaps. 1 and 7.

known that sacred Scripture has three ways of conveying meaning—namely, history, allegory, and tropology."[2]

These variances are interesting in their own right yet need not concern us here. For our purposes, what matters is that for the medieval mind, there was always *Letter* and *Spirit*. One needed to go beyond the literal to grasp the greater mysteries, to arrive at the fullest meaning of the inspired Word. Regardless of the terminology used to describe them, or of their enumeration, this conviction was common ground in the ancient and medieval ages.

Unfortunately, in the present age, the Four Senses are often viewed as distinct, alternative approaches at best. One might explore this or that sense as interest warrants, yet with no particular direction or aim beyond "checking it out." This is not at all the way ancient and medieval readers considered them. And so, in place of such fanciful, modern impressions, we argue that the Four Senses of Sacred Scripture truly are a pathway and a progression toward the face of the Lord.

Appropriating Christ through the Four Senses—Objectively and Subjectively

Filling out this thesis is the ancient and medieval notion that the Four Senses were *connected*. By following Andrew Willard Jones's extended description of their dynamic relationship, we can see that, viewed collectively, they sort of ran along a continuum (see fig. 1). One begins, as always, with the literal sense. Once it is sufficiently grasped, one moves further along the continuum, into the Spirit of the text—through the allegorical, tropological, and anagogical senses. In this integrated model, each of the Four Senses is vital to the fullest discovery of meaning in a given biblical text.[3]

One begins with the literal sense, which is always the starting point. Once the author's intentions are better understood, one looks beyond history, beyond the things referred to in the text. One goes through it,

2. Hugh of St. Victor, "To the New Student of Sacred Scripture," 159.

3. In this section, I follow closely Andrew Willard Jones's exposition of the relationship between the senses and between those senses and the reader of Scripture. See his "The Liturgical Cosmos: The Worldview of the High Middle Ages (Part 1 of 3)," YouTube video, 1:01:37, posted by Franciscan University of Steubenville, January 15, 2016, https://www.youtube.com/watch?v=GpdD6a-TYss.

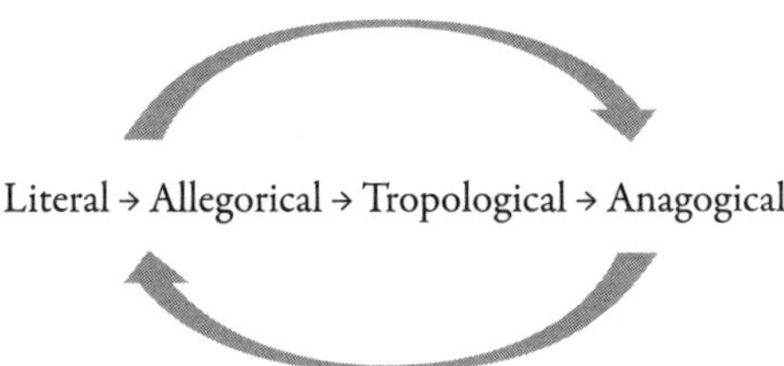

FIGURE 1. The pathway and progression through the Four Senses of sacred Scripture. The author wishes to express his gratitude to historian and author Andrew W. Jones for being an inspiration regarding the visual depiction of the Four Senses. See *Before Church and State*. See also *Word Became Flesh*; Jones and Hillaire, *Evidence of Things Unseen*.

beyond it. One peers into the spiritual senses, which hold a plentitude of riches for the faith-filled reader to gradually draw out of the Word. One can deal only with the Letter and stop there. This approach is not fruitless; one has arrived at the "first instruction," at the historic level of meaning. Yet for the sweetest honey to be tasted, one must cross over from the Letter to the Spirit. Here, one advances beyond the literal, passing through it into the allegorical sense (see fig. 1).

This is the first and most crucial move of all. Here, one has transcended the Letter and passed over into the Spirit. In the allegorical, one encounters the person of Christ. Each of the spiritual senses reveals another dimension of Christ. Allegory holds up the person of Christ. That is, Christ in his Incarnate life on earth, Christ in his teaching and healing, and, above all, Christ in his Passion, death, and Resurrection. Once Christ is seen in the text through the allegorical, the progression continues to the next stage—the tropological.

In the allegorical sense, one encountered Christ himself in the text—the person of Christ, Jesus of Nazareth, walking along the shore. The next sense is different. Now in the tropological, one encounters Christ within the soul. Not the objective person of Christ, but the *subjective experience* of Christ in an interior way. This differentiation cannot be stressed enough. Here, the text preaches to the reader, so that Christ is poured from the preached Word into one's heart. So, in the tropological, one moves from contemplating the person of Christ, to Christ-lived-in-the-virtuous-life. Experiencing Christ tropologically leads to conversion of heart and leads the soul toward moral perfection.

A contrast emerges here between the allegorical and the tropological. And this contrast must be kept clear. It was already mentioned but needs to be stressed. Specifically, the allegorical sense represents one's objective encounter with the person of Christ, and the tropological represents one's subjective encounter with Christ within the soul. There is something of a circular movement between these two senses. One begins by encountering the Person of Christ in the allegorical sense. This leads to a truer understanding of Christ himself, objectively speaking. As one moves from the allegorical and into the tropological sense, one encounters Christ within the soul (see fig. 1). Arriving at a deeper knowledge of Christ with one's intellect in the allegorical leads into the tropological. There, one does not merely grow in the knowledge of Christ in his Person. One develops morally and in the virtues. This interiority is what makes it subjective. Through the tropological, the Person of Christ is *transfigured* in one's soul, through the will that is conformed to him.

As indicated, one may cycle between the objective (allegorical) to the subjective (tropological) and back to the objective again, and repeatedly so. It is not simply a matter of "pushing through" from one sense to another. No—armed with a greater depth of moral perfection within the soul subjectively, *one returns to the objective* and contemplates the person of Christ with the intellect more readily. Re-approaching the text tropologically a second or third time may strengthen one's resolve to invite the person of Christ—who has just been experienced more intimately through the allegorical—into one's interior life.

The larger aim is unity with Christ. Immersing oneself in Scripture with all Four Senses, one journeys along the interpretative continuum toward the divine Son. Along this pathway is the dynamic movement between the objective and the subjective, between the allegorical and the tropological (see fig. 1). And this is not a mere cerebral exercise. It is not passive reading. Along this "path of instruction," *one's whole being participates and is progressively transformed.*

The literal sense—though entirely necessary—is but the first stage. Once one leaps from the literal to the allegorical, the true "ascent to Christ" has begun. The literal is, in some sense, confined to a horizontal encounter of Christ, historically. In contrast, the spiritual senses are collectively a vertical encounter of Christ, and one that steadily ascends both objectively and subjectively.

The spiritual sense has a tremendous advantage over the literal sense: one's whole being is involved in the sacred text—mind, soul, and body. The entire affective dimension is exposed to the Spirit. With the literal sense, one reads and searches for the intentions of the author. With the spiritual sense, *one is read, searched,* and contemplates *one's own intentions* in the light of Christ. Conformity to Christ within the soul is what precisely distinguishes the literal from the spiritual sense. The literal provides the reader with knowledge, with understanding. Yet it does not aim at an objective encounter with the person of Christ (*allegory*)—much less an experience of Christ in an interior way (*tropology*). But there is more to it than this.

Along the "path of instruction," this dynamic pattern continues—back and forth between the objective and subjective encounter with Christ. The reader participates in the truth that the Spirit pours out and experiences progressive deeper levels of conversion. As this perfecting of the soul continues, the space between them diminishes (see fig. 1). The "closing of this gap"—between *the objective understanding of Christ* and *the subjective appropriation of Christ*—is the true hallmark of the spiritual sense.

As the allegorical and tropological senses converge, the distance between the objective Christ (allegorical) and the subjective Christ (tropological) diminishes. This is the aim! This is the fruit of the spiritual senses working together in the life of the believer, indeed, in the life of the Church. As two converge, there is less differentiation between one's knowing about Christ objectively and performing as Christ subjectively in one's own being. This dynamic process between the objective and the subjective—between the allegorical and the tropological—leads to one's ascent toward God. *This movement toward this heavenly longing is anagogy.*

The anagogical sense is the fruit of the uniting of the objective and the subjective encounters with Christ, as one ascends along the pathway, making progress toward the contemplation of God. Accordingly, the anagogical sense is a bringing together of the allegorical and the tropological *in a perfecting way*. One does not experience true perfection in the here and now; nevertheless, one is on the path, drawing nearer to the heavenly Christ. In a manner of speaking, this movement through the senses, leading to the anagogical, has a decidedly eschatological quality to it. One's ultimate aim is the contemplation of the Resurrected and Ascended Christ, in his heavenly glory. And not only the glorified Christ, but also the communion of saints with him.[4] In an epistle, the great St. Cyprian even has in mind the "saints" of the Old Testament:

> What will be the glory and how great the joy to be admitted *to see God*, to be honoured to receive with Christ, thy Lord God, the joy of eternal salvation and light—to greet Abraham, and Isaac, and Jacob, and all the patriarchs, and prophets, and apostles, and martyrs—to rejoice with the righteous and the friends of God in the kingdom of heaven, with the pleasure of immortality given to us—to receive there what neither eye hath seen, nor ear heard, neither hath entered into the heart of man! For the apostle announces that we shall receive greater things than anything that we here either do or suffer, saying, "The sufferings of this present time are not worthy to be compared with the glory to come hereafter which shall be revealed in us."[5]

Even so, this pathway through the Four Senses is not merely eschatological. Spiritually, one ascends toward perfection, and with God's grace truly grows in perfection, approaching the end of the anagogical, the Beatific Vision. As St. Basil writes,

> Through the Holy Spirit comes our restoration to Paradise, our ascension into the kingdom of heaven, our return to the adoption of sons, our liberty to call God our Father, our being made partakers of the grace of Christ, our being called children of light, our sharing in eternal glory, and, in a word, our being brought into a state of all "fulness of blessing," both in this world and in the world to come, of all the good gifts that are in store for us, by promise whereof, through faith, *beholding the reflection of their grace as though they were already present, we await perfect enjoyment.*[6]

4. See Heb 12:1.

5. St. Cyprian of Carthage, *Epistle* LV. See Rom 8:18.

6. St. Basil of Caesarea, "Book of Saint Basil on the Spirit." We have not had much to say about the sacramental economy in the book. Not because it is not important—it is vitally so. Yet the topic has not been relevant, strictly speaking. The graces that we are discussing (i.e., that flow from Scripture) are "stirred" in the believer from one's participation in the sacraments. In fact, it is difficult to imagine one's "ascent" toward the face of the Lord apart from frequent reception of the sacraments. This was certainly the case for Basil. What he discusses here is the *fruit of Christian Baptism*, not Scripture alone. Basil writes: "If such is the earnest, what the perfection? If such the first fruits, what the complete fulfilment? Furthermore, *from this too may be apprehended the difference between the grace that comes from the Spirit and the baptism by water:* in that John indeed baptized with water, but our Lord Jesus Christ by the Holy Ghost" (emphasis added).

Eschatologically speaking, this process is not fully complete during one's earthly pilgrimage. The journey toward God is precisely that—a journey that involves a pathway and a progression toward the heavenly Christ. Temptation and sin may contravene one's forward progress. But only for a time. As one confesses sin, repents, and is renewed in Christ through the sacraments, the path that leads to the anagogical is again opened. This continual movement of ascent, bringing about a continuous perfecting of the soul, infuses the believer with increased levels of the theological virtue of hope, even as, in St. Augustine's words, our earthly journey continues:

> And what tongue can tell, or what imagination can conceive, the reward He will bestow at the last, when we consider that for our comfort in this earthly journey He has given us so freely of His Spirit, that in the adversities of this life we may retain our confidence in, and love for, *Him whom as yet we see not*; and that He has also given to each gifts suitable for the building up of His Church, that we may do what He points out as right to be done, not only without a murmur, but even with delight?[7]

Accordingly, the appropriation of the anagogical sense is not merely a future-oriented endeavor. Rather, the believer steps into the eschatological mysteries of the heavenly Christ, and union with Christ in heaven, and through the sacraments, brings more of it gradually into one's life, as Augustine says, "with delight."

The pathway through the senses may now be fully summarized. (1) The reader diligently searches for the text's meaning, as expressed by the sacred author. (2) Moving beyond the literal and "historical" sense, one crosses the threshold into the spiritual. In the allegorical sense, one meets the person of Christ in an *objective* way. (3) Arriving at the tropological sense, one moves beyond the objective and into the interior, and meets Christ in a *subjective* way. (4) In circulating between the allegorical and tropological senses, the gap between them diminishes—and deeper conversion is the result. The ascent to Christ rises higher until (5) finally, through the convergence of the objective and subjective, one ascends in growing perfection. This prepares one for the last stage, anagogy. Here, one does not merely reflect on the "heavenly" Christ but *participates in* Christ through the Spirit in a continually "perfecting" way.

7. St. Augustine, *On Christian Doctrine*, I.XI.XIV, in *St. Augustin's City of God*, 526; emphasis added.

The larger aim is clear. Through the Four Senses, one ascends higher and higher, knowing Christ and experiencing him in an interior way. This is the pathway and progression through the Four Senses—toward the face of the Lord. Ultimately, one aspires to climb to the true contemplation of the risen and glorified Christ: *Ad quod et vocavit vos per evangelium nostrum in acquisitionem gloriae Domini nostri Iesu Christi.*[8]

The Full Flowering of the Four Senses in the Second through Thirteenth Centuries

The above thesis, now fully developed, will guide the investigation of the encounter scenes in Part II of this volume. But is this claim sound? Does it, broadly speaking, reflect the reality of things in ancient and medieval biblical interpretation? Is it merely speculative, or is there a legitimate basis for it? In this section, I provide historical and literary support from both the patristic and medieval periods that support these claims. We first examine data from the patristic period, beginning with Origen himself. After a few patristic examples, we turn to others from the medieval period, specifically the High Middle Ages.

A word of clarification is necessary here. Many wrongly confine the full flowering of the Four Senses to the age of the primitive Church. But this is not accurate. In Western Europe, the High Middles Ages of the eleventh through the thirteenth centuries were a time of rebirth or renaissance. As one medieval historian summarizes, there was an "improvement in economic and social conditions, a new productive and organizational vitality in urban centers, and a greater openness in commercial relations, as well as a perceptible parallel increase in intellectual activity and literary production in every field ... This awakening was to a great extent fostered, as in all renaissances, by a return to antiquity that included the rediscovery of philosophical, logico-grammatical, and scientific texts and exegetical texts of the patristic period."[9]

8. 2 Thes 2:14: "To this he called you through our gospel, so that you may obtain the glory of our Lord Jesus Christ."

9. D'Onofrio, *History of Theology*, 164. In Western Europe, the eleventh to the thirteenth centuries were generally a time of social rebirth and renaissance. There was an "improvement in economic and social conditions, a new productive and organizational vitality in urban centers, and a greater openness in commercial relations, as well as a perceptible parallel increase in intellectual activity and literary production in every field ... This awakening was to a great extent fostered, as in all renaissances, by a return to antiquity

As Jones has argued, the High Middle Ages were equally a time of tremendous *reform* in the Church, and not only in the patristic age. Well beyond it, the Four Senses dominated biblical exegesis and biblical preaching. They held powerful sway over virtually every sphere of life. The pathway and progression through the Four Senses—from the literal to the spiritual—*were the optics by which all of life was lived in this period.* By the twelfth century, the Four Senses were at the foundation of the entire sacramental vision of life, from the Chair of Peter to the poorest farmer, and everyone in between.[10]

Additionally during this time, there was a renewed interest in retrieving beliefs from antiquity, including the patristic age. The monastic movement, well underway near the end of the patristic age, took on new fervor and import. Monks and monasteries populated Western Europe as never before. Their role in the Church and in society ought never be reduced to an entrenchment or hunkering down. Rather, the monastery mediated a kind of restoration of Christian society. The continuous prayer, liturgy, manual labor, and silence within its walls not only

---

that included the rediscovery of philosophical, logico-grammatical, and scientific texts and exegetical texts of the patristic period." Prior to these two pivotal centuries, the Church witnessed the splitting of the Roman Empire into the Latin Church in the West and Byzantium in the East; St. John Damascene and the close of the patristic period; the Carolingian revival and the proliferation of monasteries; the Cluniac movement across Europe; and St. Anselm's *Proslogion*, to name a few historical highlights. The period was a time of intense renewal and reform within the Church. Monasticism flourished more than ever before. It was the age of Scholasticism, Peter Lombard, the retrieval of Aristotle, and the *Doctor Angelicus*, St. Thomas Aquinas. It was in this age that the Cathedral Schools developed along with the mendicant orders; notably, the Dominicans and the Franciscans. St. Bernard of Clairvaux produced his *Commentary on the Canticle of Canticles,* and the "New Augustine," Hugh of St. Victor, led a remarkable movement of new exegesis involving mysticism and philosophical reason.

10. The same period witnessed a convergence of achievements realized with the Church. It was the time of the launch of the First Crusade, which brought new hope and optimism about the liberation of the Holy Land. It was age of the Cluniac movement and of increased monastic influence upon both Church and society. It was the age of SS. Thomas Aquinas and Bonaventure, and of an epoch-making Church Council, Lateran IV in 1215 AD. See Andrew Willard Jones's "The Liturgical Cosmos: The Worldview of the High Middle Ages (Part 1 of 3)," YouTube video, 1:01:37, posted by Franciscan University of Steubenville, January 15, 2016, https://www.youtube.com/watch?v=GpdD6a-TYss; "The Liturgical Cosmos: The Worldview of the High Middle Ages (Part 2 of 3)," YouTube video, 1:01:29, posted by Franciscan University of Steubenville, January 15, 2016, https://www.youtube.com/watch?v=wdy6PjqTgyc&t=3s; "The Liturgical Cosmos: The Worldview of the High Middle Ages (Part 3 of 3), YouTube video, 1:06:43, posted by Franciscan University of Steubenville, January 15, 2016, https://www.youtube.com/watch?v=XA1C7U8TdbM. See also his "The Preacher of the Fourth Lateran Council," *Logos* 18, no. 2 (Spring 2015): 121–49.

formed the community of monks. It was also a witness and a hope to the Christian society beyond its walls.[11]

During the High Middle Ages, there were new methods of biblical interpretation in comparison with the earlier patristic age or even the Early Middle Ages.[12] More than ever, the Four Senses of Scripture held sway in this period. And not only over the interpretation of Scripture, but also in preaching, liturgy, and over the whole of reality. If ever there were a time in which the Four Senses triumphed—in which the Four Senses as a pathway and progression to God was considered possible—it was undoubtedly within this period. For all these reasons, we consider examples from the early patristic period through the High Middle Ages (and not the earlier patristic period alone) to further substantiate this thesis.

Exemplum: Patristic and Medieval Examples That Reinforce the Thesis

In this section, ten *Exempla* ("examples") are presented: (1) Origen, (2) St. Jerome, (3) St. Augustine, (4) St. Gregory the Great, (5) Honorius of Autun, (6) Guigo II, (7) St. Bernard of Clairvaux, (8) Hugh of St. Victor, (9) Allain of Lilly and Dante Alighieri, and (10) Joachim of Fiore. These examples reflect a range of scholarship from the second through the thirteenth centuries.[13]

The data from these various ancient and medieval sources are by no means exhaustive, but rather merely representative of the time frame we are looking at. Moreover, the individual cases, intriguing in their own right, ought not be seen as prescriptive. Rather, they are descriptive of the logic and reasonability of our thesis. Various points may be drawn from the data, individually. Taken together, however, these sources represent over one thousand years of reflection, and as such a fair sample of

11. "The Liturgical Cosmos: The Worldview of the High Middle Ages (Part 2 of 3)," YouTube video, 1:01:29, posted by Franciscan University of Steubenville, January 15, 2016, https://www.youtube.com/watch?v=wdy6PjqTgyc&t=3s.

12. The patristic period is often described as the period from the second to the eighth centuries. Although a matter of debate, the eighth through the tenth centuries are generally considered the Early Middle Ages.

13. Origen (184–253); Jerome (347–420); Augustine (354–430); Gregory the Great (540–604); Honorius (1080–1154); Guigo (ca. 1083–1128); Bernard (1090–1153); Hugh (1096–1141); Allain (1128–1203); Dante (1265–1361); Joachim (1135–1202).

data.[14] Collectively, this historical and literary evidence demonstrates the enduring and continual reference to the literal and spiritual senses as much more than "alternative approaches" to biblical interpretation.

From the details brought forth in the following illustrations, the reader is asked to especially note three larger patterns: (1) This thesis (the Four Senses as a pathways and progression) is amply corroborated across an array of ancient and medieval thinkers of both East and West, and over a period of one thousand years. (2) The texts chosen support the thesis in diverse ways. No two are alike, yet the notion of moving through the senses in an ascending pattern was is clearly evident. (3) "Ascent" to God through the senses is progressive, not in such a way that the previous senses are eclipsed or eradicated. Rather, both the Letter and the Spirit are preserved.[15]

Additionally, the following examples illustrate a key point made previously. Specifically, the Four Senses were not deployed in exegesis in a slavish fashion. Historically, this was not ever the case, as far as can be attested. In fact, one or more of the senses may be absent or alluded to only indirectly. A given author may stress a point in the context of one sense more explicitly than the others. This does not diminish our thesis, as one might imagine. In fact, the liberty with which ancient and medieval thinkers engaged the Scriptures demonstrates that their primary aim was exegeting texts, not following certain rules in a mechanical fashion. They expressed their confidence in the value of the senses in independent and distinct ways.

Finally, this thesis does not rest solely upon the *exempla* included here. Reams of data could be added. Nevertheless, the logic and direction of the thesis are amply undergirded by the collective witness of the historical and literary evidence that follows.

14. It is beyond the scope of this book to engage in lengthy explanations of each example. Instead, they are presented as concisely as possible. These examples could be developed into chapters (or books) of their own, along with a sifting through of various secondary opinions on the texts with debate and analysis—not to mention extensive annotation and bibliographic materials. Such is not my purpose, as it would be unwieldy and not contribute to the larger aim of the book. Even so, these brief examples are of merit and deserve to be included. Together, they demonstrate the logic and reasonability of our thesis, i.e., *seeking the face of the Lord through the pathway and progression of the Four Senses.*

15. This last point becomes clear in Joachim of Fiore, and certain overreaches and flaws in his philosophy of history.

1. *Unum Exemplum*: Origen

Origen of Alexandria was not only one of the earliest practitioners of Christian allegory. He was one of the greatest masters of it, ever. There should be no dispute about this. All subsequent allegorical interpretation of Scripture looks back to this prolific writer as its true pioneer. As Jerome once quipped about Origen, "Who has ever managed to read all that he has written?"[16] Moreover, despite certain controversies that plague his happy memory, there have been modern efforts to reclaim Origen's monumental stature as the one of the Church's grandest theologians.[17] As Pope Benedict XVI put it, Origen "truly was a figure crucial to the whole development of Christian thought."[18]

But it may come as a surprise that in no way did Origin limit himself to the allegorical sense. First, and importantly, he was well aware of the literal sense and dealt with it in expositing biblical texts. In his *Commentary on the Gospel According to Saint John*, he treats Jesus's temple action as recorded in chapter 2. There, St. John presents the objection of the Temple authorities: "The Jews then said, 'It has taken forty-six years to build this temple, and will you raise it up in three days?'" (v. 20). Concerning this text, Origen writes: "We are not able to say how the Jews declare that the temple was built in forty-six years, *if we follow the literal sense*."[19] Setting aside the particulars of why he moves beyond the literal sense here,[20] what is important is that Origen clearly sees it as the

16. St. Jerome, *Epistle* 33, in *St. Jerome*, 46. According to Jerome, Origen composed 320 books and 310 homilies.

17. See esp. de Lubac, *History and Spirit*; Martens, *Origen and Scripture*; Radner, *Time and the Word*, chaps. 1–2.

18. Pope Benedict XVI, *General Audiences of Benedict XVI*. He adds, "Theology to him was essentially explaining, understanding Scripture; or we might also say that his theology was a perfect symbiosis between theology and exegesis. In fact, the proper hallmark of Origen's doctrine seems to lie precisely in the constant invitation to move from the letter to the spirit of the Scriptures, to progress in knowledge of God. Furthermore, this so-called 'allegorism,' as von Balthasar wrote, coincides exactly 'with the development of Christian dogma, effected by the teaching of the Church Doctors,' who in one way or another accepted Origen's 'lessons.' Thus, Tradition and the Magisterium, the foundation and guarantee of theological research, come to take the form of 'scripture in action.'"

19. Origen, *Commentary on the Gospel According to John, Books 1–10*, 311; emphasis added.

20. Origen explains: "And in the fourth year, in the second month, when king Solomon was ruling over Israel, the king commanded, and they brought great precious stones for the foundation of the house, and unhewn stones. And the sons of Solomon and the sons of Hiram hewed them and laid them in the fourth year, and they laid the foundation of the

starting position and in this instance looks to an allegorical meaning. Other examples of Origen's handling the literal sense are found in this commentary as well as in other works.[21]

The previous example highlighted Origen's work with the literal sense. While it is true that allegory predominates his commentary on the Gospel According to St. John,[22] our second example involves anagogy. Although it may be a surprise to some, Origen carefully delineated between the various spiritual senses. He did not merely resort to the allegorical in his treatment of biblical texts. He was well aware that the allegorical yields the person of Christ in his *earthly* life, whereas the anagogical brought attention to the *heavenly* Christ.

In his treatment of the raising of Lazarus in John,[23] Origen turns to anagogy to describe the restoration of those who have sinned after Baptism. Jesus wants these people, he says, who have been restored to life by his prayer to come forth from the tomb and to be released from the bonds with which they have been bound. He writes, "*The anagogical sense concerning the passage* is not difficult in consequence of what we have already explained. For he asked that the one who had sinned, after becoming his friend [i.e., baptized], and had become dead to God return to life by divine power. And he obtained it and saw movements of life in such a one for which he gave thanks to the Father."[24]

While more texts could be added along similar lines, the point should be clear enough; the pioneer and greatest purveyor of allegory did not limit himself to it, even though the allegorical was clearly his preference. He knew the literal and the other spiritual senses, and the examples given underscore that he didn't neglect them. Where he felt the need, he appropriated them accordingly.

As de Lubac states, Origen had "perfect mastery over his own thought."[25] We can add to de Lubac's right assessment this way: Origen was strategic in his concentration on the allegorical sense. Far from ne-

house of the Lord in the month Nisan and the second month. In the eleventh year, in the month Baal, which was the eighth month, the house was completed in its whole plan and in its whole arrangement." *Commentary on the Gospel According to John, Books 1–10*, 311.

21. See Origen, *Commentary on the Gospel According to John, Books 1–10*, 43, 96, 160, 214–15; Origen, *Commentary on the Gospel According to John, Books 13–32*, 153, 167.

22. See Origen, *Commentary on the Gospel According to John, Books 13–32*, 33, 313.

23. See Jn 11:1*ff.*

24. Origen, *Commentary on the Gospel According to John, Books 13–32*, 302.

25. De Lubac, *Medieval Exegesis*, vol. 3, 365.

glecting or ignoring the other senses, he aimed to proclaim the person of Christ, primarily in the Hebrew Scriptures and in his commentaries on the New Testament. One can make an argument that his appropriation of both the Literal and Spiritual senses reflects both his respect for the multiplicity of meaning in Scripture and his acceptance of the legitimacy of both as well as an understanding of the believer's growth within the pathway of the senses, and not merely from one sense alone.

2. *Exempli Gratia Duas*: St. Jerome

The next example is from St. Jerome and his *Commentary on the Psalms*. There, he deals with the first two verses in Psalm 75: "In Judah God is known, his name is great in Israel. His abode has been established in Salem, his dwelling place in Zion." In his exegesis on this biblical text, Jerome begins, "In peace is his 'abode': for which the Hebrew has 'in Salem.' You see, therefore, *the literal translation* is Jerusalem—that is Salem—which first was called Salem, later Jebus, and finally, Jerusalem. This is that Salem in which Melchizedek was king. We read: 'You are a priest forever, according to the order of Melchizedek' (Ps 110:4). The psalmist did not say according the order of Aaron, but Melchizedek."[26]

Here, Jerome has dealt with the text through the literal sense, drawing on key terms and pointing out their etymology and drawing on the Hebrew terms that Psalms 75 and 110 have in common. Yet in continuing his explanation, he moves from the literal to the allegorical, and then to the tropological and anagogical senses. Jerome comments on the phrase "His dwelling is in Zion" according to the latter two spiritual senses: "A literal interpretation permits us to say of Jerusalem and Zion, that the Temple was there, but in a tropological and anagogical sense, we mean that the dwelling of God is in Zion. Now Zion means stronghold or watchtower; hence, where there is in the soul the knowledge of Scripture and its doctrine, that soul is the dwelling place of God."[27]

Three distinct observations may be made about the above selection. First, Jerome has given us what we stressed was indeed rare; namely, a commentary on a biblical text according to all Four Senses of Scripture. Second, he begins from the literal sense and moves to the spiritual sens-

26. St. Jerome, Psa 76:1–2, in *Homilies of Saint Jerome*, 62–63.

27. St. Jerome, Psa 76:1–2, in *Homilies of Saint Jerome*, 63.

es. Finally and importantly, Jerome's commentary clearly appropriates the Four Senses as a pathway and progression within the spiritual life. On this last point, notice that "the dwelling place of God" is for Jerome both the Temple in Jerusalem in the literal sense *and the soul of the believer* in the tropological/anagogical senses. This is an excellent example of the movement of ascent through the senses of Scripture.

3. *Exempli Gratia Tres*: St. Augustine

While any number of texts could be drawn upon from St. Augustine, a few examples drawn primarily from his *De Doctrina Christiana* (*On Christian Doctrine*) will suffice. In Book I of *De Doctrina Christiana*, Augustine writes:

> Since we are to enjoy to the full that Truth which lives without change and since, in that Truth, God the Trinity, the Author and Founder of the universe, takes counsel for the things which He has created, the mind must be cleansed in order that it may be able to look upon that light and cling to it when it has seen it. Let us consider this cleansing as a sort of traveling or sailing to our own country. We are not brought any closer to Him who is everywhere present by moving from place to place, but by a holy desire and lofty morals.[28]

Here, in dealing with God's immutable and unchangeable truth revealed in Scripture, Augustine explains the necessity for the believer's soul to be purified to have the spiritual capacity to perceive the light of God's truth in the soul and to rest in this truth once it is perceived.

Although he has not mentioned any of the senses directly, Augustine is dealing with the biblical text anagogically. His "traveling" metaphor is striking, as it relates to the Four Senses. He describes the process of spiritual purification as "a kind of journey or voyage to our native land," by which he means our heavenly home. The destination of the voyage of purity is heaven itself. There is a kind of *exitus/reditus* idea here, that is, of the soul's origin in God and return to God. This text from *De Doctrina Christiana* supports the thesis of the Four Senses as a pathway and a progression toward the contemplation of God. Clearly, Augustine sees assimilation of Scriptural truth as integral to our continual purification and this takes place in the soul as a process.

A second example is seen in *De Doctrina*, Book III. There, Augus-

28. St. Augustine of Hippo, *On Christian Doctrine*, I.10, in *Christian Instruction*, 34.

tine warns against occasions for lust. One is to avoid it, whatever the cost. His explanation of the distinctions between "things" and "signs" in Book I[29] prepared his readers to understand how to discriminate between that which is sin and that which may not be. Consequently, he cautions,

> we must prudently take into account what is proper for places, circumstances, and persons, so that we may not indiscreetly convict them of sin. It is possible for a wise man to eat the most delicious food without any sin of sensuality or gluttony, while a fool is ravenous for the meanest food with a raging hunger that is most unseemly. Any sane man would rather eat fish as the Lord did, than eat lentils as did Esau,[30] Abraham's grandson, or barley the way oxen do. The fact that they are fed upon coarser food does not indicate that most animals are more self-restrained than we. For, in all cases of this kind, it is not the quality of the things we use, but our motive in using them and our way of striving for them, that causes our actions to be either commendable or reprehensible.[31]

As he goes on to explain, "The things which seem almost wicked to the unenlightened, whether they are only words or whether they are even deeds, either of God or of men whose sanctity is commended to us—*these are entirely figurative*. Their latent kernels of meaning must be extracted as food for charity."[32] For Augustine, that which is figurative in Scripture has a distinct purpose. Ultimately, it is to help us grown in charity.

Throughout the text, he distinguishes between true Christian interpretation—with its proper use of figural readings—and superstitious pages, who misappropriate signs and distort the meaning of things:

> When such a meaning is elicited that its uncertainty cannot be explained by the unerring testimonies of the Holy Scriptures, however, it remains for us to explain it by the proof of reason, even if the man whose words we are seeking to understand were perhaps unaware of that meaning. *This, however, is a dangerous practice. It is much safer to walk by means of the Holy Scriptures.* When we are trying to search out those passages that are obscured by figurative words, we may either start out from a passage which is not subject to dispute, or, if it is disputed, we may settle the question by employing the testimonies that have been discovered everywhere in the same Scripture.[33]

29. See St. Augustine, *On Christian Doctrine*, I.1–11, in *Christian Instruction*.

30. See Lk 24:43; Gn 25:34.

31. St. Augustine, *On Christian Doctrine*, III.12, in *Christian Instruction*.

32. St. Augustine, *On Christian Doctrine*, III.12, in *Christian Instruction*; emphasis added.

33. St. Augustine, *On Christian Doctrine*, III.28, in St. Jerome, *Select Letters*; emphasis added.

All of Scripture, by virtue of its divine inspiration by the Holy Spirit, has the capacity to lead the believer upward to the face of God. This is the case whether it is through the plain sense of the Word or through figural means, unpacked through sound rules of interpretation. Regardless, the devout reading of Scripture is, for Augustine, how we grow into perfect charity, and in that respect how we ascend toward the face of God.

Elsewhere, in *On Christian Combat*, Augustine explains:

> Let us be fed in Christ, nourished by the milk of a simple and unaffected faith. While we are children, let us not long for the food of adults. But, let us grow in Christ by wholesome nourishment, by the acquisition of good habits, and by Christian righteousness, wherein the love of God and neighbor is made perfect and strong. In this way each one of us can win an interior victory over the hostile Devil and his angels, being united with Christ whom we have put on. Perfect charity harbors neither covetousness nor fear of the world, that is to say, perfect charity is neither covetous to acquire temporal goods nor fearful of losing them.[34]

He goes on to describe covetousness fear as "the two doors through which the enemy gains entrance and obtains the ascendancy over us. He must be driven out; first by the fear of God, then by love. We ought, then, to long more eagerly for the clear and distinct knowledge of Truth, according as we see ourselves advancing in charity, having hearts made pure by its simplicity, for it is by the eye of the soul that Truth is perceived."[35]

He concludes his remarks, citing both Jesus and Paul: "'Blessed,' indeed, 'are the pure of heart,' says Christ, '*for they shall see God*.'[36] 'So that, being rooted and grounded in love,' we may be able 'to comprehend with all the saints what is the breadth and length and height and depth, to know also the surpassing knowledge of the love of Christ, in order that we may be filled unto all the fullness of God.'"[37]

In the above texts, Augustine's hermeneutic of charity is clearly evident. Yet it is especially in how one avails himself of charity, and how

34. St. Augustine, "On Christian Combat," 33, in *Christian Instruction*, 352–53. See Eph 3:17–19.

35. St. Augustine, "On Christian Combat," 33, in *Christian Instruction*, 352–53.

36. Mt 5:8; emphasis added.

37. St. Augustine, "On Christian Combat," 33, in *Christian Instruction*, 352–353. See Eph 3:17–19.

one grows in it that is central to discussion. Charity is that virtue by which the Christian believer is able to understand the Scriptures, if he is to understand them at all. Likewise, charity is the virtue that one seeks to grow in, to develop, through reading Scripture. Without charity, one cannot understand Scripture. And, at least theoretically, if one acquired perfect charity, one would not need the Scriptures at all. Not that Augustine believed that it was logically possible for a believer to do so in this earthly life, least of all himself. His point is rather that charity is the believer's spiritual matrix. We begin by being filled with charity by the Holy Spirit at Baptism. We continue to grow in charity toward our *telos*, our end. In all of these examples, Augustine engages the Scriptures with both the Letter and the Spirit.

4. *Exemplum Quattuor*: St. Gregory the Great

The last example from the patristic period is from St. Gregory the Great and his masterful *Moralia in Iob*. Gregory takes up the discussion of Job 33:26: "He shall pray unto God, and he will be favorable unto him: *And he shall see his face with joy*."[38] Concerning this text, Gregory writes:

> But yet this unsubstantial and hasty vision, which results from contemplation, or rather, so to speak, this semblance of a vision, is called the face of God. For we, who recognize a person by his face, not unnaturally call the knowledge of God, His face. When Jacob says, after he had struggled with the Angel, "*I have seen the Lord face to face*."[39] As though he were to say, I know the Lord, because He Himself has deigned to know me. But Paul declares that this knowledge will take place most completely in the end, when he says, "*Then shall I know, even as I am known*."[40]

First, notice that Gregory's argument is itself scriptural. He draws upon both Genesis and 1 Corinthians. The former is Jacob's theophany, the latter St. Paul's eschatological conclusion to his chapter on divine charity. Second, Gregory explains the original text from Job ("And he shall see his face with joy") in an anagogical fashion, with help from Paul: "Then shall I know, even as I am known." Third, Gregory's ana-

38. Job 33:26, King James Version (emphasis added).

39. Gn 32:30; emphasis added.

40. St. Gregory the Great, *Moralia in Iob*, 24.12, in *Morals on the Book of Job*, 57–58; emphasis added. See 1 Cor 13:12.

gogical explanation of the text in Job is not a future reality, an eschatological hope on the distant horizon. Rather, the anagogical is *appropriated in the present*, as Gregory connects the contemplation of God in the heavenly sense with the soul of the believer in the present.

Specifically, Gregory counsels that the man who faces temptations successfully, and remains faithful, is not only rewarded in the future. He is also able to harness the power of the future hope in overcoming temptations now: "Because then, after the contests of labors, after the waves of temptations, the soul is often caught up in rapture, in order that it may contemplate a knowledge of the Divine Presence (a Presence which it can feel, but which it can never fully enjoy), it is well said of this man who is tempted, after his many labors, *He will see His face in exultation. But because the more a man contemplates heavenly things, the more he amends his earthly doings*, after the grace of contemplation he fitly adds the righteousness of his doings."[41]

The critical thing to see is the way that the anagogical sense has a dual function. On one hand, Gregory deals with the contemplation of the face of God, eschatologically speaking. It is the believer's future hope. On the other hand, Gregory connects the anagogical to the tropological. The future hope provides the believer with the courage and confidence to overcome temptations with God's grace and so add to "the righteousness of his doings."

Here again, we see how the Four Senses are appropriated in a cohesive way. There is a reciprocal dynamic between the spiritual senses. In concise order, Gregory deals with the spiritual senses as a pathway and a progression toward the face of God. Note the pattern of ascent. With Gregory, the reader encounters St. Paul's eschatological text. In so doing, one meditates on *the future contemplation of the face of God* and the joy that it will yield. This instills in the reader the theological virtue of hope, which in turn "fuels" the believer to grow in the theological virtue of charity. As a result, his temptations are more readily overcome through anagogy; hope is born in the soul, giving rise to an increase in charity and moral perfection. All of this takes place within a few lines on Gregory's commentary on Job, which is a tropological commentary on the text, concerned with the moral dimension of the Christian life.

41. St. Gregory the Great, *Moralia in Iob*, in *Morals on the Book of Job*, 24.12; emphasis added.

5. *Exemplum Quinque*: Honorius of Autun

We turn from the above patristic examples to those from the latter, medieval period, beginning with Honorius of Autun.[42] In explaining chapter 5 of the Song of Songs, Honorius writes: "The reason, moreover, why this lament finds a place in this song of love is that the faithful soul, the Bride of Christ, is joined to him by penitence; and 'There will be joy among the angels of God over one sinner who does penance.'[43] This lament belongs more to the tropological than to the allegorical sense, because in it the Church exhorts the penitent to good morals. Hence the allegorical sense is missing in this passage."[44]

First, Honorius's commentary deals with all the spiritual senses.[45] His primary move is a subjective one, that is, conveying Christ within the soul, rather than a purely objective focus on the person of Christ. In this way, Honorius brings the reader to the face of the Lord in a tropological way. Once accomplished, however, Honorius pivots and considers the possibility that the biblical text simultaneously has an anagogical dimension—the heavenly Christ.

In the extended quote below, I have emphasized terms from the

42. Honorius of Autun was also known as Honorius Augustodunensis. "At the end of his work *On the Luminaries of the Church*, an otherwise nameless monk of the Benedictine order who flourished in the first half of the 12th century identified himself as 'Honorius,' located himself in Autun [in Burgundy], and described himself as a priest and a scholar. There is little doubt that this account of himself, for whatever reason, deliberately falsified both his name and his place of residence. The likelihood is that the greater part of his writing career was spent at the abbey of St. James at Ratisbon in Germany, a Benedictine house of British foundation where the monks were permitted to be solitaries in the Celtic manner. He may well have been of British origin, and he may have begun his monastic life at Canterbury under the tutelage of Anselm. His—complete and systematic—commentary on *The Song of Songs* was only one of a large number of works in which, without seeking originality, he sought to summarize and synthesize the theological learning of his day." Norris and Wilken, *Song of Songs*, 300.

43. Lk 15:10.

44. Honorius, *Commentary on the Song of Songs*, 5.7, in Norris and Wilken, *Song of Songs*, 208.

45. For example, in his *Commentary on the Song of Songs*, Honorius treats the theme of "marriage" according to all Four Senses. Regarding the literal, he describes the "mingling" of male and female flesh, in the natural sense. Allegorically, he allows two possibilities: (1) the incarnation of the Logos—i.e., joined to the flesh—or (2) the union of Christ with the Church. Tropologically, the text is read as a dialogue between Christ the Bridegroom, joined to the soul of the believer, that is, the Bridegroom. Finally, Honorius reads the text anagogically: the new man ascends to heaven after the Resurrection, to be joined with the whole Church in heavenly glory. See Levy, *Introducing Medieval Biblical Interpretation*, 122.

Song of Songs, with which Honorius is interacting in discussing the anagogical sense:

> If it be taken in the anagogical sense, the pilgrim Church is sleeping with her heart ... awake when she is insensible to things earthly and transitory and aspires solely to things heavenly. The voice of the Beloved hammers upon her when he summons her to her heavenly fatherland by bodily ills and the approach of death. She quickly opens to him because she gratefully accepts his calling. For she is brought into the Lord's inheritance as his *sister*; she is admitted into heavenly mysteries as his *friend*; she is enlightened by the Holy Spirit as a *dove*; and as one who is *spotless* she is established in the bedchamber of the Bridegroom. She removes her *mantle* when she lays down the body. She bathes her *feet* when, by her final act of penance, she washes off the fine dust of distracting thoughts. The Beloved puts out his *hand* when he touches her with the pangs of death. But her *belly* trembles at his touch because by her slightest sins, which she committed through the frailty of the flesh, she has merited the judge's sentence. Nevertheless, she rises up to open to him because she wishes to have the vision of him who dwells on high. His hands drip with myrrh because it stands for the works by which she has mortified herself here in order that for them she may receive eternal rewards.[46]

Honorius's commentary, penned as it was in the High Middle Ages, underscores how biblical texts continued to be broken open according to two or three of the spiritual senses. Additionally, in moving from the tropological to the anagogical senses, his commentary exemplifies the pathway and progress of the believer in the ascent toward God. Not only does he deal with the moral dimension of the text, but he also looks forward to eschatological realities. Importantly, Honorius appropriates the heavenly hopes and then anchors them in the experience of the believer within the present age.

6. *Exemplum Sex*: Guigo II

The Ladder to from Earth to Heaven is a classic text from the High Middle Ages, and today it is often considered as a sort of primer on *Lectio Divina*, as it leads the reader through a fourfold sequence of spiritual reading.[47] Yet

46. Honorius, *Commentary on the Song of Songs*, 5.7, in Norris and Wilken, *Song of Songs*, 208; emphasis added.

47. "Guigo II [d. 1188] was the ninth prior of the Carthusian motherhouse, the Grande Chartreuse, in the second half of the twelfth century. Neither he nor his order were much concerned to leave a record about his life, and in the history of the order he is largely

our specific interest is not with Guigo's methodology of *Lectio Divina*. It lies with the pattern of ascent involved in such an approach to the reading of Scripture.

Early in the meditation, Guigo writes, "One day, while I was busy with the bodily labor of the hands, I began to think about man's spiritual exercise, and four spiritual steps suddenly presented themselves to my pondering soul: *reading, meditation, prayer,* and *contemplation*. This is the ladder of cloistered monks whereby they are lifted up from earth into heaven; although it is divided into only a few steps, its length is nonetheless immense and incredible. *Its lower part rests on the earth, but its upper part penetrates the clouds and probes the secrets of heaven*."[48]

It may be something of a leap to impose a direct correlation between his four stages of spiritual reading (reading, meditation, prayer, and contemplation) and the Four Senses. Caution is therefore necessary in this respect. Even so, the essential parallel between them should not be disregarded. Notice that Guigo explains that this ladder extends from heaven to earth: "Its lower part rests on the earth, but its upper part penetrates the clouds and probes the secrets of heaven." Here, one thinks of the general movement from the literal to the anagogical, which is clearly a pattern of ascent. Additionally, Guigo's first rung, the earthly one (i.e., reading), has a general correspondence with the historical dimension of the literal sense. Similarly, the final rung of the ladder "penetrates the clouds and probes the secrets of heaven." Here, too, one thinks of the anagogical sense, which deals with the heavenly Christ and is the destination of the Four Senses overall.

Later in the text, after providing several biblical texts to further illustrate his point, Guigo discusses the process of climbing the ladder as follows:

---

overshadowed by his predecessor, Guigo I. As a result, the work here translated, his *Scala Claustralium* [i.e., 'The Ladder of Monks'], has been attributed to various authors over time, including St. Augustine and St. Bernard of Clairvaux. Its popularity has endured, and today it is seen as a classic work in *lectio divina*, or the technique of reading sacred Scripture accompanied by prayer. My translation is based on the critical edition of Guigo's work, Guigo II, *Lettre sur la vie contemplative (l'échelle des moines), Douze méditations*, Sources Chrétiennes 163, eds. Edmund Colledge and James Walsh [Paris: Éditions du Cerf, 1970]. After the translation was complete, I compared it with the translation given by Colledge and Walsh in Guigo II, *The Ladder of Monks and Twelve Meditations*, Cistercian Studies Series 148 [Kalamazoo, MI: Cistercian Publications, 1981]." This is a note of the translator, Jeremy Holmes, in "Ladder from Earth to Heaven," 175.

48. Guigo II, *Ladder from Earth to Heaven*, 176; emphasis added.

> For reading comes first, being as it were the foundation, and once it has given us the subject matter it sends us on to meditation. Meditation then inquires more diligently about what should be desired, and like a man digging in the ground it finds a treasure and displays it; but when it cannot obtain [the treasure] on its own, it sends us on to prayer. Raising itself to God with all its powers, prayer begs for the desirable treasure, the sweetness of contemplation. When this comes, it rewards the labors of the three previous [steps], as it inebriates the thirsty soul with the dew of heavenly sweetness.[49]

Again, the aim is not to superimpose a one-to-one correspondence between the stages of ascent in Guigo's *Ladder from Earth to Heaven* and the Four Senses. Nevertheless, note that Guigo describes reading as the "foundation," which corresponds to the primary characteristics of the literal sense. The next two rungs of meditation and prayer share, in a collective sense, the attributes of the allegorical and tropological senses. These two rungs have a kind of interplay between them that rings familiar as it relates to the allegorical and tropological senses. One desires a thing but cannot obtain it as one's own.

In Guigo's explanation of the middle rungs of meditation and prayer, we recall the discussion of allegory as objective and tropology as subjective. Finally, Guigo's ladder of ascent is only complete with the last rung of contemplation. As he poetically describes, it is contemplation that "inebriates the thirsty soul with the dew of heavenly sweetness" (fig. 2).

Guigo's classic text illustrates the value of the Four Senses in this age. As he writes, "By means of the distinctions made here one can perceive the properties of the aforementioned steps, *how they are interrelated, and what each of them does in us*."[50] Not only this, the ladder itself is a fitting image of the Four Senses as a pathway and progression toward the face of God. Guigo's text is a significant example. For our purposes, it is a profoundly rich and clear articulation of how the Four Senses collaborate in the hand of the attentive reader of Scripture. Together, they lead the soul upward toward the contemplation of the divine Son, which is the ultimate end of all true exegesis.

This is evident in the following excerpt. Guigo's overall aim is nothing else than contemplating the "God of gods." He writes, "The one who has labored on the first step, has pondered on the second, has been de-

49. Guigo II, *Ladder from Earth to Heaven*, 183–84.
50. Guigo II, *Ladder from Earth to Heaven*, 185–86; emphasis added.

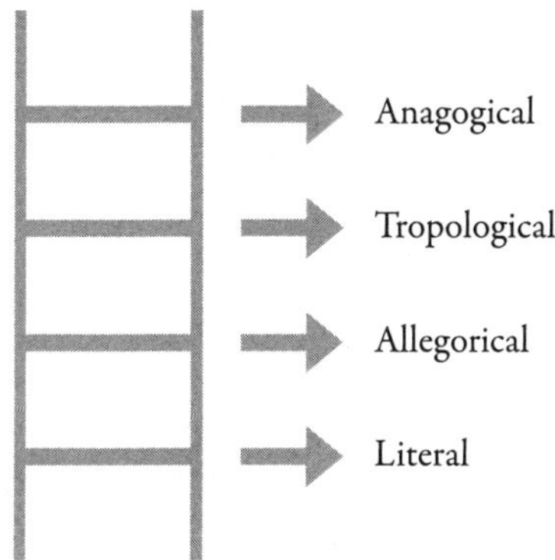

FIGURE 2. Guigo II and the "ladder" of the Four Senses of Scripture.

voted on the third, and has been lifted above himself on the fourth—by these ascents which he has arranged in his heart he ascends from strength to strength until he sees the God of gods in Zion."[51]

7. *Exemplum Septem*: St. Bernard of Clairvaux

Next, we turn to St. Bernard of Clairvaux's *In Praise of the New Knighthood*. Bernard composed this letter to encourage the Knights Temple in the Holy Land at the start of the Crusades. By way of introduction to Bernard, a few words need to be said about his immeasurable contributions to the study of the Sacred Page according to the Four Senses. One cannot broach his extensive *Commentary on the Canticle of Canticles* without immediately recognizing his appropriation of the spiritual senses. He engaged Scripture tropologically most especially. Even so, numerous examples of anagogy are found, too. Like so many other figures from the period, Bernard was conversant with all of the senses and drew upon them accordingly: "There is a very sweet drink in history; but still sweeter in allegory; most sweet, however, in [tropology]; but incomparably sweetest by far, the one in anagogy, i.e., in contemplation."[52]

Bernard's sustained examination of Song of Songs through the Four

51. Guigo II, *Ladder from Earth to Heaven*, 186.
52. St. Bernard, cited in de Lubac, *Medieval Exegesis*, vol. 3, 177.

Senses leads the reader into a pattern of ascent. For Bernard, this unfolds in Song of Songs through the dynamic interchange between Christ, the Bridegroom, and his union with the Bridegroom. The tropological sense has the lead here, and as Bernard unpacks the sacred text, he magnifies *Christ within the soul of the surrendered believer.*

As de Lubac observes, the vivid images of Song of Songs are poetically paralleled by Bernard's own words: "Bernard, like Gregory [the Great], and even more than he, had the words 'honey,' 'smoothness,' 'delectation,' 'sweetness' on his lips ... When the Word comes to the soul, it is to instruct her in wisdom, and this union of the soul with the Word 'has nothing imaginary' about it."[53] At times, the original words of Scripture are so beautifully interwoven with Bernard's own ruminations that it can be difficult to separate them. This is not a result of Bernard attempting to step on the toes of Scripture. Rather, it is a sign of his own delight with Scripture. His words reflect the state of his heart as he meditates on the Sacred Page. In the process of humble, prayerful contemplation on the Word, *his own words are transformed.*

For Bernard, "the mystical signification is beautiful and delightful ... all things are full of the supernatural mysteries and they redound each other with heavenly sweetness."[54] It is this "smoothness of the Spirit"[55] that lies at the epicenter of Bernard's biblical interpretation of Song of Songs. As a result of this rich synthesis, his commentary is, as de Lubac remarks, a "mystical tropology."[56]

For many today, Bernard is known for his work on Song of Songs. But he was a busy abbot, reformer, and spiritual director, among other roles. Bernard's written influence was likewise prolific beyond his commentaries and homilies, beyond his influence in the founding of the Cistercian order, and beyond his denouncements of Peter Abelard at the Council of Sens in northern France in 1141.

In his modest position as abbot of Clairvaux, a daughter of Cîteaux that he himself established in 1115, he was almost a pope without a tiara. He practically says this of himself when writing in 1145 to Pope Eugene III, who had been his disciple, to congratulate him on his election:

53. De Lubac, *Medieval Exegesis*, vol. 3, 173–74, with a citation from St. Bernard; emphasis added.

54. De Lubac, *Medieval Exegesis*, vol. 3, 175.

55. De Lubac, *Medieval Exegesis*, vol. 3, 175, citing St. Bernard.

56. De Lubac, *Medieval Exegesis*, vol. 3, 175.

"They say that I, not you, are the pope." In the work known as *On Consideration*, Bernard's influence and his plain talk to Eugene are clear:

> I loved you when you were poor, I will love you now that you are the father of both rich and poor. For if I know you well, you have not in becoming the father of the poor lost your poverty of spirit. I am sure that the change in your circumstances has come to you: it has not been sought by you; and I am no less certain that your promotion has left you what you were before, though something be added thereto. I will, accordingly, admonish you, not as a schoolmaster, but as a mother, at all events as one who loves you. Perhaps the fonder I am, the more foolish I may seem. If so, it will be in the eyes of him who loves not and does not feel the power of love.[57]

Even so, the greatest work of his literary extensive literary output is unquestionably his *Commentary on the Canticle of Canticles.* It is a supreme example of the interpretation of Scripture according to the spiritual senses.

So heightened is his spiritual honey that some mistakenly assume Bernard had no use for the literal sense. Or, worse yet, that he had no grasp of its necessity or its benefits. This is a gross distortion of Bernard and indeed of ancient and medieval interpreters writ large. Bernard was highly confident, incredibly well read, and erudite in many fields of knowledge. He was, to say the least, fully competent in treating a biblical text according from the literal and could perform this task as well as any, if not better than most.

This point must be understood to fully appreciate his interpretative strategy with Song of Songs. Bernard was not operating outside of the literal. He wasn't ignorant of it, or any such thing.[58] This is, simply put, an uninformed and inaccurate assessment of Bernard. Even in his voluminous appropriation of the tropological sense, he knew *exactly what he was doing.* And he did not neglect the literal: "Now we have to try and discover what is the spiritual signification of these storerooms, as the literal sense of the text is manifest enough from the foregoing observations."[59]

Examples of Bernard's grasp of all Four Senses abound: "This is the

57. St. Bernard of Clairvaux, *Ad Considerationem*, prologue in *Saint Bernard on Consideration*, 11–12; emphasis added.

58. Sadly, one gets that impression when discussing his work with some modern readers.

59. St. Bernard of Clairvaux, *Ad Considerationem*, *Sermon* XXIII, in *Saint Bernard on Consideration*.

meaning of the words added, 'My vineyard I have not kept.' As if she wanted to explain how it happened that she is now appointed keeper, not of one, but of many vineyards. *Such, I take it, is the literal sense of the text*."[60] "Therefore, His companions also, who have remained with her, address her in words of gracious kindness and offer her presents, knowing this to be the will of their Lord. Hence, it is to them that she directs her answer. *Such, I think, is the literal sense* and the sequence of our present text."[61] "*The literal signification of this verse*, my brethren, may be presented as follows."[62] "*Such is the play of the literal sense*. Why should I not call it a play, since if we stop at it *and go not beyond the surface meaning*, it is impossible to discover in these words anything like a serious purpose. Indeed, as they sound on the external ear, they suggest nothing even worthy to be heard, unless the Holy Spirit shall deign to strengthen with His interior light the weakness of our understanding."[63]

That said, Bernard's exposition of Song of Songs is deeply tropological. Throughout it is clear that, for Bernard, every facet of human knowledge is the result of spiritual contemplation. The aim is to be "united with truth." The believer cannot be united with truth without devotion to true knowledge, which for Bernard is nothing less than Sacred Scripture—along with the Fathers of the Church and Sacred Tradition.[64] In other words, for Bernard, knowledge is not its own reward. Rather, true knowledge has as its *telos* the purification of the soul. In his view of things, "theological knowledge can only end in a state of mystical contemplation of the truth that faith alone can make intelligible and interiorly vitalizing to the soul of the believer."[65]

With these remarks in mind, we turn to a far lesser known text from Bernard—*In Praise of the New Knighthood*.[66] Bernard wrote the

60. St. Bernard of Clairvaux, *Ad Considerationem*, *Sermon* XXX, in *Saint Bernard on Consideration*; emphasis added.

61. St. Bernard of Clairvaux, *Ad Considerationem*, *Sermon* XCII, in *Saint Bernard on Consideration*; emphasis added.

62. St. Bernard of Clairvaux, *Ad Considerationem*, *Sermon* XCIX, in *Saint Bernard on Consideration*; emphasis added.

63. St. Bernard of Clairvaux, *Ad Considerationem*, *Sermon* CIX, in *Saint Bernard on Consideration*; emphasis added. Numerous examples of this sort may be added to the ones provided here.

64. See D'Onofrio, *History of Theology*, 225.

65. D'Onofrio, *History of Theology*, 226.

66. St. Bernard of Clairvaux, *In Praise of the New Knighthood*.

text, modest in length, out of his support for the Knights Templar, also known as the Order of Solomon's Temple.[67] In the introduction, historian Malcolm Barber provides the necessary context: "If, therefore, the polarization between monk and warrior remained acute in the second decade of the thirteenth century, it can be seen that when Bernard of Clairvaux wrote his treatise *In Praise of the New Knighthood* sometime around 1130, he was indeed entering new territory—which fully justified his statement that his subject was that of 'a new kind of knighthood and one unknown to the ages gone by.'"[68]

As Barber continues, the text begins with Bernard drawing "a distinction between two kinds of warfare: the spiritual, characteristics of monks and fought against the invisible forces of evil, and the physical, undertaken by [warriors] against terrestrial and material enemies."[69] Yet the Templars were "involved in a battle 'hitherto unknown' in that they fight in both ways, a role which gives them a double armour and means they need fear neither life nor death."[70]

It was the worldly warrior that stood in opposition to these holy Knights Templar, "who, in contrast to the double protection of the Templar, runs a double risk: if he dies himself he suffers a physical death; while if he kills another, he dies a spiritual death."[71] The key distinction was "motivation, or in [Augustinian] terms, right intention. Pride, revenge, or self-defence, are unjustifiable reasons for killing; only when the motive is pure can the fighting not be considered evil."[72] To be clear, *In Praise of the New Knighthood* does not operate on precisely the same level as his commentary. Even so, the two texts do share three elements in common: frequent allegorizing, reference to the Scriptures (including the Old Testament), and figural readings of history.

67. It is beyond the scope of this book to engage in the history of the Crusades and the Knights Templar. The Knights Templar were founded by Pope Innocent by papal bull in 1139 (*Omne Datum Optimum*) to defend the Holy Land and to restore Christian order and rule in Jerusalem. There has been much ink spilled on the topic, much of it of the spurious sort, for popular consumption. A few studies are recommended: Barber, *New Knighthood*; Nicholson, *Knights Hospitaller*; and Nicolle, *Knights of Jerusalem*. At a more popular level, yet still historically grounded, *God's Battalions* by Rodney Stark is a panegyric volume that seeks to correct modern myths about the Crusades.

68. Barber, "Introduction," in *New Knighthood*, 9.

69. Barber, "Introduction," in *New Knighthood*, 14; emphasis added.

70. Barber, "Introduction," in *New Knighthood*, 14.

71. Barber, "Introduction," in *New Knighthood*, 14; emphasis added.

72. Barber, "Introduction," in *New Knighthood*, 14.

So, in his exhortation to the Knights Templar, as in his commentary on Song of Songs, Bernard sees a deeper mystery at play in history. There is much more happening than one can visibly see in the battles for Jerusalem. For example, at one point, Bernard refers to the Muslim armies as "the children of disobedience,"[73] drawing upon St. Paul's description of sinful man in Ephesians.[74] He turns again to Ephesians and describes the Crusader battle for Jerusalem as "a twofold combat, against flesh and blood and against a spiritual host of evil in the heavens."[75] Again, in this last citation, Bernard is cognizant of the historical battle. He makes reference to literal even as he presses into the spiritual senses.

Drawing the lines ever closer between the holy cleric and holy warrior, Bernard writes, "And when war is waged by spiritual strength against vice or demons [literal, spiritual], this too, is nothing remarkable, though I consider it praiseworthy, *for the world is full of monks.*"[76] In addition to his continual references to the New Testament, Bernard draws upon the Old Testament, and not merely for context. For Bernard, it is the true spiritual foundation for the logic and direction of the battle to which the Knights Templar are summoned. In responding to the reality of the death of some of the soldiers, he looks to Ezekiel 18: "Behold, all souls are mine; the soul of the father as well as the soul of the son is mine: the soul that sins shall die" (v. 4).

Here, Bernard employs an Old Testament text to shore up the connection between the Knights Templar and the martyrs of Israel's battles that Ezekiel refers to: "Precious indeed in the sight of the Lord is the death of His holy ones, whether they die in battle or in bed, but death in battle is more precious as it is glorious . . . How truly holy and secure this knighthood and how entirely free of the double risk run by the kind of men who are at risk, but who do not fight for Christ's cause."[77]

One last point may be added to what has been discussed here. For Bernard, the location of the battle itself—the city of Jerusalem—is brought up out of the Old and New Testaments in a manner of spiritual ascent (see fig. 3). This city that they fight for is *the same one* in which the Temple of Solomon was built. The Knights Templar battle to regain

73. St. Bernard of Clairvaux, *In Praise of the New Knighthood*, 33.

74. See Eph 2:2.

75. St. Bernard of Clairvaux, *In Praise of the New Knighthood*, 33. See Eph 6:12.

76. St. Bernard of Clairvaux, *In Praise of the New Knighthood*, 33; emphasis added.

77. St. Bernard of Clairvaux, *In Praise of the New Knighthood*, 34–35; emphases added.

FIGURE 3. St. Bernard: "Jerusalem" in the Old Testament and in 1130.

the ground upon which Christ cleansed the Temple. Therefore it is not merely a medieval battlefield. It is a quest to restore the Promised Land. It was not lost on Bernard that the headquarters of the Templars themselves stood atop the ground of the house of the Lord:

Rejoice Jerusalem and recognize right now the time of your visitation! Be glad and give praise all at once ... The Lord has bared His arm in the sight of all of the nations. O virgin Israel, you had fallen and there was no one to raise you up.[78] Rise up now and shake off the dust, O virgin, O captive daughter of Zion[79] ... Do you not see how often these ancient witnesses authorize the new Knighthood? Surely what we have heard, we have now seen in the city of the Lord of hosts.[80]

Although more could be added, three points may be drawn from Bernard's *In Praise of the New Knighthood* as it bears upon our study. First, Bernard's appropriation of the Four Senses of Scripture, as in his commentary on Song of Songs, is evident here. He deals with history in a way that is literal yet, in looking beyond it, profoundly spiritual.

78. See Am 5:2: "The virgin of Israel is fallen; she shall no more rise: She is forsaken upon her land; there is none to raise her up" (KJV).

79. See Isa 52:2: "*Shake thyself from the dust; arise, and sit down, O Jerusalem*: Loose thyself from the bands of thy neck, O captive daughter of Zion" (KJV; emphasis added).

80. St. Bernard of Clairvaux, *In Praise of the New Knighthood*, 41–42. Adding a note of caution, Bernard writes: "At the same time, of course, we must not let *this literal interpretation* blind us to *the spiritual meaning of texts, for we must live in in eternal hope* in spite of such temporal realizations" (42; emphasis added).

Second, his exhortation draws upon both the Old and New Testaments in allegorizing events current to his age. This is a distinctive move. We will learn about another example of this sort in Joachim of Fiore (below). Yet, in contrast to Joachim, Bernard is on firm ground. Even in his allegorizing, he keeps the literal and spiritual distinct, for example, "*for we must live in in eternal hope in spite of such temporal realizations*" (emphasis added). Bernard has no appetite for mixing the senses. He does not sacrifice the one for the other, nor is the literal subsumed into the spiritual in such a way that it is lost. Nor does his allegorizing allow him for a moment to lose sight of the true eternal hope that is only realized through Christ himself. These are serious problems for Joachim of Fiore.

Third and finally, there is unquestionably a notion of ascent throughout the exhortation. This is especially the case as the holy Knights Templar—fighting in both the natural and supernatural realms—whom he contrasts with the merely earthly warriors, "who are at double risk," at the literal level and at the spiritual level. "The world is full of monks," Bernard wrote. And he summoned them to a new knighthood and a new battle that would be fought according to both the Letter and the Spirit.

8. *Exemplum Octo*: Hugh of St. Victor

We turn next to Hugh of St. Victor's "To the New Student of Sacred Scripture." Hugh begins his instruction as follows: "To the eager student, first of all it ought to be known that sacred Scripture has three ways of conveying meaning—namely, history, allegory, and tropology."[81] As Hugh continues, he is careful not to force any of the senses upon a biblical text. Nor does he subject Scripture texts to this process, so that they have to be explained according to all the senses. "To be sure, all things in the divine utterance must not be wrenched to an interpretation such that each of them is held to contain history, allegory, and tropology all at once. Even if a triple meaning can appropriately be assigned in many passages, nevertheless it is either difficult or impossible

81. Hugh of St. Victor, "To the New Student of Sacred Scripture," 159. As noted above, Hugh maintains three, not four, senses of Scripture: the literal, allegorical, and tropological. This in no way implies a negation of the anagogical. Rather, anagogy is the natural outgrowth of the ascent that transpires within the dynamic between the allegorical and the tropological. (See fig. 1.)

to see it everywhere. It is necessary, therefore, so to handle the sacred Scripture that we assign individual things fittingly in their own places, as reason demands."[82]

Next, Hugh develops an extended metaphor—that of constructing a building. In so doing, he illustrates how the Four Senses work in a dynamic fashion. One builds upon the other in such a way that the former is not dissolved. Rather, it is *subsumed* into the ascending senses. Hugh writes, "In the order of study of sacred Scripture, *history precedes allegory and tropology*. In this question it is not without value to call to mind what we see happen in the construction of buildings—where first the foundation is laid, then the structure is raised upon it, and finally, when the work is all finished, the house is decorated by the laying on of color."[83]

First, as expected, Hugh insists that the literal sense proceeds the allegorical and tropological senses. Through the metaphor of the raising of a building, the Four Senses are not replacing those previously laid down; rather, they build upon one another in an orderly fashion. Next, Hugh provides examples of how the Old Testament needs to be read allegorically. He even specifies which books should be read first: "I think the ones to be studied most are: Genesis, Exodus, Joshua, the Book of Judges, and that of Kings, and Chronicles."[84]

Notably, Hugh does not ask the new student of Scripture to wait until his studies of the Old Testament are completed before proceeding to the New Testament. Rather, it is more a question of gaining as much perspective about Christ in the Old Testament through allegorical reading: "I am not now saying that you should first struggle to unfold the figures of the Old Testament and penetrate its mystical sayings before you come to the gospel streams you must drink from. But just as you see that every building lacking a foundation cannot stand firm, so also is it in learning."[85]

82. Hugh of St. Victor, "To the New Student of Sacred Scripture," 159.

83. Hugh of St. Victor, "To the New Student of Sacred Scripture," 160; emphasis added.

84. Hugh of St. Victor, "To the New Student of Sacred Scripture," 161.

85. Hugh of St. Victor, "To the New Student of Sacred Scripture," 161. "The foundation and principle of sacred learning is history, from which, like honey from the honeycomb, the truth of allegory is extracted. As you are about to build, therefore, lay first the foundation of history; next, by pursuing the 'typical' meaning, build up a structure in your mind to be a fortress of faith. Last of all, however, through the loveliness of morality, paint the structure over as with the most beautiful of colors."

Finally, as Hugh continues to instruct the new Scripture student, he points the entire building metaphor at the soul of the reader as something to be interiorized: "See now, you have come to your study. You are about to construct the spiritual building, the spiritual structure. Already the foundations of history *have been laid in you. It remains now that you found the bases of the superstructure.*"[86] What does Hugh have in mind for the student to do, to build on the foundations of history from the literal sense? To move into spiritual senses—the allegorical and the tropological, to flesh out the "superstructure" (see fig. 4).

Then, as one moves into the spiritual senses, Hugh adds one additional piece of instruction: "The very bases of your spiritual structure are certain principles of the faith—principles which form your starting point. Truly, the judicious student ought to be sure that, before he makes his way through extensive volumes, he is so instructed in the particulars which bear upon his task and upon *his profession of the true faith*, that he may safely be able to build onto his structure whatever he afterwards finds."[87]

Hugh invites the student of Scripture to apply *the infused virtues*, by nature of his Baptism in Christ, to bear on the interpretation of Scripture. The truths of the faith that one has received, through instruction and through the liturgy, are brought to bear on the interpretation of Scripture. He then lists a number of Catholic doctrines, beginning with the mystery of the Trinity: "First learn briefly and clearly what is to be believed about the Trinity, what you ought unquestionably to profess and truthfully to believe."[88] From the Trinity, he continues: "Thus should you do concerning the mystery of the altar, thus concerning the mystery of baptism, that of confirmation, that of marriage, and all which were enumerated for you above."[89] Notice that, to the Blessed Trinity, Hugh adds the sacramental order; first, the Eucharist (i.e., the mystery of the altar) followed by the other sacraments (i.e., Baptism, Confirmation, and Marriage).

In conclusion, this example from Hugh of St. Victor substantiates our thesis in at least two significant ways. First, Hugh insists upon engaging the Scriptures according to both the *Letter* and the *Spirit.* Both

86. Hugh of St. Victor, "To the New Student of Sacred Scripture," 164; emphasis added.
87. Hugh of St. Victor, "To the New Student of Sacred Scripture," 164; emphasis added.
88. Hugh of St. Victor, "To the New Student of Sacred Scripture," 164.
89. Hugh of St. Victor, "To the New Student of Sacred Scripture," 164.

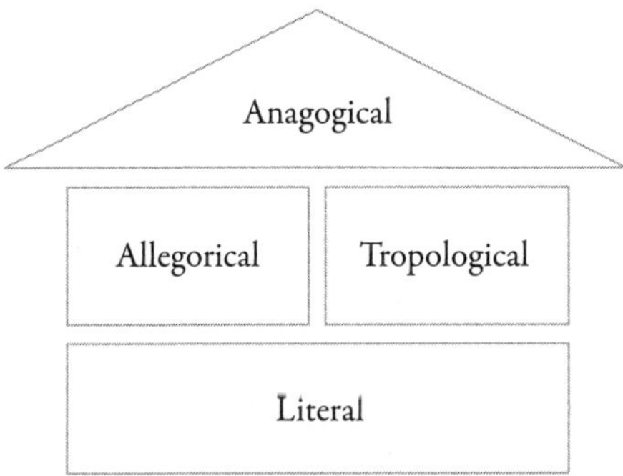

FIGURE 4. Hugh of St. Victor and the "Superstructure" of the Four Senses.

are necessary. And it is not merely his inclusion of both that is significant. It is also that his building metaphor makes it plain that the senses of Scripture represent a pathway and progression for spiritual growth. According to Hugh, without this movement—from the literal to the spiritual—such progress is not possible. Second, Hugh's instruction, brief as it is, brings the reality of the Sacraments to the interpretation of Scripture. His hermeneutic is entirely Trinitarian and Eucharistic. The grace of the sacraments assists one's growth in faith, charity, and hope. Hugh's instruction is a melding of the senses of Scripture with the theological virtues, flowing out of one's cooperation with the grace of God.

9. *Exemplum Novem*: Alain of Lilly and Dante Alighieri

This penultimate example presents itself from two distinct poetic sources; namely, Alain of Lilly[90] and Dante Alighieri. What they share in common is the way the logic of the Four Senses is extended beyond Scripture and into artistic interpretation. Key distinctions are noted as it pertains to biblical exegesis. Nevertheless, the example they offer is worthy of inclusion here.

Alain of Lilly was a French theologian and poet, widely known as Doctor Universalis. Alain pushed back against the rising tide of Scho-

90. "Lilly" is pronounce *lēēl.*

lasticism and was characterized by both mysticism and reason. He was likely educated by Peter Abelard, and is said to have attended the Third Lateran Council in 1179. His comfort with allegory is evident in the following quote: "Poetry's lyre rings with vibrant falsehood *on the outward literal shell* of a poem, but interiorly it communicates *a hidden and profound meaning* to those who listen."[91] Notice that this movement—from the literal and outer meaning to the inner, hidden one—is not, as in previous examples, in relation to Sacred Scripture. Rather, he is describing a *poem*. Alain's example, which is extrabiblical in nature, requires a few additional remarks to more fully understand the basis upon which his comments on poetry.

To begin with, this appropriation of the Four Senses of Scripture—and more specifically the allegorizing of biblical texts—was made possible because of the broader sacramental worldview of the time. This was the case across Christianized Europe. It was especially true in Alain's city of Lilly, in the northern region of French Flanders, prior to the Hundred Years' War.[92] The purveyors of High Middle Ages not only accepted the *l'ordre sacramentel* of the patristic period. They also applied and extended it further than before. This even pertained to nonbiblical texts, such as Alain's poem. Alain's comments are at home within this framework. At approximately the same time, Hugh of St. Victor rather famously remarked, "The whole sense-perceptible world is like a sort of book written by the finger of God."[93] Hugh's description is an apt one and well summarizes the sacramental worldview, particularly in the High Middle Ages. This view of reality, in which the Church (and indeed the entire world) is, in some sense, a sacrament was undergirded and supported by the Four Senses of Scripture.[94]

The Scriptures alone are the inspired Word of God, yet the mindset of deeper mysteries and signification is nonetheless at play, even in a poem. This sacramental worldview was firmly established long before

91. Alain de Lille, *De planctu naturae* (*The Complaint of Nature*), cited in Chenu, *Nature, Man, and Society*, 117; emphasis added.

92. For more on this period of Catholic history in France, see Rider and Murray, *Galbert of Bruges*; Jones, *Before Church and State*.

93. Cited in Chenu, *Nature, Man, and Society*, 117.

94. This motif of *sacrement du monde* turns up in the theological anthropology of St. Pope John Paul II. He writes, "*The sacrament of the world*, and the sacrament of man in the world, comes forth from the divine source of holiness and is instituted, at the same time, for holiness." *Man and Woman He Created Them*, 204.

the time of Alain, Dante, and Hugh of St. Victor. In his important study of early patristic exegesis, *The Bible and the Liturgy*, Daniélou described how figures and shadows of the Old Testament prefigured the realities in the New Testament. Nevertheless, many biblical scholars have discussed biblical typology in similar ways. What distinguishes Daniélou's work from most others (especially Protestant studies of typology) is that he did not stop with the New Testament antitype. Rather, he traced this typological paradigm through, into the history of the primitive Church.

In a fascinating study of Christian Baptism and baptismal rites, the Eucharist, Confirmation, and other topics, Daniélou showed that *typology did not end in the Gospels.* Rather, biblical typology carried through into the sacramental life of the primitive Church: "The sacraments carry into our midst the *mirabilia*, the great works of God in the Old Testament and in the New."[95] In other words, the sacraments are by extension the continuation of the great works of God of the Old and New Testaments, into history itself: "So, the sacraments were seen as the great events in sacred history, the *mirabilia* which fill the space of between the *gloriosa Ascensio* and the glorious Parousia."[96] This sacramental understanding of the world pervaded the patristic and medieval periods. It was intimately connected to and supported by the Four Senses of Scripture. Even the above example from the High Middle Ages, Alain's description of a poem as containing a hidden and profound meaning beyond its "outer shell" is best understood in this light.

95. Jean Daniélou, *The Bible and the Liturgy*, 5. Elsewhere he writes: "The sacraments are conceived in relation to the acts of God in the Old Testament and the New. God acts in the world; His actions are the mirabilia, the deeds that are His alone. God creates, judges, makes a covenant, is present, makes holy, delivers. These same acts are carried out in the different phases of the history of salvation. There is, then, a fundamental analogy between these actions. *The sacraments are simply the continuation in the era of the Church of God's acts in the Old Testament and the New*. This is the proper significance of the relationship between the Bible and the liturgy. The Bible is a sacred history; the liturgy is a sacred history. The Bible is a witness given to real events; it is a sacred history. There is a profane history, which is that of civilizations, witnessing to the great deeds done by men. But the Bible is *the history of divine actions*; it witnesses to the great deeds carried out by God. It is all for the glory of God. And so it is the proper object of faith. For 'to believe' does not mean only to believe that God exists, but also that He intervenes in human life. Faith is wholly concerned with these interventions of God: the covenant, the incarnation, the resurrection, the diffusion of the Spirit. And the Old Testament in particular is already essentially a sacred history." Daniélou, "Sacraments and the History of Salvation," in *The Liturgy and the Word of God*, 28; emphases added.

96. Daniélou, *The Bible and the Liturgy*, 199.

Before directing our attention to medieval Florence, and therefore to Dante, one more remark needs to be added about Alain. Reminiscent of descriptions of the spiritual senses of Scripture, he writes, "The man who reads with penetration, *having cast away the outer shell of falsehood, finds the savory kernel of truth wrapped within*."[97] The careful reader may have detected something of a dichotomy in Alain, with his outer shell of falsehood versus the savory kernel of truth within. This paradox in his poetry is not representative of the unified progression in truth, in the literal-to-anagogical framework of the Four Senses of Scripture.

With this we turn from Alain to Dante Alighieri and *La Divina Commedia*. Dante expressed the importance of the distinction between the inspired Word. Literary compositions such as poetry were merely human: *veritade ascosa sotto bella menzogna*. Translated from Italian, it is the idea of a "truth hidden beneath a beautiful lie."[98]

Dante scholar Prue Shaw explains, "The poet *invents a fiction*—makes up a story—in order to convey a truth. Poets' allegory differs from allegory as understood by theologians precisely in this respect—that is, in the relationship of the literal meaning to truth or fact. The distinction is a crucial one."[99] Even so, such poetic examples demonstrate how allegory was in no way limited to the Sacred Page. It was infused in poetry and other forms of art and literature: "The same men who read the Grail story and the homilies of St. Bernard, carved the capitals of Chartres and composed bestiaries, allegorized Ovid and scrutinized the typological senses of the Bible, or enriched their christological analysis of the sacraments with naturalistic symbols of water, light, eating, marriage."[100] Chenu asks directly, "How can one write the history of Christian doctrines, let alone that of theological science, without taking into consideration this recourse to symbols—to symbols drawn from nature, from history, from liturgical practice—which continually nourished both doctrine and theology?"[101]

97. Alain de Lille, *De planctu naturae*, in Chenu, *Nature, Man, and Society*, 99; emphasis added. Similarly, Congar writes: "For the Fathers and the early Middle Ages, the sacred actions performed in the Church, according to the forms of the Church, and are rigorously sacred as such. But their subject is God, in an actual and direct way." *Tradition and Traditions*, 135.

98. Dante, cited in Shaw, *Reading Dante*, 160–69 (Canto 16).

99. Shaw, *Reading Dante*, 80; emphasis added.

100. Chenu, *Nature, Man, and Society*, 101.

101. Chenu, *Nature, Man, and Society*, 101.

In addition to the work of Alain of Lilly, poetic examples of this sort are evident in Dante, who was not averse to such descriptions. Consider Canto IX from his *Inferno*. Anthony Esolen offers a concise bit of context about this canto: "Waiting for the angel from Heaven, the poets see the Furies upon the ramparts and hear them call for the Gargon, Medusa, the sight of whom could turn a man to stone. Virgil shields Dante from looking at her. At last the angel arrives and opens the gates. Dante and Virgil now enter the sixth circle, where the heretics are confined to the tombs of fire."[102]

As Medusa stares down at the two of them, Virgil shuts Dante's eyes, to assure he does not gaze upon her in a moment of weakness.[103] In the following lines, Dante writes,

> O voi ch'avete li'ntelletti sani,
> mirate la dottrina che s'asconde
> sotto 'l velame de li versi strani.[104]

Esolen translates these lines as follows:

> O you whose intellects see clear and whole,
> Gaze on the doctrine that is hidden here
> Beneath the unfamiliar verses veil.[105]

Commenting on this text, Dante scholar Guy Raffa explains, "When Dante interrupts the narrative to instruct his (smart) readers to 'note the doctrine hidden under the veil of the strange verses,' he calls upon the popular medieval of allegorical reading. Commonly applied to sacred texts (namely, the Bible), allegory, in its various forms, assumes that other, deeper levels of meaning (often spiritual) lie beneath the surface, in addition to (or in place of) the literal meaning of the words."[106] Raffa's assessment is helpful and mostly correct, although one clarification is necessary. Patristic and medieval interpreters of Scripture did not seek to replace the literal meaning with the spiritual senses. To the contrary, as St. Thomas stressed, the literal sense is the foundation of biblical exegesis. The move to the spiritual senses does not proceed without it.[107]

102. This is Esolen's comment, pertaining to Dante's *Inferno*, 87.
103. See Dante, *Inferno*, Canto 9, ll. 52–59.
104. Dante, *Inferno*, Canto 90, ll. 61–63.
105. Dante, *Inferno*, Canto 90, ll. 61–63.
106. Raffa, *Complete Danteworlds*, 44.
107. See chap. 2 in this volume.

There is meaning at *all levels* of the text, and one does not supplant the Letter (as if it is devoid of meaning) with the Spirit. Rather, one works through the text and discovers the literal meaning. Then and *only* then, one moves from the literal to the spiritual sense, confident that the inspired Word has still greater mysteries to be revealed to the reader with the eyes of faith. This clarification notwithstanding, Raffa correctly asserts that in the text from Canto IX, Dante's comment "Gaze on the doctrine that is hidden here / Beneath the unfamiliar verses veil" presupposes that there is a deeper allegorical meaning *in his poem*, just as there is in the veil of biblical texts.

Added to this intriguing text from the *Inferno* is a letter from the age of Dante concerning the interpretation of his *Purgatorio.*[108] There is debate among Dante scholars over the letter's authorship. Some scholars have concluded that it was penned by Dante himself. Others believe it was a scholarly figure other than Dante, from within his circle of friends.[109] I am convinced, however, upon the scholarship of Richard Lansing, of its authenticity with regard to authorship by Dante himself.[110] Regardless, the content of the letter is relevant to the present *Exemplum*.

Contextually, in Canto II of the *Purgatorio*, the souls are singing a text from the Psalms, "When Israel went out of Egypt."[111] Regarding this biblical text, the "Dante letter" reads as follows:

> Now if we look at the *letter* alone, what is signified to us is the departure of the sons of Israel from Egypt during the time of Moses; if at the allegory, what is signified to us is our redemption through Christ; if at the moral sense, what is signified to us is the conversion of the soul from the sorrow and misery of sin to the state of grace; if at the anagogical, what is signified to us is the departure of the sanctified soul from bondage to the corruption of this world into the freedom of eternal glory.[112]

108. Specifically, the letter concerns Canto 2, ll. 46–48 of Dante's *Purgatory*.

109. See Raffa, *Complete Danteworlds*, 134; Shaw, *Reading Dante*, 205–62.

110. See "Dante on Allegory," in Lansing, *Dante Encyclopedia*, 26–27.

111. See *Purgatory*, Canto 2, 46–48. The biblical text is from Ps 114: "When Israel went forth from Egypt, the house of Jacob from a people of strange language."

112. Haller, *Literary Criticism of Dante*, 99; emphasis added. This letter is known as *Epistle* X of Dante, also known as "The Letter to Can Grande." See also Raffa, *Complete Danteworlds*, 134–35.

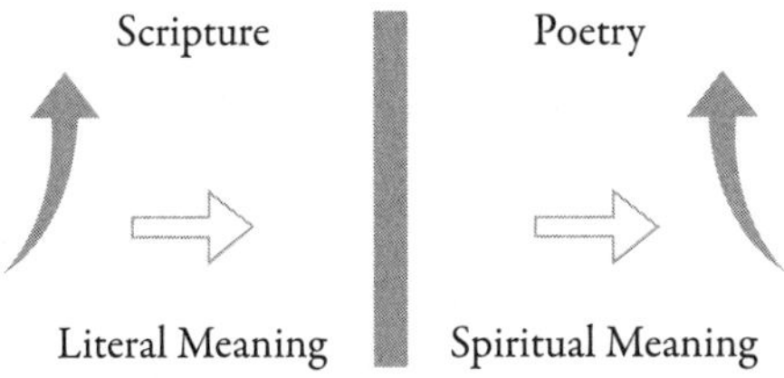

FIGURE 5. The literal and spiritual senses in Scripture and Dante.

St. Thomas's viewpoint in the *Summa* seems to rule out any notion of any humanly composed writing on having within it an allegorical or figural sense, the way that the inspired Scriptures do: "The multiplicity of these senses does not produce equivocation or any other kind of multiplicity, seeing that these senses are not multiplied because one word signifies several things; but because the things signified by the words can be themselves types of other things. Thus, in Holy Writ no confusion results, *for all the senses are founded on one—the literal—from which alone can any argument be drawn, and not from those intended in allegory*, as Augustine says (*Epistle* xlviii)."[113] Nevertheless, Thomas is careful to add, "nothing of Holy Scripture perishes because of this, since nothing necessary to faith is contained under the spiritual sense which is not elsewhere put forward by the Scripture in its literal sense."[114]

In summarizing Thomas's perspective, Lansing writes, "Only God could write signification into history and into created things and . . . human writers could only write a literal sense that contained the whole intention of the author (including any figurative language) should have ruled out a 'figurally' composed *Commedia*"[115] (see fig. 5). In other words, Dante's use of the fourfold sense of Scripture in the *Epistle* "appeared to many as a provocative appropriation *by a human author of a technique Aquinas reserved for Scripture.*"[116] Regardless of such debates,

113. St. Thomas Aquinas, *ST* I, q. 10, a. 10, ad 1; emphasis added.

114. St. Thomas Aquinas, *ST* I, q. 10, a. 10, ad 1.

115. "Dante's Allegory and the Critics," in Lansing, *Dante Encyclopedia*, 28.

116. "Dante's Allegory and the Critics," in Lansing, *Dante Encyclopedia*, 28; emphasis added. Even so, "early commentators, like Guido da Pisa, and Dante's son Pietro, *ratify the appropriation . . . and open the way to later assertions by Boccaccio and Petrarch that poetry is the peer of theology*" (28; emphasis added).

Lansing correctly judges the broader implications as it pertains to this study: "The prominence of allegory in Dante's work is, ultimately, a reflection of the prominence of allegorical thinking in the Middle Ages. The centrality of the notion of the 'book as symbol' to medieval culture was long ago pointed out ... and the centrality of both allegory and language to Dante's project is implicit in *Dante's choice of the use of a book to express how all of Creation is held, in archetype, in the mind of God* ... Dante's poem is at once *theological* and *logo-logical:* in the beginning *and in the end is the Word.*"[117]

Finally, the texts of Alain of Lilly and Dante, like the previous example from St. Bernard of Clairvaux, are a departure from the array of patristic and medieval examples provided here in that they involve extrabiblical elements such as poetry and warfare. These examples, along with the final one below, were included precisely for this reason: they illustrate that the pathway and progression through the Four Senses was not limited to Scripture alone. Rather, such biblical exegesis—from meaning to deeper meaning, from the Letter to the Spirit, ascending upward toward the contemplation of God—had a remarkable influence in the first millennium, flowing out of the Scripture and into the larger sacramental worldview in this period.

10. *Exemplum Decem*: Joachim of Fiore

In this final example, we look to the schema of history as proposed by Joachim of Fiore, the twelfth-century monk and founder of the order of San Giovani in southern Italy. Joachim had an intense conversion while on pilgrimage to the Holy Land in 1159. As one medieval historian observes, these spiritual experiences "were destined to have a notable influence on the religious world and the theological ideas of the next century."[118] Joachim's worldview was founded on the Sacred Scriptures. But

117. "Allegory in All Things," in Lansing, *Dante Encyclopedia*, 32; emphases added. "Inevitably, the book in God's mind is mirrored i*n Dante's poem, the book that records it, each being an allegory of the other*" (emphasis added). See Dante, *Paradise*, Canto 33, ll. 84–87.

118. D'Onofrio, *History of Theology*, 248. "Many factors, including his own immediate personal experiences, fused to produce Joachim's unique spiritual and prophetic vocation. These were *the missionary spirit of the crusader ideal, the longing for monastic perfection*, and the pauperism of *the popular religious movements* and the impulse to evangelical revival that inspired them. But there were also influences from *the lively movement of reform* that swept through Byzantine monasticism in the eleventh and twelfth centuries ... A detailed

he developed his own language on the basis of the sacred text. D'Onofrio finds that Joachim's reading of biblical texts is "not of a rational and conceptional kind; rather, it adheres closely to *the revealed truth* and is therefore *profoundly visionary*."[119] Moreover, he did not embrace the classical framework of the three spiritual senses; rather, he held to at least five spiritual or mystical senses.[120]

In a series of four related works on the Scriptures, and particularly on the Book of Revelation,[121] Joachim developed a symbolic vision of history, the chief aim of which was to draw the reader nearer to God himself. Most controversial was his schema of history. It not only built upon the symbolic meaning of the Old Testament, transferred into the New. But it also rested upon the *New Testament itself.* Joachim's approach was modeled upon the Blessed Trinity. Accordingly, there were three "concords" (spiritual ages): the Age of the Father, prior to the advent of Christ; the Age of the Son; and the Age of the Spirit, the latter of which was the time from the Ascension of Christ until his future Parousia.[122]

This was a revolutionary appropriation of the New Testament that transgressed the way it had been handled nearly universally until this time. Eventually, Joachim's esoteric and speculative ideas about the Trinity were condemned at the Fourth Lateran Council in 1215. Even so, Dante interestingly placed him in Paradise in the *Commedia*.[123] Joa-

knowledge of the Fathers and of the early monastic ascetical tradition served to unify several elements of this synthesis by rooting them directly in the fruitful, integrative earth that feeds all of Christian truth, *namely Sacred Scripture*" (249).

119. D'Onofrio, *History of Theology*, 251; emphasis added.

120. See de Lubac, *Medieval Exegesis*, vol. 3, 329.

121. The main works of Joachim, in which he developed his schema of history, are *Concordia novi et veteris Testamenti* (*Concord, Old and New Testament*); *Expositio in Apocalypsim* (*Exposition of the Apocalypse*); *Psalterium decem chordarum* (*Harp of Ten Strings*); and *Super quatuor evangelia* (*The Four Gospels*). "There is no room to look for an evolution of any importance in his thought, which is systematically expressed in all four texts . . . A few differences in terminology or presentation do not undermine their coherence." De Lubac, *Medieval Exegesis*, vol. 3, 328.

122. See de Lubac, *Medieval Exegesis*, vol. 3, 327*ff.* Joachim's larger schema is complex, and its many details need not concern us here. Only a few key details may be sketched out here. First, Joachim articulated his understanding of history as a "concord of the letter" (*concordia litterae*), composed of three essential states: "before grace" (i.e., before Christ"), "under grace" (i.e., the time of Christ"), and "fuller grace" (i.e., the future time which he soon expected, in which "spiritual man" would be guided to perfection by the Spirit. The entire schema was Trinitarian in nature.

123. See Dante, *Paradise*, Canto 33, 115–20; Richard K. Emmerson, "Joachim of Fiore," in Lansing, *Dante Encyclopedia*, 537–38.

chim's notion of the eternal Gospel was particularly circumspect and detrimental to Christian orthodoxy. He posited that in the future, in the Age of the Spirit,

> The eternal gospel would bring humanity a future of peace and of understanding of the divine will through an understanding that is spiritual because it is given by the Spirit . . . The Age of the Spirit [was] the goal and resolution of the entire theology of history: a complex system of [numeric] calculations based on the data of Scripture, together with an authentic interpretation of the Old and New Testament prophecies, led the prophet to foretell the end of all wars, punitive coercions, and earthly sovereignties and the triumph of peace through the establishment of a new order, that of spiritual human beings who find their true freedom in the truth, and the model of Christ.[124]

In de Lubac's assessment, Joachim's vision of history was "properly trinitarian . . . There are three states of the world because there are three persons of the divinity."[125] Problematically, however, Joachim's schema is a kind of progressive pedagogy in that God "guides his elect by stages 'from virtue to virtue' and 'from clarity unto clarity.'"[126] Particularly troublesome was Joachim's understanding of the Four Gospels as *inchoative*, that is, the beginning of a state that would later be completed or perfected. Only in the coming Third Age of the Spirit would the mysteries of both the Old and New Testaments be realized by those belonging to the Spirit: "Then what had till then remained hidden within these Four Gospels will come to light for all . . . Only then will the kerchief that covers the head of Jesus be removed . . . Then, as in the third day at Cana, this third period will be the time for wedding: the Church, made new again, will be joined to her heavenly Spouse."[127]

Joachim truly believed that in this coming Third Age a new religion would begin. In the process, a purified and virginal Church would emerge, "a Church not of scholars or doctors *but of contemplatives*."[128] In prophetic jubilation, Joachim wrote: "Happy the men who will no longer have any desire for worldly things! Happy the Church in this third state! *A Church completely free at last* . . . where there will no longer be laboring and groaning, but repose and leisure and abundance of peace!

124. D'Onofrio, *History of Theology*, 251.
125. De Lubac, *Medieval Exegesis*, vol. 3, 339.
126. De Lubac, *Medieval Exegesis*, vol. 3, 338, citing Joachim.
127. De Lubac, *Medieval Exegesis*, vol. 3, 338–39.
128. De Lubac, *Medieval Exegesis*, vol. 3, 339; emphasis added.

O universal joy! O fulfillment of our perfection! ... O third heaven! O happy time of Rachel! O time of the effusion of the Spirit! To sum up: O time of spiritual understanding... *of the beginning of 'the anagogical understanding' which ought to be that of eternity.*"[129]

As the discussion of this final example draws to a close, several questions emerge: (1) What is one to make of Joachim's prophetic and apocalyptic schema of history, with his divisions of time into the Three Ages? (2) What does it say about our thesis, of the Four Senses as a pathway and progression toward the face of God?

As to the first question, his spiritual arithmetic did not curry favor with the Church. As indicated, a number of his concepts were refuted at Lateran IV. Many of his ideas were so innovative yet so unorthodox that de Lubac sets Joachim of Fiore apart from "all others, whether ancient or medieval."[130] Whereas the collective voice of the Church used symbolism in a chiefly theological or moral way, Joachim pressed it into service as a prophetic vision of history from his age until the end of time.[131]

De Lubac underscores the singularity of Joachim in this respect, stating that he had "not merely pressed further but ... radically changed the traditional idea ... The concord that he sings is not the same as the one sung before him."[132] As de Lubac summarizes, what Joachim had developed crossed a threshold that had theretofore not been crossed: "It is no longer the correspondence of history to the mystery, of the figure to the deep reality, or of the letter to the spirit."[133]

The second question, as to the import of Joachim on our thesis, requires additional comment. First, his errors notwithstanding, Joachim's

129. Joachim of Fiore, cited in de Lubac, *Medieval Exegesis*, vol. 3, 339; emphases added.

130. De Lubac, *Medieval Exegesis*, vol. 3, 342.

131. See de Lubac, *Medieval Exegesis*, vol. 3, 342.

132. De Lubac, *Medieval Exegesis*, vol. 3, 342.

133. De Lubac, *Medieval Exegesis*, vol. 3, 342. "The whole exegesis proceeds from *an extreme literalism*—upon which an extreme prophetic spiritualism has just been superimposed—and this spiritualism, in wanting to be realized from the beginning of this earth and within time, transforms itself once again into its contrary ... The period that he holds as idyllic is not what behind him, but the one that lies ahead. His doctrine is an 'anti-primitivism;' it is a doctrine of progress ... Naturally, he criticizes the present condition of the Church, especially that of the religious orders. The 'modern religion' seems to him to have fallen from the 'primitive form of the Church ... The first age was a dark sky; the second unfolded by the light of the moon; soon the heaven of spiritual understanding will shine on the third. Joachim also loves to recall that the young will hold sway over the old. His third age, as we have seen, is a qualified sense, will be a new religion [*nova religio*]" (344).

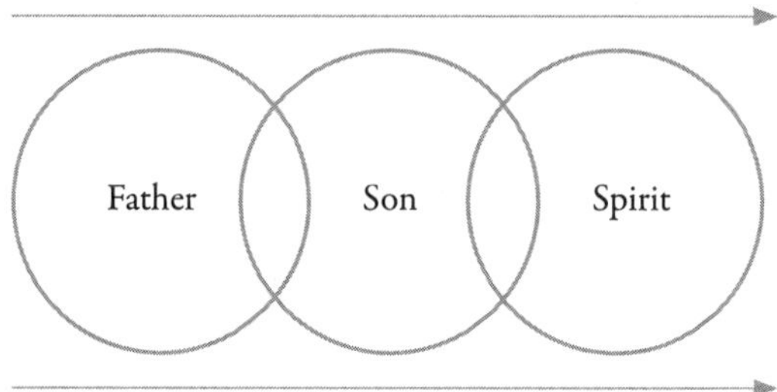

FIGURE 6. The three ages of history in Joachim of Fiore.

prophetic vision of history is undoubtedly rooted in the patristic and medieval notion of *ascent*, and the understanding of Scripture as a pathway and progression. Yet, rather than conceive of this ascent in the believer's soul (or even the entire Church), he extrapolated it into a schema of history, shrink-wrapped over reality itself. This is problematic, as is his progressive understanding of perfection within the Age of the Spirit. In fact, Joachim's understanding of a coming dispensation of the Spirit—which would surpass that dispensation of Christ himself—is deeply flawed and is the chief reason for his condemnation. Second, most patristic and medieval thinkers viewed the Four Senses in an integrated and cohesive way. As one ascended to the anagogical, sin and temptation persisted. One appropriated the hopes of heavenly glory in the soul in the here and now and yet still experienced all the pangs of the fallen world. For the ancients and medieval, anagogy really changed things. Still, the ascent to heaven continued gradually, amidst daily struggles and stumbles.

Not so for Joachim. He viewed the literal and (many) spiritual senses as a kind of sequential code that revealed Three Ages: the Age of the Father, which spanned from Creation until the Annunciation; the Age of the Son, that is, the lifetime of Jesus and his ministry on earth; and finally, the Age of the Spirit, begun at Pentecost. This last age was a mystical one in which "the spiritual man" would, in a time yet to come, reach spiritual perfection (fig. 6).

Third and finally, Joachim's problematic schema of history reflects—albeit in a negative fashion—the balance and logic, the reasonability and rationality that subsisted in orthodox thinkers in their appropriation of the Four Senses. In other words, by way of relief, Joachim's extremes underscore the stability and consistence of the appropriation of the Four Senses over a thousand-plus years. Without question, Joachim's approach is fraught with deep flaws and serious overreaches. Even so, his work brings two significant contributions to our thesis: the literal and spiritual senses are his matrix through which all of Scripture and all of reality are comprehended, and his appropriation of the Scriptures, especially through the Spiritual senses, is a pathway and progression to the face of God—despite the serious, critical flaws within his progressive, spiritualized view of history and its coming time of perfection in the Church of the future.

This brings an end to our discussion of ten *Exempla*, each of which supports our thesis and fills out the picture of its inner workings from the second to the thirteenth centuries. Next, a few remarks bring the present chapter—and the *Exordium* as a whole—to a close.

Concluding Remarks

There is a passageway that leads through the Four Senses. If pursued, it takes the student of Scripture far beyond that which may be drawn out from the literal sense alone. More specifically, our thesis is that, collectively, the Four Senses are a pathway and a progression in the contemplation of the face of God in a threefold movement. The starting point of this thesis is the decisive move from the literal to the spiritual senses, from history into mystery (Movement 1). As de Lubac insisted, "We do not have the right through 'negligence' to deprive ourselves of the many allegories of which history is so full."[134]

The next stage involves both the allegorical and the tropological senses. The former contemplates the person of Christ. The latter, Christ within the soul. Here, a spiraling pattern is detected between the objective Christ and the subjective Christ, and back again in a repetitive fashion (Movement 2). Deeper conversion is the result of this symbiosis between the allegorical and tropological senses. Finally, as the allegorical and tropological begin to converge, perfection deepens in the soul, through the theological virtues of faith and charity. This momentum of ascent is the chief characteristic of the anagogical sense (Movement 3).

134. De Lubac, *Medieval Exegesis,* vol. 1, 84.

Gradually, the soul makes progress in the pathway to God, aided by the theological virtue of hope.[135]

Throughout the first millennium of Church history and into the second, there was vast—in fact, virtually universal—acceptance that the optimal approach to the Scriptures was "from the seen to the unseen," that is, from the literal and into the spiritual senses. The latter part of the chapter presented ten examples from the early patristic period through the High Middle Ages. Accordingly, our thesis does not rest upon speculation. It is substantiated by the history of the ancient and medieval exegesis, evidenced through a breadth of diverse sources. Our thesis is firmly anchored and may be restated: *the Four Senses of Scripture are a pathway and progression leading to the face of God* himself.

This completes the *Exordium* and Part I. In Part II, *Vetus Testamentum*, we turn to the biblical encounter scenes—five in all, from across the canon of the Old Testament. There, our thesis is further demonstrated as specific texts in Scripture are broken open according to the Four Senses. At the outset of *Vetus Testamentum*, a few words of orientation assist the reader in understanding the manner and method by which all the encounter scenes are examined.

135. Figures 1–4 offer a visual framework in which to see the pathway and progression from the literal to the anagogical senses. The reader is encouraged to return to them as often as needed. They not only inform the present discussion but also serve as a visual reference for subsequent study. See also "The Liturgical Cosmos: The Worldview of the High Middle Ages (Part 1 of 3)," YouTube video, 1:01:37, posted by Franciscan University of Steubenville, January 15, 2016, https://www.youtube.com/watch?v=GpdD6a-TYss.

PART II

Vetus Testamentum

Introductory Remarks

This chapter is a decisive turning point in the book. In Part I (*Exordium*), the reader was introduced to the topic of "seeking the face of the Lord" (chap. 1). Following this, I provided a detailed discussion of the Four Senses of Scripture and their import for this study (chap. 2). There, the primary thesis of the book was presented: that the Four Senses of Sacred Scripture represent a pathway and a progression toward the face of the Lord. This thesis was further clarified and corroborated with data from ten literary examples. Finally, we came to understand the unity of Four Senses as a totality, and the way they help us ascend to the face of the Lord (chap. 3).

Now we turn directly to the Scriptures themselves, with the fuller calculus of all the Letter and the Spirit and not merely one or the other to guide us toward the meaning of the text. Here, we apply the knowledge gained through the *Exordium* to a number of encounter scenes within the Old Testament. Before turning to the first, a few remarks will be helpful for the reader, to give an idea as to (1) the overall method involved in the discussion of this scene (and all subsequent ones) and (2) the format of these discussions.

First, as to our methodology, the overall approach that is embraced here is that of Catholic biblical interpretation, and our hermeneutic is animated by faith, not "suspicion." It is not necessary to further delineate what is and is not involved in such an approach. The lodestar that guides our hermeneutic is *Dei Verbum*. Elsewhere, I have articulated the particular principles of such an approach, which similarly need not be repeated here.[1]

Each encounter scene is examined from the literal before moving to the spiritual senses. The literal sense is intrinsic to every search for meaning in the text—and historical inquiry is "indispensable" in this regard.[2] The primary objective of our work within the literal sense will be *to locate the author's intentions in a given text—What is it that the author expressed in these biblical words?*

We will not succumb to the postmodern fallacy that texts mean whatever the reader determines, nor its dysfunctional corollary, that

1. See Smith, *Word of the Lord*; idem, *House of the Lord*, 23–25, 213–15.
2. See Ratzinger, *Jesus of Nazareth*, xv.

texts do not have/do not need authors. Texts do not organically evolve on their own. They are the product of authors, and we search diligently for the meaning intended by the biblical authors. To ascertain what a text *means*, we agree (to a point) with Raymond Brown, that we must first determine what a text *meant*. Here, we must establish the context—those facts crucial to understanding of the biblical text as it is presently before us. For example, to approach Genesis 32 intelligently, a basic discussion of the book's authorship and dating is necessary, as is an understanding of its overall structure and dominant themes. Initially, our contextual questions concern the Book of Genesis as a whole. Then, the focus turns to the passage under investigation (Gn 32).

Both the general and the particular are necessary and will be dealt with accordingly. Yet several words of clarification are necessary. For starters, we will not overly concern ourselves with speculative reconstructions of the text "diachronically," as it may have developed over time, prior to the canonical form. The hermeneutical approach adopted here is more synchronic than diachronic. Rather than engaging in source-critical theories of the text's supposed evolution, or in hypotheses involving extensive redaction, our focus will be upon "the text as we have it" at the canonical stage. The study of the text adopted here is anchored in the canon of Scripture.

That a canonical approach is considered controversial today—and it is, in certain circles—only underscores the reality of the relatively "widespread disenchantment with the so-called biblical theology movement."[3] The rise of redaction criticism and various postmodernist lenses have only magnified such tendencies in academia: "Fragmentation and suspicion of a 'grand narrative' are hallmarks of postmodern thought."[4] Yet even those less comfortable with the confines of canonical approaches would hopefully agree to the necessity of some fashion of a biblical canon, at least "to mark out the circumference of acceptable diversity."[5] Above and beyond this, a canonical approach is not in the

3. Anthony Thistelton, "Canon, Community and Theological Construction," in Bartholomew et al., *Canon and Biblical Interpretation*, 1.

4. Thistelton, "Canon, Community and Theological Construction," in Bartholomew et al., *Canon and Biblical Interpretation*, 1.

5. See Thistelton, "Canon, Community and Theological Construction," in Bartholomew et al., *Canon and Biblical Interpretation*, 1, citing Dunn, *Unity and Diversity in the New Testament*, 376. As Thistelton points out, an increasing number of highly respected modern theologians engaged or are engaging in biblical theology from a canonical

least uncritical. Kevin Vanhoozer, following Brevard Childs, argues that "the Canon of the Old and New Testaments, as well as that of the Bible as a whole, *encloses a space within which texts deemed authoritative can interact with and inform one another*."[6] As Vanhoozer explains, "Canon confirms intertextuality by showing it at work. New Testament texts refer directly and indirectly to certain Old Testament texts; the Meaning of the Synoptic Gospels is in part a function of their differences from one another; later texts are shot through and through with a vocabulary and themes of earlier texts. In short, the books within the canon *form a 'separate cognitive zone'* and are '*interrelated like the parts of a single book.*' The canon encourages a play of meaning, as it were, but only within carefully prescribed boundaries."[7]

The canonical approach in this book is not "running interference" against the historical-critical method. Rather, it provides a kind of counter-balance necessary today, from historical-critical over-reaches. Canonical criticism may keep it in check when it proves necessary: "*The canonical approach has not turned its back on the findings of historical-critical inquiry, but it has put it under a hot light and asked what is really being said that sheds light on the plain or literal sense of the text.*"[8]

It is simply not possible (nor desirable) to engage all the contemporary literature (e.g., commentaries, monographs, articles) on a biblical book of passage. As the proverb goes, "Of making many books there is no end, and much study is a weariness of the flesh."[9] Without apology, the examination of the text according to the literal sense will be selective. I am interested in the most balanced, most helpful, and most persuasive arguments, wherever they are found and to whomever they

---

perspective, including Brevard Childs, James Sanders, Gordon Wenham, Denis Farkasfalvy, and the like.

6. Vanhoozer, *Is There a Meaning in This Text?*, 134; emphasis added. "The ordering of the tradition for this new [canonical] function involved a profoundly hermeneutical activity, the effects of which are now built into the structure of the canonical text." Childs, *Introduction to the Old Testament*, 60.

7. Vanhoozer, *Is There a Meaning in This Text?*; emphases added.

8. Christopher R. Seitz, "The Canonical Approach and Theological Interpretation," in Bartholomew et al., *Canon and Biblical Interpretation*, 102; emphasis added. "A canonical approach can detect something like a kindred set of concerns linking the reading of Aquinas and its own sense of what is crucial in interpretation, and *it is persuaded this capacity is crucial to its own success as a method for our day, because of and not in spite of historical-critical questions*" (102–3; emphasis original).

9. Eccl 12:12.

belong. I am not interested in the thickest commentaries—unless they have something valuable to contribute. Nor am I interested in impressing the reader with supposedly erudite studies, unless their contributions are crucial to establishing the meaning at the literal level.

Recent studies of a reliable nature are prudently enjoined as we discuss contextual questions pertinent to understanding the biblical text.[10] Where it is warranted, the reader will be alerted to secondary literature befitting further study on the biblical text. All the while, the solitary aim is to concisely establish the literary and historical meaning of *the text as we have it*. This is the aim, not a guarantee. I aspire to approximate the intentions of the biblical author as best as I am able.[11]

Given that historical methods and the commentaries that rely upon them are employed, a few more words about them are necessary. Here, we think of Pope Benedict XVI's recent reflection on "the overall value" of historical-critical methods. While his comments are specifically focused upon the Four Gospels, they apply more broadly to the entire canon: "Certainly to interpret Jesus' words, historical knowledge is necessary, which teaches us to understand the time and the language at that time. But that alone is not enough if we are really to comprehend the Lord's message in depth."[12]

Indeed, it is not enough. Another false crutch is the extra-thick commentary. Simply because it weighs as much as a shelf of books does not necessitate that it is more helpful: "Anyone who today reads ever-thicker commentaries on the Gospels remains disappointed in the end. He

10. Although a number of modern authors and a variety of commentaries and monographs were consulted, a few were particularly valuable and are worth mentioning here. First, regarding the Old Testament, the works of Robert Alter—especially in providing fresh translations—were immeasurably helpful. Likewise, James Kugel's reference works that present ancient Jewish and early Christian commentary on biblical texts were frequently consulted. In terms of commentaries, a number were engaged here: *Word Biblical Commentary* and *Anchor Bible Commentary*, as well as the *Hermeneia* series, along with a few others. The *Eerdmans Dictionary of Early Judaism* was near at hand throughout my research. In terms of the New Testament, a wide array of scholarly views was consulted from the aforementioned commentary series. Additionally, I regularly looked to Dale Allison, Gregory Beale, Craig Keener, Erasmo Leiva-Merikakas, Joseph Ratzinger, Peter Williamson, and N. T. Wright, among others. In regard to the New Testament, the *Commentary on the New Testament Use of the Old Testament* was useful, as were the various Bible dictionaries from InterVarsity Academic Press. (The above list is merely a sample of sources used. For a complete listing of authors and works consulted, see the bibliography.)

11. See the discussion of *Dei Verbum* in chapter 2.

12. Pope Emeritus Benedict XVI, "Afterword," in Sarah, *Power of Silence*, 243.

learns a lot that us useful about those days and a lot of hypotheses that ultimately contribute nothing at all to an understanding of the text. In the end you feel that in all the excess of words, something essential is lacking: entrance into Jesus' silence, from which his word is born. If we cannot enter into this silence, we will hear the word only on the surface and thus not really understand it."[13]

Once the meaning of the encounter scene has been properly established at the literal level, the discussion turns to the mystery of the text within the spiritual senses. Here, we depart from the methodological approach of, say, Raymond Brown to ponder what the text means at the spiritual, even mystical level.[14] Here, the ascent truly begins—from the allegorical and tropological to the anagogical—toward the face of the Lord. As with the literal sense, I am selective regarding commentary on biblical texts. Preference is given to those patristic and medieval voices that help illuminate the text through one or more of the spiritual senses.[15]

I do not intend to include everything that has been said about Genesis 32 (or other biblical texts). Likewise, no attempt will be made to represent East and West, nor every century between 200 and 1300 AD.

13. Benedict XVI, "Afterword," in Sarah, *Power of Silence*, 243.

14. I am not suggesting Brown did not hold to *sensus plenior* in biblical texts. That would be unfair, as he did not reject it. As Barron's essay points out, however, Brown mostly set aside discussion of the spiritual sense. For this reason, I am precise in my terminology in speaking of Brown's "methodological approach" as opposed to his personal beliefs. This may seem like hair splitting. Yet Brown was careful to distinguish between his personal assent to Catholic doctrine and tradition on one hand and his scholarly approach, which was heavily governed by historical-critical principles, on the other. In no way do I wish to disparage Brown, one of the most significant biblical scholars of the last century. The issue is one of emphasis, i.e., of what he stressed and what he didn't. In fairness, Brown undoubtedly affirmed *sensus plenior* and the spiritual sense as a Catholic priest and believer. But it did not play much of a role in his biblical commentaries. Rather, he seems content to set it aside for pastoral use. We should defend rather than blame Brown. Along with like-minded exegetes Joseph Fitzmyer and Roland Murphy, he was operating in the "spirit of a new age" in the aftermath of Pius XII's 1943 encyclical *Divino Afflante Spiritu* (*DAS*). Such scholars were the first wave of Catholics engaging the historical-critical methods, newly permissible with the dawn of *DAS*. In the decades following *DAS*, source-critical approaches—along with textual criticism, archeological discoveries, and an array of related studies—took center stage. Meanwhile, the spiritual senses fell on hard times. More recently, and especially following Vatican II, the latter has been brought forward a bit more.

15. Like modern sources, various collections of ancient and medieval sources were consulted, such as: The Fathers of the Church, Ancient Christian Commentary, The Church's Bible, Loeb Classical Library, the various works of Origen, SS. Augustine and Thomas Aquinas, Hugh of St. Victor, the Dead Sea Scrolls, and the sources compiled by James Kugel. For a complete listing of authors and works consulted, see the bibliography.

To the degree possible, however, each encounter scene includes an ample amount of patristic and medieval impressions of the biblical text. Above all, texts related to the spiritual senses were chosen upon two criteria. First is their contribution to the allegorical, tropological and/or anagogical understanding of the text and the degree to which they embody the pattern of ascent discussed above.

Second, the above will suffice in terms of the method of approach going forward. Before turning to the first encounter scene, a few brief words are necessary as to the format adopted here. For the sake for uniformity, the style of presentation applies to all five encounter scenes and not merely to the present chapter.[16] As deep and pervasive as the Four Senses were in the patristic and medieval ages, few commentators adhered to them in a perfunctory way. Neither will our own engagement of the Four Senses be executed in a mechanical fashion.

The discussion of each encounter scene is organized in a twofold manner. First, we establish the *Sensus Litteralis* (literal sense). Second and immediately following is a discussion of the text according to the *Sensus Spiritualis* (spiritual sense). For the sake of clarity and continuity, these headings (*Sensus Litteralis, Sensus Spiritualis*) appear before these respective discussions. In each encounter scene, the literal sense is engaged first, followed by the spiritual sense. As the various senses are engaged, the reader will encounter Christ in history (literal), the Person of Christ (allegorical), Christ within the soul (tropological), and the heavenly Christ (anagogical), in this sequence. Note that not every scene presents all three spiritual senses under the *Sensus Spiritualis* heading. Some will, others may not.

The primary objective is not to show evidence that biblical texts were regularly engaged according to all Four Senses. This is well documented at this point in the book. Rather, the objective is *to contemplate the divine Son in Scripture through the Four Senses.* What's more, regardless of how many senses are involved in a given discussion, the pattern and progression toward the face of the Lord remain consistent. The reader should concentrate on the pattern of ascent through the Four Senses, regardless of how many are technically involved in a given discussion.

16. The *Meditationes* are the exception to this rule. Each meditation will unfold as an essay in its own right and is not, strictly speaking, subject to the methodological rubrics or formatting conventions as in the encounter scenes.

Finally, it is not only the Four Senses that help the reader ascend toward the face of the Lord. In addition, the content of the biblical encounter scenes themselves—each carefully selected—involve a kind of seeing. Each scene is another tile in the mosaic portrait of the divine Son. It is not suggested that together they yield a biblical Christology nor a complete portrait. Nevertheless, a clearer picture of the face of the Lord will begin to emerge over the course of our investigation.[17]

17. This is hinted at in the chapter titles and will become increasingly evident as the book progresses.

CHAPTER 4

Contemplating the Face of the Brotherly Christ with Jacob (Genesis 32–33)

Jacob wrestled the angel
and the angel was overcome.

—U2

Having provided foundational comments on method and format, we turn now to the analysis of the first encounter scene according to the Four Senses, that of "Jacob Wrestling with the Angel" (Gn 32:24–30):

> The same night he arose and took his two wives, his two maids, and his eleven children, and crossed the ford of the Jabbok. He took them and sent them across the stream, and likewise everything that he had. And Jacob was left alone; and a man wrestled with him until the breaking of the day. When the man saw that he did not prevail against Jacob, he touched the hollow of his thigh; and Jacob's thigh was put out of joint as he wrestled with him. Then he said, "Let me go, for the day is breaking." But Jacob said, "I will not let you go, unless you bless me." And he said to him, "What is your name?" And he said, "Jacob." Then he said, "Your name shall no more be called Jacob, but Israel, for you have striven with God and with men, and have prevailed." Then Jacob asked him, "Tell me, I pray, your name." But he said, "Why is it that you ask my name?" And there he blessed him. So Jacob called the name of the place Peniel, saying, "For I have seen God face to face, and yet my life is preserved."

Sensus Litteralis

The majority of critics have subjugated the text of Genesis to much fragmentary analyses, according to the four sources of the Documentary Hypothesis. And while it has been attempted with this particular episode, no clear consensus has been reached. In fact, "Recent exegesis agrees for the most part that the text of Gen 32:23–33 cannot be separated into two literary sources but has been subsequently expanded into a unity."[1] The geography of the scene is at the Jabbok Ford, which is a tributary of the Jordan River. Unlike the Jordan, which runs north to south, the Jabbok crosses it, running east to west.[2] Among the many riddles within this brief text is why Jacob was "left alone" here, apart from his family: "Was it duty, or anxiety, or simply to inform us that there was none of his party with him when he was attacked?"[3]

A mysterious figure suddenly appears, seemingly from nowhere, and wrestles or struggles with Jacob. The term *yēʾābēq* occurs only twice in the Hebrew Bible, in verses 24 and 25. There is likely significance to this term, which is "clearly a play on *yăbbōk*" (i.e., Jabbok), and it is etymologically close to his own name (Jacob) as well.[4]

Another mystery concerns the dialogue between the two in verse 26, "Then he said, 'Let me go, for the day is breaking.' But Jacob said, 'I will not let you go, unless you bless me.'" Although various scholarly proposals have been suggested about the "man's" insistence that Jacob let go, most are unsatisfactory, as they find merely human parallels or, worse, *non-Jewish ones.*[5] What is more likely is that the angelic figure's countenance[6] is theophanic—a bodily representation of God himself: "Jacob's

1. Westermann, *Continental Commentary*, 515. "Contrary to many earlier critics who attempted to distinguish two sources, it is now recognized following the work of Barthes that the tale is a substantial unity conforming to the outline of many folk tales, with perhaps a few later additions." Wenham, *Genesis 16–50*, 294.

2. As Alter notes, "The Word for 'ford' (Heb, *ma'avar*) is a noun derived from the reiterated verb *'avar*, 'to cross over.'" *Five Books of Moses*, 179n23.

3. Wenham, *Genesis 16–50*, 295.

4. See Wenham, *Genesis 16–50*, 295. Westermann agrees: The word used for the struggle . . . found only in vv. 25, 26 (another word is used in the addition v. 29), is certainly chosen because of the name of the river." *Continental Commentary*, 519.

5. Among other aberrant suggestions is a dependence upon a saying attributed to the Roman god Jupiter has been suggested. See Wenham, *Genesis 16–50*, 296.

6. "The unrecognized foe is the Lord or his angel, and often in Genesis the Lord is equated with El." Wenham, *Genesis 16–50*, 295.

question about the name in v. 30 would make no sense if he knew that his opponent was God."[7] A few verses later, the figure declares, "Your name shall no more be called Jacob, but Israel," explaining that Jacob has "*striven with God and with men and have prevailed*" (v. 28; emphasis added).

This name change is profoundly significant: "instead of merely blessing him," his opponent changes Jacob's name, thus announcing Jacob's new character and destiny. Similarly, Abram's name was changed to Abraham and Sarai's to Sarah to presage the long-awaited fulfillment of the promise of the birth of a son (17:5, 15). Here Jacob's rebaptism as Israel is equally significant, for Israel is of course the name of the nation, and in granting it, Jacob's opponent reveals the true import of the encounter: "you have struggled with God and with men and have overcome."[8] Following this all-important name change, the figure blesses Jacob (v. 29). At the climax of the scene, Jacob names the place of the theophany, "For I have seen God face to face, and yet my life is preserved." In Hebrew, *Peni'el* (or the derivative, *Penuel*) means "face of God."[9] This verse is at the center of our analysis of the text according to the spiritual sense.

What does Jacob mean in saying that his life was *tinnāsēl* (Hebrew for "preserved") in verse 30? The most plausible answer is that his life is spared from the Angel of the Lord, as it is later spared from his estranged brother Esau: "The phrase 'was rescued' harks back to v 11, and so Jacob confesses that his prayer for deliverance from Esau is answered. If he has survived meeting God, he will survive his meeting with Esau."[10] Before further discussing the context in Genesis 32, and in keeping with our methodology, I offer broader comments concerning the Book of Genesis, in which our theophany is located.

Today, the study of Genesis is in something of a state of flux. To approach Genesis at the literal level, discussion must first take place about the state of modern criticism of the book. This may not seem relevant or

7. Westermann, *Continental Commentary*, 519.

8. Wenham, *Genesis 16–50*, 297. "Whenever his descendants heard this name, or used it to describe themselves, they were reminded of its origin and of its meaning, that as their father had triumphed in his struggle with men (i.e., Esau and Laban) and with God, so they too could eventually hope to triumph. Within this episode, of course, his new name is a guarantee of a successful meeting with his brother Esau."

9. The form "Penuel" appears in Jgs 8:8–9 and 1 Kgs 12:25.

10. Wenham, *Genesis 16–50*, 297. Gn 32:11: "*Deliver me, I pray thee, from the hand of my brother, from the hand of Esau*, for I fear him, lest he come and slay us all, the mothers with the children" (emphasis added).

vital to our discussion, yet it is warranted. At the outset, I should stress that I am not interested in persuading the reader one way or another in terms of the major schools of thought about the formation of the Pentateuch.[11] This part takes the reader through of the main turns in source criticism of the Five Books of Moses (i.e., the Pentateuch) and therefore of Genesis. Here the aim is not to drench the reader in superfluous details but to aid in becoming reasonably conversant with the state of affairs today. And this requires some backtracking to nineteenth-century Old Testament criticism and the so-called Documentary Hypothesis (DH).

The DH posits that the Five Books of Moses evolved over about five hundred years. Originally, these biblical books were not, as the theory goes, a unified text. Rather, they gradually developed out of four older textual traditions known as the *Jahwist*, *Elohist*, *Deuteronomist*, and *Priestly* sources (or J, E, D, P). According to German source critic Julius Wellhausen, its primary proponent, the J and E sources—which he identified through philological and literary criteria—are the oldest strata. Gradually, from approximately 950 BC through postexilic Judaism (400s BC), two other schools, the D and P sources, were intricately interwoven with the J-E tradition. This was slowly and intricately woven into a single source document over time, yielding the J-E-D-P amalgamation that is now known as the Pentateuch (Greek for "five volumes").

While theories of such literary formation and dating vary even among source critics, there is general consensus that these documents represent divergent interests, distinct Judaisms, plural. Without getting into the details too deeply, one school represented more of the moralistic, social code (D), whereas other schools represented the priestly elite in Jerusalem (P), which promoted centralized, sacrificial worship, and so on. These Judaisms competed for control of the narrative represented by the emerging document. These developments brought about shifting emphases, as they redacted and arranged the text in a manner that augmented their "way of being Jewish." Oddly, all of this vying for theological control of the larger narrative did not cause later schools (D, P) to entirely omit or reject those points of view of competing views. Rather, the previous views were, for the most part, preserved. But they were preserved in such a way that the present source's own view subtly

11. Discussion of this material is limited to that which is most pertinent to our examination of the text of Gn 32, in which our encounter scene is located.

emerges as the dominant and correct one, the right way of living Jewishly. This is a drastic oversimplification of the DH both past and present. Yet it is not inaccurate.

While such approaches persist, there is less and less agreement today as to what texts belong to J or P, and so on. It has gotten to the point where even small segments of text, even a word or two within a sentence, are scrutinized. From a Catholic biblical perspective, source criticism in and of itself is not off limits or to be entirely avoided. In the words of Ratzinger, however, the historical-critical method appears "to have yielded its essential fruit" over the past hundred or so years. Biblical exegesis needs a revitalization in methodology if there is to be a true theological engagement of the book of Genesis (or any biblical text), and not merely more fragmentation and deconstruction.

In fairness, I have my own criticism of the DH. The hypothesis has yielded countless insights and cannot be discounted as irrelevant even if one does not accept its primary line of reasoning or if one is not persuaded by the evidence that supports it. Even so, there is a counterargument that the DH is on life support today, in need of serious reprisal. There are a few scholars that have successfully pushed back against the tide of the DH. Again, the point is not necessarily to coax the reader away from one approach or toward another. Rather, it is to suggest that the DH is "not the only game in town" and that there are other arguments that advocate a more unified reading of Genesis.[12]

On the one hand, source-critical approaches have dominated the field for the better part of the past 150 years. The legacy of Wellhausen's DH that postulated at least four independent written sources behind the Books of Moses continues to dominate Pentateuchal studies to the present day. This need not be discussed at great length here.[13] Most academic commentaries and monographs on Genesis—though certainly not all—adhere to the general precepts of the DH. But a number of voices have pushed back against the deconstruction of the text through

12. My approach leans in the direction of a unified text. This approach, which considers "the text as we have it," is supported by serious scholarship but is unquestionably a minority view today. Such synchronic approaches are overwhelmingly dwarfed by some variation of the DH or an altogether different source-critical approach.

13. See Smith, *House of the Lord*, 4–6, 78. For a recent introduction to the substance of the DH as well as its history and development in Old Testament studies, see esp. "The Rise of the Documentary Hypothesis," in Alexander, *From Paradise to the Promised Land*, 7–31.

increasingly fragmented approaches to Genesis (and the remainder of the Pentateuch).

Two scholars are worth nothing here. First, Umberto Cassuto (1883–1951), a voice of early opposition to the DH, is significant for at least three reasons. (1) Cassuto, who was an Italian Jew and chief rabbi in Florence, overlapped with Wellhausen (1844–1918). The DH was blossoming in his own lifetime. He witnessed its popularity and growing influence, and as an orthodox rabbi and a highly trained scholar of the Hebrew Bible, he raised specific issues with the DH, and although diminished by many, his challenges did not go unheard—then or now. (2) Cassuto gave a series of eight lectures, later published,[14] in which he critiqued the DH and its internal inconsistencies. Cassuto criticized the DH for its use of the divine names (i.e., Yahweh, Elohim) as a key determinant of multiple and divergent sources. In contrast, he interpreted the text in a unitive fashion. He proposed that the use of the names was not evidence of two (or more) sources. Rather, it signified theological distinctions represented by these divine names; namely, divine immanence (Yahweh) and divine transcendence (Elohim). Additionally, Cassuto identified serious difficulties of the DH and its dependence upon language, style, repetitions, and other criteria to foster its source-critical view. (3) Finally, while his lectures were surmountable challenges to the DH and its ability to explain the state of the Pentateuch as we have it, what was nevertheless needed was a positive approach to the Five Books of Moses in a more unified and cohesive way.

To this end, Cassuto eventually developed two commentaries that worked along such lines. In them he did not seek to negate the results of the DH. Rather, in closely following the logic of the Hebrew text, he put forth alternative explanations that pointed to a unified Pentateuch. One dealt with the first twelve chapters of Genesis[15] and the other with the Book of Exodus.[16] Cassuto's work on the Pentateuch in these commentaries, while not exhaustive, demonstrated that it was possible to interpret the text in a critical way, using all the tools of philology and other tools pertaining to language, yet in a manner that does

14. Cassuto, *Documentary Hypothesis*. Later, Cassuto taught at the Hebrew University of Jerusalem, where he served as the chair of the biblical studies department.

15. Cassuto, *From Adam to Noah*; idem, *Commentary on the Book of Genesis*.

16. Cassuto, *Commentary on the Book of Exodus*. Cassuto's commentary on Genesis does not include the text in question (Gn 32) and will not be engaged here.

not set out to deconstruct the text. Perhaps the chief contribution of his commentaries is the manner in which he demonstrated—from the text itself—the unity and cohesiveness of Genesis and Exodus, in a technically sound and persuasive manner.

More recently, Anglican scholar T. Desmond Alexander has provided up-to-date analysis of source-critical studies of the Pentateuch and the unraveling of the DH, at least theoretically. In a series of essays, Alexander, like Cassuto, assessed the continual problems of the DH in a factual way. Unlike Cassuto, Alexander had the advantage of looking back, from his twenty-first-century vantage point, over the many developments of the DH which increasingly threaten its viability. Among other contributions, Alexander explains significant, alternative voices to the DH, such as R. Norman Whybray, Rolf Rendtdorff, John Van Seeters, among others.[17] Although none of these scholars' works has individually or collectively supplanted the DH, it signifies that the tide may be turning in a new, yet unspecified direction in the future.[18]

I remain unconvinced as to the logic or necessity of the DH, either in its original Wellhausian form or in any of its more recent derivatives. My approach, like Cassuto's, rests upon a conviction of the essential unity of both the text of the Pentateuch and well as its inner theological consistency. I do not hold that the text was "set in stone" at the time of Moses, nor that it was necessarily composed by one and only one author at that time. Rather, I agree with Ratzinger that the text developed over the centuries, and the text of the Pentateuch likely reached its final, canonical shape around the time of the Babylonian exile.[19] At the same time, while we do not exclude moderate amount of arrangement or editing of the Pentateuch as a whole, we are more persuaded, along with Cassuto, of a stable oral tradition—carefully preserved from the time of the historic Moses until its canonical shape sometime around

17. "The Documentary Hypothesis under Threat," in Alexander, *From Paradise to the Promised Land*, 42–53. For a recent defense of the DH, see Baden, *Composition of the Pentateuch*. Van Seeters was a critic of the DH, yet he himself was skeptical as to the historicity of the tradition.

18. "Alternatives to the Documentary Hypothesis," in Alexander, *From Paradise to the Promised Land*, 54–63. See also Carbajosa, *Faith*, esp. "Calling the Documentary Hypothesis Into Question," 56–70.

19. See Ratzinger, *"In the Beginning . . . ,"* 10–11. "The moment when creation became a dominant theme occurred during the Babylonian Exile. It was then that the account that we have just heard—based to be sure on very ancient traditions–assumed its present form."

the 400s AD. Regardless, and in keeping with the stated methodological approach, we will examine Genesis (and all biblical texts) according to "the text as we have it" in its final, canonical stage.

What about the chronology of the book, or at least of the patriarchs, since Abraham's grandson Jacob is of primary interest? Wenham summarizes: "The chronology of Genesis dates Abraham about 2000 B.C. and his descendants in the following centuries. Between Joseph and the time of Moses, it places a long interlude of four generations (15:16) or four centuries (15:13; Ex 12:40–41)."[20]

If Genesis developed out of an essential unity rather than disparate sources, what are the main theological themes of the book? There are two interrelated concepts that work hand in hand throughout the book: Creation and Covenant. The former is the central theme in Genesis 1–11; the latter predominates the remainder of the book (Gn 12–50). Yet even in the early chapters of the Creation narratives, the theme of covenant is implicit in Genesis. "In the beginning" (Gn 1:1). Here, God creates and calls all of Creation—and particularly Adam and Eve—into relationship with himself. Later, in the undoing of the fallen and sinful Creation, God again covenants with Noah.[21]

Things come to a crescendo in Genesis 11, where the Tower of Babel incident symbolizes the ascent of a fallen humanity to the throne of God as a problem and a challenge. This climactic moment of sinful disobedience leads to a new beginning for all of humanity, in God's initiation of a universal and worldwide covenant with Abram in Genesis 12.[22] The remainder of Genesis unfolds the Abrahamic covenant in his descendants—through the child of the covenant, Isaac, and then to his son, Jacob. Not only this, the covenantal narrative in Genesis is foundational to the remainder of the Pentateuch and the whole of the Hebrew Bible that follows. Gordon Wenham summarizes:

20. Wenham, *Genesis 16–50*, xx–xxi.

21. See Gn 8–9.

22. See esp. Gn 12:1–7; 15:10–21; 17:1–19; 22:1–18. "In this chapter it is argued that, while there is essentially one covenant relationship with Abraham, this covenantal relationship undergoes development. The basic covenant in Genesis 15 is expanded and reconfigured in Genesis 17, and then again in Genesis 22. These three covenants are successive and cumulative, each building on the previous one(s). The succession of these three covenants is foreshadowed in Genesis 12:1–3, God's initial blessing of Abraham. Each of the three main elements of this blessing are taken up and given covenantal solemnity in Genesis 15, 17, and 22 respectively." Hahn, *Kinship by Covenant*, 102–3.

[Genesis] does not stand on its own, but rather contains essential background for understanding those events *which constituted the nation of Israel as the LORD's covenant people*. It would therefore not be surprising to find adumbrations of the later national history in the story of the patriarchs. In turn, too, the primeval history (chaps. 1–11) must be seen in this perspective. *It is also essentially preparatory in function and puts the patriarchs into their cosmic context.* The God who called Abraham was no local divinity but the creator of the whole universe. The succession of catastrophes that befell humanity prior to Abraham's call show just why the election of Abraham, and in him, Israel, was necessary.[23]

In a comparable way, bioethicist and Hebrew scholar Leon Kass underscores the theme of covenant in Genesis and its implications for the remainder of the biblical story. Commenting on the "binding of Isaac" and God's testing of Abraham in chapter 22, Kass writes, "Abraham, called by God to be the father of a new nation that will carry God's righteous ways to the rest of the world, is educated by God Himself in the proper role of father and founder, and proves his readiness in the final test."[24]

These contextual remarks about the Book of Genesis and the question of the development of the Pentateuch to which it belongs will suffice. We now turn to a close-up look at chapter 32, specifically, at verses 24–30.

We begin with the person of Jacob himself: "[He] was the third of the great Hebrew patriarchs and second born of the twins of Isaac and Rebekah. He is presented as a man who sometimes manifested flashes of great faith and in his later years showed a deep spirituality. But de-

23. Wenham, *Genesis 1–15*, xxii; emphases added. In *Genesis 16–50*, Wenham adds: "The theme of the whole Pentateuch, the partial fulfillment of the promises to Abraham of land, descendants, covenant, and blessing to the nations, is set out first in 12:1–3. And all the subsequent stories in Genesis explain the fulfillment of these promises. This statement of the divine promises thus sets the agenda for the whole of Genesis 12–50" (169).

24. Kass, *Beginning of Wisdom*, 348. Though trained as a bioethicist, Kass taught the Hebrew Bible at the University of Chicago (x–xv). Out of that coursework he developed this highly regarded text. Kass's exegesis is based on close readings of the Hebrew text, while at the same time yielding fresh insights on Genesis: "It is time for us to take stock ... Father Abraham, I submit, is the model father, both of his family and of his people—yes, even in his willingness to sacrifice his son—because he reveres God, the source of life and blessing and the teacher of righteousness, more than he loves his own. He is a model not because all fathers should *literally* seek to imitate him; almost none of us could, and fortunately, thanks to him, none of us has to. He is a model, rather, because he sets an admirable example for proper paternal rule, *in which the love of one's own children is put into service of the right, the good, and the holy*" (347–48; emphases added).

TABLE 1. The Palistrophic Structure of the Jacob Cycle (Gn 25:19–35:29)

Genesis Verse	*Episode*	*Corresponding Pairs*
25:19–34	First encounters of Jacob and Esau	A
26:1–33	Isaac and the Philistines	B
26:34–28:9	Jacob cheats Esau of his blessing	C
28:10–22	Jacob meets God at Bethel	D
29:1–14	Jacob arrives at Laban's house	E
29:15–30	Jacob marries Leah and Rachel	F
29:31–30:24	Birth of Jacob's sons	G
30:25–31:1	Jacob outwits Laban	F^1
31:2–32:1	Jacob leaves Laban	E^1
32:2–3	Jacob meets angels of God at Mahanaim	D^1
32:4–33:20	Jacob returns Esau's blessing	C^1
34:1–31	Dinah and the Hivites	B^1
35:1–29	Journey's end for Jacob and Isaac	A^1

spite these excellent qualities, Jacob was an unusual hero. Especially in his early life, he fluctuated between godliness and worldliness."[25] In the larger schema of Genesis, the Jacob cycle spans nearly ten chapters and "consists of a number of biographical episodes that constitute almost all of the generations [*tôlĕdōt*] of Isaac."[26]

Structurally, Wenham has amply demonstrated that the entire Jacob cycle is composed palistrophically, that is, as an extended chiasm (table 1).[27] Before discussing the palistrophic nature of the Jacob-cycle, three preliminary remarks are necessary about these intentional chiastic arrangements. First, Wenham has identified several chiastic arrangements throughout the Book of Genesis. Such identification is not foolproof, as Wenham readily admits. Yet painstaking analysis of numerous texts across the canon of the Hebrew Bible has sufficiently demonstrated that such structural arrangements are not the product of scholarly imagination.[28] Not all are as extensive as the one above. In fact, some chiasms

25. R. O. Rigsby, "Jacob," in Alexander and Baker, *Dictionary of the Old Testament*, 461.
26. Rigsby, "Jacob," in Alexander and Baker, *Dictionary of the Old Testament*, 461.
27. Wenham, *Genesis 16–50*, 169.
28. See Alter, *Art of Biblical Narrative*; Berlin, *Poetics and Interpretation of Biblical Narrative*; Fokkelmann, *Narrative Art in Genesis*; Wenham, "Coherence of the Flood Narrative"; Beauchamp, *Création et séparation*.

in Genesis are rather minute, involving one or two verses. Others extend over several chapters.[29]

Second, the most significant palistrophe in Genesis, aside from the Jacob narrative, is the flood narrative. Specifically, Genesis 6:9–9:19 has been composed in a clear chiastic form structure.[30] The center of the chiasm—which unlike the remaining pairs does not have a mirror image—is what reveals episode's main theological point. In this case, the center of the flood narrative is Genesis 8:1a,[31] which in the Vulgate reads: *recordatus autem Deus Noe*. At the literal level, this theme of God's *recordatus*, that is, "recollecting, or remembering" Noah, is the central thought of the flood narrative (table 2). Wenham's literary analysis is not only sound but also helps to underscore a theme that has been too often overlooked in studies of the flood in modern criticism; namely, God's election and covenanting with Noah and his family.

Put simply, the flood narrative in Scripture is not primarily about God's undoing of Creation due to sin or divine wrath. Rather, chapters 6 through 9 are about the "righteous man,"[32] whom God remembers, spares, and later invites into a holy covenant.[33] Close analysis of the Hebrew text, along with careful attention to the chiastic patterns as described here, dislodges a common misperception of what these early chapters of Genesis are really communicating to the reader.

29. Wenham explains the chiasm in Gn 1:24 as follows: "Note the chiasmus between command (v 24) and fulfillment:

A cattle and creeping things
B wild animals
B1 wild animals
A1 cattle ... creeping things." *Genesis 1–15*, 25. Additionally, see his commentary on Gn 2:4 (46, 55), 4:2 (94), 6:5–8 (137), and 9:18–19 (194).

30. "Note how each feature in the first half of the story matches a corresponding feature in the second half to create a mirror-image structure (3//8, 4//7, 5//6, etc.) with its center '*God remembered Noah*' in 8:1." Wenham, *Genesis 1–15*, 156; emphasis added.

31. Gn 8:1: "But *God remembered Noah* and all the beasts and all the cattle that were with him in the ark" (emphasis added).

32. "God's words reflect a frequently used technique of biblical narrative, in which the narrator's report or evaluation is confirmed by a near verbatim repetition in dialogue, or vice versa. The judgement that Noah is 'righteous in this generation' explicitly expresses the narrator's declaration in 6:9 that Noah is 'a righteous man' ... blameless in his time' (the Hebrew word for 'time' is literally 'generations')." Alter, *Five Books of Moses*, 42n1. Alter's remark concerns Gn 7:1, which he translates as "And the Lord said to Noah, 'Come into the ark, you and all your household, for *it is you I have seen righteous before Me in this generation*'" (emphasis added).

33. See Gn 9:8–11.

TABLE 2. The Palistrophic Structure of the Flood Story Cycle (Gn 6:9–9:19)

Transitional introduction (6:9–10)
- 1. Violence in creation (6:11–12)
  - 2. First divine speech: resolve to destroy (6:13–22)
    - 3. Second divine speech: "enter ark" (7:1–10)
      - 4. Beginning of flood (7:11–16)
        - 5. The rising flood (7:17–24)
          - *God remembers Noah* (8:1a)
        - 5A. The receding flood (8:1–5)
      - 4A. Drying of the earth (8:6–14)
    - 3A. Third divine speech: "leave ark" (8:15–19)
  - 2A. God's resolve to preserve order (8:20–22)
- 1A. Fourth divine speech: covenant (9:1–17)

Transitional conclusion (9:18–19)

Source: See Wenham, *Genesis 1–15*, 156. Here, Wenham follows Anderson, "From Analysis to Synthesis."

The sacred author is not portraying a wrathful Deity. Such is the intent of the pagan accounts of the flood. Instead, they reveal a compassionate God. Forsaking the vengeance due him from a mutinous Creation, God's anger turns to compassion, in seeing the righteous man. God remembers the one who remembers him. Rather than a focus on past sins, this God is future-building and covenant-planning—resting his precarious project upon a single man, who along with his family will turn the story forward.

Life is not extinguished but spared. Humanity is not despised but cleansed and offered a fresh start. And Noah is a safe bet. Like Daniel and Job, Noah remains true to God in a darkened, hopeless generation.

For the prophet Ezekiel, it is this rare human quality—nearness to God when all others are far off—that unify these three biblical figures: "And the word of the Lord came to me: 'Son of man, when a land sins against me by acting faithlessly, and I stretch out my hand against it, and break its staff of bread and send famine upon it, and cut off from it man and beast, even if these three men, Noah, Daniel, and Job, were in it, they would deliver but their own lives by *sidqāt* ("their righteousness"), says the Lord GOD.'"[34]

34. Ezek 14:14. Most of the English versions of the text translate *sidqāt* as "their righteousness." The New Jerusalem Bible is close, yet slightly different, with "uprightness."

Here is the key point: the author of Genesis has arranged the entire narrative in such a way that its meaning is centrally placed, even as it is hidden in plain sight. Recent studies of chiastic structures have had a positive effect. Whereas many historical-critical studies tend to deconstruct Genesis in a fragmentary way, these insights help to recover the inherent unity of the text, and in so doing better identify the theological coherence of the book as a whole.

A third point may be added. Wenham's literary analysis suggests other principal elements of the flood narrative that are often overlooked. The first and last pair of the structure are Genesis 6:11–12 and 8:20–22. In the first text, the violence in the antediluvian world, prior to the flood, is pronounced: "Now the earth was corrupt in God's sight, and the earth was filled with violence. And God saw the earth, and behold, it was corrupt; for all flesh had corrupted their way upon the earth" (6:20–22).

Strikingly, in its literary pair, nearly the same language describes the violence of men after the flood. There, God vows, "I will never again curse the ground because of man, for the imagination of man's heart is evil from his youth; neither will I ever again destroy every living creature as I have done" (8:21). The chiastic linkage of 6:20–22 with 8:21 is indisputable and undergirds our point: the flood narrative of Genesis is not principally about a wrathful God castigating a sinful humanity. This careful literary and textual analysis turns the story right-side-up. In his age, Noah stands apart as a man of *tsedāqāh*—of honesty and justice, of righteousness.

But we must be careful in describing the scene. To be precise, it is not Noah's remembering God that saves the day. Such would turn the entire episode into a kind of Pelagian utopia of heroism and vanity. No—it is "*God's remembering*" and not Noah's faith upon which the flood story hinges and moves determinedly forward. True, Noah *zakar* (remembers) God in all his ways. This is what sets him apart from the remainder of humanity. And like Daniel and Job, Noah continues to remember God when all around him turn their backs on God. He is, after all, the first in Scripture to build a *mizbēah* (altar),[35] where he performs a decidedly priestly duty and offers up a burnt offering to God.

Nevertheless, it is God who recognizes *hă nîhōhă rêah* (the pleasing

35. Gn 8:1.

aroma) of the sacrifice.[36] The center of the flood story is indeed God's recollecting the righteous Noah, with whom he enters into a covenant. It is God's saving action, God's remembering Noah, upon which the narrative moves, upon which total disaster is abruptly and gracefully averted. This insight is not to be overlooked, as it sharpens our understanding of what is really happening over the course of Genesis 6–9. Unfortunately, this is not the state of affairs today, especially at a popular level. What is more commonly believed about the flood story of Genesis is derived from more of a Calvinist interpretation of the text, that is, of God's punishment of sin and his purging of all wickedness from the antediluvian world. And this would be entirely wrong.

We are now in a position to summarize this literal analysis. Our structural analysis of the flood story has revealed a number of insights about Genesis 6–9 and underscores the value of sound literary analysis. Specifically, it appears that the author of Genesis has intricately composed the book with deeply interwoven structural arrangements. Closer study of such chiastic compositions suggests that they operate as carefully chosen literary arrangements in service of the theological meaning of the text: "To search out the intention of the sacred writers, attention should be given, among other things, to 'literary forms.' For truth is set forth and expressed differently in texts which are variously historical, prophetic, poetic, or of other forms of discourse. The interpreter must investigate what meaning the sacred writer intended to express and actually expressed in particular circumstances by using contemporary literary forms in accordance with the situation of his own time and culture."[37]

Similar chiastic analysis is crucial to a proper understanding of the Jacob cycle (Gn 25–35), to which we now return. Here, three insights emerge more readily from such careful study of the text according to the literal sense.

36. Gn 8:20–22: "Then *Noah built an altar to the Lord*, and took of every clean animal and of every clean bird, and offered burnt offerings on the altar. And when the Lord smelled *the pleasing odor*, the Lord said in his heart, 'I will never again curse the ground because of man, for the imagination of man's heart is evil from his youth; neither will I ever again destroy every living creature as I have done. While the earth remains, seedtime and harvest, cold and heat, summer and winter, day and night, shall not cease'" (emphasis added).

37. *Dei Verbum*, 12; see *Verbum Domini*, 34.

1. The center panel (G) of the chiasm is in Genesis 29:31–30:24 (table 1). The subject of that text is "The Birth of Jacob's Sons." In these two chapters at the center of the Jacob cycle, what stands out is not merely the telling of the births of his twelve sons but the human treachery with which is comes about.

Reminiscent of his grandfather Abraham, who fathered children with two women, Sarah and Haggar,[38] Jacob too engaged in polygamy. His twelve sons are the offspring of he and his two wives, Leah and Rachel, and their two maidservants, Bilhah and Zilpah, respectively. As Wenham summarizes, "It is into this most bitterly divided family that the forefathers of the twelve tribes were born. Fathered by a lying trickster and mothered by sharp-tongued shrews, the patriarchs grew up to be less than perfect themselves. Yet through them the promises to Abraham took a great step toward their fulfillment, showing that it is divine grace not human merit that gives mankind hope of salvation."[39]

2. This center panel of the Jacob cycle shares a feature with the previous palistrophe we examined, that of the flood narrative:

> The central scene (G), the birth of Jacob's sons—more precisely, the birth of a son to Rachel (30:22–24)—is the turning point of the story. As soon as this happens Jacob asks Laban for permission to return home (30:25). Though, of course, he prevaricates and uses various excuses to detain Jacob, it is clear that in Jacob's eyes it is the birth of Joseph to the only woman he regarded as his wife that signals it is time for him to go home. The flood story is another prime example of a palistrophe in Genesis. It is noteworthy that both palistrophes have a similar comment at the turning point (God remembered Rachel/Noah, 30:22; 8:1) to emphasize that it is God who controls events and saves his people.[40]

3. A third and final insight emerges from our palistrophic ("chiastic") analysis. The theophany scene we are concerned with is in Genesis 32, where Jacob wrestles with the angel and prevails (vv. 22–32). Structurally, this is located within panel C^1 (Gn 32:4–33:20), "Jacob Returns Esau's blessing." This may not appear particularly striking at first glance, until one realizes that this panel is the mirror of panel C (Gn 26:34–28:9), "Jacob Cheats Esau of His Blessing." The theophany scene is introduced

38. Abraham had two wives, Sarah and later Keturah (see Gn 25:1*ff.*), and he fathered Ishmael with Sarah's maidservant Haggar prior to the "miraculous" birth of Isaac to he and Sarah.

39. Wenham, *Genesis 16–50*, 250.

40. Wenham, *Genesis 16–50*, 170.

at a critical stage of the entire Jacob-cycle, prior to their reconciliation!

At the climax of the theophany scene, Jacob is renamed "Israel" by the angel. He is one "who struggles with God and men and prevails" (32:29). Immediately afterward, Jacob/Israel renames the place of divine encounter: "So Jacob called the name of the place Peniel, saying, '*For I have seen God face to face*, and yet my life is preserved'" (v. 30; emphasis added).

Next, the action shifts from Jacob's dramatic encounter with the angel in Genesis 32 to *another* dramatic encounter in the following chapter—with his brother Esau, from whom he is estranged. The chapter begins with on this tense note: "And Jacob lifted up his eyes and looked, and behold, Esau was coming, and four hundred men with him" (33:1a). Kass's literary analysis makes sense of the denouement of the entire Jacob cycle: "We try to imagine ourselves in Esau's place. What a strange and moving sight. My hated brother, my rival, the conniving supplanter paying me supreme homage, abasing himself supremely. Is this not a confession of his guilt, an acknowledgement of my rightful standing? See how he places himself at my mercy, trusting me with his life. And look how he has aged and limps along!"[41]

Surprisingly, then, Esau embraces Jacob: "But Esau ran to meet him, and embraced him, and fell on his neck and kissed him, and they wept."[42] Here, five active verbs summarize the action in this reunion scene: ran, embraced, fell, kissed, and wept. Strikingly, the first panel (A) of the Jacob cycle[43] concludes with five active verbs: "Then Jacob *gave* Esau bread and pottage of lentils, and he *ate* and drank, and *rose* and *went* his way. Esau *despised* his birthright" (Gn 25:34; emphasis added). Whereas the first panel (A) ends with Esau 'despising,' here in the resolution scene, "both Jacob and Esau 'wept'—together."[44]

Sensus Spiritualis

Regarding Jacob wresting with the angel, we now move from the Letter to the Spirit, from the first to the second instruction, from "history to

41. Kass, *Beginning of Wisdom*, 467.
42. Gn 33:4.
43. Gn 25:1–34 ("First Encounters of Jacob and Esau").
44. Kass, *Beginning of Wisdom*, 467n16.

mystery." How was this text engaged at the earliest stages of the Tradition—and what is the oldest known commentary on the Jacob episode? It appears that the oldest commentary on Jacob's wrestling with the angel in Genesis 32 is also biblical, from the prophet Hosea: "In the womb he took his brother by the heel, and in his manhood, he strove with God. He strove with the angel and prevailed, he wept and sought his favor. He met God at Bethel. There God spoke with him—the Lord the God of hosts, the Lord is his name."[45] The prophet alludes to a few traditions within the Jacob cycle, including the birth of Jacob and Esau,[46] Jacob's wrestling with the angel,[47] and the naming of Bethel.[48]

Other early Jewish commentaries on the scene stress that the *îsh* (man) of verse 24 is to be identified with the "angel(s) of God." Here, we can begin with what are known as the "targums," a term that means "translation" in Aramaic. Targums are translations of the Hebrew text of Scripture into its sister Semitic language of Aramaic, once termed "Chaldee."[49] There is an array of *targumim*, and each should be considered on its own merits. They begin to emerge in about the mid-first century AD and continue for many centuries afterward.[50] They are highly valuable not only as early Jewish translations of Scripture, but also for their interpretative decisions. They are some of the earliest translations of Scripture, and "the type and purpose of the rendering involved in Ju-

45. Hos 12:3–5.

46. Gn 25:24.

47. Gn 25:24.

48. Gn 35:8.

49. Aside from sayings in the Gospels, several sections of Ezra are in Aramaic (see Ez 4:8–6:18, 7:12–26). A large chunk of Daniel is in Aramaic (2:4–7:28), which has led to robust scholarly debate as to when Daniel was composed. Although this part of the book may have been composed earlier, some critics assert that it was written around 164 BC, with the apparently older Hebrew portions originating in the sixth century BC. There are an array of positions on just when Daniel was composed, and to what end. For a review of this position, see Hartman and Di Lella, *Book of Daniel*, 12–18; Goldingay, *Daniel*, xxv–xl. For a recent review of the question, and a positive reconsideration of the "sixth century hypothesis," see "Historical Issues in Daniel," in Pitre and Bergsma, *Catholic Introduction to the Bible*, 892–97.

50. "The earliest Targum is *Targum Onqelos,* made some time between the first and fifth centuries A.D. The more expansive *Targum Pseudo-Jonathan* was completed sometime after the rise of Islam. In 1956 A. Díez Macho announced the discovery of a previously unknown targum now known as *Targum Neofiti,* which is contained in a manuscript dating from A.D. 1504 but with a text dating back at least to the mid-first millennium A.D." P. J. Williams, "Textual Criticism," in Alexander and Baker, *Dictionary of the Old Testament*, 838.

daism was distinctive."[51] Generally speaking, the targums "share translation features such as the avoidance of anthropomorphisms with reference to God, the updating of geographical place names and expansions inspired by subtle triggering phrases in the original text.[52]

Yet it is difficult to assess just how ancient they really are. The earliest written targum, *Targum Neophyti*, may date back to the first century AD. The targums emerged orally, however, as the Hebrew Scriptures were spoken in the Aramaic vernacular in synagogues during the centuries during the Babylonia exile. This continued for centuries after, among those Jews that returned to Judea as well as among those in the Diaspora.

Targum Neophyti on Genesis 32:28 reads: "He said, 'Your name shall no more be called Jacob, but Israel, for you have made yourself *great with angels of God* and with men and you have overcome them.'"[53] Josephus likewise follows this line of approach: "In the Hebrew Tongue, this signifies the adversary of *the angel of God.*"[54] Similar statements are found in the *Peshitta* on Genesis 32:28 ("for you have been strong *with an angel*") and the *Samaritan Targum* ("for you have made yourself great with *angels of God* and with men").[55] These early remarks about the identity of the "man" with whom Jacob wrestles are not insignificant, and we will return to the angelic dimension of the text. Additionally, in these early Jewish texts, Jacob is not said to struggle with God himself. Rather, he wrestles with his angelic representative. This cosmic figure, the "angel of the Lord," is God's mediatorial agent:

> Many consider the appearances of the angel of the Lord as constituting theophanic events. There are justifiable reasons for viewing these appearances as theophanies, especially since the angel of the Lord is frequently equated with God. The deity of this unique angel is suggested by the facts that he (1) is identi-

51. Bruce Chilton, "Rabbinic Literature: Targumim," in Evans and Porter, *Dictionary of New Testament Background*, 902.

52. Williams, "Textual Criticism," in Alexander and Baker, *Dictionary of the Old Testament*, 838.

53. In Kugel, *Traditions of the Bible*, 387; emphasis added. *Targum Jonathan*, from about the same period, is similar: "And he said, Thy name shall be no more called Jakob but Israel, because thou art magnified with the angels of the Lord and with the mighty, and thou hast prevailed with them" (*waʾămar lāʾ yaʿăqḇ ʾîṯĕʾamar ʿôḏ šĕmāḵ ʾĕlāhēn yišrāʾēl ʾărûm ʾiṯraḇraḇt ʿim malʾāḵayāʾ ḏayyā wĕʿim ḡûḇĕrayāʾ wiyḵālt lĕhôm*).

54. Josephus, *Antiquities*, 1.333; emphasis added.

55. In Kugel, *Traditions of the Bible*, 387; emphasis added.

fied as God,[56] (2) is recognized as God,[57] (3) is described in terms befitting the Deity alone,[58] (4) calls himself God,[59] (5) receives worship,[60] and (6) speaks with divine authority.[61] The angel of the Lord who appeared in the burning bush[62] not only says he is God[63] but is designated as God by the text.[64] The angel of the Lord received sacrifice,[65] and Gideon feared his life because he had gazed at God.[66] The angel who wrestled with Jacob[67] was recognized to be God.[68] The angel-of-the-Lord theophanies are linked with major statements in redemptive history, including the Abrahamic and Mosaic covenants.[69]

Elsewhere, *Targum Onqelos*, which dates from the second century AD, adapts Jacob's new name, given by the angel. The Hebrew reads "striven with God," yet *Targum Onqelos* adapts this to "*you are a prince before the Lord*" (emphasis added). This alleviates the anthropomorphistic image of the man Jacob physically wrestling with God—or even the "Angel of the Lord," which is noncorporeal.[70] While Genesis itself states that Jacob had seen God "face-to-face," later Targums clarify the matter. For example, the third-century *Targum Jonathan* reworks the original text as follows: "And Jakob called the name of the place Peniel; for he said, I have seen *the Angels of the Lord face to face,* and my life is saved."[71]

Two things are striking about this first-century translation of Genesis 32.[72] First and most important, it is not the Lord that sees face-to-

56. See Gn 16:7–13, 18:2, 18:10, 18:13, 22:10–12, 22:15–18; Ex 3:2–6, 3:14, 3:18; Jgs 2:1, 2:5, 6:11, 6:14, 6:16.

57. See Gn 16:9–13; Jgs 6:22–24, 13:21–23; cf. Gn 32:24–30 with Hos 12:4–5.

58. See Ex 3:2–9, 3:14; 23:20–23; Jos 5:15.

59. See Gn 31:11, 3:13 (in reference to the "angel of God"); Ex 3:2, 3:6, 3:14.

60. See Jos 5:14; Jgs 2:4–5.

61. See Jgs 2:1–5.

62. See Ex 3:2.

63. See Ex 3:6.

64. See Ex 3:4.

65. See Jgs 6:21.

66. See Jgs 6:22.

67. See Hos 12:4.

68. See Gn 32:30.

69. M. F. Rooker, "Theophany," in Alexander and Baker, *Dictionary of the Old Testament*, 36. See also Jeremias, *Theophanie*; von Rad, *Old Testament Theology*, 2.19–21.

70. Cathcart et al., *Aramaic Bible*, Gn 32:29: "The Hebrew: 'for you have striven with God,' is a gross anthropomorphism, which the Targum circumvents by connecting the Hebrew word for "you have striven"—*sarîtā* with *sr*—"a prince, a great one," and substituting *qdm* for Hebrew *'Im.*"

71. *Targum Jonathan* on Gn 32:30 (*ûqĕrāʾya ʿăqḇ šĕmāʾ ḏĕʾaṯrāʾ pĕnîʾēl ʾărûm ʾāmar ḥămîṯî malʾāḵayāyʾ ḏayyā ʾappîn kāl qĕḇêl ʾappîn wĕʾîštĕzîḇaṯ nap̄šî*). This is my translation of the text; emphasis added.

72. A clarification: the term "life" is, in the Hebrew of Genesis, *nephesh*. It is nearly

face. It is God's *angelic mediator*. It is as if the Aramaic targum is sensitive to the theological conundrum of the biblical text and repairs its starkness. In the translation (and, obviously, interpretation), Jacob's theophany is retrofit to an encounter with the angel of God. Problem solved.

Second, and relatedly, is the plural: Jacob declares that he has seen "the angels of the Lord face-to-face." At first glance, this seems to multiply the theophany—from one to many angels. Technically, this is the case. In reality, this diffuses the directness of the theophanic encounter. Jacob did not see one specific "angel." Rather, he saw the faces of angels. In other words, his stature has been raised to the dignity of the angels, to that of the angelic host.

Let us move forward, from early Jewish to early Christian interpretation of the scene. Spiritual exegesis of Genesis 32 was not limited to the *allegorical* in the patristic age, though certainly it was predominant. Perhaps earliest of all, St. Justin Martyr draws an allegorical connection between the "wounding of Jacob's thigh"[73] and the crucifixion of Jesus: "But since our Christ was also to grow numb (or put out of joint), namely in toil and in the sense of suffering at the time He was to be crucified, [Scripture] proclaimed this also beforehand by having Jacob's thigh be touched and making it grow numb."[74] To be sure, allegorical interpretation of the Old Testament does not always look to the Passion of Christ as in this early example of Justin. As the Crucifixion is the pinnacle of story of Jesus in the Gospels, however, neither should such alignment with the Cross surprise the reader.

Later, in the fourth century, St. Augustine engaged the theophany scene in a number of his writings. Like his predecessors, he did so in

---

identical to the Aramaic term in *Targum Jonathan*. In both instances, the term may be translated as "life" or "soul." The latter is used in many English translations of Ps 23:1, i.e., "He restores my *soul*." This is time honored and beautiful, yet technically imprecise. The difficulty with translating *nephesh* as "soul" is that, in a Christian sense, it conjures up the life of the soul apart from the body. Yet the notion of "body and soul" in ancient Judaism is complex. They are bound together, and really inseparable. In the most ancient Jewish understanding, when one dies, one's whole being dies. One goes to *Sheol*. But it is not as though the being in Sheol can be reunited with one's body. This is not the understanding of death in ancient Judaism. Rather than a "separation" of body from soul (as in the early Christian understanding), the experience renders death to the person in a holistic way. And so applying this clarification to Ps 23:1 would yield "*he restores my life*" in the sense that the person *has been spared death*, he has been saved from the possibility of death. Likewise, in Gn 32:30, it is Jacob's *life* that has been spared from death.

73. See Gn 32:25, 31–32.

74. St. Justin Martyr, *Dialogue with Trypho*, 125.5.

a highly allegorized way. In Book XVI of *The City of God*, Augustine comments on the name Israel, given to Jacob after their contest: "As I just mentioned, Jacob was also called Israel, which became the special name assumed by the people descended from him. It was the name given to him by the angel who wrestled with Jacob during the return journey from Mesopotamia. This angel was another manifest symbol of Christ."[75]

"Actually," Augustine continues, "Jacob wins the victory over the angel who willingly submitted to defeat. This, of course, dramatizes a mystery. It is a foreshadowing of Christ's passion, in which the Jews are the seeming victors over Christ."[76] Notice how Augustine puts it as he brings the Old and New Testaments together: Genesis dramatizes the mystery of the Gospel. One might think of such a performative action to come after the original event. By necessity. For example, one thinks of movies about the life of President Lincoln, the American Civil War, or the 1969 moon landing. Such films are only developed after the original events that they look back upon. Yet such sequential ordering is not an issue for the biblical allegorists. The Christ event is dramatized by Genesis, even though the Gospels were written long after the Book of Genesis. As is true with biblical typology, so it is the case with allegory: first comes the shadow, and then the reality to which the shadow's presence decisively points forward.

Again, the pliability of time relative to the Old Testament preceding the New Testament is no difficulty for Augustine. Nor was it the case with other patristic and medieval interpreters, for whom the ultimate author is the Holy Spirit who inspired Scripture. This alleviates problems raised by chronology. And so it is no difficulty for Origen, Augustine, or the entire array of early Christian exegetes that the "dramatization" precedes the historical event.[77]

75. St. Augustine, *City of God* 16.39, in *City of God, Books VIII–XVI*, 558.

76. St. Augustine, *City of God* 16.39, in *City of God, Books VIII–XVI*, 558.

77. See *Dei Verbum* 11–12. See also *Verbum Domini*, 18: "We see clearly, then, how important it is for the People of God to be properly taught and trained to approach the sacred Scriptures in relation to the Church's living Tradition, and to recognize in them the word of God. Fostering such an approach in the faithful is important from the standpoint of the spiritual life. Here it might be helpful to recall the analogy drawn by the Fathers of the Church between the word of God which became 'flesh' and the word which became a 'book.' The Dogmatic Constitution *Dei Verbum* takes up this ancient tradition which holds, as Saint Ambrose says, that 'the body of the Son is the Scripture which we have

Here we are reminded of *Dei Verbum*'s nonnegotiable precept, echoed in Pope Benedict XVI's *Verbum Domini*, that "God speaks" to us in the inspired Scriptures. Benedict's words echo that of the rabbis and Church Fathers, as Kugel has shown. All of this undergirds the historicity and the constancy of the Catholic doctrine of biblical inspiration. Elsewhere, in one of his homilies, St. Augustine looks beyond the literal to the allegorical meaning: "Therefore it is a mystery, a sacrament, a prophecy, a figure; let us therefore understand it . . . Some high meaning is here."[78] Notice the adjective used here; not merely another meaning but a *high* meaning. The spiritual senses always point *upward*.

Reading Jacob's wrestling with the man in light of the Gospel, Augustine draws out an allegorical meaning in which Christ is prefigured: "And when the man had prevailed against the Angel, he kept hold of Him; yes, the man kept hold of Him Whom he had conquered. And said to Him, I will not let thee go, except thou bless me. When the conqueror was blessed by the conquered, *Christ was figured*."[79]

As is common in allegory, many of the details are set aside. Then one, possibly two details that are most useful in drawing out the Christological meaning are spotlighted. In this instance, it is Jacob's relentless grip, overcoming the more powerful angel, that symbolizes Christ blessing the persistent believer. As he develops the homily, Augustine makes the reader aware of Jacob's accessible proximity to the face of God, to recall Guardini's apt phrase. Augustine's treatment of the theophany is allegorical: "So great power had this conquered one (i.e., the angel) as to touch the thigh, and make lame. It was then with his own will that he was conquered. For he had power to lay down his strength, and he had power to take it up."[80]

Next, drawing on Christ's own words in John, Augustine makes the

---

received,' and declares that 'the words of God, expressed in human language, are in every way like human speech, just as the word of the eternal Father, when he took on himself the weak flesh of human beings, became like them.' When understood in this way, sacred Scripture presents itself to us, in the variety of its many forms and content, as a single reality. Indeed, 'through all the words of sacred Scripture, God speaks only one single word, his one utterance, in whom he expresses himself completely (cf. Heb 1:1–3).' Saint Augustine had already made the point clearly: '*Remember that one alone is the discourse of God which unfolds in all sacred Scripture, and one alone is the word which resounds on the lips of all the holy writers*'" (emphasis added). See *VD* for full citations.

78. St. Augustine, *Sermon* LXXII, in *Sermons on Selected Lessons*, 516–17.

79. St. Augustine, *Sermon* LXXII, in *Sermons on Selected Lessons*.

80. St. Augustine, *Sermon* LXXII, in *Sermons on Selected Lessons*.

allegorical connection even more concrete. He does so by focusing attention on Christ's divine will, aligned with the Father's and his laying down of his life freely: "He is not angry at being conquered, *for He is not angry at being crucified*."[81] This lack of anger, resentment, vengeance, or stubborn refusal sets Christ apart from all who prefigure him throughout salvation history. This is divine love of the Son, poured out for his own, having "loved them to the end" (*in finem dilexit eos*). For Augustine, this is what distinguishes Jesus Christ from Jacob, David, and all the figures that stretch across the biblical narrative and across our own horizon.

About a generation after St. Augustine, in what is today the southern region of Provence, France, St. Caesarius of Arles (468–542 AD) provides a similar treatment of the theophanic scene in a homily. Caesarius's allegorical interpretation is more developed than Augustine's (who influenced his thought): "In that struggle Jacob prefigured the people of the Jews; the angel with whom he wrestled signified our Lord and Savior ... 'Let me go,' said the angel, 'it is dawn.' This prefigured the Lord's resurrection, for the Lord, as you know very well, is read to have risen before dawn."[82]

Not surprisingly, for Caesarius, the angel signifies Christ. Yet Caesarius extends the allegory beyond Christ and the Resurrection, drawing a connection between Jacob and the Jewish people at the time of Christ: "Jacob wrestled with the angel *because the Jewish people were to wrestle with Christ even to death*. However, not all the Jews were unfaithful to Christ, as we said above, but a considerable number of them are read to have believed in his name, and for this reason the angel touched Jacob's thigh, which began to be lame. That foot with which he limped typified the Jews who did not believe in Christ; the one that remained uninjured signified those who received Christ the Lord."[83] In addition to the allegorical, early Christian interpreters examined this pivotal scene in the Jacob cycle tropologically. Let us consider some examples.

First, there is St. Clement of Alexandria, who writes of the angel as a pedagogical instructor of Jacob: "And he most manifestly appears as Ja-

81. St. Augustine, *Sermon* LXXII, in *Sermons on Selected Lessons*; emphasis added. Jn 10:18: "No one takes it from me, but I lay it down of my own accord. I have power to lay it down, and I have power to take it again; this charge I have received from my Father."

82. St. Caesarius of Arles, *Sermon* 88.5.

83. St. Caesarius of Arles, *Sermon* 88.5; emphasis added.

cob's instructor. He says accordingly to him, 'Lo, I am with thee, to keep thee in all the way in which thou shalt go; and I will bring thee back into this land: for I will not leave thee till I do what I have told thee.'[84] He is said, too, to have wrestled with him."[85] Going on, Clement explains, "And Jacob was left alone, and there wrestled with him a man [the Instructor] till the morning.' *This was the man who led, and brought, and wrestled with, and anointed the athlete Jacob against evil.*"[86] Here, the Alexandrian father sees a kind of ethical pedagogy in the theophany scene: it is the angel-teacher who guides Jacob the "athlete" toward moral purity.

What Clement writes subsequently integrates the tropological with the allegorical. The angel prefigures Christ the Logos, the divine Instructor. Even so, the primary emphasis of Clement's commentary is again the moral dimension: "It was God, the Word, the Instructor, who said to him again afterwards, 'Fear not to go down into Egypt.'[87] See how the Instructor follows the righteous man, and how He anoints the athlete, teaching him to trip up his antagonist."[88]

In similar fashion, the great pupil of Clement, Origen, deals with this theophany scene in a primarily tropological fashion. Origen sees a "moral battle," yet not as one might expect. Rather than an adversary, fighting against Jacob, Origen sees the angel as fighting *on behalf of* Jacob, for his moral purity:

> The angel is said to have wrestled with Jacob. Here, however, I understand the writer to mean, that it was not the same thing for the angel to have wrestled with Jacob, and to have wrestled against him; but the angel that wrestles with him is he who was present with him in order to secure his safety, who, after knowing also his moral progress, gave him in addition the name of Israel, i.e., he is with him in the struggle, and assists him in the contest; seeing there was undoubtedly another angel against whom he contended, and against whom he had to carry on a contest.[89]

Elsewhere, Origen makes an intrinsic connection between the moral challenges of the Christian life and the spiritual powers beyond the

84. See Gn 28:15.
85. St. Clement of Alexandria, "The Instructor," 1.7.
86. St. Clement of Alexandria, "The Instructor," 1.7; emphasis added.
87. Gn 46:3.
88. Clement, "The Instructor," 1.7.
89. Origen, *De Principiis*, 8.25.

veil that threaten the believer. Summoning St. Paul in Ephesians 6, he writes: "Finally, Paul has not said that we wrestle with princes, or with powers, but against principalities and powers. And hence, although Jacob wrestled, it was unquestionably against one of those powers which, Paul declares, resist and contend with the human race, and especially with the saints. And therefore, at last the Scripture says of him that 'he wrestled with the angel and had power with God' so that the struggle is supported by help of the angel, but the prize of success conducts the conqueror to God."[90]

Later, St. Ambrose interpreted the scene along tropological lines. Yet, unlike Origen, the man who was Augustine's bishop and mentor is content to see the figure as *God himself.* As Jacob wrestles with God, he struggles to forsake the things of this world and, in imaging God, being filled with virtue: "Therefore Jacob, who had purified his heart of all pretense and was manifesting a peaceable disposition, first cast off all that was his, then remained behind alone and wrestled with God. For whoever forsakes worldly things comes nearer to the image and likeness of God. What is it to wrestle with God, *other than to enter upon the struggle for virtue, to contend with one who is stronger and to become a better imitator of God than the others are?*"[91]

For Ambrose, then, it is precisely this accessible proximity to God that leads to grappling with one's life decisions in light of this divine encounter. And this "wrestling" is the path that leads to the virtuous life. For Ambrose, Jacob's wrestling with the angel presents the Church with an image of every Christian's daily struggle: it is only when we wrestle with the texts of Scripture that we are blessed with a new name, be it *servant, truth-teller, peacemaker*, and so on. In other words, for Ambrose, every time the Scripture is read with such divine expectancy, there is the possibility that the Christian's name may, like Jacob's, be changed to reflect the growth and transformation in moral development in the believer.

Although the next part of Ambrose's meditation is a continuation of his tropological interpretation of the scene, there is a sense in which is also anagogical in nature: "Because Jacob's faith and devotion were un-

90. Origen, *De Principiis*, 8.25. Eph 6:10–20.

91. St. Ambrose, *Jacob and the Happy Life*, 2.7.30, in *Seven Exegetical Works*, 163–64; emphasis added.

conquerable, the Lord revealed His hidden mysteries to him by touching the side of his thigh. For it was by descent from him that the Lord Jesus was to be born of a virgin, and Jesus would be neither unlike nor unequal to God."[92] Homing in, he writes, "The numbness in the side of Jacob's thigh foreshadowed the cross of Christ, who would bring salvation to all men by spreading the forgiveness of sins throughout the whole world and would give resurrection to the departed by the numbness and torpidity of His own body. On this account the sun rightly rose on holy Jacob, *for the saving cross of the Lord shone brightly on his lineage, and at the same time the Sun of Justice rises on the man who recognizes God, because He is Himself the Everlasting Light.*"[93]

Like Justin writing long before them, for both Augustine and Caesarius, the first movement in this text is undoubtedly of an allegorical sort. The wounding of Jacob's thigh again signifies Christ and his crucifixion. In the next movement, however, there is a path of ascent *toward the heavenly Christ* in splendor. The image of the sun rising on Jacob leads Ambrose to contemplate the believer in relation to the "Sun of Justice." This image and that of God as "everlasting Light" go beyond descriptions of the Resurrection and toward the eschatological reality of the believer being united with Christ in glory.

Finally, Genesis 32:22–32 appears to have been probed less from the *anagogical* sense than the allegorical or tropological senses. There is an explanation for the seeming lack of anagogy attached to this seminal text. First, we must distinguish between early Jewish and early Christian interpretations of the text. In Second Temple Judaism, the entire scene did evoke—let us not refer to them as anagogical interpretations—"mystical" meanings. As Kugel summarizes, "There is considerable evidence of an ancient [Jewish] belief that one of God's angels was named Jacob or Israel. The origins of such an idea are diverse. Certainly, the very name *Israel* and its explanation in Gen 32:28 were important factors … if *Israel* really meant 'man who saw God,' then perhaps the 'man' in question was not the earthly Jacob but *an angelic Israel* who, dwelling in heaven, might quite naturally *see God* on a regular basis."[94]

Several ancient Jewish texts seem to bear this out. First, Philo of Alex-

92. St. Ambrose, *Jacob and the Happy Life*, 2.7.30, in *Seven Exegetical Works*.

93. St. Ambrose, *Jacob and the Happy Life*, 2.7.30, in *Seven Exegetical Works*; emphasis added.

94. Kugel, *Traditions of the Bible*, 397; emphasis added.

andria writes that "God's firstborn, the logos, who holds eldership among the angels ... and many names are his, for he is called 'the Beginning' ... the Man after His image, and 'he that sees God.'"[95] Another Jewish text that seems to assert the notion of an "angelic Jacob" is the first-century text known as the *Prayer of Joseph*, composed in Aramaic. Here, Jacob/Israel is not merely an angel but a ruling archangel. The fragment in question reads, "I Jacob, who am speaking to you, *am also Israel, an angel of God and a ruling spirit.* Abraham and Isaac were created before any work. But I, Jacob, whom men call Jacob but whose name is Israel, am he who God called Israel, which means a man seeing God, because I am the firstborn of every living thing to whom God gives life ... and I, Israel, *the archangel of the power of the Lord and chief captain among the sons of God*, am I not Israel, *the first minister before the face of God*?"[96]

Lastly, the Jewish pseudepigraphal book known as 1 Enoch may allude to this Jacob-angel tradition in several passages. If so, the reference is indirect, as the book does not name Jacob/Israel. But it identifies an archangel known as *Phanuel*, an alternative spelling of *Peniel*, the very name of the place renamed by Jacob in Genesis 32: "And I saw angels who could not be counted, a thousand thousands, and ten thousand times ten thousand, encircling that house; and Michael, and Raphael, and Gabriel, *and Phanuel, and the holy angels who are above the heavens, go in and out of that house.*"[97] Earlier in 1 Enoch, the angel Phanuel is associated with those who will receive eternal life: "And he said to me: 'This first is Michael, the merciful and long-suffering: and the second, who is set over all the diseases and all the wounds of the children of men, is Raphael: and the third, who is set over all the powers, is Gabriel: and the fourth, who is set over the repentance unto hope of those who inherit eternal life, is named *Phanuel*.'"[98]

These examples from 1 Enoch may or may not confer an angelic identity upon Jacob/Israel. Yet the texts from Philo and the *Prayer of Joseph* most certainly do. Given this angelic speculation in Jewish tradition—many of which were contemporary with earliest Christianity—it is understandable why patristic figures may have sought to avoid the

95. Philo of Alexandria, *Confusion of Tongues*, in *Vol. IV*, 146.

96. *Prayer of Joseph*, Fragment 1, in Kugel, *Traditions of the Bible*, 398; emphasis added. See also idem, *Ladder of Jacob*, 3:3; 4:1–3.

97. *1 Enoch* 71:8, in Charles, *Pseudepigrapha of the Old Testament*, 236; emphasis added.

98. *1 Enoch* 40:9, in Charles, *Pseudepigrapha of the Old Testament*.

anagogical sense and given priority to the allegorical and tropological senses as it concerned Jacob.

There is a New Testament text that may indirectly refer to Jacob's claim to have "seen God face-to-face." It is a text we encountered earlier in the book, John 1:18: *Deum nemo vidit umquam; unigenitus Deus, qui est in sinum Patris, ipse enarravit*—"No one has ever seen God; the only Son, who is in the bosom of the Father, he has made him known." There is no question that this text, the concluding verse of St. John's opening prologue, has Moses in mind. The prior verse reads: "For the law was given through Moses; grace and truth came through Jesus Christ."

Although Jacob's role in John is less pervasive compared with Moses, Jacob is referenced in several places. At the end of chapter 1, Jesus tells Nathanael that he will see "heaven opened, and the angels of God ascending and descending upon the Son of man,"[99] a clear reference to Jacob's vision of *angels* "ascending and descending" upon the ladder reaching from earth to heaven.[100] Additionally, Jesus's encounter with the Samaritan woman occurs at "Jacob's well."[101] These references to the great patriarch in the early chapters of John are not incidental. His claims of seeing God "face-to-face" is memorialized in Genesis and is again presented in *Targum Jonathan*, the Aramaic translation (and interpretation) of Genesis. These Jacobian motifs in John suggest that the Apostle's proclamation that "no one has seen God" in 1:18 is a double reference, first to Moses, the Lawgiver, and second to Jacob, the father of Israel. If so, St. John may be the best example of an anagogical meaning being applied to the scene of Jacob wrestling with an angel.

Consider Jacob's claim: "I have seen God face-to-face, yet my life is preserved."[102] In contrast, St. John declares, "No one has ever seen God; the only Son who is in the bosom of the Father, he has made him known."[103] Once again, Guardini's wisdom is sound. It is man who seeks. Yet it is God who makes himself known. *Sapientia vero ubi invenitur? Et quis est locus intellegentiae? Nescit homo structuram eius, nec invenitur in terra viventium.*[104]

99. Jn 1:51.
100. See Gn 28:12.
101. See Jn 4:6.
102. Gn 32:30.
103. Jn 1:18.
104. Job 28:13: "But where shall wisdom be found? And where is the place of understanding? Man does not know the way to it, and it is not found in the land of the living."

Reading St. John's prologue now presents us with an arresting possibility that, in addition to his referring to Moses and God's speaking to Moses face-to-face, St. John may be alluding to Jacob. Moreover, given early Jewish traditions, which gave voice to the speculative claim that Jacob/Israel was a kind of angel or angelic figure—and the "*first minister before the face of God*,"[105] St. John may be countering such mystical claims in his prologue. Given the complexity, depth, and breadth of John's Logos Christology, such a multivalent possibility (i.e., both Moses and Jacob in view) should not be entirely surprising.

Final Remarks: Seeing the Face of the Brotherly Christ

Our first theophanic scene—of Jacob wrestling with the angel—has yielded remarkable insights. The most salient are summarized here. First, according to the literal sense, structural and palistrophic analysis reveals key contextual clues about Genesis 32 in relation to the larger Jacob cycle. The theophany scene is a climactic moment in the larger sequence, as it concerns Jacob's familial relationships, especially with his wives and most of all with his brother Esau. Second, the history of spiritual exegesis of the text suggests a definitive pattern: the passage was explored according to the allegorical and tropological senses rather than the anagogical sense. Most frequently, in the allegorical sense, the angel prefigures the Crucified or Resurrected Jesus. Tropologically, Jacob signifies the righteous believer, whose virtue is tested and shaped through trial.

As to the relative lack of anagogical exegesis of the text, I suggested a possibility, that early Jewish angel speculation in which Jacob/Israel was identified with an (arch)angel figure may have restrained early Christian interpretation from such problematic assertions about one of the patriarchs. Jacob's accessible proximity to the Divine may have brought angels to the fore in ancient Judaism—yet the Christian interpreters avoided such interpretations. St. John possibly may have such traditions in mind in his prologue and may countering them in his proclamation that "No one has seen God except God the only Son."[106] If so, the the-

105. *Prayer of Joseph*, Fragment 1, in Kugel, *Traditions of the Bible*, 398; emphasis added. See also idem, *Ladder of Jacob*, 3:3; 4:1–3.

106. See Jn 1:18.

ophanic text is being summoned up *anagogically*. It is a refutation that neither Moses nor Jacob nor any figure from Israel's past (nor any other person) has in fact seen God except Jesus, the divine Son of God.

Drawing these observations together from both the literal and spiritual senses, one final comment is offered. It concerns Jacob's estranged relationship with his brother, Esau. As discussed, Jacob's wrestling with and prevailing over the angel should not be viewed in isolation from the larger cycle. Rather, his prevailing "with God and men" in Genesis 32 informs the substance of the brothers' reconciliation in the following chapter. With St. John, we may dispense with the notion that Jacob *actually saw God*. He did not, as the Apostle makes clear.[107] Yet his theophanic encounter with the angel of God did transform Jacob. It summoned all his strength, perseverance, and courage, and he caused him to endure Christ-like suffering from the episode.

His conquering spirit was honored by God, however, and Jacob's faith conferred upon him a new name—*Israel*, one who struggles with God and men and prevails. He memorializes the place, as he did earlier at Beth-el, with a new name as well: *Peni'el*. As he stresses, "I have seen God face to face, yet my life is preserved." Whatever Jacob "saw" and encountered, it had the effect of healing his estranged relationship with Esau, with whom he was alienated: "Jacob said, 'No, I pray you, if I have found favor in your sight, then accept my present from my hand; for truly to see your face is like seeing the face of God, with such favor have you received me.'"[108]

As Kass summarizes, Jacob may possess a crafty disposition and the use of flattery. Yet the comparison "of seeing Esau's face with seeing the face of God cannot be for Jacob simply artful" or calculating. Jacob is calculating—but not here.[109] Rather, he offers to Esau "his own profound understanding of the connection between the two encounters."[110]

In the previous scene, Jacob stood *facie ad faciem*—"face-to-face" with God—and was forever changed. Now, he is *facie ad faciem* with Esau. Like the theophanic scene, with its dramatic nature, the relation-

107. See Jn 1:18; Ex 32:20.

108. Gn 33:10.

109. Kass, *Beginning of Wisdom*, 469; emphasis added. I agree with Kass. Jacob's response to Esau's request, that Jacob keep what he has (Gn 33:9–10), is not a "work of calculation," as Nahum Sarna infers. It is profoundly sincere. See Sarna, *Genesis*, 230.

110. Kass, *Beginning of Wisdom*, 469.

ship of Jacob and Esau has been marked by a similar sort of life-and-death struggle. As Jacob is brought low in the mystery of seeing God, so too is his own brother's unexpected graceful opening *a mystery* that transforms Jacob before our eyes:

> The mystery that is Esau, like the mystery that is God, inspires awe and reverence. *Jacob sees another divine image, the equal god-likeness of his equal brother.* Further, he sees *the majesty of divine likeness*, with its powers to forgive, and bestow favor but also to judge and to take life. Jacob has looked into the depths, recognized his unworthiness, faced the possibility of his own deserved death, *and experienced the unmerited superhuman display of grace* from the one who stood ready and able to destroy him. What Cain learns only after he murdered Abel, Jacob discovers as fratricide is wonderfully avoided.[111]

Kass's analysis is astute and compels one to reflect upon the Jacob–Esau relationship in light of the Cain–Abel one earlier in Genesis.[112] In a sense, the dynamic between Jacob and Esau redeems that between Cain and Abel. Jacob's encounter with "the majesty of divine likeness"—in the angel of God *and in his estranged brother*—brings about a fraternal healing that is violently lacking in the narrative of Cain and Abel. More than this, Jacob's wrestling with the angel, when examined from all Four Senses, allows us to ascend toward the face of the Lord. Even though anagogical impressions of the text are scant, the movement is decidedly upward. What is lacking in Cain is filled in Jacob. Even so, what is lacking in Jacob—in all men—is perfected in Jesus. Finally, this theophanic scene points us beyond Jacob and the angel—beyond Jacob and Esau to *the brotherly Christ.*

This phrase—Christ, our brother—leaves some wanting. In contemporary Christianity, it can regrettably conjure up malformed images of "Christ the social justice warrior" of liberation theology. This need not be so, nor is this our point of reference. Rather, Christ is our brother in light of the Incarnation—the Word became flesh and in so doing became our divine Brother. Christ is our brother! Not in a back-slapping way that lessens his divinity, nor in a hermeneutic of false liberation. No—Christ is the crucified Brother of humanity.

As St. Paul teaches us, though we were helpless sinners, "in due time," Christ our Brother died for us, his ungodly brothers (and sisters).[113] This

111. Kass, *Beginning of Wisdom*, 469–70; emphases added.
112. See Gn 4:1*ff.*
113. See Rom 5:6, KJV.

is no human brotherhood—though we are united with him in his flesh. No—it is Christ, the only Son of God, and his death on the Cross, that alone heals our wounds and restores us to his Father, our Father: "For if, when we were enemies, we were reconciled to God by the death of his Son, much more, being reconciled, we shall be saved by His life."[114]

Jacob and his wrestling with the angel—opened through the Four Senses—helps us ascend to Christ, our divine Brother. Christ, who died for us and rose for us, will restore us to the Father in heaven. In Jacob—in relief—we gaze upon the Brotherly Christ, who alone has seen God and reveals him to us for our sake and our salvation. Christ's brotherly perfection is the model, the icon, for us to grow in our own perfection as brothers and sisters, as children of God: "Not that I have already obtained this or am already perfect; *but I press on to make it my own, because Christ Jesus has made me his own.* Brethren, I do not consider that I have made it my own; but one thing I do, forgetting what lies behind and straining forward to what lies ahead, I press on toward the goal for the prize of the upward call of God in Christ Jesus."[115]

This examination of this first theophany scene has opened fresh insights upon a familiar passage and has revealed more of the face of the Lord through the Four Senses. But our portrait of Jesus is just coming into focus. There is much more to see. In chapter 5, we turn from Jacob to Moses and with him contemplate the glorious Christ.

Meditatio

The "lonely planet" is a common motif in science fiction.[116] Even those who are not diehard fans of the genre can imagine Luke Skywalker or a character from *Star Trek* traipsing across a sand-filled horizon. There is nothing or no one for as far as the eye can see. The hero is isolated from society and in some sense even from himself. He must get across this barren place and discover his true purpose. While the genre of science fiction is relatively recent, the motif is quite old. It reverberates in stories of the high seas and in various myths. One thinks of Sam and Frodo heading across the wastelands of Middle Earth toward Mordor in *The Lord of the Rings.* They must complete Gandalf's task and "unmake" the Ring of Power.

114. Rom 5:10, KJV.
115. Phil 3:12–14; emphasis added.
116. See esp. Lewis, *Space Trilogy*.

Jacob too inhabits a lonely planet. And it is not merely the geographic wilderness of the deserts he crosses, from Beer-sheba to Bethel, from Bethel to Shechem, and on to Peni'el. The lonely planet Jacob walks across is alienation from God. His early life is characterized by struggle, his very birth by "grasping."[117] The prophet Jeremiah surely has the younger twin Jacob in mind when he warns, "Let everyone beware of his neighbor, and put no trust in any brother; for every brother is a supplanter (*aqôb*), and every neighbor goes about as a slanderer."[118] As the story of the grasping Jacob unfolds, he orders his world with his own brute strength. He seizes his brother's birthright and flees to his uncle Laban, a fugitive now from Esau's murderous threats. Even in this wasteland, however, God reassures Jacob of protection and his eventual return: "*so that I come again to my father's house in peace, then the Lord shall be my God*."[119]

Paradoxically, it is this same trait that characterized his "war in the womb"—grasping—that brings him into a life and death battle with God.[120] In the theophany scene, Jacob grips the angelic figure and refuses to "let go" until he is blessed.[121] There, at Peni'el, he meets God "face-to-face." Interiorly, Jacob's life was a kind of lonely planet. How could it not have been? Despite all of his exterior might, skills, and determined will, Jacob's relationships were not characterized by light and life. They were not filled with hope but with fear. In all of his striving, running, and wandering, the barren place in his heart yearned for the spiritual determination of the psalmist, who cries: "*My soul thirsts for God, for the living God. When shall I come and behold the face of God?*"[122]

In the Gospels, Jesus meets another soul, weary from walking across a lonely planet of her own. Of all places, Jesus meets her at *Jacob's well:* Jesus "left Judea and departed again to Galilee. He had to pass through Samaria. So he came to a city of Samaria, called Sychar, near the field that Jacob gave to his son Joseph. Jacob's well was there, and so Jesus, wearied as he was with his journey, sat down beside the well. It was about the sixth hour. There came a woman of Samaria to draw water.

117. See Gn 25:26.
118. Jer 9:4.
119. Gn 28:21; emphasis added.
120. See Gn 25:23.
121. Gn 32:26.
122. Ps 42:2; emphasis added.

Jesus said to her, 'Give me a drink.'"[123] Throughout this poignant encounter at the well of Jacob, the woman, a Samaritan, "wrestles" with Jesus in her questioning: "How is it that you, a Jew, ask a drink of me, a woman of Samaria?"[124] "From where do you get this living water," she asks, and "Are you greater than *our father Jacob*?"[125]

Like her forefather Jacob, she is alienated from her community and herself. Like Jacob, there is a barren place in her heart that longs to see the face of God. In the Eastern Orthodox liturgy, this Jacobean figure, this spouseless soul, is identified as St. Photini. At Peni'el, God meets Jacob, the "supplanter," and gives him a new name: Israel, *one who struggles with God and men, and prevails.*

In John, Jesus seeks out this weary Samaritan, knowing that the lonely planet she inhabits has brought her to a place of emptiness. She is waiting to be filled with Living Water, with grace. Although the Evangelist does not identify her name, her "wrestling with God" is beautifully preserved in the Gospel. Whatever her name was prior to her Peni'el-like moment, she receives a new name. Like Jacob, she was given "accessible proximity" to the face of the Lord. Whereas Jacob wrestled with the Angel of the Lord, however, she spars with the divine Son himself and receives him as her true Bridegroom. Now she is no longer a lost soul at a sun-scorched well at midday. Once baptized, she becomes *Photini*, a "luminous one." And many more came to believe in Jesus through this light-bearer.[126]

Every page of Scripture is an invitation. To drop our buckets and to drink of Living Water. Jacob's might and Photini's questions are no match against the grace of God. Nothing can pin down the divine Son, who is waiting to wrestle us in his word, and make us more luminescent.

> How can I sing to You, O Luminous and Holy One?
> For it is only the mouth that is pure and luminous
> and which resembles you, Lord, that shall sing to You
> —the luminous to the Luminous One,
> —the pure to the Pure One,
> For it is his voice that is pleasing to You.
>
> —St. Ephrem

123. Jn 4:3–7.
124. Jn 4:9.
125. Jn 4:11–12; emphasis added.
126. See Jn 4:39.
Epigraph. St. Ephrem the Syrian, in Brock, *Luminous Eye*, 74.

CHAPTER 5

Contemplating the Face of the Glorious Christ with Moses (Exodus 33)

> [Moses] shone with glory. And although lifted up through such lofty experiences, he is still unsatisfied in his desire for more. He still thirsts for that which he consistently filled himself to capacity, as if he had never partaken, beseeching God to appear to him, not according to his capacity, but according to God's true being.
>
> —St. Gregory of Nyssa

The last encounter scene focused on Jacob, who wrestled with God in Genesis. Our next scene is taken from the Pentateuch, too. We turn to the life of the great Lawgiver, Moses, in a climactic moment in the narrative of Exodus:

> And the Lord said to Moses, "This very thing that you have spoken I will do; for you have found favor in my sight, and I know you by name." Moses said, "I pray thee, show me thy glory." And he said, "I will make all my goodness pass before you, and will proclaim before you my name 'The Lord'; and I will be gracious to whom I will be gracious, and will show mercy on whom I will show mercy. But," he said, "you cannot see my face; for man shall not see me and live." And the Lord said, "Behold, there is a place by me where you shall stand upon the rock; and while my glory passes by I will put you in a cleft of the rock, and I will cover you with my hand until I have passed by; then I will take away my hand, and you shall see my back; but my face shall not be seen."[1]

1. Ex 33:17–23.

Sensus Litteralis

Before moving directly to a discussion of the literal sense, a few words are necessary about the sources consulted in this study of Exodus. Sifting through modern research on Exodus presents several challenges. Two may be mentioned. First, the scholarly literature pertaining to the Book of Exodus is vast.[2] A good deal of this material is in the form of monographs and essays, and many are of a technical sort.[3] Second, the majority of commentaries on Exodus embrace the source critical approach. This is not to say they should not be consulted, but such commentaries often forego much discussion of the unity of the text, not to mention its role in the biblical canon. Many technical commentaries more or less abandon these crucial topics altogether. In their place are discussions of source-critical minutiae that only specialists or the most pedantic reader may appreciate.

Close analysis of texts is welcome and much needed. Yet, too often, such approaches do not serve the curious reader.[4] Such commentaries do not expound on the meaning of, say, Exodus 32, as much as they stake out turf on source critical theories. They tend to operate in a microanalytical way that ends up fragmenting the text. Elements of history and authenticity are emphasized over theological concerns, and one is often left with more questions than answers, yet no wiser about the essence of it all, the text's meaning.

2. Although there are many full-length commentaries that deal with the book, the extant of such literature is dwarfed by those dedicated to Genesis. Significant modern commentaries on Exodus include: Childs, *Book of Exodus*; Cassuto, *Commentary on the Book of Exodus*; Cole, *Exodus*; Dozeman, *Exodus*; Driver, *Exodus*; Durham, *Exodus*; Fretheim, *Exodus*; Hamilton, *Exodus*; Janzen, *Exodus*; Noth, *Exodus*; Propp, *Exodus 1–18*; idem, *Exodus 19–40*; Sarna, *Exodus*.

3. A sampling of the massive number of technical studies pertaining to the Book of Exodus includes: Bietak, "Comments on the 'Exodus'"; Davies, "Was There an Exodus?"; Hayward, "St. Jerome and the Meaning of the High-Priestly Vestments"; Hendel, "Sacrifice as a Cultural System"; Hess, "Divine Name Yahweh"; Hoffmeier, *Israel in Egypt*; Hoffmeier and Magaly, *Did I Not Bring Israel Out of Egypt?*; McCarthy, "Exodus 3:14"; Rendsburg, "Date of the Exodus"; Van Seeters, "Law and the Wilderness Rebellion Tradition"; Weinfield, "The Decalogue." For recent, extensive bibliographies, see both Hamilton, *Exodus*, 623–66, and Propp, *Exodus 19–40*, 37–97.

4. Some of this "inside baseball" discussion might be more suitable at an academic conference among scholarly peers. There, a dozen or so linguists and source critics can gather and engage in such discussions. It is unclear how much benefit this is for the general reader, however.

I have consulted many of these works to be thorough, always on the lookout for nuggets of exegetical insight. Yet I have refrained from foisting them upon the reader to appear erudite. A few exceptions stand out from the population described. Four or five commentaries are especially useful for my purposes, and I provide the reader with a brief explanation as to their selection.

First, William Propp's Anchor Bible commentary is source critical in nature, and his approach is more anthropological than theological. Once one recognizes these limitations, the value of the massive (850 pp.) commentary on Exodus 19–40 comes through.[5] His mastery of biblical Hebrew and close reading of each verse offers countless insights. Second, Victor Hamilton, a contemporary Evangelical scholar, provides a counterweight to Propp.[6] He emphasizes the unity of the text, divine authorship, and so on. What both of these Old Testament scholars share is a trained eye for detail and extensive discussion of the text itself.

Third, and similar to Hamilton, is John Durham, a Protestant scholar whose commentary on Exodus is highly regarded. His translation is worthy of close consideration.[7] Like the aforementioned, Durham provides in-depth analysis of the text. Hebrew and other ancient languages are engaged, but in a way that is not off-putting to those without such access.

Fourth, and on the subject of Bible translation, we look to Jewish scholar Robert Alter's work in *The Five Books of Moses* for expertise on the text itself and, as always, thought-provoking translations.[8] Every serious student of the Old Testament should become acquainted with Alter's translations of the Hebrew Bible.[9] Those without knowledge of the original language will benefit by reading the text in his fresh translations, with a keen eye to the original Hebrew. Alter's expertise brings out elements of the biblical text that are hidden in the colloquiums and nuances of biblical poetry. English-only readers of the Bible are urged,

5. Propp, *Exodus 1–18*.
6. Hamilton, *Exodus*.
7. Durham, *Exodus*.
8. Alter, *Five Books of Moses*.
9. Alter's life work has been a translation of the entire Hebrew Bible. Various volumes have been published over the years, dealing with the Pentateuch, the Psalms, Wisdom books, and so on (see the bibliography). Happily, Alter's massive project, titled *The Hebrew Bible*, is now complete and was recently released in a large, three-volume set of the entire Tanak.

as much as possible, "to do something" with the original languages.[10] Short of that, periodically consulting multiple English translations is advised. At the least, doing so reminds one that the Bible did not drop from heaven in the Revised Standard Version.

Aside from these heavily consulted sources, one additional commentary proved valuable and deserves mention. The work of rabbi and Hebrew scholar Umberto Cassuto (1883–1951) was pivotal to my engagement of the text. Cassuto distinguished himself from the overwhelming majority of European biblical critics in the early twentieth century. Not only did Cassuto mount a decisive critique of the *Documentary Hypothesis* (DH),[11] but he also then set out a positive vision of exegesis of the biblical text from the standpoint of the integrity of the text—and believability of the its divine origins and roots in the Mosaic tradition.[12]

In the preface to his commentary, Cassuto states three guiding principles for the proper interpretation of Exodus. We adhere closely to these following aims. First, Cassuto writes, "This commentary on the Book of Exodus is entirely new, being based on new exegetical principles. Its aim is to expound [it] scientifically, with the help of all the resources that modern scholarship puts at our disposal today. To achieve this purpose, its approach differs considerably from that of most of contemporary scientific commentaries . . . In their opinion, the study of the sources takes precedence over that of the book as we have it."[13] He continues, "To my mind, the reverse view is the more reasonable. A scientific exposition of any literary work should aim at elucidating and evaluating the work itself; whereas the dissection of its sources is only a means to this end . . . Ultimately, we must realize that this is the book

10. Aside from university courses, there are a number of helpful resources for nonspecialists to engage the original biblical language, including online courses, books and CDs, YouTube videos, and the like.

11. Recall that in a series of prominent lectures, Cassuto critiqued the DH and its five major tenets. These lectures were later published as *The Documentary Hypothesis and the Composition of the Pentateuch.*

12. Cassuto, *Commentary on the Book of Exodus.*

13. Cassuto, *Exodus*, 1: "The primary differences between the present commentary and others are, in the main, three, to wit: The commentaries written in our generation on any book of the Pentateuch are, in most instances, chiefly devoted to investigating the sources and to determining the process by which they have been fitted together. They annotate the documentary fragments that they discern in the book rather than the book itself. The great importance attached by exegetes to the question of the sources diverts their attention from the study of the work that has grown out of these documents."

whose significance is so great in the history of Israel and of all mankind, and that it alone has factual existence, not the imaginary work that rests on mere conjecture."[14]

The next point Cassuto makes is along similar lines: "One of the principal sources—possibly the principal source—was, if I am not mistaken, an ancient heroic poem, an epic dating back to earliest times, that told at length the story of the Egyptian bondage, of the liberation and of the wandering of the children of Israel in the wilderness. In the course of my commentary I frequently indicate, in detail, the use made of this poem, and I point out the traces of the epic still perceptible in the Scriptural text."[15] This point of Cassuto's is somewhat speculative, and his detractors would suggest the theory fills his need for an early written corpus of some sort. This is a fair critique in and of itself. Yet it is an ironic criticism, raised by scholars who embrace the DH, which itself is a speculative reconstruction of written sources. The DH has held sway for well over a century, yet, strictly speaking, the source traditions upon which the theory rests have not been unearthed.[16]

There is an array of possibilities for how the text may have developed over the centuries prior to the Exile. The vast majority of Pentateuchal scholars now admit to a great deal of diversity in the sources and composition of the Pentateuch; most are unconvinced of Mosaic authorship. Cassuto did not insist on Mosaic authorship, strictly speaking. His larger point is that the Pentateuch reflects far more unity than disunity. It is this particular assertion—of a broadly unified text, admittedly out of vogue today—with which I agree.

Many of the critics of Cassuto's day overlooked insights from "the literature and culture of the neighbouring nations of Israel."[17] At the outset, he states his intentions to engage such materials to help illuminate the biblical text. "It is impossible to gain a correct understanding of Scripture without continual reference to the environment in which

14. Cassuto, *Exodus*, 1.

15. Cassuto, *Exodus*, 2: "The sources of the Book of Exodus are not in my view those recognized by the current hypothesis, namely, P (Priestly Code), E (Elohist), J (Jahwist) and their different strata."

16. To be fair, simply because the J, E, D, and P sources are not extant does not mean that they did not exist. Moreover, the lack of documentation does not invalidate the DH, which rests upon considerable literary data. Our point is simply that there is an irony here, in that it is *source critics* who often dismiss Cassuto's argument about alternative sources of influence.

17. Cassuto, *Exodus*, 2; emphasis added.

the Israelites lived and worked, and in which the books of the Bible were composed."[18] Cassuto's approach cuts against the grain of much source criticism: "My commentary is concerned with the plain meaning of the text. I have aimed to explain the natural sense of Scripture according to its original import ... Our task is obviously to search out, to the utmost of our capacity, the true meaning of the Scriptural text."[19]

The merits of the above five sources help guide the analysis that follows. We now turn to contextual remarks about the book as a whole, before considering the particulars of Exodus 33:17–23.

Helpfully, Hamilton frames his discussion of the Book of Exodus in light of its place in the canon: "Before the book of Exodus begins to narrate an *exodus* ("a way out") of Hebrews from Egypt, it first describes an *eisodus* ("a way into") of a Hebrew family from Egypt."[20] Durham likewise emphasizes its continuity with the Book of Genesis: "This opening passage of Exodus functions as a compact transitional unit that summarizes that part of the preceding Genesis narrative that is essential to what follows, states a new and discontinuous situation, and anticipates the progress of the family of Jacob/Israel toward their birth, in exodus and at Sinai, as the people of God."[21]

These remarks may be somewhat obvious, yet they are necessary. Without this acknowledgment, of the place of the book within it larger structure, any discussion of Exodus risks running adrift from the narrative in which it is located. Establishing this canonical framework helps reveal the true theme of the book. If Exodus was primarily interested in explaining how the Lord delivered his people from bondage in Egypt, the book might have well ended with the Song of Moses in Exodus 15, which celebrates the Crossing of the Red Sea.[22] Instead, the book moves well beyond, with the journey through the wilderness,[23] the ratification of the covenant and giving of the Law at Sinai,[24] and the divine instructions for the construction of the Tabernacle.[25]

18. Cassuto, *Exodus*, 2: "In this commentary, on the other hand, I have paid constant attention to the literary works of these peoples, as well as to all that archaeological research has taught us regarding their cultural achievements."

19. Cassuto, *Exodus*, 2.

20. Hamilton, *Exodus*, xxi.

21. Durham, *Exodus*, 2–3.

22. See Ex 14:1–30.

23. See Ex 16–18.

24. See Ex 19–24.

25. Ex 25–40.

What, then, is the book primary about? Hamilton sums up: "Israel's misery is not the Lord's primary motivating factor" in acting on their behalf, in delivering His people from Egypt.[26] Rather, "It is to fulfill the covenant he has made with Abraham, Isaac, and Jacob ... *The covenant at Sinai is not distinct from the covenant God has made with Abraham.* Rather, it fulfills that covenant. There is not one covenant with the patriarchs and another covenant with their offspring four centuries later. What God has started in Gen 12 he is bringing to completion in Exod 19–24."[27] Hamilton is essentially correct in his larger point of the covenantal continuity that exists between Genesis and Exodus. What God began with Abraham back in Genesis 12 is playing out in Exodus 19–24 (Law) and 25–40 (Tabernacle). What had begun in Genesis with a simple command to "Go" is now greatly expanded in Exodus. Now, Abraham's many descendants are graced with the knowledge of right living (Law) and right worship (Tabernacle).

These are all helpful insights. Upon closer inspection, however, a few things are missing from Hamilton's analysis that must now be stressed. Drawing upon the careful study of the characteristics of and differences between ancient covenants,[28] I add the following four remarks.

1. There are various types of covenants in the ancient Near East. It is important to be as precise as possible in describing the nature of those between God and his people, as found in the Old Testament. Strong literary evidence suggests that the covenantal scenes in Genesis and Exodus[29] are of a familial sort, with relational dimensions and household dynamics, rather than a "one-way" legalistic obligation, as in a vassal treaty.[30]

26. Hamilton, *Exodus*, xxi.

27. Hamilton, *Exodus*, xxi, xxiv; emphasis added.

28. See Hahn, *Kinship by Covenant*; Cross, "Kinship and Covenant in Ancient Israel," in *From Epic to Canon*.

29. Additionally, there are numerous connections between the covenantal scenes in Genesis and Exodus, particularly regarding the Abrahamic and Sinai covenants: "For all these reasons I would draw a line between the 'covenant-between-the-pieces' and the Sinai covenant. The initial covenants with Abraham and Israel have been described in such a way as to reflect each other. Both concern the nationhood of Israel, but notably absent from both Genesis 15 and Exodus 20–24 are references to an Israelite monarchy ("great name") and the blessing to all nations. These elements of the Abrahamic promise will be taken up in later covenants with Israel." Hahn, *Kinship by Covenant*, 113–14.

30. "It should be apparent from the discussion of the history of covenant research above that the very definition of 'covenant' [Hebrew = *bĕrît* or Greek = *diathēkē*) in the

2. This sort of familial covenant is often characterized by ritual and cultic acts like sacrifice, meal-sharing, and especially oath-making. Such characteristics are found throughout the covenantal scenes in the Pentateuch.[31]

3. "Divine covenants are unique. God is not merely invoked, he actually enters into kinship bonds by covenant."[32] One would expect the key members of each family or tribe to enter a covenant cast in kinship terms. What is surprising is that *God does so.*

4. Finally, in Exodus, a familial (or kinship-type) covenant "is cast in terms of a father-son relationship."[33] This is first expressed in Exodus 4:22, where God refers to Israel as his *bekōr* (Hebrew for "firstborn") and culminates in the Sinai covenant: "The covenant ritual at Sinai represents an act of national initiation. Israel publicly witnesses to a solemn acceptance of God's vocation to serve as 'a kingdom of priests' (Ex 19:6). The climactic scene in which Israel's elders draw near and eat a meal with the God of Israel (24:9–11) vividly conveys the newly-formed covenant communion and family fellowship."[34]

Considering all the above, a concise thematic summary of the book can be offered as follows*:* Exodus narrates the ongoing story of the Abrahamic covenant, in which the living God liberates Israel from slavery in Egypt, restoring them as his "firstborn," with a priestly and redemptive

---

Old and New Testaments is a matter of controversy. As we have seen, biblical scholars divide roughly into two camps on this issue. On the one hand, there are those who view covenant in a unilateral perspective, as synonymous with 'obligation' in the legalistic sense (e.g., Wellhausen, Kutsch, Perlitt, Nicholson). On the other hand, there are those who recognize that a covenant is always bilateral in some sense and serves to establish or renew a (kinship) relationship between two parties (McCarthy, Freedman, Kalluveettil, Cross, etc.). It is not the purpose here to rehearse this debate and argue step-by-step for a certain definition of covenant. This has been done at length and competently by others, most notably Frank Moore Cross and Gordon Hugenberger. It must suffice here to indicate that we are firmly in the camp of those who understand covenant in bilateral, relational categories." Hahn, *Kinship by Covenant*, 28.

31. Many references could be cited here. See esp. Ex 24:9–11, after the ratification of the Sinai covenant: "Then Moses and Aaron, Nadab, and Abihu, and seventy of the elders of Israel went up, and they saw the God of Israel; and there was under his feet as it were a pavement of sapphire stone, like the very heaven for clearness. And he did not lay his hand on the chief men of the people of Israel; *they beheld God and ate and drank*" (emphasis added).

32. Hahn, *Kinship by Covenant*, 48. Also, see his analysis of the "covenant-between-the-pieces" in Abraham's strange dream sequence in Gn 15 (102–15).

33. Hahn, *Kinship by Covenant*, 48. See Ex 4:22: "And you shall say to Pharaoh, 'Thus says the Lord, Israel is my first-born son.'"

34. Hahn, *Kinship by Covenant*, 48.

role in the salvation of the world. Miraculously set free in body, Yahweh covenants with his people through Moses at Sinai, entering a familial bond with the children of Jacob/Israel, through giving of the Torah and the Tabernacle. These two divine gifts of Torah and Tabernacle further the covenantal bond between God and his people, offering redemption to their minds and hearts as well as their bodies. Despite persistent disobedience and trials in the wilderness, the Law and Tabernacle continually remind Israel of God's ever presence with them, lovingly guiding them into right morality and right worship. Before turning to the text at hand (Ex 33:17–23), a few remarks are necessary as to the book's significance in the canon of the Old and New Testaments.

First, as to the Hebrew Scriptures, Exodus is, along with Genesis, the foundational story of Creation, Fall, and Redemption. It played a perpetual and vital role in the life, liturgy, and theology of ancient Israel. The exodus from Egypt—and the Passover feast—is re-presented and retold repeatedly: in the other books of the Pentateuch,[35] in historical books,[36] in the Psalter,[37] in the Wisdom tradition,[38] and not least in Israel's prophets.[39]

Second, in the New Testament, Exodus is one of the most cited books of the Old Testament. It follows Psalms and Isaiah, both of which are much longer works. In the Gospels, Jesus's entire life is, in some sense, mapped out as the fulfillment of the exodus narrative. Jesus brings about (and is) the New Exodus. A wealth of data supports this claim. In Luke, Mary's Magnificat echoes themes in the Songs of Moses.[40] Jesus, like the children of Israel, is *called out of Egypt*.[41] Similarly, He is tempted for *forty days*, echoing Israel's *forty years* in the wilderness.[42] Even

35. See Dt 26:5–9, 28:68, 32:12–14.

36. See Jos 24:2–13; Jgs 11:15–18; 1 Sm 12:6–18.

37. Ps 74:2, 74:12–15, 77:16–20, 78:9–16, 80:8, 81:1–16, 103:8, 105:23–45, 106:6–33, 114:1–8, 136:10–16.

38. Wisdom of Solomon 10–18 represents the exodus narrative, with the key distinction that it is "Lady Wisdom"—not Moses, that is the mediator and agent of delivery on behalf of God.

39. See Isa 11:15–16, 35:1–10, 43:15–21, 51:9–11, 63:10–15; Jer 31:31–34, 32:18–23, 32:40; Ezek 20:33–38; Amos 2:10; Jl 2:13; Jn 4:2; Hos 8:13, 9:3–6, 11:5; Mi 4:1:1–15.

40. Cf. Lk 1:46–47 with Ex 15:1–2; Lk 1:52 with Ex 15:6–7.

41. Cf. Mt 2:15 with Hos 11:1. Recall in Ex 4:22 that Israel is called God's *firstborn* son: "For those whom he foreknew he also predestined to be conformed to the image of his Son, in order that he might be the first-born among many brethren" (Rom 8:29).

42. See Mt 4:1–11.

the "slaughter of the innocents" echoes the treatment of the Israelites by Pharaoh in Exodus.[43] Above all, however, it is in the Passion of Jesus that the Book of Exodus is recapitulated and brought forward: "Jesus not only celebrates the Passover meal[44] but, in a remarkable theological extension, is himself identified as the 'Passover lamb'[45] and the 'supernatural rock' who followed Israel in the wilderness."[46]

The connection between Exodus and the Passion of Jesus cannot be emphasized strongly enough: "Luke alone of the Synoptic Gospels specifies the cup as the '*new covenant in my blood*,'[47] which alters the most immediate OT reference from Exodus 24:6–8 (the Sinaitic Covenant) to Jeremiah 31:31. The new covenant of Jeremiah 31:31 is explicitly said to be unlike the broken covenant of Sinai."[48] In fact, the New Covenant in Luke is linked with both the Sinaitic covenant and the Davidic one. As the Passover feast was the unifying liturgical event of the Mosaic covenant, so is the Last Supper the climactic liturgical bond between Jesus and his apostles.

Also, by identifying the chalice with the New Covenant, Jesus marks this meal—the Eucharistic "breaking of bread" to be continued "in remembrance" of him—as a solemn meal enacting a covenant bond. St. Luke's readers would have understood that when they participated in the Eucharistic cup, they reaffirmed their place within the Kingdom that Jesus inaugurated. What they experienced in the Eucharist was the transfiguration of the Mosaic and Davidic covenants. What happened on the Cross was the completion of these liturgical actions in the Upper Room. The Cross is diminished when detached from the Last Supper, and the Last Supper is sensible only in light of the Cross.[49] And both events—the Last Supper and the Cross—are *transhistoric actions* of the divine Son, bound up in his person and mission. To understand these

43. Cf. Mt 2:16–18 with Ex 1:15–22. Brown has catalogued many parallels between Matthew and Exodus. Regarding Mt 2:16, he writes: "The verb *empaizein* has a tone of mockery or ridicule. The chief other use of it in Matthew (27:29, 31, 41) is for the mockery of Jesus as king during the passion narrative—another point of contact between that narrative and the infancy narrative." *Birth of the Messiah*, 204.

44. Mt 26:17, 26:26–28; Mk 14:12–25.

45. 1 Cor 5:7, 11:25. See Jn 19:36.

46. Fretheim, *Exodus*, 257. See 1 Cor 10:4; cf. Ex 17:6.

47. Lk 22:20; emphasis added.

48. Hahn, *Kinship by Covenant*, 226. See Jer 31:32.

49. Hahn, *Kinship by Covenant*, 226; emphasis added. See Pitre, *Jesus, the Tribulation, and the End of the Exile.*

twin sacrificial events at the deepest levels of meaning is to understand that they are the threshold to the New Exodus.

Finally, beyond the tradition of the Gospels, Exodus plays a continual and decisive role in the remainder of the New Testament, above all in the Book of Revelation.[50] As to how the book itself is organized, there is considerable debate today. A number of scholars look to the book's geography as clues to its structure; for example, Israel in Egypt, Its Deliverance by God, and Its Response (Ex 1:1–15:21); Israel in the Wilderness and God's Providence (Ex 15:22–18:27); and Israel at Sinai (Ex 19:1–40:38).[51] Others have deduced a narrative structure to Exodus, as a "story in two acts." Act One narrates Israel's Oppression, Redemption, Covenant (Ex 1–31). This is followed by Act Two, which narrates Israel's Sin, Redemption, Covenant (Ex 32–40).[52]

Other outlines are unnecessarily complex, such as Hamilton's rhyming scheme.[53] Among the array of opinions, the geographical approach-

50. Cf. Rv 1:6 with Ex 19:10; Rv 2:17 with Ex 16:31–34; Rv 5:10 with Ex 15:13; Rv 7:15 with Ex 25:8; and the "plagues" of Rv 8:7–11:19 with Exod ch. 8–11. "John leaves almost no OT stone unturned in the course of Revelation, but six OT books in particular have overarching conceptual significance for the composition of his work. The creation/fall accounts of Genesis are foundational for Revelation, in terms of both antithesis (the dissolution of the created order in John's visionary material) and fulfillment (the blessings of the new Jerusalem as eschatological fulfillment of Eden). The accounts of the plagues in Exodus are the source of some of the most startling imagery in Revelation, and the theme of liberation from oppressive rulers is the predominant motif in both books." Beale and McDonough, "Revelation," in *Commentary on the New Testament*, 1082. "The exodus plagues, now universalized through the judgments of the trumpets and bowls, form the background for the end-time woes upon the earth; the vision of four living creatures worshiping God in heaven combines images from Ezekiel and Isaiah; the association of stars and angels (Rv 1:20) hearkens back to OT texts such as Jgs 5:20. Examples could be multiplied" (1086).

51. See T. E. Fretheim, "Exodus, Book of," in Alexander and Baker, *Dictionary of the Old Testament*, 250–51; Durham, *Exodus*, xxx.

52. See Janzen, *Exodus*, vii–viii. Janzen's narrative structure is slightly more nuanced than presented here, for the sake of simplicity. His approach is chiastic in nature. Although story based, it contains geographic overtones: "Planning for a Place of Presence" (chaps. 25–31) and "Preparing for a Place of Presence" (chaps. 35–40).

53. "*Oppression* (1:1–2:25); *Trepidation* (3:1–4:31); *Rejection* (5:1–23); *Reaffirmation* (6:1–30); *Confrontation* (7:1–12:30); *Liberation* (12:31–14:31); *Celebration* (15:1–21); *Itineration* (15:22–17:15); *Administration* (18:1–27); *Legislation* (19:1–24:18); *Specification* (25:1–31:18); *Deviation* (32:1–33:23); *Reconciliation* (34:1–35); *Construction* (35:1–40:33); *Glorification* (40:34–38)." Hamilton, *Exodus*, xxviii–xxix. Such arrangements, while echoing key movements in the book are, in the end, overworked ("itineration"?) and decidedly modern guesswork about the book's structure. In fact, most contemporary approaches to the structure of Exodus are a bit of a disappointment, for two reasons. Primarily, the aim of structural analysis is not simply to "say something new" or in a "fresh way" but, as with

es are among the better options. Yet even these are satisfactory at best, as they tend to focus on *Israel's movements* rather than on *God's saving actions*.[54] The ancient Jewish author did not conceive of the book as being primarily about "Israel." Rather, it is about Israel's God and his saving deeds on behalf of Israel. Adhering to such structural aids could shift the focus away from where it primarily belongs. Clean, simple outlines that follow the natural logic of the text, rather than imaginative proposals, are best. Make no mistake: a good outline is worth its weight in gold. Yet discretion is called for in their selection.

Let us stay with the book's geographical features for the moment. Contextually, Exodus 33:17–23 is located within the Sinai geography. Following the giving of the Law[55] and the ratification of the covenant,[56] the narrative moves to the instructions for God's holy Tabernacle.[57] All of this occurs at the Israelites' basecamp at Sinai (or above it, as Moses ascends). Next, after Exodus records instructions for the curtains of the Tabernacle,[58] the Altar of Burnt Offering,[59] the priestly vestments,[60] the Levitical priesthood,[61] the Altar of Incense and other elements,[62] the narrative is suddenly interrupted by the report of Israel's great apostasy: the Golden Calf.[63] "Exodus 32 describes Israel's archetypal apostasy at God's own mountain, scant weeks after ratifying the Covenant. Having brought them to Yahweh's abode in the wilderness, Moses disappears, perhaps as part of the 'test' mentioned in 20:20."[64] As Hamilton comments, "The shift in atmosphere from Exod 1–31 to Exod 32 is jarring."[65]

In what follows, Moses the great Lawgiver acts as the great Interces-

---

close-up exegesis of a text, to attempt to ascertain the *intentions of the author.* Commentaries that adopt rhyming schemes (*in English*) or similarly minded approaches ought to be set aside.

54. Note that in our thematic summary, the name of *Moses*, critical as he is to the narrative, is mentioned once; *God/Yahweh* is mentioned four times and alluded to indirectly numerous others. This is not mere semantics.

55. Ex 19:1–23:33.

56. Ex 24:1–18.

57. Ex 25–40.

58. Ex 26.

59. Ex 27.

60. Ex 28.

61. Ex 29.

62. Ex 30–31.

63. Ex 32:1–6.

64. Propp, *Exodus 19–40*, 566.

65. Hamilton, *Exodus*, 531.

sor, praying on behalf of God's "stiff-necked people."[66] In a most pivotal text, it is Moses's uttering the Abrahamic covenant that brings about divine mercy, as God "relents" and forges ahead with a disobedient people: "*Remember Abraham, Isaac, and Israel, thy servants, to whom thou didst swear by thine own self*, and didst say to them, 'I will multiply your descendants as the stars of heaven, and all this land that I have promised I will give to your descendants, and they shall inherit it forever.'"[67]

Quickly, however, Moses's intercession *for* Israel turns to indignation *at* Israel, as he returns down to the camp: "And as soon as he came near the camp and saw the calf and the dancing, Moses' anger burned hot, and he threw the tables out of his hands and broke them at the foot of the mountain. And he took the calf which they had made, and burnt it with fire, and ground it to powder, and scattered it upon the water, and made the people of Israel drink it."[68] After confronting his brother Aaron,[69] he renders judgment upon the guilty party,[70] executed by the Levites, a testimony to their faithfulness.

This leads to Moses's final intercession.[71] Altar's translation of Moses's plea in verses 31–32 reads as follows: "I beg you! This people has committed a great offense, they have made for themselves gods of gold. And now, if you would bear their offense ... and if not, wipe me out, pray, from Your book which You have written."[72] As Alter correctly notes, "I beg you!" in Hebrew is a single word (*'ana*), and he admits that "please" is accurate but "not sufficiently imploring."[73] Additionally, he comments on the broken conditional clause, which he translates as "if you would bear their offense ..." Alter explains his suspended translation with ellipses as follows: "The thought is left incomplete, perhaps because Moses is uncertain of what to say."[74] In any event, Cassuto adds this caution: "Some exegetes have regarded this request as a suggestion

66. Ex 32:7–14.

67. Ex 32:13; emphasis added.

68. Ex 32:19–20. "Unidentified here, the water is characterized in the duplicate account of Deuteronomy 9:21 as 'the brook that comes down from the mountain.' This implies a single source of water for the entire camp, the idea being, apparently, that no individual could escape drinking the mixture." Sarna, *Exodus*, 207.

69. Ex 32:21–24.

70. Ex 32:25–29.

71. Ex 32:30–35.

72. Alter, *Five Books of Moses*, 499; emphasis added.

73. Alter, Five Books of Moses, 499.

74. Alter, *Five Books of Moses*, 499; emphasis added.

by Moses to receive the punishment instead of his people. Such a proposal would undoubtedly have been very noble on Moses' part, but this does not appear to be the actual meaning of the text."[75]

As chapter 33 opens, it yet appears that the children of Israel, now expunged of their apostate brethren, will move on—without God and his holy presence (vv. 1–11). Here, Alter translates Exodus 33:11 as "And the Lord would speak to Moses *face to face,* as a man speaks to his fellow."[76] Helpfully, in his comment, Alter stresses that this idiom "*cannot be literally true* because of the burden of what follows in this chapter . . . *that no man, not even Moses, can see God's face.*"[77]

Just prior to the theophany scene, Moses speaks to God about his presence with his people:

Moses said to the Lord, "See, thou sayest to me, 'Bring up this people'; but thou hast not let me know whom thou wilt send with me. Yet thou hast said, 'I know you by name, and you have also found favor in my sight.' Now therefore, I pray thee, if I have found favor in thy sight, show me now thy ways, that I may know thee and find favor in thy sight. Consider too that this nation is thy people." And he said, "My presence will go with you, and I will give you rest." And he said to him, "If thy presence will not go with me, do not carry us up from here. For how shall it be known that I have found favor in thy sight, I and thy people? *Is it not in thy going with us, so that we are distinct, I and thy people, from all other people that are upon the face of the earth?*"[78]

The entire scene is climactic in the larger context of Exodus 32–34.[79] Commenting on the text, Cassuto summarizes:

For how shall it be known that I have found favour in Thy sight, I and Thy people? Is it not in Thy going with us? It were better for us not to go forth from here, for it is only by Thy going with us that the world will know that we have found grace in Thine eyes and that Thou hast chosen us, *so that we are dis-*

75. Cassuto, *Exodus*, 423.

76. Alter, *Five Books of Moses*, 503; emphasis added.

77. Alter, *Five Books of Moses*, 499n11; emphases added.

78. Ex 33:12–16; emphasis added.

79. "In a brief passage, displaying profound insight and presented with the consummate skill of a literary genius, the composite narrative of Exod 32–34 is brought to its zenith. Moses focuses the real issue of the aftermath of Israel's sin with the calf. Though Israel has cancelled any possible claim to a continuation of the gift of Yahweh's Presence, deserving only the Absence Yahweh has promised, Israel cannot continue to exist without that Presence. The entire great undertaking, made possible from beginning to end by Yahweh's Presence, is about to come to a humiliating and complete finish because of Yahweh's Absence." Durham, *Exodus*, 448.

tinct—separated thereby to our advantage—*I and Thy people, from all the people that are upon the face of the earth*. The distinction that Thou hast already made between Israel and the Egyptians ... will have no real value unless it persists also in the future. For the third time Moses emphasizes here the expression *Thy people*, and again he associates himself with his people.[80]

This leads directly into the core of the theophany itself, which is dialogical in nature:[81]

And the Lord said to Moses, "This very thing that you have spoken I will do; for you have found favor in my sight, and I know you by name." Now, "Moses begins his speech as would a man addressing his friend,"[82] with the direct petition, "*I pray thee, show me thy glory*." And he said, "I will make all my goodness pass before you and will proclaim before you my name 'The Lord'; and I will be gracious to whom I will be gracious and will show mercy on whom I will show mercy. But," he said, "*you cannot see my face; for man shall not see me and live*." And the Lord said, "Behold, there is a place by me where you shall stand upon the rock; and while my glory passes by I will put you in a cleft of the rock, and I will cover you with my hand until I have passed by; then I will take away my hand, and you shall see my back; *but my face shall not be seen*."[83]

Given the careful contextual analysis above, exhaustive exegesis of the text is not called for. Instead, we will focus on the essence of the dialogue: *I pray thee, show me thy glory* / "*you cannot see my face; for man shall not see me and live*." First, the term "glory" (Hebrew = *kavōd*) is critical, given its theological significance in Exodus, which is in its entirety, a revelation of God's glory. Cassuto adds, "The signification of the word *glory* in this verse, as above (16:7, 10; 24:16, and in several other pentateuchal passages), is '*theophany*.'[84] In the Septuagint, the Hebrew term *kavōd* is brought into the Greek as *doxa*. This is noteworthy, as is the entire phrase, *deixōn moi tēn seautou dōxan* ('Show me your glory') recalls the Greek of Jn 14:8, 'Show us the father' (*eixon hēmin ton pantera*)."[85]

80. Cassuto, *Exodus*, 434–35; emphasis original.

81. "In order to comprehend the dialogue in this paragraph properly, heed must be paid to the fact that this conversation is not conducted in accord with Greek or modern processes of logical thinking, but follows the pattern of eastern dialogues, which convey the intention of the speakers more by way of allusion than through explicit statements." Cassuto, *Exodus*, 432.

82. Cassuto, *Exodus*, 432.

83. Ex 33:17–23; emphasis added.

84. Cassuto, *Exodus*, 435; emphasis added.

85. Hamilton, *Exodus*, 567, note on 33:18.

As striking as Moses's question to God is, there are numerous clues that the entire text functions on a metaphoric level:

> From this point till the end of the paragraph it is clear from the wording that a number of things are expressed metaphorically. This is to be observed immediately in the answer given to Moses' last request. *Although the reply is positive, yet it contains a certain reservation:* as far as a human being can understand. It is possible for you to hear the voice of the Lord speaking to you as one hears that of his friend (v. 11), *but as far as seeing is concerned, that is to say, in regard to the comprehension of the Divine attributes, there is a boundary that man cannot cross.*[86]

Cassuto continues, "It is impossible for you to contemplate My attributes as one contemplates the face of his fellow who stands before him. You will be able to achieve no more than this: *I will make all My goodness*—all My virtues (it is already implied here that fundamentally the Divine qualities are compassionate)—*pass before you*, that is, I shall not cause them to stand before you, so that you may contemplate them, but I shall make them pass before you in a momentary flash, whilst you stand at the side."[87] Four concluding remarks may be offered as to the encounter scene as it relates to the literal sense.

First, in Exodus 33:12, Moses prays, "Now therefore, I pray thee, if I have found favor in thy sight, *show me now thy ways*, that I may know thee and find favor in thy sight." The man who could not look straight at the Burning Bush (3:6) now requests a full vision of Yahweh's Glory (although he already experienced a theophany in 24:9–11).[88]

While Moses's prayer to see God's face remains unanswered, the particular petition of his knowing God's "ways" *is* granted: "The Lord passed before him, and proclaimed, 'The Lord, the Lord, a God merciful and gracious, slow to anger, and abounding in steadfast love and faithfulness, keeping steadfast love for thousands, forgiving iniquity and transgression and sin, but who will by no means clear the guilty, visiting the iniquity of the fathers upon the children and the children's children, to the third and the fourth generation.'"[89]

86. Cassuto, *Exodus*, 435; emphases added.

87. Cassuto, *Exodus*, 435; emphases added.

88. Propp, *Exodus 19–40*, 606; emphasis added.

89. Ex 34:6–7. Cassuto breaks this down further, into a fivefold revealing of God's ways: "1) First and foremost *a God compassionate and gracious*—the moral qualities of grace and compassion, which had already conceded Moses' requests on behalf of the people (compare also 33:19: 'And I will be gracious to whom I will be gracious, and show compassion to whom

Second, in verses 14–15, God declares to Moses, "*My presence will go with you, and I will give you rest.*" This promise was a consolation for Moses himself, as the "you," occurring twice in the verse, is in the *singular*, referring to Moses himself. In responding "If thy presence will not go with me, do not carry us up from here," Moses took a risk, effectively saying, "Do not make us leave from here *unless* your Face is going." It would seem that, just as he earlier offered his own life (32:32), now Moses risks the entire people's fate. "*Better they should drop dead in the desert, at the foot of Yahweh's mountain, than traverse the wilderness and inhabit Canaan without the divine presence.*"[90]

Third, while Moses is not given a vision of *the face of God*, the Lord does offer Moses a "glimpse" at his divine glory[91] and in so doing allows him closer than any *person* in salvation history: "And while my glory passes by I will put you in a cleft of the rock, and I will cover you with my hand until I have passed by; then I will take away my hand, and you shall see my back; *but my face shall not be seen.*"[92]

Hamilton sees a link between this scene and the previous scene of the Passover in Exodus 12: "Twice in Exodus the Lord 'passes' (*'abar*) by something. In conjunction with the Passover, he says in Exod 12:12, '*I will pass through Egypt*' ... Here, in Exod 33:22, he will cause his goodness to pass before Moses ... *The earlier 'passing' was in judgement, the second passing is in benevolence.*"[93]

I will show compassion'); 2) *Slow to* [literally, 'long of'] *anger*, that is, His anger prolongs itself and is not quick to inflict punishment on the sinner, in order that he may repent, as happened on this occasion; 3) *Abounding in lovingkindness and truth*: this is a single attribute, since lovingkindness and truth are dual elements of a unitary quality—lovingkindness of truth, true and faithful lovingkindness. He keeps, with complete faithfulness, His promises to shew loving kindness and bestow good, and so, in fact, he is fulfilling them in this instance; 4) *Keeping lovingkindness for the thousands*: He continues to shew His lovingkindness even for thousands of generations, to the distant descendants of those to whom the promises were made, and thus He will do on this occasion to the people of Israel; 5) *Forgiving iniquity, and transgression and sin*, even as God had answered Moses' entreaty when he prayed to Him to forgive Israel's sin (32:32)." Cassuto, *Exodus*, 439–40.

90. Propp, *Exodus 19–40*, 605; emphasis added.

91. "This story qualifies others indicating that Moses obtained a full, frontal view of God (24:11; 33:11; Num 12:8; Deut 34:10). In this vignette, the divine Face may not be experienced. The fullest vision flesh and blood can sustain is of the divine back, still part of God's essence but a side less fraught with his dangerous aura than his Face or front side. *The context suggests that Yahweh's Face is constituted by his attributes of mercy and punishment, through which he interacts with humanity* (34:6–7)." Propp, *Exodus 19–40*, 608; emphasis added.

92. Ex 33:22–23.

93. Hamilton, *Exodus*, 570; emphasis added.

Fourth and finally, the entire theophany scene brings about a "complete forgiveness"[94] for Israel's transgression from its earlier apostasy. And because this has been achieved, "it is now possible to renew the Covenant that had been broken by the people's guilt; and together with the renewal of the Covenant there would take place the Revelation promised to Moses—the revelation of God's attributes in so far as a human being could comprehend them."[95] We now turn from the interpretation of the text from the Letter to the Spirit, from the literal sense to the spiritual senses.

Sensus Spiritualis

To begin, we look to the Aramaic *Targum Neofiti*, whose specific date is unclear and was composed sometime between the first and fourth centuries. Regardless, it makes an interesting adjustment to Exodus 33:18–19. The Hebrew reads, "And he said, 'I will make all my goodness pass before you, and will proclaim before you my name "The Lord"; and I will be gracious to whom I will be gracious, and will show mercy on whom I will show mercy. But,' he said, 'you cannot see my face; *for man shall not see me and live*.'" In contrast, *Targum Neofiti* reads, "And he said, 'Behold, I made the entire measure of my goodness pass before you, and I will have pity on *whoever is worthy of pity*, and I will have mercy on *whoever is worthy of mercy*.' And he said, 'You will not be able to see my face, because *it is not possible that a son of man see my face and live*.'"[96]

It is unclear who is referred to by the phrases "whoever is worthy of pity" and "whoever is worthy of mercy." When read in light of "a son of man," however, it is likely that *Targum Neofiti* shifts the seeing of God away from humanity but leaves the possibility open for the angels of God. Elsewhere in Isaiah, the angel *yĕḵasse p̄ānāy*, "covered his face."[97] Even so, the "burning ones," the seraphim, stood in the presence of God. *Targum Neofiti* seems to take the entire experience away from Moses, or *any* of "son of man."

Targum Pseudo-Jonathan, which cannot be safely dated before the early Islamic period, retains the language of the earlier *Targum Neofiti*. Yet it modifies the end of Exodus 33 as follows:

94. Cassuto, *Exodus*, 437; emphasis added.
95. Cassuto, *Exodus*, 437.
96. *Targum Neofitii*, Ex 33:19–20, in Cathcart et al., *Aramaic Bible*; emphasis added.
97. Isa 6:2.

> And the Lord said: "Behold, [there is] a place set aside beside me, and you shall stand in readiness upon the rock. And it shall come to pass that when the Glory *of my Shekinah* passes by, I shall place you in a cleft of the rock. And I shall spread my palm over you until *the troops of angels, which you will see*, pass by. *And I will make the troops of angels pass by, and they will stand and minister before me*, and you will see *the dibbera* (word) *of the glory of Shekinah, but it is* not *possible that* you see the face *of the Glory of my Shekinah.*"[98]

The "word of the Glory" is more elegant than "hind parts" and pushes the theophany in a mystical direction. Additionally, it is *not the Lord himself who "passes by"* but rather "troops of angels." Again, we can see how the Targums alter the sacred text of Exodus, and in some sense remove the anthropomorphisms and direct contact with God.

We now turn from the targums to the New Testament. Like Moses, St. Paul had his own experience of "accessible proximity" to the face of the God, during his theophany on the road to Damascus. This is where we continue our examination of our theophany scene according to the Spirit.[99] It is more likely that Paul is referring to his own experience rather than Moses. Even so, his language in 1 Corinthians is at least worth mentioning here: "For now we see in a mirror dimly, but then *face to face*. Now I know in part; then I shall understand fully, even as I have been fully understood."[100] Whether or not St. Paul intends a Mosaic reference here, the Apostle seems to gather up the various theophanies of the Old Testament inasmuch as he yearns with Jacob, Moses, and the others, the one and same desire to *go beyond seeing to the eschatological hope of being seen and being known* by the one, true, revelatory God.

Regardless, it is without doubt that the great Cappadocian father St. Gregory of Nyssa, in his *Life of Moses*, draws a connection between the theophany of Moses and St. Paul. In Philippians, Paul writes: "Brethren, I do not consider that I have made it my own; but one thing I do, forgetting what lies behind and straining forward to what lies ahead, I press on toward the goal for the prize of the upward call of God in Christ Jesus."[101] Concerning this text, St. Gregory writes, "The text seems to signify some such understanding, '*Whereas, Moses, you desire for "what is still to come"* has expanded and you have not reached

98. *Targum Neofitii*, Ex 33:21–23, in Cathcart et al., *Aramaic Bible*; emphasis added.
99. See Act 9.
100. 1 Cor 13:12; emphasis added.
101. Phil 3:13–14.

satisfaction in your progress but and whereas you do not see any limit to the Good, but your yearning always for more, the place with Me is so great that one running in it is never able to cease from his progress.'"[102]

It is natural to view this scene according to the anagogical sense. There is little doubt that it is, at least in part. Gregory fuses Moses's theophany with Paul's statement and asserts that Moses yearns for that which is *still to come*. Gregory understands that, like Paul, Moses's experience of the glory of Christ is *in part and not in full*—in a "mirror dimly" within the present age and face-to-face in the heavenly splendor of the age to come.

Upon closer examination, however, Gregory's text has a tropological dimension to it. Several clues suggest this possibility. First, the entire text of *The Life of Moses* is for Gregory a moral meditation, intended to guide the Christian believer toward an increase in virtue. This is especially true of the latter half of the work; after Gregory provides a concise summary of Moses's life in Book I, he then "uses only the story of Moses to illuminate nearly everything we need to understand to live a virtuous, faith-filled life"[103] in Book II.

Second, in the text, note that Gregory indicates that Moses does not "see any limit to the Good." This is a classical, Greek way of speaking of virtue and the virtuous life. The connection between the tropological and the anagogical becomes clear: Moses, who saw God, "in part" longs for him in his fullness. This holy yearning, though never satisfied in this life, suggests a pattern of ascent and pulls him toward that day when Moses will see God "face-to-face."

This anagogical hope spurs his desire to grow in charity and the other virtues: "Truly this is the vision of God: never to be satisfied in the desire to see him. But one must always, by looking at what he can see, rekindle *his desire to see more*. Thus, no limit would interrupt *growth in the ascent to God, since no limit to the Good can be found*, nor is the increasing of desire for the Good brought to an end because it is satisfied."[104] Here again, the Pauline desire is expressed: *to see more of God and to continue seeing*. In other words, as much as anagogy lifts us upward, toward the heights of heaven, the upward ascent does not end until one truly beholds the face of God. All else is the journey, the upward ascent.

102. St. Gregory of Nyssa, *Life of Moses*, Book II, 107; emphasis added.
103. Silas House, from the foreword in St. Gregory of Nyssa, *Life of Moses*, x.
104. St. Gregory of Nyssa, *Life of Moses*, Book II, 106; emphasis added.

Allegorical interpretations are found elsewhere in the primitive Church. They abound in St. Cyril of Jerusalem, among others. In his *Catechetical Lectures*, Cyril writes, "Moses says to him, 'Show me yourself.' You see that the prophets saw Christ, that is, in the measure each was able. 'Show me yourself, that I may see you clearly.' But he said, 'No one sees me and still lives.' *Therefore, because no one could see the face of the Godhead and live, he assumed the face of human nature, that seeing this we might live.*"[105]

For Cyril, then, the theophany of Moses is likened to the various visions of the prophets who saw Christ "in the measure each was able."[106] It is not only the words of the prophets that rise the allegorical interest of the early Christian interpreters. Given the intense persecution, and in fact the offering up of the lives of many of the biblical prophets, it is understandable how Cyril, along with numerous others of the period, saw in them the figural Crucified and Risen Jesus. A similar allegorical treatment appears in St. Augustine's *On the Trinity*. His description surpasses the great Cyril in its colorful detail: "As a matter of fact the words which the Lord later says to Moses ... are commonly and not without reason understood *to* prefigure the person of our Lord Jesus Christ. Thus, the back parts are taken to be his flesh, in which he was born of the Virgin and rose again, whether they are called the *back parts* because of the posteriority of his mortal nature or because he deigned to take it near the end of the world, that is, at a later period."[107]

Here, Augustine suggests a Christophanic reading, to use Bucur's terminology. Specifically, Augustine makes a correlation with the "back parts" (Latin = *posteriora*) of the Lord passing by Moses to be the enfleshed Christ, prefigured in Exodus. Additionally, Augustine raises several fascinating possibilities from his close semantical study of the Latin text of Moses's theophany. The first possibility is that "back parts" refers to the human nature of Christ, in contrast to his divine nature. A second possibility is that the term should be taken *eschatologically*, since Christ's taking upon himself a human nature occurred at a "later period" (Latin = *posterius*). Regardless, both intriguing options are rooted in Augustine's allegorical reading of Exodus.

105. St. Cyril of Jerusalem, *Catechetical Lecture*, 10.7, in *Works of Saint Cyril of Jerusalem*; emphasis added.

106. Daniélou would categorize these examples as "typologies" rather than "allegories."

107. St. Augustine, *The Trinity*, 2.17.28.

Finally, in one of his letters, Augustine draws out *entirely anagogical* readings of the text. In the first, he interprets Exodus 33 as prefiguring Christ, and not only him but the Church, too:

> Again, in ancient times, in the case of the faithful servant of God, Moses, who was destined to labor on this earth and to rule the chosen people, it would not be surprising that what he asked was granted: that he might see the glory of the Lord, to whom he said, "If I have found favor before you, show me yourself openly." He received an answer adapted to present conditions: that he could not see the face of God, because no man could see him and live. *Thus, God made clear that the vision belongs to another and better life. In addition to that, the mystery of the future church of Christ was foreshadowed by the words of God.*[108]

Augustine's thought characterizes the mystery of anagogy: one reflects on the face of God and in some sense may come near to it. Yet it is ultimately a grace that belongs to another and better life, for it is in the reality of heaven that one can truly gaze upon the face of the Lord. Augustine, like many in the primitive and medieval Church, did not consider dwelling upon this heavenly hope as fruitless. To the contrary, such anagogical meaning in the text prepares the heart for the presence of God. It opens one's eyes to gaze upon him *now*. Such seeing, in the here and now, is incomplete. Even so, it is *sanctified gazing* as it pulls the soul upward. It spurs sanctity in the heart of the believer, reminding him of the ultimate purpose of true discipleship.

Earlier in the same letter, Augustine emphasizes the glorious vision of God enjoyed by the saints in heaven:

> The saintly Moses, his faithful servant, showed the flame of this desire of his when he said to God, with whom he spoke face to face as to a friend: "If I have found favor before you, show me yourself." What, then? Was it not himself? If it were not himself, he would not have said "Show me yourself" but "Show me God"; yet, if he really beheld his very nature and substance, he would have been far from saying "Show me yourself." It was himself, therefore, under that aspect in which he willed to appear (but he did not appear in his own very nature) which Moses longed to see, *inasmuch as that is promised to the saints in another life.*[109]

Here, Augustine's interest is more precisely upon the idea of the "eschatological promise," the heavenly vision that Moses confidently await-

108. St. Augustine, *Letter* 147.32; emphasis added.
109. St. Augustine, *Letter* 147.20; emphasis added.

ed, which carried him over the waves of uncertainty in daily travails. Augustine's anagogical move is not merely for the reader to honor and respect this forward looking hope of the great Lawgiver, but to imitate Moses—to put his stalwart hope into practice in one's own life. In this respect, we can say that anagogy has a faith-building aspect to it, as well as a moral dimension.

In the nascent Church, the text was read in a *tropological* fashion. For instance, the man known as Gaius Marius Victorinus,[110] a more obscure patristic figure from the period, was nonetheless a fervent opponent of the Arians. In one of Victorinus's third-century texts, he speaks of "life and death," although the concepts are more closely tied with moral rather than physical life: "No one sees the power itself alone, for 'no one has ever seen God' (Jn 1:18). And since power is life at rest and knowledge at rest but life and knowledge are actions, *if someone were to see God he must die, because the life and knowledge of God remain in themselves and are not in act. But every act is exterior*. Indeed, for us to live is to live externally [in a body]; to see God is therefore a death."[111]

Here, Victorinus is speaking about the kind of knowledge of God that leads to self-knowledge and self-mastery. God is *being* and not an act. Human life is bodily and human actions are performed in the flesh, in an exterior way. In contrast, God's life is incorporeal and spiritual; he remains in and of himself. All of this may sound philosophical rather than moral, but that is not the case. Victorinus's argument is not merely about metaphysics but is deeply tropological. Our acts are exterior and intrinsically spiritual at the same time. As one puts the substance of his argument into practice, one is compelled to weigh moral actions in light of eternity, and our human acts in light of God's eternal being.

Finally, another tropological approach to Exodus 33 comes from St. Ambrose:

110. Marius Victorinus (ca. 280–363 AD) "A fourth-century grammarian, rhetorician, philosopher, and theologian, born in Africa about the year 300. In pursuance of his profession as teacher of rhetoric he migrated to Rome where he attained such fame and popularity that in a statue was erected in his honor in the Forum of Trajan. Details regarding his life come almost entirely from Jerome or Augustine, the latter of whom calls him a man of the highest learning and thoroughly skilled in the liberal arts." *Theological Treatises on the Trinity*, 4.

111. Victorinus, *Against Arius* 3.3.1, in *Theological Treatises on the Trinity*; emphasis added.

"Who shall see my face and live?" Scripture said, and rightly so. For our eyes cannot bear the sun's rays, and whoever turns too long in its direction is generally blinded, so they say. Now if one creature cannot look upon another creature without loss and harm to himself, how can he see the dazzling face of his eternal Creator while covered with the clothing that is this body? For who is justified in the sight of God, when the infant of but one day cannot be clean from sin and no one can glory in his uprightness and purity of heart?[112]

Final Remarks: Seeing the Face of the Glorious Christ

Like the previous theophany scene with Jacob, Moses's "accessible proximity" to the face of the Lord in Exodus 33 yields a number of insights from all Four Senses. By way of commonality, what both scenes share is that they are perhaps best understood as *metaphoric* in nature. This is not to dispute the historical dimension of these biblical traditions. Rather, it is to emphasize that neither Jacob nor Moses *actually* saw God. Jacob wrestled with the "angel of the Lord," and Moses was gifted with a glimpse of God's presence "passing by"—from behind, tucked safely in the cleft of the rock.

As significant as Jacob and his theophany at *Peni'el* are in terms of salvation history, however, the theophany of Moses surpasses it in a few ways. First, and more generally, while Jacob's life contains a number of "spiritual visions," the life of Moses in Scripture is, in some sense, one theophany after another: the Burning Bush,[113] the pillar of cloud[114] and pillar of fire,[115] his numerous encounters with God atop Sinai,[116] and this scene.[117] Additionally, *Yahweh* reveals his holy name first to Moses,[118] to whom he "spoke" many times.[119]

112. St. Ambrose, *Death as a Good*, 11.49, in *Hexameron, Paradise, and Cain and Abel.*
113. See Ex 3:1–10.
114. See Ex 13:21, 13:22, 14:19, 14:24, 33:9–10; Num 12:5, 14:14; Dt 31:15.
115. See Ex 13:21–22, 14:24; Num 14:14; Wis 18:3.
116. See Ex 19–24, 34.
117. See Ex 3:1–22.
118. See Ex 3:13–15.
119. See Ex 6:1, 6:2, 6:10, 6:13, 6:29, 7:1–19, 8:1–20, 9:1–22, 10:1–21, 11:1–9, 12:1, 12:43, 13:1, 14:1, 14:11, 14:15, 14:26, 17:5, 17:14, 19:9–10, 19:21, 20:19, 20:22, 25:1, 30:11, 30:17, 30:22, 30:34, 32:7, 32:9, 32:17, 32:33, 34:1, 34:27, 36:5, 40:1; Lv 4:1, 5:14, 6:1, 6:8, 6:19, 6:24, 7:22, 7:28, 9:1, 10:19, 11:1, 12:1, 13:1, 14:1, 14:33, 15:1, 16:2, 17:1, 18:1, 19:1, 20:1, 21:1, 21:16, 22:1, 22:17, 22:26, 23:1, 23:9, 23:23, 23:26, 23:33, 24:1, 24:13, 25:1, 27:1; Num 1:48, 2:1, 3:5.

All of these encounters, theophanic and otherwise, demonstrate the elevated the figure of Moses—the Deliverer, Law Giver, Mediator and Shepherd—above all others. "The Sinai theophany was accompanied by cataclysmic events, although it is emphasized that when God spoke to Moses no form was seen.[120] The revelation of God to Moses and then to the nation of Israel at Mt. Sinai was the watershed event in Israelite history and as such marked a change in the way God would manifest himself in theophanies."[121] Clearly, the Bible depicts Moses and his mission as unique and utterly distinct. He is the seminal figure in the Old Testament, perhaps surpassed only by David. So, it should come as no surprise that in the New Testament, Moses looms over all other figures in salvation history, with the exception of David.

In light of this, St. John's prologue comes sharply into focus once again, specifically John's selection of Moses as the figure he chose to highlight and contrast with Jesus: "For the law was given through Moses; grace and truth came through Jesus Christ. *No one has ever seen God*; the only Son, who is in the bosom of the Father, he has made him known."[122]

In his Apostolic Exhortation *Verbum Domini*, Pope Benedict draws on John's prologue and in fact uses it as his organizing principle in the document.[123] Three of his observations are worth including here.

First, as he summarizes patristic and medieval reflection on the pro-

120. See Dt 4:12, 4:15.

121. M. F. Rooker, "Theophany," in Alexander and Baker, *Dictionary of the Old Testament*, 861.

122. Jn 1:17–18.

123. "With this Apostolic Exhortation I would like the work of the Synod to have a real effect on the life of the Church: on our personal relationship with the sacred Scriptures, on their interpretation in the liturgy and catechesis, and in scientific research, so that the Bible may not be simply a word from the past, but a living and timely word. To accomplish this, I would like to present and develop the labours of the Synod by making constant reference to the *Prologue of John's Gospel* (Jn 1:1–18), which makes known to us the basis of our life: the Word, who from the beginning is with God, who became flesh and who made his dwelling among us (cf. Jn 1:14). This is a magnificent text, one which offers a synthesis of the entire Christian faith. From his personal experience of having met and followed Christ, John, whom tradition identifies as 'the disciple whom Jesus loved' (Jn 13:23; 20:2; 21:7, 20), 'came to a deep certainty: Jesus is the Wisdom of God incarnate, he is his eternal Word who became a mortal man.' May John, who 'saw and believed' (cf. Jn 20:8) also help us to lean on the breast of Christ (cf. Jn 13:25), the source of the blood and water (cf. Jn 19:34) which are symbols of the Church's sacraments. Following the example of the Apostle John and the other inspired authors, may we allow ourselves to be led by the Holy Spirit to *an ever-greater love of the word of God*." Pope Benedict XVI, *Verbum Domini*.

logue, he underscores the Incarnation and how the *enfleshment* of Jesus is an unprecedented development in light of the Old Testament: "The patristic and medieval tradition, in contemplating this 'Christology of the word,' employed an evocative expression: *the word was 'abbreviated.'*[124] 'The Fathers of the Church found in their Greek translation of the Old Testament a passage from the Isaiah that Saint Paul also quotes to show how God's new ways had already been foretold in the Old Testament. There we read: 'The Lord made his word short, he abbreviated it.'"[125] Elsewhere he writes, "The Son himself is the Word, the *Logos*: the eternal word became small—small enough to fit into a manger. He became a child, so that the word could be grasped by us. Now the word is not simply audible; not only does it have a *voice*, now the word has a *face*, one which we can see: that of Jesus of Nazareth."[126] Although Benedict is referring to the plethora of times that "God spoke" across the Old Testament in general, it is difficult not to think of the many times he did so with Moses in particular. Evidently, the pope did so as well.

Later in the text, he makes explicit the connection between Moses and Jesus as he discusses the holy Eucharist: "The profound unity of word and Eucharist is grounded in the witness of Scripture, attested to by the Fathers of the Church, and reaffirmed by the Second Vatican Council. Here we think of Jesus' discourse on the bread of life in the synagogue of Capernaum,[127] with its underlying comparison between Moses and Jesus, *between the one who spoke face to face with God*[128] *and the one who makes God known*."[129] Here, Benedict contrasts the way in which God merely spoke to Moses[130] with Jesus, the Logos, who really was "with God" in the beginning, and who alone *exēgēsato* ("has manifested/revealed") God the Father.[131]

Next, Benedict looks to Moses again, this time to contrast the Law with Jesus, *the Law in person*:

124. Here, Benedict is referring to Origen's *First Principles (De Principiis)*, I.II.8; emphasis added.

125. Benedict XVI, *Homily on the Solemnity of the Birth of the Lord*. See Isa 10:23; Rom 9:28.

126. Benedict XVI, *Verbum Domini*, 12.

127. See Jn 6:22–69.

128. See Ex 33:11.

129. Benedict XVI, *Verbum Domini*, 54; emphasis added. See Jn 1:18.

130. See Dt 34:10: "And there has not arisen a prophet since in Israel like Moses, *whom the Lord knew face to face*"; emphasis added.

131. See Jn 1:1, 1:18.

At the "Jesus" discourse on the bread speaks of the gift of God, which Moses obtained for his people with the manna in the desert, which is really the Torah, the life-giving word of God.[132] In his own person Jesus brings to fulfilment the ancient image: "The bread of God is that which comes down from heaven and gives life to the world" ... "*I am the bread of life*."[133] Here "*the law has become a person*. When we encounter Jesus, we feed on the living God himself, so to speak; we truly eat 'the bread from heaven.'"[134] In the discourse at Capernaum, John's Prologue is brought to a deeper level. There God's *Logos* became flesh, but here this flesh becomes "*bread*" given for the life of the world,[135] with an allusion to Jesus' self-gift in the mystery of the cross, confirmed by the words about his blood being given as *drink*.[136]

As Benedict concludes, "The mystery of the Eucharist reveals the true manna, the true bread of heaven: it is God's *Logos* made flesh, who gave himself up for us in the paschal mystery."[137] In an ecclesial sense, Benedict connects our seeing of the face of God in Jesus with *the virtue of hope*: "What the Church proclaims to the world is the *Logos of Hope*;[138] in order to be able to live fully each moment, men and women need 'the great hope' which is '*the God who possesses a human face and who "has loved us to the end."*'"[139]

In interpreting Exodus 33 according to the literal sense, two final remarks may be added. First, from our initial analysis of the text, it is clear that, like Jacob, Moses's theophanic experience, real as it is, ostensibly serves as a metaphor of Moses's intimacy with God and not as an optic encounter, a genuinely visual experience of "seeing" the face of the Lord. As gracious as God is, he does not even allow the great Lawgiver to see him "face-to-face" but, to borrow a New Testament image, "through a glass darkly."[140]

Second, and in turning from the literal to the spiritual sense, the greater theological import of this theophany scene began to unfold. *No one* surpassed the great Moses in encountering God in the most intimate

132. See Ps 119; Prv 9:5.

133. Jn 6:33–35; emphasis added.

134. See Ratzinger, *Jesus of Nazareth*, 268; emphasis added.

135. See Jn 6:51; emphasis added.

136. Benedict XVI, *Verbum Domini*, 54; emphasis added.

137. Benedict XVI, *Verbum Domini*, 54.

138. See 1 Pt 3:15.

139. Benedict XVI, citing Encyclical Letter *Spe Salvi* (November 30, 2007), 31, in *Verbum Domini*, 54. See Jn 13:1.

140. 1 Cor 13:12.

of ways. Allegorically, his life and example of yearning for God point forward to Christ in the flesh. Tropologically, Moses's prayer *Show me Thy glory* highlights the need for virtue in the life of every believer who longs to *truly* "see God." Anagogically, several possibilities presented themselves.

Only when Exodus 33 is read in the light of Christ, however, is the true heavenly import known. Moses's theophanic encounter is a singularly important stage of the Old Covenant, in the ascent to God. It is not merely that Moses's divine encounter in Exodus 33 is pedagogical; Moses's entire life is a pedagogy, as Gregory of Nyssa has demonstrated. Moses's theophanic encounter—and his entire life—point forward to the New Moses, to the One who was "with God in the beginning" and "through whom all things were made."[141] St. John proclaims that "the eternal life which was with the Father . . . was made manifest to us" in the flesh.[142] Here is the anagogical center of Moses's encounter: "No one has ever seen God; the only Son, who is in the bosom of the Father, he has made him known."[143]

In this holy scene, in Moses's encounter with God, we see through him to the true Moses, who continually gazes at the glory of the Father, from all eternity. And in this way, we see beyond Moses to *the face of the glorious Christ:*

> Who will not give thanks to the Hidden One, most hidden of all,
> who came to open revelation, most open of all
> for He put on a body, and other bodies felt him
> —though minds never grasped Him.[144]

In chapter 6, we turn to the prophet Isaiah and so move beyond theophany, strictly speaking. In his *Servant Songs*, however, we encounter another aspect of the face of the Lord—the face of the suffering Christ. Once again, will examine it according to the Four Senses of Scripture.

Secundo Meditation

The following meditation, "The Mountain of Divine Knowledge," is from St. Gregory of Nyssa's *The Life of Moses* (91–94):

141. See Jn 1:2, 1:3.
142. 1 Jn 1:2.
143. Jn 1:18.
144. St. Ephrem the Syrian, in Brock, *Luminous Eye*, 28.

Again the Scripture leads our understanding upward to the higher levels of virtue. For the man who received strength from the food and showed his power in fighting with his enemies and was the victor over his opponents is then led to the ineffable knowledge of God. Scripture teaches us by these things the nature and the number of things one must accomplish in life before he would at some time dare to approach in his understanding the mountain of the knowledge of God, to hear the sound of the trumpets, to enter into the darkness where God is, to inscribe the tablets with divine characters, and, if these should be broken through some offense, again to present the hand-cut tables to God and to carve with the divine finger the letters which were damaged on the first tables.

It would be better next, in keeping with the order of the history, to harmonize what is perceived with the spiritual sense. Whoever looks to Moses and the cloud, both of whom are guides to those who progress in virtue (Moses in this place would be the legal precepts, and the cloud which leads, the proper understanding of the Law), who has been purified by crossing the water, who has put the foreigner to death and separated himself from the foreigner, who has tasted the waters of Marah (that is, the life removed far from pleasures) which although appearing bitter and unpleasant at first to those tasting it offers a sweet sensation to those accepting the wood, who has then delighted in the beauties of the palm trees and springs (which were those who preached the Gospel, who were filled with the living water which is the rock), who received the heavenly bread, who has played the man against the foreigners, and for whom the outstretched hands of the lawgiver became the cause of victory foreshadowing the mystery of the cross, he it is who then advances to the contemplation of the transcendent nature.

His way to such knowledge is purity, not only purity of a body sprinkled by some lustral vessels but also of the clothes washed from every stain with water. This means that the one person who would approach the contemplation of Being must be pure in all things so as to be pure in soul and body, washed stainless of every spot in both parts, in order that he might appear pure to the One who sees what is hidden and that visible respectability might correspond to the inward condition of the soul.

For this reason the garments are washed at divine command before he ascends the mountain, the garments representing for us in a figure the outward respectability of life. No one would say that a visible spot on the garments hinders the progress of those ascending to God, but I think that the outward pursuits of life are well named the "garment."

When this had been accomplished and the herd of irrational animals had been driven as far from the mountain as possible, Moses then approached the ascent to lofty perceptions. That none of the irrational animals was allowed to appear on the mountain signifies, in my opinion, that in the contemplation of the intelligible we surpass the knowledge which originates with the senses. For it is characteristic of the nature of irrational animals that they are governed by the senses alone divorced from understanding. Their sight and hearing often lead them to what stimulates their appetites. Also, all other things through which sense perception becomes active assume an important place in irrational animals.

The contemplation of God is not affected by sight and hearing, nor is it comprehended by any of the customary perceptions of the mind. For *no eye has seen, and no ear has heard*, nor does it belong to those things which usually enter *into the heart of man*. He who would approach the knowledge of things sublime must first purify his manner of life from all sensual and irrational emotion. He must wash from his understanding every opinion derived from some preconception and withdraw himself from his customary intercourse with his own companion, that is, with his sense perceptions, which are, as it were, wedded to our nature as its companion. When he is so purified, then he assaults the mountain.

The knowledge of God is a mountain steep indeed and difficult to climb—the majority of people scarcely reach its base. If one were a Moses, he would ascend higher and hear the sound of trumpets which, as the text of the history says, becomes louder as one advances. For the preaching of the divine nature is truly a trumpet blast, which strikes the hearing, being already loud at the beginning but becoming yet louder at the end.

The Law and the Prophets trumpeted the divine mystery of the incarnation, but the first sounds were too weak to strike the disobedient ear. Therefore the Jews' deaf ears did not receive the sound of the trumpets. As the trumpets came closer, according to the text, they became louder. The last sounds, which came through the preaching of the Gospels, struck their ears, since the Spirit through his instruments sounds a noise more loudly ringing and makes a sound more vibrant in each succeeding spokesman. The instruments which ring out the Spirit's sound would be the Prophets and Apostles whose *voice*, as the Psalter says, *goes out through all the earth: and their message to the ends of the world.*

CHAPTER 6

Contemplating the Face of the Suffering Christ with Isaiah (Isaiah 52–53)

> [Isaiah] should be called an evangelist rather than a prophet because he describes all the mysteries of Christ and the church so clearly that one would think he is composing a history of what has already happened rather than prophesying what is to come.
>
> —St. Jerome

Sensus Litteralis

The next encounter scene is taken from the last of four Servant Songs[1] in the Book of Isaiah (Isa 52:13–53:12). In moving directly to the literal sense of the text, four critical distinctions need be made as it pertains to this scene and two that were previously examined. First, we have moved from the first part of the Hebrew Bible, the Law (*Torah*), to the second part, the Prophets (*Nebi'im*). There are significant distinctions between the two parts of the canon. The backdrop of the prophetic books is not Moses or the exodus narrative. Rather, it is David, the Temple, and the Babylonian exile. There are other differences, too—not least of which are the literary forms that are encountered in each. We must account

1. The four Servant Songs in the second half of the book are: Isa 42:1–4, 49:1–6, 50:4–9, and 52:13–53:12. The first scholar to identify this was Lutheran theologian Bernhard Duhm (see *Das Buch Jesaia*, 3:189.

for these distinctions as we examine the text, which leads directly to a second point. This scene is in the literary form of Hebrew poetry,[2] in contrast to the narrative of Jacob's wrestling with the angel in Genesis[3] or the discourse between God and Moses petitioning to see the glory of the Lord in Exodus.[4] To this point, we have not directly dealt with Hebrew poetry and the particular characteristics that distinguish it from either narrative or discourse.

Third, the present chapter examines a substantially larger text compared with those previously considered (Isa 52:13–53:12). There is no way to compress the text further without eliminating essential context. In any event, owing to its length, it will not be reproduced here. The reader is advised to read the biblical passage in its entirety along with our discussion of it here. Fourth, the present text should not be, strictly speaking, characterized as a theophany.[5] Rather, it is part of the author's broader prophetic vision—a vision largely about the "Servant of Yahweh."[6] It is as if this text works in the opposite direction of the encounter scenes examined earlier. This is most clear in the following portion: "He was despised and rejected by men; a man of sorrows, and acquainted with grief; and *as one from whom men hide their faces* he was despised, and we esteemed him not."[7] Rather than expressing a desire *to see* the face of God (Moses), or boasting that he has done so (Jacob),

2. "We have already seen 'the servant' mentioned in 42:1–9; 49:1–7; and 50:4–9. *These three poetic units*, together with our present text, have been regarded by many interpreters as a distinctive group of texts, commonly referred to as 'the Servant Songs.'" Brueggemann, *Isaiah 40–66*, 141; emphasis added.

3. See Gn 32:22–33.

4. See Ex 33:17–23.

5. Yet other passages within Isa 40–55 (Second Isaiah) contain *the rhetoric of theophany*: "Now the servant is for the moment disregarded. Now it is all Yahweh, no proximate agents. The whole earth and all its creatures are invited to sing along with Israel in exuberant praise of Yahweh. *The language is the rhetoric of theophany* (an appearance of God) that anticipates the radical coming of Yahweh to work a newness." Brueggemann, *Isaiah 40–66*, 45 (emphasis added). Other scholars see theophanic elements across the text of Isa 40–55. See esp. Baltzer, *Deutero-Isaiah*.

6. "Although the primary faith line of chapters 40–55 is clear enough, special notice may be made of one particular problem, 'the servant of the Lord.' For a century, scholars have suggested that the 'servant songs' of 42:1–9; 49:1–7; 50:4–9; and 52:13–53:12 are a quite distinct literary grouping, referring to a special character identified as 'the servant of the Lord.' More recently, some scholars have concluded that this literature does not form a distinct part of Isaiah; rather, each text needs to be taken in its own immediate literary context." Brueggemann, *Isaiah 40–66*, 13.

7. Isa 53:3.

Isaiah's poetic vision expresses the reverse intention: "*And we hid as it were our faces from him.*"[8]

As the discussion unfolds, the distinctions between this scene and previous ones cannot be overlooked. In fact, the reader will better appreciate the logic that explains such incongruities—and why, despite them, this scene belongs here every bit as much as any of the others. To begin with, all four of Isaiah's Servant Songs have long been considered an essential Old Testament backdrop to contemplating the Passion narratives of the Four Gospels and indeed the face of the *suffering Christ.* The opening words of the chapter, in which St. Jerome describes Isaiah as more evangelist than prophet, contain a conviction widely shared among patristic and medieval theologians.

Among numerous examples that could be brought forth is that of St. Augustine, who in his *Confessions* writes, "And by letters I wrote my Bishop, the holy man Ambrose ... desiring him to advise me what part of the Scriptures were best for my reading, to make me readier and fitter for the receiving of so great a grace. He recommended Isaiah the Prophet to me: for this reason, I believe, for that he is a clearer foreshadowing of the Gospel, and of the calling of the Gentiles, than are the rest of the Prophets."[9] Moreover, the notion of Isaiah as sort of proto-evangelist has persisted over the centuries, and even contemporary scholars have not hesitated to refer to Isaiah as "the Fifth Gospel."[10] And not merely because of the content of the Servant Songs: "Just as Isaiah 53 was virtually universally understood as a reference to the passion of Christ, the early church interpreted the march from Edom by the bloodied and vengeful warrior in Isaiah 63 as a reference to the ascended *Christus victor*. The early church also saw in Isaiah validation that the *pax Romana* represented the triumph of Christianity over Judaism."[11]

Yet clear evangelical reverberations within Isaiah may be one of the few points of genuine agreement among modern Christian scholars. As one moves into questions of a contextual nature, any singlemindedness about the book itself begins to evaporate. Recent studies on the Book of Isaiah have been unnecessarily bogged down by debates about both its

8. Isa 53:3, KJV; emphasis added.

9. St. Augustine, *Confessions*, IX.5; translation slightly modified.

10. See Sawyer, "Daughter of Zion and Servant of the Lord in Isaiah"; idem, *Fifth Gospel.*

11. B. H. Lim, "Isaiah: History of Interpretation," in Boda and McConville, *Dictionary of the Old Testament*, 386.

authorship and literary unity, not to mention the historical backdrop in the age of the Assyrian and Babylonian empires, which loom large in the background of the book. These two elements go hand in hand, as most scholars do not view the book as the product of a single author. Rather, it is seen as a composite of two or three independent sources over a span of time that exceeds the suggested lifespan of the prophet Isaiah.

A detailed discussion of the book's setting need not be taken up here.[12] But a basic grasp of the historical condition facing Israel in the time of Isaiah is necessary. Specifically, three national crises cast a shadow over the book, all of which appear to inform the author's theological message throughout the book.[13] First, there was the unwillingness of Ahaz to heed Isaiah's interdict. Ahaz reigned in Isaiah's lifetime[14] as king of Judah (ca. 744–728 BC). God's message to his king was that Ahaz was to take no action against rising northern aggression. Syria and northern Israel formed a defensive coalition, concerned as they were with Assyrian imperialism under the powerful leadership of Tiglath-Pileser: "The circumstances throughout the ancient Near East changed dramatically in 745 BC ... when Tiglath-Pileser III took the throne of Assyria. He immediately undertook a series of campaigns designed to reassert control over the full extent of the empire."[15] Isaiah had expressly conveyed God's word to Ahaz: *do nothing*. "Take heed, be quiet, do not fear, and do not let your heart be faint because of these two smoldering stumps of firebrands."[16]

In the prophetic voice of Isaiah, the Lord spoke to Ahaz: "*It shall not stand, and it shall not come to pass.* For the head of Syria is Damascus, and the head of Damascus is Rezin. (Within sixty-five years Ephraim will be broken to pieces so that it will no longer be a people.) And the head of Ephraim is Samaria, and the head of Samaria is the son of Rema-

12. For a brief overview of the historical setting, see Baltzer, *Deutero-Isaiah*, 26–33. For a discussion of the audience of Isaiah, see Goldingay and Payne, *Critical and Exegetical Commentary on Isaiah 40–55*, 26–44.

13. Here, we draw especially on Moyter, *Isaiah*, 22–32.

14. The extent of time of Isaiah's prophetic ministry is debated. It likely extends from the death of Uzziah, in ca. 739 BC, and that of King Hezekiah in 686 BC. See H. G. M. Williamson, "Isaiah: Book of," in Boda and McConville, *Dictionary of the Old Testament*, 364; Schultz, "How Many Isaiahs Were There and What Does It Matter?," 150–70.

15. B. E. Kelle, "Israelite History," in Boda and McConville, *Dictionary of the Old Testament*, 404.

16. Isa 7:4.

liah. If you will not believe, surely you shall not be established.'"[17] Yet Ahaz bought Assyrian protection with treasure from the house of the Lord, rather than listening to Isaiah or the Lord.[18]

The second crisis followed on the heels of the first, during the reign of Hezekiah, who reigned as king of Judah from approximately 715 to 686 BC. When the Assyrian king Sennacherib moved against Judah in the early 700s, Hezekiah, unlike Ahaz, heeded Isaiah's prophetic word. Communicating with Hezekiah's servants, Isaiah instructs, "Say to your master, 'Thus says the Lord: Do not be afraid because of the words that you have heard, with which the servants of the king of Assyria have reviled me. Behold, I will put a spirit in him, so that he shall hear a rumor, and return to his own land; and I will make him fall by the sword in his own land.'"[19] After receiving a letter from Isaiah, Hezekiah turned to the Lord in prayer, and his faithfulness signaled the defeat of the Assyrians—they would not lay hold of Jerusalem: "Therefore thus says the Lord concerning the king of Assyria: He shall not come into this city, or shoot an arrow there, or come before it with a shield, or cast up a siege mound against it. By the way that he came, by the same he shall return, and he shall not come into this city, says the Lord. For I will defend this city to save it, for my own sake and for the sake of my servant David."[20]

Third and finally, Isaiah prophetically announced the coming siege of Jerusalem by Babylon, there success in conquering the city and its king, its plundering and destroying the Temple, and the captivity of many: "Then Isaiah said to Hezekiah, 'Hear the word of the Lord of hosts: Behold, the days are coming, when all that is in your house, and that which your fathers have stored up till this day, shall be carried to Babylon; nothing shall be left, says the Lord. And some of your own sons, who are born to you, shall be taken away; and they shall be eunuchs in the palace of the king of Babylon.'"[21] It is this third and most dramatic crisis that undergirds Isaiah 52–53. Prior to the Fourth Servant Song (52:13–53:12), the prophet writes: "For thus says the Lord: 'You were sold for nothing, and you shall be redeemed without money. For thus says the Lord God: My people went down at the first into Egypt to sojourn there, and the As-

17. Isa 7:7–9; emphasis added.
18. See 2 Kgs 16:1–9.
19. Isa 37:5–7.
20. Isa 37:33–35.
21. Isa 39:5–7.

syrian oppressed them for nothing. Now therefore what have I here, says the Lord, seeing that my people are taken away for nothing? Their rulers wail, says the Lord, and continually all the day my name is despised.'"[22]

The shift from "Lord" (v. 3) to "Lord God" (v. 4) juxtaposes Israel's past defeats with God's true sovereignty and utmost ability to redeem her from the present calamity.[23] This leads to this strong and personal affirmation in verse 6: "Therefore my people shall know my name; therefore in that day they shall know that it is I who speak; here am I."[24] Here, it is as if all of the calamitous circumstances Israel finds herself in serve the greater purpose: "Now God is using the entire historical process of defeat and deportation to make his people aware of himself, to know his name, and to recognize his call for attention. YHWH's central goal is repeated. *He wants a people who know him and his name*. He wants them and all peoples to be aware of his presence and of his return to Zion."[25]

One of the things that these crises share in common is Israel's governance and the way the nation was threatened by it, both from within and without. Whether through defiant monarchs or the threat of destruction from imposing overlords, Israel's hopes hung in the balance. Or so it seemed. Israel had indeed "wearied" the Lord,[26] yet for Isaiah, a future judgment of the wicked—and a full restoration of a beleaguered nation—was inevitable, and it would come about in precisely the way and time of the Lord's choosing. And it would come about through a *ḥōter yishāy*, a shoot of Jesse: "There shall come forth a shoot from the stump of Jesse, and a branch shall grow out of his roots."[27]

In the mid-twentieth century, one of the significant monographs on this subject was that of Scandinavian scholar Sigmund Mowinckel, a student of form critic Hermann Gunkel.[28] In many ways, Mowinckel's *He That Cometh* is a watershed text in modern biblical theology.[29] Expansive in scope, *He That Cometh* traces the roots of the messiah concept in early Jewish eschatology. Not limiting his study to the Old Tes-

22. Isa 52:3–5.
23. See Moyter, *Isaiah*, 371.
24. Isa 52:3–6.
25. Watts, *Isaiah 34–66*, 775; emphasis added.
26. See Isa 7:12–13.
27. Isa 11:1.
28. Gunkel, *Legends of Genesis*; idem, *The Psalms*; idem, "Israelite Prophecy from the Time of Amos," 48–75; idem, "Israelite Literary History," 31–41.
29. Mowinckel, *He That Cometh*.

tament, Mowinckel broke new ground in contextualizing such Jewish hopes considering its historical and political environment in the ancient near East,[30] and particularly the relationship of the prophet in relation to liturgy and cult.[31]

As groundbreaking as his proposals were, however, they were rapidly critiqued, even by his mentor, Gunkel, who maintained that "that the conjunction of prophets and priest was not cultic, since other texts of a similar nature include other functionaries as well who are not cultic figures.[32] The presence of prophets at a cultic site does not establish their cultic duties. Rather, they may be present simply because of their desire, as pious individuals, to be present, or if they spoke prophetically, it was only because a cultic site would assure them of an audience, and the message need not be related to the cult."[33]

Similarly, in his examination of "son of man" in Daniel, Mowinckel argued that the gist of the concept is not rooted in Jewish eschatology. Rather, they were adapted from Indo Iranian myths.[34] Elsewhere, he examined the Psalter[35] for clues as to the "day of the Lord"[36] concept

30. "The idea that the prophets were closely connected with the cult arises first with the work of S. Mowinckel." Phinney, "Call/Commission Narratives," 69.

31. "Among the many scholars who advocated for extensive involvement by OT prophets in the cult, S. Mowinckel and A. Johnson stand out. Their primary evidence is as follows: (1) prophets were active at festivals and cultic sites (1 Sam 3:21; 10:5; 19:19–24; 1 Kg 18:16–39; 19:10; 2 Kg 2:3; 4:22–25, 38); (2) there was a close association between prophets and priests (Isa 28:7; Jer 6:13; 8:10; 14:18; Lam 2:20; 4:13; Mic 3:11; Zech 7:3); (3) Jeremiah and Ezekiel are of priestly descent (Jer 1:1; Ezek 1:3); (4) the book of Jeremiah describes his ministry in the temple and relates his ministry to priests and other prophets who were there (Jer 23:11; 26:7; 27:16; 29:26; 35:4); (5) in addition to the prophetic ministry of the Levites (1 Chron 25:1), there is an extended description of the intercessory role of a Levite who prophesies in response to a royal lament (2 Chron 20:5, 14)." Hilber, "Liturgy and Cult," in Boda and McConville, *Dictionary of the Old Testament*, 515–16.

32. See, e.g., Jer 4:9, 8:1, 18:18; Mi 3:11.

33. Hilber, "Liturgy and Cult," in Boda and McConville, *Dictionary of the Old Testament*, 516.

34. "Mowinckel contended that 'son of man' was actually understood as a title meant to identify a heavenly messiah figure that would come to earth to judge the earth.... More recent work has noted the use of the term in late Jewish literature, in particular 4 Ezra and the Similitudes of Enoch, suggesting that this literature appropriates the Danielic 'one like a son of man' in new ways, linking it to a reinterpreted notion of a messiah, and even the vindication of a messianic figure (N.T. Wright)." W. D. Tucker Jr., "Daniel: History of Interpretation," in Boda and McConville, *Dictionary of the Old Testament*, 126.

35. Mowinckel, *Psalms in Israel's Worship*. For additional background on the topic, see Cross, "Divine Warrior in Israel's Early Cult," 11–30; von Rad, "Origin of the Concept of the Day of the Lord," 97–108; Everson, "Days of Yahweh," 329–37.

36. There are a dozen and a half occurrences of *yôm yhwh* ("day of the Lord") in the

in the biblical prophets.[37] In a close study of proposed parallels between numerous royal psalms with Babylonian and Canaanite texts, he concluded that the latter influenced the development of an Enthronement festival of Yahweh as king in Israel.[38] Here again, though, Mowinckel's attempt to locate the origins of the day of the Lord in such non-Jewish materials was met with "significant challenges from those who question the existence of the enthronement festival and argue that it relies too much on Babylonian cultic practices."[39] This is quite true. Is it plausible that a nation driven by monotheism, a nation eager to cordon itself off from its polytheistic neighbors, would import its religious feasts and festivals in such an axiomatic fashion?[40]

---

biblical prophets: Isa 13:6, 13:9; Ezek 13:5; Jl 1:15, 2:1, 2:11, 2:31, 3:14, 4:14; Am 5:18, 5:20; Ob 15; Zep 1:7, 1:14 (two times); Mal 3:1. The concept should *not* be limited to these specific texts, however.

37. "The Day of the Lord is a significant recurring theme in the prophetic literature of the OT. At its essence, it refers to *a time of Yahweh's unmistakable and powerful intervention*. It appears in a variety of contexts in prophetic literature and draws together a wide array of images. The prophets employ the specter of the Day of the Lord to offer both warning and hope, announcing both disaster and salvation." J. D. Barker, "Day of the Lord," in Boda and McConville, *Dictionary of the Old Testament: Prophets*, 132; emphasis added.

38. "Various references to the Day of the Lord in prophetic literature play significant roles in this discussion. S. Mowinckel is a key figure in the discussion of the origins of the Day of the Lord, which he locates in harvest celebrations and an annual festival of enthronement in which Yahweh took his place as the rightful ruler over Israel. This festival would occur at the end of the agricultural cycle, when the earth hovered on the brink of returning to chaos and only the renewed presence of Yahweh could restore prosperity and fertility ... The Day of the Lord, in this understanding, reestablishes Yahweh's governance over Israel and pointed to his great acts as a means of cementing his position. This perspective is rooted in comparisons with practices from Babylonian and Canaanite practices that celebrate a ritual enthronement of deities." J. D. Barker, "Day of the Lord," in Boda and McConville, *Dictionary of the Old Testament: Prophets*, 134.

39. Barker, "Day of the Lord," in Boda and McConville, *Dictionary of the Old Testament: Prophets*, 134. "The presumed relationship between the Temple cult and literary form is far less certain in the current scholarly study of the hymns, prayers, and psalms dated from the time of Alexander's conquest through the Bar Kokhba Revolt (ca. 321 b.c.e.–135 c.e.). *While older scholarship may have confidently situated this type of literature within a specific context of worship, the automatic relationship between prayer literature and the cult is less frequently assumed today*." Angela Kim Harkins, "Hymns, Prayers, and Psalms," in Collins and Harlow, *Eerdmans Dictionary of Early Judaism*, 755; emphasis added.

40. This requires qualification. I am not suggesting that there is an impenetrable wall between Israel and its neighbors. Frankly, that would be naïve. Yet Mowinckel's proposal seems to bypass the "law of diminishing returns" with respect to the manner in which ancient Israel distinguished herself from Canaanite counterparts. Was there an adaptation of *the form* of "Enthronment" feasts, such that they were fitted to primitive, emerging liturgies in the early monarchial period? Perhaps. To suggest as he does, however, that the *substance*

For all the above reasons, Mowinckel's text must be engaged with prudence. On the one hand, his understanding of the messiah in Jewish texts is clearly substantial, and *He That Cometh* is among the most important modern studies on the Servant Songs in *Isaiah*. Yet the extent to which he grounds his larger argument in the adaptation of non-Jewish sources by the biblical prophets is overstated[41] and far better supported by the breadth of Jewish eschatology.

Additionally, his conclusions about the nature of Jewish messianism are overly sociopolitical in nature and leave little to no room for the burgeoning complexity of *Jewish* eschatology.[42] In turn, such misunderstandings of the biblical prophets may lead to disastrous results as it concerns the apocalypticism found in the New Testament, particularly in the Four Gospels.[43] For example, Michael Bird, in *Are You the One to Come: The Historical Jesus and the Messianic Question*,[44] offers a critique of Fitzmy-

---

of these Canaanite ceremonies was brought into the religious festivals of the cult of Yahweh, is much more problematic.

41. "The Messiah of the Jewish future hope and of Jewish eschatology is ... a figure who belongs to the this-worldly, political side of the hope of restoration and deliverance, but who must, of course, be understood in the light of the general religious outlook, like everything else of significance in Israelite life. *Religion and politics were not two distinct spheres, but politics was regarded as an outcome of man's place in the world as defined by religion* ... For Deutero-Isaiah, the picture of Yahweh's glorious royal 'appearance' and salvation overshadows all the concrete details of everyday experience. It is only incidental that he mentions that it also involves the re-establishment in Israel of the kingly rule of the Davidic line: *he takes it for granted.* It is through the gloriously endowed kind, who will inherit the covenant promises made to David, that the kingly rule of Yahweh will be exercised in the daily life of the future ... The scion of David *is so natural an element* in the description of the future, that he is often *not mentioned but tacitly assumed*." Mowinckel, *He That Cometh*, 169–70; emphases added.

42. "It is against the background of the hope of national restoration (*which is essentially this-worldly and political*) that we must consider the Messianic expectation of early Judaism ... *The Messiah is simply the king in this national and religious future kingdom*, which will only be established by the miraculous intervention of Yahweh." Mowinckel, *He That Cometh*, 155; emphases added. His proposal is not false, yet neither is it wholly correct. Mowinckel emphasizes the fall of the "state" of ancient Israel in its political context while in many ways ignoring or downplaying its religious context, e.g., the destruction of the Temple and the latter corruption of its priesthood. While it is true that the religious and political were in interwoven in the ancient Jewish worldview, Mowinckel unnecessarily subjugates the former to the latter.

43. For an introduction to apocalypticism, see Brant J. Pitre, "Apocalypticism and Apocalyptic Teaching," in Green et al., *Dictionary of Jesus and the Gospels*, 23–33. See also Allison, *Jesus of Nazareth*; Aune, *Apocalypticism, Prophecy, and Magic*; Bird, *Are You the One Who Is to Come?*; and Wright, *Jesus and the Victory of God*, vol. 2.

44. Bird, *Are You the One to Come?*

er's work on the same topic.[45] Bird ascribes to him "the mistake of an older generation" of biblical scholars on the issue of the extant of messianism within the pages of the Old Testament. In Bird's view, "Fitzmyer (following Sigmund Mowinckel) opts for a definition of a messianic text as one that contains a reference to 'an awaited or future anointed agent of God.' Thus, Fitzmyer sees messianic texts in the Old Testament as quite strictly limited to the use of the word [*mashiach*] (anointed one) in connection with the teaching about a continuing Davidic dynasty in the subsequent history of Israel."[46] The concern with Fitzmyer's approach—that is, to texts in which *mashiach* is present—is that it limits messianism such that "it is seen as a postexilic phenomenon."[47] This approach represents "a rather narrow lexical approach to the matter, and one wonders if Fitzmyer has exchanged the elastic rubber-band definition of messianism for one that is caught up in a linguistic straight-jacket."[48]

More will be said about the prophet's depiction of the Servant in Isaiah chapters 52–53. For now, a few comments about structure are needed. As far as the structure of Isaiah 52:13–53:12 is concerned, and its place in the book, one scholar characterizes the nature of Isaian studies as "a casualty of historical-critical scholarship."[49] This may sound harsh but is not inaccurate. An example of such criticism is seen in the commentary on Deutero-Isaiah (i.e., Second Isaiah) by Hebrew scholar Shalom Paul: "Contemporary scholars tend to divide the book as a whole into three parts (chaps. 1–39, 40–55, and 56–66); these were edited expanded, and combined by a redactor whose purpose was to create a work of unique ideas, images, and language."[50] For his part, Paul divides the book between chapters 1–29 and 40–66. Parting company from the Trito-Isaiah school, he writes, "I maintain that chaps. 40–66 are one coherent opus composed by a single prophet."[51]

45. See Fitzmyer, *The One Who Is to Come*.

46. Bird, *Are You the One to Come?*, 34–35. See Fitzmyer, *The One Who Is to Come*, 7, 11–13; Mowinckel, *He That Cometh*, 155–56.

47. Bird, *Are You the One to Come?*, 35.

48. Bird, *Are You the One to Come?*, 35. "When we come to messianic hopes biblical and post-biblical, we see that functions and roles are often more important than a single title . . . What is more, messianic figures could go by a variety of names other than 'Messiah': including *Son of David, Son of God, Son of Man, the Prophet, Elect One, Prince, Branch, Root, Scepter, Star, Chosen One, Coming One*, and so forth" (emphasis added).

49. Clines, *I, He, We, and They*, 25.

50. Paul, *Isaiah 40–66*, 12.

51. Paul, *Isaiah 40–66*, 12.

Paul is correct in viewing the latter part of the book as an integrated composition, characterized not by disunity but by its wholeness, the result of a single author's work. Even so, whether one is persuaded by arguments calling for a twofold division (1 – 39 + 40 – 66) or a threefold division of the book (1 – 39 + 40 – 55 + 56 – 66), the larger integrity of *the whole book* has been set aside by most contemporary Isaian scholars, beginning with Samuel Driver.[52] The arguments for a division between the two (or three) books between chapters 39 and 40 need not be reiterated here.[53]

In keeping with our stated methodology, the examination of biblical books from which all encounter scenes are drawn from the text as we have it. Our canonical approach to Isaiah, while not embraced by the majority of contemporary scholars, is certainly not repudiated by all recent efforts. This is largely the case with regard to John Goldingay and David Payne. In their massive commentary on chapters 40–55, Goldingay and Payne state their approach as follows: "In this commentary we sometimes note the implications of redaction-critical theories for particular sections and have used exegetical insights that emerge from them, *but we have taken the text broadly in the form that we have it as the basis for the commentary*."[54]

Among the many pieces of evidence suggesting an essential unity of the text, a particularly significant one is the fate of the city of Jerusalem: "A theological theme that runs through the whole book is *the destiny of*

52. One of the earliest modern scholars to argue for a Deutero-Isaiah model was Samuel Driver in *Introduction to the Literature of the Old Testament*. Taken as a whole, the structure of the text is complex: "The book of Isaiah is long and, at first sight, bewildering in its variety" (Williamson, "Isaiah: Book of," in Boda and McConville, *Dictionary of the Old Testament*, 364). Williamson discusses the variety of approaches to the structure of Isaiah (364–72).

53. "Historically, the interrelationship of the book's parts is simple to state in outline but impossible to determine in detail. Isaiah 1–39 contains a number of explicit references to the Judah of the eighth century BC when Assyria was the great middle-eastern power, and to the activity of a prophet called Isaiah ben Amoz in that period. Isaiah 40–55 contains a number of explicit references to the circumstances of the sixth century BC when Babylon was the great power. *The Babylonian period is spoken of not as future, as if Isaiah were prophesying it, but as present, as if the prophecies come from someone who is contemporary with it* ... Different parts of the book (particularly within chapters 1–39) may presuppose other contexts such as the imminent collapse of Assyria in the seventh century BC, or later developments in the Second Temple period." Goldingay and Payne, *Critical and Exegetical Commentary on Isaiah 40–55*, 1–2; emphasis added.

54. Goldingay and Payne, *Critical and Exegetical Commentary on Isaiah 40–55*, 7; emphasis added.

Jerusalem / Zion ... Chapters 40–55 and 56–66 reaffirm all the aspects of the way this motif is handled in chapters 1–39 and declare that God's commitment will have the last word ... The need to see chapters 40–55 as part of a whole can thus be argued on both a diachronic and a synchronic basis. We have assumed that the nature of a commentary lends itself to study that is synchronic and also linear."[55]

With such views, Goldingay and Payne are among the more conservative of academic scholars working on Isaiah today.[56] Overall, their approach is congruent with ours and offers much, particularly at the literal level. With respect to their approach to the authorship, however, there are differences, too. Based on scant stylistic clues, Goldingay and Payne conjecture that chapters 40–55 are the product of a female author: "Israel's having a number of women prophets would allow for the possibility that Second Isaiah was a woman, which might be another reason for letting the poems remain anonymous. The commission of a *məbaśśeret*, which suggests a woman herald (40:9), might then be her commission."[57] Although such hypothesizing is unnecessarily speculative, there are many salient contributions within their commentary.[58]

Goldingay's other commentary on Isaiah, written not from a source-critical but from a literary and theological approach, is equally if not more useful here.[59] In it, Goldingay provides a sound working structure of Isaiah 40–55, which we will adopt here:[60]

55. Goldingay and Payne, *Critical and Exegetical Commentary on Isaiah 40–55*, 4; emphasis added.

56. For an overview of the history of interpretation of Isaiah, see B. H. Lim, "Isaiah: History of Interpretation," in Boda and McConville, *Dictionary of the Old Testament*, 378–91.

57. Goldingay and Payne, *Critical and Exegetical Commentary on Isaiah 40–55*, 48. They add: "On the other hand, the testimony in 50:4–9 comes from someone who apparently has a beard to pull (presumably literally). Further, we take the portrayal of the servant in 52:13–53:12 as a description of the prophet's own actual or potential experience, and that is the portrait of a male. The implication is that the prophet wants to be thought of as a man. †Schmitt suggests that the portrayal of Yhwh as mother derives from the motif of Zion as mother, but more likely it is part of the evidence that the author was conscious of the nature of many of a woman's distinctive experiences. If the poet was a man, then at least this was a man who knew about the nature of many of a woman's distinctive experiences, had reflected on them, and knew how to use them theologically and pastorally. But to leave open the question about the prophet's gender, we will seek to avoid referring to this prophet-poet as 'he.'"

58. It is beyond the scope of this book to venture into the complex issue of Isaiah's authorship. Given that such a discussion would occupy many pages, it will be set aside. Regardless, our examination of Isaiah involves a synchronic approach at the final, canonical stage.

59. Goldingay, *Message of Isaiah 40–55*.

60. Goldingay, *Message of Isaiah 40–55*, v–vi.

Part I	Introduction (40:1–31)
Part II	Yhwh's Vindication and Deliverance (41:1–44:23)
Part III	Yhwh's Work with Cyrus (44:24–48:22)
Part IV	The Servant and Zion (49:1–52:12)
Part V	Yhwh's Act of Restoration and Transformation (52:13–55:13)

With respect to Part V, Goldingay subdivides this material as follows: "The Fruitfulness of the Servant's Ministry,"[61] "The Renewing of the Abandoned Woman/City,"[62] and "The Broadening of the Covenant Commitment."[63] And so Isaiah 52:13–53:12 is in the *concluding section* of chapters 40–55 overall. Yet the Fourth Servant Song[64] is at the *beginning* of the unit dealing with Yahweh's "Act of Restoration and Transformation"[65] and is followed upon by two closely related scenes, all of which are characterized by *anonymity*.

Goldingay highlights a literary feature of this section of Isaiah; namely, anonymity: "The servant of 52:13–53:12, the woman-city addressed in 54:1–17a, and the covenanted people addressed in 54:17b–55:13 are all unidentified. The prophet makes promises about an *unnamed servant*, speaks of an *unidentified 'many'* and for an unidentified 'we,' encourages an *unnamed woman-city*, and issues an invitation to *unnamed hungry and thirsty*. This anonymity is then one of the features that link 52:13–55:13 with chs 55–66."[66] He discusses possible connections between these anonymous elements of chapters 52–55 and previous sections within the Book of Isaiah[67] yet wisely refrains from iden-

61. Isa 52:13–53:12.

62. Isa 54:1–17a.

63. Isa 54:17b–55:13. See Goldingay, *Message of Isaiah 40–55*, 461–58. For different and more detailed structural outlines of Isa 40–55, see Oswalt, *Book of Isaiah*, 16. An even more extensive one is found in Baltzer, *Deutero-Isaiah*, viii–xv. Paul's commentary does not include a structural outline. He does present a "literary sequence" of the text, with literary breaks being determined by the author's employment of "many of the same phrases, terms, and motifs in consecutive units ... These links weave together the entire work from beginning to end, chapter by chapter" (Paul, *Isaiah 40–66*, 31). Paul's literary sequence is detailed on pp. 31–42 of the commentary.

64. Isa 52:13–53:12.

65. Isa 52:13–55:13.

66. Goldingay, *Message of Isaiah 40–55*, 463; emphases added.

67. "We know from earlier chapters that *the servant is Jacob-Israel and is the prophet*, but not using the name here signals that the servant may also be more (or less) than that ... *The woman city is the Jerusalem of the 540s,* but the promises made to this woman-city are not explicitly related to the Jerusalem of that period. Indeed, the link between her portrayal and

tifying them too closely. Instead, he leaves open the distinct possibility that, for the prophet, they extend beyond earlier references.

In terms of the structure of the Fourth Servant Song, a chiastic arrangement is evident (see list below). The entire unit of chapters 52–53 presents the humiliation and exaltation of Yahweh's servant: "The significance of the servant's exaltation is that he is *extraordinarily transformed from failure to success*, from humiliation to exaltation, from object of horror to sacrament, from object of abuse to cause of confounding."[68]

13–15 My Servant will triumph despite his suffering
  1 Who could have recognized Yhwh's arm?
    2–3 He was treated with contempt
      4–6 The reason was his suffering for us
    7–9 He did not deserve his treatment
  10–11a By his hand Yhwh's purpose will succeed
11b–12 My servant will triumph because of his suffering[69]

The promise of exaltation begins in 52:13: "Behold, my servant shall prosper, he shall be exalted and lifted up, and shall be very high." On the other end of the chiastic frame, in 53:12a–b, the exaltation is echoed, but only *after* the suffering of this same servant: "Therefore I will divide him a portion with the great, and he shall divide the spoil with the strong." Yet his exaltation, earlier hinted at but now concrete, is only after the servant's willingness to "suffer for" the many: "because he poured out his soul to death and was numbered with the transgressors; *yet he bore the sin of many and made intercession for the transgressors.*"[70] As Walter

---

that of the servant suggests that *she can be embodies elsewhere . . . The covenanted people is the deportee community of the 540s*, but it too *is not confined to those who represent Jacob-Israel* in that place at that moment. Indeed, the invitation to 'everyone' *suggests* it might reach *far beyond that*." Goldingay, *Message of Isaiah 40–55*, 464; emphasis added.

68. Goldingay, *Message of Isaiah 40–55*, 493; emphasis added. "The whole may be expressed as a chiasm that moves from the prospect of triumph to the contrast of suffering and on the reasons for this suffering, then back again. As is the nature of chiasm, special significance attaches to the central subsection and to the final one" (470).

69. Adopted from Goldingay, *Message of Isaiah 40–55*, 469.

70. Isa 53:12c–e; emphasis added. See the Aramiac translation of Isa 53:10–12, known as *Targum Jonathan*, which adds this interpolation to the text: "And it was the pleasure of the Lord to refine and to purify the remnant of his people, in order to cleans their souls from sin, *that they might see the kingdom of their messiah* (*ûmin qŏḏām yĕyā hăwāṯ ra ʿăwā ʾ lĕmiṣrap̄ûlĕḏakkā ʾâ yaṯ šĕ ʾārā ʾ ḏĕ ʿamēh bĕḏîl lĕnaqā ʾâ mēḥôḇîn nap̄šêhôn yeḥĕzûn bĕmalḵûṯ mĕšîḥêhôn yisḡûn bĕnîn ûḇĕnān yôrĕḵûn yômîn wĕ ʿāḇḏê ʾôrayṯā ʾ ḏayyā bir ʿûṯēh yiṣlĕḥûn*)." This inclusion of "kingdom of the messiah" is an important theological development in

Bruggemann summarizes, this thematic text "voices the ultimate resolve of Yahweh that the servant ... will succeed in every way, will be honored and exalted. This motif at the beginning of the poem is matched by a concluding affirmative assertion about the exaltation of the servant (53:10–12). These affirmations form the final conclusion *and assert the destiny of the servant.* It is unmistakably clear, however, that such anticipated well-being is only at the end. Before that glorious culmination, the remainder of the poem details the life of the servant, a life of suffering and humiliation."[71]

As indicated above, Isaiah 52:13–53:12 is not a theophany, strictly speaking, as was the case with texts discussed previously in the book. Even so, the Fourth Servant Song contains elements of "encounter" in the form of a prophetic vision. Questions remain. With whom? Who is this "servant of Yahweh"? While every detail of the text cannot be dealt with here, a few finer points must mentioned as they relate to our study.

First, 52:15a demands attention and clarification. Most English translations render the phrase as "so shall he startle many nations"[72] or "sprinkle the nations."[73] The latter follow the King James Version in preserving "sprinkle" rather than "startle." Yet neither possibility truly captures the Hebrew term *nāzāh*, which is better rendered as *splatter:* "'Splatter' (*nāzāh*) denotes the splashing of blood, oil, or water over people or objects in connection with their dedication or cleansing."[74] In the vast majority of its twenty-four occurrences in the Old Testament, *nāzāh* has clear priestly connotations.[75] Twelve of these occur in the Book of Leviticus,[76] where *nāzāh* refers to the "splattering of blood" in relation to priestly actions in the Temple: "Then he shall kill the goat of the sin offering which is for the people, and bring its blood within the veil, and do with its blood as he did with the blood of the bull, *splattering* it upon the mercy seat and before the mercy seat."[77] Here, *nāzāh*

---

the targum and represents a bringing together of the Suffering Servant motif with a direct correlation of messianic expectation as it relates to Isaiah's prophecy.

71. Brueggemann, *Isaiah 40–66*, 141–42; emphases added.

72. Isa 52:15, RSV.

73. Isa 52:15, NAB, ESV, New International Version.

74. Goldingay and Payne, *Isaiah 40–55*, 294.

75. Ex 29:21; Lv 4:6, 4:17, 5:9, 6:27, 8:11, 8:30, 14:7, 14:16, 14:27, 14:51, 16:14, 16:15, 16:19; Num 8:7, 19:4, 19:18, 19:19, 19:21; Isa 52:15, 63:3. The occurrence at 2 Kgs 9:33 is distinct from this list and has a nonpriestly connotation.

76. Lv 4:6, 4:17, 5:9, 8:11, 8:30, 14:7, 14:16, 14:27, 14:51, 16:14, 16:15, 1619.

77. Lv 16:15; see vv. 14 and 19.

describes the action of the priest splattering the blood of the goat upon the mercy seat in the Holy of Holies, at the culmination of the Day of Atonement liturgy. The remaining occurrences in Leviticus all relate to blood being splattered by priests in the Temple—with one exception: "Then Moses took some of the anointing oil and of the blood which was on the altar, *and splattered it* upon Aaron and his garments, and also upon his sons and his sons' garments; so, he consecrated Aaron and his garments, and his sons and his sons' garments with him."[78]

Yet this too is striking, as here *nāzāh* refers back to anointing of the altar with *oil and blood* in the priestly instructions given to Moses in the Book of Exodus: "Then Moses took some of the anointing oil and of the blood which was on the altar, and *splattered* it upon Aaron and his garments, and also upon his sons and his sons' garments; so he consecrated Aaron and his garments, and his sons and his sons' garments with him."[79]

They are part of the collective priestly instructions, specifically given in regard to the Aaron and his sons, as an *atoning sacrifice* for the "many" in Israel: "Thus you shall do to Aaron and to his sons, according to all that I have commanded you; through seven days shall you ordain them, and every day you shall offer a bull as a sin offering for atonement. Also, you shall offer a sin offering for the altar, when you make atonement for it, and shall anoint it, to consecrate it."[80] Looking at the use of *nāzāh* in Isaiah 52:13, Goldingay concludes, "Instead of God's servant splattering oil on altar and priest, *as himself an anointed one he is splattering the nations.*"[81]

A second observation concerns the center of the chiasm.[82] In verses 2–3, Isaiah's poem

> offers a life story of the servant from birth ("grow up"; v. 2) to death ("buried"; v. 9). The beginning point is *birth and growth*. It was, however, not an auspicious beginning. Indeed, the servant began in something like humiliation—out of dry ground, no form, no majesty, nothing to notice or admire or value. These sentences interpret 52:14. He was *a rejected person, not valued, perhaps ostracized, perhaps disabled, of whom nothing was expected. This is not, and never*

78. Lv 8:30; emphasis added.
79. Lv 8:30.
80. Ex 29:35–36.
81. Goldingay, *Message of Isaiah 40–55*, 492; emphasis added.
82. Specifically, Isa 53:2–3, 53:4–6, and 53:7–9.

was, one of the great ones of the earth. This is one of the little ones, surely of no consequence.[83]

This leads to the next panel, verses 4–6, with its opening verse point directly to the humiliation of Yahweh's servant: "Surely he has borne our griefs and carried our sorrows; yet we esteemed him stricken, smitten by God, and afflicted." There are several possible connotations of the verb *nāsā'* (i.e., bore): one is *to carry or take away*. The other is *to lift,* including the lifting up of petitions to God.[84] In either case, "the servant *bore with* the pains of other people, independent of any pains of his own ... Like the suffering of someone such as Jeremiah, the servant's suffering issues from *his identification* with the lot of the people as a whole."[85] The other verb of special interest in v. 4 is *nākâ* (i.e., smitten). "Here it is explicit that God is the agent."[86]

Several additional verbs deserve our attention in verse 5: "But he was *wounded* for our transgressions, he was bruised for our iniquities; upon him was the chastisement that made us whole, and with his stripes we are *healed*" (emphasis added). The first, *hōlāl* is not adequately captured by translations such as "wounded," but requires something starker, as in "pierced." On a technical note, the conjunction "but" that begins the verse is known as a "disjunctive waw" and contrasts the Servant (he) from the many (we). "We had thought God was punishing this man for his own sins and failures, but in fact he was *pierced through* because of our rebellion; he was *crushed* because of our twistedness. The images have now shifted from illness to injury and have become more severe."[87]

It is by the "piercing" of Yahweh's servant that the many are healed (*rāpā'*). This term is often translated "we are healed." Yet it is expressed as third-person perfect and is more like "there was healing for us."[88] This term, like the earlier "splatter" is closely linked with Exodus, where *Yah-*

83. Brueggemann, *Isaiah 40–66*, 145; emphases added.

84. See Goldingay, *Message of Isaiah 40–55*, 500.

85. Goldingay, *Message of Isaiah 40–55*, 501; emphases added.

86. "In such phrases the word for God sometimes suggests a superlative, so that the phrase might mean 'dreadfully beaten.' But it would be pointless for the speakers to say that they esteemed him dreadfully beaten when there was no question of that; what is new in their confession is their recognition of the cause of this, not the fact of it." Goldingay and Payne, *Isaiah 40–55*, 305.

87. Oswalt, *Isaiah 40–66*, 387; emphases added. "While 'pierced through' is not always specifically said to result in death, it is typically used in contexts with death (22:2; 51:9; 66:16; Ps 69:27."

88. Goldingay and Payne, *Isaiah 40–55*, 307.

weh himself is called healer: "If you will diligently hearken to the voice of the Lord your God, and do that which is right in his eyes, and give heed to his commandments and keep all his statutes, I will put none of the diseases upon you which I put upon the Egyptians; *for I am the Lord, your healer.*"[89] Here, in the Fourth Servant Song, it is not Yahweh but his servant who provides such healing and "suggests the restoration of a broken nation."[90]

One last point needs to be mentioned about this scene, before turning from the literal to the spiritual sense: the thrust of Isaiah 53:7–9 makes clear that Yahweh's servant *did not deserve such treatment*:

> He was oppressed, and he was afflicted, yet he opened not his mouth; like a lamb that is led to the slaughter, and like a sheep that before its shearers is dumb, so he opened not his mouth. By oppression and judgment, he was taken away; and as for his generation, who considered that he was cut off out of the land of the living, stricken for the transgression of my people? And they made his grave with the wicked and with a rich man in his death, although he had done no violence, and there was no deceit in his mouth.

Here, as Brueggemann stresses, "He is the righteous sufferer of whom the Psalter endlessly sings. Consequently, he is 'cut off' (excommunicated), the ultimate humiliation. No, penultimate! The ultimate humiliation is that he is buried among the wicked, that is, outside the cared-for space where the righteous dead are kept and cherished. *He is utterly rejected, treated to the end as utterly guilty, treated in death even as he had been in life.* He is buried among 'the rich.'"[91] Above all, what is most astonishing is the "silence" of the one who was like *a lamb led to slaughter:* "Silence is an odd stance ... This servant would not open his mouth. For all the passive verbs so far (*touched, struck, afflicted, hurt, crushed*) ... suffering was not simply *imposed upon him.* He 'bore' and 'carried' *not because he had to but because he agreed to.* So, there was no basis for logic or protest. To put it another way, *he was at every point a victim, but he maintained a form of control of his destiny,* not letting anyone else determine his reaction to it."[92]

89. Ex 15:26; emphasis added.

90. Goldingay, *Message of Isaiah 40–55*, 503.

91. Brueggemann, *Isaiah 40–66*, 147; emphasis added. The reference to "the rich" is likely a reference to the Babylonians, who have deposed Israel of her city, her Temple, and her possessions, in the exile.

92. Goldingay, *Message of Isaiah 40–55*, 506; emphasis added.

And it is precisely because of this freedom with which the Servant of the Lord was willingly "put to grief"[93] that he "poured out his soul to death," and so made *many* to be accounted as "righteousness,"[94] that Yahweh gave him a "portion of the great."[95] We now turn from the Letter to the Spirit, from the literal to the spiritual sense of Isaiah 52:13–53:12.

Sensus Spiritualis

The *Targum Isaiah* has several interesting interpretative developments. Where the text of Isaiah 52:13 has "behold my servant (Hebrew = *ʿăbdi*)", the targum has messiah (Hebrew = *māšîaḥ*): Behold, my servant, *the Messiah*, shall prosper, he shall be exalted and increase, and shall be very strong."[96] Likewise, near the conclusion of the Fourth Servant Song, another key modification is evident. The text of Isaiah 53:10 reads, "Yet it was the will of the Lord to bruise him; he has put him to grief; when he makes himself an offering for sin, he shall see his offspring, he shall prolong his days; the will of the Lord shall prosper in his hand." Meanwhile, *Targum Isaiah* modifies the text as follows: "Yet before the Lord it was a pleasure to refine and to cleanse the remnant of his people, in order to purify their soul from sins; *they shall see the kingdom of their Messiah*, they shall increase sons and daughters, they shall prolong days; those who perform the law of the Lord shall prosper in his pleasure."[97]

Several things call for attention here. First and foremost is the addition of *māšîaḥ*, in place of the pronoun "he/him" in Isaiah 53:10, a reference to the "servant." Note, too, that it is part of the larger phrase "kingdom of the messiah." Second, the biblical text indicates that the servant will "prolong his days," and the will of the Lord shall "prosper in his hand." In contrast, in *Targum Isaiah*, it is not the servant (or *māšîaḥ*) who prospers but "the remnant." It is they who "shall prolong days"—provided they "*perform the law of the Lord*." In these modifications, the biblical text is reworked: on one hand, introducing the messiah concept into the text, in place of Isaiah's "servant." On the other hand, the targum looks beyond the messianic figure to a restored remnant of Israel—

93. Isa 53:10.
94. Isa 53:11.
95. Isa 53:12.
96. *Targum Isaiah*, Isa 52:13, in Cathcart et al., *Aramaic Bible*.
97. *Targum Isaiah*, Isa 53:10, in Cathcart et al., *Aramaic Bible*; emphasis added.

it is not he but they who "prosper" as a result of his testing by the Lord.

In the primitive Church, the interpretation of Isaiah was largely Christological in nature. In light of this hermeneutic, the prophet Isaiah was recognized as a proto-evangelist more than a prophet. St. Augustine couldn't help but see "accessible proximity" to the face of the Lord in Isaiah's Suffering Servant. This was all the more true once he understood the book in its totality. Augustine's logic of the book, as a portrait of the suffering Christ, written about him in advance, may be credited in part to St. Ambrose. About this, Augustine writes that St. Ambrose "recommended Isaiah the Prophet; I believe, because he foreshows more clearly than others the Gospel, and the calling of the Gentiles. But I, not understanding the first portion of the book, and imagining the whole to be like it, *laid it aside, intending to take it up hereafter, when better practiced in our Lord's words.*"[98]

This fuller discovery of Christ in the prophet Isaiah, which led to Augustine's pronounced "astonishment," is clear in what he writes elsewhere, in *The City of God:* "The prophecy of Isaiah is not in the book of the twelve prophets, who are called the minor from the brevity of their writings, as compared with those who are called the greater prophets because they published larger volumes. Isaiah belongs to the latter, yet I connect him with the two above named, because he prophesied at the same time."[99]

For Augustine, the whole of the book portrayed Christ. And not only Christ, but also his holy Church: "Isaiah, with his rebukes of wickedness, precepts of righteousness, and predictions of evil, also prophesied much more than the rest about Christ and the Church, about the King and that city which he founded; so that some say he should be called an evangelist rather than a prophet ... Speaking in the person of the Father, he says, '*Behold, my servant shall understand, and shall be exalted and glorified very much.* As many shall be astonished at Thee.'[100] This is about Christ."[101]

In this text from *The City of God,* Augustine stops short of outrightly calling Isaiah an "Evangelist." Still, one gets the impression that he might not be too uncomfortable with such a description since, accord-

98. St. Augustine, *Confessions*, V.13; emphasis added.
99. St. Augustine, *City of God*, 29.1.
100. Isa 52:13, 53:11, cited in full by Augustine.
101. St. Augustine, *City of God*, 29.1; emphasis added.

ing to his reading of Isaiah, it is all "about Christ." This was the case not just for Augustine, but also for virtually all patristic interpreters and the vast majority of medieval figures after them. In fact, more than any other book of the Hebrew Bible, in the primitive Church, Isaiah's Servant was primarily interpreted as an image of the face of the *suffering* Christ. Not surprisingly, then, most of patristic and medieval interpretations were of an allegorical sort, which is reflected in the discussion that follows. Even so, the tropological and anagogical were certainly not neglected, as will be indicated, too.

Let us look to Origen and his handling of the text. The Alexandrian master frequently drew upon Isaiah and sought to demonstrate the truth of Christ and his Passion. For example, early in Book I of his commentary on the Gospel According to St. John, Origen treats the various titles of Christ used by St. John, including *Agnus Dei—Lamb of God*:[102]

> And although the Father says it was great, the fact that he became a servant was moderate indeed compared to the fact that he became an innocent little lamb ... For the Lamb of God became as an innocent little lamb led to be slaughtered that he might take away "the sin of the world." He who bestowed speech on all is compared to a lamb dumb "before his shearer," that we might all be cleansed by his death which is distributed like a drug against the adverse influences and against the sin of those who wish to receive the truth. For the death of Christ has made the powers which war against the human race ineffectual, and, by an ineffable power, has brought the life in sin in each believer to an end.[103]

We previously discussed Augustine's interpretation of Jacob wrestling with the angel, in Genesis 32. There, we noted that his sense of time is shaped by his understanding of biblical revelation—as all of Scripture, no matter the who the chosen human writer is, ultimately is a Word poured out by the Spirit. Accordingly, Jacob's wrestling is a holy story, one that "dramatizes" the Crucifixion, long before the Annunciation of the conception of Jesus. Time is conditioned by God's Word. With Origen, there is likewise a revelatory handling of the notion of "time." Specifically, for Origen, the mystery of the Lamb continues to unfold across time, and through the Holy Spirit, *throughout the age of the Church*, until Christ's glorious return:

102. Jn 1:29, 1:36.

103. Origen, *Commentary on the Gospel According to John, Books 1–10*, I.235–38. See 1 Cor 15:28.

And because he takes away sin until all his enemies are abolished, and death is the last indeed, that the whole world might be without sin, John points to him and says, "Behold the Lamb of God who takes away the sin of the world." He does not say he who will take it away but is not already also taking it away; nor he does he say who took it away but is not still taking it away. For the "taking away" affects each one in the world until sin be removed from all the world and the Savior deliver to the Father a prepared kingdom in which there is no sin at all, a kingdom which permits the Father's rule and again admits all things of God in its whole and total self, when the saying is fulfilled: "That God may be all in all."[104]

Three points in Origen's commentary deserve mention. First, he brings together the perfection, the blamelessness of Christ ("innocent little lamb") with the sacrificial image of the sacrificial Lamb of God, who takes away the sin of the world. Specifically, he does so in his use of Isaiah 53:7: "like a lamb that is led to the slaughter, and like a sheep that before its shearers is dumb, so he opened not his mouth," applying this to Christ, silent before his accusers. Second, Origen emphasizes the complete efficacy of Christ the Lamb's sacrificial death *as a perfect oblation with ongoing effects:* "He does not say he who will take it away but is not already also taking it away; nor he does he say who took it away but is not still taking it away."[105] Third and finally, he associates the sacrifice of Christ with the eschatological Kingdom in which sin has been obliterated and the formerly sinful have been perfected under the total reign of God. Here, Origen's allegorical impression does not exclude the anagogical but in some sense incorporates it as well.

Later, in Book VI, Origen again returns to the title "Lamb of God." There, his largely allegorical impression of Isaiah now takes on a tropological dimension: "This is why in the Apocalypse, too, a little lamb is seen '*standing as though slain.*'[106] This lamb, indeed, which was slain in accordance with certain secret reasons, has become the expiation of the whole world.[107] In accordance with the Father's love for man, he also submitted to slaughter on behalf of the world, purchasing us with

104. Origen, *Commentary on the Gospel According to John, Books 1–10*, I.235–38.

105. Origen, *Commentary on the Gospel According to John, Books 1–10*, I.234.

106. Rv 5:6.

107. Rv 5:9–10: "And they sang a new song, saying, 'Worthy art thou to take the scroll and to open its seals, for thou wast slain and by thy blood *didst ransom men for God from every tribe and tongue and people and nation,* and hast made them a kingdom and priests to our God, and they shall reign on earth'" (emphasis added).

his own blood from him who bought us when we had sold ourselves to sins."[108] By bringing in the Book of Revelation, Origen makes a connection between the Lamb of God in John, and the image of the lamb "standing as though slain." Note that in doing so, Origen bears witness to and extols the virtue of "true devotion" of Christian martyrs. Like Jesus, they are willing offer up their lives to God: "We hold then that the death of the holy martyrs destroys the evil powers. Their endurance and their confession even to the point of death, and their zeal for true devotion, blunt, as it were, the sharp point of the treachery of their enemies against their victims."[109]

In *The Lord*, Guardini ventures into the Book of Revelation and like Origen sees a salvific dimension in lives of the saints: "Human existence often seems deserted, God appears not to exist. Men are able to act against his will with impunity. They blaspheme, they say that God is dead, and no thunderbolt falls from heaven. Sometimes it seems as if really there were nothing outside this world."[110]

Guardini continues:

The Book of Revelation shoes [God] above things; not isolated in Olympian remoteness, where blissful in himself, he strolls over the clouds, disdainful of the miserable swarms below, *but walking among his congregations* ... Those who on earth were found foolish because they believed in him are placed after death in eternity, *in the presence of God.*[111] Earthly powers may seem to be their own lords; history may appear as the workings of human will. In reality it is Christ *who is the Lord of both* ... Nothing can harm the golden light-bearer: no enemy, no event, no accident ... "To him who overcomes, I will give the hidden manna, and I will give him a white [stone], and upon [it] a new name ... He who overcomes I will make a pillar in the temple of my God ... He who overcomes,

108. Origen, John VI.274, in *Commentary on the Gospel According to John, Books 1–10*, 242; emphasis added.

109. Origen, *John* VI.284, in in *Commentary on the Gospel According to John*, 245. "Now we have occupied ourselves with the discussion about the martyrs and the account concerning those who have died because of a state of pestilence, in order to see the distinctive character of him who was led as a sheep to slaughter and was dumb as a lamb before its shearer. For if these stories are not told in vain by the Greeks, and if the stories about the martyrs who became the refuse of the world, and about the apostles who were called the 'offscourings of all' for the same reason, have been related correctly, *what must we understand, and of what magnitude, about the Lamb of God who was sacrificed that he might take away the sin, not of a few, but of the whole world, for which also he has suffered?*" (Origen, *Commentary on the Gospel According to John, Books 1–10*, VI.284; emphasis added).

110. Guardini, *The Lord*, 564.

111. See Wis 3:1–7.

I will permit him to sit with me upon my throne; as I also have sat with my Father on his throne."[112]

Long after the time of Origen, we see another allegorical move by a patristic interpreter of the Suffering Servant text. Specifically, St. Gregory the Great makes a correlation between the lamb of Isaiah's Fourth Servant Song and the sacrifice of Christ. In the process, Gregory makes an additional connection:

> Abel, Isaiah, and John lived at different times. They were separated in time but not in what they preached. Abel offered up a lamb for sacrifice, typifying the passion of our Redeemer.[113] Of him Isaiah says: "as a lamb is silent before its shearer, so he does not open his mouth."[114] And John exclaims: "Behold, the Lamb of God, who takes away the sin of the world!"[115] Behold, they were sent at different times indeed, and yet they were one in thinking that the redeemer was innocent. But they spoke *of the same Lamb, John by pointing to him, Isaiah by foreseeing him, and Abel by offering him.* The one whom John set forth by pointing to him and Isaiah proclaimed in his words, Abel held as a type in his hands.[116]

Here, Gregory's analysis involves a *progression.* His interpretation need not be limited to biblical typology, although typology is certainly in play here, as well. But this is not an example of biblical typology, pure and simple. It is more complex than that. To be clear, Gregory's *Moralia in Iob* is a rich example of patristic allegory that rests not only upon two texts but *three*—the first from the Pentateuch, the second from the Prophets, and the third from the Gospel. Typology, in stark contrast, typically involves two (and only two) biblical texts, with the earlier "type" corresponding to and prefiguring a later "antitype." Such is the essence of biblical typology. There is usually a strict one-to-one correspondence.

Gregory's analysis is a bit different, resting upon three particular Scriptures. And each text adds another layer of meaning to the biblical motif of the sacrificial lamb. Masterfully brought together by Gregory, there is a rich synthesis of scriptural texts that work in successive ways,

112. Guardini, *The Lord*, 566–69; emphases added. See Rv 2:17, 3:12.

113. See Gn 4:4.

114. Isa 53:7.

115. Jn 1:29.

116. St. Gregory the Great, *Moralia on Job* 29.69, in Wilken et al., *Isaiah*, 428; emphasis added.

folding forward and culminating in the Gospel According to St. John. And so Gregory's exegesis goes beyond the more familiar type/antitype sequence and represents a rich example of patristic allegory drawn from three distinct sections of the biblical canon.

For his part, Tertullian makes a connection between Isaiah's Servant, who "bore our griefs and carried our sorrows," and the divine healing brought about by Christ: "He did himself touch others, upon whom He laid His hands, which were capable of being felt, and conferred the blessings of healing, which were not less true, not less un-imaginary, than were the hands wherewith He bestowed them. *He was therefore the very Christ of Isaiah, the healer of our sicknesses*. 'Surely' says he, 'He hath borne our griefs and *carried* our sorrows.'"[117]

Interestingly, Tertullian subtly changes the meaning of a Greek term from the Septuagint of Isaiah 53 to make a poignant point about belonging to Christ: "Now the Greeks are accustomed to use for *carry* a word which also signifies to *take away*.[118] A general promise is enough for me in passing. Whatever were the cures which Jesus effected, *He is mine*."[119] No mere parsing of terms, Tertullian's commentary is both Christological and deeply personal. Such allegorical exegesis, so prevalent in patristic and medieval Christian interpretation of Isaiah, while rooted in Christ, occasionally has a point of reference *other than Christ*, as in that of St. Ephrem the Syrian: "'Listen to me, my people, and give ear to me, my nation; for a law will go forth from me.' And how could it go forth now, if it were the same law that went forth in the days of Moses? *But it is evident that here he mystically signifies the spiritual law, which is the New Testament*. 'And my justice is a light to the peoples,' that is, my sacrament. He also means that the conscience of the Gentiles, which is now clouded by idolatry, will be enlightened after all their gods are condemned by the divine sentence."[120]

Commenting upon Isaiah 51:4,[121] Ephrem, who is believed by many

117. Tertullian, *Against the Marcionites*, IV.8; emphasis added.

118. Isa 53:4 (LXX; emphasis added), *phérō*, "to carry" or "to take away."

119. Tertullian, *Against the Marcionites*, IV.8; emphasis added.

120. St. Ephrem the Syrian, *Commentary on Isaiah*, 51.4; emphasis added. It is possible that Ephrem has in mind the literal rather than allegorical sense. Among modern scholars—e.g., Daniélou—this might likely be categorized as typology rather than allegory. Even so, the example is included for the sake of illustration.

121. Isa 51:4: "Listen to me, my people, and give ear to me, my nation; for a law will go forth from me, and my justice for a light to the peoples."

to be a deacon, has in mind the written rather than the Living Word of God. Even so, allegorical interpretation of the Old Testament, insofar as it may refer to a variety of things, *is rooted in Christ and is all about Christ.* All such references, then, whether they point to the New Testament, the Apostles, the proclamation of the Gospel message, the sacraments, the Church itself, or something else, are in fact allegorical since they are all contained in the one Mystery, that is, Jesus Christ. Even so, Ephrem retains that patristic sense of Christ's hiddenness and our inability to see him of our own accord. It is he alone who reveals himself to us, aided by the grace of faith he offers us: "You are entirely a source of amazement, from whatever side we may seek You: You are close at hand, yet distant—*who shall reach You*? Searching is quite unable to extend its reach to You: when it is fully extended trying to attain to You *then it is cut off and stops short*, being too short to reach Your mountain. *But faith gets there, and so does love with prayer.*"[122]

Turning from the allegorical to the other spiritual senses, it is evident that the Fourth Servant Song was interpreted tropologically from St. Clement of Alexandria until at least the time of St. Thomas Aquinas. In his treatise *Christ the Educator*, Clement writes, "Isaiah says [about Christ], 'The Lord has laid on him the iniquity of us all,' that is, to correct our iniquities and set them right. For that reason, he alone is able to forgive our sins, he who has been appointed by the Father of all as our educator, for he alone is able to separate obedience from disobedience."[123]

With respect to Isaiah 53:6, Clement shifts away, however slightly, from the prevalent "Lamb of God" imagery in the text, focusing attention instead upon *the pedagogy of Christ.* Through his efficacious sacrificial death, Clement begins, Christ "is able to forgive our sins." From this, he reasons that he is the divine educator of our souls, "for He alone is able to separate obedience from disobedience."

Clement's text does not neglect the allegorical dimension but is in dialogue with it. Nevertheless, in a way that would not be as readily clear apart from an allegorical foundation, Clement points to the "interiority" of Christian experience, the necessity of conforming one's actions, and one's one while life to that of Christ. Allegory gives way

122. St. Ephrem, in Brock, *Luminous Eye*, 70; emphases added.

123. St. Clement of Alexandria, *Christ the Educator*, 1.8.67–68.

to tropology, as the suffering Christ educates the soul of the believer, so that "obedience is separated from disobedience," bringing our soul into greater union with his.

Another early Christian text, known as the *Apostolic Constitutions*,[124] reveals a decidedly tropological orientation. Here, the text admonishes bishops, above all, to imitate Christ in their ministry:

For as yours is the burden, so you receive as your fruit the supply of food and other necessities. For you imitate Christ the Lord; and as he "bore the sins of us all on the tree"[125] at his crucifixion, the innocent for those who deserved punishment, *so also you ought to bear the sins of your own people.* For concerning our Savior it is said in Isaiah, "He bears our sins and is afflicted for us"[126] ... For do not you imagine that the office of a bishop is an easy or light burden.

Similar to the passage in Clement, this text places the allegorical and tropological dimensions of Isaiah in conversation with the unmistakable end of conformity to Christ: "so also you ought to bear the sins of your own people." Here, every bishop is instructed *to imitate Christ*, bearing the sins of his own people, like he—allegorically present in Isaiah—does for all his people.

A final example of tropological interpretation of the Fourth Servant Song is seen in a much later text, from St. Thomas and his commentary on the Gospel According to St. John:

Jesus, because he chose to, did not give an answer, so that he might show that he was unwilling to overwhelm by words and to make excuses, since he had come to suffer. At the same time he is for us an example of patience, and fulfilled what is found in Isaiah: "Like a sheep that before its shearers is dumb, so he opened not his mouth."[127] It says, "like a sheep," to show that the silence of Jesus was not that of a man convicted of sin and aware of his evil, but the silence of a gentle person being sacrificed for the sins of others.[128]

Here, Thomas takes up the subject of silence, specifically two distinct types of silence. One sort is that of the guilty man who, aware of

124. The *Apostolic Constitutions* was also known as *Constitutions of the Holy Apostles* and thought to be redacted by Julian of Neapolis. It is divided into eight books and is primarily a collection of and expansion on previous works such as the *Didache* (100 AD) and the *Apostolic Traditions*. Book VIII ends with eighty-five canons from various sources and is elsewhere known as the *Apostolic Canons.* It dates from approximately 380 AD.

125. Isa 53:12.

126. See Isa 53:7–8.

127. Isa 53:6.

128. St. Thomas Aquinas, *Commentary on the Gospel of John*, 230–31.

his own sinfulness, does not dare to diverge from a truthful account of his wrongdoing, but in silence offers his own quiet assent. The other sort, however, is that of godly innocence, as typified by Christ himself. It is the meekness, the innocence of the sheep that is highlighted by Thomas, that is, "the silence of a gentle person being sacrificed for the sins of others."

Elsewhere, in the *Summa Theologica*, Thomas deals with the virtue of patience as it pertains to suffering evil:

> It seems that it is possible to have patience without grace. For the more his reason inclines to a thing, the more is it possible for the rational creature to accomplish it. Now it is more reasonable to suffer evil for the sake of good than for the sake of evil. Yet some suffer evil for evil's sake, by their own virtue and without the help of grace; for Augustine says that "men endure many toils and sorrows for the sake of the things they love sinfully." Much more, therefore, is it possible for man, without the help of grace, to bear evil for the sake of good, and this is to be truly patient.[129]

To this apparent objection, however, Thomas responds, "On the contrary, it is written '*From Him*, that is, from God, *is my patience*.'"[130] Drawing on the thought of Augustine, he continues, "'the strength of desire helps a man to bear toil and pain: and no one willingly undertakes to bear what is painful, save for the sake of that which gives pleasure.'[131] The reason of this is because *sorrow and pain are of themselves displeasing to the soul*, wherefore it would never choose to suffer them for their own sake, but only for the sake of an end."[132] And so it stands to reason that "the good for the sake of which one is willing to endure evils *is more desired and loved* than the good the privation of which causes the sorrow that we bear patiently."[133] All of this necessitates for Thomas the virtue of patience "caused by charity," and so "it is clearly impossible to have patience without the help of grace."[134]

Lastly, and notwithstanding additional examples of a tropological nature, the Fourth Servant Song was interpreted according to the *ana-*

129. St. Thomas Aquinas, *ST* II-II, q. 136, a. 3, obj. 1. See St. Augustine, *On Patience*, III.

130. St. Thomas Aquinas, *ST* II-II, q. 136, a. 3, sed contra; emphasis added. See Ps 61:5: "For God alone my soul waits in silence, for my hope is from him."

131. See St. Augustine, *On Patience*, IV.

132. St. Thomas Aquinas, *ST* II-II, q. 136, a. 3, resp; emphasis added.

133. St. Thomas Aquinas, *ST* II-II, q. 136, a. 3, resp; emphasis added.

134. St. Thomas Aquinas, *ST* II-II, q. 136, a. 3, resp.; see 1 Cor 13:4; Rom 5:5.

gogical sense. St. Gregory of Nyssa puts the text of Isaiah 53:9[135] to use in such a way.[136] By way of context, Gregory is dealing with a difficult text in 1 Corinthians: "When all things are subjected to him, then the Son himself will also be subjected to him who put all things under him, that God may be everything to everyone."[137]

First, he clarifies what St. Paul is teaching; namely, that "some time evil will recede into non-being and be completely eradicated and that God's perfect goodness will enfold in itself every rational being, and nothing God has made will be cast out of his kingdom. This will come to be when all the evil mixed in with what exists has been consumed, like dross, by the purifying fire, and everything God has made will be as it was at the beginning before evil entered the world."[138]

Next, Gregory goes on to explain that, for Paul, "all this happens in the following way: the pure, perfect divinity of the only Son entered into human nature, which is subject to death. The human Christ came to be from the mingling of the divine with human nature as a whole, a kind of '*first fruits*' from the one '*lump of dough*,' and by this all humanity was attached to the godhead."[139]

Finally, citing Isaiah, Gregory concludes, "'*nor was there any deceit in his mouth*'—and in him death, which follows sin, was also totally wiped out, since there is no other cause of death except sin. Thus, both the obliteration of evil and the dissolution of death had their beginning in him."[140] Here, then, Gregory of Nyssa uses a text from the Fourth Servant Song in an anagogical way: Christ, in his perfection, as evidenced by the absolute truth and purity of his words, achieves the final victory over sin and death, such that "*God's perfect goodness will enfold in itself every rational being, and nothing God has made will be cast out of his kingdom*."[141]

Yet another anagogical interpretation of Isaiah's Servant Songs is evident in St. Jerome, who writes: "[Isaiah] gives the historical sense for the Jews [the Red Sea overcoming Pharaoh], yet this includes an-

135. Isa 53:9: "And they made his grave with the wicked and with a rich man in his death, although he had done no violence, and there was no deceit in his mouth."

136. See St. Gregory of Nyssa, *Treatise on 1 Corinthians 15:28*.

137. 1 Cor 15:28.

138. St. Gregory of Nyssa, *When All Things Will Be Subject to Him*.

139. St. Gregory of Nyssa, *When All Things Will Be Subject to Him*; emphasis added. See 1 Cor 15:20; Rom 11:16.

140. St. Gregory of Nyssa, *When All Things Will Be Subject to Him*. See Rom 5:12.

141. St. Gregory the Great, *Moralia on Job* 29.69.

other sense, since the One who did these things now also leads those redeemed and freed by your blood into Zion and into the heavenly Jerusalem—into the church that you have prepared by your blood.... This is what [Isaiah] teaches."[142] Here, Jerome distinguishes between the historical (literal) sense and "another sense," which is undoubtedly the anagogical. Christ, St. Jerome explains, had delivered Israel through the Red Sea. Now, by what he achieved upon his Cross, an eschatological deliverance is in view, as the risen Christ "leads those redeemed and freed by your blood into Zion and *into the heavenly Jerusalem—into the church that you have prepared by your blood*." This, Jerome adds, is what "Isaiah teaches."[143]

A final example of anagogical interpretation is seen in a homily of St. Augustine dealing with Paul's admonition that "we for we walk by faith, not by sight."[144] "What," Augustine asks, "does 'by sight' mean? His form was a beautiful sight beyond 'the sons of men.'[145] Because 'in the beginning was the Word, and the Word was with God, and the Word was God.'[146] 'Whoever loves me, he says, keeps my commandments, and whoever loves me, shall be loved by my Father, and I myself will love him. And what will you give him? *And I will show myself to him*.'"[147] A clear pattern of ascent emerges in St. Augustine's approach. First, note how scriptural his homiletic explanation is, as his immediate response consists of no less than three biblical texts. Second, Augustine begins to develop a theme, drawn from the Gospel According to St. John, "And I will show myself to him." This theme continues in the homily: "There will be sight when he does what he said, *And I will show myself to him*. There you will see God's impartiality, there you will read the Word without a book. So, *when we see him as he is*,[148] our journey will be over. After that we will rejoice with the joy of the angels."[149]

Next, Augustine brings in the text of Isaiah's Fourth Servant Song,

142. St. Jerome, *Commentary on Isaiah*, 14.10. See Isa 51:10.

143. Jerome adds another literal note: "The rest of the meaning is found through reading the Septuagint concerning Jerusalem, that is, the sinful soul is provoked to put on the strength of God's arm and to take on the former works such as it did before the fall, when the soul was illumined" (*Commentary on Isaiah*, 14.10).

144. 2 Cor 5:7.

145. Ps 45:2.

146. Jn 1:1.

147. St. Augustine, Sermon 27.6, in Wilken et al., *Isaiah*, 423–24. See Jn 14:21.

148. 1 Jn 3:2.

149. St. Augustine, Sermon 27.6, in Wilken et al., *Isaiah*, 423–24.

to contrast the Christian's future life with Christ in heaven, "when we will see him as he is," and the present age: "Now we are still on the way. What is the way? It is faith. For the sake of your faith Christ became deformed,[150] yet Christ remains beautiful. When we have come to the end of our journey, his form will be seen as a beautiful sight beyond the sons of men.[151] But how is he seen now, in faith? *And we saw him, and he did not have any beauty nor comeliness, but his face was abject, and his strength deformed . . . a man beset with calamity and knowing how to bear infirmities.*"[152] By the conclusion of his homily, St. Augustine has used several texts of Isaiah 53 to undergird his anagogical and pastoral challenge, to embrace the Sign of the Cross:

> It is Christ's deformity that gives form to you. For if he had been unwilling to be deformed, you would never have gotten back the form you lost. So, he hung on the cross deformed; but his deformity is our beauty. Therefore, in this life let us hold fast to the deformed Christ. What do I mean the deformed Christ? Far be it from me to glory except in the cross of our Lord Jesus Christ, through whom the world has been crucified to me, and I to the world. That is the deformity of Christ. Have I ever spoken to you about anything except that way? This is the way to believe in the crucifix. We carry the sign of this deformity on the forehead.[153]

Although more texts could be added from other commentators, the Fourth Servant Song (Isa 52:13–53:12) was clearly a treasure trove of Christological insight. Throughout the patristic and medieval periods, Isaiah's vision of the Suffering Servant was re-presented as an "accessible proximity" to Christ—specifically, the face of the *suffering* Christ. These riches were drawn out both according to the allegorical sense and from the tropological and anagogical senses.

One of the earliest of theologians to present the suffering Christ is from the pen of a somewhat obscure figure, the second-century saint Melito of Sardis.[154] Even more than Gregory's weaving together of three texts in an allegorical fashion, Melito weaves together an exquisite tapestry of *the suffering Christ* from a cacophony of Old Testament texts

150. Isa 53:2.

151. Ps 45:2.

152. St. Augustine, Sermon 27.6, in Wilken et al., *Isaiah*, 423–24; Isa 53:2–3.

153. St. Augustine, Sermon 27.6, in Wilken et al., *Isaiah*, 423–24.

154. Little is known of Melito, Bishop of Sardis. According to Polycrates, he was Jewish by birth. Among his numerous works is a liturgical document known as *On Pascha* (ca. 160–177). As a Quartodeciman, and one intimately involved in that controversy, Melito celebrated Pascha on the fourteenth of Nisan in line with the custom handed down from Judaism.

and motifs. The result is one of the most striking examples of this sort from the entire patristic age, and it is with his words that we conclude the present chapter.

> This is the one who comes from heaven onto the earth for the suffering one and wraps himself in the suffering one through a virgin womb and comes as a man.
> He accepted the suffering of the suffering one,
> through suffering in a body that could suffer,
> and set free the flesh from suffering.
> Through the spirit that cannot die he slew the manslayer death.
> He is the one led like a lamb and slaughtered like a sheep;
> he ransomed us from the worship of the world
> as from the land of Egypt, and he set us free from slavery of the devil
> as from the hands of Pharaoh, and sealed our souls with his own spirit,
> and the members of our body with his blood.
> This is the one who clad death in shame and,
> as Moses did to Pharaoh, made the devil grieve.
> This is the one who struck down lawlessness
> and made injustice childless, as Moses did to Egypt.
> This is the one who delivered us from slavery to freedom,
> from darkness into light, from death into life,
> from tyranny into eternal kingdom, and made us a new priesthood,
> and a people everlasting for himself.
> This is the Pascha of our salvation:
> this is the one who in many people endured many things.
> This is the one who was murdered in Abel,
> tied up in Isaac, exiled in Jacob, sold in Joseph,
> exposed in Moses, slaughtered in the lamb,
> hunted in David, dishonored in the prophets.
> This is the one made flesh in a virgin,
> who was hanged on a tree, who was buried in the earth,
> who was raised from the dead, who was exalted to the heights of heaven.
> This is the lamb slain, this is the speechless lamb,
> this is the one born of Mary the fair ewe,
> this is the one taken from the flock, and led to slaughter.
> Who was sacrificed in the evening, and buried at night;
> who was not broken on the tree, who was not undone in the earth,
> who rose from the dead and resurrected humankind from the grave below.[155]

155. St. Melito of Sardis, *On Pascha*, 66–71.

Tertio Meditation

The Fourth Servant Song is read in its entirety in the liturgy for Good Friday. It is proclaimed just before the Passion of the Lord, in the Gospel According to St. John.[156] The Servant Song signifies the Crucifixion of Jesus Christ in such profound ways that to not include it here would seem a capital mistake. It is fitting and highly appropriate to read it in anticipation of the Gospel—and to read the Passion in John in light of the servant who "shall be exalted and lifted up, and shall be very high."[157]

In between the two readings is the Responsorial Psalm, taken from Psalm 31.[158] A portion of it reads, "My times are in thy hand; deliver me from the hand of my enemies and persecutors! *Let thy face shine on thy servant; save me in thy steadfast love!*"[159] Like other psalms of petition, it expresses the needful cry of the afflicted soul. Yet, when read (sung) liturgically, "between" Isaiah's Suffering Servant and John's Passion, it takes on a deeply Christological significance.

In the Sacred Liturgy, the psalm unites the Old And New Testaments, calling directly to God in the first person. Here, on Good Friday, every word of the psalm is taken beyond its original meaning. It is as it is shaken by the earth, with the Cross firmly planted within it, to crucify the divine Son.[160] Between the Servant of Isaiah and the Christ of the Gospel, the psalmist cries, "In thee, O Lord, do I seek refuge; let me never be put to shame."[161] And though "despised and rejected by men"—indeed, but all humanity—The Father's Christ is not put to shame.[162] In perfect confidence upon the Cross, the divine Son says with the psalmist, "Be thou a rock of refuge for me, a strong fortress to save me!"[163]

Amid the agony and the jeers were not these "words of David" foremost of Christ's thought: "Yea, I hear the whispering of many—terror on every side!—as they scheme together against me, as they plot to take my life."[164] Indeed, at the last breath of his earthly ordeal, Jesus makes

156. Isa 52:13–53:12; see also Jn 18:1–19:42.
157. Isa 52:13.
158. Ps 31:2, 31:6, 31:12–13, 31:15–17.
159. Ps 31:15–16.
160. See Mt 27:54.
161. Ps 31:1.
162. Isa 53:3.
163. Ps 31:2.
164. Ps 31:13.

David's utterance his own, at the point of death: "Into thy hand I commit my spirit; thou hast redeemed me, O Lord, faithful God."[165] Yet Jesus adds something important to the phrase from Psalm 33: "*Father* ..." Jesus's cry is directed to his Father, the One whom the divine Logos gazed upon from all eternity. With these words of consolation, Jesus breathes his last.

The Servant Song again reverberates at Calvary: "Therefore I will divide him a portion with the great, and he shall divide the spoil with the strong; because he poured out his soul to death, and was numbered with the transgressors; yet he bore the sin of many, and made intercession for the transgressors."[166] In silence, the Father gazes at Jesus, whose will is perfectly united with him, even in death. Here, in the darkness of the tomb, the psalmist's words accompany the crucified Son: "Let me not be put to shame, O Lord, for I call on thee; let the wicked be put to shame, let them go dumbfounded to Sheol."[167] Not only do these words of the psalmist "anoint" Jesus at Golgotha, but they also speak hope to his disciples, frightened and dismayed. Yet only in his Resurrection could they hear they with clarity, peace, and new resolve: "Be strong, and let your heart take courage, all you who wait for the Lord!"[168]

There are many portraits of Christ in the Old Testament—but only one face of the Lord. To look upon him, to really stare with eyes unabated at the divine Son, is to see his Cross. Though tempted to look away, or even run and hide from it, it is there that we see the radiant beauty and boundless love of his face. And it is from there that he looks at us, and in the words of David, he speaks to us, "*Be strong, and let your heart take courage, all you who wait for the Lord!*"[169]

165. Ps 31:5.
166. Isa 53:12.
167. Ps 31:17.
168. Ps 31:24.
169. Ps 31:24.

CHAPTER 7

Contemplating the Face of the Bridegroom Christ with the Shulamite (Song 4:1–5:1)

> Hear my soul speak. Of the very instant that I saw you,
> Did my heart fly at your service.
>
> —William Shakespeare, *The Tempest*

Sensus Litteralis

The previous Old Testament encounter scenes were from the Torah (Jacob, Moses) and the *Nevi'im*—the Prophets (Isaiah). Now we prepare to shift to yet another division of the canon. The remaining two scenes are drawn from the *Ketuvim* of the Hebrew Bible, that is, the Writings. The present chapter involves *Shîr Hashrîm*, the Song of Songs. Chapter 8 covers the enigmatic Book of Job. These choices were deliberate, as they allow the reader to engage all three divisions of the *Tanak*, the Hebrew Bible.

The proper interpretation Scripture depends upon a number of factors: historical context, theological features, literary genre, structure, interplay with other books of the canon, and so forth. The same is true with Song and Job. But approaching these last two books requires additional skills, such as competency in Hebrew poetry, an understanding of the Jewish wisdom tradition, and the nature of *theodicy*,[1] which is not to be

1. "Theodicy is discourse about the justice of God in the face of indications to the contrary—the presence in the world of evil in all its forms." J. Davies, "Theodicy," in Longman and Enns, *Dictionary of the Old Testament*, 808.

confused with theophany. There are mountains of literature written about these two books. In fact, there is more commentary about Song and Job than almost any twelve biblical books put together. And there are legitimate reasons for this seeming disparity.[2] To the extent that these complexities bear upon the interpretation of these texts, they will be discussed. To the extent that they don't, I omit them or point the reader to the relevant secondary literature, so that the focus remains on the Bible itself.[3]

The first thing that needs to be said about Song concerns the selection process. Which passage from the book should be evaluated? This is no simple matter. From beginning to end, Song is, in some sense, one long encounter scene. It is an encounter set in lyrical form—in Hebrew verse—between the Lover and his Beloved.[4] Interestingly, the word "encounter" is frequently used in numerous commentaries: "The best starting point for theological appreciation is to look behind the Temple building itself to the spiritual reality for which it stands. The Song points to the possibility of *intimate encounter with God in this world*. More than that, it attests that such *encounter* is necessary for a truly human life in this world (every Israelite was commanded to make pilgrimage to the Temple each year, once or several times)."[5] Concluding her remarks, Davis writes, "Meditating on the Song might give us eyes to see that this 'pale blue dot,' the planet Earth, is in fact nothing other than the Garden of God, *where God invites us into delighted encounter,* which God has charged and privileged us 'to serve and to keep' (Gn 2:15)."[6]

2. "During the later patristic period and the rest of the Middle Ages, Christian interpreters wrote more works on the Song of Songs than on any other individual book of the Old Testament." Murphy, *Song of Songs*, 21. In light of this, and to keep the chapters of this book uniform, such discussions are presented as concisely as possible. The reader will be referred to secondary sources accordingly.

3. Judgment is called for in weighing the secondary literature and determining if a fact needs to be included in our discussions. On one hand, if key data are excluded, our analysis—and the reader's understanding—will suffer. Excessive or irrelevant data would cause our study to become unwieldy. I have sought to make prudent editing decisions, aiming to be thorough while admitting only those facts that make a meaningful difference for the reader. As the book approaches its conclusion, the reader is advised to review the bibliography.

4. Some might feel that this is an exaggeration or not follow this far. Yet I am confident about this assessment, which is echoed in a good deal of the secondary literature written about Song.

5. Davis, *Proverbs, Ecclesiastes, and the Song of Songs*, 271–72; emphasis added. Similarly, see Bergant's commentary, *Song of Songs*, 18, 21, 22, 27, 32, 65.

6. Davis, *Proverbs, Ecclesiastes, and the Song of Songs*, 272; emphasis added.

Given the array of possibilities, numerous texts presented themselves for consideration. The choice was narrowed down to three candidates, which are mentioned briefly here. Each of them would have made a suitable choice, given the intimate dialogue and evocative phraseology involved. First, there is the opening scene of Song, with its familiar and evocative phraseology, "*O that you would kiss me with the kisses of your mouth*!"[7] This is perhaps the most familiar turn of phrase in the book. Its vocative start, impassioned plea, and facial emphasis all beg to be explored in greater detail. Second, and at the opposite end, is the book's culminating song. It too has its own visceral beauty in spoken words of love: "Set me as a seal upon your heart, as a seal upon your arm; for strong as death is love, fierce as Sheol is jealously. Its sparks are fiery sparks, a fearsome flame."[8] The deliberate juxtaposition of the rhyming (and nearly homophonic) *'ăhăbā* ("love"), *'ăzzāh* ("strong"), and *ămāwēt* ("death") is striking. The entire phrase—*love is strong as death*—pushes the dialogue in a heavenly direction. Third and finally, a passage in Song 2 explicitly uses the term of "face" twice: "O my dove, in the clefts of the rock, in the covert of the cliff, let me see your *măre(h)* ("face"), let me hear your voice, for your voice is sweet, and your *face* is comely."[9] Additionally, the phrase "in the cleft of the rock" is evocative of that previous encounter scene from Exodus, in which Moses's appeal to the Lord, *to see his face.*[10]

To these three, others certainly could be added. Nevertheless, the text that has been chosen is the following from Song, chapter 4:

Behold, thou art fair, my love; behold, thou art fair; thou hast doves' eyes within thy tresses: thy hair is as a herd of goats, that have swept down Mount Gilead. Thy teeth are like a flock of sheep that are even shorn, that have come up from the washing; whereof everyone bear twins, and none is barren among them. Thy lips are like a thread of scarlet, and thy words enchanting: thy cheekbones are like cut pomegranate within thy locks. Thy neck is like the Tower of David built as a fortress, whereon there hang a thousand bucklers, all shields of mighty men.

Thy two breasts are like two young fawns that are twins, that graze among the lilies. Till morning's breeze blows, and the shadows flee, I will go to the

7. Song 1:2; emphasis added.
8. Song 8:6, in Alter, *Strong as Death Is Love*, 50.
9. Song 2:14.
10. See Ex 33:18–20.

mountain of myrrh, and to the hill of frankincense. Thou art wholly fair, my love; there is no blemish in thee. Come with me from Lebanon, my spouse, with me from Lebanon: look from the top of Amana, from the peak of Senir and Hermon, from the lions' dens, from the mountains of the leopards.

Thou hast ravished my heart, my sister, my bride; thou hast ravished my heart with one glance of thine eyes, with one bead of thy necklace. How beautiful is thy loving, my sister, my bride! how much better is thy love than wine! and the smell of thine ointments than all spices! Thy lips, O my bride, drip as the honeycomb: honey and milk are under thy tongue; and the smell of thy garments like Lebanon's scent.

A garden enclosed is my sister, my spouse; a locked well, a sealed spring. Thy branches, an orchard of pomegranates, with luscious fruits; cypress, with spikenard. Spikenard and saffron; cane and cinnamon, with every tree of frankincense; myrrh and aloes, with every choice perfume: A fountain of gardens, a well of living waters, and streams from Lebanon. Awake, O north wind; and come, thou south; blow upon my garden, let its perfume flow. Let my beloved come into his garden and eat his luscious fruits.

I have come into my garden, my sister, my bride: I have gathered my myrrh with my perfume; I have eaten my honeycomb with my honey; I have drunk my wine with my milk: eat, O friends; drink, yea, drink abundantly, O beloved.[11]

This text is an ideal choice for closer analysis. It is one of the most astonishing encounters in the book, for at least three reasons. First, Song 4:1–5:1 has an explicit nuptial motif throughout; that is, the language is evocative not just of two lovers but also of a *bridegroom and bride.* In Guardini's phraseology, the accessible proximity to the face of God flows from the dialogue between lovers. This is true throughout Song, yet it is at its most explicit here. In short, this text is an encounter scene rooted in spousal love.[12] Second, it contains all three "voices" pres-

11. Song 4:1–5:1. Translating the Song of Songs is a complex undertaking, and there are numerous approaches, each of which has strengths and limitations. The above is my own translation, looking first to the original Hebrew. I relied upon the King James Version as a base text, given its sheer beauty, poetic clarity, and predominant stature among English bibles. Because today many are less accustomed to formal translations, I made linguistic revisions to the text. Along with the New Jerusalem Bible, I looked to Alter's *Strong as Death Is Love*. Alter's work on Song is essential reading, and he frequently brings fascinating but overlooked nuances to light, though at times his translations appear labored or unnecessarily eclectic. The overall strength of his translation far outweighs any limitations, however, and one is remiss to ignore them. Along with Alter, Blaise Arminjon's translation of Song was consulted. Arminjon was provincial of the Jesuits in Lyon and France and was a highly regarded retreat master. His achievement on Song is, in my opinion, among the most valuable modern commentaries on the text.

12. Some critics argue for parallels between Song and pagan love poetry, such as "tavern/

ent in Song: the Lover (Solomon), the Beloved (the "Shulamite"), and the Poet/Narrator.[13] This third voice often recedes, compared with the two active voices, but it mustn't be forgotten.[14] It is an *exchange* of metaphors in poetic discourse. This is significant, because the "encounter" dynamic is best heard dialogically in this unique, sacred book. Third and most importantly, Song 4:1–5:1 contains imagery that is hard to discount as messianic. This will become more evident as we analyze texts such as this: "Thy neck is like the Tower of David built as a fortress, whereon there hang a thousand bucklers, all shields of mighty men."[15] Although Song contains many simultaneous layers of meaning, among them are messianic reverberations.

Before engaging Song 4:1–5:1 in further detail, contextual remarks are necessary about the book as a whole. Chief among the many questions about it is the "whether" question. That is, whether Song should be interpreted on a literal or a spiritual level. On the one hand, the book is replete with "erotic language and themes, the name of God is nowhere mentioned or alluded to. The Song neither possesses a notion of salvation history or divine law nor offers explicit moral guidelines."[16] On the other hand, it appears to be recognized as part of the Hebrew canon by Jewish authorities as early as the first century, if not well prior. Many early rabbis spoke of Song in the most reverent tones, even comparing it to the Holy of Holies![17]

---

drinking" songs. This wildly mischaracterizes the sort of love described in the text. In his academic commentary, Roland Murphy writes: "A number of strikingly similar topoi are attested in the Sumerian love poems and Song. However, it is equally important to observe that several of the Sumerian compositions ... share with the biblical Song use of the literary device of dialogue, *whose absence is conspicuous in the otherwise comparable Egyptian collections surveyed earlier*. These topoi and the common use of dialogue seem quite intelligible as belletristic features; there is, in any case, *no compelling reason to posit a fertility cultus or specifically liturgical transmission as the primary link between them*." *Song of Songs*, 55; emphases added. Scholars asserting a "tavern song" approach include Michael V. Fox, "The Entertainment Song Genre in Egyptian Literature," in Groll, *Egyptological Studies*, 268–316; Davis, "Cairo Love Songs." See Murphy's bibliography for more details.

13. Lover, 4:1–15; Beloved, 4:16; Poet/Narrator, 5:1. More will be said about the structure and voices in the poem below. In the New Jerusalem Bible, these headings are included throughout the text of Song.

14. This point, about the significance of the narrator's voice, applies to *all* biblical books.

15. Song 4:4.

16. R. Beaton, "Song of Songs 3: History of Interpretation," in Longman and Enns, *Dictionary of the Old Testament*, 760.

17. "The traditional position [is] that the Song achieved canonical status in the OT

Moreover, the book has been long associated with King Solomon himself.[18] Whatever is to be made of that, its close association with well-established texts of the Solomonic corpus (Proverbs, Ecclesiastes, etc.) was undoubtedly beneficial. Liturgically, Song came to be associated with the Feast of Passover in Jewish communities by the third century. Based on textual data, the rabbis interpreted the book as an allegory of the exodus narrative.[19] Subsequently, the book was one of "Five Scrolls" of the *Megillot*.[20] "Though previously read privately, by

---

because it was read symbolically/allegorically, depicting Israel's relationship to the Lord. There are a few early traditions that may affix a symbolic, though not necessarily allegorical ... reading by the first and early second century AD. That the well-known Rabbi Aqiba thoroughly knew and highly esteemed the Song suggests that it had already been considered Scripture for some time: '*Whoever sings the Song of Songs with a tremulous voice in a banquet hall and so treats it as a sort of ditty will not participate in the world to come*;' and '*Had not the Torah been given, Canticles would have sufficed to guide the world*.' Perhaps the most important tradition related to the issue of canonicity is ... cited in the Mishnah: '*God forbid!—no man in Israel ever disputed about the Song of Songs that it does not render the hands unclean, for all the ages are not worth the day on which the Songs of Songs was given to Israel; for all the Writings are holy, but the Song of Songs is the Holy of Holies*.' The phrase 'render the hands unclean' affirmed the canonicity of a document ... From Aqiba's perspective, not to include the Song in the canon was unthinkable. These quotes provide evidence that a respected rabbi deemed Song worthy of its canonical status and indicate that *there was probable broad acceptance of the Song's inclusion into the canon early, at the latest by AD 100, and likely much earlier*, since Aqiba's death is dated to AD 135." Beaton, "Song of Songs 3: History of Interpretation," in Longman and Enns, *Dictionary of the Old Testament*, 761; emphases added.

18. See Song 1:1.

19. "The exegetical traditions that connect Song of Songs with the events surrounding the exodus from Egypt are first attested in the third century AD. Primary among these traditions was the interpretation of Song 1:9, '*To a mare of the chariots of Pharaoh I compare you, my beloved*,' as referring to the crossing of the Red Sea (Ex 14). Once Song was understood as referring allegorically to the narrative of Israel's salvation history, other connections with the Passover and the exodus emerged. For example, Song 2:9, which refers to looking through windows and lattices, often was placed in the context of the Destroyer passing through on the night of the tenth plague (Targum of Song 2:9). Other themes probably reinforced the association of Song with the season of Passover. Both are set in the springtime, and the prophets' characterization of Israel as God's bride provided a strong parallel as well." in B. C. Gregory, "Megillot and Festivals," in Longman and Enns, *Dictionary of the Old Testament*, 459.

20. "*Megillot*, which simply means 'scrolls' in Hebrew, is used in a more specific sense to refer to the collection of the five smallest books of the Writings of the OT. The concept of the Megillot as a group developed over a long period and was closely tied to the emerging usage of these five books during the festivals of the Jewish liturgical year. The Megillot is comprised of the Song of Songs, Ruth, Lamentations, Ecclesiastes, and Esther. The Jewish festivals in which they are read in their entirety are, respectively, Passover, Pentecost, the Ninth of Av, Tabernacles and Purim." Gregory, "Megillot and Festivals," in Longman and Enns, *Dictionary of the Old Testament*, 458.

the close of the Talmudic period (eighth century) the books of Ruth, Lamentations and Song of Songs had been incorporated into the liturgy of the synagogue."[21]

Song was the last book to be added to the canon of the Hebrew Bible. Despite the book's problematic content, replete with strikingly erotic imagery, other factors overtook it, and in the end, Song prevailed. Factors include Song's association with Solomon and the Solomonic corpus, as well as its liturgical use in the synagogue and Jewish life. These factors contributed favorably, and the book eventually acquired its hard-won place in both the Jewish and Christian canons of inspired texts.

Yet—and here is crucial point—the hinge upon which Song's canonical status hung was not the above factors, but something else: the proliferation of and preference for allegorical readings of the text. This is true in ancient Jewish circles and in the primitive Church. Allegory—and allegorical interpretation of Song—was decisive in overcoming the barriers it faced at the literal level. This is because any interpretation Song at the literal level of meaning put the book at odds with the rest of the canon. It "seemed" as though the book did not belong with sacred texts like Genesis and Exodus. On the surface, it appeared as though it was merely a book of erotic love poetry between a man and a woman. One scholar puts it this way: "The traditional position, if one exists, maintains that the Song achieved canonical status in the OT because it was read symbolically/allegorically, depicting Israel's relationship to the Lord. There are a few early traditions that may affix a symbolic, though not necessarily allegorical in the strict sense, reading by the first century and early second century AD."[22]

Roland Murphy agrees: "The factors leading to the canonization of the Song remain obscure. Despite this, there has been no lack of assumptions regarding how the Song achieved canonical status—for example, because of its supposed Solomonic authorship, its cultic significance, or an alleged 'allegorical' interpretation of it. Whatever the precise reasons and process, the fact of canonization is firmly supported by both ancient Jewish and Christian traditions."[23]

21. Gregory, "Megillot and Festivals," in Longman and Enns, *Dictionary of the Old Testament*, 463.

22. Beaton, "Song of Songs 3: History of Interpretation," in Longman and Enns, *Dictionary of the Old Testament*, 761.

23. Murphy, *Song of Songs*, 5–6.

However one looks at it, there's little doubt that Song's admittance to the canon was in large measure dependent upon the allegorical way it was (broadly) received in Judaism and early Christianity. The romantic imagery in the book paved the way for a plethora of allegorical pathways that blossomed over the centuries, in a whole new direction. It is an irony, then, that a book that barely made it into the canon became one of the most—*if not the most*—commented on books in the whole of Scripture.

There are an array of images and motifs in the book. As the book grew in acceptance, these were mined as allegorical gold. But among all the others, the nuptial imagery of the Lover/Bridegroom and Beloved/Bride came to signify various theological realities. Three primary ones may be mentioned here. The first allegorical pathway is one in which Song represents the marriage of Yahweh, the Bridegroom, to his chosen Bride, Israel. This one functions on both a Jewish and Christian level, but more so with the former. The other two are Christian interpretations, through and through. The second allegorical pathway is one in which Song represents Christ the Bridegroom of the Church, his beloved Bride. The third is a variation of the previous one, in which Song represents Christ the Bridegroom of the believer's soul and "dwelling place" of the Bridegroom. Whereas the second pathway involves the nuptial union in more of the corporate dimension, the third one involves more of the personal dimension. Even so, it is mistaken to suggest an either/or position regarding the literal and spiritual interpretation of the book. As we have stressed all along, the literal sense cannot be dispensed with but is the starting place for all biblical interpretation, including the spiritual senses.

This raises questions. Is a literal explanation available that could find acceptance among orthodox theologians and believers alike—while not disrupting the intrinsic nuptial mystery located within the allegorical mode? If this is possible, how? Song cannot now be separated from (nor should it) its allegorical heritage, whether one takes it as an allegory of Yahweh and Israel, Christ and the Church, or Christ and the Soul.

Yahweh, the Bridegroom → Israel, His Chosen Bride (Jewish/Christian)
Christ, the Bridegroom → The Church, the Bride of Christ (Christian)
Christ, the Bridegroom → The Believer's Soul (Christian)

Put directly, does a genuine literal reading of the text, diminish, distance, or even undermine Song on the spiritual level? As we press on, our answer is unequivocally no. In fact, we can—and must—read the text at both the literal and spiritual levels if we are to more fully comprehend it and its depth of possible meanings. Along the way, I will help the reader navigate from the literal to the spiritual in a way that respects both and, above all, respects the text itself.

In the introduction to *The Cantata of Love*, Arminjon addresses the either/or question and wisely understands it for what it is—a false and unnecessary dichotomy.[24] His work exhibits great sensitivity and respect for the received tradition of Song along with a careful eye for details. Arminjon cuts through the confusion and replaces it with both/and clarity. There is both a literal and a spiritual interpretation to the book. But not all literal solutions are equal in merit. In fact, some are dreadful. As Arminjon explains, the real dilemma is not whether there is a literal meaning of Song. Of course there is, or the book would be *senseless*. Rather, it is whether the explanations offered at the literal level really work or not. And, indeed, many are far less helpful than others. Here, Arminjon critiques secular approaches that interpret the book in a merely erotic way, which he deems the "naturalistic" approach: "Some of the so-called naturalistic school see the Song as a mere poem, or better yet a collection of poems, not inspired by religion at all, but purely secular if not indeed erotic. 'The free sheaf of songs celebrates only one thing: the splendid, radiant and terrifying glory of *eros* between man and woman' ... *Eros* itself vibrates without any purpose than natural love ... *Eros* is sufficient unto itself. *The eros of the Song is not the agape of God*."[25] Such naturalistic approaches are not uncommon in modern secular scholarship. Though, in truth, they are hardly new. Theodore of Mopsuestia (ca. 350–428)[26] developed an approach that may be called "naturalist" in the late fourth century. He was subsequently condemned for it and for other heresies at the Second Council of Constantinople in 553.

As Martin Pope summarizes,

24. See Arminjon, *Cantata of Love*, 31–45.

25. Arminjon, *Cantata of Love*, 32–33 (emphasis added), citing Gillis Gerleman, *Ruth*, 63–77. See also von Balthasar, *La gloire et al croix*, 3:115–16, 124.

26. See Smalley, *Study of the Bible in the Middle Ages*, 14–20.

Theodore, bishop of Mopsuestia, at the end of the fourth century wrote a commentary on the Song of Songs in which he rejected allegorical meaning and read it in its literal and plain sense, as an erotic song. Theodore theorized that Solomon's subjects had criticized his marriage with an Egyptian princess and that the king responded to the protest by boldly singing of his love in this Song. Unfortunately, Theodore's commentary did not survive and is known only from the attacks on it. His great learning, no doubt, discouraged debate during his lifetime. In little more than a century after Theodore's death, at the Council of Constantinople in 550, his views were condemned as unfit for Christian ears.[27]

Whether it is unfortunate that Theodore's commentary on Song did not survive is perhaps debatable. Regardless, his ideas about how to interpret Song outlived him and his condemnation and have resurfaced in modernity. Murphy offers salient analysis:

By the end of the fifth century, Origen's quest for the spiritual meaning of the Song was an established tradition, especially in western Christendom, having won the enthusiastic endorsement of such influential patristic authors as Gregory of Nyssa, Jerome, Ambrose, Theodoret, and Cyril of Alexandria. We cannot pass over this era, however, without mentioning an alternative approach to the Song which came to be associated almost exclusively with the views of Theodore, bishop of Mopsuestia in Cilicia from 392–428. As the intellectual figurehead of the so-called Antiochene school of exegesis and theology, Theodore epitomized resistance to the allegorical emphasis of Alexandrian hermeneutics in general and Origen's exegetical work in particular.[28]

Murphy goes on to explain Theodore's legacy and subsequent influence on interpretation of the book:

As far as we know, Theodore never authored a comprehensive study of the Song, but his perspective on the biblical work seems to be cogently represented in the extracts of a letter he had written to a friend . . . According to these extracts, Theodore vigorously rejected the notion that the Song should be un-

27. Pope, *Song of Songs*, 49–50; Longman, *Song of Songs*, 38–39; Exum, *Song of Songs*, 73. Fragments of Theodore's commentary on Song (*Expositio in Canticum canticorum*) are extant. One example is seen in J. P. Migne's *Patrologia Graeca*, 66, Column 46, pp. 699–700 (see the HathiTrust website, accessed January 23, 2020, https://babel.hathitrust.org/cgi/pt?view=image;size=100;id=mdp.39015008467477;page=root;seq=356). The text of the Second Council of Constantinople is available at Papal Encyclicals Online, accessed December 2, 2019, http://www.papalencyclicals.net/Councils/ecum05.htm. For a discussion of Theodore's commentary on Song and their import in the Council proceedings, see Pirot, *L'oeuvre exégétique de Théodore de Mopsueste*, 131–37; and Vosté, "L'oeuvre exégétique de Théodore de Mopsueste," 394–95.

28. Murphy, *Song of Songs*, 21.

derstood as Solomonic prophecy of the spiritual relationship between Christ and the church. Rather, he suggested, for the contemporary Christian reader the Song had only limited didactic and apologetic relevance, the work being comprised of love poetry that Solomon had apparently written in response to popular criticism of his marriage to the dark-skinned daughter of pharaoh. While this example of Theodore's "literal" exegesis was only peripheral to the charge that he was "the father of Nestorianism," his condemnation by the Second Council was unfortunately to cast a long shadow over the subsequent history of the Song's interpretation.[29]

One wonders if Murphy placed the term literal in quotation marks to highlight Theodore's questionable approach. Regardless, his analysis is sound. Theodore rejected allegorical readings in favor of his own nonallegorical and speculative interpretation. Whether Theodore's approach was properly literal remains questionable, but it is less central to our discussion. The key point is that Theodore's approach brought intense scrutiny upon similar approaches. Meanwhile, allegory continued to flourish. And, given the immeasurable value of *any* of the three major allegorical interpretations mentioned above, it's no surprise that Song would continue for many centuries thereafter, to be interpreted primarily with the spiritual senses, with the literal sense in recession.

St. Pope John Paul II's *Man and Woman He Created Them: A Theology of the Body* is, for a number of reasons, a massive achievement. Among its many contributions, it represents something of a case study in approaching Song in a literal way. This is so for at least two reasons. First, it reflects a genuine respect for the long tradition of reading Song allegorically.[30] Second, it urges for a restoration of the literal sense, yet one in which purely naturalistic approaches are set aside. The difference between *Man and Woman He Created Them* and most secular approaches to Song is that the former is rooted in Christian anthropology, whereas most of the latter are not. John Paul II examines human love in Song from within the framework of its Divine origins: "In relation to the rereading of the language of the body in the truth, and thus also in relation to the reality of the sacramental sign of marriage, we should an-

29. Murphy, *Song of Songs*, 21–22. As to the extracts in question, Murphy explains that they were "preserved as part of the evidence brought against Theodore when he was posthumously condemned by the Second Council of Constantinople in 553" (22).

30. This does not, of course, exclude the possibility of speaking about a "fuller meaning" of the Song of Songs." St. Pope John Paul II, *Man and Woman He Created Them*, 548n95.

alyze, even if only in summary fashion, also that entirely special book of the Old Testament, namely, the Song of Songs. *The theme of the spousal love that unites man and woman connects this part of the Bible in some way with the whole tradition of the 'great analogy,' which flows through the writings of the prophets into the New Testament and especially into Ephesians.*"[31]

In *Man and Woman He Created Them*, the primary background for reading Song is not the so-called love poetry from pagan texts. Instead, it is salvation history as recorded in Scripture. This is a crucial difference. It is not only that John Paul II's approach is biblical and canonical, though it is both. It is that his study of human love in Song—at the literal level—is not tainted by a downgrading of Song into mere eroticism. Seen in this light, the nuptial love in Scripture derives its greater meaning in light of *what it images*, the love between Christ and the Church. This is not to say that John Paul II's literal approach is allegory by another name. Such would be self-contradictory, and to miss the point. No—his literal approach is *analogical*—it is rooted in the Great Analogy of marriage expressed by St. Paul in Ephesians 5.

And so, reading analogously, John Paul II is truly interested to study *human* love, informed by—but outside of—the Great Analogy, as he describes: "One should immediately add, however, that in the Song of Songs the theme is not treated within the sphere of the analogy of the love of God toward Israel (or the love of *Christ for the Church in Ephesians*). *The theme of spousal love in this singular biblical 'poem' lies outside*

31. St. Pope John Paul II, *Man and Woman He Created Them*, 548; emphases added [*Theology of the* Body, 108, from an undelivered written address]. With regard to the "Great Analogy," John Paul II is referring to St. Paul's teaching in Eph 5:21–33: "In the text of Ephesians, the encounter presents itself first of all as a great *analogy*. We read, 'Wives, be subject to your husbands *as* you are to the Lord.' This is the first component of the analogy. 'For the husband is the head of the wife *as* Christ is the head of the Church.' This is the second component that clarifies the first and shows its cause. 'And *as* the Church is subject to Christ, *so* also wives ought to be subject to their husbands.' The relationship of Christ with the Church, which had been presented earlier, is now expressed as a relationship of the Church with Christ, and the next component of the analogy is contained here. Finally, 'And you, husbands, love your wives, *as* Christ loved the Church and gave himself for her.' *This is the final component of the analogy. The remainder of the text of the letter develops the underlying thought contained in the passage just quoted, and the whole text of Ephesians 5:21–33 is permeated by the same analogy: that is, the reciprocal relationship between the spouses, husband and wife, should be understood by Christians according to the image of the relationship between Christ and the Church*" (475; emphasis added) [*TOB* 89, General Audience of August 11, 1982].

that great analogy. The love of bridegroom and bride in the Song of Songs is a theme by itself, and in this lies the singularity and originality of that book."[32]

For John Paul II, it is not a question of allowing for either the spiritual or the literal interpretation of Song. Along with Arminjon and Murphy, he embraces the text in a both/and fashion. As to the literal meaning of Song, John Paul II suggests reading the text in a canonical way: "Although the analysis of the text of this book obliges us to situate its content outside the sphere of the great prophetic analogy, *it is not possible to separate it from the reality of the primordial sacrament*."[33] By "primordial sacrament" he is referring to Adam's spousal expression in the early chapters of Genesis.[34] He continues, "It is not possible to reread [Song] *except along the lines of what is written in the first chapters of Genesis*, as a testimony of the 'beginning'—of that beginning—to which Christ appealed in his decisive conversation with the Pharisees ... *The Song of Songs demonstrates the richness of this language, whose first sketch is already found in Genesis 2:23–25*."[35] According to his reading of the text, locating the literal meaning is not a calamitous process that potentially ends in a reduction of Song to a pagan tavern poem, celebrating sexuality and eroticism apart from God.[36] No—the logic of the text, John Paul II explains, is sensible in light of the Book of Genesis.

32. Pope St. John Paul II, *Man and Woman He Created Them*, 548; emphases added [*TOB* 108, undelivered]. He adds, "'The Song of Songs is thus to be taken simply as what it manifestly is: a song of human love.' This sentence by J. Weinandy, OSB, expresses the conviction of a growing number of exegetes. J. Weinandy, *Le Cantique des Cantiques: Poéme d'amour mué en écrit de Sagesse* (Tournai, Paris, and Maredsous: Casterman/Maredsous, 1960), 26" (548n95).

33. Pope St. John Paul II, *Man and Woman He Created Them*, 550–52; emphasis added [*TOB* 108, undelivered].

34. See Gn 2:23–24.

35. Pope St. John Paul II, *Man and Woman He Created Them*, 550–52; emphasis added [*TOB* 108, undelivered]. See Mt 19:4: "The Song of Songs is certainly found in the wake of this sacrament, in which, through the 'language of the body,' the visible sign of man and woman's participation in the covenant of grace and love offered by God to man is constituted."

36. For an insightful critique of the fallacious notion that the religion of the Old Testament "poisoned" *eros*, or that *eros* and *agape* are opposed in Scripture, see Pope Benedict XVI, *Deus Caritas Est*: "*Did Christianity really destroy eros?* Let us take a look at the pre-Christian world. The Greeks—not unlike other cultures—considered eros principally as a kind of intoxication, the overpowering of reason by a 'divine madness' which tears man away from his finite existence and enables him, in the very process of being overwhelmed by divine power, to experience supreme happiness ... In the religions, this attitude found

Drawing first on the opening words of Song,[37] John Paul II describes the way in which Song is in dialogue with Genesis, intentionally expanding its concise meaning of the nuptial love of the original Man and Woman: "These words lead us immediately into the atmosphere of the whole 'poem,' in which the bridegroom and the bride seem to move in the circle traced by the inner irradiation of love. The words, movements, and gestures of the spouses, their whole behavior, correspond to the inner movement of their hearts. It is only through the prism of this movement that one can understand 'the language of the body.'"[38]

Rooted in St. Paul's Great Analogy (Eph 5:32), John Paul II is able to transcend naturalistic approaches and the difficulties one encounters when human love is separated from its Source. As he writes, "This discovery—already analyzed on the basis of Genesis 2—clothes itself in the Song of Songs with all the richness of the language of human love. What was barely expressed in the second chapter of Genesis (vv. 23–25) in a few simple and essential words is developed here in a full dialogue, or rather in a duet, in which the bridegroom's words are interwoven with the bride's, and they complete each other."[39] These insights amply demonstrate that a sound literal reading of Song is not only plausible but also essential. When grounded not in needless speculation but in the context of Scripture and salvation history, the literal sense secures the book's meaning. More than this, it *strengthens* the place of the book in the canon of Scripture.

---

expression in fertility cults, part of which was the 'sacred' prostitution which flourished in many temples. Eros was thus celebrated as divine power, as fellowship with the Divine. *The Old Testament firmly opposed this form of religion, which represents a powerful temptation against monotheistic faith, combating it as a perversion of religiosity. But it in no way rejected eros as such; rather, it declared war on a warped and destructive form of it, because this counterfeit divinization of eros actually strips it of its dignity and dehumanizes it. . . . An intoxicated and undisciplined eros, then, is not an ascent in 'ecstasy' towards the Divine, but a fall, a degradation of man. Evidently, eros needs to be disciplined and purified if it is to provide not just fleeting pleasure, but a certain foretaste of the pinnacle of our existence, of that beatitude for which our whole being yearns. . . .* Man is truly himself when his body and soul are intimately united . . . *Only when both dimensions are truly united, does man attain his full stature. Only thus is love—eros—able to mature and attain its authentic grandeur*" (4, 5; emphases added).

37. Song 1:1–2, 1:4: "Let him kiss me with the kisses of his mouth! For your love is better than wine . . . Draw me after you, let us make haste . . . We will exult and rejoice for you; we will remember your tender caresses."

38. Pope St. John Paul II, *Man and Woman He Created Them*, 552; emphasis added [*TOB* 108, undelivered].

39. Pope St. John Paul II, *Man and Woman He Created Them*, 552 [*TOB* 108, undelivered].

Now, the charges of modern biblical criticism against Song appear much weaker and indeed baseless. When complemented by a proper understanding of *eros* in relation to *agape*, the secular vision of Song becomes even more difficult to maintain in light of such a canonical approach to the text. Yet this canonical approach does not depend merely on papal writings. Alongside the thought of John Paul II and Benedict XVI, prominent voices in Protestant biblical scholarship on the Song of Songs may be added. Two such scholars advocate a reading of the book on a literal level, and both suggest that a canonical approach to the text carries us further than noncanonical approaches. The first of the two is Ellen Davis. In her commentary on Song, Davis argues against the modern tendency to read the text as secular love poetry. Like John Paul II, she locates the literal meaning of Song alongside Genesis:

> The approach taken in this commentary is that the Song of Songs is, in a sense, the most biblical of books. That is to say, *the poet is throughout in conversation with other biblical writers.* The Song itself is a comparatively late composition. Despite the ascription to Solomon, the linguistic evidence indicates that it is to be dated between the fourth and the second centuries B.C.E. As we shall see, the Song is thick with words and images drawn from earlier books. By means of this "recycled" language, the poet places this love song firmly in the context of God's passionate and troubled relationship with humanity (or, more particularly, with Israel), which is the story the rest of the Bible tells.[40]

Davis's canonical hermeneutic distinguishes her commentary from the naturalistic approaches. "Far from being a secular composition, the Song is profoundly revelatory. Its unique contribution to the biblical canon is to point to the healing of the deepest wounds in the created order, and even the wounds in God's own heart, made by human sin. Most briefly stated, *the Song is about repairing the damage done by the first disobedience in Eden, what Christian tradition calls 'the Fall.'*"[41]

As Davis continues, this thesis

> requires some explication. According to the third chapter of Genesis, the consequence of that disobedience was a threefold rupture in the original harmony of creation. In the highly condensed language of myth, Genesis acknowledges that our fallen world is characterized by three fundamental forms of tension or alienation. First is the asymmetry of power between woman and man. Wom-

40. Davis, *Proverbs, Ecclesiastes, and the Song of Songs*, 231; emphasis added.
41. Davis, *Proverbs, Ecclesiastes, and the Song of Songs*, 231; emphases added.

en in ancient Israel would have heard the hard truth in God's warning to Eve: *"Your desire shall be for your husband, and he shall rule over you."*[42] The second level of alienation is between humanity and nature, represented in the cursing of the fertile soil[43] and the enmity between the snake and the woman.[44]

Davis further probes the scene:

Third and most terrible, there is now a painful distance between humanity and God. The great mythic symbol of this is the expulsion of Adam and Eve from Eden, the delightful garden where they lived in God's presence and joined in God's evening stroll.[45] From a biblical perspective, the sadness in our world stems from what happened in the Garden of Eden. That mythic exile is mirrored in the most dreadful event of Israel's history, the exile to Babylon following the fall of Jerusalem in 587 B.C.E. Virtually all the books of the Bible bear traces—one might say "scars"—of the great and terrible experience of exile as a result of disobedience to God.[46]

Getting to the heart of the connection between Song and Genesis, Davis explains, "The theological importance of the Song is that *it represents the reversal of that primordial exile from Eden.* In a word, it returns us to the Garden of God. There, through the imaginative vehicle of poetry, we may experience the healing of painful rupture at all three levels. First, woman and man embrace in the full ecstasy of mutuality. Two people, equally powerful, are lost in admiration of one another—or, more accurately, in admiration they truly find themselves and each other."[47] Going on, Davis sees two other implications: "Second, the natural world rejoices with them. It is alive with birdsong and rampant bloom. The lovers' garden of delight is the very opposite of the harsh world into which Eve and Adam 'fell,' where snakebite threatens the heel[48] and thorns and thistles choke the good seed.[49] Third and finally, as I shall try to show, *the lover's garden is subtly but consistently represented as the garden of delight that Eden was meant to be, the place where life may be lived fully in the presence of God.*"[50]

42. Gn 3:16.
43. Gn 3:17.
44. Davis, *Proverbs, Ecclesiastes, and the Song of Songs*, 231. See Gn 3:15.
45. In Gn 3:8; "Eden" means "delight."
46. Davis, *Proverbs, Ecclesiastes, and the Song of Songs*, 231.
47. Davis, *Proverbs, Ecclesiastes, and the Song of Songs*, 232; emphasis added.
48. Gn 3:15.
49. Gn 3:18.
50. Davis, *Proverbs, Ecclesiastes, and the Song of Songs*, 232; emphasis added.

The details of Davis's argument are unpacked in the remainder of her commentary, and her thesis is well supported and compelling throughout. Also, Davis's analysis is not identical to that of John Paul II. The two are distinct, operating within different frameworks of biblical exegesis and philosophical anthropology, respectively. Yet they provide rational, biblically grounded arguments that complement one another as two distinct ways of explaining Song on a literal level and within its canonical framework.

One more voice may be added to John Paul II's aside from Davis, that of James Hamilton. In a provocative essay, "The Messianic Music of the Song of Songs," he offers a "non-allegorical interpretation" of the book.[51] Hamilton describes his thesis as follows: "In academic discussions of the Song of Songs, the nearest thing to a discussion of the Messiah in the Song is a nod to the Christian, allegorical reading of the Song which interprets the poetry with reference to Christ and the church".[52] He adds, "I have yet to find a discussion of the Song of Songs which highlights the interlocking messianic themes of the Song's music: *the Song is about Israel's shepherd king, a descendent of David, who is treated as an ideal Israelite enjoying an ideal bride in a lush garden where the effects of the fall are reversed*."[53]

Hamilton's treatment of the book is a bit different than John Paul II's and Davis's approach. Like theirs, however, it rests upon reading Song within a canonical framework. What is distinct about Hamilton is that his canonical approach attempts to identify and call attention to a number of "messianic threads." These become clear only when Song is read within the canon of Scripture: "When the Song is heard in the context of the three-movement symphony of *Torah, Neviim*, and *Ketuvim*, this lyrical theme, the sublime Song proves to be an exposition of the messianic motif of the OT. I am suggesting that the Song of Songs, read in the context of the OT, is messianic music that we do not need allegorically imaginative ears to hear."[54]

51. Hamilton, "Messianic Music of the Song of Songs."

52. Hamilton, "Messianic Music of the Song of Songs," 331; emphasis added. Murphy suggests early messianic readings were not uncommon: "The third expository sections explicitly follow 'along the paths of the Midrash [Rabbah]'; *here he explores figurative senses* that reveal the Song's imagery to depict the history of the covenantal relationship between Israel and God, from the call of Abraham through the messianic age still to come" (Murphy, *Song of Songs*, 32).

53. Hamilton, "Messianic Music of the Song of Songs," 331; emphasis added.

54. Hamilton, "Messianic Music of the Song of Songs," 332. Again, Hamilton stresses that his messianic reading is at the literal, not the allegorical, level.

Pushing against the allegorical tide, Hamilton argues that a reading of Song on a purely literal (and canonical) level reveals that the author's intentions are clearly messianic in nature. His proposal an attempt to "read the Song as it might have been understood originally, that is, 'prior to the allegorizations introduced by both the Rabbis and the early Christians.'"[55] This thesis may raise questions as to its veracity. As intriguing as it sounds, is such an approach to Song warranted, or does it ring of "messianic" predilection and bias? Are his conclusions substantially supported by the text, or is he culpable for introducing eisegesis, merely reading his own messianic point of view into Song of Songs? The answer depends, to an extent, upon how much credence one gives to canonical approaches in general. Hamilton's messianic approach to Song is less conspicuous, less tenable, until it is put alongside other key texts in the Old Testament. Then and only then does the "messianic music" rise to an audible level, to be weighed accordingly. This places a certain burden upon a canonical reading for his messianic thesis to hold water.

Here is why: the messianism in the text, as Hamilton sees it, does not emerge as clearly unless the book was originally placed in dialogue with or, let's say, it was playing with other books in the canon. There are two possibilities that present themselves. (1) It was the human author who deliberately meant for Song to be read messianically, with the most supportive columns coming from *outside the book*, that is, from other books of the canon. (2) The Divine author "hid" these messianisms within the book, for example, similar to the manner in which Isaiah 7:13–14 was reinterpreted by later Christian interpreters, in a manner that was beyond the prophet's own knowledge.

We would not rule out the latter. And we have no objections to messianic readings of the Old Testament—none at all. There are numerous significant messianic texts in the Old Testament. As to the question of an operative pattern of messianism in Song, there are few efforts that have argued as convincingly.[56] It is my observation that some contemporary evangelical scholarship overreaches in this regard, proposing an overabundance of rather thin "messianic sureties" in the Old Testament.[57] In fairness to Hamilton, such does not appear to be the case in

55. Hamilton, "Messianic Music of the Song of Songs," 342; emphasis added.

56. At least none that I am aware of at present.

57. I do not wish to paint evangelical scholarship with a broad brush in this respect. Such "overreach" is generally not found and is an exception to the rule. I am appreciative of

his essay. The textual data that he marshals is impressive, and there are few loose ends.

Let us return to the two possibilities mentioned above. The nature of what Hamilton describes does not appear to be the sort of messianism that emerged later. In other words, if the messianisms are present in the book as he proposes, the human author *could not have been unaware* of their presence. I make this assertion on the basis of Hamilton's own argument. Such an orchestration of texts in a messianic direction—from Song and other canonical texts—could not have lain dormant and been "hidden" under the human author's own nose. There are too many, and they are too intricate to postulate that the "messianic reverberations" were the design of the divine Author alone, that is, *sensus plenior*. Such a development is not dispositive. It is untenable to suggest that they were placed there, beyond the human author's conscious awareness. In other words, if there are messianic motifs in Song, the human author was somehow involved. He deliberately shaped the text in this particular way and was somehow responsible for them.[58]

With that said, Hamilton makes a compelling case, when all the pertinent data points are gathered together. The strength of his argument rests upon a several pieces of literary evidence from Song and connections between it and other parts of the Old Testament. Two of these are discussed here.[59]

---

many significant contributions in recent Protestant scholarship, in particular for its attention to the rise of Jewish messianism and its implications for reading the New Testament, and especially the Four Gospels. Moreover, I am indebted to the many brilliant contributions of Protestant/evangelical scholars, among them, especially in regard to messianic motifs in the Old Testament, Michel Bird and Craig Keener. See esp. Bird, *Jesus Is the Christ*; idem, *Are You the One Who Is to Come?*; Bock, *Messiah in the Passover*; idem, *Gospel According to Isaiah 53*; Kaiser, *Messiah in the Old Testament*; Bauckham, *Jesus and the Eyewitnesses*; Hengel, *Studies in Early Christology*; Hurtado, *Lord Jesus Christ*; Fletcher-Louis, *All the Glory of Adam*; idem, "God's Image"; Keener, *Historical Jesus of the Gospels*. In addition to the above Protestant scholars, see the following texts by Catholic scholars: Meyer, *Aims of Jesus*; Collins and Collins, *King and Messiah as Son of God*; Fitzmyer, *The One Who Is To Come*.

58. A fair-minded critique of Hamilton's thesis is warranted, as a fair portion of his supporting evidence is *beyond* Song itself. Accordingly, his argument rests as heavily upon other canonical texts, as it does upon the Song of Solomon. To be clear, this is not the case with John Paul II's or Davis's intertextual reading. Therefore we proceed with care.

59. Those interested in a fuller treatment of the subject are encouraged to read Hamilton's monograph *Song of Songs*. For the sake of concision, we deal with his essay here. The book goes beyond it, yet the argument there is essentially the same. See also his *God's Glory in Salvation through Judgment*; *With the Clouds of Heaven*; and *God's Indwelling Presence*.

Despite the challenges raised above, Hamilton makes an interesting case when the data are gathered together. Yet it is either quite right or quite wrong; there is little room for middle ground here. Although the reader is free to decide for him- or herself, the following data are worthy of consideration.[60] The strength of his argument rests upon a few pieces of literary evidence from Song and literary connections between it and other parts of the Hebrew Bible. Two of these are discussed here.

First, among the strongest planks upon which Hamilton's thesis rests are royal and Davidic motifs that permeate Song and that have paral lels throughout the canon. Our criticism notwithstanding, these should not be quickly discarded. Hamilton traces the motif of kinship that runs through the Old Testament from Genesis onward.[61] He looks to the David story and argues for a "Davidic background of Gen 3:15,"[62] looking especially to the Royal Psalms: "David is addressed as God's 'anointed' or 'messiah'[63] whose 'seed' will endure forever under God's favor.[64] As Yahweh has crushed the ancient serpent 'Rahab,'[65] so now David and his sons will crush their enemies in the dust beneath their feet."[66]

There is more to his Davidic approach in addition to the above remarks. After unpacking further evidence that supports the royal motif, Hamilton turns to the "son of David," Solomon himself. He suggests that scholars have long overlooked the symbolic importance of Solomon, which saturates Song of Songs. He asserts that Solomon's role in the book is by no means superfluous and that his prominence in Song

60. Those interested in a fuller treatment of the subject are encouraged to read Hamilton's monograph *Song of Songs*. For the sake of concision, we deal with his essay here. The book goes beyond it, yet the argument there is essentially the same. See also his *God's Glory in Salvation through Judgment*; *With the Clouds of Heaven*; and *God's Indwelling Presence*.

61. "The OT is much concerned with kingship. Genesis readies readers for a monarch. It would seem that even Adam is presented in royal terms, for, having stated that man and woman are to be in his own image and likeness, God's first statement about them is, 'Let them rule' (Gn 1:26, 28)." Hamilton, "Messianic Music of the Song of Songs," 334.

62. Hamilton, "Messianic Music of the Song of Songs," 335.

63. See Ps 89:21, 89:39; 2 Sm 22:51.

64. See Ps 89:5, 89:30, 89:37.

65. See Ps 89:11.

66. See Ps 89:24; 2 Sm 22:37–43. Hamilton, "Messianic Music of the Song of Songs," 335, citing Wifall, "Gen 3:15: A Protoevangelium?": "Other 'royal' Psalms tend further to establish the Davidic background of the Yahwist's portrait in Gen 3:15. In Psa 72:9, the foes of the Davidic king are described as 'bowing down before him' and 'licking the dust.' In the familiar 'messianic' Psalms, God is described as having placed 'all things under his feet' (Psa 8:6) and will make 'your enemies your footstool' (Psa 110: l)."

is not merely to add authorial weight behind it. Hamilton discusses the role of Solomon and the Jerusalem Temple in the Davidic covenant and how they are crucial to understanding Song at a literal level. In his reading, it is the presence of Solomon—and all that his presence entails—that makes Song into a verse of "messianic music." As Hamilton explains:

> The Song is in harmony with this [messianic] expectation, for it names Solomon in its opening verse. The only Solomon in the OT is the son of David, third king over Israel. Whatever view one takes of the lamed prefixed to the name "Solomon" in Song 1:1 ... *the person who is the immediate referent of the promises to David concerning his "seed"*[67] *is invoked.* It is generally agreed that "beginning with the time when the oracle of Nathan fixed the hope of Israel on the dynasty of David,[68] each king issuing from him became the actual "Messiah" by whom God wished to fulfill His plan with regard to His people."[69]

Hamilton's literal reading of the text runs counter to that of most modern scholars, such as Martin Pope, who treats the Solomonic reference as purely allegorical. Aware of this, Hamilton pushes back: "For the allegorists the king is either YHWH or Christ; for proponents of dramatic theories, it is Solomon."[70] In a similar fashion, other modern scholars, following Pope's allegorical line of reasoning, suggest that when the "lover" is referred to as "king," it is merely a term of endearment and nothing more.[71] As Hamilton correctly points out, however, this does not appear likely: "The option that Pope does not name is the interpretation taken here: *the king is the son of David, presented as Solomon. But the Solomonic king here represents the ultimate expression of David's royal seed.*"[72] "In other words," he continues, "for it to be established that the designation 'king' is used as a 'term of endearment,' examples of this usage in the OT would be necessary. This does not appear, however, to be a meaning of [*mĕlĕk*, "king"] attested in the OT. Thus, the door is open to the possibility that *the male in the Song is presented as the Davidic king, with all the messianic connotations that status*

67. See 2 Sm 7.

68. See 2 Sm 7:12–16.

69. Hamilton, "Messianic Music of the Song of Songs," 336, emphasis added, citing Bonnard and Grelot, "Messiah."

70. Pope, *Song of Songs*, 303.

71. Weems, *Song of Songs*, 380; Hamilton, "Messianic Music of the Song of Songs," 337.

72. Hamilton, "Messianic Music of the Song of Songs," 337; emphasis added.

carries."[73] Indeed, Song does refer to the male speaker numerous times as *molech* ("king") and in one instance as *nādîb* ("prince").[74] Song is replete with references to *shelōmōh* ("Solomon"), and twice it mentions *hămĕlĕk shelōmōh* ("King Solomon").[75]

A second line of evidence related to the above involves the motif of Jerusalem and its Temple. Like the Davidic/Solomonic motif, the "centrality of Jerusalem" runs throughout the text of Song. It too suggests that Hamilton represents much more than the logical geographic setting for the poem—it is teeming with messianic symbolism. He begins by noting that Song's setting is in a certain *îr* ("city") and that the most obvious point of reference is *Jerusalem*. Moreover, Song refers to the *benōt tsiyyôn* ("daughters of Zion"), which directly links one of the subjects of the text with the Temple of Solomon and, in Hamilton's view, messianism.[76] In addition, the motif of *găn* ("garden") is central to Song. Regardless of what one makes of Hamilton's thesis, the Edenic symbolism here clearly cannot be discounted: "The recurrent tragedy of biblical history is that human love and responsiveness to God repeatedly weakens and fails. The Song of Songs answers that tragic history, stretching all the way back to Eden."[77]

Similarly, Davis asserts, "*There is an Edenic quality to the description of the blooming land, here and throughout the Song.* The lovers imagine the land of Israel in its fullest bloom, but beyond that they imagine an exotic landscape, fragrant with the scents of distant lands.[78] This supernaturalistic picture, which exceeds the bounty of any one place on earth, may be seen as *an imaginative return to paradise, the Garden of God.*"[79]

Like Davis, Hamilton interprets Song as a reversal of the Fall in Eden and a kind of recapitulation and restoration of the human love that God intended "in the beginning." As he explains, "This theme is introduced in the first words of the Song, where the woman longs for the

73. Hamilton, "Messianic Music of the Song of Songs," 337; emphasis added.

74. See Song 1:4, 1:12, 7:6.

75. See Song 1:5, 3:7, 3:9, 3:11, 8:11, 8:12.

76. See Song 3:2, 3:3, 5:7. "Though I do not explore it further in this article, I should note that the Song is in part set in a city (e.g., 3:2–4; 5:7), *and the most natural interpretation is that the city is Jerusalem* (cf. the reference to 'daughters of Zion' in 3:11). *Zion is, of course, also associated with messianism* (cf., e.g., Psa 2:6; Pss. Sol 17:22, 30; Sir 24:9–12)." Hamilton, "Messianic Music of the Song of Songs," 331n2; emphases added.

77. Davis, *Proverbs, Ecclesiastes, and the Song of Songs*, 234.

78. See Song 4:13–14.

79. Davis, *Proverbs, Ecclesiastes, and the Song of Songs*, 250–51; emphases added.

kisses of the king.[80] She yearns for the intimacy she is not presently experiencing. Somehow the love depicted here is love in which it is 'right' … for others to indulge.[81] I would suggest that it is upright for all the righteous to admire the Davidic king and to benefit from the depicted glories of the idealized relationship between the hoped-for Messiah and his splendid bride."[82]

By way of summary, Hamilton's reading sees Song as interacting and engaging with Genesis, such that the original intimacy of the Man and Woman, though thwarted by sin, is now being restored in Song. Overcoming this "alienation," as he puts it, is not merely represented by any two lovers. It is experienced by Solomon and the Shulamite. In other words, Solomon is the "son of David," or "messiah." The Shulamite is a postexilic Israel longing for her Lover, the Solomonic king: "Israel's king, depicted here as a good shepherd, overcomes the fears and shame of his beloved with reassuring compliments."[83]

Looking to the early chapters of Genesis, Hamilton adds: "By her confident response and exultation in the king (1:12–14), and through their mutual affirmation and enjoyment of the health of their relationship, *the Song's audience experiences their edenesque enjoyment*.[84] The Song then seems to go from verse to refrain, as the daughters of Jerusalem are urged not to stir up love until it pleases."[85] Later in the text, Hamilton argues, "The king comes *to his wedding in glory*[86] … and upon his arrival he sings a song of praise to his beloved,[87] followed by a declaration of both her beauty and his desire.[88] *She invites him to put an end to separation and alienation*,[89] and when he announces that he has done so[90] the return to intimacy is celebrated."[91]

80. Song 1:2–4.
81. Song 1:3c, 1:4c.
82. Hamilton, "Messianic Music of the Song of Songs," 340.
83. Hamilton, "Messianic Music of the Song of Songs," 340. See Song 1:8–l 1.
84. Song 1:15–2:6.
85. Hamilton, "Messianic Music of the Song of Songs," 341; emphases added. See Song 2:7.
86. Song 3:6–11.
87. Song 4:1–5.
88. Song 4:6–16.
89. Song 4:16b.
90. Song 5:1a.
91. Hamilton, "Messianic Music of the Song of Songs," 341; emphases added. See Song 5:lb.

At the end of the essay, Hamilton concludes that such a messianic reading is "the most plausible interpretation of the Song given its canonical context" and that the exegetical implications are "far-reaching."[92] Citing Murphy, he explains, "'Recent critics have been unable to establish an objective exegetical basis for decoding the Song along the lines of patristic and medieval Christian exposition. While this does not negate the value of the expository tradition in its own right, it leaves us without empirical criteria by which to assess the possible connection between "original" authorial intent and subsequent creations of hermeneutical imagination.'"[93] So, if the nonallegorical messianic interpretation of the Song proposed here is correct, it would appear to explain the allegorizations "produced by both Jewish and Christian interpreters after the life of Jesus of Nazareth."[94] In other words, Hamilton is suggesting that if the thesis is correct, then this *literary* meaning—the author's original intentions, gave way even more readily to Jewish and Christian interpretations at the *allegorical* level. Although such cannot be proven, this is a most intriguing argument.

We are now in a position to consolidate our research on Song. Adding up the findings from John Paul II, Davis, and Hamilton, we are in a firm position to clarify our own approach to the text. Song is a book that challenges the reader on numerous levels. Even determining the literal meaning can be daunting. We are not suggesting a once-for-all solution to the book's many riddles. Yet three points may be asserted with a fair degree of confidence.

1. The richest, newer approaches to the book work primarily within the literal meaning of the text and in a canonical framework. Setting aside secular and "naturalistic" interpretations, Song appears to have a clear and coherent message at the literal and not merely allegorical level. Its message appears highly attuned to Genesis as well as other Old Testament texts. Whatever Song's true logic, it appears likely that a *literal reading brings us far closer to the author's intentions of the book* than previously imagined. Despite impressions that Song is miles apart from the

92. Hamilton, "Messianic Music of the Song of Songs," 343, citing Murphy, *Song of Songs*, 94.

93. Hamilton, "Messianic Music of the Song of Songs," 343, citing Murphy, *Song of Songs*, 94.

94. Hamilton, "Messianic Music of the Song of Songs," 343.

rest of the canon, our research suggests that it may be in fact be one of the most canonically dependent books in the collection.

2. A strong literary relationship between Song of Songs and the early chapters of Genesis appears probable. In fact, it is not unreasonable to posit a kind of intertextual dialogue taking place between Song of Songs and Genesis 1–3. Whether one investigates these connections on an anthropological level (John Paul II) or on a level of biblical theology (Davis, Hamilton), there are sufficient connections between the two traditions that some sort of interchange between them cannot—and should not—be entirely set aside but thoughtfully considered.

3. There is a shared quality to all three scholars and their work on Song. Despite the distinctions in their work, all three hold in common a reading of Genesis and Song that involves some kind of restoration—specifically of the former by the latter. All three scholars hear a note of recapitulation, sending the reader back to the "Adamic Garden." Elements of Song heal, reconcile, or reorder something intrinsic to the original Garden. And it is all "worked out" in the new, Solomonic one. That John Paul II, Davis, and Hamilton all affirm this (in distinct ways) is significant and worth further study.

Up to this point, we have primarily addressed the book as a whole and not engaged Song 4:1–5:1 in great detail. Nor have we dealt with contextual questions, such as that of the book's authorship and dating, as well as the book's structure. Having broached the "literal–spiritual divide," we suggested three fresh approaches to the book overall. We are now better situated to home in and deal with the passage in question. To begin, the first two contextual questions—of authorship and dating—do not bear as heavily on our discussion as one might imagine.

First is the question of authorship. We may dispense with it rather quickly. We are committed to dealing with this text "as we have it," that is, at the final, canonical stage. Additionally, as Murphy correctly states, there is vast disagreement among scholars as to whether "the work a collection of disparate poems, variously authored over the course of several centuries, or should the individual units of poetry be attributed to a single author."[95] Murphy is correct when he asserts, "The question of

95. Murphy, *Song of Songs*, 3.

authorship is complicated by the issue of the unity of the Song."[96] And so, on authorship, we could dig quite a bit and not necessarily find a convincing answer, certainly not one that would satisfy many.

Second is the book's date of composition. Unlike authorship, there is wide consensus today about its relative date. Much like Proverbs and Ecclesiastes, Song appears to have originated in a post-Solomonic context. Much later still, it was likely composed in a *postexilic context*, feasibly in or near Jerusalem: "Many scholars date Song of Songs to the Persian period. Linguistic arguments have been the chief justification put forward for maintaining a late date for the Song."[97]

This rapidly moves us beyond authorship and dating to the question of the book's overall structure, which requires a bit of discussion to unpack adequately. Additionally, looking at "structure" will help situate 4:1–5:1 in our detailed discussion that follows. Murphy correctly states that there is vast disagreement among scholars as to whether "the work a collection of disparate poems, variously authored over the course of several centuries, or should the individual units of poetry be attributed to a single author."[98] For his part, however, Murphy is persuaded—and we along with him—that Song is not characterized not disunity. Rather, a cohesive wholeness characterizes the entire work.[99] As it happens, if the book emerged from a postexilic author, say, in Jerusalem, this only supports Hamilton's messianic thesis, or at least makes it more plausible when Jewish messianism was on the rise. As to the literary structure of Song, this too is hotly debated, given the above. Yet a few authors have come to recognize a chiastic framework along the lines of the list below.[100]

96. Murphy, *Song of Songs*, 3.

97. Garrett, *Song of Songs*, 16. "Linguistic criteria are all we can go on in determining the general period of the Song's composition. The language of the Song resembles mishnaic Hebrew in many ways" (187). Fox goes on to list 'characteristically mishnaic words and constructions that demand a late date for the Song'" (citing Fox, " Cairo Love Songs").

98. Murphy, *Song of Songs*, 3.

99. Murphy, *Song of Songs*, 3. He adds, "To be sure, this unity may be contrived, reflecting the efforts of a later redactor or editor who is perhaps also responsible for the superscription in 1:1. But there is equal merit to the view that the poet who authored most if not all of the individual love poems preserved in the Song *also designed the composition as a whole.* While no certainty can be reached in such matters of authorship, *the collection of poems within the Song is not haphazard*" (emphases added).

100. See Garrett, *Song of Songs*, 32.

Superscript (1:1)
A I. Chorus and soprano: the entrance (1:2–4)
B II. Soprano: the virgin's education I (1:5–6)
C III. Soprano and chorus: finding the beloved (1:7–8)
D IV. Tenor, chorus, and soprano: the first song of mutual love (1:9–2:7)
E V. Soprano and tenor: the invitation to depart (2:8–17)
F VI. Three wedding-night songs (3:1–5; 3:6–11; 4:1–15)
F a. Soprano: the bride's anxiety (3:1–5)
F b. Chorus: the bride comes to the groom (3:6–11)
F c. Tenor: the flawless bride I (4:1–15)
G VII. Soprano, tenor, and chorus: the consummation (4:16–5:1)
F VIII. Three wedding-night songs (5:2–16; 6:1–3; 6:4–10)
F a. Soprano, tenor, and chorus: the bride's pain (5:2–8)
F b. Chorus and soprano: the bride recovers the groom (5:9–6:3)
F c. Tenor and chorus: the flawless bride II (6:4–10)
E IX. Soprano, chorus, and tenor: leaving girlhood behind (6:11–7:1)
D X. Tenor and soprano: the second song of mutual love (7:2–8:4)
C XI. Chorus and soprano: claiming the beloved (8:5–7)
B XII. Chorus and soprano: the virgin's education II (8:8–12)
A XIII. Tenor, chorus, and soprano: the farewell (8:13–14)

Three additional remarks are necessary here on Song's literary structure, and they open our specific analysis of 4:1–5:1.

1. The logic of Garrett's proposal is "that the Song of Songs is a unified work with chiastic structure and is composed of thirteen individual songs, or cantos, for presentation by a male and a female soloist with a chorus."[101]

101. Garrett, *Song of Songs*, 31–32.

2. Next, he builds his structure independently. But he does so with reference to and interaction with other scholars who agree that Song has some sort of chiastic structure. In his discussion of their structural proposals, he notes the wide variety of views. Yet he adds that at "one point they agree . . . Song 4:12–5:1, the garden metaphor, is the climax of the whole poem. This is hardly surprising since it is here that the man and woman consummate their relationship."[102]

3. Garrett places this text at the heart of the chiasm: "Canto VII[103] is the centerpiece of the chiasmus and describes the sexual union of bride and groom on their wedding night. It is an appropriately balanced set of twelve lines, with strophes of four lines, two lines, four again, and two again."[104]

That our text is the central panel of the book's chiastic structure is significant and should not be overlooked. As we have it, the nature of palistrophes (biblical or otherwise) necessitates special attention be paid to the absolute middle and end of the chiasm to unlock the fuller meaning of the whole. We will return to this point later.

Accordingly, 4:1–5:1[105] can be described as follows: 4:1–15 is given in the voice of the Lover, the male speaker, and depicts "the flawless bride."[106] This is the third of "Three Wedding-night songs."[107] Following the flawless bride sequence is "the consummation" in 4:16–5:1. This section includes the voice of both the Lover and Beloved—as well as the narrator.[108]

Garrett's analysis is complemented by Murphy's genre analysis of 4:1–5:1, and it too is commendable. Murphy writes:

This section can be divided into separate poems: 4:1–7, the man's description of the woman's physical beauty; v 8, his invitation to her to come from Lebanon,

102. Garrett, *Song of Songs*, 31; emphasis added.

103. Song 4:16–5:1.

104. Garrett, *Song of Songs*, 35.

105. "A new section begins in 4:1, which has no connection with the preceding passage dealing with Solomon's procession, and finds a natural ending in the invitation of 5:1 to eat and drink of the fruits of the 'garden.' This unit is clearly separate from the woman's second description of her experience in seeking her lover." Murphy, *Song of Songs*, 158.

106. Garrett refers to the Lover/male speaker as the "tenor," the Beloved/female speaker as the "soprano," and the voice of the narrator as the "chorus." See Garrett, *Song of Songs*, 32.

107. See Song 3:1–5, 3:6–11, and 4:1–15. This is followed by three *more* "Wedding Night Songs" in 5:2–16, 6:1–3, and 6:4–10. See list above.

108. In Garrett's terminology, "soprano, tenor, and chorus." *Song of Songs*, 32.

which serves as a prelude to vv 9–11, a song of admiration; 4:12–5:1, the garden song. These divisions are based on genre and content. The dialogue pattern running through these verses is clear enough to give them a unity that should be honored: the man speaks of her beauty (vv 1–7) calls for her presence (v 8), and expresses his admiration, (vv 9–16a); in v 16b she invites him to the garden, and in 5:1 he affirms his acceptance of the invitation.[109]

Arminjon's analysis of this section of Song works in a slightly different way. He begins the unit at 3:6,[110] although both scholars identify 5:1 as the conclusion of the unit. Arminjon terms this section as "The Summer of the Wedding."[111] He laments of the predicament of the Beloved and the Bride to this point in Song: "How can one fail to be sad, if we consider that after having already risen in so many love ascents … the soul does not seem to have grasped what it is seeking."[112] Within a few verses that follow, the name of Solomon is invoked twice: "Look, *Solomon's bed*—sixty warriors round it of the warriors of Israel. A [pavilion] did King *Solomon* make from Lebanon wood. Its posts made of silver, its padding gold, its curtains crimson, its inside paved with love by the daughters of Jerusalem."[113]

These references to the king, along with the *benôth tsiyyôn* ("daughters of Jerusalem"), bolster Hamilton's thesis. These recurring Solomonic themes appear to signify something more than a basic association of the book with his royal name. About the imagery in 3:6, Davis explains, "In the Song, the bride is redolent with myrrh and frankincense. Yet here is another piece that doesn't fit. Ancient women wore perfume made of myrrh,[114] but *frankincense was not a cosmetic. It was reserved for sacred use, to accompany sacrificial offerings and make a 'pleasing odor to the Lord.'*[115] It seems, then, that the poet is picturing Israel as itself a sacrificial offering to its God."[116]

109. Murphy, *Song of Songs*, 158.

110. Song 3:6: "What is that coming up from the wilderness, like a column of smoke, perfumed with myrrh and frankincense, with all the fragrant powders of the merchant?"

111. Arminjon, *Cantata of Love*, 201.

112. Arminjon, *Cantata of Love*, 201, citing St. Gregory of Nyssa, *In Canticum Canticorum*, Homily 6.

113. Song, 3:7, 3:9. Alter's translation, *Strong as Death Is Love*, 21–22; emphases added. Note the slight variation: instead of "pavilion," Alter has "palanquin" for the Hebrew term *'apiryon* (22n9).

114. See Est 2:12.

115. See Lv 6:15.

116. Davis, *Song of Songs*, 261; emphases added.

Davis continues:

That implication is reinforced by the fact that the verb "come up" also has strong associations with sacrifice. The offering burnt on the altar "comes up" to God. But the associations are even more complex. The same verb also regularly designates the journey of the pilgrim ascending to the Jerusalem Temple, on the crest of the Judean Hills on the edge of the wilderness: "Rise, let us *come up to Zion*, to the Lord our God."[117] The woman who is "coming up" thus appears in a dual aspect, as both the one who offers sacrifice to God and the perfumed offering itself.[118]

For Davis, then, the clear connection between the "Lover" and "King Solomon," along with "Zion/Temple"–related motifs, is part of a larger body of evidence in Song that supports her thesis. True, unlike Hamilton, Davis does not put forth a messianic reading of the text. Yet both scholars agree that the role of Solomon in Song is anything but incidental. Additionally, both assert that the book's author is, in one way or another, using the figure of Solomon. Specifically, they suggest his presence is part of its deeper theological intentions that can only be fully grasped when Song is read in light of the canon, particularly in light of Genesis. This is a significant point of agreement, and one that is even more persuasive, given that Davis and Hamilton deal with the particulars of Song in discrete ways.

Returning to the chiastic structure of Song (see above) brings our attention back to 4:16—5:1, which both Garrett and Murphy identify as the centerpiece of the entire book. The latter's insights on this section of Song is especially relevant to our discussion because Murphy identifies additional literary motifs beyond the Solomonic ones discussed here. In particular, he looks to symbolic language related to king's Bride. Consider 4:9 and 12 in particular: "You have ravished my heart, my sister, my bride, you have ravished my heart with a glance of your eyes, with one jewel of your necklace … A garden locked is my sister, my bride, a garden locked, a fountain sealed." This imagery followed upon by 4:16–5:1a, the lovers' "consummation."[119] It reads as follows: "Awake, O north wind, and come, O south wind! Blow upon my garden, let its fragrance be wafted abroad. Let my beloved come to his garden and eat

117. See Jer 31:6; Ps 122:4.
118. Davis, *Song of Songs*, 261; emphases added.
119. See list above.

its choicest fruits. *I come to my garden, my sister, my bride,* I gather my myrrh with my spice, I eat my honeycomb with my honey, I drink my wine with my milk" (emphasis added).

At the climax of the chiastic centerpiece[120] is the conclusion of the verse, which presents the voice of the Chorus/Narrator: "Eat, O friends, and drink: drink deeply, O lovers!"[121] Murphy points to the following evidence: "Central to the poem of admiration in 4:9–16a is comparison of the woman to a luxuriant 'garden' (*gan*) that produces choice fruits and spices."[122] Along with this motif "is the imagery of vines and vineyards that appears throughout the Song."[123] While not all of Murphy's analysis is equally persuasive,[124] the stronger part of his exegesis is that "The point of 'garden enclosed' is that the woman belongs to the man alone. One is moving in the same world of thought as Prov 5:15–19 … [both texts] mean the same thing, although the metaphors (sealed fountain, well) differ. *She is his exclusive water source, and a source in the garden which he describes.*"[125]

120. See Song 4:16–5:1.

121. Alter agrees that despite the chapter break, 5:1 is "clearly the conclusion of this poem." *Strong as Death Is Love*, 29. His translation of 5:1b is slightly different: "Eat, friends, and drink, *be drunk with loving.*" He explains, "The concluding line of the poem is formally anomalous because a third person is now speaking, urging the two lovers to revel in the consummation of their love … the bride and groom are exhorted by a wedding guest or by a kind of chorus to enjoy the pleasures of love."

122. Murphy, *Song of Songs*, 78. See Song 4:12–16.

123. Murphy, *Song of Songs*, 78. This motif is pervasive; see Song 1:6, 1:14, 2:13, 2:15, 6:11, 7:9, 7:13, 8:11–12.

124. Murphy is a highly credible guide to reading Song, yet we are not persuaded by the following point: "This garden is unreal, in the sense that no garden in the ancient Near East would have nourished such a wide variety of plants and trees. Gerleman rightly calls it a 'utopian, fantasy-garden,' that contains the precious aromatic plants of the ancient world. One suspects that the terms are chosen for sound and exotic qualities, rather than for botanical reasons." See Gerleman, *Ruth*. At issue is Murphy's unnecessary "comparative religions approach." Regarding the metaphors in Song, the analysis of John Paul II is refreshingly illuminating: "The fact that in this approach the feminine 'I' is revealed for the bridegroom as 'sister'—and that *she is bride* precisely *as sister*—has a particular eloquence. The expression 'sister' speaks of union in humanity and at the same time of feminine diversity, of the originality of this humanity. This difference and originality exists not only with regard to sex, but to the very way of 'being a person' … The 'sister' in some sense helps the man to define and conceive himself, she becomes, I would say, a challenge in this direction … The bridegroom … accepts this challenge and gives a spontaneous answer. When [he] addresses the bride with the word 'sister,' this expression signifies *a specific rereading of the 'language of the body.'* This rereading is unfolded explicitly in the duet of the spouses." *Man and Woman He Created Them*, 563–64; emphases original [*Theology of the* Body, 109, 4–5, from an undelivered written address].

125. Murphy, *Song of Songs*, 158; emphases added. See Prv 5:15–19: "Drink water from

In contrast, Hamilton's take is that all of the garden imagery in Song is best understood in light of that other canonical garden, that is, Eden: "The question posed in 5:9[126] provides the bride with an opportunity to extol her king, and the first characteristic named is that he is 'ruddy,'[127] *bringing David to mind.*[128] After the virtues of the king are sung,[129] another question is posed as to the location of the king.[130] It is remarkable here that the king with Davidic characteristics has gone *to his garden,*[131] where he enjoys the intimacy of his bride.[132] *If the music is in a messianic key, it has an edenic pitch.*"[133] There is too much in this quotation to offer a detailed commentary. Five points are worthy of discussion as our discussion of the literal sense nears its end.

First, the connection to David appears to be on firmer ground than Hamilton suggests. Song 5:9 describes the Bridegroom as *ʾādôm* ("ruddy"). He is correct to suggest that this mention recalls David. The same term is used twice to describe the physical appearance of David. The first occurrence is in a crucial text in 1 Samuel. There, the prophet and priest of God, Samuel, visits the house of Jesse. He is sent there by the Lord to find his anointed one: "And [Jesse] sent, and brought him in. Now he was *ʾādômonî* ("ruddy"), and had beautiful eyes, and was handsome. And the Lord said, 'Arise, anoint him; for this is he.'"[134] Here is the same Davidic term, *ʾādôm*, used in 1 Samuel and in Song. But this particular observation is only part of the picture.

There is more to commend it, and at least two points of support should be mentioned. The first is the context in which it occurs in 1 Sam-

---

your own cistern, flowing water from your own well. Should your springs be scattered abroad, streams of water in the streets? Let them be for yourself alone, and not for strangers with you. Let your fountain be blessed, and rejoice in the wife of your youth, a lovely hind, a graceful doe. Let her affection fill you at all times with delight, be infatuated always with her love."

126. Song 5:9: "What is your beloved more than another beloved, O fairest among women? What is your beloved more than another beloved, that you thus adjure us?"

127. See Song 5:10: "My beloved is all radiant and ruddy, distinguished among ten thousand."

128. See 1 Sm 16:12, 17:42.

129. See Song 5:10–16.

130. See Song 6:1: "Whither has your beloved gone, O fairest among women? Whither has your beloved turned, that we may seek him with you?"

131. Here, Hamilton is referring to Song 6:2: "My beloved has gone down to his garden, to the beds of spices, to pasture his flock in the gardens, and to gather lilies."

132. See Song 6:3: "I am my beloved's and my beloved is mine; he pastures his flock among the lilies."

133. Hamilton, "Messianic Music of the Song of Songs," 341; emphases added.

134. 1 Sm 16:12.

uel. Immediately following this description of David as "ruddy," the Lord commands Samuel, "Arise, anoint him; for this is he." The term occurs within the call narrative of the future King David. The ruddy one is in fact the same person as the future king, about to be anointed by Samuel. A second point is this passage in 1 Samuel contains other royal imagery with messianic overtones. Specifically, Samuel is told to *mishāchē* ("anoint") the ruddy David. It is from this term that the English word "messiah" is derived.[135] The next scene depicts the actual anointing of David: "Then Samuel took *the horn of oil* and anointed him in the midst of his brothers; and the Spirit of the Lord came mightily upon David from that day forward."[136]

Hamilton's literary reading of Song is decidedly messianic in nature. The Lover/Bridegroom is "Israel's hoped-for Messiah," presented through the original "son of David," Solomon.[137] But how does he account for the garden/bride imagery, and what does it signify at the literal level? As he explains, the Beloved refers the literal bride of the messiah, restored by the Solomonic "son of David," her Messiah/Lover: "So if we ask whom the female symbolizes if the male is the Messiah, the simplest answer is that *she is the Messiah's beloved*. If it is true that the sons of David who were anointed king over Israel were in a sense Israel's Messiah, then it would seem plausible to suppose that the developing messianic expectation could have extended to the Messiah's most intimate relationship."[138] As he concludes, "The Song sings that the Messiah will attain intimacy, and that overcoming the obstacles thereto is as triumphant as the subjugation of the nations. *Why would Israel's expected messianic king not have a queen*? And why would their relationship not be worthy of the most majestic Song?"[139]

This brings the discussion of the literal sense to a close. Our search for meaning has taken us on an extensive trek. There is in fact more evidence worthy of scrutiny, yet space does not permit further engagement.

135. "The English word *messiah* is based on the Hebrew *māšîach*, an adjective related to a verb meaning 'to anoint' or 'to [smear] with oil.'" D. G. Firth, "Messiah," in Boda and McConville, *Dictionary of the Old Testament*, 538. Of course, the Greek term *Christos* ("Christ") is the corollary to the Hebrew term meaning *anointed one*, i.e., messiah.

136. 1 Sm 16:13. In terms of "the Spirit of the Lord coming mightily upon David," one recalls the Spirit descending upon Jesus in the scene of his baptism (see Mk 1:10 and parallels).

137. Hamilton, "Messianic Music of the Song of Songs," 342.

138. Hamilton, "Messianic Music of the Song of Songs," 342; emphasis added.

139. Hamilton, "Messianic Music of the Song of Songs," 342; emphasis added.

The above discussion will have to suffice, as we move on to the spiritual sense of the passage. Before we do, and by way of summation, five brief remarks are offered on the above discussion.

1. Song is undoubtedly one of the most complex books to interpret within the Hebrew Bible, and our analysis is by no means exhaustive. Even so, it is clear enough that the text demands to be read at both the literal *and* the spiritual levels of meaning, beginning of course with the former. This point should stand upon its own, without further support. Every book of the Bible needs to be engaged at the literal and spiritual level. It is, in some sense, "truer" in Song than the rest, for all of the reasons described in this chapter.

2. Three scholars—John Paul II, Ellen Davis, and James Hamilton—diverge in their interpretations of the book. Yet all of them stand in agreement that a secular/naturalistic approach to Song is untenable. Indeed, it is not a viable way of interpreting this sacred, poetic text. The collective wisdom of these three commentators demonstrates that to get at the literal meaning of Song, a canonical approach is not only viable. It yields the richest array of potentialities.

3. John Paul II's *Man and Woman He Created Them* is not a biblical commentary. Even so, his close reading of Song sheds important light on our study. Above all, two points stand out. First, he rightly states the need to recover the literal meaning of Song. Moreover, the literal meaning is not to be found in naturalistic, secular readings of the book. Second, his *Theology of the Body* bought us briefly into contact with Ephesians 5, Paul's "Great Analogy." This sent us back to Genesis, where John Paul II drew out the connection between Song and Genesis, in the motif of spousal love.

4. Ellen Davis's reading of the text is, like Hamilton's, canonical in orientation. Whereas he sifts through many details and brings them together into an extensive messianic symphony, however, Davis's proposal relies upon less restrictive parallels between Song and Genesis. And the upshot for Davis is not messianism, but cosmic and earthly renewal. In her view, the author of Song is offering a more universal message—a new Eden and a new hope for a restoration of God's relationship with humanity and also a restoration of interpersonal relationships.[140]

140. In fact, Davis also envisions in Song a restoration between *humanity and nature*, which along with the Divine-human and interpersonal divides was likewise breached at

5. Finally, we are intrigued by Hamilton's messianic exegesis of the text. This is especially the case since his proposal is worked out at the *literal*, not the allegorical, level of meaning. In fact, it'd be easier to dismiss *if it were at the allegorical level.* But it isn't, and his argument, while complex, is not without merit. Although we subjected his argument to reasonable criticism, the textual basis on which he puts it forth is not as far-fetched as it may have appeared at the outset. Song was likely composed sometime in the postexilic period, and its messianic themes would be at home alongside other messianic-minded texts, such as Zechariah, Daniel, and the Servant Songs of Isaiah. Whether or not one is persuaded by his entire argument, it is worthy of consideration.

In short, the contributions of the scholars engaged in this chapter offer fresh insights into Song. The above discussion is intended to present the reader of Song with an understanding of the book at the literal level. Some approaches may require further reflection and scrutiny. Nevertheless, with respect to the author's original intentions, it should be clear that canonical approaches offer much and generate more optimism than noncanonical ones.

The former lead us back to Genesis and beyond, presenting an array of possibilities that illuminate the text at the literal level. The latter—and those that depend upon naturalistic, "comparative religion" approaches—misalign Song with erotic pagan poetry and in so doing do not adequately illuminate the text at the literal level. We now turn to an examination of Song according to the "second instruction," that is, the spiritual sense.

Sensus Spiritualis

To begin with, St. Theodoret of Cyr once wrote, "It is not possible by any other way, you see, to come to know the meaning of the divine Scripture, especially the Song of Songs, than having the very one who inspired those composers illuminate our vision by sending rays of grace and give a glimpse of the hidden sense."[141] This is a fantastic claim, yet

"the Fall." As she writes, "The second level of alienation is between humanity and nature, represented in the cursing of the fertile soil (3:17) and the enmity between the snake and the woman (3:15)." *Song of Songs*, 232.

141. St. Theodoret of Cyr (393–466), *Commentary on the Song of Songs*, 4.

the history of interpretation of Song from Origen onward serve to vindicate Theodoret's pronouncement.

As noted, Song has generated ream upon ream of exegetical engagement over the centuries, and it was and is one of the most commented on of all the books in the biblical canon. In no way will this discussion engage the vast ocean of spiritual exegesis of Song over the centuries. What is presented here are but a few droplets from the period of roughly 200–1300 AD. Nevertheless, this discussion will be more than adequate to orient the reader to the general logic of reading Song through to the spiritual senses. Recall that our primary aim is to seek "the face of the Lord" through the Four Senses, the Bridegroom Christ in the Song of Songs.

We begin with the allegorical and then move to tropological and finally anagogical interpretations of Song 4:1–5:1. St. Bernard of Clairvaux is dealt with separately, only after covering three spiritual senses. The reason for this exception is that Bernard's approach is complex, and his *Commentary on the Song of Songs* tends to operate on a number of spiritual levels of meaning nearly simultaneously, or at least in a more fluid fashion than others.

We turn first to St. Augustine. Although he did not pen a commentary on Song, Augustine did manage in his voluminous works to engage it in intriguing ways. In his masterpiece *On Christian Doctrine*, he makes a point using one of our texts: "Your teeth are like a flock of shorn ewes that have come up from the washing, all of which bear twins, and not one among them is bereaved."[142] In puzzling about its meaning, Augustine admits a question: "Does the hearer learn anything more than when he listens to the same thought expressed in the plainest language, without the help of this figure?"[143] Augustine is not leaping over the literal or plain meaning of the text. Rather, he recognizes that there are numerous mysteries in the text. He is open to the possibility that figural elements of the poem may illuminate that which remains obscure at the literal level. For Augustine, the meaning of Song becomes most salient when read at an allegorical level. It does not only point to Christ. Along with him, it signifies the Sacrament of Baptism and to his commandment to love God and neighbor: "And yet, I don't know why,

142. Song 4:2.
143. St. Augustine of Hippo, *On Christian Doctrine*, II.6, 537.

I feel greater pleasure in contemplating holy men, when I view them as *the teeth of the Church*, tearing men away from their errors, and bringing them into the Church's body, with all their harshness softened down, just as if they had been torn off and masticated by the teeth."

Augustine continues, "It is with the greatest pleasure, too, that I recognize them under the figure of sheep that have been shorn, laying down the burthens of the world like fleeces, *and coming up from the washing, i.e., from baptism, and all bearing twins, i.e., the twin commandments of love*, and none among them barren in that holy fruit."[144] Note how Augustine describes the Church's theologians and apologists as the "teeth that tear men away from error," bringing them into the light of truth. Here, one verse from *Song* is explained in a threefold allegorical manner. Elsewhere, in the *City of God*, Augustine returns to chapter 4 of Song. Again he approaches it in an allegorical fashion, and again it signifies Christ's Church: "This account can be even better read *as an allegory of the church*, prophetical of what was to happen in the future. Thus, the garden is the Church itself, as we can see from the Canticle of Canticles; the four rivers are the four Gospels; the fruit-bearing trees are the saints, as the fruits are their works; and the tree of life is, of course, the Saint of saints, Christ."[145] Like the previous example in *On Christian Doctrine*, Augustine's allegorical interpretation is multifaceted, with associations drawn between Song and the Four Gospels, the saints and their good works, and even Christ himself.

Augustine's bishop and mentor, St. Ambrose, employed a similar allegorical approach: "Christ, then, feeds his church with these sacraments, by means of which the substance of the soul is strengthened, and seeing the continual progress of her grace, he rightly says to her, 'How comely are your breasts, my sister, my spouse, how comely they are made by wine, and the smell of your garments is above all spices. A dropping honeycomb are your lips, my spouse, honey, and milk are under your tongue, and the smell of your garments is as the smell of Lebanon. A garden enclosed is my sister, my spouse, a garden enclosed, a fountain sealed.'"[146] For Ambrose, the "garden enclosed" and "fountain sealed" signify the virtues of a modest, quite life: "The mystery ought to remain

144. St. Augustine of Hippo, *On Christian Doctrine*, II.7; emphasis added.
145. St. Augustine, *City of God*, XIII.21.
146. St. Ambrose, *On the Mysteries*, IX.5, in *Seven Exegetical Works*. See Song 4:12–15.

sealed up with you, that it be not violated by the deeds of an evil life, and pollution of chastity, that it be not made known to you, for whom it is not fitting, nor by garrulous talkativeness it be spread abroad among unbelievers. Your guardianship of the faith ought therefore to be good, that integrity of life and silence may endure unblemished."[147]

A clear pattern of ascent is evident here. Ambrose first deals with Christ *allegorically*, made present to the Church by means of the sacraments he instituted as means of grace. From this Ambrose moves to the *tropological*, applying the twofold garden/fountain motif of Song, forward into the age of the Church. Believers are encouraged to live chastely, avoiding all forms of immorality, such as gossip and slander. Like the Bride of Song, the Bride of Christ is to entrust the custodian of her soul, the Bridegroom, with her very being, and so make progress in a life of integrity.[148]

For St. Ephrem, to contemplate the Church as Bride is to receive the invitation to the Eucharistic wedding feast and to praise the Bridegroom Christ there. It is in the taking of the wine that a new dimension of "beholding" occurs:

> I have invited You, Lord, to a wedding feast of song,
> but the wine—the utterance of praise—at our feast has failed.
> You are the guest who fills the jars with good wine,
> fill my mouth with your praise.

147. St. Ambrose, *On the Mysteries*, IX.5. See Song 4:12–15.

148. Similarly, see St. Cyril of Alexandria, who interprets the garden/fountain motif of Song allegorically, with an eye to the Sacrament of Baptism: "[This garden] is closed to the world but opened to the heavenly bridegroom. And the fountain where we are anointed after baptism was sealed by the Holy Spirit." *Fragments in the Commentary on the Song of Songs*, 4.12 (available via the Internet Archive, accessed December 26, 2019, https://archive.org/stream/PatrologiaGraeca/Patrologia%20Graeca%20Vol.%20069#page/n665/mode/2up).

Fragments in the Commentary on the Song of Songs, 4.12. Similarly, see St. Cyprian of Carthage, *LXIX*, 2. Elsewhere, John Paul II anchors his discussion in the literal sense: "We cannot limit ourselves to a summary glimpse of the poetic beauty of these metaphors. It is not only a beauty of language, but a beauty of the truth expressed by this language' ... The metaphors just quoted, 'a garden closed, a fountain sealed,' reveal *the presence of another vision of the same feminine 'I.'* From the 'beginning,' in fact, femininity determines the mystery about which Genesis speaks in relation to the man's 'knowledge,' that is, to 'union' with the man (Gn 4:1) ... The bride *presents herself to the eyes of the man as the master of her own mystery*. One can say that both metaphors, 'garden closed' and 'fountain sealed,' express the whole *personal dignity of the sex*—of that femininity which belongs to the personal structure of self-possession ... of the personal gift." *Man and Woman He Created Them*, 571–72 (emphases original) [*TOB*, 110 undelivered].

The wine that was in the jars was akin to and related to
This eloquent Wine that gives birth to praise
from those who drank it and beheld the wonder.
You who are just, if at a wedding feast not Your own,
You filled six jars with good wine,
do You at this wedding feast fill, not the jars,
but the ten thousand ears with its sweetness.
Jesus, You were invited to a wedding feast of others,
Here is Your own pure and fair wedding feast:
gladden Your rejuvenated people,
for Your guests too, O Lord, need Your songs:
let Your harp utter.
The soul is Your bride, the body Your bridal chamber,
Your guests are in the senses and the thoughts.
And if a single body us a wedding feast for You,
how great is Your banquet for the whole Church![149]

In addition to the Church and the Sacraments, Song 4:1–5:1 was fertile soil for allegorical and figural interpretations involving the Holy Scriptures themselves. In an extended discussion of the text, Honorius of Autun develops such a line of thought in light of the "tower of David" motif: "Now the neck joins head and body, while a tower protects the inhabitants of a city from their enemies. Hence the Church's neck is those who are instructed and knowledgeable in the Scriptures—who join the Church to Christ by word and example."[150] Honorius believes this signifies the strength of the future Church. For him, a key building block of its holy might is Scripture itself, which is rightly handle by the Church: "Just as David's tower is impregnable, that is, just as the primitive Church is like a tower constructed by Christ the true David, the one who is desirable and strong of hand, against persecutors and heresies, and fortified by the gifts of the Holy Spirit, so too these persons are strengthened by Christ *with the rampart of the Scriptures*, for the purpose of defending the buildings of the faith and repelling the darts of its enemies."[151]

Still dealing with the same verse, Honorius turns to the motif of the "tower built with ramparts." This too is brought into his allegorical

149. St. Ephrem in Brock, *Luminous Eye*, 123–24; emphases added.

150. Honorius of Autun, *Expositio*, 2 (see Song 4:4). The aim of the Scriptures, he explains, "is to protect the ordinary citizens of Jerusalem, untutored as they are, from the citizens of Babylon—heretics, Jews, pagans, and false Christians."

151. Honorius of Autun, *Expositio*, 2; emphasis added.

discussion. He suggests two related possibilities. It signifies either "the impregnable teachings of the Scriptures" or the Apostles, "in that they fought against the faithless on behalf of the Church with the weapons of patience."[152] Next, Honorius lifts out of the biblical text the twin motifs of the "thousand shields" and "weaponry of mighty men." Here, he points to the saints of martyrs of valiant courage who defended the Church with "unnumbered defenses drawn from the Scriptures and from rational argument."[153] Strikingly, all these points from Honorius's allegorical treatment are drawn from a single verse of Song.

Honorius continues to work through other texts in Song in a similar fashion. Occasionally, he offers alternative possibilities for a text, as in the above example. Yet this is not a weakness of Honorius or the spiritual senses. Modern biblical interpretation is too often characterized with putting forth an airtight argument at the expense of the range of potential meanings of a text. Honorius's approach is more, not less, convincing, given his humility before the mystery of the Word.

Other patristic figures look to the tropological sense in their interpretation of our text in Song. Not surprisingly, in a letter to priests, Ambrose makes a connection between the garden/fountain motif and chastity: "A 'garden enclosed' [is virginity] because it is shut in on all sides by the wall of chastity. A 'fountain sealed up' is virginity, for it is the fount and wellspring of modesty that keeps the seal of purity inviolate, in whose source there may shine the image of God, since the pureness of simplicity coincides with the chastity of the body."[154] Similarly, St. Gregory of Nyssa deals with the text tropologically. In his *Homilies of the Song of Songs*, he repeatedly looks to the text to describe the virtuous Christian life: "Because a seal protects the inviolability of whatever it guards, it scares off thieves; everything not stolen remains unharmed for the master. Praise of the bride in the Song would then testify to her excellence in virtue because her mind remains safe from enemies and is guarded for her Lord in purity and tranquility. Purity seals this fountain while the radiance and transparency of the bride's heart is unclouded by no mire of evil thoughts."[155]

Turning to Song 4:3, Gregory develops a tropological interpretation

152. Honorius of Autun, *Expositio*, 2. The distinction between Honorius's two possibilities is not that great, as it is the Apostles who proclaimed the Scriptures with Divine authority.

153. Honorius of Autun, *Expositio*, 2.

154. St. Gregory of Nyssa, *Homilies on the Song of Songs*, 9. See Song 4:12.

155. St. Gregory of Nyssa, *Homilies on the Song of Songs*, 9.

that sees in the pomegranate a symbol of the Word that issues forth from the Bride (i.e., the Church), which toughens the believer: "The pomegranate is difficult for a thief to grasp because of its thorny branches, and its fruit is surrounded and protected by a rind bitter and harsh to the taste. Once the pomegranate ripens in its own good time, and once the rind is peeled off and the inside revealed, it is sweet and appealing to the sight much like honey to the taste; its juice tastes like wine and affords much pleasure to the palate."[156] Here, Gregory has in mind the Christian believer who listens attentively to the words of Scripture, poured out by the Church, and in so doing does not "become soft by indulgence and enjoyment of this present life. Rather, we should choose a life that has become toughened by continence. Thus, virtue's fruit is inaccessible to thieves and is protected by the bitter covering of self-control. Surrounded by a solemn, austere way of life, it wards off as though by spiny thorns those who approach the fruit with evil intent."[157]

Working through the same text, Theodoret of Cyr develops his own tropological approach. In it, the pomegranate does not signify the Church's Scripture. Rather, it signifies *her members* who live according to the virtue of charity, through their distinct vocational callings. As he writes, "'Pomegranate' is to be taken figuratively as love, since countless seeds are contained together within the one skin, pressed together without squeezing or ruining one another, remaining fresh unless one of the seeds in the middle goes bad."[158]

Theodoret lists the various stations of life in which believers found: "We see many ranks also among the saved, one of virgins, one of ascetics, one of those drawing the yoke of marriage, and of the affluent, one of those living a life of poverty, one of slaves in love with godliness, one of masters exercising lordship lawfully. The pomegranate, too, then, has walled off compartments, as it were, separating its seeds into certain divisions. This is the reason he compares the presents of the bride to 'an orchard of pomegranates.'"[159] In other words, Theodoret's tropological approach deduces a moral witness of Christian vocations. For him, the seeds signify Christian believers in all their diversity, "an orchard of pomegranates" emanating out of the fruit of the one holy Church.

156. St. Gregory of Nyssa, *Homilies on the Song of Songs*, 9.
157. St. Gregory of Nyssa, *Homilies on the Song of Songs*, 9.
158. Theodoret of Cyr, *Commentary on the Song of Songs*, 4.
159. Theodoret of Cyr, *Commentary on the Song of Songs*, 4.

Looking ahead to the Church of the High Middle Ages, additional features of Song 4:1–5:1 are used by Rupert of Deutz and members of the Victorine school. Like their predecessors, they do so in a largely tropological fashion. Rupert explains: "What then are your perfumes, O my sister, my Bride? *Your acts of mercy,* which you have performed on my behalf. My friends hear and will hear of a certain woman who poured oil over the head and the feet of your Beloved as he was reclining at table, and they say that "the house was full of the scent of the perfume," and they understand that woman to represent our Church, which pours her perfumes over my feet *and dispenses their sweet smells as often as she performs acts of mercy for the benefit of our poor.*"[160]

Rupert's discussion makes rich use of Song as well as the Gospel According to St. John, as he discusses the corporeal works of mercy performed within the Church.[161] By linking them to the perfumes being lavishly and generously poured out, he has made an appeal to beauty, as well as truth, in the goodness of the corporeal works of mercy; not only are they right acts, they are fragrant, aromatic acts performed on behalf of Christ. One also thinks of the expensive perfume poured out over the feet of Jesus in the Gospels.[162] Moreover, these scenes are intimately connected with the Passion of Jesus, for example, in the Johannine account: Jesus said, "Let her alone, let her keep it for the day of my burial. The poor you always have with you, but you do not always have me" (Jn 12:7–8).

For his part, Hugh of St. Victor hears Christ in the voice of the Bridegroom—urging believer toward moral uprightness: "You are all fair, my love; there is no flaw in you."[163] Hugh contrasts two type of souls, one turned toward Christ and the other turned away: "Every soul is either turned away from God or turned toward God. Of those souls that are turned away, however, one is far removed, while another is as

160. Rupert of Deutz, Libri Commentariorum, 3; emphasis added. "For these are the precious perfumes, the truly sweet smells—to feed any one of my enemies who is hungry, to give drink to one who is thirsty, to take in the stranger or the traveler, to clothe the naked, to visit the sick, and to go to see those who are in prison (Mt 25:35–36). But the fragrance of your perfumes is above all these sweet smells—that is to say, the sweetness of your acts of mercy; for you have manifested your unmeasured generosity not merely in my physical members but in my very self."

161. See Song 4:10, 4:14; Jn 12:3.

162. See Jn 12:1–8; also Mk 14:3–9; Mt 26:6–13; Lk 7:36–50.

163. Song 4:7.

far removed as possible. On the other hand, of the souls that are turned toward God, one is close, while another is as close as possible."[164]

With the text as his guide, Hugh continues his tropological interpretation: "That person is altogether fair in whom no element of beauty is lacking. That person is altogether fair *in whom there is no element of moral unsightliness.* I am altogether fair because everything beautiful is within me. You are altogether fair because there is nothing unsightly within you. There is no spot upon you."[165] Hugh's close reading of the text turns to Song 4:8a, "Come with me from Lebanon, my bride; come with me from Lebanon." In the Vulgate, it reads: *Veni de Libano, sponsa, veni de Libano, ingredere.*[166] Here, Hugh notices the repetition of *veni* ("come").

As his comments involve both the tropological and the anagogical, a pattern of ascent is evident. He writes, "But why does he say come twice?"[167] In his response, he points out the Lover—that is, the Lord—is *above us*, calling us up to himself. "So that the person who is outside himself may first of all return to himself, and so the person who is in himself may rise up beyond himself. First of all, *he is within us*, and he warns transgressors to return to the heart; *but then he is above us*, that he may invite the justified to come to himself. Come, he says, come! 'Come out inwardly to yourself! Come within, farther within, wholly within, above yourself to me!'"[168]

One more example of tropology is seen in Hugh's student Richard of St. Victor as he looks to Song 4:5: *Duo ubera tua sicut duo hinnuli, capreae gemelli, qui pascuntur in liliis.*[169] Richard sees in the two breasts of the Bride "a twofold compassion, one corporeal and the other spiritual. The soul possesses these when she shares the suffering of those who struggle because of bodily need or some adversity, or when she devotes prayer or consolation to those who find themselves in some sin or temptation."[170] Integrating the book's vivid bodily imagery into his moral

164. Hugh of St. Victor, *De Amore Sponsi ad Sponsam*.

165. Hugh of St. Victor, *De Amore Sponsi ad Sponsam*; emphasis added.

166. Song 4:8a; emphasis added: "Come with me from Lebanon, my bride; come with me from Lebanon."

167. Hugh of St. Victor, *De Amore Sponsi ad Sponsam*.

168. Hugh of St. Victor, *De Amore Sponsi ad Sponsam*.

169. Song 4:5: "Your two breasts are like two fawns, twins of a gazelle, that feed among the lilies."

170. Richard of St. Victor, *In Cantica Canticorum Explicatio*.

reading, Richard writes: "She possesses these breasts when she knows how to rejoice with those who rejoice and weep with those who weep, to be weak with those who are weak, to burn with those who have been made to stumble. Beautiful are the breasts of that soul who shares the suffering of all out of goodwill and is unable, without sorrow of heart, to pass by the sorrows of anyone."[171]

Turning to the last of the three senses, the nuptial imagery in Song lent itself to anagogical interpretation. We return to Gregory of Nyssa and his *Homilies on Song of Songs* for three examples. In the first, Gregory draws upon Song's repeated references to the Beloved as *soror mea, sponsa*: "You have ravished my heart, *my sister, my bride*."[172] He writes, "The voice of the Word is always a voice of power. Hence just as in the first creation the light shone forth even as the command was given, and the firmament in its turn came into being simultaneously with the word of command, and all the rest of the creation was in the same way manifested simultaneously with the creative Word—so too now, *when the Word commands the soul in her new-found goodness to come to him, she is instantly empowered by the command and comes to be what the Bridegroom willed*."[173]

Notice that, for Gregory, it is the Word that "commands" the soul of the Beloved, compelling the Beloved, newly baptized ("new found goodness") to respond, to come to him. Thus the grace of Baptism works *anagogically*, leading her to live out, to become "what the Bridegroom willed." He continues, "She is changed into something more divine, and on account of her happy alteration she is changed from the glory she has already attained to a higher glory, with the result that she becomes a source of wonder to the chorus of angels about the Bridegroom."[174] Here again, baptismal theology lies under his interpretation. "She," the new believer, becomes something more divine. The initial "spark of divinity" is infused into the believer's soul at the baptismal regeneration. The believer is now brought "to a higher glory" by responding to the

171. Richard of St. Victor, *In Cantica Canticorum Explicatio.*

172. See Song 4:9, 4:10, 4:12, 5:1.

173. St. Gregory of Nyssa, *Homilies on the Song of Songs*, 8; emphasis added. In what follows, Gregory has the angels singing an eschatological response to the Bride: "That is why they say to her, 'You have given us heart, O Bride our sister; and you are honored with each of these titles in its fullest sense. Our sister you are in virtue of our kinship in impassibility, and Bride you are in virtue of being joined to the Word.'"

174. St. Gregory of Nyssa, *Homilies on the Song of Songs*, 8.

Voice of the Bridegroom. All of this works through Gregory's anagogical reception of the text.

In the final two examples, a clear pattern of ascent is detected in Gregory's appropriation of Song, beyond allegory, beyond tropology, to the anagogical destination. First, homing in on the fragrances of *turiferis* and *myrrha* ("frankincense and myrrh"), Gregory writes, "*When the Word raises his bride to such a point through her ascents,* he leads her even further, saying that her garments have the scent of frankincense. Scripture testifies that Christ is clothed with this frankincense. *The end of a virtuous life is participation in God, for frankincense manifests the divinity.* The soul is not always led by the Word *to what is higher* by means of honey and milk, but after having been compared with the scent of frankincense, the garden becomes an image of paradise."[175] Here, Gregory sees in the frankincense a life surrendered to Christ. By living the virtues, the soul is transfigured into the image of the risen Christ. Like a fragrant offering in the Temple, the soul *rises up to God,* being raised to perfection.

Next, Gregory turns from those individual believers whose "end of a virtuous life is participation in God" to the Church as a whole. Up to this point, "the Word" has been pronouncing the praise of the Church's individual members. Now, in what follows, Gregory contrives an encomium on the whole body of Christ, since "through death he destroyed him who has the power of death."[176] He writes, "she was restored again to the glory proper to the Godhead, which he possessed from the beginning, before the cosmos existed ... Therefore the One who says, 'You are beautiful through and through, my close one,'[177] there is no flaw within you, and who introduces the mystery of his suffering under the figure of myrrh and then makes mention of frankincense—this One is instructing us that the person who shares myrrh with him will also fully share in his frankincense."[178] Where the frankincense signifies the fragrant offering of a holy life, for Gregory, the myrrh signifies *the suffering Church:* "The one who suffers with him will be fully glorified with him; and the one who has once for all entered into the divine glory becomes all beautiful, having been separated from the inimical flaw."[179]

175. St. Gregory of Nyssa, *Homilies on the Song of Songs*, 9; emphasis added.
176. See Heb 2:14.
177. See Song 4:7.
178. St. Gregory of Nyssa, *Homilies on the Song of Songs*, 7.
179. St. Gregory of Nyssa, *Homilies on the Song of Songs*, 7.

We turn now from the array of figures mentioned above to one final and significant commentator. Specifically, we look to one of the great spiritual masters of Song, St. Bernard of Clairvaux. It is fair to say that Bernard's interpretation of Song is ingenious. It is sort of the platonic example of the pattern of ascent discussed earlier in the book. In Bernard's commentary, allegory, tropology and anagogy converge in one seamless, poetic outpouring of biblical wisdom. When Song is read with Bernard, one encounters the person of Christ in the Gospels; Christ, the Bridegroom of the soul; and Christ, the heavenly Groom awaiting his Bride in glory.

This Bernardian synthesis is evident from his opening remarks about Song: "You, my brethren, require instruction different from that which would suit people living in the world, and if not in matter, in manner, at least. For a teacher who would follow the example of Saint Paul, should give *them* 'milk to drink, not meat.' But more solid food must be set before spiritual persons, as the same Apostle teaches us by his practice. 'We speak,' he says, 'not in the learned words of human wisdom, but in the doctrine of the Spirit, comparing spiritual things with spiritual.'"[180] Bernard then turns this Pauline exhortation toward his monastic brothers: "'We speak wisdom among the perfect'—such, my brethren, as I believe you to be, unless, indeed, it is to no purpose that you have been so long engaged in the study of spiritual things, in mortifying your senses, and in meditating day and night on the law of God."[181]

Integrating St. Paul and Song as few can, Bernard prepares them in decidedly allegorical terms: "So now open your mouths to receive not milk, but bread. It is the bread of Solomon and is exceedingly good and palatable. For the Book entitled the Canticle of Canticles is the bread I speak of, which may now, if you please, be brought forth to be broken."[182] Along similar lines, Bernard adds, "I think, my brethren, you already recognize in your own experience those canticles, which in the Psalter are not called the Canticle of Canticles, but the 'Canticles of the Steps.' *For at every advance you make towards perfection, according to the 'ascents' which each has 'disposed in his heart,'* a particular canticle has to

180. St. Bernard of Clairvaux, *St. Bernard's Sermons on the Canticle of Canticles*, 1. See 1 Cor 3:1–2: "But I, brethren, could not address you as spiritual men, but as men of the flesh, as babes in Christ. I fed you with milk, not solid food; for you were not ready for it."

181. See 1 Cor 2:6.

182. St. Bernard of Clairvaux, *St. Bernard's Sermons on the Canticle of Canticles*, 1.

be sung to the praise and glory of Him Who advances you."[183] Notice that both the idea and the language of "ascent" are already invoked at the beginning of the commentary.

With these initial remarks, we turn to Bernard's discussion of our encounter scene. Bernard takes up the motif of the *hortorum* ("garden"), which we have seen is prevalent in Song 4:1–5:1. He explains:

> This applies in varying senses to Our Lord Jesus Christ. He is the Flower of the garden, inasmuch as He is a virgin Blossom produced from a virgin stem. He is the Flower of the field because He is a martyr, the Crown of martyrs, and the Model of martyrs. For He was led forth from the city... He was lifted up on the cross, in the sight of all, for the mockery of all. He is finally the Flower of the Chamber, being the Example and Pattern of all well-doing... But if the Lord Jesus is thus each of the three flowers, what motive can He have for choosing to call Himself the Flower of the field rather than the flower of the garden or the flower of the chamber?[184]

The reason, Bernard argues, is that "He desires to animate His Spouse to patient endurance, as knowing that she would have to suffer persecution, since she wished 'to live godly in Christ.' Therefore, He presents Himself to her *under the type of that in which He particularly wants her to imitate Him*."[185] In other words, Christ appears in Song in a hidden and mysterious way. He is present *allegorically*, in the motif of the Flower, so that, as the Bridegroom, he may draw the Bride into this same image, being conformed to him through suffering and death. *Tropologically*, the flowers (plural) begin to imitate the One True Flower through lives of charity, even as they are poured out in death as he was. In the process of their imitation, however, these flowers are none other than the Bride herself and are so being perfected for the consumma-

183. St. Bernard of Clairvaux, *St. Bernard's Sermons on the Commentary on the Canticle of Canticles*, Homily 1: "It is for the experienced, therefore, to recognize it, and for others to burn with the desire, not so much of knowing, as of feeling it; since this canticle is not a noise made by the mouth but a jubilee of the heart, not a sound of the lips but a tumult of internal joys, not a symphony of voices but a harmony of wills. It is not heard outside, for it sounds not externally. The singer alone can hear it, and He to Whom it is sung, namely, the Bridegroom and the Bride. *For it is a nuptial song, celebrating the chaste and joyous embraces of loving hearts, the concord of minds, and the union resulting from reciprocal affection*" (emphasis added).

184. St. Bernard of Clairvaux, *St. Bernard's Sermons on the Canticle of Canticles*, Homily 48.

185. St. Bernard of Clairvaux, *St. Bernard's Sermons on the Canticle of Canticles*, Homily 48; emphasis added.

tion of Divine love between the Bridegroom and his Bride in an anagogical way.

Final Remarks on Christ the Bridegroom in Song of Songs

In his examination of Song 4:1–5:1, Arminjon calls attention to the Hebrew word for "bride," *kallah*, pointing out that it translates more precisely as "promised bride."[186] Why is this significant? As he explains, there is a twofold reason: "first, even though she is so wonderfully loved and admired, *the Bride has not yet reached the stage that will be hers when she attains perfect union.* Thus, however dazzling it is, her face is *still veiled as that of a promised bride.*"[187]

To read Song according to all Four Senses—and particularly according to the spiritual senses—one sees both the "promised bride" on the way to her Bridegroom, to Christ, and the eschatological "perfected bride," as Arminjon explains. He writes, "the Lord is revealing the ever absolutely new and incredible nature of his love, independently of the past, for her *who never ceases to be betrothed while being bride,* as we will hear at the end of the Scriptures in the Revelation of John: 'Come here and I will show you *the bride of the Lamb that has been married.*' The love of Yahweh for his bride is always a *betrothal love*, young, ardent, and pure as he is."[188]

Perhaps it is this tension, of the already-but-not-yet, that makes Song one of the most compelling and mysterious books of the canon. Throughout the book, there is a continual longing, an unmet desire. It is a yearning that both Lover and Beloved experience in half measures and even in their lamentations and longing. This desire is "fulfilled only at the end of the poem, but the desire itself is already a kind of fulfillment. *The very longing for Heaven is Heaven.*"[189] Even today, though the text

186. Arminjon, *Cantata of Love*, 219; see Song 4:1, 4:3.

187. Arminjon, *Cantata of Love*, 219; emphases added.

188. Arminjon, *Cantata of Love*, 219–20; emphases added.

189. Kreeft, "Song of Songs: Life as Love," in *Three Philosophies of Life*, 112, emphasis added. See Song 8:5. Kreeft adds: "Dmitri Karamazov, in Dostoyevsky's novel, tells God that if he should put him in Hell, he would sing to God the hymn of joy even from Hell, 'the hymn from the underground.' That would transform Hell (or the Siberian salt mines) into Heaven. *The song of love makes Heaven. Heaven does not make God's love lovely; God's love makes Heaven heavenly*" (emphasis added).

of Song has been overly dissected from a strictly historical point of view, there are still voices that, in the manner of Bernard, Origen, Augustine, and Gregory, beckon the reader to look deeper within the text. Stepping into the poetic Garden in such a way, one hears the Lover summoning his fragrant Beloved, as is called to a "perfecting of love" that involves the whole self.

Fleming Rutledge writes:

> Since God's love *is perfect and will be perfected in the saints,* we can affirm the message of the Song of Songs: Human love that is *both* passionate *and* faithful is an image of the covenant God made with us. It is a covenant distinguished by its unconditional nature—for better, for worse; for richer, for poorer; in sickness and in health—and then, in the humanly unimaginable word that comes to us from beyond death, God is faithful to us, beyond our deserving, even unto the Resurrection to eternal life, for "my Love, the Crucified, is raised to life this morrow." He welcomes you to this banqueting table; his banner over you is love.[190]

Quarto Meditation

Abraham Heschel, who had a way with words about the Bible, wrote, "There are no proofs for demonstrating the beauty of music to a man who is both deaf and insensitive."[191] How true this is. In our previous meditation, we looked at Psalm 31. Like Psalms, the Song of Songs is among the most lyrical of texts in Scripture. To encounter the face of the Lord, we have dealt with a number of biblical texts—narrative, prophecy, poetry, and so on. All of them are beautiful in their own way, yet none surpass Song of Songs, with its resplendent canticles exchanged between the Bridegroom and his Beloved.

St. Pope John Paul II took us to the Apostle's Great Analogy and with it back "to the beginning," to the original Man and Woman of Genesis. With its nuptial imagery, Song pulls us forward to the New Testament and the "Wedding of the Lamb" in the Book of Revelation: "Then I heard what seemed to be the voice of a great multitude, like the sound of many waters and like the sound of mighty thunderpeals, crying, 'Hallelujah! For the Lord our God the Almighty reigns. Let us rejoice and exult and give him the glory, for the marriage of the Lamb has come, and his Bride has made herself ready; it was granted her to

190. Rutledge, *And God Spoke to Abraham*, 218; emphasis added.

191. Heschel, *God in Search of Man*, 233.

be clothed with fine linen, bright and pure'— for the fine linen is the righteous deeds of the saints."[192]

Let us contemplate this New Testament canticle, which recalls that the Song of Songs yet is remarkably different. Like the cantos in Song, this text from St. John's *Apocalypse* is arranged as a wedding song filled with nuptial imagery. It speaks of the "wedding of the Lamb" and of the "bride" who has readied herself for the solemn event. Even the *lampron* ("bright") and *katharon* ("pure") linens of the bride recall similar motifs in Song. Yet St. John breaks into the figural language, interrupting it with an account of what it signifies: "for the fine linen is the righteous deeds of the saints."[193] It is as if the urgency of first-century persecution—the setting of the Book of Revelation—necessitates that the metaphor momentarily leave. In its place is the stark reality of an immense crisis: many with the Church face violent pressure and terrible oppression "from without" (Roman imperialism) and "from within" (Jewish synagogal opposition). Many were killed; others committed apostasy or were on the verge.

On this dark and perilous occasion, *John sings.* His song is not foolhardy, nor are his glasses rose colored. His song is one of defiance and of countercultural resolve. His song is the Book of Revelation, and strange as it seems to modern ears, it was perfectly attuned for the ancient Jewish and early Christian ears of those who faced such ugliness and pain. One might think that only a madman sings when the Church is on fire. And this is partly right. John is mad—mad with *agape*. He is utterly mad in his joyful testimony of the "*lamb, standing as though slain*"—a cryptic yet sensible image of the crucified and risen Jesus.[194]

Like St. Paul, John's message is *Christos Kyrios*—Jesus is Lord. Caesar (whether Nero or Domitian or whoever) is not. Revelation would have sounded like nonsense to the Church's enemies and even to some within who broke ranks and fled. Yet to the faithful ones who pressed on, *it was their song, the Church's song*: "Let us rejoice and exult and give him the glory, for the marriage of the Lamb has come, and his Bride has made herself ready."[195] And for those who wish to follow Christ today, the mystical vision of Revelation must become their song anew. Until

192. Rv 19:6–8.
193. Rv 19:8.
194. Rv 5:6; emphasis added.
195. Rv 19:7.

Christ's Second Coming, the Church will have its share of "beasts from the sea," and yes, many will have their "white robes" washed in blood red. Yet, in the end, the victory belongs to the Bridegroom, who awaits his glorious Bride.

"Amen. Come Lord Jesus."[196]

196. Rv 22:20.

CHAPTER 8

Contemplating the Face of the Merciful Christ with Job (Job 38–41)

> Pain and suffering are always inevitable for a large intelligence and a deep heart. The really great men must, I think, have great sadness on earth.
>
> —Fyodor Dostoyevsky, *Crime and Punishment*

This chapter deals with a rather extensive text: chapters 38 through 42 of the Book of Job. For reasons that will become more clear, the encounter scene is really a larger poetic speech of Yahweh, identified as the voice that addresses the man Job *min hă seʿārāh*, "from the Whirlwind."[1]

Sensus Litteralis

Of all the books within the Hebrew Bible, there are few that contain more puzzles than the Book of Job.[2] Robert Alter explains why, and it has a lot do with its poetic majesty: "The Book of Job is in several ways the most mysterious book of the Hebrew Bible. Formally, as a sustained debated in poetry, it resembles no other text in the canon ... *Its astounding poetry* eclipses all other biblical poetry working in the same formal system but in a style that is often distinct both lexically and imagistically

1. Job 38:1.

2. This is not to say Job is the only puzzling book in the canon; Ecclesiastes comes immediately to mind, especially for its content, which is frequently opaque.

from its biblical counterparts."[3] In addition to the poetical reason, Alter adds the theological: "As a radical challenge to the doctrine of reward for the righteous and punishment for the wicked, [Job] dissents from a consensus view of biblical writers—a dissent compounded by its equally radical rejection of the anthropocentric conception of creation that is expressed from Genesis onward."[4]

Most of Alter's assessment as to what makes Job so unlike all other books in the Hebrew Bible is accurate. As to the poetical, we find nothing to quibble about. And while others investigate the book through the lens of prose—which can be accomplished—the book becomes most sensible when one sticks closely to its many poetic clues.[5] Later, I highlight the most important ones that Alter calls attention to in his translation and commentary. As to the theological, Alter is correct—mostly. The book is certainly a "radical challenge to the doctrine of reward for the righteous and punishment for the wicked." As St. Thomas put it long before him, the riddle put forth in the Book of Job is the idea that "there is no sure order apparent in in human events. For good things do not always befall the good, nor evil things the wicked."[6] As Thomas identifies, this problem, known as "theodicy," is a challenge to our intelligence and human reason: "This idea causes a great deal of harm to mankind. For if divine providence is denied, *no reverence or true fear of God will remain among men.* Each man can weigh well how great the propensity for vice and the lack of desire for virtue which follows from this idea. For nothing so much calls men back from evil things and induces them to good as much as the fear and love of God."[7] And so, for Thomas, the core riddle of the book involves the providence of a

3. Alter, *Wisdom Books*, 3; emphasis added.

4. Alter, *Wisdom Books*, 3.

5. "We may distinguish between the *framework* of the book and its *core* or *center*, using the image of a painting surrounded by a frame. The book itself suggests this view of its shape through its use of *prose* and *poetry*. The *framework* of the book is *prose*, the *core* is *poetry*; and since the framework is naive (or so it seems) and the core is sophisticated, the distinction between the relatively cheap and unimportant frame of a painting and the painting itself sounds a convincing analogy. We can also distinguish framework from core by noticing that the *framework* of Job is *narrative,* and the *core* is *didactic poetry*. The book as a whole is thus both a *narrative* and an *argument*, or, perhaps more precise, an *argument* set within the context of a *narrative*." Clines, *Job 1–20*, xxxv; emphases added. See also Sarna, "Epic Substratum in the Prose of Job"; Brenner, "Job the Pious?"

6. St. Thomas Aquinas, "Prologue," in *Commentary on the Book of Job*, 8.

7. St. Thomas Aquinas, "Prologue," in *Commentary on the Book of Job*, 8; emphasis added.

good and gracious God—and how the problem of "bad things happening to good people" seems to undo, or at least threaten, his providence.

In the end, the Book of Job does not shirk from these tensions. On the contrary, its author embraces this apparent contradiction. And in pushing through it, he exposes the quid pro quo fault line of Job's three "friends." Over the course of the book, their knowledge of the divine is exposed as an insufficient theological construct. Over and against these "worthless physicians,"[8] these "miserable comforters,"[9] Yahweh's providence and goodness is wholly vindicated. As is Job's innocence. Near the start of the book, it appears as if "the satan" is the central antagonist. His taunts occupy the space of chapter 2, in the heavenly court scene.[10] As it turns out, however, this "accuser" disappears from the book, dropping out of sight altogether. By the end of Job, it is not "the satan" that is triumphed over but something much more earthly than this enigmatic, cosmic accuser. Indeed, God bests him handily by the end of the book.

Why is it this "accuser" is not mentioned beyond the prologue? Because he is a literary and theological foil. Once the heavenly dialogue is over, he's not heard from. But we hear *a good deal* from Job's friends. And, in a sense, it is these friends who become the book's real adversaries. At least we can say that they represent the conventional worldview of ancient Jewish culture.

Something needs to be stressed here, in talking about Job's friends and their role in the book. Through them, it is not the older wisdom of the patriarchs nor the Pentateuch that is being critiqued—assuming the Pentateuch was written before Job (another unanswered question). No, it is the street-level view of God that is being critiqued. Yet, through the cycles of dialogical debates between Job and the three friends, their fault lines appear, first as cracks and then eventually as huge chasms. The author is brilliantly guiding the reader *away from their flawed idea of God, of divine retribution*—and toward the perfect justice of the sovereign God.

Again, in the end, it is not "the satan" that is defeated (though he is). It turns out that he was merely the universal foil that sets up the gauntlet

8. Job 13:4.
9. Job 16:2.
10. See Job 2:1–6.

that Job faces, and it is the theological view of Job's friends that is condemned. This subtle shift—from the foil of *satan* to the true opponents, Job's friends—is a brilliant tactic of the author. The reader is free to receive them as helpful at the start of the book, but by the end the reader *must part company with them.* They have not "spoken well of God."[11] And speaking properly about God is at the heart of this book.

Throughout its complex narrative, the Book of Job masterfully deals with one of the greatest of human questions—theodicy. And it does so with theocentric grandeur. The book is much more about God and the eternal wisdom of his divine providence than it is about Job's sufferings. Paradoxically, since it is about God and not man, Job's true suffering is ultimately worked out in a way that is mysterious yet deeply satisfying.

Here, St. Thomas's exposition of Scripture is far more satisfying than Alter's. In *The Wisdom Books*, Alter asserts that the previously composed books of the Hebrew canon held to an "anthropocentric conception of creation . . . expressed from Genesis onward." It would require too much ink to engage Alter's assertion with the philosophical and theological rigor it should be met with here. But a few remarks are necessary.

First, Alter's anthropocentric view of Genesis is partially correct. True, given that Genesis focuses on the centrality of Man in the creation narrative of chapter 2, it is anthropocentric. Yet the account is preceded by chapter 1, which is overwhelmingly theocentric, even with the inclusion of verses 26–31. Taken together, Genesis chapters 1–2 present creation in both theocentric *and* anthropocentric emphases. And this is an important clarification. Whether Alter's description is deliberate—that is, representative of his particular interpretation of the text—or simply the result of imprecise language, we do not assent to it.

Despite numerous strengths of Alter's commentary on *The Five Books of* Moses, as well as the contributions of his larger translation project, it would be negligent to ignore the shortcomings of this remark. Genesis—with its spectacular portrayal of Yahweh Elohim, the creating, calling, covenanting, and delivering God of Abraham, Isaac, and Jacob—should not be thought of as anthropocentric but as theocentric. Likewise, the main character of Exodus is not the Lawgiver Moses. Rather, it is the God who liberates them from the clutches of Pharaoh. The same should equally be said for the rest of the Law and the Proph-

11. See Job 42:8.

ets, as well as the Psalter, the oldest stands of which may predate the composition of Job.[12]

Second, the Book of Job is not entirely alone in presenting its unassailable questions of theodicy, such as it does. There are elements of theodicy in a number of books in the Hebrew Bible. One thinks of Ecclesiastes, to which Job is often compared. Or perhaps one of St. Augustine's favorite psalms, which works in a somewhat similar (yet far less sustained way) as Job. In Psalm 73, the psalmist yearns to understand why the unrighteous avoid God's justice. He begins: "Surely God is good to Israel, To those who are pure in heart! But as for me, my feet came close to stumbling, My steps had almost slipped. For I was envious of the arrogant, *As* I saw the prosperity of the wicked."[13]

Although a much more compact text compared with the expansive Job, the experience of the two subjects shares certain parallels:

> Let the day perish wherein I was born, and the night
> which said, "A man-child is conceived." (Job 3:3)
>
> For I have been stricken all day long
> and chastened every morning. (Ps 73:14)

Yet this psalm develops the theme of theodicy differently than the epic book in which our encounter scene is located. Again, Job is engaged by his three "friends" in a series of dialogues. These friends' protestations are designed to show the Job the error of his apparently wicked ways. Their prescription? Fall upon your face, admit your sins, and beg God's forgiveness. In contrast to this public contest, the psalmist struggles through pain internally. He does not speak about it to anyone, though he is tempted.[14] Even though their situations are different, both the psalmist and Job do suffer immensely. And in their own way, each does encounter God, and each finds peace in the nearness and justice of God.[15] Again, in different ways.

None of this is to dispute Alter's point about the distinctive theol-

12. Although I offer a few remarks about the possible dating of Job below, this topic is yet another elusive puzzle pertaining to the book, and one not easily resolved. Nevertheless, I suggest that the Book of Job was likely composed sometime in the postexilic period, perhaps in the fifth or fourth century BC.

13. Ps 73:1–3. I have presented the NAB-RE rather than the RSV in this instance, as the latter translates *yisrāʾēl* as "the righteous" in v. 1; more accurately, the former has "Israel."

14. See Ps 73:15–16.

15. See Ps 73:17–28, esp. vv. 17–18, 28.

ogy in Job, which uniquely and perhaps "radically" challenges the doctrine of reward for the righteous and punishment for the wicked. I agree with this point but do not concur that the remainder of the Hebrew canon is essentially anthropocentric. Perhaps a better way to unlock at least one of Job's manifold mysteries is through Thomas's *Commentary on Job*. This is because he does not pit anthropocentricism over and against theocentrism as Alter's commentary seems to do.

To begin, many nonspecialists may be somewhat surprised to discover that Thomas composed a trove of full-length works on the Scriptures. "Even within Thomistic circles they have not received the kind of attention accorded the 'major' works, the *Summa Theologiae* and *Summa Contra Gentiles.*"[16] According to reliable reconstructions, Thomas's *Literal Exposition on Job* was composed between 1261 and 1265, during his time in Orvieto.[17] By way of introduction, not all of his commentaries are of a piece in terms of how they were developed: "All his commentaries have come down to us either as notes taken by a student—often Thomas' colleague (*socius*), Reginald of Piperno—as Thomas lectured, or else directly from Thomas. The lecture notes (*reportatio*) were sometimes corrected and expanded by Thomas, sometimes not. If a commentary is a *reportatio*, its Latin title is usually *Lectura*, as the commentary on Matthew, *Lectura super Matthaeum.* On the other hand, if the commentary was written or dictated by Thomas himself, it is called an *Expositio.*"[18]

So, it appears that the *Literal Exposition on Job* was written (or dictated) by Thomas, not compiled by one of his students. Before discussing his commentary, however, it is crucial to grasp how Thomas appropriated literal sense and interpreted Job. Four remarks are called for.

16. Nicholas M. Healy, "Introduction," in Weinandy et al., *Aquinas on Scripture*, 1. There is a misperception concerning Thomas as "the prime example of that form of traditional Catholic theological inquiry which emphasizes philosophical reasoning, in contradistinction to the Scripture-based tradition of the Reformers and their heirs" (1). On top of this general lack of appreciation of Thomas as biblical commentator, the virtual nonexistence of English translations of his works more or less assured that Thomas's treatment of Job, Isaiah, Matthew, John, the Pauline corpus, and Hebrews remained unread. Fortunately, as Healy explained, "the perception shows signs of change, as does the underlying lack of interest in or awareness of Thomas' exegesis that helped produced it" (1). Emmaus Academic Press is currently completing a translation project that began in the past ten years. These are encouraging signs. It is hoped that future generations will have easier access to the works than past students of Scripture.

17. John Yocum, "Aquinas' Literal Exposition on Job," in Weinandy et al., *Aquinas on Scripture*, 22. See also Torrell, *St. Thomas Aquinas*, 1:117–41.

18. Healey, "Introduction," in Weinandy et al., *Aquinas on Scripture*, 11.

First, for Thomas, "faith" is the fundamental criteria for the proper understanding of sacred Scripture. Faith is a gift from the Holy Spirit to the believer, poured out in the Church's preaching of the Scriptures. Indeed, faith "is distinguished from all other things pertaining to the intellect.[19] As Healy explains, for Thomas, "Christianity is a way of life founded upon the assent of believers *to what they have heard of God's revelation* ... Revelation is the necessary basis for Christianity because Christians are oriented to a goal that is *beyond our natural capacities* not only to attain, but even to know anything about."[20]

Second, the medieval understanding of the literal sense was, comparatively speaking, more pliable and accommodating than the understanding of it today. For instance, there is nothing to suggest that by literal Thomas meant *nontheological* or *natural.* It was not reducible to the merely historical, as is often the case with modern, empirical approaches. Moreover, the literal sense did not exclude the use of metaphor or other forms of literary symbolism. So, when the Scriptures speak of God anthropomorphically—for example, his "right hand"—this was within the purview of the literal. *The literal sense is that which the words of Scripture conveyed, according to the author.* Not so fast. There is a wrinkle that needs to be recognized, in following Thomas as he unpacks the literal meaning of a biblical text: Thomas firmly believed that everything in salvation history—from Genesis onward—revealed *Jesus Christ.*"[21] And so the literal meaning of text *begins* with the meaning of the biblical words and phrases and *ends* in a revelation of Jesus Christ.

Third, Thomas explains further what is contained by the literal sense in the first chapter. Commenting on Job 1:6, he writes: "The literal sense is that which is intended by the words, *whether they are used properly or figuratively.*" Or figuratively, he stresses. "Therefore," as Yocum observes,

19. *ST* II, q. 4, a. 1, resp.

20. Healy, "Introduction," in Weinandy et al., *Aquinas on Scripture*, 13; emphases added.

21. Healy, "Introduction," in Weinandy et al., *Aquinas on Scripture*, 16; emphasis added. "Thomas' conception of the primacy of the literal sense does not require him to say that Scripture is 'literally' true in any modern sense of the word, or of its description of things that would nowadays fall under the purview of the hard sciences. Thomas seems to have thought that most of it was accurate in that way. But like earlier exegetes, he was willing to reinterpret a passage when it seemed to assert something he knew could not be true on logical, historical, or scientific grounds. His basic principle was: '*nothing false can ever underlie the literal sense of Scripture.*' So, when Scripture appears to be claiming something clearly untrue, its divine author *must intend a meaning other than the apparent, one that can be true. The interpreter's responsibility is to find that meaning*" (17; emphases added).

"the literal sense includes metaphors and other poetic devices. This is important for Thomas' interpretation of Job, because a good deal of his effort is directed at unpacking *the poetic figures* Job uses to describe his condition or to make his argumentative points."[22]

Fourth, and more broadly, Thomas made sense of Job as a unified work and avoided "the 'atomization' of the text that Robert Alter deplores in historical-critical exegesis … Thomas' interpretation struggles with the text as it is, and employs a subtle anthropology and a profound metaphysics of God as author, dispenser and end of all things."[23] Yocum rightly describes Thomas's approach to Job as *traditional but unconventional*: traditional because he engages the text in the light of Tradition and unconventional in that he did not conform to earlier spiritual readings of the book, such as Gregory the Great and his tropological *Moralia in Iob.*[24]

For instance, Thomas does not describe Job as a type of Christ as Gregory does. Rather, he interprets Job in light of other revealed truths in the whole canon of Scripture. This is not the same—not at all—as Gregory's tropological reading of Job. This canonical hermeneutic allowed Thomas to see hints of the resurrection of the body in Job, even though it was elucidated far more elaborately and explicitly in Paul's letter to the Corinthians.[25]

Yocum clarifies that "This could suggest an arbitrary approach to the text that Thomas claimed he will interpret according to the letter; *but this impression would be imbalanced.*"[26] Rather, "Thomas finds indications of what further doctrines–such as the resurrection of the body–are germane to the book of Job itself, within the book of Job itself."[27] Moving closer to the book itself, Thomas views the literal sense of Job as a kind of "theological corrective" to the heart of man. Because of this, Job occupies a place of preeminence in the third part of the Old Testament,

22. Yocum, "Aquinas' Literal Exposition on Job," in Weinandy et al., *Aquinas on Scripture*, 26.

23. Yocum, "Aquinas' Literal Exposition on Job," in Weinandy et al., *Aquinas on Scripture*, 41. See Alter, *Art of Biblical Narrative*.

24. See Yocum, "Aquinas' Literal Exposition on Job," in Weinandy et al., *Aquinas on Scripture*, 40–41.

25. See 1 Cor 15.

26. Yocum, "Aquinas' Literal Exposition on Job," in Weinandy et al., *Aquinas on Scripture*, 28; emphasis added.

27. Yocum, "Aquinas' Literal Exposition on Job," in Weinandy et al., *Aquinas on Scripture*, 28.

the Writings: "So after the promulgation of the Law and the Prophets, *the Book of Job occupies first place in the order of the Holy Scripture*."[28]

Why does Thomas assign Job such a leading status? Because of its aim: "The whole intention of this book is directed to this: to show that human affairs are ruled by divine providence using probable arguments."[29] This is markedly different than Alter's assertion—that all other biblical books prior to Job were anthropocentric in their theology of creation. For Thomas, the beauty of Job is that it brings God and humanity "face-to-face" to correct this specific dimension of man's view of Providence.

The Book of Job does not assert that all of humanity is irreformable in this regard. True, neither Job's wife nor his three friends Eliphaz, Bildad, and Zophar show any sign of understanding the truth about God. And for this, the three friends are later rebuked by God for misrepresenting him.[30] Neither does Job truly comprehend this. Even so, he remains *tām wiyāshār*, "blameless and upright" in his person.[31] In other words, it is the actions of Job, his righteous character, that prove his innocence, not his mind nor his speech. Nor his background for that matter! Job is a non-Israelite from the east, the land of Uz.[32]

28. St. Thomas Aquinas, "Prologue," in *Commentary on the Book of Job*, 8; emphasis added.

29. St. Thomas Aquinas, "Prologue," in *Commentary on the Book of Job*, 8.

30. See Job 42:7–10: "After the Lord had spoken these words to Job, the Lord said to Eliphaz the Temanite: 'My wrath is kindled against you and against your two friends; *for you have not spoken of me what is right, as my servant Job has*. Now therefore take seven bulls and seven rams, and go to my servant Job, and offer up for yourselves a burnt offering; and my servant Job shall pray for you, for I will accept his prayer not to deal with you according to your folly; for you have not spoken of me what is right, as my servant Job has.' So Eliphaz the Temanite and Bildad the Shuhite and Zophar the Naamathite went and did what the Lord had told them; and the Lord accepted Job's prayer" (emphasis added). See also C. L. Seow: "Yet, how do the friends lie for God? They do so, Aquinas says, by pointing to human frailty on the one hand and divine excellence on the other, so that it might seem more likely that the human is sinful rather than God unjust. *They make Job look bad in order to make God look good. Their God is much too small; their God is much too easily manipulated.* As Job points out, the friends should not assume God is on their side just because they presume to be on God's side (13:9–12)" (*Job 1–21*, 96; emphasis added).

31. Job 1:1.

32. "The narrator sets the story in a distant land, perhaps meaning to avoid a particularistic reading of the story. Job is, in a sense, anyone who believes in God but suffers for no apparent reason. Nevertheless, the narrator's Yahwistic faith is belied by the framework. Despite the fact that all the human speakers in the dialogue refer to the deity in generic epithets that are at home in the Transjordan, the narrator is clear that YHWH is responsible for the cosmos and all that happens therein. It is YHWH who presides over the divine

Somehow, despite all of Job's protesting of innocence, *it is not enough* for his friends, who assume the role of "the foil" in the narrative,[33] holding firm to the ideas that the book itself is critiquing: *there is perfect justice in the Godhead. The God of heaven is living and just, despite whatever material evidence appears on earth to the contrary.* This is the theological core of the book, not Job's just suffering nor his innocence. In fact, his vindication is only to serve the larger principle—there is justice in the God of Israel, *perfect, divine justice.*

Thomas brings out this nuance in the presentation of Job in a number of places in his literal[34] commentary on Job. That is, the idea that Job's *rûach dâ'ât*, "windy knowledge,"[35] however eloquent it is, cannot and does not overcome accusations of his three friends, blind though they are. For example, in chapter 16, Job answers Eliphaz the Temanite, who accuses Job of empty words in the form of "hot air," and that be-

---

council. Thus, when the man from Uz praises the deity, it is the name of YHWH that is mentioned (1:21). Even in the poetry, where other names of the deity are used, Job attributes all that is and that happens to 'the hand of YHWH' (12:9b). *There is no theological dichotomy, then, between the God who gives and the God who takes away (1:21), the God who gives good and the God who gives evil (2:10). Rather, the God of the narrator is a dialectical God responsible for both weal and for woe.*" Seow, *Job 1–21*, 105; emphasis added.

33. All three friends have traditional Jewish names, while Job is depicted as the "righteous man from the east." So, it is possible that the Job Poet is critiquing a strand of rabbinic wisdom which posits a quid pro quo view; e.g., God rewards the just and punishes the weak. Intrinsic to this view is that a "righteous" man could determine who is a sinner by merely looking at the surface of things. This idea of divine retribution was not unique to Israel but was widespread in ancient Near Eastern cultures. Positioning Job as the "upright and blameless" outsider suggests that cracks were developing in this theological construct. As to Alter's charge of anthropocentrism within the Hebrew Bible, I disagree. True, there are instances of divine retribution in the wisdom literature, especially in the axiomatic Book of Proverbs. But Proverbs is sapiential, not legal, material. Accordingly, Alter's claim is vastly overstated. On the presentation of Job and his friends and the portrayal of Job as a "righteous Gentile," see Tremper Longman III, "Job 4: Person," in Longman and Enns, *Dictionary of the Old Testament*, 371–75. "Accordingly, Job is a Gentile, though he worships the true God, much as Melchizedek (Gn 14) and Jethro do. And as with these two other non-Hebrew worshipers of the true God, we do not know how Job came to know and worship him" (372).

34. In commenting on the literal sense of previous encounter scenes, I have not, for the most part, relied upon patristic and medieval thinkers but modern and contemporary ones. As discussed earlier in the book, Thomas deliberately aside the spiritual sense in his *Commentary on Job.* He did so not because of any discomfort with it, but as an act of sheer humility. He sought to pay homage to "blessed pope Gregory" (St. Pope Gregory the Great) and his masterful *Moralia in Iob*. Thomas believed that he so adequately explained "the mystical sense ... that nothing further need be added to this sort of commentary." See Thomas, "Prologue," in *Commentary on Job*, 8.

35. Job 15:2.

neath his hollow rhetoric lies an impious sinner.[36] Regrettably, all that Job can offer to Eliphaz, entrenched as he is in a quid pro quo conception of God's justice, are words. Even so, Job persists:

> Earth, O do not cover my blood,
> And let there be no place for my scream.[37]
> Even now, in the heavens my witness stands,
> One who vouches for me up above.
> My advocates, my companions!
> Before God my eye shed tears.
> Let a man dispute with God
> and a human with his fellow.
> For a handful of years will come,
> and on the path of no return I shall go.
> My spirit is wrecked,
> My days flicker out.
> Graves are what I have.[38]

Who is this *'ēdi*, this "witness" in heaven? For Thomas, and a host of others, it is God himself. This is interesting, as God,

> who has been portrayed as Job's enemy in the preceding stanza, *is at once the accused, the witness, and the judge.* Yet when God is called "witness" elsewhere in the Bible, it is always in the sense of a hostile witness, not a friendly one.[39]

36. Alter's translation of the 15:2 reads as follows: "Will a wise man speak up ideas of *hot air* and the east wind fill his belly?" He explains that "The literal sense of the Hebrew is 'wind' . . . It is noteworthy that in this second round of the debate, Eliphaz, whose first speech (ch. 4) began diplomatically, *launches a full frontal assault against Job, denouncing him as a juggler of empty words and then an impious sinner* (verses 4–6)." *Wisdom Books*, 66; emphasis added.

37. "The conjunction of the earth's not covering the blood and not muffling the scream is probably a reminiscence of God's words to Cain, 'Your brother's blood cries out [the same verbal root used here] from the soil' (Genesis 4:10). The allusion would implicitly cast God in the role of the archetypal murder." *Wisdom Books*, 73n18. Seow agrees: "*The language in v. 18 recalls the unjust murder of Abel by his brother Cain—a murder that results in the blood of the victim crying out from the ground (Gn 4:10), meaning no doubt blood that is not covered up*. And just as the cry of his blood reaches God, Job insists that 'even now' he has a witness in heaven, as if he has already been unjustly murdered, which is not surprising, given his description of God's overkill in the preceding stanza. On earth, Job's physical condition arises as a false witness against him (v. 8). All who see him, the friends included, conclude from his obvious afflictions that he must be guilty. Job imagines, however, a countervailing testimony, not one given before humans on earth, but a witness in heaven, indeed, a truth-telling witness." *Job 1–21: Interpretation and Commentary*, 738; emphasis added.

38. Job 16:18–22, Alter's translation. See *Wisdom Books*, 73–74.

39. See, e.g., 1 Sm 12:5; Jer 29:23, 42:5; Mi 1:2.

Moreover, while Job portrays the injustice of a moral universe where God is at once judge and litigant,[40] a clear conflict of interest, there is no suggestion anywhere in these poems of God playing a role in any way supportive of Job.[41]

According to Seow, this leads to the sense of urgency in Job's pleas:

Job's call to Earth not to cover his blood, as if he has already been unjustly murdered, builds on his depiction of divine violence against him in the preceding stanza. He speaks of the restlessness of his cry, as if referring to the cry of the blood for justice to be done. *Yet he is not satisfied imagining a postmortem protest in heaven. He is not interested in justice that is deferred till after one is physically dead. Rather, he speaks of the confrontation in heaven "even now"* (v. 19). *There is urgency on the matter, for his life on earth is ephemeral—his years to come are but few* (v. 22a)—and one who dies cannot come back to see justice done.[42]

In other words, the struggle Job is faced with is not one merely of false accusation. It is one of *conscience* and something that no amount of words, however eloquent, can remedy. As Thomas puts it, "The witness of heaven is greater than the frailty of the earth."[43] Armed with the Vulgate, from which he primarily worked, Thomas's interpretation becomes clear, as it translates Job 16:19[44] as *Ecce enim in caelo testis meuset conscius meus in excelsis*: "for behold, my witness is in heaven, my conscience is from above." This is quite different from the translation of either the Hebrew or Septuagint of the second part of the verse, which is something like "And my advocate is on high." Without further parsing of the textual variations, it is clear that *conscius meus*—my conscience—is known only by God. Here, Thomas concludes, "The witness of heaven is fittingly used here because [Job] even investigates *the secret intention of conscience,* and so he says *my conscience is above,* for my cry cannot find a place to hide on earth below *because my conscience is known above in heaven.*"[45]

All of the above has plunged us directly toward the theological core of the Book of Job—and its aims overall. This was by design: to help the reader acclimate to the gist of the book, and to not lose sight of it amidst the array of contextual questions that are part of the larger task of get-

40. See Job 9:32–35, 13:3–16.

41. Seow, *Job 1–21*, 738.

42. Seow, *Job 1–21*, 740; emphasis added.

43. St. Thomas Aquinas, *Commentary on the Book of Job*, 199.

44. Job 16:19: "Even now, behold, my witness is in heaven, and he that vouches for me is on high."

45. St. Thomas Aquinas, *Commentary on the Book of Job*, 199; emphasis added.

ting at the literal meaning. Even so, our discussion of the book's theology has taken us a considerable way in attending to the literal sense. It has also well positioned us to grasp the meaning of the encounter scene, that is, "the Voice from the Whirlwind" (Job 38–41). Additional aspects of the literal sense of this text are required before turning to the spiritual sense. While there are an array of contextual issues that could be discussed, from matters of textual criticism to the history of interpretation of the book, including its reception in Islam, we will limit our discussion to crucial historical issues and several literary features.

First, among the many historical questions that loom over the Book of Job,[46] none are more crucial than the author, audience, and dating of the book. These are not merely a matter of historical curiosity but are central to the interpretation of the book. Yet it is easier to talk about the style and intention of the author than any historical figure behind the book. Early rabbinic tradition held that Moses was the book's author, and a text from the Babylonian Talmud provocatively asserts that "Moses wrote his own book and part of Balaam and Job" and even more provocatively that "The length of Job's life was from the time that Israel entered Egypt until they left!"[47]

Others held that if Moses did not write all (or part) of the book, perhaps it still originated in the time of Moses or even earlier. The case for the early, written origins of Job is not without evidence. It tends to rest upon certain patriarchal features of the book, such as Job's status as the "priest" of his family as well as his longevity and wealth being measured in cattle.[48] Such features do not demand an early composition of the book, however.

46. For a recent and thorough discussion of these and other contextual issues—including Job's placement in the canon, its unity or disunity, its genre(s), the personification of wisdom, its narration, and the role of *śāṭān* ("the satan"), etc.—see the lengthy "Introduction," in Seow, *Job 1–21*, 1–248. Each unit of discussion has its own distinct bibliography. For an overview of the history of the interpretation of Job, see J. Allen, "Job 3: History of Interpretation," in Longman and Enns, *Dictionary of the Old Testament*, 361–71. On the use of *śāṭān* in the Book of Job and in the Old Testament, see J. H. Walton, "Satan," in Longman and Enns, *Dictionary of the Old Testament*, 714–17.

47. *Baba Batra*, in Neusner, *Babylonian Talmud*, 57. "Many different opinions existed among the rabbis as to the date and location of Job's life. These differing opinions were brought about by the lack of specificity in the canonical book itself. Job was believed by some to have lived in Egypt during the period of Moses and, in fact, to have been (along with Jethro and Balaam) one of Pharaoh's advisors." Allen, "Job 3," in Longman and Enns, *Dictionary of the Old Testament*, 365.

48. See Job 1:3, 11:4, 42:12.

Similarly, another thesis posits King Solomon as the book's author. Given Job's primary genre, that of a sapiential book, and the Jewish wisdom tradition being closely associated with Solomon, this too is circumstantial and not necessarily convincing. Still, many ancient Jewish commentators were unwilling to date the book after the time of the death of Solomon as a result. Such ancient proposals of Mosaic or Solomonic authorship cannot be proven or disproven. More than likely, such ascriptions are reverential and not necessarily historical. Although other theories of authorship have been put forth, both ancient and modern, the riddle remains unsolved.

It is not implausible that the roots of the book are deep in the soil of oral tradition and quite ancient. Exactly when an oral Job was developed into written form is unclear. However, some weaving together of discreet tradition with the bulk of the narrative appears likely. Among the independent textual traditions that were brought together include the prologue (1:1–2:13), the epilogue (42:1–17), and possibly the Elihu section (32:1–37:24).

This is not to suggest that the book's author—or Job himself—cannot be fixed in history: "That the book of Job places Job in historically known places (e.g., Uz), makes reference to historical parties (however slight—e.g., Sabeans, Chaldeans)[49] and reputes him to be a well-known sage suggests that the wisdom piece is based on the life and experiences of a historical person. As in the case of the other wisdom pieces, however, the genre typically operates by means of an author building a wisdom piece around the recognized character."[50]

49. See Job 1:15, 1:17.

50. J. H. Walton, "Job 1: Book of," in Longman and Enns, *Dictionary of the Old Testament*, 336. "It is common to hear that the chronological setting for the narrative frame is as early as the patriarchal period or even earlier. *The actual evidence for this conclusion, however, is slight.*

- Wealth measured by cattle and flocks
- Patriarch serving as priest for the family
- Longevity (Job's 140-year lifespan)
- No reference to covenant, Torah, exodus, etc.
- Roving Sabaean and Chaldean tribesmen.

Most of these, however, can be explained by the non-Israelite setting. Job's longevity is striking, but also it could simply be exceptional. The Chaldeans' early history is too little known (they first appear in the first millennium BC), and the Sabeans are not identified with confidence, though as a North Arabian tribe they are more at home in the first millennium BC as well. The unit of money is obscure. None of these provide convincing evidence,

As to the person of Job, Thomas, like some (but by no means all) patristic commentators, affirmed his historicity. As to the book's literal meaning, however, Thomas did not believe that the intentions of the book hinged upon the truth of the matter: "But there were some who hold that Job was not someone who was in the nature of things, but that this was a parable made up to serve as a kind of theme to dispute providence, as men frequently invent cases to serve as a model for debate. *Although it does not matter for the intention of the book whether or not this is the case, still it makes a difference for the truth itself.*"[51]

In *Summa*-like fashion, Thomas answers that "this aforementioned opinion seems to contradict the authority of Scripture. In Ezekiel, the Lord is represented as saying, 'if there were three just men in our midst, Noah, Daniel, and Job, these would free your souls from injustice.'"[52] And so Thomas concludes that "Clearly Noah and Daniel really were men in the nature of things and so there should be no doubt about Job who is the third man numbered with them. Also, James says, behold, we bless those who persevered. You have heard of the suffering of Job and you have seen the intention of the Lord (Jas 5:11). Therefore, one must believe that Job was in the nature of things."[53]

Setting aside the book's authorship (Alter is content to refer to him as the "Job poet"), a few remarks about the audience and dating of the book are called for. As to the audience, it seems clear that whatever audience the book aimed at reaching, the larger aim is that of overturning—or at least enlarging—Jewish beliefs of a quid pro quo dynamic in regard to divine justice (see above). Of course, with the question of authorship open as it is, pinning down an era in which the book emerged remains a challenge.

In the early to mid-twentieth century, it was common to hear of Job being the oldest book of the Hebrew canon. While certainly possible, given its reference to Genesis 4:10, it seems unlikely that Job predates Genesis. However old it may be in its origins,[54] most scholars today

---

though little circumstantial evidence from the content would offer support of a later setting for the events either. This position is usually maintained by traditional scholars" (344; emphases added).

51. St. Thomas Aquinas, "Prologue," in *Commentary on the Book of Job*, 8; emphasis added.

52. St. Thomas Aquinas, "Prologue," in *Commentary on the Book of Job*, 8. See Ezek 14:14.

53. St. Thomas Aquinas, "Prologue," in *Commentary on the Book of Job*, 8.

54. Our own approach is that the Pentateuch—the Five Books of Moses—have their

date the completion of the Pentateuch, including Genesis, to around the time of the Babylonian exile, or shortly thereafter (fifth–fourth centuries BC).

That being the case, it would seem logical to date the written Book of Job—which seems to include a clear reference to the Book of Genesis—to about the same time or sometime thereafter. That would place Job alongside Genesis, in the postexilic period. Additionally, the "accuser"—that is, the *śātān* figure in Job—is presented in a way that is similar to the prophetic book of Zechariah, which most certainly dates from the sixth century (ca. 520–518 BC).[55] It is beyond the scope of this book to attempt to resolve such historical questions. Based upon the above, I offer a modest proposal: the Book of Job is an ancient Jewish composition of wisdom literature. Although unprovable, the book is likely ancient, perhaps originating in a primitive oral form sometime prior to the Israelite monarchy. This leaves open the question of dating, but it is probable that Job was brought into its canonical form around the time of the exile in Babylon or shortly thereafter. No matter when it developed, or who was responsible for its contents, the following is clear as to the aims of this inspired book of Scripture. It aims to challenge conventional theological beliefs held by members of the audience.

---

historic roots in the historical figure of the man called "Moses" in the 1400s BC. The question of the development of the Pentateuch, including its oral and written history, is a complex one. Ratzinger asserts that the Pentateuch reached its final stages of composition in the postexilic period. See *"In the Beginning . . .,"* Homily One.

55. Compare Job 1:12 and 2:1–7 with Zec 3:1 and 3:2. His role is in fact slight; once God allows *śātān* to test Job, he disappears from the book. It may seem as though the *śātān* figure is the antagonist in the book. This reads a New Testament understanding of "Satan" upon the *śātān* figure back into the earlier text of Job. The true antagonists are Job's three friends, who represent the flawed theology of divine providence that the author of the book is seeking to overcome. They—not *śātān*—are rebuked at the end of Job. After chapters 1–2, *śātān* does not reappear in the book.

"Apart from the terrestrial adversaries, there are four passages in the Bible that refer to a celestial *śātān*, although not necessarily the same figure throughout. The earliest of these is the Balaam Oracles, where a divine being—called *mal'ak yhwh*—is deployed by the angry deity as a *śātān* to hinder Balaam (Num 22:22, 32). There is no indication, though, that antagonism was the particular function of the divine agent, and nothing suggests that the intermediary was in any way hostile to YHWH. The *mal'ak yhwh* was simply acting on behalf of YHWH as an adversary against a certain group of people. At the end of the sixth century B.C.E., however, one finds the form with the definite article, *haśśātān*, 'the Adversary,' used as an appellation of a particular divine being who stands next to the *mal'ak yhwh* to play an adversarial role (Zec 3:1–2), perhaps a judicial role (compare Ps 109:6)." Seow, *Job 1–21*, 272–73.

This quid pro quo belief involved a dynamic of divine retribution; God rewards the just and punishes the wicked.

There are several literary features of the book that require attention: the first of which concerns the structure of the book, the second its poetic style. Table 3 offers a proposal regarding the structure of Job.

For our purposes, two points are crucial about the structure of the book. First, the overall framework of the book follows the dialogical nature of its contents. Following the book's prologue[56] and Job's Opening Lament,[57] the book pivots upon a threefold cycle of debates between each of the three friends and Job, in sequence.[58] Following this is an interlude in the literary form of a Wisdom Hymn[59] and a series of poetic protestations by Job, in the form of soliloquy rather than dialogue.[60] Next, the author introduces a fourth friend, the enigmatic Elihu, who in some sense speaks for and provides a transition to the speech of God.[61] This is followed by the speech of God himself as "the Voice from the Whirlwind.[62] Subsequent to this is Job's response to God,[63] and finally the book's Epilogue.[64]

From this larger structure, the texts we are concerned with are chapters 38–41 and 42. They clearly represent our encounter scene, but before turning to them, one last literary feature deserves to be included here, that of the poetic style of Job. The strength of the composition of Job is nearly unsurpassed in the history of literature. The Book of Job is a poetic masterpiece, filled with linguistic treasures and elegiac beauty. Yet we need not concern ourselves with the many fascinating details and complexities of Job as poetry.

Only one overarching pattern needs to be mentioned here. As explained at the beginning of this chapter, the Book of Job is a "*theological argument conducted in poetry*."[65] In this respect, one of the most significant contributions of Alter's translation and commentary of *The*

56. Job 1–2.
57. Job 3.
58. Job 4–27.
59. Job 28.
60. Job 29–31.
61. Job 32–37.
62. Job 38–41.
63. Job 42:1–6.
64. Job 42:7–17.
65. Alter, *Wisdom Books*, 6; emphasis added.

TABLE 3. Narrative Structure of the Book of Job

Description	*Verse*
Prologue: Heaven and Earth	1–2
Job's Opening Lament	3
Cycle One: Job 4–14	
Eliphaz	4–5
Job	6–7
Bildad	8
Job	9–10
Zophar	11
Job	12–14
Cycle Two: Job 15–21	
Eliphaz	15
Job	16–17
Bildad	18
Job	19
Zophar	20
Job	21
Cycle Three: Job 22–27	
Eliphaz	22
Job	23–24
Bildad	25
Job	26–27
Interlude: Wisdom Hymn, Job 28	
Series One: Job 29–31	
Job: Reminiscences	29
Job: Affliction	30
Job: Oath of Innocence	31
Series Two: Job 32–37	
Elihu: Introduction and Theory	32–33
Elihu: Verdict on Job	34
Elihu: Offense of Job	35
Elihu: Summary	36–37
Series Three: Job 38–41	
Yahweh: Maintaining Roles/Functions in Cosmic Order	38–39
Yahweh: Harnessing Threats to Cosmic Order	40:6–41:34
Narrative Frame: Job 42	
Job's Closing Statements	42:1–6
Epilogue: Heaven and Earth	42:7–17

Source: Adapted from John Walton, "Job 1: Book Of," in Longman and Enns, *Dictionary of the Old Testament*, 334. Seow's structure is also recommended; see *Job 1–21*, 73–74. See also Sawyer, "Authorship and Structure of the Book of Job," 253–57; Westermann, *Structure of the Book of Job*.

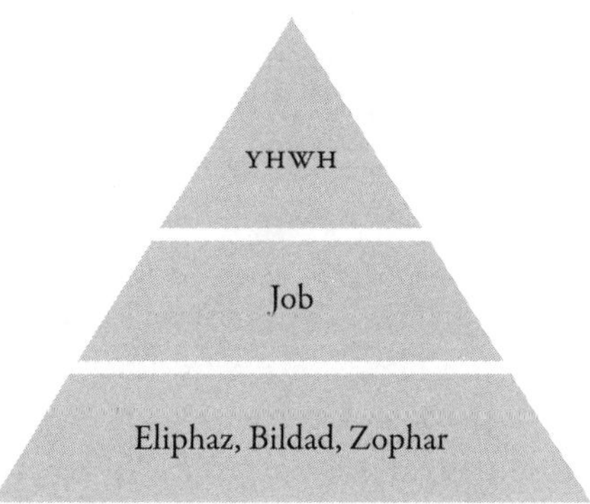

FIGURE 7. Three levels of poetry in the Book of Job. Adapted from Walton, "Job 1: Book Of," in Longman and Enns, *Dictionary of the Old Testament*, 334. Seow's structure is also recommended. See *Job 1–21*, 73–74. See also Sawyer, "Authorship and Structure of the Book of Job."

Wisdom Books is his explanation of the way that the poetical form serves the theological content of the book: "The debate between Job and his three adversarial friends and then God's climactic speech to Job exhibit *three purposefully deployed levels of poetry.*"[66]

In other words, within the language of the Book of Job, there are decisive clues as to whose "voice" is to be heeded. Although it involves more complexity than can be relayed here, there is a kind of "hierarchy" among the various speakers in Job. These range from more foolish at the lowest portion of the hierarchal pyramid, to Job in the middle portion, who is wiser (or better, *less foolish*) than they are. Finally, at the top of the pyramid is "the Voice from the Whirlwind," Almighty God. Elihu is a sort of human representative of God. He is beneath God in this hierarchy, but we can set him aside for our purposes.

This poetic structuring is not incidental. It is foundational for understanding what's really going on in the book. Once again, this knowledge rests upon a sound principle of biblical interpretation: *form is at the service of content*. This is true elsewhere in Scripture, and it is the case here in Job. This "leveling up" in poetic diction and poetic sophistication aids the reader in discerning which speaker is the one true champion of the moral debate.

66. Alter, *Wisdom Books*, 6; emphasis added.

In the case of the three friends and their respective contests with Job, their poetry may be described as "adequate." It is not poor—none of Job's poetry is poor. Still, their poetry is more elemental in comparison to his, with commonly used phrases and simpler terms. Job's own poetical phrases are more pleasing. They are filled with irony and other literary subtleties, rich vivid descriptions, and a sophisticated command of speech. These sorts of linguistic clues support the author's overall aims; namely, to underscore Job's innocence before their charges. More subtly, yet still at the core, is the idea that there is something inherently flawed in the friends' responses. As Alter explains, "In keeping with the conventional moral views that they complacently defend, the poetry they speak abounds in familiar formulations closely analogous to what one encounters in Psalms and Proverbs.[67] What this means is that *much of their poetry verges on cliché.*"[68]

Again, it is not to say it is altogether poor—no. That would create a straw man, which the book's author certainly does not do: "The Job poet is too subtle an artist to assign *bad verse* to them."[69] And so, as Alter continues, "There are moments when *their poetry catches fire*, conveying to us a sense that *even the spokesmen for wrongheaded ideas may exercise a certain power of vision.*"[70] Several examples of such vision, where the poetry of the friends "breaks out" and rises above conventionality, include "For we are but yesterday, unknowing, for our days are a shadow on the earth" and "Whose faith is mere cobweb; spider's house his trust. He leans on his house and it will not stand, he grasps it and it does not endure."[71]

Additionally, the Job poet knows his audience and recognizes that many among them share (at least some of) the theological views of the three friends along the lines of the quid pro quo of divine retribution.

67. The following are a few of the many examples of this sort. Zophar: "He will perish forever like his own dung; those who have seen him will say, 'Where is he?'" (Job 20:7). Eliphaz: "Is not your wickedness great? There is no end to your iniquities" (Job 22:5). Bildad: "if you are pure and upright, surely then he will rouse himself for you and reward you with a rightful habitation" (Job 8:6).

68. Alter, *Wisdom Books*, 6; emphasis added.

69. Alter, *Wisdom Books*, 6; emphasis added.

70. Alter, *Wisdom Books*, 6; emphasis added. "Throughout the speeches of Job's three critics, the poet performs a delicate balancing act in assigning them boilerplate poetry that reflects *their conventional mindset* and giving them *some striking lines* in which his own extraordinary poetic powers are manifest" (39; emphases added).

71. Alter's own translation of Job 8:9 and 14–15 in *Wisdom Books*, 40; emphasis added.

The author needs to be careful here: hastily assigning to them mere cliché as poetry would only alienate those he is attempting to persuade. This insight further helps to explain, at least in part, why the satan is the antagonist at the beginning of Job. Were it clear from the outset of the book that the three friends were the true antagonists—*and it is not*—it would be easier for the book's audience to unhitch their theological wagons from Eliphaz, Bildad, and Zophar. Make no mistake: the author desires this outcome. But not yet. He needs the audience to go along for the ride and to "figure it out" gradually over the course of the book. Their poetry is sound and adequate, yet nowhere near as elegant as Job's responses.

In other words, the level of sophistication of Job's poetry—over and against that of his friends—corresponds to his objective innocence, his righteousness. In turn, their *lesser poetry*, compared with Job's, corresponds to their *lesser theology*. This provides a linguistic road map for reading through the extensive discourses. And long before the book's climax, it hints at Job's eventual vindication before God. And so the lowest or bottom level of the book's poetry is that of the accusatory discourses of the three friends (see fig. 7 above).

In contrast to his friends, with their occasionally less-than-pedantic verse, Job's poetry continually rises far above their attempts to render him speechless. His elegance confounds their protests: "*The stubborn authenticity* of Job's perception of moral reality is firmly manifested in the power of the poetry he speaks clearly transcends the poetry of his reprovers."[72] Perhaps the best example of this is seen in Job's opening lament, in chapter 3:

> Perish the day on which I was born and the night that told of a boy conceived. May that day be darkness, may God on high have no thought for it, may no light shine on it. May murk and shadow dark as death claim it for their own, clouds hang over it, eclipse swoop down on it. See! Let obscurity seize on it, from the days of the year let it be excluded, into the reckoning of the months not find its way. And may that night be sterile, devoid of any cries of joy! Let it be cursed by those who curse certain days and are ready to rouse Leviathan. Dark be the stars of its morning, let it wait in vain for light and never see the opening eyes of dawn.[73]

72. Alter, *Wisdom Books*, 7; emphasis added.
73. Job 3:3:9, NJB.

As Clines remarks, "In this speech we are suddenly plunged out of the epic grandeur and deliberateness of the prologue into the dramatic turmoil of the poetry, from the external description of suffering to Job's inner experience. This beautiful and affecting poem is built upon a dynamic movement from the past to the future and from the experience of the man Job outwards to the experience of humankind."[74] About Job's inaugural speech, Clines writes,

> This poem, one of the great masterpieces of the work, is striking above all for its restraint. Not for the restraint of Job's emotions, which are deep, raw, and terrifying, as he showers with maledictions every aspect of the world that gave him existence or continues to support it. That excessive and surreal rejection of life that imagines the night of his conception being swallowed up by the underworld (v 6) or that depicts the world-weary as grave-robbers desperately digging their way into Sheol as into a treasure-house (vv 21–22) is a quintessential instance of the vitality of the human spirit when freed from the bounds of custom, decorum and prosaic reality.[75]

Clines concludes that "The restraint that makes this a poem of world stature is the exclusive concentration on feeling, without the importation of ideological questions. For a book that is so dominated by intellectual issues of theodicy, it is amazing to find here *not one strictly theological sentence, not a single question* about the meaning of his suffering, not a hint that it may be deserved, not the slightest nod to the doctrine of retribution."[76] As Clines describes, all of that will come in good time. At present, however, "we are invited to view the man Job in the violence of his grief Unless we encounter this man with these feelings we have no right to listen in on the debates that follow; with this speech before us we cannot overintellectualize the book, but must always be reading it as the drama of a human soul."[77]

It is not exaggeration to claim that "Anger has rarely been given more powerful expression" than this text in Job.[78] Job's heartfelt cries ascend into the air—seemingly unheard—through spiraling patterns of "intensification" and semantic parallelism. Strikingly, Job wishes that he was never born and that he could even obliterate the moment of his

74. Clines, *Job 1–20*, 77–78.
75. Clines, *Job 1–20*, 104.
76. Clines, *Job 1–20*, 104; emphases added.
77. Clines, *Job 1–20*, 104.
78. Alter, *Wisdom Books*, 7.

conception. Yet he does so in this monologue and in all his subsequent debates with his friends, such that his poetry—indeed, the heart of his thoughts—rises high above theirs. It is as if the splendid quality of his speech makes up for his utter "lack of evidence." Again, this pattern of "besting" Eliphaz, Bildad, and Zophar is repeated over and over through the body of the book. And here is a critical point about the literal meaning of the encounter scene: these poetic rhythms reveal, at least in part, the "pattern of ascent" toward the face of God. But how?

We have not yet heard the highest forms of poetry in the book, from the "Voice from the Whirlwind." Yahweh's speech transcends *all other voices* in the book. Still, Job's sufferings, expressed in refined speech, *lifts off the ground,* the ground of the everyday poetry where his friends dwell (see fig. 7 above). Job's poetry contains elements of the transcendent, and his words "float," ascending toward the divine, toward the voice and face of God, able to trounce his human counterparts. Job's poetry will prove no match for YHWH.

Still, and this is the main point, Job's sophisticated poetry is legitimately beautiful, far surpassing the best efforts that his friends can collectively throw at him. The author's aim is clear: Job's advanced poetry is illustrative of his elevated character. And it serves a vital theological purpose, *galvanizing the trueness of his words,* in contrast to their earthbound protestations. Even so—and this next point takes us to the immediacy of the encounter scene in chapters 38–41, *Job's poetic speech is utterly insufficient compared with the divine speech of YHWH.* And this brings us close to the theological core of the encounter scene and the entire book. Again, Job's lyrical responses disarm the threatening poetics of his friends, but he is no competition for the transcendent and holy Voice from the Whirlwind. God's ways are above man's ways. His Word is utterly perfect in both form and content, unsurpassed in what it says and how it is said. As there was no true comparison between the poetry of Job's friends and Job, there is none to be made between the "upright and blameless" Job and the Lord God.

Were there any proximity between the speech of Job and that of the Voice, it would undermine the author's message. Yet the Job poet is no "proto-Arian" and does not portray Job as more than mortal, as if his innocence were some sort of godlike quality. No—when God speaks, Job can do nothing but prostrate himself and listen to the Voice of Creation, to the Voice from the whirlwind:

Who is this who darkens counsel
in words without knowledge?
Gird your loins like a man,
that I may ask you, and you can inform Me.
Where you there when I founded the earth?
Tell, if you know understanding…
Who hedges the sea with its double doors,
when it gushes forth from the womb,
when I made cloud its clothing,
and thick mist its swaddling bands?[79]

The sheer power of the Voice from the *se'ārah*, the Whirlwind, is indeed likened to a "tempest"[80] and is aptly translated as *de turbine* in the Vulgate. This disputation speech,[81] which unfolds over four chapters, does so in a twofold manner. In between its preface[82] and conclusion[83] are two larger units. The first unit is composed of thirty-five lines and concerns God's omnipotence over his creation.[84] The second unit is made up of thirty-three lines and deals with God's majestic power over all living things.[85]

Nothing that came before—not the poetry of Eliphaz, Bildad, and Zophar, nor that of Job, nor even the mysterious Elihu—can compare with the magnitude of poetic eloquence on display in these chapters: "The poet, having given Job such vividly powerful language for the articulation of his outrage and his anguish, now fashions still greater poetry for God." As Alter describes, "The wide-ranging panorama of creation in the Voice from the Whirlwind shows a sublimity of expression, a plasticity of description, an ability to evoke the complex and dynamic interplay of beauty and violence in the natural world, and even an originality of metaphoric inventiveness, that surpasses all the poetry, great as it is, that Job has spoken."[86]

As to the potency of the divine speech, Alter stresses, in contrast to

79. Job 38:1–4, 8–9. Alter's own translation, *Wisdom Books*, 158–59.

80. Clines, *Job 38–42*, 1087. Alter argues that "storm" is more accurate. Even so, he follows the KJV since it has been "so deeply embedded in the imagination" of English speakers (*Wisdom Books*, 158n1).

81. Clines, *Job 38–42*, 1087.

82. Job 8:2–3.

83. Job 40:1–2.

84. Job 38:4–38.

85. Clines, *Job 38–42*, 1085; Job 38:39–39:30.

86. Alter, *Wisdom Books*, 10; emphasis added.

critics, that "God's thundering challenge to Job is not bullying. Rather, it rousingly introduces a comprehensive overview of the nature of reality that exposes the limits of Job's human perspective, anchored in the restricted compass of human knowledge and the inevitable egoism of suffering. The vehicle of that overview is *an order of poetry created to match the grandeur—or perhaps the omniscience—of God.*"[87]

As to the necessity of this "divine tornado" of poetic speech, St. Thomas explains, "Because human wisdom is not sufficient to understand the truth of divine providence, it was necessary that the dispute should be determined by divine authority."[88] In all of this, Job is utterly silent. Finally, in chapter 40, he utters a few words in his first, feeble response: "My words have been frivolous: what can I reply? I had better lay my hand over my mouth. I have spoken once, I shall not speak again; I have spoken twice, I have nothing more to say."[89] This is the shortest speech of the book, but it is a crucial one for understanding the significance of the encounter. It is not a withdrawal of Job's complaint, for none of his protestations were addressed by the Voice from the Whirlwind. Here, one wonders "whether Job has been listening very carefully to Yahweh. Yahweh's chief concern has been to sketch his conception of the universe, and Job responds by saying, 'Behind, I am of little account.' He has taken the divine speech personally, and heard nothing in it but the admittedly reproachful remarks of Yahweh."[90]

Even so, As Clines underscores, "Making Job feel small *has not been Yahweh's main intention* … It has not been Yahweh's purpose in his speech to humiliate Job, not even to stress Job's incapacity. His purpose seems rather to expound his intentions for the universe he created."[91] Following Job's slight response, YHWH continues: "Brace yourself like a fighter, I am going to ask the questions, and you are to inform me! *Do you really want to reverse my judgement, put me in the wrong and yourself in the right?* Has your arm the strength of God's, can your voice thunder as loud? Come on, display your majesty and grandeur, robe yourself in splendour and glory."[92]

87. Alter, *Wisdom Books*, 10; emphasis added.
88. St. Thomas Aquinas, *Commentary on the Book of Job*, chap. 38, Lecture 1, 373–74.
89. Job 40:4–5, NJB.
90. Clines, *Job 38–42*, 1085.
91. Clines, *Job 38–42*, 1139; emphasis added.
92. Job 40:7–10, NJB; emphasis added.

Here, St. Thomas explains the theology under the encounter scene before us: "The Lord demonstrated his wisdom and power by recalling the marvelous things which appear in his effects, *so that he might make clear that no man can contend with God either in wisdom or in power.*"[93] The next words of God to Job are crucial: "Let the fury of your anger burst forth, humble the haughty at a glance! At a glance, bring down all the proud, strike down the wicked where they stand. Bury the lot of them in the ground, shut them, everyone, in the Dungeon. *And I shall be the first to pay you homage, since your own right hand is strong enough to save you.*"[94]

Again, God is not attempting to humiliate Job. Rather, he is *conveying Job of his need for divine mercy.* As Thomas indicates, "The Lord has treated these things first as proper to his own works. *It is proper to him also to not need anyone else's help.*"[95] Yet prideful man—and the "upright and blameless" Job is not without pride—does need the help of another, God. According to Thomas, it as if the Job poet is saying, to Job and to all of his audience, "If you can do these works which are proper only to God, *you can reasonable attribute to yourself that you do not need divine help to be saved.* But as you cannot do the former, you cannot do the latter."[96]

This insight of St. Thomas Aquinas takes us to the deepest depths of the literal meaning of the encounter scene between God and Job. Poetically, Job's former speeches carried him aloft, above all his oppositional "friends" seeking to keep him earthbound in the quid pro quo of their fallible human reasoning. Job's true innocence rises out of his lungs. His voice is the one thing Satan apparently spared him of, and it repeatedly vindicated him. Yet not before the Creator and Power and Lord of heaven and earth, and all living things. And that is precisely the point of the encounter scene—and the point of the author. Job, and all who live and breathe, must only attribute to God that which he—and he alone—is capable of doing; namely, redeeming us from our suffering, as he is wont to do.

93. St. Thomas Aquinas, *Commentary on the Book of Job*, chap. 40, Lecture 1, 399; emphasis added.

94. Job 40:11–15, NJB; emphasis added.

95. St. Thomas Aquinas, *Commentary on the Book of Job*, chap. 40, Lecture 1, 403; emphasis added.

96. St. Thomas Aquinas, *Commentary on the Book of Job*, chap. 40, Lecture 1, 403; emphasis added.

Throughout the thick verbal debates with his friends, Job's poetic diction surpasses theirs at each turn. Even so, he is powerless to persuade them of what he needs them to realize: that true justice will only be accomplished at the final judgment, *after the resurrection of the dead.* For Thomas, Job's fundamental error is not his temper or his complaining. It is that, in his pedagogical discourse, Job fails to make himself clear regarding the resurrection of the dead and the final judgment. Therefore his friends remain in a stupor, baffled by his "lofty words." Eliphaz, Bildad, and Zophar are unable to see what Job sees and are therefore confused as to what he is laboring to say. These tensions are only addressed in the book's epilogue, by the Voice himself: after the Lord had spoken these words to Job, the Lord said to Eliphaz the Temanite, "My wrath is kindled against you and against your two friends; for you have not spoken of me what is right, as my servant Job has."[97]

Finally, then, in Job 42:1–6, which is the theological climax of the encounter, Job speaks in language reminiscent of those *who saw—and not merely heard—something of God.* His words recall Jacob and Moses who, in Guardini's words, were granted "accessible proximity" to the face of God. In a strange and mysterious way, realized through intense holy suffering, Job is now aware of God's nearness. Through his suffering, Job has been brought near to God, gifted with a rare, "accessible proximity" to the divine voice. He bested his friends and capably stood his ground. Still, his life was aimless, accused as he was. But now he understands that before God he is *qăllōti*—I am "frivolous, of no account."[98]

Finally, Job is able to be *fully receptive* of God's mercy:

> This was the answer Job gave to Yahweh: I know that you are all-powerful: what you conceive, you can perform. I was the man who misrepresented your intentions with my ignorant words. You have told me about great works that I cannot understand, about marvels which are beyond me, of which I know nothing. (Listen, please, and let me speak: I am going to ask the questions, and you are to inform me.) Before, I knew you only by hearsay *but now, having seen you with my own eyes, I retract what I have said, and repent in dust and ashes.*[99]

97. Job 42:7. See also the NJB's translation, which in some sense captures the Lord's anger: "When Yahweh had finished saying this to Job, he said to Eliphaz of Teman, '*I burn with anger against you and your two friends*, for not having spoken correctly about me as my servant Job has done.'"

98. Job 40:4. See the RSV and NJB.

99. Job 42:1–6, NJB; emphasis added.

Here, at the end of the encounter scene, and indeed throughout the entire book, it is highly significant that Job repents "in dust and ashes" and is delivered by God. Yet it is only here and now that he can exclaim *nunc autem oculus meus videt te*—"but now my eye sees thee." Even so, like Moses, Job's "seeing" God is yet veiled:

> The seeing of the eye is a testimony to the persuasive power of the poetry that God has spoken to Job out of the whirlwind. Through that long chain of vividly arresting images, from the swaddling bands of mist drifting over the primordial sea at creation to the fearsomely armored Leviathan, whose eyes are like the eyelids of dawn, Job has been led to see the multifarious character of God's vast creation, its unfathomable fusion of beauty and cruelty, and through this he has come to understand the incommensurability between his human notions of right and wrong and the structure of reality. *But he may not see God Himself because God addresses him from a storm-cloud.*[100]

All of these insights from the encounter scene point forward to the *merciful* Christ. He is the only One who has truly "seen God"[101] yet longs to save us from our pain. He is the One who gazes at the beauty of the Father yet mounts the Cross of mercy. He is the One who gazes at Life itself yet gives up his own to redeem ours.

Sensus Spiritualis

Once again, among the earliest of texts that should be consulted are the Aramaic Targumim. *Targum Jonathan* on the Book of Job has several interesting variants worth mentioning as it pertains to chapters 38–41. First, here is the English translation of Job 38:12–13 in the Hebrew Bible: "Have you ever in your life given orders to the morning or sent the dawn to its post, to grasp the earth by its edges and shake the wicked out of it?" Regarding the same text, *Targum Jonathan* reads: "Have you, since your days [began], commanded the morning to be? Have you made known to the dawn its place[102] that it might take hold of the borders of *the land of Israel,* and the sinners be shaken from it?"[103] Here, the

100. Alter, *Wisdom Books*, 177; emphasis added.

101. Jn 1:18.

102. A variant of *Targum Jonathan* on this verse reads, "Were you in the days of the beginning, and did you command the morning to be? Did you make known to the dawn what its place was?"

103. Mangan et al., *Aramaic Bible*, Job 38:12–13; emphasis added.

inclusion of "the land of Israel" situates the geographic and theological context of the book *within the Promised Land.* I have suggested above that the man Job is only identified as a man from Uz, in the east, beyond Israel. This text does not dispute his origins; rather, it guides the reader toward the place of *the reception of the book*, that is, within Israel. This small phrase raises more questions than can be answered: is one meant to think of the Abrahamic, Mosaic, or Davidic covenants, of Israel's fall from grace, leading up to the Exile? Or is the *Targum* simply rooting the narrative to "all of Israel" and its inhabitants?

A similar addition added by *Targum Jonathan* is found in 38:17. Whereas the Tanakh reads, "Have you been shown the gates of Death, have you seen the janitors of the shadow dark as death?" the *Targum* modifies the end to "the shadow of death of *Ghenna*."[104] Too much should not be made of this Second Temple term for "hell," yet it does call to mind Jesus's statements of fiery judgment upon the unrighteous.[105] A third variation between the Hebrew Bible and the Aramaic *Targum Jonathan* is seen in 38:18: "Have you comprehended the expanse of the earth? Declare, if you know all this." In its translation of the same verse, however, *Targum Jonathan* adds a key phrase: "Have you perceived as far as the expanse of the land of *the garden of Eden?* Reveal [it] if you know it all."[106] The mentioned of Gehenna is of interest. Here, the *Targum* pushes the entire speech—and in some sense the entire Book of Job—into dialogue with Genesis. It is as if the man Job is reminded by Voice that he is a descendant of Adam and of one who ultimately overstepped his mortal ranks.

Targum Jonathan is recapitulating the Creation narrative of Genesis in the speech to underscore the chasm between the man Job and Yahweh—and to hint at the "re-creation" of Job that is about to take place in the Epilogue of the book. There, Job is "remade" by Yahweh: his "fortunes" are restored, and his entire life has been remapped in light of his repentance.

104. Similarly, see *Targum Jonathan* on Job 38:23 (emphasis added): "The snow which I have reserved for the time of trouble in *Gehenna*, and the hail for the day of the war of Pharaoh and the fight of the Egyptians."

105. See, e.g., Mt 5:22, 5:29, 5:30; Mk 9:43, 9:45, 9:47; Lk 12:5; emphasis added. Also, see the Epistle of James, which includes this sharp warning for those whose speech is impure or untrue: "And the tongue is a fire. The tongue is an unrighteous world among our members, staining the whole body, setting on fire the cycle of nature, and set on fire by hell" (Jas 3:6).

106. Mangan et al., *Aramaic Bible*, Job 38:18; emphasis added.

In the Septuagint (LXX)—the Greek translation of the Hebrew Bible—significant modifications to the text are found. Above all, the LXX shortens the text considerably, into what Seow calls a more "reader-friendly" version.[107] As he explains, the LXX is "*literary rather than literal*, as it seeks to be unencumbered by confusing poetic lines and redundancies. Such poetic license in translation may say something about the authority of the book. Unlike the Pentateuch and the Psalter, which were used in the synagogue and hence translated in ways that adhered closely to the original, *Job* appears to have been treated as a literary composition intended to have wide appeal in Hellenistic Alexandria."[108] In the LXX, Job 40:4 is nearly identical to the Book of Job at this point: "Or is there for you an arm like the Lord's, or do you thunder with a voice like his?"[109] No attempt is made to cover the anthropomorphism of "the Lord's arm." In what follows, however, the LXX adds an angelic dimension not present in Job. Following Job 40:10,[110] it inserts "*And send forth angels in ange*r, and humble every haughty person."[111] Near the end of the Lord's speech, "angels" are again inserted into the narrative. Referring to Leviathan, the LXX reads, "There is not anything upon the earth like it, *being made to be mocked at by my angels*."[112]

Given the rise of angelology in Second Temple Judaism, these additions are not a complete surprise. I mention these changes to the original biblical text as being noteworthy in themselves. But that this may be another instance of angelic mediation in an encounter scene. The first instance seems to refer to the disobedient Lucifer and his demonic host that the Lord "sends forth in anger." In the second one, just mentioned, it is God's holy angels that "mock" the power of the earthly Leviathan. With regard to the encounter scene in Genesis 32, the Aramaic targums make clear that it was the angel(s), not God, with whom Jacob wrestled. The LXX is not clear-cut as the targums, yet the very insertion of the angels is intriguing. It may well be that their inclusion in the LXX

107. Seow, *Job 1–21*, 111.

108. Seow, *Job 1–21*, 111; emphasis added.

109. Job 40:4: "Have you an arm like God, and can you thunder with a voice like his?"

110. Job 40:10: "Deck yourself with majesty and dignity; clothe yourself with glory and splendor."

111. My translation; emphasis added. The LXX of Job 40:11 reads: *aposteilon de angelous orgē, pan de hybristēn tapeinōson* (Rahlfs, *Septuaginta*).

112. My translation; emphasis added. The LXX of Job 40:10 reads: *ouk estin ouden epi tēs gēs homoion autō, pepoiēmenon enkatapaizesthai hypo tōn angelōn mou* (Rahlfs, *Septuaginta*).

of Job is unrelated to the theophanic nature of the speech and merely incidental. Even if this is the case, it highlights how Jewish angelology played an increasingly important role in Second Temple Judaism and in the reinterpretation of the Hebrew Bible.

Turning to the primitive Church, and as soon as one thinks of interpreting Job according to the spiritual sense, St. Gregory the Great comes immediately to mind. With his massive *Moralia in Iob*, he loomed over the book so much so that St. Thomas dared not even interpret the text from the spiritual sense. Rather, in a kind of holy respect, Thomas kept strictly to the literal.

In what follows, we will encounter Gregory's insights into the mysteries of Job. Joining the discussion of Gregory are texts from Origen, Chrysostom, Ephrem the Syrian, and Augustine, all of whom exegete the text through the allegorical, the tropological, and the anagogical senses. Collectively, their commentaries on Job 38–41 reflect the "pathway and progression" toward the face of the Lord that we have seen throughout the book.

First, we turn to allegorical interpretations pertaining to Job 38–41, beginning with Gregory the Great. He is most remembered for his moral contributions to the book. As St. Bernard's *Commentary on the Song of Songs* is by no means strictly allegorical, however, *Moralia in Iob* is not merely tropological. True, the allegorical and tropological are the defining features of the commentaries of Bernard and Gregory, respectively. Like his counterpart from the High Middle Ages, however, Gregory moves in and through the various spiritual senses as he interprets Scripture. In a number of instances in the *Moralia*, Gregory sees the Church allegorically prefigured in the Book of Job. For instance, in 38:4—"Where were you when I laid the foundation of the earth?"—Gregory perceives an image of the Church's preachers: "In the holy Scriptures, the foundations represent the preachers. The Lord first put them in the church, and on them the structure of the building was developed. That is the reason why the priest, by entering the tabernacle, had to wear twelve stones on his breast, because our high priest, who offers himself for us, giving us from the beginning firm preachers, wore twelve stones under his head in the upper part of his body."[113] Signifying the Lord's Apostles, these stones "constitute the main ornament

113. St. Gregory the Great, *Moralia in Iob*, 28.14.

of the breast *and are the foundations that make the building firm on the ground*. . . . When holy Scripture does not speak of different foundations but of a single foundation, it refers to the Lord himself, who supports our weak and fickle hearts with the power of his divinity."[114]

Gregory's interpretation rests upon the inspired Word of God, and it is upon their foundation that the preacher exposits and teaches the truth of the Gospel. Additionally, Gregory draws upon the instructions of the priestly garments in Exodus 28, and it is clear that the preachers he speaks of are the Church's priests. Finally, it is Christ that is the "one foundation" about which the Scriptures speak. Later, in dealing with the "fishing" motifs in regarding to Leviathan in chapter 41, Gregory again sees an image of the church allegorically prefigured: "What is designated by 'nets' or a 'cabin of fish' *except the churches of the faithful that make one universal church*? Hence it is written in the Gospel, 'The kingdom of heaven is like a net cast into the sea and gathering of every kind of fish.'"[115]

Before extending his commentary further, in a similar direction, Gregory interrupts the allegorical flow with more of an anagogical impression: "The church is in truth called the kingdom of heaven, for while the Lord exalts its conduct to things above, it already reigns herself in toward the Lord by heavenly conversation." Long before Gregory, Origen's commentary on Job, which today amounts to mere fragments of the text, looked to the colorful description of the Leviathan as a motif of Satan. From there, he interprets the "limbs" of the creature as those heretics against whom he mounted rigorous opposition, such as Marcion and Valentinus: "I believe that all the impious teachers of immoral doctrines are properly the limbs of the dragon. What are the names, if you want to listen, of the limbs of the dragon? *The mouth of the dragon can be figurally interpreted as the main limb, because all the dangerous speeches come from it.*"[116]

In this next example from Gregory, he turns from the allegorical to the tropological of Job 38:16: "Have you entered into the springs of the sea, or walked in the recesses of the deep?" He explains the text in terms of the "sea of humanity," drenched in sin and in need of Christ's redemption: "'Have you entered into the depth of the sea?' *The 'sea' is the mind*

114. St. Gregory the Great, *Moralia in Iob*, 28.14; emphasis added.
115. St. Gregory the Great, *Moralia in Iob*, 33.34; emphasis added. See Mt 13:47.
116. Origen, *Älteren griechischen Kommentar zum Buch Hiob*, 28.114; emphasis added.

of humankind, and God enters its depths when it is roused from its inmost thoughts to lamentations of penitence through its knowledge of itself, and when he calls to its memory the wickedness of its former life and rouses the mind, which is agitated by its own confusion."[117]

Next, he turns to the cleansing action of God, who, through the Sacrament of Reconciliation, washes away sin and reorders the heart toward charity:

God penetrates the depth of the sea when he changes hearts that are in despair. For he goes into the sea *when he humbles a worldly heart.* He enters the depth of the sea when he does not disdain to visit minds that are even overwhelmed with sins ... From the gates of death are wicked thoughts that we open to God when we confess them with weeping in penitence. He beholds them even when not confessed, but he enters into them when confessed. He then in truth opens a way for himself in the gates of death when we have put aside evil thoughts, *and he comes to us after confession.*[118]

In dealing with the image of the Leviathan, Origen again looks to the Devil. But unlike the previous example, which involved him in an allegorical interpretation of heretics, here it is not so much the Devil as it is the "mask of deceit" with which the Devil tempts the believer, away from virtue to vice: "Why did he not say, '*Who can disclose his face*?' What is the purpose of these doors? 'Who can open,' he says, 'the doors of his face?' In order to understand what is said here, let us take the example of the actors, who wear masks not in order to show what they are but in order to show what they want to look like. Indeed, those who play a certain character on the scene wear masks, so that they sometimes play the role of a general or a king, and often of a woman."[119]

Origen explains:

their real *face is concealed, and they do not show what they are, while only what they want to look like is seen.* The dragon acts in the same way. He never shows his face, but by assuming a mask in order to deceive humankind, he takes advantage of it. The enemy has many masks and wears a mask of virtue for any vice. And who can detect the mask that he wears? Who can disclose and show how the dragon is inside? Such are also his other followers, 'who come to you in sheep's clothing but inwardly are ravenous wolves.[120]

117. St. Gregory the Great, *Moralia in Iob*, 29.27; emphasis added.
118. St. Gregory the Great, *Moralia in Iob*, 29.27; emphasis added.
119. Origen, *Älteren griechischen Kommentar zum Buch Hiob*, 28.95.
120. Origen, *Älteren griechischen Kommentar zum Buch Hiob*, 28.95.

A unique text from St. Ephrem the Syrian involves Job 39 and its mention of many wild animals: mountain goats, donkeys, ostriches, horses, and eagles. Verse 9 reads as follows: "Is the *wild ox* willing to serve you? Will he spend the night at your crib?" The Hebrew term *rêm'* is best translated as "wild ox" as in the Revised Standard Version. Yet the Vulgate (and the Septuagint) had translated it less accurately as *volet Taurus*, a "unicorn."[121]

Following suit, Ephrem commented on the text, with the image of the unicorn in place of the ox:

> This animal, as is reported, is similar to an ox and is found in the austral regions, armed with a single horn. In the unicorn, whoever is not subjected at all to the bondage of the world is covertly represented. It is said to be provided with a single horn, because there is only one truth for the righteous. *Again the human soul is compared with the unicorn, and it must be defined as endowed with a single horn if it is led by a single movement to the top*. Moreover, it is said that the unicorn cannot be caught as its strength and dangerousness are extreme. However, the virgin hunter can win it, after being captured by the pleasure of beauty. So the soul is caught by the things that it has loved.[122]

Critics of the spiritual sense may be inclined to point out that Ephrem's tropological interpretation is rendered invalid by its translation that describes a unicorn instead of an ox. But I make no apology for his exegesis. Ephrem bases his commentary on the best available translations of his time. Regardless, his sublime commentary on the text works, even though the ox has two horns to the one of the "unicorn."

One final example of tropology concerns military images, and of waring armies, in Job 39:19–24. Gregory writes:

> Concerning the exhortation of the captains and the howling of the army, th*e tempting vices that fight against us in invisible contest in behalf of the pride that reigns over them,* some of them go first, like captains, others follow, after the manner of an army. For all faults do not occupy the heart with equal access. But while the greater and the few surprise a neglected mind, the smaller and the numberless pour themselves upon it in a whole body. For when pride, the queen of sins, has fully possessed a conquered heart, she surrenders it immediately to the seven cardinal sins, as if to some of her generals, to lay it waste. And an army follows these generals, because doubtless there spring up from them importunate hosts of sins.[123]

121. For an explanation of this textual issue, see Clines, *Job 38–42*, 1123.
122. St. Ephrem the Syrian, *Commentarii in Job*, 39.35; emphasis added.
123. St. Gregory the Great, *Moralia in Iob*, 31.87; emphasis added.

This type of image works perfectly in *Moralia in Iob*, given that, for Gregory, resisting vice and taking up virtue is a spiritual battle. But it was a battle that *all the members of our body* were actively engaged in. And, characteristic of Gregory, it is not merely the "generals" that one needs to be wary of. It is not the big sins, but "the smaller and numberless soldiers." To Gregory, these signify venial sins. They appear harmless at first. Yet, in time, they progressively overwhelm the person as much as a horde of warriors spring upon and overtake a soldier caught off guard. This encounter scene in Job was mined as richly in the anagogical sense as in the other spiritual senses.

In Job 40:6–8, God for a second time says to Job, *Accinge sicut vir lumbos tuos; interrogabo te, et edoce me*: "Gird up your loins like a man; I will question you, and you declare to me" (v. 7). About this text, Origen leads the believer toward eschatological fulfillment: "*The perfect rewards of the struggles are reserved after this life to those who fought bravely.* The grace of God nevertheless offers a sort of pledge to the athletes. For this reason, Job faced the hardest fights; while losing his riches, he praised him who gave him these afflictions. After losing his children, he glorified him who had taken them away. While realizing that worms grew out of his body, he was not defeated by his diseases. God gave him the firstlings and the pledge of his fights by speaking to him out of the clouds and the whirlwind."[124]

As Origen explains, after Job listened to his friends' speeches, it is as if he is spent, with nothing left to say to God in the crucial moment. Origen even suggests that Job "did not know yet what would have been written by Moses, 'Moses spoke, and God answered him with a voice.'"[125] Beautifully, Origen concludes that Job was a person who "did not know that he did not want to answer God. But God granted him forgiveness to speak. The benevolence of God is such that he does not play the role of the judge but that of the lawyer, who discusses the case with a man."[126] This is all the more interesting, since "the satan" plays the role of the accuser, the prosecuting attorney. Origen knows this and describes God as the wise and compassionate divine counsel.

What Origen wrote in the second century is echoed much later, in what Thomas explained in greater detail. Recall that Thomas dealt

124. Origen, *Älteren griechischen Kommentar zum Buch Hiob*, 28.7.
125. Origen, *Älteren griechischen Kommentar zum Buch Hiob*, 28.7.
126. Origen, *Älteren griechischen Kommentar zum Buch Hiob*, 28.7.

with Job's hesitant speech, and how God's eloquent speech of creation dwarfed his human reasoning, stopping it short. Yet Thomas recognized *the merciful Christ* in God's commanding presence and not a humiliation of Job. Similarly, Origen discerns that it is the benevolent mercy of God, who "comes alongside Job" as a divine Advocate rather than as the Judge. Beneath the logic of both Origen and Thomas is the Johannine theology of "the God who is greater than our own hearts, who does not condemn us."[127]

Elsewhere, in his *Commentary on Job*, St. John Chrysostom looked to heavenly realities and brought out an anagogical interpretation of the text. In Job 38:1, Chrysostom saw Heaven itself in the "storm cloud" out of which the Voice speaks to Job: "In my opinion, he has placed at this stage a cloud over this righteous man in order to raise his thoughts and to persuade him that 'that voice' came 'from above,' as [in the case] of the 'mercy seat placed upon the ark of the Covenant.' *Since the cloud is a symbol of heaven, it is as if God wanted to place heaven itself over Job, as if he had moved his throne near him.*"[128]

"This is what also happened," Chrysostom continues, "it seems to me, 'on the mountain,' when 'the cloud' settled on it, so that we might learn that 'the voice came from above.' Let us listen carefully, because it is the common Master of the universe who speaks. Let us see how he exhorts Job. Does he do it with the same vehemence of humankind? Not at all. Now we find a very clear solution to all the previous, disquieting questions, dear friends, which Job asked and to which we have tried to find a solution."[129] Putting forth a solidly biblical case, Chrysostom refers back to the experience of Moses and the Israelites at Mt. Sinai and the Glory Cloud covering the mountain. He recognized then the parallel experience of Moses and Job. In both cases, God "shielded" them from his face, from his holy presence, even as he brought each of them nearer to himself than the rest of humanity.

Yet another example of anagogical exegesis is seen in Gregory's *Moralia*. He deals with Job 38:8, "The mountains are the pastures that [the Lord] ranges in quest of anything green."[130] Moving through this

127. See 1 Jn 3:20.
128. St. John Chrysostom, *Kommentar zu Hiob*, 38.1.
129. St. John Chrysostom, *Kommentar zu Hiob*, 38.1.
130. Job 39:8, NJB.

text as Chrysostom before him, Gregory discusses the motif of Heaven in a similar fashion:

> Holy Scripture calls "pasture" that green place of eternity where our nourishment will never be spoiled by any drought. About this pasture the psalmist says, "The Lord is my shepherd, and I will never lack anything. In a green place, there he gave me rest."[131] And again, "We are his people and herd of his pasture."[132] And the Truth himself says about *these pastures, "If one enters through me, he will be saved and will get out and will find pasture."*[133] *They go to pasture because, after going out of their body, they find the eternal green pastures.* They go out and do not go back to them, because, *after being received in that joyful contemplation,* they do not need to hear the words of those who teach.[134]

He concludes, "And so, after going out they do not go back to them, because after escaping the afflictions of life, they do not seek to receive any longer from the doctors the doctrine of life."[135]

A final anagogical text comes from Book XXII of Augustine's *City of God.* There, Augustine interprets Job 42:5 ("I had heard of thee by the hearing of the ear, but now my eye sees thee") in light of the resurrection of the body: "The eye, then, shall have a vastly superior power—the power not of keen sight, such as is ascribed to serpents or eagles, for however keenly these animals see, they can discern nothing but bodily substances—but the power of seeing things incorporeal." What does this signify? "Possibly," Augustine says, "*it was this great power of vision which was temporarily communicated to the eyes of the holy Job* while yet in this mortal body, when he says to God, 'I have heard of Thee by the hearing of the ear; but now mine eye seeth Thee: wherefore I abhor myself, and melt away, and count myself dust and ashes.'"[136]

The first thing Augustine explains is that "seeing" refers to the eyes of the heart and not a physical seeing.[137] After providing additional examples, he returns to the text from Job and continues, "As for the words of the above-mentioned Job, as they are found in the Hebrew manuscripts, 'And *in my flesh* I shall see God,' *no doubt they were a prophecy of*

131. Ps 23:1.
132. Ps 95:7.
133. Jn 10:9.
134. St. Gregory the Great, *Moralia in Iob*, 30.49.
135. St. Gregory the Great, *Moralia in Iob*, 30.49.
136. St. Augustine, *City of God*, XXII.29.4.
137. See Mt 5:8.

the resurrection of the flesh; yet he does not say '*by* the flesh.' And indeed, if he had said this, it would still be possible that Christ was meant by 'God'; for Christ shall be seen *by the flesh in the flesh*."[138]

Concluding Remarks

Several distinctive elements characterize our investigation of this encounter. First, I drew a great deal upon St. Thomas Aquinas to get at the literal meaning of the text. This may have come as something of a surprise to some, yet it ought not. The patristic and medieval masters of Scripture knew and made use of the literal sense regularly. Yet most did not, so they restrict themselves to the literal alone. For Thomas and all the great ancient and medieval masters, the literal was the foundational sense from which one launched out into the deeper mysteries of Scripture, only accessible through the spiritual senses of the allegorical, the tropological, and the anagogical.

A second distinction of this particular encounter scene has to do with the literal sense. In this analysis, we saw that the poetics of the book play an instrumental role in the "ascent to God." The prior encounter scene, from the Song of Songs, also involved poetry. But the poetry in Job actually reveals the theological architecture of the book—especially the relation of Job to his three friends—and of Job (and all of humanity) in relation to the "Voice from the Whirlwind," to God. What sets apart the poetry of Job from other books is the way that it is carefully calibrated to the speaker and their nearness—or lack thereof—to the truth of God.

Through all Four Senses, a recurrent pattern was evident: *mercy*. Here, then, is another surprise in studying the Book of Job. Many are quick to associate the book with suffering or Job's patience through his many trials. These themes do register throughout the book, but the primary question in the book is not really "Why do bad things happen to good people?" but rather "Is there justice in the Godhead?"

The book's author carefully overturned the conventional quid pro quo understanding about divine retribution or reward and punishment as it relates to human sin. Along these lines, we discovered that while "the satan" does pay a decisive role in the book, it is only in the prelim-

138. St. Augustine, *City of God*, XXII.29.5.

inary stages of the book. By the end of the book, he is nowhere to be found. Instead, the true antagonists—who had also been present from the beginning—emerge: Eliphaz, Bildad, and Zophar. It is not that they are "bad" people. At the onset of his trial, they do comfort him, weeping and tearing their robes. They remain with him for seven days, and beautifully "spoke not a word, for they saw that his suffering was very great."[139]

As the cycle of respective debates between these antagonists and Job unfolds, however, it becomes clearer and clearer—both theologically and poetically—that the "upright and blameless" Job does not bend or break before them. Rather, he withstands their barrage of insolent words, all aimed at getting Job to repent his sins and beg for God's forgiveness. Job *more than withstands* their assaults; he triumphs over them, stubbornly, shortsightedly, and at times impatiently. Yet, in the end, he escapes their "net of causality," for the one thing Job knows is that he truly is innocent of any wrongdoing.

And so, in the end, Job stands before God. And he must simply listen. Gradually his mouth is silenced, and his heart is opened before the One who "laid the foundations of the earth,"[140] who "shut in the sea with doors,"[141] who "loosed the cords of Orion"[142] before the One who "gives the horse its might"[143] and "draws out Leviathan with a fishhook."[144] And in this silence and stillness, Job is offered mercy as God comes near.

Through this "accessible proximity," Job meets the One—and only One—who can redeem him. Even though his "intimate friends abhor" him,[145] even though his heart "faints within" him,[146] he is not alone. His *gōʾel*—his redeemer—truly does live,[147] One that hears and sees, and in his mercy forgives. And so Job can in freedom cry, *Miseremini mei, miseremini mei*—"have mercy on me, have mercy on me"[148]—

139. See Job 2:11–13.
140. Job 38:4.
141. Job 38:8.
142. Job 38:31.
143. Job 39:19.
144. Job 41:1.
145. Job 19:19.
146. See Job 19:27.
147. See Job 19:25.
148. Job 19:21.

not to his friends, for there is little mercy to be found there—but to YHWH, who is the *miqôr chăyyîm*, the fountain of life.[149]

Meditatio Quinta

As with so many theophanies and encounter scenes in Scripture, there are often more questions than answers. This is certainly the case with the Book of Job. According to Peter Kreeft, there is one question, above all others, that Job asks: "The greatest of all questions, the question that includes all other questions, is the one Job asks God in Job 10:18: 'Why did you bring me out of the womb?' In other words, *what kind of a story am I in?*"[150] Kreeft's response once again brings Moses back into the picture:

> It is Ecclesiastes' question, too, but Job gets an answer, while Ecclesiastes does not. Pascal calls them the two greatest philosophers, and I agree. *But why did Job get an answer and Ecclesiastes not?* For the same reason Moses got an answer to the questions about which philosophers had speculated endlessly and fruitlessly for ages: Who is God? What is his name? What is his nature? Moses had the good sense to ask him![151] Ecclesiastes is like Job's three friends: endlessly philosophizing *about* God. Job is like Moses: Job asks *God*; he seeks God's face. And "all who seek, find."[152]

Job seeks God's face. And he is not disappointed, for he sees the face of Mercy. It is a mercy that points to Christ himself, as we saw in chapter 7. "This world is 'a vale of soul making,' a great sculptor's shop, and we are the statues. To be finished, the statues must endure many blows of the chisel and be hardened in the fire. This is not optional. Once we lost our original innocence, the way back to God *has* to be painful, for the Old Man of sin will keep on complaining and paining at each step toward his enemy, goodness."[153] Figuring out "what sort of story we are in," as Kreeft puts it, ought to be right up there with food, clothing, and shelter, in the hierarchy of human needs. Yet for a host of reasons—many that we have no control over, others of which we do—this quest gets pushed aside as we pursue "the tyranny of the urgent."

In truth, few things are more urgent, more demanding than under-

149. Ps 36:9.
150. Kreeft, *Three Philosophies of Life*, 84; emphasis added.
151. See Ex 3:14.
152. Kreeft, *Three Philosophies of Life*, 84; emphases added.
153. Kreeft, *Three Philosophies of Life*, 85; emphases added.

standing the story in which we live, move, and cash checks. In Scripture, there are essentially two types of persons. There are those who "get it" and those who don't in terms of what's happening and what is called for by God. There are of course the immediate examples that spring to mind: Moses gets it, Pharaoh doesn't. Peter gets it, Judas doesn't. Mary and Joseph get it. Herod does not.

But it's not always as obvious as one might think. it's not a matter of one's "tribe"—Ruth gets it, as does Rahab. Joseph of Arimathea *shouldn't* get it, but he does. As does Nicodemus. Many of Jesus's nearest relatives in Nazareth apparently do not. One's station in life, family of origin, wealth, or lack thereof, gender, religious beliefs—none of these things are as important as answering the question, *What sort of story am I in?* This why theophanies and other encounter scenes are so valuable, such teachable moments. In them, *the veil is pulled back*, and ordinary human beings peer at "the face of the Lord." Whatever they see, sense, or hear, they are brought up "into the mystery."

Take for example our first scene with Jacob. This stubborn, crafty, and shrewd "heel grabber" is transformed into "one who struggles with God and men, and prevails." His close encounter not only cements his relationship with the Lord but also may have saved him from the hands of his brother! And that is precisely the point. We shouldn't read such scenes because they feature burning bushes, lightning, glowing faces, or other special effects. We should be interested in them because of what they tell us about God—that he is real, that he is present, and that he desires to be known by us. Theophanies are not only theologically rich for what they reveal about God. They also contain a great amount of insight into the human condition. Jesus's Transfiguration on Tabor is one of the most spectacular moments recorded in the Gospels. And though it can't be easily proven, one suspects that it was one of the things that "steadied" Peter after Jesus's Crucifixion. It was not until the risen Jesus meets him and the others on the shore of the Sea of Galilee that things change dramatically, when Jesus "reinstates" and commissions Peter to "feed My sheep."[154] Yet the moment on Mt. Tabor, when Jesus momentarily revealed his divine glory, was a decisive turn for Peter, James, and John.

Theophanies and encounter scenes are a special gift to us in Sacred Scripture. Through them we see the invisible glory of God, manifest in

154. Jn 21, esp. v. 17.

visual and palpable ways. They are clothed with mystery and saturated in Christological meaning. Whether it is Jacob wrestling with the angel, Moses on the mountain, Isaiah's Servant, the poetic exchanges of the Bridegroom and his Beloved, or Job's encounter with the Voice, these remarkable scenes bring us near to the face of the Lord. The help us to contemplate the divine Son. They remind us all of what story of story we are in. And they restore our humanity by reminding us that *we need faces to see his face.*

Peter Kreeft sums it up this way: "Saying 'not my will but thine be done' was ecstatic joy in Eden and will be in Heaven, but it is life's most difficult (and most necessary) task now. Without it, we have no face with which to face God. Why could Job see God face to face and live? Because Job got a face through his suffering faith. As C. S. Lewis says at the end of his novel *Till We Have Faces*, '*How can we meet the gods face to face till we have faces*?'"[155]

155. Kreeft, *Three Philosophies of Life*, 85; emphases added.

PART III

Finis

CHAPTER 9

Finalis Meditatio Mea

The Face of Christ in the Old Testament

> We have too restricted a sense of the revelation of the Triune God found in the Law and the Prophets. If the God of Abraham, Isaac, and Jacob is truly the Father of our Lord Jesus Christ, then the witness of the entire Scripture is a seamless garment.
>
> —Fleming Rutledge, *And God Said to Abraham*

Seeking the Face of God in Faith

Walter Moberly, English scholar and professor of biblical interpretation at Durham University, once wrote, "To be Christian means, at least in part, the acceptance and appropriation of certain theological doctrines and patterns of living. Yet the task of reading the Bible 'critically' has regularly been defined precisely in terms of the exclusion of these doctrines and patterns of living from the interpretive process."[1] This book has sought to bridge this gap—a chasm about which Moberly is appropriately concerned. This project involved approaching Scripture with the *Letter* and the *Spirit* in a manner that sought to respect both dimensions of biblical interpretation—that is, critically and theologically. There really is no truer way to "put on"[2] the Scriptures: "The Christian receives the letter and the spirit like a double garment."[3] As

1. Moberly, *Bible, Theology, and Faith*, 5.
2. See Col 3:10–12, 3:14.
3. De Lubac, *History and Spirit*, 205.

stressed at the outset, the reader will determine what degree of success was achieved in the investigation.

All of our efforts have put the reader on a journey and (at least Scripturally speaking) nearer to *the face of the Lord*. From the great patriarch Jacob to the lawgiver Moses and on to the holy prophet Isaiah, we have observed in Guardini's words their "accessible proximity" to God in and through various encounter scenes. Not limiting ourselves to the Torah and *Nebi'im* (Law and Prophets), we engaged the section of the Hebrew canon known as the *Kethubim* (Writings). There, we peered at the face of the Lord in Song with the Bridegroom and Bride, and with the "blameless and upright" Job.

In the process, we too have been granted accessible proximity to the face of the Lord through the inspired Scriptures. At the conclusion of our journey, this is a critical point not to be missed, in part because of the mystery of the Scriptures themselves. They do not merely *record* encounters with the face of the Lord—they *are* an encounter with the face of the Lord. And not merely one encounter, but many. Every reader who peers out with Moses, from the cleft of the rock, experiences *a distinct encounter with the face of God*. The text itself does not change, but the reception of it does. It is born anew in the reader's mind and heart. There, one "wrestles" the angel alongside Jacob and "hears" the Voice from the Whirlwind with Job. In addition, each reading of the text—even by the same reader—brings new sightings of the One, True, Living God.

How is this possible? How can such countless variations reveal God to us, as diverse individuals yet as the one "assembly of the faithful" (Ps 149:1)? And even now, at the end of our contemplation of the encounter scenes, it is worth asking again: *How is it even possible?* The Old and New Testaments are of one accord on the matter: "You cannot see My face" (Ex 33:20) and "No one has seen God" (Jn 1:18).

Our topic is mysterious. All of the "answers" that presented themselves over the course of our study somehow elude us, remaining just out of grasp. Like the very name of God, *I AM*, every attempt to "conclusively define" him evades us. Even so, our search was far from fruitless. Jesus is the Logos Incarnate, the God-Man, the divine Son made manifest in the flesh. With Jesus, we really do see the face of the Lord. *He who has seen Me has seen the Father.*[4]

4. Jn 14:9.

When we *stay with Christ*, we are near to the face of the invisible God. As Ratzinger explains, the Hebrew word *pānîm*—"face"—is "a term that describes relationships."[5] And since all of these encounter scenes involve, one way or another, "seeing" the face of God, something new of our relationship with God is revealed in the process. "Let us be sure of this: the Hebrew term *pānîm* recognizes God as a person, a being concerned about us, who hears and sees us, speaks to us, and can love us and be angry at us—as the God who is above all and yet still has a face."[6]

Because the God revealed in the Scriptures has a face and a name, he is knowable and knows us: "In this, man is similar to him; man is his *image; from the face, man can recognize who and what and how God is. He is referred to this face; in his innermost being he is in search of it.*"[7] Here, near the end, we press a point made earlier in the book. Although Jacob, Moses, and the others "searched for God," like the Parable of the Prodigal Son, it is the Father who *first searches out us* and invites us to search for him. What compelled Jacob to wrestle the angel?[8] What was it that led Moss to cry out, "*Show me Your Glory*"?[9] And what of Isaiah's *Servant Songs* and the *Suffering Servant* revealed there?[10] What led the "Shulamite" to find the one "whom *my soul loves*"?[11] How did Job withstand so much, to yet stand and exclaim, "*I had heard of thee by the hearing of the ear, but now my eye sees thee*?"[12] Was it not the God who saw them "yet at a distance," who ran to them and embraced and kissed them?[13]

There is a decisive trait among by those in Scripture to whom God came near. They were gifted with the privilege of *seeing* him in a clearer and closer way. This quality goes by different names. In the New Testament, it is usually associated with the word "faith." In the Old Testament, it is often referred to as "righteousness." This seems to be the necessary ingredient, the common denominator that allowed each of them

5. Ratzinger, *On the Way to Jesus Christ*, 18.
6. Ratzinger, *On the Way to Jesus Christ*, 19–20.
7. Ratzinger, *On the Way to Jesus Christ*, 20; emphasis added.
8. See Gn 32:24.
9. Ex 33:20; emphasis added.
10. See esp. Isa 53:1*ff*.
11. Song 3:4; emphasis added.
12. Job 42:5; emphasis added.
13. See Lk 15:20.

to, in some sense, "see" the face of the Lord. This characteristic—of faith or righteousness—opens up humanity more fully to the presence of God, to the Person of God, the face of God. In Scripture, God comes near to Noah, to Abraham, to Hannah and Ruth, and to countless others in the Old Testament—some of whom we have discussed here.

Over the pages of this book, we have contemplated the face of God. We have peered over the shoulder of Jacob and all the others. And although it was God who *initiated contact* in each biblical episode, a kind of tenacious faith was instrumental, crucial in receiving this gift. By faith, and only by faith, they encountered the face of the Lord. Thinking about these biblical "giants" calls to mind a contrast. By highlighting those who did see the face of the Lord, those who did not see are brought into sharp relief. After all, it was Moses—not Pharaoh—who cried out, "*I pray, show me Thy glory*" (emphasis added). And it was Jacob—not Esau—who summoned the courage to grapple with the angel. In order for Isaiah to be given his prophetic vision of the *One Who is to Come*, he first needed to acknowledge to God that he was a "man of unclean lips."[14]

It was not Eliphaz, Bildad, or Zophar who "heard" the Voice speaking from the whirlwind. It was Job. Likewise, it was not Herod, Caiaphas, nor Pilate who really "saw" Jesus. It was Peter, Zacchaeus, the Samaritan woman. This may provoke a certain fear, but it should elicit hope: *hoi katharoi tē kardia*—it is *the pure in heart* who shall "see God."[15] One doesn't need to be the firstborn, Esau. We simply need to be willing *to "not let go" until God blesses us.*[16]

If asked to "put out into the deep," we need to do so.[17] And if we even *think we see him*, we need to leap into the sea.[18] If asked to received Jesus into our house, we need to get down from our tree.[19] And open the door.[20] And if he is standing in front of us offering "living water," we need to drink it lavishly.[21] And invite others to do the same.[22]

14. Isa 6:4.
15. Mt 5:8.
16. See Gn 32:26.
17. See Lk 5:4.
18. See Jn 21:7.
19. See Lk 19:5–5.
20. See Rv 3:20.
21. See Jn 4:13–15.
22. See Jn 4:39–42.

To see the face of the Lord, we must *stay with Jesus.* Indeed, to "see" God is to see Love, to see Life, Freedom, Truth, Mercy, and Grace.

When God turns his face toward Abraham, and toward each of us, it is Beauty that is seen. Yet the opposite is true: "Wherever God turns away his face, everything eventually returns to dust. Therefore the petition that God not hide his countenance is *a prayer for life itself, for the power of sight, without which nothing can be good.* God's silence, the concealment of his countenance, is punishment in and of itself. Of course, when God hides himself, the sinner may experience a false sense of security: it seems that God does not exist at all. One can safely live without him, in opposition to him, turning one's back upon him—*or so it seems.*"[23] According to Ratzinger, it is "Precisely this security of the godless man [that] is his most serious trouble. In times when God is silent, in a time when his face seems to have become unrecognizable, should we not reflect with some alarm upon the significance of God's concealment? *Should we not view it as the true fate to which the world is doomed and call upon God all the louder and more urgently for him to show his countenance?* Is not the search for his face that much more urgent in this situation?"[24]

The Many Faces of the One Christ

Through the encounter scenes examined in this book, at least five portraits of Christ were revealed. Working with both the literal and the spiritual senses, we have sought to first ascertain, as best as possible, the intentions of the author of the text. Not stopping there, however, we have sought to ascend further into the mystery. With Origen, we recognize that "*the spirit is in the letter like honey in its honeycomb.*"[25]

First, in Jacob's encounter (Gn 32–33) we met *the brotherly Christ.* In his struggle with the angel, Jacob sees "the face of God," yet as with Moses after him, God's face remains veiled. Even so, Jacob's experience is not a falsification or a mere boast. God "came near" to him, and Jacob's life was transformed. His name is changed to Israel, for he "strove with God and prevailed." And all who come after him, identified by that

23. Ratzinger, *On the Way to Jesus Christ*, 24; emphases added.
24. Ratzinger, *On the Way to Jesus Christ*, 24; emphases added.
25. Origen, cited in de Lubac, *History and Spirit*, 205; emphasis added.

name—Israel—bear something of Jacob in their own lives. Not merely as their great ancestor. As an exemplar, as one *who would not let go of God*, no matter what adversity is encountered. Defined this way, it is not only the Israelites who "belong" to Jacob but also all who call on God's name. In Baptism, the Christian is given a new name, for a new birth has begun in Christ, the New Jacob.

A second way in which Jacob's life was changed at Peni'el was in relation to Esau, his brother. The animosity between these twins from the womb need not be recalled here. By all logic and human reasoning, their brotherly strife, marked by a long and painful absence, should have culminated in a decisive battle. Instead, their reunion was met with an unexpected peace, on both sides. Nothing but Jacob's encounter with "the face of God" could so transform his stony heart into one of compassion—and—joy—at the sight of his estranged brother. Upon seeing him Jacob cries out, "*for truly to see your face is like seeing the face of God.*"[26] Because the face of the Lord is tender, compassionate, longsuffering, and above all illumined with *reconciling grace*, one cannot gaze upon him and not be radically changed.

Perhaps what is most astonishing is that Jacob did not *actually* gaze upon the face of God. In his humanity, however, he is so lifted up by the encounter, beyond his own frailty. Jacob was touched not only at "the hollow of his thigh"[27] but also in his thorny heart. Though it was consumed by pride, jealousy, fear, and anger, Jacob's heart was touched by divine love. Christ's light shone in the darkness there, enlarging it and making new relationships possible, between him and God and between him and his brother. Christ is *more than a brother*—he is Lord, he is God, he is Savior. But he is not *less than a brother*. In his Incarnation, we are met by the God-Man, and one who alone can teach us what it means to be loved with divine love, that we too might love one another "with brotherly affection" (Rom 12:10). The New Jacob has not kept his face from us but gazes at us from his Cross and beckons to behold "the one whom they have pierced."[28]

Christ, the divine Son, who extends to us his brotherly grace, has now reconciled us "in his body of flesh by his death," to present us holy

26. Gn 33:10; emphasis added.
27. Gn 32:25.
28. Jn 19:37; see Zec 12:10.

and blameless and irreproachable before him.[29] It is through Christ that a new brotherhood—conceived not by human reasoning or human efforts but by the grace poured out by the New Jacob—is entirely possible. It is open for all who look upon him with the eyes of faith. That we too may rise up and exclaim to another, *seeing you is like seeing the face of God.*

A second portrait of Christ was revealed in Moses's theophanic experience (Ex 33). Whereas the previous scene illuminated the brotherly Christ of a new humanity, this episode accentuated the *glorious* Christ. Throughout salvation history, recorded in the Old Testament, the *kavôd* of God, the glory of God shone upon his people. From Adam's experience in Eden, to Moses atop Sinai, to the Pillar of Fire through many long wilderness nights, God did not withhold his glory from his people. Yet neither were they allowed to look directly upon it. As God's agent, Moses was drawn closer to the *kavôd* of God than any other before or after him—until the appearance of the New Moses.

Only because of Christ can the Apostle John announce that "*the eternal life which was with the Father and was made manifest to us*."[30] However magnificent the experience of Moses, as recorded in the Book of Exodus, St. John's encounter surpasses it; he truly "*beheld His glory*."[31] Peter, John, and all of the Apostles did not merely see him in the eyes of their heart or in the cleft of the rock. Rather, *quod vidimus oculis nostris*—"with our eyes."[32] It is the *enfleshed Christ*—Christ in the feeding trough at Bethlehem, Christ in the Temple, and atop Tabor, Christ atop the Mount of Beatitudes in Galilee, and above all Christ pierced to the Cross at Golgotha—that Mary and the Apostles saw. This is "the hour," the moment in time and space, "for the Son of Man to be glorified."[33] For this reason, John concludes his prologue this way: "*For the law was given through Moses, but grace and truth came through Jesus Christ*."[34]

Reflecting on these key distinctions between Moses and Christ, the author of Hebrews writes that Christ "was faithful to him who appoint-

29. Col 1:22.
30. 1 Jn 1:2; emphasis added.
31. Jn 1:14c.
32. 1 Jn 1:1.
33. Jn 12:23.
34. Jn 1:17; emphasis added.

ed him, as Moses was faithful in God's house. Yet Jesus has been counted worthy of *hoson pleinos doxēs* ("as much more glory") than Moses as the builder of a house has more honor than the house ... Now Moses was faithful in all God's house as a servant, to testify to the things that were to be spoken later, but Christ was faithful over God's house as a son."[35]

"Christ is not merely the servant of God's house. He is the Son and Lord over it. Christ is not merely the agent of God. He is the divine Agent, the Logos-Son who was *with* God in the beginning."[36] Moses prayed, *Lord, show me Your glory.* And God granted him "accessible proximity" as he passed by. Yet *Christ is the glory of God:* "He reflects the glory of God and bears the very stamp of his nature, upholding the universe by his word of power."[37] To see the face of God, we must *stay with* the New Moses.

Moses's experience of nearness to God was, in the Old Covenant, unsurpassed. And his encounter in the wilderness, tucked safely in the rock, was not the only one. God appeared to him at the Flaming Bush Not Consumed by Fire. He revealed his name to Moses.[38] And, after receiving the Law at Sinai, Moses, along with Aaron and his sons, and the elders of Israel, "beheld God, and ate and drank."[39]

Upon his death on the mountains of Moab, however, there was still more of the face of God yet to behold. Mysteriously, on Mt. Tabor, along with Elijah, Moses would gaze—along with Peter, James, and John—upon the One who from all eternity gazed upon the Father. In his commentary on the Transfiguration scene in the Gospel According to Luke,[40] St. Cyril of Alexandria explains Moses's presence: "For it is true that the Law was given through Moses, and the teaching of the holy prophets, revealed in advance of the Mystery of Christ: Moses suggesting *only in images and shadows, as if in a painting* ... that he would be seen in time *in a form like ours*, and that for the well-being and life of all of us he would not refuse to suffer on a cross."[41]

Later, Leo VI, the emperor of Byzantium (866–912) and known as

35. Heb 3:2–6a.
36. Jn 1:1; emphasis added.
37. Heb 1:3.
38. See Ex 3–4.
39. Ex 24:9–10.
40. Lk 9:28–36.
41. St. John Chrysostom, *Homily 51 on Luke*, in Daley, *Light on the Mountain*, 101; emphasis added.

"Leo the Wise," wrote a homily of a similar sort. Drawing together what was learned about the "pathway and progression" to the face of God in the encounter scene in Exodus, with the Transfiguration of the Lord, we conclude our remarks on the "glorious" Christ with his words:

> But for now, let us go up with the Master as he climbs the mountain, and share with him in the Mysteries he accomplished there. Let no one be left behind by his own choice, nor remain inactive because he is unable to climb; *for Christ does not want anyone to remain below, buts wants us to ascend and be initiated into the Mystery he experiences. Let eyes feast upon this sight, until which even today the sun has not witnessed.* Let them gaze on the one who is "wrapped in light as a cloak," radiating light from his garments, and illuminating his earthly covering with sparks of immaterial light. Let us stand and participate in the choicest words of the disciples and the prophets, and let us become sharers in these delights with them.[42]

A third portrait of Christ, seen in the divine tapestry of the Old Testament, was offered by the prophet Isaiah. His fourth Servant Song[43] reveals the face of the "suffering Christ." This depiction of the One Who Is To Come, however painful and even grotesque, is a vital encounter scene in the Old Testament and a shadow of the reality of Christ in the New Testament. Christ's mission can never be separated from his Cross. In his first epistle to the Corinthian Church, St. Paul makes this clear:

> Where is the wise man? Where is the scribe? Where is the debater of this age? Has not God made foolish the wisdom of the world? For since, in the wisdom of God, the world did not know God through wisdom, it pleased God through the folly of what we preach to save those who believe. For Jews demand signs and Greeks seek wisdom, but we preach Christ crucified, a stumbling block to Jews and folly to Gentiles, but to those who are called, both Jews and Greeks, Christ the power of God and the wisdom of God. For the foolishness of God is wiser than men, and the weakness of God is stronger than men.[44]

Fleming Rutledge aptly remarked, "there is theological gold in Isaiah 53."[45] As she explains, this chapter "gives strong support to the affirmation that *the suffering of the Messiah* is part of the plan of God for

42. Leo the Emperor, "A Homily on Christ the King," in Daley, *Light on the Mountain*, 239; emphasis added.

43. See Isa 52–53.

44. 1 Cor 1:20–25.

45. Rutledge, *Crucifixion*, 475.

salvation revealed proleptically to ancient Israel."[46] Paradoxically, Isaiah 52–53 contains yet another facet of the face of the Lord, aside from the obvious "suffering Christ," that we have reflected upon. In and through the song of the *Suffering Servant* is true beauty—the face of the "beautiful Christ." As Ratzinger explains,

> When we turn to the text from Isaiah, a question arises at first of whether or not Christ was beautiful, a question that interested the Fathers of the Church. Implied here is the more radical question of whether beauty is true or whether perhaps ugliness leads us to the actual truth of reality. Whoever believes in God, in the God who revealed himself precisely in the distorted figure of Christ crucified as Love "to the end,"[47] knows that *beauty is truth and truth beauty;* but in the suffering Christ he also learns that the beauty of truth also involves wounds, pain, and even the obscure mystery of death and that this can only be found in accepting pain, not in ignoring it.[48]

In our own search for the true and the beautiful, it is the Passion of Christ that grounds us firmly in them. There, above all, the true and the beautiful are painfully yet graciously interwoven. It is not as though suffering has been obliterated, or thwarted, from causing humanity harm, despair, and death. Rather, suffering has been *transcended:* "In the Passion of Christ ... the experience of the beautiful has received a new depth and a new realism. The One who is beauty itself let himself be struck in the face, spat upon, crowned with thorns—the Shroud of Turin can help us realize this in a moving way. Yet precisely in this Face that is so disfigured, there appears the genuine, the ultimate beauty: the beauty of love that goes 'to the very end' and thus proves to be mightier than falsehood and violence."[49] To see the face of the Lord, we must *stay with*—and embrace—the Father's Suffering Servant.

We can only but mention the last two—the Song of Songs and of the Book of Job. In these poetic encounter scenes, we gaze upon the "bridegroom Christ" and the "merciful Christ." It is fitting that they are united here: he who is the faithful Lover is the face of Mercy in person. The fourth encounter scene in Song reminds us that the Church is always more than what is seen, more than a visible institution. It is at the same time "mystery," a great sacrament and sign of God's love in the

46. Rutledge, *Crucifixion*, 475; emphasis added.
47. Jn 13:1.
48. Ratzinger, *On the Way to Jesus Christ*, 34; emphasis added.
49. Ratzinger, *On the Way to Jesus Christ*; 39.

world. She is the mystical Body whose Head is the divine Bridegroom. The Church is his Beloved, and she belongs to her Spouse. The love of the Bridegroom is *oblative*, *sacrificial*, and *eternal*. It cannot be bought or sold. It "bears all things, believes all things, hopes all things, endures all things."[50] This *agape* of the nuptial Christ, the Lover of the Church and the Lover of the soul, held him upon the Cross so that he might present his beloved to himself "in splendor, without spot or wrinkle or any such thing, that she might be holy and without blemish."[51] To see the face of God, we must *stay* with Jesus and allow ourselves to be held in the holy arms of the divine Bridegroom.

Lastly, the fifth encounter scene in Job leads us to the face of the "merciful Christ." Only by coming to the end of himself is Job able to truly hear the Voice from the Whirlwind. At first, it appears as though this Voice has only bewildered Job, rendered him silent. Yet it is in his *silence* that Job is able to hear Mercy speak to him. Through all of his trials, Job talks and talks and talks. But his "windy words" are not able to give him what he needs most: *saving*. To be silent is to be *vulnerable*, which is one of the reasons the ancient and medieval theologians saw in Job a shadow of Jesus himself, silent before his accusers.

Job learns that there is a difference between hearing and seeing, and more specifically between *hearing of* and *being seen*. Only in his silence, fully exposed and naked, is he able to hear the Voice of Mercy. Finally, Job grasps that he is *seen* and not merely heard. And in this vulnerability Job mysteriously sees the face of the Lord: "I had heard of thee by the hearing of the ear, *but now my eye sees thee*."[52]

To see the face of the Lord, we must attune our ears to hear the Voice of Mercy. In these five ways, and countless others not touched upon in this book, the Scriptures do provide an answer to our great question, *Can we see the face of the Lord?* What begins as a whisper grows louder and clearer, until it thunders like a chorus of the archangels themselves. Yes—yes we can gaze upon the face of the Lord. But to arrive at our destiny, we must *stay with Jesus*.

Oh Jesus, help us to stay with you. For to behold you is to behold the face of God.

50. 1 Cor 13:7.
51. Eph 5:27.
52. Job 42:5; emphasis added.

Ascending the Ladder to the Face of God

These five scenes have paid many dividends with respect to contemplating the divine Son in Sacred Scripture: *the brotherly Christ*, *the glorious Christ*, *the suffering Christ*, *the Bridegroom Christ*, and *the merciful Christ.* But they are by no means the only portraits of the face of the Lord in the Old Testament. What portrait is revealed in the experience of Adam in the Garden? Of the slain Abel? Of Isaac, placed upon the wood of the altar? And of Aaron, arrayed in his priestly garments? What of David, the shepherd? Of Jonah, in the stomach of the whale? Of Daniel, Jeremiah, and even Lady Wisdom? What of the Psalmist and each of their hymns? The Lamb of the Passover and the Ark of the Covenant? Of the Temple we have already spoken, and in *The House of the Lord* were portraits of the New Temple, the True Priest, the Spotless Victim. To these countless more could be added from the Old Testament.

As the New Testament opens, *a new world* appears, revealing vivid portraits of Jesus in the flesh. No longer are the portraits monochromatic, mere echoes. Now, they are *the living reality* of the Face of God in Person. So new is the world of the New Testament that the nature of the Four Senses are themselves transformed. As indicated at the beginning of the book, it is as if the raison d'être of the allegorical sense fades into the sea, as the Word become flesh speaks, and says, "*He who has seen me has seen the Father.*"[53]

Bucur's recent work *Scripture Re-envisioned* is a significant step forward in articulating what is happening when such Old Testament texts are read in light of Christ. Rather than Ephraim Radner's term of figural readings, de Lubac's allegory, or Daniélou's preference for typology, Bucur describes the exegesis of such texts as *Christophanic:*

> Neither "allegory" nor "typology" (nor the more recent terms of "figural" and "figurative") capture the epiphanic claim underlying the identification of Jesus Christ with the divine manifestation to the patriarchs and prophets of Israel... The term "rewritten Bible" is also inadequate, because the Christian "rewriting" of theophanies does not express itself in the production of a new text, but in a new reading of the existing texts. I have therefore used the term "Christophanic exegesis" to designate this performative, experientially (liturgically) located

53. Jn 14:9; emphasis added.

exegesis that discerns and affirms the presence of Christ—not a literary reality but an epiphanic "real presence"—in the theophanic accounts of the Old Testament and in the very act of exegeting such texts.[54]

The thesis of this book is that the Four Senses of Sacred Scripture represent a pathway and a progression toward the face of the Lord. Through the encounter scenes of the Old Testament, we have gazed upon his face. We have seen that the Four Senses are not merely various ways of interpreting the Scriptures. Collectively, they truly represent something more than that. When coupled together, one *ascends the ladder of God*, to borrow the monk Guigo's phrase. And while there are other portraits yet to look upon, and to contemplate, the Four Senses have opened up countless insights into the Christ of the Old Testament. Finally, it is hoped that as one moves from the Old to the New Testament, this book deepens one's curiosity, as well as one's appetite, to gaze on the face of Jesus Christ, the divine Son in Scripture.

Ultima Dicta: Final Impressions on the Completion of a Trilogy

This book is the conclusion of a trilogy. All three volumes deal with Sacred Scripture. This volume, as well as the previous one, *The House of the Lord*, might not have become what they are without the seven principles of Catholic Scripture study, as sketched out in the first volume, *The Word of the Lord.* As important as these concepts are, however, principles are merely the foundation upon which to build. In numerous ways, *The House of the Lord* and *The Face of the Lord* are the produce of the tree from which they steadily grew. Whatever fruit this trilogy offers to the reader—and I hope there is a bounty—there is one significant point to mention, something that I have sought to convey in many ways across this trilogy: Sacred Scripture is a great mystery. It is in fact an unfathomable chain of mysteries linked together by narrative and by the Spirit. It can never be reduced to history alone, nor to the intellect alone, yet that has been a characteristic of much modern criticism. Fortunately, such was not always the case.

As Wilken writes, "Early Christian thinkers moved in the world of the Bible, understood its idiom, loved its teaching, *and were filled with*

54. Bucur, *Scripture Re-envisioned*, 276.

awe before its mysteries. They believed in the maxim, 'Scripture interprets Scripture.' They knew something that has largely been forgotten by biblical scholars."[55] Wilken's analysis is prescient. Still, this trilogy has not advocated a return to the patristic or medieval ages in a nostalgic or sentimental way. Rather, it has sought to encourage a new hermeneutical momentum going forward. The hermeneutic of these books rests upon sound Catholic principles. It also rests upon the idea of mystery.

Because Scripture is indeed a great mystery, it must be ever encountered anew. And so the distinctive advantages of biblical criticism today can be wedded to the wisdom of the ages. Our examination of the five episodes from Scripture in the present volume, according to all four senses of Scripture, is but one modest effort in this regard. My vision is that the wise integration of exegesis and theology may together usher forth new and delicious fruit from the Master's vineyard, leading us to the face of Jesus Christ.

Oh Jesus, help us to stay with you. For to behold you is to behold the face of God.

55. Wilken, *Isaiah*, xi.

BIBLIOGRAPHY

In addition to the sources listed below, the reader is advised to consult William Harmless's "Bibliographies for Theology" at the website for the *Journal of Religion and Society*, accessed December 14, 2019, http://moses.creighton.edu/JRS/toc/bibliographies.html. See also the Sant'Agostino website, accessed December 14, 2019, www.augustinus.it/latino/index.htm.

Alexander, T. Desmond. *From Paradise to the Promised Land: An Introduction to the Pentateuch*. Grand Rapids, MI: Baker Academic, 1995, 2002, 2012.

Alexander, T. Desmond, and David W. Baker, *Dictionary of the Old Testament: Pentateuch*. Downers Grove, IL: InterVarsity Press, 2003.

Allison, Dale. *Jesus of Nazareth: Millenarian Prophet*. Minneapolis: Fortress Press, 1998.

Altaner, B., and A. Stuiber. *Patrologie*. Freiburg: Herder, 1960.

Alter, Robert. *The Art of Biblical Narrative*. New York: Basic Books, 1981.

———. *The Five Books of Moses: A Translation with Commentary*. New York: W. W. Norton, 2004.

———. *Strong as Death Is Love: The Song of Songs, Ruth, Esther, Jonah, and Daniel. A Translation with Commentary*. New York: W. W. Norton, 2015.

———. *The Wisdom Books: Job, Proverbs, and Ecclesiastes: A Translation with Commentary*. New York: W. W. Norton, 2015.

———. *The Hebrew Bible: A Translation with Commentary*. 3 vols. New York: W. W. Norton, 2018.

Ambrose of Milan, St. *Hexameron, Paradise, and Cain and Abel*. Translated by John J. Savage. Fathers of the Church 42. Washington, DC: Catholic University of America Press, 1961.

———. *Seven Exegetical Works*. Edited by Bernard M. Peebles. Translated by Michael P. McHugh. Fathers of the Church 65. Washington, DC: Catholic University of America Press, 1972.

Anderson, B. W. "From Analysis to Synthesis: The Interpretation of Gen 1–11." *Journal of Biblical Literature* 97 (1978): 29–39.

Anderson, Gary A. *Christian Doctrine and the Old Testament: Theology in the Service of Biblical Exegesis*. Notre Dame, IN: Notre Dame University Press, 2015.

Arminjon, Blaise. *Cantata of Love: A Verse by Verse Reading of the Song of Songs*. San Francisco: Ignatius, 1988.

Armstrong, Chris A. *Medieval Wisdom for Modern Christians: Finding Authentic Faith in a Forgotten Age with C. S. Lewis*. Grand Rapids, MI: Brazos Press, 2016.

Arnold, Duane W. H., and Pamela Bright, eds. *De Doctrina Christiana: A Classic of Western Culture*. Christianity and Judaism in Antiquity. Notre Dame, IN: University of Notre Dame Press, 1995.

Augustine, St. *Sermons on Selected Lessons of the New Testament*. Library of Fathers of the Holy Catholic Church, Anterior to the Division of the East and West 2. Oxford: John Henry Parker, 1844–45.

———. *On Christian Doctrine*. In *St. Augustin's City of God and Christian Doctrine*, ed. Philip Schaff, trans. J. F. Shaw. Select Library of the Nicene and Post-Nicene Fathers of the Christian Church 2. First Series. Buffalo, NY: Christian Literature Co., 1887.

———. *St. Augustine's Confessions*. Vol. 2, *Latin Text*. Edited by T. E. Page and W. H. D. Rouse. Translated by William Watts. Loeb Classical Library. New York: Macmillan, 1912.

———. *On Christian Doctrine*, I.10. In *Christian Instruction; Admonition and Grace; The Christian Combat; Faith, Hope and Charity*, 2nd ed., ed. Roy Joseph Deferrari, trans. John J. Gavigan et al. Fathers of the Church 2. Washington, DC: Catholic University of America Press, 1950.

———. *The City of God, Books VIII–XVI*. Edited by Hermigild Dressler. Translated by Gerald G. Walsh and Grace Monahan. Fathers of the Church 14. Washington, DC: Catholic University of America Press, 1952.

———. *Confessions*. Edited by Roy Joseph Deferrari. Translated by Vernon J. Bourke. Fathers of the Church 21. Washington, DC: Catholic University of America Press, 1953.

———. *Letters (131–164)*. Edited by Roy Joseph Deferrari. Translated by Wilfrid Parsons. Fathers of the Church 20. Washington, DC: Catholic University of America Press, 1953.

———. *The Trinity*. Edited by Hermigild Dressler. Translated by Stephen McKenna. Fathers of the Church 45. Washington, DC: Catholic University of America Press, 1963.

———. *Quaestiones evangeliorum* [Questions on the Gospels]. Corpus Christianorum 44B. Brepols: Turnholti, 1980.

———. *Tractates on the Gospel of John*. Translated by John W. Rettig. Fathers of the Church 78, 79, 88, 90, and 92. Washington, DC: Catholic University of America Press, 1988–95.

———. *Confessions*. Edited by Michael J. Foley. Translated by F. J. Sheed. Introduction by Peter Brown. Cambridge, MA: Hackett, 2006.

Aune, David E. *Apocalypticism, Prophecy, and Magic in Early Christianity*. Wissenschaftliche Untersuchungen zum Neuen Testament 199. Tübingen: Mohr Siebeck, 2006.

Baden, Joel S. *The Composition of the Pentateuch: Renewing the Documentary Hypothesis*. Anchor Yale Bible Reference Library. New Haven, CT: Yale University Press, 2012.

Balthasar, Hans Urs von. *La gloire et al croix*. Vol. 3. Paris: Aubier, 1972.

———. *Henri de Lubac*. Einsiedeln: Johannes Verlag, 1976. [English translation: *The Theology of Henri de Lubac*. San Francisco: Ignatius Press/Communio, 1991.]

Baltzer, Klaus. *Deutero-Isaiah: A Commentary on Isaiah 40–55*. Edited by Peter Machinist. Hermeneia—A Critical and Historical Commentary on the Bible. Minneapolis: Fortress Press, 2001.

Barber, Malcolm. *The New Knighthood: A History of the Order of the Temple*. Cambridge: Cambridge University Press, 2012.

Barclay, James M. G. *Jews in the Mediterranean Diaspora*. Edinburgh: T & T Clark, 1996.

Barna Research Group. *Barna Trends 2018: What's New and What's Next at the Intersection of Faith and Culture*. Grand Rapids, MI: Baker Books, 2017.

Barrett, C. K. "The Allegory of Abraham, Sarah, and Hagar in the Argument of Galatians." In *Rechtfertigung: Festschrift fur E. Käsemann*, ed. J. Friedrich, W. Pohlmann, and P. Stuhlmacher, 1–16. Tübingen: Mohr-Siebeck, 1976.

———. "John and the Synoptic Gospels." In *Expository Rethinking the Gospel Audiences*, ed. R. Bauckham, 147–71. Grand Rapids, MI: Eerdmans, 1998.

———. *The Testimony of the Beloved Disciple: Narrative, History, and Theology in the Gospel of John*. Grand Rapids, MI: Baker Academic, 2007.

Barron, Bishop Robert. "Biblical Interpretation and Theology: Irenaeus, Modernity, and Vatican II." *Letter & Spirit: Liturgy and Empire. Faith in Exile and Political Theology* 5 (2009): 173–92.

Bartholomew, Craig, et al., eds. *Canon and Biblical Interpretation*. Scripture and Hermeneutic Series. Waynesboro, GA: Paternoster Press, 2006.

Basil of Caesarea, St. "The Book of Saint Basil on the Spirit." Chapter 14 in *St. Basil: Letters and Select Works*, ed. Philip Schaff and Henry Wace, trans. Blomfield Jackson. Select Library of the Nicene and Post-Nicene Fathers of the Christian Church 8. Second Series. New York: Christian Literature Company, 1895.

Bauckham, Richard. *Jesus and the Eyewitnesses: The Gospels as Eyewitness Testimony*. Grand Rapids, MI: Eerdmans, 2006.

Beale, G. K. *The Temple and the Church's Mission: A Biblical Theology of the Dwelling Place of God*. Downers Grove, IL: InterVarsity, 2004.

Beale, Gregory K., and Benjamin L. Gladd. *Hidden but Now Revealed: A Biblical Theology of Mystery*. Downers Grove, IL: InterVarsity Press, 2014.

Beale, Gregory K., and Sean M. McDonough. *Commentary on the New Testament Use of the Old Testament*. Grand Rapids, MI; Baker Academic, 2007.

Beauchamp, P. *Création et séparation*. Paris: Desclée, 1969.

Bechard, Dean, ed. *Scripture Documents: An Anthology of Official Catholic Teachings*. Collegeville, MN: Liturgical Press, 2002.

Benedict XVI, Pope. *Deus Caritas Est*. Vatican City: Libreria Editrice Vaticana, 2005.

———. *Verbum Domini*. Vatican City: Libreria Editrice Vaticana, 2010.

———. *General Audiences of Benedict XVI, Wednesday, April 7, 2007*. Vatican City: Libreria Editrice Vaticana, 2013.

———. *Homily on the Solemnity of the Birth of the Lord, December 24, 2006*.

Berardino, A. di, ed., *Encyclopedia of the Early Church*. 2 vols. New York: Oxford University Press, 1992.

Bergant, Dianne. *The Song of Songs*. Edited by David W. Cotter, Jerome T. Walsh, and Chris Franke. Berit Olam Studies in Hebrew Narrative and Poetry. Collegeville, MN: Liturgical Press, 2001.

Berlin, Adele. *Poetics and Interpretation of Biblical Narrative*. Sheffield: Almond Press, 1983.

Bernard of Clairvaux, St. *Saint Bernard on Consideration*. Translated by George Lewis. Oxford: Clarendon Press, 1908.

———. *St. Bernard's Sermons on the Canticle of Canticles*. 2 vols. Translated by a Priest of Mount Melleray. Dublin: Browne and Nolan, 1920.

———. *In Praise of the New Knighthood*. Translated by M. Conrad Greenia, OSCO. Trappist, KY: Cistercian, 2000.

Bernthal, Craig. *Tolkien's Sacramental Vision: Discerning the Holy in Middle Earth*. Oxford: Second Springs Press, 2014.

Bickerman, Elias J. *The Jews in the Greek Age*. Cambridge, MA: Harvard University Press, 1988.

Bietak, Manfred. "Comments on the 'Exodus.'" In *Egypt, Israel, Sinai: Archaeological and Historical Relationships in the Biblical Period*, ed. Anson F. Rainey, 163–71. Tel Aviv: Tel Aviv University Press, 1987.

Bird, Michael M. *Are You the One Who Is to Come? The Historical Jesus and the Messianic Question*. Grand Rapids, MI: Baker Academic, 2009.

———. *Jesus Is the Christ: The Messianic Testimony of the Gospels*. Downers Grove, IL: InterVarsity, 2013.

Boccaccini, Gabriele. *Middle Judaism: Jewish Thought, 300 B.C. to 200 C.E.* Minneapolis: Fortress Press, 1991.

Bock, Darryl. *The Gospel According to Isaiah 53: Encountering the Suffering Servant in Jewish and Christian Theology*. Grand Rapids, MI: Kregel, 2012.

———. *Messiah in the Passover.* Grand Rapids, MI: Kregel, 2017.

Boda, Mark J., and Gordon J. McConville. *Dictionary of the Old Testament: Prophets*. Downers Grove, IL: InterVarsity, 2012.

Boersma, Hans. *Heavenly Participation: The Weaving of a Sacramental Tapestry*. Grand Rapids, MI: Eerdmans, 2011.

———. *Nouvelle Theologie and Sacramental Ontology: A Return to Mystery*. Oxford: Oxford University Press, 2013.

———. *Scripture as Real Presence: Sacramental Exegesis in the Early Church*. Grand Rapids, MI: Baker Academic, 2017.

Boethius. *I Commentarii; De Interpretatione*. Edited by G. Meiser. Leipzig, 1887–80.

———. *On Aristotle; On Interpretation 1–3*. Ancient Commentators on Aristotle. Translated by Andrew Smith. Reprint. New York: Bristol Classical Press, 2014.

Boismard, Marie-Émile. *St. John's Prologue.* Westminster, MD: Newman Press, 1956.

Bonnard, Pierre-Emile, and Pierre Grelot. "Messiah." In *Dictionary of Biblical Theology*, ed. Xavier Léon-Dufour, trans. P. Joseph Cahill, 312. London: Geoffrey Chapman, 1967.

Borgen, Peder. *Philo of Alexandria: An Exegete for His Time*. Supplements to Novum Testamentum 86. Atlanta: Society of Biblical Literature, 2005.

Boulding, Maria, trans. *Confessions: Works of Saint Augustine I/1*. Hyde Park, NY: New City Press, 2002.

Bouyer, Louis. "The Word of God Lives in the Liturgy." In *The Liturgy and the Word of God*, ed. A. G. Martimort. Collegeville, MN: Liturgical Press, 1959.

Brenner, A. "Job the Pious? The Characterization of Job in the Narrative Framework of the Book." In *The Poetical Books: A Sheffield Reader*, ed. D. J. A. Clines, 298–313. Biblical Seminar 41. Sheffield: Sheffield Academic Press, 1997.

Brock, Sebastian. *The Luminous Eye: The Spiritual World Vision of Saint Ephrem the Syrian*. Kalamazoo: Cistercian, 1985.

Brown, Peter. *Augustine of Hippo: A Biography*. New ed. with epilogue. Oakland: University of California Press, 2000.

Brown, Raymond E. *The Community of the Beloved Disciple: The Life, Loves and Hates of an Individual Church in New Testament Times*. New York: Paulist Press, 1978.

———. *The Birth of the Messiah: A Commentary on the Infancy Narratives in the Gospels of Matthew and Luke*. Rev. ed. New York: Doubleday, 1993.

———. *The Gospel According to John (I–XII): Introduction, Translation, and Notes*. Anchor Bible Series 29. New Haven, CT: Yale University Press, 2008.

Brown, Raymond, Joseph Fitzmyer, and Roland Murphy. *The New Jerome Biblical Commentary*. Englewood Cliffs, NJ: Prentice Hall, 1970, 1990.

Brown, Raymond E., and Francis J. Moloney. *An Introduction to the Gospel of John*. Anchor Bible Reference Library. New York: Doubleday, 2003.

Bruggemann, Walter. *Isaiah 40–66*. Edited by Patrick D. Miller and David L. Bartlett. Westminster Bible Companion. Louisville, KY: Westminster John Knox Press, 1998.

———. *The Creative Word: Canon as a Model for Biblical Education*. Minneapolis: Fortress Press, 2015.

Bucur, Bogdan Gabriel . *Scripture Re-envisioned: Christophanic Exegesis and the Making of a Christian Bible*. Leiden: Brill Academic, 2018.

Bultmann, Rudolf. *Die Geschichte der synoptischen Tradition*. 2nd ed. Forschungen zur Religion und Literatur des Alten und Neuen Testaments 29. Gottingen: Vandenhoeck & Ruprecht, 1931.

———. *History of the Synoptic Tradition*. Translated by John Marsh. New York: Harper, 1963.

Caesarius of Arles, St. *Saint Caesarius of Arles: Sermons (1–238)*. Edited by Hermigild Dressler and Bernard M. Peebles. Translated by Mary Magdeleine Mueller. Fathers of the Church 31. Washington, DC: Catholic University of America Press, 1956–73.

Carbajosa, Ignacio. *Faith, the Fount of Exegesis: The Interpretation of Scripture in the Light of the History of Research on the Old Testament*. Translated by Paul Stevenson. San Francisco: Ignatius Press, 2013.

Cathcart, Kevin, Michael Maher, and Martin McNamara, eds. *The Aramaic Bible: The Targum Onqelos to Genesis*. Vol. 6. Translated by Bernard Grossfeld. Collegeville, MN: Liturgical Press, 1990.

Catholic Church. *Catechism of the Catholic Church*. 2nd ed. Washington, DC: United States Catholic Conference, 2000.

Cassuto, Umberto. *The Documentary Hypothesis and the Composition of the Pentateuch*. Jerusalem: Shalom Press, 1941, 1961.

———. *A Commentary on the Book of Genesis, Part 2: From Noah to Abraham, Genesis VI 9–XI 32, with an Appendix: A Fragment of Part III*. Jerusalem: Magnes Press, 1961.

———. *From Adam to Noah: A Commentary on the Book of Genesis I–VI, Part 1*. Jerusalem: Magnes Press, 1961.

———. *A Commentary on the Book of Exodus*. Jerusalem: Magnes Press, 1951, 1967, 1997.

Chadwick, Henry, trans. *Saint Augustine: Confessions*. Oxford World's Classics. New York: Oxford University Press, 1992.

Chantraine, G. "Beyond Modernity and Postmodernity: The Thought of Henri de Lubac." *Communio* 17 (1990): 207–19.

Charles, Robert Henry, ed. *Pseudepigrapha of the Old Testament*. Vol. 2. Oxford: Clarendon Press, 1913.

Chenu, Marie-Dominic. *Nature, Man, and Society in the Twelfth Century: Essays on the New Theological Perspectives in the Latin West*. Edited and translated by Jerome Taylor and Lester K. Little. Chicago: University of Chicago Press, 1957, 1968.

Childs, Brevard S. *The Book of Exodus: A Critical, Theological Commentary*. Old Testament Library. Philadelphia: Westminster, 1974.

———. *Introduction to the Old Testament as Scripture*. Philadelphia: Fortress Press, 1979.

———. *Biblical Theology of the Old and New Testaments: Theological Reflection on the Christian Bible*. Minneapolis: Fortress Press, 2011.

Chrysostom, St. John. *Kommentar zu Hiob*. Patristische Texte und Studien 35. Edited by Ursula and Dieter Hagedorn. Berlin: de Gruyter, 1990.

Clement of Alexandria, St. "The Instructor." In *Fathers of the Second Century: Hermas, Tatian, Athenagoras, Theophilus, and Clement of Alexandria*, ed. Alexander Roberts, James Donaldson, and A. Cleveland Coxe. Ante-Nicene Fathers 2. Buffalo, NY: Christian Literature Co., 1885.

Clifford, R. J. *Creation Accounts in the Ancient Near East and in the Bible*. Catholic Biblical Quarterly Monograph Series 26. Washington, DC: Catholic Biblical Association of America, 1994.

Clines, D. J. A. *I, He, We, and They*. Journal for the Study of the Old Testament Supplement 3. Sheffield: Journal for the Study of the Old Testament Press, 1976.

Clines, David J. A. *Job 1–20*. Word Biblical Commentary 17. Dallas: Word, Inc., 1998.

Clines, David J. A. *Job 38–42*. Word Biblical Commentary 18B. Grand Rapids, MI: Zondervan, 2011.

Cole, Alan. *Exodus*. Tyndale Old Testament Commentary. Downers Grove, IL: InterVarsity, 2008.

Collins, A. Y., and J. J. Collins. *King and Messiah as Son of God: Divine, Human, and Angelic Messianic Figures in Biblical and Related Literature*. Grand Rapids, MI: Eerdmans, 2008.

Collins, John J. *Between Athens and Jerusalem: Jewish Identity in the Hellenistic Diaspora*. New York: Crossroad, 1986.

———. *The Bible after Babel: Historical Criticism in a Postmodern Age*. Grand Rapids, MI: Eerdmans, 2005.

Collins, John J., and Daniel C. Harlow. *The Eerdmans Dictionary of Early Judaism*. Grand Rapids, MI: Eerdmans, 2010.

Congar, Yves. *The Mystery of the Temple*. Translated by Reginald F. Trevett. Westminster, MD: Newman, 1962.

———. *Tradition and Traditions: The Biblical, Historical, and Theological Evidence for Catholic Teaching on Tradition*. Translated by Michael Naseby and Thomas Rainborough. San Diego: Basilica Press, 1966.

Coolman, Boyd Taylor. *The Theology of Hugh of Saint Victor: An Interpretation*. Cambridge: Cambridge University Press, 2013.

Crawford, Jason. *Allegory and Enchantment: An Early Modern Poetics*. Oxford: Oxford University Press, 2017.

Cross, Frank Moore. "The Divine Warrior in Israel's Early Cult." In *Biblical Motifs: Origins and Transformations*, ed. A. Altmann, 11–30. Cambridge, MA: Harvard University Press, 1966.

———. *From Epic to Canon: History and Literature in Ancient Israel*. Baltimore: Johns Hopkins University Press, 1998.

Cyprian of Carthage, St. *Epistle LV*. In *Fathers of the Third Century: Hippolytus, Cyprian, Novatian, Appendix*. Edited by Alexander Roberts, James Donaldson, and A. Cleveland Coxe. Translated by Robert Ernest Wallis. Ante-Nicene Fathers 5. Buffalo, NY: Christian Literature Co., 1886.

———. *Epistle LXIX*. In *Fathers of the Third Century: Hippolytus, Cyprian, Novatian, Appendix*. Edited by Alexander Roberts, James Donaldson, and A. Cleveland Coxe. Translated by Robert Ernest Wallis. Ante-Nicene Fathers 5. Buffalo, NY: Christian Literature Co., 1886.

Cyril of Jerusalem, St. *The Works of Saint Cyril of Jerusalem*. Edited by Roy Joseph Deferrari. Translated by Leo P. McCauley and Anthony A. Stephenson. Fathers of the Church 61. Washington, DC: Catholic University of America Press, 1969.

Dahan, Gilbert. "The Commentary of Thomas Aquinas in the History of Medieval Exegesis on Job: *Intentio et Materia*." Translated by David L. Augustine. *Nova et Vetera* 17, no. 4 (2019): 1053–75.

Daley, Brian E., trans. *Light on the Mountain: Greek Patristic and Byzantine Homilies on the Transfiguration of the Lord*. Popular Patristics Series 48. New York: St. Vladimir's Press, 2013.

D'Ambrosio, Marcellino. "Henri de Lubac and the Recovery of the Traditional Hermeneutic." PhD diss., Catholic University of America, 1991.

———. "*Ressourcement* Theology, *Aggiornamento* and the Hermeneutics of Tradition." *Communio* 18 (1991): 530–55.

———. "The Spiritual Sense in de Lubac's Hermeneutics of Tradition." *Letter & Spirit: Reading Salvation: Word, Worship, and the Mysteries* 1 (2005): 154.

Daniélou, Jean. *Les divers sens de l'écriture dans la tradition chrétienne primitive* [The different meanings of writing in the early Christian tradition]. Paris: Desclée De Brouwer, 1948.

———. *Bible et liturgie: La théologie biblique des sacrements et des fêtes d'après les Pères de l'Église*. Paris: Cerf, 1951. [English translation: *The Bible and the Liturgy*. Liturgical Studies 3. Notre Dame, IN: University of Notre Dame Press, 1956.]

———. "The Sacraments and the History of Salvation." In *The Liturgy and the Word of God*, edited by A. G. Martimort. Collegeville, MN: Liturgical Press, 1959.

———. *Les manuscrits de la Mer Morte et les origines du Christianisme*. Paris: L'Orante, 1957. [English translation: *The Dead Sea Scrolls and Primitive Christianity* Westport, CT: Greenwood, 1979.]

———. *Théologie du Judéo-Christianisme: Histoire des doctrines chrétiennes avant Nicée*. Vol. 1. Tournai: Desclée, 1958. [English translation: *The Theology of Jewish Christianity*. Edited and translated by John A Baker. London: Darton, Longman and Todd, 1964.]

———. *From Shadows to Reality: Studies in the Biblical Typology of the Fathers*. Translated by Wulstan Hibberd. London: Burns & Oates, 1960.

———. *Christ and Us*. New York: Sheed and Ward, 1961.

———. *The Lord of History: Reflections on the Inner Meaning of History*. Translated by Nigel Abercrombie, 1958. [Reprint, Cleveland, OH: Meridian, 1968.]

Daniélou, Jean, and James G. Colbert. *Philo of Alexandria*. [Reprint, Eugene, OR: Cascade Books, 2014.]

Dante. *Inferno*. Translated by Anthony Esolen. New York: Random House, 2003.

———. *Purgatory*. Translated by Anthony Esolen. New York: Random House, 2003.

———. *Paradise*. Translated by Anthony Esolen. New York: Random House, 2007.

Davies, Graham. "Was There an Exodus?" In *In Search of Pre-Exilic Israel: Proceedings of the Oxford Old Testament Seminar*, ed. John Day, 23–40. Journal for the Study of the Old Testament 406. London: T & T Clark, 2004.

Davis, Ellen F. *Proverbs, Ecclesiastes, and the Song of Songs*. Westminster Bible Companion. Edited by Patrick D. Miller and David L. Bartlett. Louisville, KY: Westminster John Knox Press, 2000.

Davis, Ellen F., and Richard B. Hays, eds. *The Art of Reading Scripture*. Grand Rapids, MI: Eerdmans, 2003.

Davis, Virginia. "The Cairo Love Songs." *Journal of Oriental Studies* 100 (1980): 101–9.

Dodd, C. H. *Historical Tradition in the Fourth Gospel*. Cambridge: Cambridge University Press, 1963.

D'Onofrio, Giulio. *History of Theology: The Middle Ages*. Vol. 2. Translated by Matthew J. O'Connell. Collegeville, MN: Liturgical Press, 2008.

Dozeman, Thomas. *Exodus*. Eerdmans Critical Commentary. Grand Rapids, MI: Eerdmans, 2009.

Dreher, Rod. *The Benedict Option: A Strategy for Christians in a Post-Christian Nation*. New York: Sentinel Press, 2018.

Drescher, Elizabeth. *Choosing Our Religion: The Spiritual Lives of America's Nones*. Oxford: Oxford University Press, 2016.

Driver, Samuel R. *Exodus*. Cambridge: Cambridge University Press, 1911.

———. *An Introduction to the Literature of the Old Testament*. 9th ed. Edinburgh: T & T Clark, 1913.

Duhm, Bernhard. *Das Buch Jesaia*. 1st ed. Handkommentar Zum Alten Testament 3. Göttingen: Vandenhoeck & Ruprecht, 1897.

Dunn, James D. G. *Unity and Diversity in the New Testament*. London: SCM Press, 1977.

Durham, John. *Exodus*. Word Biblical Commentary. Waco, TX: Word, Inc., 1987.

Durrwell, F. X. "The Sacrament of Sacred Scripture." *Letter & Spirit: Reading Salvation. Word, Worship, and the Mysteries* 1 (2005): 167.

Ehrman, Bart D. *Jesus, Interrupted: Revealing the Hidden Contradictions in the Bible and Why We Don't Know about Them*. New York: Harper One, 2010.

———. *Jesus before the Gospels: How the Earliest Christians Remembered, Changed, and Invented Their Stories of the Savior*. New York: Harper One, 2016.

Ephrem the Syrian, St. *Commentarii in Job*. In *Sancti Patris Nostri Ephraem Syri Opera Omnia* 2. Edited by J. S. Assemani. Rome, 1740.

———. *Hymns*. Edited by Bernard McGinn. Translated by Kathleen E. McVey. Classics of Western Spirituality. Mahwah, NJ: Paulist Press, 1989.

Evans, Craig A., and Stanley E. Porter Jr. *Dictionary of New Testament Background: A Compendium of Contemporary Biblical Scholarship*. Downers Grove, IL: InterVarsity, 2000.

Evans, G. R. *The Language and Logic of the Bible: The Earlier Middle Ages*. Cambridge: Cambridge University Press, 1984.

Everson, J. A. "The Days of Yahweh." *Journal of Biblical Literature* 93 (1974): 329–37.

Exum, Cheryl. *Song of Songs*. Old Testament Library. Louisville, KY: Westminster John Knox, 2005.

Farkasfalvy, Denis. *Inspiration and Interpretation: A Theological Introduction to Sacred Scripture*. Washington, DC: Catholic University of America Press, 2010.

———. *A Theology of the Christian Bible: Revelation–Inspiration–Canon*. Washington, DC: Catholic University of America Press, 2018.

Feldman, Lawrence J. *Jew and Gentile in the Ancient World*. Princeton, NJ: Princeton University Press, 1993.

Ferguson, Everett, ed. *Encyclopedia of Early Christianity*. New York: Garland, 1990.

Fitzmyer, Joseph A. *The One Who Is to Come*. Grand Rapids: Eerdmans, 2007.

Fleiger, Verlyn. *Splintered Light: Logos and Language in Tolkien's World*. Kent, OH: Kent State University Press, 2002.

———. *Tolkien on Fairy Stories*. New York: HarperCollins, 2014.

Fletcher-Louis, Crispin. *All the Glory of Adam: Liturgical Anthropology in the Dead Sea Scrolls*. Studies on the Texts of the Desert of Judah. Leiden: Brill, 2002.

———. "God's Image, His Cosmic Temple and the High Priest: Towards an

Historical and Theological Account of the Incarnation." In *Heaven on Earth: The Temple in Biblical Theology*, ed. T. D. Alexander and S. Gathercole, 81–99. Carlisle, UK: Paternoster, 2004.

Fleteren, Frederick van, and Joseph C. Schnaubelt, eds. *Augustine: Biblical Exegete*. New York: Peter Lang, 2001.

Fokkelmann, J. P. *Narrative Art in Genesis*. Assen: Van Gorcum, 1975.

Fox, M. V. "The Cairo Love Songs." *Journal of the American Oriental Society* 100 (1980): 101–9.

Francis de Sales, St. *Introduction to the Devout Life*. San Francisco: Ignatius Press, 2015.

Fretheim, Terrence. *Exodus*. Interpretation Series. Louisville, KY: John Knox, 1991.

Garrett, Duane. *Song of Songs/Lamentations*. Word Biblical Commentary 23B. Dallas, TX: Word, Inc., 2004.

Gavigan, John J., trans. *Christian Instruction*. Fathers of the Church 2. Washington, DC: Catholic University of America Press, 1947.

Gerleman, Gillis. *Ruth: Das Hohelied*. Biblischer Kommentar Altes Testamen 18. Neukirchen-Vluyn: Neukirchener, 1965.

Goldingay, John. E. *Daniel*. Word Biblical Commentary 30. Dallas, TX: Word, Inc., 1989.

———. *The Message of Isaiah 40–55: A Literary-Theological Commentary*. London: T & T Clark, 2005.

———. *Key Questions about Biblical Interpretation: Old Testament Answers*. Grand Rapids, MI: Baker Academic, 2011.

Goldingay, John, and David Payne. *A Critical and Exegetical Commentary on Isaiah 40–55*. Edited by G. I. Davies and G. N. Stanton. International Critical Commentary 1. London: T & T Clark, 2006.

Goodenough, Erwin R. *Jewish Symbols in the Greco-Roman Period*. 13 vols. New York: Pantheon, 1953–68.

Gorman, Michael. *Participating in Christ: Explorations in Paul's Theology and Spirituality*. Grand Rapids, MI: Eerdmans, 2019.

Grant, Robert M., with David Tracy. *A Short History of the Interpretation of the Bible*. 2nd ed. Philadelphia: Fortress Press, 1984.

Green, Joel B., Jeannine K. Brown, and Nicholas Perrin. *Dictionary of Jesus and the Gospels*. 2nd ed. Downers Grove, IL: InterVarsity, 2013.

Green, R. P. H., ed., *Augustine: De doctrina christiana*. Oxford Early Christian Texts. Oxford: Oxford University Press, 1995.

———, trans. *Saint Augustine: On Christian Teaching*. Oxford World Classics. New York: Oxford University Press, 1997.

Gregory the Great, St. *Morals on the Book of Job*, vol. 3. Oxford: John Henry Parker, 1847–50.

———. *Moralia on Job*. In *Corpus Christianorum*. Series Latina 143B:1482. Turnhout (Belgium): Brepols, 1953*ff*.

Gregory of Nyssa, St. *Commentary on the Song of Songs*. Translated by Casimir McCambley. Brookline, MA: Hellenic College Press, 1987.

———. *Treatise on 1 Corinthians 15:28: Opera Dogmatica Minora*. Edited by J. Kenneth Downing. Leiden: Brill, 1987.

———. *The Life of Moses*. Translated by Abraham Malherbe and Everett Ferguson. New York: Harper One, 2006.

Groll, Sarah Israelit, ed. *Egyptological Studies*. Scripta Hierosolymitana 26. Jerusalem: Magnes/Hebrew University, 1982.

Guardini, Romano. *The Spirit of the Liturgy*. New York: Sheed and Ward, 1931.

———. *Jesus Christus: Meditations*. Translated by Peter White. Chicago: Regnery Press, 1959.

———. *Letters from Lake Como: Explorations on Technology and the Human Race*. Ressourcement: Retrieval and Renewal in Catholic Thought. Grand Rapids, MI: Eerdmans, 1994.

———. *The Lord*. Washington, DC: Regnery Press, 1996. [Originally published in 1954.]

———. *The End of the Modern World*. Rev. ed. Wilmington, DE: Isi Books, 2001.

Guigo II. "*The Ladder from Earth to Heaven*." Translated by Jeremy Holmes. *Letter & Spirit: The Authority of Mystery. The Word of God and the People of God* 2 (2006): 175–88.

Gunkel, Hermann. *The Legends of Genesis*. Translated by W. H. Carruth. Chicago: Open Court, 1901.

———. *The Psalms: A Form-Critical Introduction*. Translated by T. Horner. Biblical Series 19. Philadelphia: Fortress Press, 1967.

———. "The Israelite Prophecy from the Time of Amos." In *Twentieth Century Theology in the Making*. Vol. 1, *Themes of Biblical Theology*, ed. J. Pelikan, 48–75. London: Fontana, 1969.

———. "Israelite Literary History." In *Water for a Thirsty Land: Israelite Literature and Religion*, ed. K. C. Hanson, 31–41. Minneapolis: Fortress Press, 2001.

Hahn, Scott. *Kinship by Covenant: A Canonical Approach to the Fulfillment of God's Saving Promises*. New Haven, CT: Yale University Press, 2009.

———, ed. *Catholic Bible Dictionary*. New York: Doubleday, 2009.

Haidt, Jonathan. *The Righteous Mind: Why Good People Are Divided by Politics and Religion*. New York: Vintage Press, 2013.

Haller, Robert S., ed. and trans. *Literary Criticism of Dante*. Lincoln: University of Nebraska, 1977.

Hamilton, James M. *God's Indwelling Presence: The Holy Spirit in the Old and New Testaments*. NAC Studies in Bible and Theology. Nashville: B & H Academic, 2006.

———. "The Messianic Music of the Song of Songs: A Non-Allegorical Reading." *Westminster Theological Journal* 68 (2006): 331–45.

———. *God's Glory in Salvation through Judgment: A Biblical Theology*. Wheaton, IL: Crossway Books, 2010.

———. *With the Clouds of Heaven: The Book of Daniel in Biblical Theology*. New Studies in Biblical Theology. Downers Grove, IL: InterVarsity, 2014.

———. *Song of Songs: A Biblical-Theological, Allegorical, Christological Interpretation*. Fairn, Scotland: Christian Focus on the Bible Press, 2015.

Hamilton, Victor P. *Exodus: An Exegetical Commentary*. Grand Rapids, MI: Baker Academic, 2011.

Hartman, Louis F., and Alexander A. Di Lella. *The Book of Daniel: A New Translation with Notes and Commentary on Chapters 1–9*. Anchor Bible Series 23. New Haven, CT: Yale University Press, 2008.

Hays, Richard B. *Echoes of Scripture in the Letters of St. Paul*. New Haven, CT: Yale University Press, 1993.

Hayward, R. "St. Jerome and the Meaning of the High-Priestly Vestments." In *Hebrew Study from Ezra to Ben-Yehuda*, ed. W. Horbury, 20–105. Edinburgh: Clark, 1999.

Hendel, R. S. "Sacrifice as a Cultural System: The Ritual Symbolism of Exodus 24, 3–8." *Zeitschrift für die alttestamentliche Wissenschaft* 101 (1989): 366–90.

Hengel, Martin. *Judaism and Hellenism*. London: SCM, 1974.

———. *The "Hellenization" of Judea in the First Century after Christ*. London: SCM, 1989.

———. *Studies in Early Christology*. London: SCM, 1995.

Heschel, Abraham J. *God in Search of Man: A Philosophy of Judaism*. New York: Farrar, Strauss, and Giroux, 1955, 1983.

Hess, Richard. "The Divine Name Yahweh in Late Bronze Age Sources." *Ugarit-Forecharged* 23 (1991): 181–88.

Hicks, Stephen R. C. *Explaining Postmodernism: Skepticism and Socialism from Rosseau to Foucault*. Tempe, AZ: Scholarly Publishing, 2004, 2011.

Hill, Edmund, trans. *Teaching Christianity*. Works of St. Augustine I/11. New York: New City Press, 1996.

Hoffmeier, James. *Israel in Egypt*. New York: Oxford University, 1996.

Hoffmeier, James, and Dennis Magaly, eds. *Did I Not Bring Israel Out of Egypt? Biblical, Archaeological, and Egyptological Perspectives on the Exodus Narratives*. Winona Lake, IN: Eisenbrauns, 2012.

Holmes, Jeremy, trans. "The Ladder from Earth to Heaven." *Letter & Spirit: The Authority of Mystery. The Word of God and the People of God* 2 (2006): 175.

Hugh of St. Victor. *De Amore Sponsi ad Sponsam*. Edited by J. P. Migne. Patrologiae Cursus Completus. Series Latina 176. Paris, 1844–64.

———. *On the Sacraments of the Christian Faith* [De Sacramentis]. Translated by R. J. Deferrari. Cambridge, MA: Mediaeval Academy of America, 1951.

———. *Didascalion: A Medieval Guide to the Arts*. Translated by Jeremy Taylor. Cambridge: Cambridge University Press, 1991.

———. "To the New Student of Sacred Scripture." *Letter & Spirit: Reading Salvation. Word, Worship, and the Mysteries* 1 (2005): 160.

Hurtado, Larry. *Lord Jesus Christ: Devotion to Jesus in Earliest Christianity*. Grand Rapids, MI: Eerdmans, 2003.

Janzen, J. Gerald. *Exodus*. Louisville, KY: Westminster John Knox, 1997.

Jeremias, Joachim. *Theophanie: Die Geschichte einer alttestamentlichen Gattung*. Wissenschaftliche Monographien zum Alten und Neuen Testament 10. Neukirchen-Vluyn: Neukirchener Verlag, 1965.

Jerome, St. *St. Jerome: Letters and Select Works*. Edited by Philip Schaff and Henry Wace. Translated by W. H. Fremantle, G. Lewis, and W. G. Martley. Select Library of the Nicene and Post-Nicene Fathers of the Christian Church 6. Second Series. New York: Christian Literature Co., 1893.

———. *Select Letters of St. Jerome*. Edited by T. E. Page, E. Capps, and W. H. D. Rouse. Translated by F. A. Wright. Loeb Classical Library. London: William Heinemann, 1933.

———. *The Homilies of Saint Jerome (1–59 on the Psalms)*. Edited by Hermigild Dressler. Translated by Marie Liguori Ewald. Fathers of the Church 1. Washington, DC: Catholic University of America Press, 1964.

———. *Commentary on Isaiah: Origen Homilies 1–9 on Isaiah*. Ancient Christian Writers: The Works of the Fathers in Translation 88. Mahwah, NJ: Paulist Press, 2015.

Jewett, Robert, and Roy David Kotansky. *Romans: A Commentary*. Edited by Eldon Jay Epp. Hermeneia—A Critical and Historical Commentary on the Bible. Minneapolis: Fortress Press, 2006.

John Paul II, St. Pope. *Man and Woman He Created Them: A Theology of the Body*. Translated by Michael Waldstein. Boston, MA: Pauline Books & Media, 2006.

Jones, Andrew W. *Before Church and State: A Study of Social Order in the Sacramental Kingdom of St. Louis IX*. Steubenville, OH: Emmaus Academic Press, 2017.

Josephus. *Antiquities: Books 1–4*. Edited by Jeffrey Henderson et al. Translated by H. St. J. Thackeray. Loeb Classical Library 4. Cambridge, MA: Harvard University Press, 1930, 1967.

Justin Martyr, St. *The First Apology, The Second Apology, Dialogue with Trypho, Exhortation to the Greeks, Discourse to the Greeks, The Monarchy or The Rule of God*. Fathers of the Church 6. Washington, DC: Catholic University of America Press, 1948.

Kähler, Martin. *The So-Called Historical Jesus and the Historic, Biblical Christ*. Edited and translated by Carl E. Braaten. Foreword by Paul J. Tillich. Philadelphia: Fortress Press, 1964.

Kaiser, Walter. *The Messiah in the Old Testament*. Grand Rapids, MI: Zondervan, 1995.

Kannengiesser, C. *Handbook of Patristic Exegesis: The Bible in Ancient Christianity*. Leiden: Brill, 2006.

Kass, Leon R. *The Beginning of Wisdom: Reading Genesis*. Chicago: University of Chicago Press, 2003.

Keating, James. *Resting upon the Heart of Christ*. Omaha: Institute for Priestly Formation, 2009.

Keener, Craig. *A Commentary on the Gospel of Matthew*. Grand Rapids, MI: Eerdmans, 1999.

———. *The Historical Jesus of the Gospels*. Grand Rapids, MI: Eerdmans, 2009.

———. *Christobiography: Memory, History, and the Reliability of the Gospels*. Grand Rapids, MI: Eerdmans, 2019.

Köster, Helmut. "Σπλαγχνίζομαι." In *Theological Dictionary of the New Testament*, ed.

Gerhard Kittel, Geoffrey W. Bromiley, and Gerhard Friedrich. Grand Rapids, MI: Eerdmans, 1964–.

Kreeft, Peter. *Three Philosophies of Life. Ecclesiastes: Life as Vanity, Job: Life as Suffering, Song of Songs: Life as Love.* San Francisco: Ignatius Press, 1989.

Krieg, Robert. *Romano Guardini: A Precursor of Vatican II.* Notre Dame, IN University of Notre Dame Press, 1997.

Kugel, James. *Traditions of the Bible: A Guide to the Bible as It Was at the Start of the Common Era.* Cambridge, MA: Harvard University Press, 1999.

———. *How to Read the Bible: A Guide to Scripture, Then and Now.* New York: Simon and Schuster, 2007.

———. *The Ladder of Jacob: Ancient Interpretations of the Biblical Story of Jacob and His Children.* Princeton, NJ: Princeton University Press, 2009.

Kysar, R. *John: The Maverick Gospel.* Atlanta: John Knox, 1976.

Lansing, Richard, ed. *Dante Encyclopedia.* London: Routledge, 2000.

La Potterie, Ignace de. "L'emploi dynamique de eis dans Saint Jean et ses incidences théologiques" [The dynamic use of *eis* in Saint John and its theological implications]. *Biblica* 43 (1962): 366–87.

Legaspi, Michael C. *The Death of Scripture and the Rise of Biblical Studies.* Oxford Studies in Historical Theology. Oxford: Oxford University Press, 2011.

Leithart, Peter. *Deep Exegesis: The Mystery of Reading Scripture.* Waco, TX: Baylor University Press, 2009.

Levenson, Jon D. *The Hebrew Bible, the Old Testament, and Historical Criticism: Jews and Christians in Biblical Studies.* Louisville, KY: Westminster John Knox, 1993.

Levering, Matthew. *Christ's Fulfillment of Temple and Torah: Salvation According to Thomas Aquinas.* Notre Dame, IN: University of Notre Dame Press, 2002.

———. *Participatory Biblical Exegesis: A Theology of Biblical Interpretation.* Notre Dame, IN: Notre Dame University Press, 2008.

———. *The Theology of Augustine: An Introductory Guide to His Most Important Works.* Grand Rapids, MI: Baker Academic, 2013.

Levy, Ian Christopher. *Introducing Medieval Biblical Interpretation: The Senses of Scripture in PreModern Exegesis.* Grand Rapids, MI: Baker Academic, 2018.

Lewis, C. S. *The Screwtape Letters.* In *The C. S. Lewis Signature Classics.* San Francisco: Harper One, 2007.

———. "Preface." In *On the Incarnation: St. Athanasius*, trans. John Behr. Yonkers: St. Vladimir's Press, 2011.

———. *The Space Trilogy (Out of the Silent Planet, Perelandra, That Hideous Strength).* New York: Simon and Schuster, 2011.

Longenecker, Richard N. *Galatians.* Word Biblical Commentary 41. Dallas, TX: Word, Inc., 1998.

Longman III, Tremper. *Song of Songs.* New International Commentary on the Old Testament. Grand Rapids, MI: Eerdmans, 2001.

Longman III, Tremper, and Peter Enns. *Dictionary of the Old Testament: Wisdom, Poetry & Writings.* Downers Grove, IL: InterVarsity, 2008.

Lubac, Henri de. *Surnaturel.* Paris: Aubier, 1946. [Paris: Desclée de Brouwer, 1991.]

———. *Catholicism*. New York: Sheed and Ward, 1950.

———. *The Sources of Revelation*. New York: Herder & Herder, 1968.

———. *The Splendor of the Church*. San Francisco: Ignatius, 1986.

———. *Théologie dans l'histoire*. Paris: Desclée, 1990.

———. *Medieval Exegesis: The Four Senses of Scripture*. Vol. 1. Translated by M. Sebanc. Grand Rapids, MI: Eerdmans, 1998.

———. *Medieval Exegesis: The Four Senses of Scripture*. Vol. 2. Translated by E. M. Macierowski. Grand Rapids, MI: Eerdmans, 2000. [Originally published as *Exégèse Médiévale: Les quatre sens de l'Écriture*. 4 vols. Paris: Aubier, 1959–64.]

———. *Medieval Exegesis: The Four Senses of Scripture*. Vol. 3. Translated by E. M. Macierowski. Grand Rapids, MI: Eerdmans, 2000.

———. *History and Spirit: The Understanding of Scripture According to Origen*. Translated by Anne Englund Nash and Juvenal Merriell. San Francisco: Ignatius Press, 2007 [1950].

Mangan, Céline, John F. Healey, and Peter S. Knobel. *The Aramaic Bible: The Targum of Job and the Targum of Proverbs and the Targum of Qohelet*. Vol. 15. Edited by Kevin Cathcart, Michael Maher, and Martin McNamara. Collegeville, MN: Liturgical Press, 1991.

Martens, Peter M. *Origen and Scripture: The Contours of the Exegetical Life*. Oxford Early Christian Studies. Oxford: Oxford University Press, 2001.

Martin, Francis. *Sacred Scripture: The Disclosure of the Word*. Ave Maria, FL: Sapientia Press, 2005.

Martyn, J. Louis. *Galatians: A New Translation with Introduction and Commentary*. Anchor Bible Series 33A. New Haven, CT: Yale University Press, 2008.

McCarthy, D. J. "Exodus 3:14: History, Philology and Theology." *Catholic Biblical Quarterly* 40 (1978): 311–22.

Melville, Herman. *Moby Dick*. Norton Critical Ed. New York: W. W. Norton, 2002.

Meyer, Ben. *The Aims of Jesus*. London: SCM, 1979.

Milgrom, Jacob J. *Leviticus 1–16*. Anchor Bible Series 3. New York: Doubleday, 1991.

Moberly, Walter. *The Bible, Theology, and Faith: A Study in Abraham and Jesus*. Cambridge: Cambridge University, 2000.

Momigliano, Arnaldo. *Alien Wisdom: The Limits of Hellenization*. Cambridge: Cambridge University Press, 1975.

Moorhead, John. *Gregory the Great*. Early Church Fathers. New York: Routledge, 2005.

Mowinckel, Sigmund. *He That Cometh, the Messiah Concept in the Old Testament and Ancient Judaism*. Translated by G. W. Anderson. New York: Abingdon Press, 1954.

———. *The Psalms in Israel's Worship*. 2 vols. Translated by D. R. Ap-Thomas. New York: Abingdon, 1962.

Moyter, J. Alec. *Isaiah*. Tyndale Old Testament Commentaries 20. Downers Grove, IL: InterVarsity, 1999.

Murphy, Roland Edmund. *The Song of Songs: A Commentary on the Book of Canticles or the Song of Songs*. Edited by S. Dean McBride. Hermeneia—A Critical and Historical Commentary on the Bible. Minneapolis, MN: Fortress Press, 1990.

Neufeld, K. H., and M. Sales, eds. *Bibliographie Henri de Lubac, S. J., 1925–1974*. 2nd ed. Einsiedeln: Johannes Verlag, 1974.

Neusner, Jacob. *Jerusalem and Athens: The Congruity of Talmudic and Classical Philosophy*. Leiden: Brill, 1997.

———. *The Babylonian Talmud: A Translation and Commentary*. Vol. 15. Peabody, MA: Hendrickson, 2011.

Nicholson, Helen. *The Knights Hospitaller*. Suffolk: Boydell & Brewer, 2006.

Nickelsburg, George W. E. *Jewish Literature Between the Bible and the Mishnah*. Philadelphia: Fortress Press, 1981.

Nicolle, David. *Knights of Jerusalem: The Crusading Order of Hospitallers, 1100–1565*. Oxford: Osprey, 2008.

Norris, Richard A., and Robert Louis Wilken, eds. *The Song of Songs: Interpreted by Early Christian and Medieval Commentators*. Translated by Richard A. Norris Jr. Church's Bible. Grand Rapids, MI: Eerdmans, 2003.

Noth, Martin. *Exodus*. Old Testament Library. Philadelphia: Westminster, 1962.

Ockholm, Dennis, and Kathleen Norris. *Monk Habits for Everyday People: Benedictine Spirituality for Protestants*. Grand Rapids, MI: Brazos Press, 2007.

Origen. *First Principles* [De Principiis]. *Fathers of the Third Century: Tertullian, Part Fourth; Minucius Felix; Commodian; Origen, Parts First and Second*. Edited by Alexander Roberts, James Donaldson, and A. Cleveland Coxe. Translated Frederick Crombie. Ante-Nicene Fathers 4. Buffalo, NY: Christian Literature Co., 1885.

———. *The Philocalia of Origen*. Translated by George Lewis. Edinburgh: T & T Clark, 1911.

———. *Homilies on Genesis and Exodus*. Translated by Ronald E. Heine. Washington, DC: Catholic University of America Press, 1982.

———. *Commentary on the Gospel According to John, Books 1–10*. Translated by Ronald E. Heine. Fathers of the Church 80. Washington, DC: Catholic University of America Press, 1989.

———. *Die älteren griechischen Kommentar zum Buch Hiob* [Older Greek commentary on the Book of Job]. Vols. 2 and 3. Patristische Texte und Studien 48 and 53. Edited by Ursula and Dieter Hagedorn. Berlin: de Gruyter, 1997–2000.

Oswalt, John N. *The Book of Isaiah, Chapters 40–66*. New International Commentary on the Old Testament. Grand Rapids, MI: Eerdmans, 1998.

Paul, Shalom M. *Isaiah 40–66, Translation and Commentary*. Eerdmans Critical Commentary. Grand Rapids, MI: Eerdmans, 2012.

Pelikan, Juroslav. *The Christian Tradition: A History of the Development of Doctrine*. Vol. 1, *The Emergence of the Catholic Tradition (100–600)*. Chicago: University of Chicago Press, 1971.

Peters, Greg. *The Story of Monasticism: Retrieving an Ancient Tradition for Contemporary Spirituality*. Grand Rapids, MI: Baker Academic, 2015.

Peterson, Jordan B. *Twelve Rules for Life: An Antidote to Chaos*. Toronto: Random House Canada, 2018.

Philo of Alexandria. *De opificio mundi* [On the creation of the world]. In *Volume I*. Loeb Classical Library 226. Cambridge, MA: Harvard University Press, 1929.

———. *Volume II*. Loeb Classical Library 227. Cambridge, MA: Harvard University Press, 1929.

———. *Volume III*. Loeb Classical Library 247. Cambridge, MA: Harvard University Press, 1929.

———. *Volume IV*. Loeb Classical Library 261. Cambridge, MA: Harvard University Press, 1932.

———. *Questions and Answers on Exodus*. Loeb Classical Library 401. Cambridge, MA: Harvard University Press, 1929.

Phinney, D. N. "Call/Commission Narratives." In *Dictionary of the Old Testament: Prophets*, edited by Mark J. Boda and Gordon J. McConville, 65–70. Downers Grove, IL: Inter-Varsity Press, 2012.

Pirot, Louis. *L'oeuvre exégétique de Théodore de Mopsueste, 350–428 après J.-C.* Scripta Pontificii Instituti Biblici. Rome: Pontifical Biblical Institute, 1913.

Pitre, Brant. *Jesus, the Tribulation, and the End of the Exile: Restoration Eschatology and the Origin of the Atonement*. Wissenschaftliche Untersuchungen zum Neuen Testament 2:204. Tübingen: Mohr-Siebeck, 2005.

———. *Jesus and the Last Supper*. Grand Rapids, MI: Eerdmans, 2017.

Pitre, Brant, Michael Barber, and John Kincaid. *Paul: A New Covenant Jew. Rethinking Pauline Theology*. Grand Rapids, MI: Eerdmans, 2019.

Pitre, Brant, and John Bergsma. *A Catholic Introduction to the Bible: The Old Testament*. San Francisco: Ignatius Press, 2018.

Pontifical Biblical Commission. *The Interpretation of the Bible in the Church*. Vatican City: Libreria Editrice Vaticana, 1993.

Pope, Martin. *Song of Songs*. Anchor Bible Commentary 7C. New York: Doubleday, 1977.

Propp, W. H. C. *Exodus 1–18: A New Translation with Introduction and Commentary*. Anchor Bible Series 2. New York: Doubleday, 1999.

———. *Exodus 19–40: A New Translation with Introduction and Commentary*. Anchor Bible Series 3. New York: Doubleday, 2008.

Putnam, Robert. *American Grace: How Religion Unites and Divides Us*. New York: Simon & Schuster, 2010.

Quasten, J. *Patrology*. Vols. 1–3. Utrecht: Spectrum, 1960.

Rabanus Maurus. *Expositio in Matthaeum*, 2 vols. Edited by B. Löfstedt. Corpus Christianorum, continuatio medievalis 174–174A. Turnhout: Brepols, 2000.

Rad, Gerhard von. "The Origin of the Concept of the Day of the Lord." *Journal of Semitic Studies* 4 (1959): 97–108.

———. *Old Testament Theology*. 2 vols. New York: Harper & Row, 1962, 1965.

Radner, Ephraim. *Time and the Word: Figural Readings of the Christian Scriptures*. Grand Rapids, MI: Eerdmans, 2016.

Raffa, Guy P. *The Complete Danteworlds: A Reader's Guide to the Divine Comedy*. Chicago: University of Chicago Press, 2007.

Rahlfs, Alfred, ed. *Septuaginta: With Morphology*. Stuttgart: Deutsche Bibelgesellschaft, 1996.

Ratzinger, Joseph (Pope Benedict XVI). *"In the Beginning . . .": A Catholic Understanding of the Story of the Creation and the Fall.* Translated by Boniface Ramsey. Grand Rapids, MI: Eerdmans Press, 1986.

———. *Biblical Interpretation in Crisis: The Ratzinger Conference on Bible and Church*. Edited by Richard John Neuhaus. Grand Rapids, MI: Eerdmans, 1988.

———. *On the Way to Jesus Christ*. San Francisco: Ignatius, 2005.

———. "Biblical Interpretation in Crisis: On the Question of the Foundations and Approaches of Exegesis Today." In *The Essential Pope Benedict XVI: His Central Writings and Speeches*, ed. John F. Thorton and Susan B. Varenne, 243–58. San Francisco: Harper San Francisco, 2007.

———. *Jesus of Nazareth: From the Baptism in the Jordan to the Transfiguration*. San Francisco: Ignatius, 2007.

———. *Jesus of Nazareth, Part Two: Holy Week. From the Entrance into Jerusalem to the Resurrection*. San Francisco: Ignatius Press, 2011.

———. *Jesus of Nazareth: The Infancy Narratives.* San Francisco: Ignatius Press, 2012.

Rendsburg, Gary. "The Date of the Exodus and the Conquest/Settlement: The Case for the 1100s." *Vetus Testamentum* 42 (1992): 510–27.

Richard of St. Victor. *In Cantica Canticorum Explicatio* 5. Edited by J.-P. Migne. Patrologiae Cursus Completus. Series Latina 196. Paris, 1844–64.

Rider, Jeff, and Alan V. Murray, eds. *Galbert of Bruges and the Historiography of Medieval Flanders*. Washington, DC: Catholic University of America Press, 2009.

Rupert of Deutz. Cantica Canticorum Commentariorum Libri 1. Vol. 26. Corpus Christianorum. Continuatio Mediaevalis. Turnhout: Brepols, 1971.

Rutgers, L. V. *The Jews in Late Ancient Rome*. Leiden: Brill, 1995.

Rutledge, Fleming. *And God Spoke to Abraham: Preaching from the Old Testament.* Grand Rapids, MI: Eerdmans, 2011.

———. *The Crucifixion: Understanding the Death of Jesus.* Grand Rapids, MI: Eerdmans, 2015.

Sailhammer, John. "The Messiah and the Hebrew Bible." *Journal of Evangelical Theological Studies* 44 (2001): 13–14.

Sanders, E. P. *Paul and Palestinian Judaism.* Minneapolis: Fortress Press, 1977.

———, ed. *Jewish and Christian Self-Definition*. Vol. 2, *Aspects of Judaism in the Greco-Roman Period*. Minneapolis: Fortress Press, 1981.

———. *The Historical Figure of Jesus.* Minneapolis: Fortress Press, 1996.

Sarah, Robert Cardinal. *The Power of Silence: Against the Dictatorship of Noise.* San Francisco: Ignatius Press, 2017.

Sarna, Nahum. "Epic Substratum in the Prose of Job." *Journal of Biblical Literature* 76 (1957): 13–25.

———. *Genesis. The JPS Torah Commentary*. Philadelphia: Jewish Publication Society, 1989.

———. *Exodus*. Philadelphia: Jewish Publication Society, 1991.

Sawyer, J. F. A. "The Authorship and Structure of the Book of Job." In *Studia Biblica 1978*, ed. E. A. Livingstone, 253–57. Journal for the Study of the Old Testament Supplement 11. Sheffield: Journal for the Study of the Old Testament Press, 1979.

———. "Daughter of Zion and Servant of the Lord in Isaiah: A Comparison." *JSOT* 44 (1989): 89–107.

———. *The Fifth Gospel: Isaiah in the History of Christianity*. Cambridge: Cambridge University Press, 1996.

Schaff, Philip, ed. *St. Augustin's City of God and Christian Doctrine*. Translated by J. F. Shaw. Select Library of the Nicene and Post-Nicene Fathers of the Christian Church 2. First Series. Buffalo, NY: Christian Literature Co., 1887.

Schultz, R. L. "How Many Isaiahs Were There and What Does It Matter? Prophetic Inspiration in Recent Evangelical Scholarship." In *Evangelicals and Scripture: Tradition, Authority and Hermeneutics*, ed. V. Bacote, L. C. Miguélez, and D. L. Okholm, 150–70. Downers Grove, IL: InterVarsity, 2004.

Schürer, Emil. *The History of the Jewish People in the Age of Jesus Christ*. 3 vols. Edited by G. Vermes, F. Millar, and M. Goodman. Edinburgh: T & T Clark, 1973–87.

Seeters, John Van. "Law and the Wilderness Rebellion Tradition: Exodus 32." In *Society of Biblical Literature 1990 Seminar Papers*, ed. D. J. Lull, 583–91. Atlanta: Scholars Press, 1990.

Seow, C. L. *Job 1–21: Interpretation and Commentary*. Illuminations. Grand Rapids, MI: Eerdmans, 2013.

Shaw, Prue. *Reading Dante: From Here to Eternity*. New York: Liveright, 2014.

Sheridan, Mark. *Language for God in Patristic Tradition: Wrestling with Biblical Anthropomorphism*. Downers Grove, IL: InterVarsity, 2015.

Simonetti, Manlio. *Biblical Interpretation in the Early Church: An Historical Introduction to Patristic Exegesis.* Translated by John A. Hughes. Edinburgh: T & T Clark, 1994.

Smalley, Beryl. *The Study of the Bible in the Middle Ages*. Notre Dame, IN: University of Notre Dame Press, 1964.

Smallwood, E. Mary. *The Jews under Roman Rule*. 2nd ed. Leiden: Brill, 1981.

Smith, D. M. *John among the Gospels: The Relationship in Twentieth-Century Research*. Philadelphia: Fortress Press, 1992.

Smith, Steven C. *The Word of the Lord: 7 Essential Principles for Catholic Scripture Study*. Huntington, IN: Our Sunday Visitor Press, 2012.

———. *The House of the Lord: A Catholic Biblical Theology of God's Temple Presence in the Old and New Testaments.* Steubenville, OH: Franciscan University Press, 2017.

Sokolowski. *Lois sacrees des cites grecques*. Paris: Boccard, 1969.

Spicq, Ceslas, and James D. Ernest. *Theological Lexicon of the New Testament*. Peabody, MA: Hendrickson, 1994.

Stark, Rodney. *The Case for the Crusades*. New York: Harper One, 2009.

Stone, Michael E. Stone, ed. *Jewish Writings of the Second Temple Period*. Compendia Rerum Iudaicarum ad Novum Testamentum 2.2. Philadelphia: Fortress Press, 1984.

Strauss, David Friedrich. *Das Leben Jesu fur das deutsche Volk bearbeitet* [A life of Jesus for the German people]. Leipzig, 1864.

Tcherikover, Victor. *Hellenistic Civilization and the Jews*. Philadelphia: Jewish Publication Society, 1961.

Tcherikover, Victor, and A. Fuks, eds. *Corpus Papyrorum Judaicarum*. 3 vols. Cambridge, MA: Harvard University Press, 1957–64.

Thérèse of Lisieux, St. *The Story of a Soul*. Washington, DC: ICS Publications, 2005.

Thomas Aquinas, St. *Catena Aurea: Commentary on the Four Gospels, Collected Out of the Works of the Fathers. St. Mark*. Vol. 2. Edited by John Henry Newman. Oxford: John Henry Parker, 1842.

———. *Summa Theologica*. Translated by the Fathers of the English Dominican Province. London: Burns Oates & Washbourne, 1947.

———. *Commentary on the Gospel of John: Chapters 1–21*. Vol. 3. Translated by Fabian Larcher and James A. Weisheipl. Washington, DC: Catholic University of America Press, 2010.

———. *Commentary on the Book of Job*. Edited by the Aquinas Institute. Translated by Brian Mullady. Lander, WY: Aquinas Institute of the Study of Sacred Doctrine, 2016.

Tobin, Thomas H. *The Creation of Man: Philo and the History of Interpretation*. Catholic Biblical Quarterly Monographs 14. Washington, DC: Catholic Biblical Association, 1983.

Tolkien, J. R. R. *The Monster and the Critics and Other Essays*. Edited by Christopher Tolkien. Boston: Houghton Mifflin, 1983.

Torrell, Jean Pierre. *St. Thomas Aquinas*. Vol. 1, *The Person and His Work*. Translated by Robert Royal. Washington, DC: Catholic University of America Press, 1996.

Tracy, David. *The Analogical Imagination: Christian Theology and the Culture of Pluralism*. Spring Valley, NY: Crossroad, 1998.

VanGemeren, W. A. *New International Dictionary of Old Testament Theology and Exegesis*. 5 vols. Grand Rapids, MI: Zondervan, 1997.

Vanhoozer, Kevin. *Is There a Meaning in This Text*? Grand Rapids, MI: Eerdmans, 1998.

Victorinus, Marius. *Theological Treatises on the Trinity*. Edited by Hermigild Dressler. Translated by Mary T. Clark. Fathers of the Church 69. Washington, DC: Catholic University of America Press, 1981.

Vosté, J. M. "L'oeuvre exégétique de Théodore de Mopsueste au IIe concile de Constantinople." *Revue biblique* 38 (1929): 394–95.

Wahlde, Urban C. von. *The Gospel and Letters of John*. 3 vols. Grand Rapids, MI: Eerdmans, 2010.

Watts, John D. W. *Isaiah 34–66*. Rev. ed. Word Biblical Commentary 25. Nashville, TN: Thomas Nelson, 2005.

Webber, Robert. *Ancient-Future Worship: Proclaiming and Enacting God's Narrative*. Grand Rapids, MI: Baker, 2008.

Webber, Robert, and Lester Ruth. *Evangelicals on the Canterbury Trail: Why Evangelicals Are Attracted to the Liturgical Church*. Atlanta: Morehouse, 2013.

Weems, Renita J. *The Song of Songs*. New Interpreters Bible. Nashville: Abingdon, 1997.

Weinandy, Thomas G. *Jesus Becoming Jesus: A Theological Interpretation of the Synoptic Gospels.* Washington, DC: Catholic University of America Press, 2018.

Weinandy, Thomas G., Daniel A. Keating, and John P. Yocum. *Aquinas on Scripture: An Introduction to his Biblical Commentaries*. New York: T & T Clark, 2005.

Weinfield, Moshe. "The Decalogue: Its Significance, Uniqueness, and Place in Israel's Tradition." In *Religion and Law: Biblical-Judaic and Islamic Perspectives*, ed. Edwin B. Firmage et al., 3–47. Winona Lake, IN: Eisenbrauns, 1990.

Wenham, Gordon J. "The Coherence of the Flood Narrative." *Vetus Testamentum* 28 (1978): 336–48.

———. *Genesis 1–15*. Word Biblical Commentary 1. Dallas, TX: Word, Inc., 1987.

———. *Genesis 16–50*. Word Biblical Commentary 2. Dallas, TX: Word, Inc., 1994.

Westermann, Claus. *The Structure of the Book of Job*. Philadelphia: Fortress Press, 1981.

———. *A Continental Commentary: Genesis 12–36*. Minneapolis: Fortress Press, 1995.

Wifall, Walter. "Gen 3:15: A Protoevangelium?" *Catholic Biblical Quarterly* 36 (1974): 361–64.

Wilken, Robert Louis. "In Defense of Allegory." *Modern Theology* 14, no. 2 (1998): 199–211.

———. "Allegory and the Interpretation of the Old Testament in the 21st Century." *Letter & Spirit: Reading Salvation. Word, Worship, and the Mysteries* 1 (2005): 11.

———. *The Spirit of Early Christian Thought: Seeking the Face of God*. New Haven, CT: Yale University Press, 2005.

Wilken, Robert Louis, Angela Russell Christman, and Michael J. Hollerich, eds. *Isaiah: Interpreted by Early Christian and Medieval Commentators*. Translated by Robert Louis Wilken, Angela Russell Christman, and Michael J. Hollerich. The Church's Bible. Grand Rapids, MI: Eerdmans, 2007.

Williamson, Peter. *Catholic Principles for Interpreting Scripture: A Study of the Pontifical Biblical Commission's The Interpretation of the Bible in the Church*. Subsidia Biblica 22. Rome: Pontifical Biblical Institute, 2001.

Wright, N. T. *Jesus and the Victory of God.* Christian Origins and the Question of God 1. London: Society for Promoting Christian Knowledge, 1996.

———. *The Resurrection of the Son of God*. Christian Origins and the Question of God 3. London: Society for Promoting Christian Knowledge, 2003.

———. *Paul and the Faithfulness of God*. Christian Origins and the Question of God 4. Minneapolis: Fortress Press, 2013.

———. *Pauline Perspectives: Essays on Paul, 1978–2013*. Minneapolis: Fortress Press, 2013.

Wright IV, William M. "Patristic Biblical Hermeneutics in Joseph Ratzinger's Jesus of Nazareth." *Letter & Spirit: The Bible and the Church Fathers. The Liturgical Context of Patristic Exegesis* 7 (2011): 191–92.

Young, Francis M. *Biblical Exegesis and the Formation of Christian Culture*. Grand Rapids, MI: Baker Academic, 2002.

INDEX

ABOUT THE ARTIST

The image on the cover of the book—*Transfiguration*—is not an icon but a carving in stone. The artist, Jonathan Pageau, carves Eastern Orthodox icons and other traditional Christian images in both wood and stone. Jonathan is one of the only professional icon carvers in North America, taking on institutional and personal art commissions from all over the world. For more information, see www.pageaucarvings.com.

Pageau is also the editor of and contributor to the *Orthodox Arts Journal*, which publishes articles and news about the revival and significance of liturgical art today (www.orthodoxartsjournal.org).

Finally, Jonathan Pageau is a noted speaker. He delivers several lectures every year at universities, conferences, and other venues around North America. He speaks on art, mostly on the symbolic structures that underlie our experience of the world. Additionally, he has collaborated with Jordan B. Peterson on a number of topics and panels related to symbolism and the Bible.

Through his YouTube channel and podcast, *The Symbolic World*, he furthers the conversation on symbolism, meaning, and patterns in everything from movies to icons to social trends (www.thesymbolicworld.com).

The author is grateful for the use of the image of this exceptional carving and for the opportunity to collaborate with such a uniquely gifted artist.

The Face of the Lord: Contemplating the Divine Son through the Four Senses of Sacred Scripture was designed in Garamond and composed by Kachergis Book Design of Pittsboro, North Carolina. It was printed on 60-pound Natures Book Natural and bound by Sheridan Books of Chelsea, Michigan.